World Music

DATE DUE

BRODART, CO.	Cat. No. 23-221

World Music
A Global Journey

Third edition

Terry E. Miller
Kent State University

and

Andrew Shahriari
Kent State University

NEW YORK AND LONDON

Senior Acquisitions Editor: Constance Ditzel
Development Editors: Felisa Salvago-Keyes
Senior Editorial Assistant: Denny Tek
Production Manager: Mhairi Bennett
Marketing Managers: Chris Bowers and Joon Won Moon
Text Design: Karl Hunt, Keystroke
Copy Editor: Janice Baiton
Proofreader: Jane Canvin
Cover Designer: Mark Lerner
Companion Website Designer: Marie Mansfield

Routledge
New York & London
Third edition published 2012
by Routledge
711 Third Avenue, New York, NY 10017

Simultaneously published in the UK
by Routledge
2 Park Square, Milton Park, Abingdon, Oxon OX14 4RN

Routledge is an imprint of the Taylor & Francis Group, an informa business

© 2012 Taylor & Francis

The right of Terry E. Miller and Andrew Shahriari to be identified as authors of this work has been asserted by them in accordance with sections 77 and 78 of the Copyright, Designs and Patents Act 1988.

All rights reserved. No part of this book may be reprinted or reproduced or utilized in any form or by any electronic, mechanical, or other means, now known or hereafter invented, including photocopying and recording, or in any information storage or retrieval system, without permission in writing from the publishers.

Trademark notice: Product or corporate names may be trademarks or registered trademarks, and are used only for identification and explanation without intent to infringe.

Library of Congress Cataloging in Publication Data
Miller, Terry E.
  World music : a global journey / Terry E. Miller, Andrew Shahriari. — 3rd ed.
    p. cm.
  1. World music—History and criticism. I. Shahriari, Andrew C. II. Title.
  ML3545.M54 2012
  780.9—dc23
                                              2011025812

ISBN: 978-0-415-88713-7 (hbk)
ISBN: 978-0-415-88714-4 (pbk)
ISBN: 978-0-415-80823-1 (pback pack)
ISBN: 978-0-203-15298-0 (ebk)

Typeset in Melior
by Keystroke, Station Road, Codsall, Wolverhampton

Printed and bound in India by Replika Press Pvt Ltd.

Contents

Preface — xiii
Scope xiii
Organization xiv
The Third Edition xv
Listening Guides xvi
   Structure of Each Listening Guide xvii
How Instructors Can Expand Course Coverage xviii
Website xix
Our Own Journey (Thus Far) xix
   Terry E. Miller xx
   Andrew Shahriari xxi

Acknowledgments — xxiv

1 Before the Trip Begins: Fundamental Issues — 1
What is Music? 2
Music: Universal Language or Culturally Specific Activity? 3
Beware of Labels 4
An Inside Look: Gerhard Kubik 7
Knowing the World's Musics 8
The Life of an Ethnomusicologist 11
Representation: What Musics Does One Study? 12
Resources for the Study of the World's Musics 12
   Reference Works 12
   Video 13
   Audio Recordings 13
   Journals 13
Questions to Consider 14
On Your Own Time 14

2 Aural Analysis: Listening to the World's Musics — 16
How to Listen to World Music 17
"Talking" about Music 18

Timbre and Medium 18
   Vocal Timbre 19
   Instrumental Timbre 19
      Aerophones: Flutes, Reeds, and Trumpets 19
      Chordophones: Lutes and Zithers 21
      Idiophones: Plucked, Struck, and Shaken 22
      Membranophones 24
      Summary 25
Pitch 25
   Tuning System 25
   Scale 27
   Interval 27
   Range 27
   Melody 28
      Melodic Contour 28
      Ornamentation 28
      Text Setting 29
Rhythm 29
   Beat and Tempo 29
   Accent and Meter 29
   Rhythmic Density 30
Phonic Structure 30
Dynamics 31
Form 32
An Inside Look: Bruno Nettl 32
Need to Know: Fundamentals of Music 33
Questions to Consider 33
On Your Own Time 34

3 Cultural Considerations: Beyond the Sounds Themselves   35
Cultural Knowledge 36
An Inside Look: Judith Becker 38
Value Systems and Hierarchies 40
Music and Identity 40
Use versus Function 42
Music and Spirituality 42
Music and Ethics 43
Music and the Environment 43
New Theoretical Perspectives 45
Music Technologies and Media 45
Music and the Arts 46
Transmission and Pedagogy 48
Notation Systems and the Creation of Music 48
Exchange and Adaptation 49
Cultural Intersections 50
A Case Study of Istanbul, Turkey: A Lesson in Geography, History, Religions, and Musical Exchange 51

Questions to Consider 59
On Your Own Time 59

4 Oceania: Australia, Papua New Guinea, Hawaii, Kiribati — 61
Background Preparation 62
Planning the Itinerary 63
Arrival: Australia 63
   Site 1: Australian Aboriginal Song with *Didjeridu* 64
Arrival: Papua New Guinea 69
   Site 2: *Susap* (lamellophone) from Papua New Guinea 70
Explore More: Singsings *of Papua New Guinea* 73
Arrival: Hawaii 74
An Inside Look: Amy Ku'uleialoha Stillman 75
Explore More: Hawaiian Steel Guitar and Ukulele 76
   Site 3: Hawaiian Drum-Dance Chant 77
Arrival: Kiribati 80
   Site 4: Group Song for *bino* (sitting dance) from Kiribati 81
Questions to Consider 85
On Your Own Time 86

5 South Asia: India, Pakistan — 89
Background Preparation 90
An Inside Look: Shanti Raghavan 94
An Inside Look: Aashish Khan 95
Planning the Itinerary 96
Arrival: North India 97
   Site 1: Hindustani (Instrumental) *Raga* 97
Need to Know: Fundamentals of Indian Classical (Hindustani) Music 107
Arrival: South India 108
   Site 2: Carnatic Classical (Vocal) *Kriti* 108
Explore More: Kathakali 115
   Site 3: Hindu *Bhajan* Devotional Song 116
Explore More: Indian Filmi Git *(Film Song)* 121
Arrival: Pakistan 122
   Site 4: *Qawwali* (Sufi Devotional Song) 123
Explore More: Bhangra 127
Questions to Consider 128
On Your Own Time 128

6 Southeast Asia: Vietnam, Thailand, Laos and Northeast Thailand, Indonesia (Java and Bali) — 131
Background Preparation 132
Planning the Itinerary 134
An Inside Look: Priwan Nanongkham 135
Arrival: Vietnam 137
   Site 1: Vietnamese Central Highlands Bronze Gong Ensemble 138

Site 2: *Nhac Tai Tu* Amateur Chamber Music 141
Arrival: Thailand 145
    Site 3: Classical *Piphat* Music 146
Arrival: Laos and Northeast Thailand 152
Explore More: The Ramayana 153
    Site 4: *Lam Klawn* Repartee Singing 155
    Site 5: *Luk Thung* popular song 159
Arrival: Indonesia (Java and Bali) 164
    Site 6: Javanese Court Gamelan 166
    Site 7: Balinese *Gamelan Gong Kebyar* 171
Explore More: Kecak—*The Balinese "Monkey Chant"* 177
Questions to Consider 178
On Your Own Time 178

7 East Asia: China, Mongolia, Korea, Japan, Tibet 181

Background Preparation 182
An Inside Look: Luo Qin 185
An Inside Look: Masayo Ishigure 186
Planning the Itinerary 187
Arrival: China 189
    Site 1: The *Guqin* (Seven-String "Ancient" Zither) 192
    Site 2: *Jiangnan Sizhu* ("Silk and Bamboo") Ensemble from Shanghai 195
    Site 3: Beijing Opera (*Jingju*) 203
    Site 4: Revolutionary Beijing Opera (*Yangbanxi*) 208
Explore More: Popular Music in East Asia 212
Arrival: Mongolia 213
    Site 5: Mongolian *Urtïn Duu* (Long Song) and with *Khöömei* (Overtone or "Throat" Singing) 214
Arrival: Korea 217
    Site 6: *P'ansori* Narrative 218
Arrival: Japan 223
    Site 7: *Sankyoku* Instrumental Chamber Music 224
Explore More: Komuso 227
    Site 8: *Kabuki* Theater 228
Explore More: Taiko 232
Arrival: Tibet 233
    Site 9: Tibetan Buddhist Ritual 234
Questions to Consider 238
On Your Own Time 239

8 The Middle East: Islam and the Arab World, Iran, Egypt, Sufism, Judaism 243

Background Preparation 244
An Inside Look: George Dimitri Sawa 246
Planning the Itinerary 247
Arrival: Islam and the Arabic World 247
    Site 1: Islamic *Adhan*, "Call to Prayer" 248

Site 2: Arabic *Taqasim* for *Ud* and *Buzuq* 253
Arrival: Iran 257
　　Site 3: *Dastgah* for *Santur* and Voice 258
Arrival: Egypt 262
　　Site 4: *Takht* Instrumental Ensemble 263
Arrival: Sufism 268
　　Site 5: Sufi *Dhikr* Ceremony 269
Arrival: Judaism 272
　　Site 6: Jewish *Shofar* and Liturgical Cantillation 274
Questions to Consider 278
On Your Own Time 278

9 Europe: Greece, Spain, Russia, Scotland, Ireland, Hungary, Bulgaria 281

Background Preparation 282
"Classical" versus "Folk" 285
Planning the Itinerary 287
Arrival: Greece 287
　　Site 1: Greek Orthodox (Byzantine) Chant 288
Arrival: Spain 291
　　Site 2: *Flamenco* 292
Arrival: Russia 297
　　Site 3: *Balalaika* Ensemble 298
Arrival: Scotland 301
An Inside Look: Morag MacLeod 302
　　Site 4: Highland Bagpipes 303
Arrival: Ireland 308
　　Site 5: *Uilleann* Bagpipes 309
Arrival: Hungary 314
　　Site 6: *Tekerölant* (Hurdy Gurdy) 314
Arrival: Bulgaria 318
　　Site 7: Bulgarian Women's Chorus 319
Questions to Consider 322
On Your Own Time 323

10 Sub-Saharan Africa: Ghana, Nigeria, Central Africa, Zimbabwe, Uganda, Senegal, The Republic of South Africa 327

Background Preparation 328
An Inside Look: Adesanya Adeyeye 331
An Inside Look: Habib Iddrisu 332
Planning the Itinerary 334
Arrival: Ghana 334
　　Site 1: Polyrhythmic Instrumental Ensemble 335
　　Site 2: "Talking Drums" 340
Arrival: Nigeria 345
　　Site 3: *Jùjú* Popular Music 345
Arrival: Central Africa 349

Site 4: Mbuti Pygmy Music from the Democratic Republic of the Congo 350
Arrival: Zimbabwe 353
   Site 5: *Mbira Dza Vadzimu* 354
Arrival: Uganda 358
   Site 6: *Akadinda* 359
Arrival: Senegal–Gambia 362
   Site 7: *Jali* with *Kora* 362
Arrival: The Republic of South Africa 366
   Site 8: *Mbube* 369
Explore More: Ladysmith Black Mambazo 371
Questions to Consider 372
On Your Own Time 373

11 The Caribbean: Haiti, Jamaica, Trinidad and Tobago, The Bahamas, Cuba, The Dominican Republic — 377

Background Preparation 378
Planning the Itinerary 379
Arrival: Haiti 379
   Site 1: *Vodou* Ritual from Haiti 380
Arrival: Jamaica 385
   Site 2: Reggae 385
Arrival: Trinidad and Tobago 390
   Site 3: Calypso 391
Explore More: Soca 397
An Inside Look: Olivia Ahyoung 398
An Inside Look: Ellie Mannette 399
   Site 4: Steel Band (Pan) 400
Arrival: The Bahamas 404
   Site 5: Rhyming Spiritual 404
Arrival: Cuba 407
   Site 6: Cuban *Son* 408
Arrival: The Dominican Republic 414
   Site 7: *Merengue* 414
Questions to Consider 418
On Your Own Time 418

12 South America and Mexico: The Amazon Rainforest, Peru, Argentina, Brazil, Mexico — 423

Background Preparation 424
Planning the Itinerary 426
An Inside Look: Martin Pereira Algarita 426
Arrival: The Amazon Rainforest 427
   Site 1: Amazonian Chant 428
Arrival: Peru 430
   Site 2: *Sikuri* (Panpipe) Ensemble 431
Arrival: Argentina 434

    Site 3: *Tango* 435
Arrival: Brazil 439
    Site 4: *Samba* 440
Explore More: Carnival 444
    Site 5: *Capoeira* Music 444
Arrival: Mexico 449
    Site 6: *Mariachi* 449
Questions to Consider 454
On Your Own Time 455

13 Canada and the United States   459

Background Preparation 460
Planning the Itinerary 461
An Inside Look: Buddy MacMaster 463
Arrival: Canada 464
    Site 1: Cape Breton Fiddling 464
Arrival: The United States of America 467
    Site 2: Ballad-Singing 468
    Site 3: Old Regular Baptist Lined Hymn 471
An Inside Look: Hugh McGraw 476
    Site 4: Singing School Shape-Note Music 476
    Site 5: Bluegrass 482
    Site 6: African-American Spiritual 488
    Site 7: African-American Gospel Choir 491
    Site 8: Country Blues 495
    Site 9: "Nuyorican" *Salsa* 499
    Site 10: Cajun Music 505
Arrival: Native American Reservations 508
    Site 11: Plains Indian Dance Song 510
    Site 12: Native American Flute 514
Explore More: Inuit Throat-Singing 517
Questions to Consider 518
On Your Own Time 518

14 Discovering Yourself Through Music   525

Music and Self-Identity 526
Researching Your Musical Roots 527
    Observation and Participant-Observation 527
    Audio Recording 527
    Video Recording 528
    Still Photography 528
An Inside Look: Nguyen Thuyet Phong 529
    Interviewing 530
    Collecting and Archiving 530
Disseminating Your Findings 531
    Teaching 531

Performance 531
Publishing 532
Where to Go from Here 532

Glossary — *534*
Resources for Further Study — *563*
Index — *572*
Recorded Examples — *583*

Preface

This textbook is inspired by a class we have taught at Kent State University for many years, "Music as a World Phenomenon." In the mid-1990s, when the university established a requirement to incorporate cultural diversity, the class was a natural fit and enrollment exploded overnight. Fifty students a semester turned into over 500 within a few years. Dissatisfied with the introductory world music textbooks offered at the time, we set out to write our own that would serve this greater number of students, few of whom had formal music training. Its success has encouraged the class to grow to nearly 1500 students per semester and is one of the most popular courses on campus. Other universities have experienced similar growth in their world music surveys. The online version of the class at Kent State, which accommodates nearly 300 students, remains full, and the textbook with its accompanying interactive website has proven an invaluable resource, especially for those students. We hope this third edition of *World Music: A Global Journey* will encourage the same enthusiasm in both instructors and students for teaching and learning about the world and its music, as it has for us at Kent State.

Scope

Anyone who attempts a book such as this should first address a few questions:

- *Breadth* or *depth*? You cannot have both, unless you want a tome that could hold down your loose papers through a hurricane. We have chosen breadth. While we recognize the impossibility of doing justice to all the world's notable and interesting musics, we also feel that doing what you can is better than doing nothing. The second major question is:
- *Geographical* or *topical organization*? As ethnomusicologists we are tempted to organize our studies topically, in order to explore such issues as identity, gender, representation, meaning, globalization, and so on, but we have found that this approach leaves most students in a state of geographical disorientation. While such a plan would make it easier to discuss many of the issues at stake in "cultural diversity" courses, it would make it difficult to communicate a coherent view of the music of a given area. Thus, we have chosen a geographical organization. A third question is:
- Should the concentration be on *music as sound* or *music as culture*? The study of world music is the focus of a discipline known as *ethnomusicology,* which seeks to understand

both music and its cultural associations. This field of scholarly research has long had a fascination with the anthropological aspects of the music studied—what we used to call "the context"—but some of our field's critics have noted a growing reluctance to discuss musical sound at all, complaining that ethnomusicologists do "everything but the music." Others scoff at ethnomusicology as eth-NO-MUSIC-ology. We have striven for a balanced approach, choosing first to emphasize music as sound because we suspect that many of the instructors using this book are situated in music departments and are naturally inclined to focus on music. However, we also include important cultural aspects, allowing teachers using this book to choose which to emphasize.

Organization

Travel is the central metaphor of the book, in part because that is often how we experienced the music we present. After three introductory chapters in which we discuss the elements of music, we present ten chapters on specific geographical areas, be they a continent (e.g., Europe) or a subcontinent (e.g., South Asia). As with any major trip, preparation is necessary before a specific area can be considered in depth.

"Background Preparation" provides the big picture giving the general lay of the land, some of an area's history, and raising certain issues related to music-making in the region. We then give an overview of music the region has to offer before landing in a particular country or area. Here we review the background information pertinent to this particular place and give the reader some feel for the locale's history and culture.

After this, we begin visiting our individual "Sites." These are the audio tracks and discussions we have chosen to represent the area—though you should always bear in mind that we have omitted many others of equal significance. As with travel, so with music: we simply cannot visit everything. Hopefully, you can return to some areas later and experience more on your own. Each Site is explored in three steps.

1. "First Impressions"—In this section we attempt to convey the impressions and associations the music might inspire in a first-time listener. These are necessarily subjective and intended to encourage readers to consider their own first impressions in comparison to ours.
2. "Aural Analysis"—Here we focus on the site in terms of musical sound, discussing whatever is most relevant. This could include the medium (instruments and/or voices) and any of the prominent musical elements that define an example.
3. "Cultural Considerations"—The final section is where relevant cultural matters are raised. These are the "contexts" and "issues" that have differentiated ethnomusicology from most other music disciplines.

This process can serve as a framework for exploring an infinite array of world music traditions. Instructors may wish to bring in some examples, based on their own focus, as a supplement to the materials provided here.

The Third Edition

Following the release of the first edition in late 2005, we were gratified so many of our colleagues in schools of all sizes and missions adopted *World Music: A Global Journey* and found it useful. Although we feel fortunate that so many chose this book over the increasing number of other choices, we continually think about how we can improve it. Hopefully, the third edition offers many of the improvements suggested by users along with those originating with the authors.

- **Updated Content**: Numerous sites have been updated, revised, or added (replacing old sites that are moved to the textbook website). These include Hawaii, Kiribati, South India, Pakistan, Thailand, Indonesia (Java), China, Mongolia, Japan, Islam, Egypt, Judaism, Scotland, Ireland, Nigeria, Senegal, South Africa, Jamaica, Trinidad, Cuba, and the United States.
- **Popular Music**: We recognize that some faculty users would prefer a more abundant mix of popular styles and have made some additions. But largely we remain faithful to our original intention: to focus on what many consider to be "traditional music". In order to incorporate more discussions of popular music, however, we have changed some sites and added several feature boxes (see below) to include a good number of types that cross into popular culture, such as Reggae, *Luk Thung*, *Jùjú*, Calypso, *Merengue*, *Tango*, *Bhangra*, *Mariachi*, *Samba*, and African-American Gospel.
- **New "Explore More" boxes**: One consideration in *not* including more popular music is the challenge of licensing commercially viable music. The payment required for royalties would force the publisher to raise the price of this book substantially. To expand our coverage of the world's music, we have added several "Explore More" feature boxes with links to iTunes tracks (which require payment) and YouTube video (which is free) available on the textbook website **www.routledge.com/cw/miller**. In cases where we have substituted new tracks, we recognize that some users might prefer to continue using the old ones, which we have moved to the textbook's website.
- **Updated "Inside Look" features**: The scholars and musicians highlighted in the "Inside Look" boxes have been updated along with a few new featured artists, such as Judith Becker and Masayo Ishigure.
- **New photos**: Approximately 25% of the photographs are new. We have drawn more extensively from professional stock footage archives, but with an eye for fieldwork-oriented images that complement our original list of figures.
- **3-CDs**: We have expanded the accompanying recordings from the original two CDs to three. This allows us to offer more complete examples of the sites, averaging three minutes per track rather than two, which often required us to edit the longer examples. The Listening Guides for new and extended tracks have been updated accordingly.
- **"On Your Own Time"** suggested resources: When traveling with a group, informed guides take you directly to the places of greatest interest for the majority of the tour. However, there is usually additional time when you are encouraged to explore a locale on your own. While you can wander off alone in any direction and probably encounter something of interest, it might be more profitable to have a few pointers to make the time more productive. At the end of each chapter we have added a short section called

PREFACE

"On Your Own Time" to suggest some possible routes of exploration, understanding that this is virtual exploration by necessity.
- **Instructors' Resources**: These have been revisited to include new presentations, exam questions, class time activities, and a more integrated website that can be used to expand course coverage.
- **Interactive Listening Guides**: Some of these have been incorporated on the website so that students can listen to streamed music at specific prompts.

Listening Guides

The purpose of the Listening Guides is to encourage *active listening*, rather than *passive listening*. Many students find they lack experience in listening actively to music. The music washes over them as a complete sound without much thought toward the details. Most everyone does this on a daily basis, such as listening to the car radio, walking through a mall, waiting in a doctor's office, or even while attending a concert. They passively "absorb" the sound without really thinking about it.

Active listening requires more than just your ears. You must focus on individual elements in the music in order to understand a variety of features, such as its organization or its rhythmic/melodic elements, its correlation to movement in dance/theatre, the sound as a manifestation of emotional/spiritual expression, etc. Such intentional listening promotes a greater appreciation of the music, which will hopefully make it more appealing, if only from an intellectual perspective.

Each listening guide focuses on key features of the example that help you identify the timbre of different instruments, important melodic and/or rhythmic elements, as well as aspects of form and variations in dynamics, if applicable. Every guide begins with an introduction to the specific example, that is, track title, chapter and site number, etc., followed by a description of the sound elements (vocal and instrumental) heard. The time outline indicates the minutes/seconds (0'00") of each "Listening Focus" item described. (These time codes may vary slightly according to the device you are using to play the example.) The guide concludes with the source for the example and an "Ethno-Challenge," (short for Ethnomusicology Challenge).

The Listening Guides will help you with the "Aural Analysis" section of the readings. Our recommendation is:

1. Listen first through the entire example *without* the guide, just to get a "First Impression" without concern over the details of the music. Compare your first impressions with those we have offered.
2. Read the "Aural Analysis" for the example.
3. Listen again *with* the guide and take note of each "Listening Focus" description. You may have to start/stop and rewind the example several times to hear each item. That's a good thing! It means you are actively listening to the music. If you get through the entire example without stopping once, this probably means you have returned to passive listening.
4. Listen through the entire example again after you feel confident that you have heard and understood all of the "Listening Focus" items. You will find you are hearing the music with a keener sense of its details. That gong sound missed before will now "jump

out" at you, or you may find yourself humming the basic melody or tapping out the fundamental rhythm.

To test your new perspective on the music, try playing the example for someone else and see if he or she notices the same details before you point them out.

We also hope that the Listening Guides will assist instructors in highlighting these key elements during lectures. To know the difference between the sound of a *tabla* and a *tambura*, for example, the instructor may have to highlight the distinction in the classroom. The time code references will help expedite searching for such "Listening Focus" items during class time.

Each guide ends with a feature called the "Ethno-Challenge". Some of these are quite simple, while others may be quite difficult. As ethnomusicologists ourselves, we tried to imagine an activity that would have benefited us in researching each music genre. This may involve library research, such as hunting down a video of Beijing Opera; learning a performance technique, such as circular breathing; or even making a musical instrument, such as a mouth harp, etc. Instructors may have their own ideas for such challenges, but the end-goal remains to encourage more active participation and understanding of the music. The challenges are also meant to be fun projects for your own enjoyment or even to present to the rest of the class.

Finally, we encourage you to add your own "Listening Focus" points to these guides. We may have overlooked or intentionally omitted features due to their repetition within the example or other factors, such as space considerations for the page layouts. You will better develop your active listening skills by adding to these guides, which will ultimately make any music you hear a more meaningful experience.

Structure of Each Listening Guide

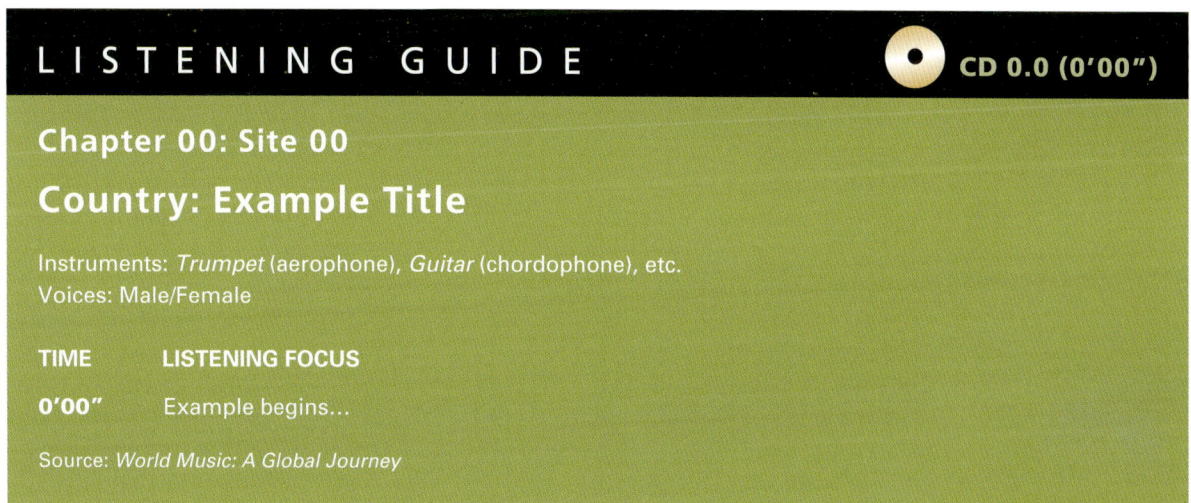

PREFACE

How Instructors Can Expand Course Coverage

"Teaching a textbook" is a widely and often effectively used method but also one that raises thorny issues. The problem with any world survey is that the authors must of necessity choose a certain set of examples and ideas based on their own thinking and experience—but course instructors may have a different view. We suggest therefore that teachers consider the following ideas when using this book:

Be selective. If you find that seventy music examples are too many for your class, then select those that suit your needs. We have attempted to provide reasonably good surveys of each area—considering the limitations of space—but for some instructors this will be too much and for others too little.

Use our plan as a model. Just as you can exclude specific sites, you can also add your own. These additions can be accomplished by either the professor or student. An excellent assignment would be for students to write about a music track not selected by us, using the three approaches employed in this book: first impressions, aural analysis, and cultural considerations. Such exercises could become class papers or presentations as well.

Research further on your own. Just as easily as additional sites can be researched and written about, those presented herein can be developed by students into class presentations that include audio examples, video/DVD clips, and even performances on substitute instruments or the real ones. Students and teachers may locate living representatives of a culture—or even musicians from the tradition under study—who can come to class to discuss the culture or perform the music live.

Consider utilizing additional resources in the neighborhood or university community. We have intentionally focused on pathways available via the Internet, but you might also consider some other areas of investigation, such as libraries and museums.

- **Libraries.** Most libraries, both public and those associated with colleges and universities, have collections of recordings and video materials. Anyone wishing to venture beyond this book might do so in places as diverse as one's local public library to world-class collections in places such as Indiana University's Archives of Traditional Music in Bloomington, Indiana, to the Library of Congress's American Folklife Center in Washington, DC. Similar collections can be found in Canada and Europe.
- **Museums.** Many large cities have excellent museums devoted to local history, culture, or general anthropology of the world. These often include displays of musical instruments, dioramas that include musical activity, and sometimes sound resources. A few have major collections of musical instruments, including the Metropolitan Museum of Art in New York City, The National Music Museum in Vermillion, South Dakota, and the Musical Instrument Museum in Phoenix, Arizona.
- **Internet.** The Internet offers virtually unlimited possibilities for exploration. Two sites relative to this book dominate: YouTube and iTunes. iTunes (and other similar sites) offer many kinds of music for paid download. These sites can be searched by genre, title, or artist; what kinds of music are offered will change constantly. YouTube similarly offers a nearly bottomless series of free video clips of most forms of music, dance, and theater known in the world. Searches of the Internet will also turn up many other kinds of information and resources. One of them is Wikipedia, a free, online encyclopedia. While many of the articles discovered (in numerous languages, too) are quite fine, users

must remember that these entries are not peer-reviewed, and their reliability varies widely since anyone (including you) can write and post entries.

Website

The website is vital to *World Music: A Global Journey*. At Kent State, the book is used for an online course, so the website has been crafted to be adaptable for all kinds of teaching situations, with audio and visual elements and numerous teaching and learning tools:

For the student

- Flashcards of vocabulary words
- Samples of the audio tracks from the accompanying CDs
- Practice quizzes
- Links to online videos
- Links to other suggested resources e.g., books, DVDs, websites, etc.
- E-Book version of the texbook

For the instructor

- Downloadable classroom presentations
- Test banks
- Additional articles and Sites from previous editions of the textbook
- Suggested classroom activities and additional projects
- Author/Instructor Interactive Portal
- E-Package materials for online course development
  www.routledge.com/cw/miller

Our Own Journey (Thus Far)

Neither author, of course, has been everywhere or heard every kind of music the world has to offer. Writing this book has been a humbling experience—only fools think they can cover the world's musics in a single volume. Regardless of our qualms, however, world music courses have become a normal part of the academic environment, and the need for such introductory courses will not go away because of philosophical reservations. If anything, the demand for them will grow. We have attempted to play to our strengths while recognizing our limitations. In the following pages of this preface we engage in a kind of "truth in advertising," by revealing some of our own personal histories with regard to the musics of the world. Perhaps after having read of our experiences, which we present separately, you will better understand why we wrote what we wrote.

PREFACE

Terry E. Miller

My first experience hearing non-Western music came during my undergraduate years at the College of Wooster (Ohio), where I was majoring in organ performance. Ravi Shankar, now India's most famous sitar player, came to the campus as part of the Community Music Series in 1964, several years before he became famous in his own right and as the teacher of George Harrison (member of the Beatles). After his performance, the music majors met with Shankar, but our attempts to understand the concept of *raga* were mostly unsuccessful. We simply had no conceptual categories with which to understand modal improvisation. Further, we had never seen a musician perform seated on the floor, or encountered incense at a music event, and we also failed to understand the significance of the *tambura* lute player and *tabla* drummer. In those days there were virtually no world music courses anywhere, and recordings other than those on the Folkways label were rare.

My next encounter with an "exotic" music did not come until after I had been drafted into the U.S. Army in 1968 and sent to the Republic of Vietnam in 1969 to help fight the war from a swivel chair in front of a Remington typewriter. As a "chairborne" soldier working at a huge base about twenty miles from Saigon (now Ho Chi Minh City), I could have ignored Vietnam entirely. Instead, I decided to explore Vietnamese music. Doing so, however, required trips to Saigon. Having no official business there and no authorization, I had to go illegally on weekends. In Saigon, I attended theatrical performances, bought instruments and recordings, and visited the Saigon Conservatory of Music, where my language abilities were too limited for effective communication. A one-week leave to Bangkok, Thailand, in January 1970 brought me into contact with Thai music. During my visit, I purchased a long, bamboo mouth-organ instrument called the *khaen*, simply because its sound resembled a pipe organ. I did not know how significant this instrument would become for my later life.

After returning to the United States, I enrolled in a Western historical musicology graduate degree program at Indiana University. In spite of the program I was in, I decided to write my master's thesis on an Ohio shape-note teacher and my doctoral dissertation on the music of northeast Thailand. With a generous grant in hand, I went with my family to northeast Thailand in late 1972, for a fourteen-month stay during which I researched that region's music. The resulting dissertation completed my Ph.D. and luckily I stumbled into a teaching position at Kent State University just as they were starting a graduate program in ethnomusicology. I taught at Kent State until my retirement in January 2005. Since that time I have remained actively engaged in research and writing, and I spend about two months a year in Thailand (wisely, during the American winter).

To make a long story short, I kept up my interest in Thailand during my tenure at Kent, but my interests also expanded in other directions. With the help of a succession of "native musician" graduate students, I started two ensembles, one to play traditional Thai music, the other to play Chinese music, and I played in both from 1979 and 1987 respectively until the ensembles were disbanded in May 2005. In 1998 the Thai Ensemble toured Thailand, performing in six cities and on most television channels. The musics of mainland Southeast Asia—Thailand, Laos, Cambodia, Vietnam, Burma, and Malaysia—remain my core interest, with the greatest emphasis being on Thailand and Laos. I also developed a now long-standing interest in orally transmitted hymnody in the West, which has led to extensive and continuing fieldwork in the United States, Scotland, Jamaica, Trinidad, and St. Vincent, the latter three being part of the English-speaking Caribbean. My third area of interest has been

Chinese music, and I have done fieldwork in China itself but much more in the overseas Chinese community of Thailand.

Lastly, I have collected material and experienced live music when possible in each country I've visited. In addition to Vietnam, Thailand, and China, these include the United Kingdom, Ireland, France, Germany, Spain, Hungary, Slovakia, Croatia, Greece, Israel, Nepal, Japan, Korea, Burma, Malaysia, Laos, and South Africa. All of these experiences have contributed to my bank of knowledge. Even so, they have exposed me to only a small percentage of the world's musics. The rest have thus far been experienced, if at all, only vicariously through audio and video recordings or at concerts given by resident or touring musicians. Naturally, knowledge gained through first-hand experience goes deeper than that gained from books and CDs, but even an introductory book like this and carefully listened-to recordings can shed some light on a corner of the world that would otherwise remain totally unfamiliar.

Co-author Terry Miller (on right) with fellow soldier while serving in the United States Army in Vietnam (1969)

Andrew Shahriari

My first recollection of an interest in "world music" is actually associated with a music that I knew quite well. As an undergraduate, I was fortunate to study abroad and to visit Russia on a two-week tour of Moscow and Leningrad (now St. Petersburg—again) in 1990, during the last days of the Soviet Union. My first revelation was that what I had previously believed about Russians was completely untrue: I had been misled all my life into thinking they were evil, American-hating Communists who would sooner spit on me than shake my hand. To the contrary, I found the people I met in Russia to be the most friendly, helpful people in Europe, with a great respect for Americans. My misconceptions were based on ignorance and on the stereotyping of people I did not know. Sadly, the negative propagandizing of other cultures by the media remains a problem today.

My second revelation came in a Moscow jazz club, where I realized that music can cross cultural barriers as effectively as speech. While music is not a "universal language," it nonetheless generally draws more on emotion than intellect. Music has the uncanny power to enable those who speak the same musical language to "connect" on a different level than is possible with the spoken word. Though conversations I had with Russians fluent in English were friendly, they were mostly superficial exchanges. In contrast, the twenty-minute "jam" my American friends and I played with the jazz club's Russian house band resulted in genuine laughter, bear hugs, and toasts in our honor for the rest of the night—without our ever even learning the names of our comrades. All of us knew we would never meet again, but for that night we were the best of friends because we spoke through music.

PREFACE

My Russian encounter inspired my interest in ethnomusicology and continues to motivate my core concerns as a scholar, educator, and musician. Cultural ignorance is the source of many stereotypes about other peoples. A primary goal of my own study and certainly of my teaching, as well as of this textbook, is to encourage an awareness of our cultural biases. You cannot learn about the world from only the nightly news and cable television. While the United States has "free" media, the stories that are presented are highly selective and strongly biased toward American interests. To think otherwise is naïve. This is true in other cultures as well. Politics and business influence the content of newspapers, books, television, movies, radio, even the Internet, all of which then shape our attitudes about others and ourselves. We cannot avoid being culturally biased, but an awareness of this reality is important to keeping an open mind, which encourages understanding of other perspectives and fosters communication rather than conflict.

After college, I spent a couple of years pursuing a career in the music business, but quickly realized that the "business" of making music greatly overwhelmed the actual creation of it. Thankfully, a professor suggested I study ethnomusicology as a graduate student due to my interest in blues and jazz. I came to Kent State in 1992 and have never looked back. I explored my diverse interests in music and discovered many new and intriguing sounds that have spurred me to travel to many new countries, experience an array of new cultures, and to meet wonderful people from all over the world. Like Terry, I became fascinated with the music and culture of Thailand and focused my studies on the northern region (Lanna), an area that no one had yet to explore in depth. I have since pursued other interests in music and spirituality, popular world music, and music therapy and traveled to numerous locales, including Mexico, China, Germany, Austria, France, Scotland, England, and throughout the United States.

Co-author Andrew Shahriari (seated at piano) and friends perform in a jazz club with local university students in Moscow, Russia (1989)

But my exploration of world music is certainly not limited to only the places I have visited. Being part of a university culture allows for a great many opportunities to learn about world music on a first-hand basis by attending concerts, meeting international musicians and local residents, as well as learning from my many students who share their world music and culture experiences with me. By studying world music, I learn about people's passions. I learn what they value, and I learn how they think. Music can reveal the deepest emotions of a people, their philosophies of life, their conceptions of death, their hopes and fears, anger and affections, desires and dreams. Music says what cannot be put into words and often adds to words what cannot be merely spoken.

I hope that each person who reads this textbook will approach each site visited with an open mind and appreciate each tradition on its own terms. Remember that appreciation is not necessarily the same thing as enjoyment. Some music is like sugar, sweet to taste and easy to take from the start. Other music is an acquired taste, and may only ever be appreciated at an intellectual level. I myself do not find all music aurally appealing, yet I strive to keep an open mind and accept that all musics (or musical sounds) are worthwhile because they are significant to someone—otherwise they would not exist. If you have read this far, I am certain you will do the same.

Terry E. Miller
Andrew Shahriari
June 2011

Acknowledgments

None of us acquire knowledge in isolation, and all of us are indebted to the many people we have encountered during our lives. Certainly we are indebted to our own formal teachers at all levels, but our knowledge of the world's musics is only possible thanks to innumerable individuals, some known first-hand, others known through performances, some only known through the Internet, who have—wittingly or unwittingly—taught us what we know. But we, not they, are responsible for that which remains unknown or misunderstood.

In particular we are indebted to the many individuals who have made it possible to offer an unprecedented seventy tracks of music, especially those who did so without payment. Similarly, we are indebted to those who appear in our photographs and to the photographers who allowed us to use their photographs. Their names are to be found in the credits for each track and each photo.

We are also indebted to our many students, who over the years have made us increasingly aware of the challenges of teaching world musics. While some of our students have been music majors, the vast majority are "non-music majors" satisfying requirements for their Liberal Education Core and for Diversity courses. As such, few have had a special interest in the world's musics, so inspiring enthusiasm in the subject matter has been an exhilarating challenge. The insights brought from teaching students with a variety of majors and levels of interest in studying the world's musics and cultures have been our greatest resource. It is these students who inspired much of our writing throughout the book.

Another motivating factor was our desire to create a book for non-specialist teachers. Based on our experience with the membership of the College Music Society, we are grateful to the many non-ethnomusicologist teachers who have been pressed into service to teach a world music survey, and shared with us their concerns and wishes.

Before this book was completed, a great number of individuals kindly offered feedback in response to four sample chapters. We found in these a remarkable amount of helpful criticism, even from those who have many "issues" with what we have done. The second edition took advantage of two years of experience in using the book. Although the audio examples remained unchanged, we then added detailed Listening Guides for each track. In preparation of the third edition we have benefitted from comments and suggestions offered by users over these past few years and by the targeted reviews made available to us by our publisher, Routledge. Although we are unable to satisfy all the suggestions we have received, we have responded to the greatest extent possible. We believe this edition is much improved thanks to these comments.

A great number of individuals offered special help, by recording tracks, offering detailed information on those tracks, supplying photos, and offering extensive corrections. For this third edition we are especially appreciative of the following: Paul Austerlitz, Mr. Balusubramaniam, Praphai Boomsermsuwong, Eliot Grasso, Kathleen Joyce-Grendahl, Roderic Knight, Mary Lawson Burke, Scott Marcus, Priwan and Siriphon Nanongkham, Phong Nguyen, Dale Olsen, Anne Prescott, K.S. Resmi, N. Scott Robinson, Ted and M. Tyler Rounds, Daniel Sheehy, and Amy Unruh. If we have omitted your name—and you will know who you are—we apologize for our oversight.

Last but not least, we must thank our families for their forbearance and their tolerance of our long periods sitting before the computer writing and revising this book. Preceding that were many long and often demanding research trips to the field, usually with our spouses or with them left behind to "hold the fort" at home.

In addition, Terry would like to acknowledge the good humor shown by his children, Sonia and Esther, who, dragged along on numerous field trips, at least contributed their charms on his "research subjects." Esther in particular thought her family's trip to Trinidad in 1990 was to visit beaches but soon discovered that they were spending up to eight hours on Sunday in Spiritual Baptist churches. Andrew apologizes in advance, expecting that his son, Cyrus, will have similar experiences in the future; but he promises to try to visit the beach at least once per field trip for the sake of his wife's sanity.

Finally, both of us would like to thank the professionals we have worked with at Routledge. These are especially Constance Ditzel, our Managing Editor, who has given special attention to this project, offered many excellent suggestions, and been especially supportive of our ideas by being flexible. Chris Bowers, our Marketing Manager, who has tirelessly promoted the book and offered great support in its dissemination throughout the globe. Denny Tek, working as a technical editor, has been consistently helpful, though while keeping a low profile behind the scenes. We are especially indebted to Karl Hunt in the UK who created the page layouts for this edition, an endless task in our opinion. It has been a pleasure working with everyone at Routledge since the inception of this book in 2002.

Map of the World

Before the Trip Begins: Fundamental Issues

1

What is Music? 2	**Resources for the Study of the World's Musics** 12	Co-author (TM) playing *yang qin* dulcimer (right) with an unknown musician playing *yeh hu* fiddle (left), Shantou, China (Sara Stone Miller)
Music: Universal Language or Culturally Specific Activity? 3	Reference Works 12	
Beware of Labels 4	Video 13	
An Inside Look: Gerhard Kubik 7	Audio Recordings 13	
Knowing the World's Musics 8	Journals 13	
The Life of an Ethnomusicologist 11	**Questions to Consider** 14	
Representation: What Musics Does One Study? 12	**On Your Own Time** 14	

What is Music?

Although virtually everyone listens to it and most libraries include books on it, music is notoriously difficult to define, describe, and discuss. While in a literal sense music is only a kind of sound vibration, it must be distinguished from other kinds of sound vibration such as speech or noise. This distinction is based not on observable acoustical differences but on the meanings we assign the sounds that become, in our minds, music. Music is thus a conceptual phenomenon that exists only in the mind; at least that is where the distinctions between "noise" and "music" occur. Graphic representations of music—notations of any sort—are only that, representations. A score is not "the music" because music is a series of sonic vibrations transmitted through the ears to the brain, where we begin the process of making sense of and finding meaning and order in these sounds.

We are normally surrounded by sounds—the sounds of nature, the sounds of man's inventions, of our own voices—but for most of us most of the time distinguishing "music" from the totality of ambient sounds around us comes "naturally." We recognize "noise" when we hear it; we recognize "music" when we hear it. Our sense of the difference between the two derives from a lifetime of conditioning. This conditioning is cultural in origin. Our own concept of what distinguishes music from noise is more or less the same as that of our overall "culture," as we were raised in an environment that conveyed to us general notions about the distinctions between the two. Therefore, definitions of "music" are of necessity culturally determined.

For example, many people make a distinction between music and singing; for them, the word *music* refers only to instrumental sounds. Some years ago we wrote to a Primitive Baptist elder (a church leader) in North Carolina regarding that denomination's orally transmitted hymn singing. We asked—naïvely—"when you sing, do you use music?" The answer was totally logical within the elder's own world: "We don't have any music in our church. All we do is sing." By *music* we meant *notation*, but for the elder music meant *instruments*. In this book, however, we use the term *music* more broadly to encompass both instrumental and vocal phenomena.

Within the vocal realm, one of the most intriguing distinctions is that between speech and song. At what point on the speech–song continuum does speech become song? The answers to this question vary widely from place to place. Listeners from one culture may easily misjudge sounds from another culture by assuming, based on their own experience, that this or that performance is "song," when the people performing consider it other than "song." A general term for such "in-between" phenomena is "heightened speech"; for example, chant. One is most likely to have trouble differentiating "speech" and "song" when experiencing the heightened speech of religious and ritual performances, especially those associated with religions that discourage or even ban the performance of "song."

In the Buddhist tradition of Thailand, for example, ordained monks are not permitted to perform song. But if you were to attend a "reading" of the great tale of Prince Wetsandawn (the Buddha's pre-final incarnation preceding *nirvana*), during which a robed monk intones a long poem describing the prince's life, you might, like most Westerners, describe the performance as "singing." After all, the monk performing the story clearly requires considerable vocal talents to negotiate such elaborate strings of pitches. From a Western perspective this performance sounds convincingly like song. From the monk's perspective, however—indeed, from that of most Thai—what he is performing cannot be song because monks are

Thai Buddhist monks chant the afternoon service at Wat [temple] Burapha, Roi-et, Thailand

prohibited from singing. The monk's performance is described by the verb *thet*, which means "to preach." Why is this performance not considered song? Because there is consensus among Thai that it is not song but rather it is preaching. Thus, this chanted poetry is simultaneously "music" from our perspective and definitely "not music" from the perspective of the performer and his primary audience. Neither perspective is right or wrong in a universal sense; rather, each is "correct" according to respective cultural norms.

Music: Universal Language or Culturally Specific Activity?

It is frequently asserted that "music is a universal [or international] language," a "metalanguage" that expresses universal human emotions and transcends the barriers of language and culture.

The problems with this metaphor are many. First, music is not a language, at least not in the sense of conveying specific meanings through specific symbols, in standard patterns analogous to syntax, and governed by rules of structure analogous to grammar. While attempts have been made to analyze music in linguistic terms, these ultimately failed because music is of a totally different realm. Second, it is questionable whether music really can transcend linguistic barriers and culturally determined behaviors, though some forms of emotional communication, such as crying, are so fundamentally human that virtually all perceive it the same way. What we see with music does not support the notion that music is a universal language, unfortunately, and we do not believe such a concept to be useful in examining the world's musics.

1 WORLD MUSIC: A GLOBAL JOURNEY

SEMIOTICS
The study of signs and systems of signs, including in music.

As will become increasingly clear as you begin your exploration of the world's vast array of musics, musical expression is both culturally determined and culturally encoded with meaning. The field of **semiotics**, which deals with signs—systems of symbols and their meanings—offers an explanation of how music works. Although semiotics was not created specifically for music, it has been adapted by Canadian scholar Jean-Jacques Nattiez and others for this purpose.

A semiotic view of music asserts that the musical sound itself is a "neutral" symbol that has no inherent meaning. Music is thus thought of as a "text" or "trace" that has to be interpreted. In a process called the *poietic*, the creator of the music encodes meanings and emotions into the "neutral" composition or performance, which is then interpreted by anyone listening to the music, a process called the *esthesic*. Each individual listener's interpretation is entirely the result of cultural conditioning and life experience. When a group of people sharing similar backgrounds encounters a work or performance of music, there is the possibility that all (or most) will interpret what they hear similarly—but it is also possible that there will be as many variant interpretations as there are listeners. In short, meaning is not passed from the creator through the music to the listener. Instead, the listener applies an interpretation that is independent of the creator. However, when both creator and listener share similar backgrounds, there is a greater likelihood that the listener's interpretation will be consistent with the creator's intended meaning.

When the creator and listener are from completely different backgrounds, miscommunication is almost inevitable. When, for example, an Indian musician performs what is called a *raga*, he or she is aware, by virtue of life experience and training, of certain emotional feelings or meanings associated with that *raga*. An audience of outsiders with little knowledge of Indian music or culture must necessarily interpret the music according to their own experience and by the norms of their society's music. They are unlikely to hear things as an Indian audience would, being unaware of culturally determined associations between, say, specific *ragas* and particular times of the day. Such miscommunication inevitably contributes to the problem of **ethnocentrism**: the assumption that one's own cultural patterns and understandings are normative and that those that differ are "strange," "exotic," or "abnormal."

ETHNOCENTRISM
The unconscious assumption that one's own cultural background is "normal," while that of others is "strange" or "exotic."

Whenever we encounter something new, we subconsciously compare it to all our previous experiences. We are strongly inclined to associate each new experience with the most similar thing we have encountered previously. People with a narrow range of life experience have less data in their memory bank, and when something is truly new, none of us has any direct way to compare it to a known experience. Misunderstandings easily occur at this point. We attempt to rationalize the unfamiliar in terms of our own experience and often "assume" the unknown is consistent with what we already know. Even if a newly encountered music sounds like something we recognize, we cannot be sure it is similar in any way. Perhaps a war song from another culture might sound like a lullaby in our culture. Knowing about this potential pitfall is the first step in avoiding the trapdoor of ethnocentrism.

Beware of Labels

The German philosopher Ludwig Wittgenstein (1889–1951) famously warned, "labels terminate thinking." But because world music is such a vast subject, it must be broken down into manageable subcategories, which are labeled for the purpose of identification. While such labels are useful, they can also mislead. In teaching the musics of the world it is often tempting to use labels as shorthand. Unfortunately, not everyone understands their meanings and limitations; furthermore, these labels are employed in a variety of ways depending on the user's background. Thus, while we prefer not to employ such labels here, we recognize that they *are* difficult to avoid. When we do use them, we will attempt to limit them to particular circumstances.

Anyone who aspires to write a music survey, especially one covering the entire planet, cannot avoid using some labels. On the one hand, we recognize the problems with labels, especially the danger of stereotyping and over-generalized statements. On the other hand, a "phenomenological" perspective allowing no possibility for generalizations—emphasizing as it does the individuality of each experience—has no limitations. We recognize the dangers of labels and generalizations but find some of them unavoidable.

Terms that can cause trouble when studying the musics of the world include *folk*, *traditional*, *classical*, *art*, *popular*, and *neotraditional*. For example, the term *folk* (from the German *volk*) carries with it a set of meanings and attitudes derived from the Romantic movement in literature, which flourished in Europe during the late eighteenth and early nineteenth centuries. During this period German scholars began exploring their own culture's roots in opposition to the dominant "classical" culture imported from France and Italy. Romanticism championed the common people over the elite, and in the early nineteenth century, writers such as the Grimm brothers and the pair Arnim von Achim and Clemens Brentano began collecting stories and song texts from the "peasants," whose wisdom was seen as equal to that of learned scholars. As a result of its origin, then, the term *folk music* carries with it a lot of nineteenth-century European baggage, which can clutter our thinking when it is applied to non-European musics.

Folk, *classical*, and *popular* are the trio of words most commonly used to categorize and distinguish among various types of music. Defining them individually is one issue; taken together they are problematic because they suggest a hierarchical value system in which *classical* is typically considered highest, *folk* of a much lower value, and *popular* at the lowest level. We would much prefer to have value-neutral terms with universally applicable definitions, but this is a difficult, if not impossible, goal within any single language. When we use terms such as *folk*, *classical*, and *popular* in this text, we mean to represent points on a continuum rather than distinct categories. We do not intend any hierarchical association, rather the terms are used merely as descriptors.

The term *classical* has several meanings and thus carries with it the potential for confusion. It may suggest connection with or influence from the styles of ancient Greece and Rome, though this usage is rarely associated with music. It also denotes a revered model or the epitome of a style or type. Thus we describe a 1956 Thunderbird as a "classic" car or certain films as "classics." In a sense many of the so-called classical musics of the world, be they European, Arabic, or Asian, conform to this second definition. A third definition, however, suggests value: it identifies *classical* as the highest form, that is, the best. Such a usage, particularly with reference to European "classical music," implies a problematic belief in a canon of "great works" created by a pantheon of "great composers"—a belief that has led to charges of cultural domination by "dead, white, European males." Finally, for commercial purposes and in the minds of many non-musicians, the word *classical* is used to refer to anything orchestral, even soundtracks and Broadway shows.

WORLD MUSIC: A GLOBAL JOURNEY

American Drum and Bugle Corps. Is it folk, popular, or classical?

Perhaps the words *folk*, *classical*, and *popular* would be more useful if defined in economic terms. *Classical,* in that case, would denote music created in contexts where there is enough surplus wealth to release musicians from the necessity of providing their own food and shelter, so that they may spend their lives practicing their art and thinking up increasingly complex and technically challenging ways of creating and performing music. Competent performances of classical music produced under these conditions generally require specialized training and years of practice. *Folk* might denote music created and performed by people of modest means whose main occupation leaves limited time for practice and whose limited income leaves little money for expensive instruments. Such music is usually simpler in process and technically less demanding because its practitioners cannot devote the time and energy to it that classical musicians devote to their type of music. As such, folk music usually requires less rehearsal to be performed proficiently and is usually learned through observation, recordings, and informal instruction.

Finally, put these words—these labels—to the test. Take as an example Drum and Bugle Corps, an offshoot of military brass bands originally created in the United States but now found world wide. Does "drum corps" exemplify folk, popular, or classical? The musicians are non-professionals and originally locally based but they perform as a large, complex ensemble after highly disciplined rehearsals playing carefully planned compositional routines. Stylistically their music is more likely to be popular in nature, though some corps play music from the Western classical tradition too. Can you realistically classify such groups under a single label?

BEFORE THE TRIP BEGINS: FUNDAMENTAL ISSUES

Gerhard Kubik

AN INSIDE LOOK

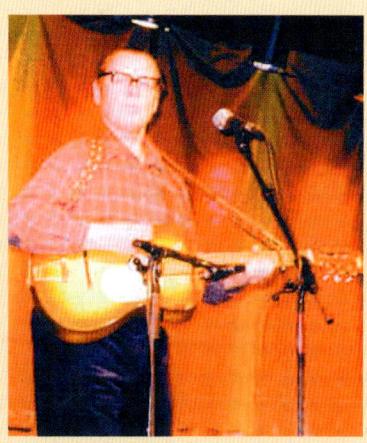

Gerhard Kubik

I became a scientist at age nine. My first exercise in data gathering was the documentation of the allied air raids on Vienna in World War II. I began to write my war diary when I was exactly eight and three-quarters years old, on August 13, 1943, under the impression of the devastating air raid on Wiener Neustadt, a small town south of Vienna. I completed my little book on April 15, 1945, just after the Russian Army had occupied the city. In 1947, when I was thirteen, I took the next step: I wrote a novel called *Im Schloss* (In the Castle) exploring my adventures with a youth gang. A year later I embarked on writing my second novel, with its plot set in China. Those original manuscripts are preserved. Music did not yet play a significant role in my life. But when it began to do so, it was jazz.

By 1948 I was addicted to Lionel Hampton, Woody Herman's "Four Brothers," Cab Calloway, Glenn Miller, and then, in 1952, I fell in love with Charlie Parker, Dizzy Gillespie, Stan Getz, Gerry Mulligan, "Bop" and "Cool." Around 1951 I began to take lessons on the clarinet. Intellectually, I was attracted to Sigmund Freud, Ludwig Klages, the poetry of Arthur Rimbaud (in French) and, somewhat later, Stefan Zweig, Arthur Schopenhauer, and George Orwell. After completing high school in 1953, I became a professional jazz musician. My band won the First Prize at the 1959 Jazz Festival in Vienna. But then it dissolved and I set out on my first long trip to Africa, walking and hitchhiking from Europe.

It took one year from October 1959 to October 1960, and I passed through twelve African countries. Studying the court music in the Kingdom of Buganda, East Africa, I made some discoveries in the field of audiopsychology; for example, the perceptual phenomenon I termed "inherent patterns" or I.P. effect. That is how I became known in the field of ethnomusicology. After many other long field trips, I completed university studies in 1971 with a Ph.D. in Cultural Anthropology (Ethnology). My dissertation was on the Mukanda boys' initiation schools I had studied in eastern Angola in 1965. In 1972 I was back to jazz, playing *kwela*, a South African jazz derivative in the band of Daniel and Donald Kachamoa of Malawi. During the 1970s we toured no less than thirty-three countries of the world with our music: in Africa, Europe, and South America.

My first visit to the United States was in 1977, thanks to an invitation by blues researcher David Evans to speak on his panel at the Musicology Congress in Berkeley, California. Ever since the 1960s I have spent about half a year's time on fieldwork in Africa or elsewhere, and the other half in Europe, writing up my notes and teaching. I have written many books on anthropological, ethnomusicological, and ethnopsychological topics, and published extensively in scholarly magazines. My recent works include *Africa and the Blues* (University of Mississippi Press, 1999) and *Theory of African Music* in two volumes (University of Chicago Press, 2010). You might also like to study my video, *African Guitar* (Stefan Grossman's Guitar Workshop, NJ, 1995).

WORLD MUSIC: A GLOBAL JOURNEY

Gypsy musicians entertain diners at an outdoor restaurant in Bugac, Hungary, a village near Kecskemet on the Great Plain (*Puszta*). From left to right: violin, *cimbalom* hammered dulcimer, string bass, viola

Popular, a term that also means many things to different people, would, in economic terms, denote music that is widely disseminated by various types of media and supported by a broad base of relatively casual consumers, whose purchases make possible productions that may reach spectacular proportions. Popular music, therefore, needs to appeal to a broad spectrum of the population to achieve financial success. Critics of popular music may see it as merely reflecting current fashions in music, but we should remember that popular music, like all music, has the potential to be politically challenging when the sentiments expressed oppose the status quo, or unifying when the words express widely held feelings.

Our discussion has to this point avoided the term *traditional*. Music that is spoken of as "traditional" is often contrasted with the individually innovative music of European classicism. It is also frequently contrasted with popular music or modernized music and is therefore considered synonymous with "folk." Traditional music is assumed to change little over time and to thereby preserve values long held by the community. Although the implication is that a special characteristic of "traditional" music is its emphasis on continuity over innovation, a great deal of music otherwise labeled as "classical" or "popular" is equally conservative or continuous in style. However, while we admit there are numerous problems with the term *traditional*, we doubt that any text on world musics can avoid its use entirely. At the very least, it can be said to be a more descriptive and less value-laden term than *folk*.

ETHNO-MUSICOLOGY The scholarly study of any music within its contemporary cultural context.

Knowing the World's Musics

What can we know about the world's musics and how do we obtain this knowledge? These are basic questions in the field of **ethnomusicology**, but there is rarely a single answer to any question. If music is a part of the culture that produces it, and both the makers and the listeners of the music share similar lifetimes of experience that give the music meaning, then how can we as outsiders experience this music?

Obviously, upon first encounter with new sounds, our own personal life experience is all we have to draw on, and the ethnocentrism we referred to earlier may intrude. The sound quality of a singer may sound unpleasantly nasal compared to vocalists trained in a Western conservatory, while the performance of a Western orchestral symphony may sound bombastic and hideous to a rural farmer from Mongolia. One of the assumptions of those who study the musics of the world is that, with additional knowledge, we can gradually overcome our ethnocentrism and accept each music on its own terms. This is each individual student's challenge.

While several fields of scholarship have included music as part of their purview, such as anthropology, sociology, and **folklore**, the main field devoted to world musics is *ethnomusicology*. In its earlier days, at the end of the nineteenth century, the field was called **comparative musicology**, or in German, *Vergleichende Musikwissenschaft*. At the time, many European colonial powers sent researchers to their growing empires to gather materials for what became the great ethnographic museums of Europe. Early ethnomusicologists worked in these museums and in archives, using as their primary source materials, recordings and other artifacts brought back from the "field" by collectors. Sometimes, however, scholars were able to work directly with foreign musicians on tour, such as when Germans Carl Stumpf and Erich Moritz von Hornbostel recorded Siamese (Thai) musicians in Berlin in 1900 for the Phonogrammarchiv, the first international archive of recordings.

Early ethnomusicologists focused on description and classification, using the rapidly accumulating materials found in European museums. Germans Curt Sachs and the aforementioned E. M. von Hornbostel, for example, drew from earlier models to evolve a comprehensive system for classifying musical instruments based on *what* vibrates to make musical sound. (This system is discussed in Chapter 2.) Scholars throughout Europe transcribed recorded music into notation and attempted classifications based on genre, scale, and other observable characteristics. This was the era of the "armchair" scholar who practiced the "science" *(Wissenschaft)* of music.

Over time, scholars began doing their own **fieldwork**, during which they recorded music in the field on cylinder, disc, wire, and later magnetic acetate tape. Many of these scholars thought of themselves as ethnographers or anthropologists. Among the greatest of these was an American woman, Frances Densmore (1867–1957), who, working directly with Native American singers and instrumentalists, wrote fifteen books and numerous articles, and released seven commercial recordings, mostly through the Smithsonian Institution in Washington, DC.

American ethnomusicology began changing dramatically in the 1960s, especially because of five men and the academic programs they influenced. Alan Merriam (1923–1980)—of Indiana University's Department of Anthropology—published in 1964 *The Anthropology of Music*, one of the most influential books ever written on the subject, in which he defined ethnomusicology as "the study of music in culture." Unlike the older school of Europeans who viewed music as sounds to be analyzed apart from their cultural context, Merriam saw music as a human behavior. Similarly, British anthropologist John Blacking (1928–1990) has defined music as "humanly organized sound."

Ki Mantle Hood (1918–2005), originally a composer, provided a musicological alternative at the University of California, Los Angeles's Institute of Ethnomusicology, by

FOLKLORE
The study of orally transmitted folk knowledge and culture.

COMPARATIVE MUSICOLOGY
An early term for the field that became ethnomusicology, when research emphasized comparisons of folk and non-Western music with Western practices.

FIELDWORK
The first-hand study of music in its original context, a technique derived from anthropology.

Frances Densmore recording a Piegan Indian c.1916 (Library of Congress)

emphasizing what he called *bi-musicality*. In this approach researchers combine learning to play the music under study with field observation. David Park McAllester (1916–2006) and others at Wesleyan University in Middletown, Connecticut, created a program in "world musics" that emphasized performance and composition taught by masters of musical traditions from around the world, especially India, Africa, and Indonesia. Finally, Bruno Nettl (b. 1930), a specialist in both Native American and Persian musics, has influenced the course of ethnomusicology over the last fifty years, both through his teaching at the University of Illinois and his numerous publications, and continues to help guide the field through a period of increasing diversification. For many, Nettl's work represents both common sense and the mainstream of the profession.

Thus, ethnomusicology has long been pulled in two directions: the anthropological and the musicological, the first centering on the study of human behavior and cultural context, the second emphasizing the sonic artifacts of human music-making. Regardless of orientation, however, most ethnomusicology programs are found in college and university departments of music. Typical programs include courses for non-majors, especially world music surveys, and more specialized courses on both broad and specific areas of the world as well as courses in research methodology. Many schools offer opportunities to play in world music performance ensembles.

Ethnomusicology today, however, has been much influenced by new ways of thinking generally subsumed under the heading *postmodernism*. A reaction against *modernism* or *positivism*, in which the establishment of "truth" is based on verifiable "facts," postmodernism de-emphasizes description and the search for absolute truth in favor of interpretation and the acceptance of the relativity of truth. A great variety of intellectual approaches, mostly borrowed from other disciplines, offer ethnomusicologists new ways to interpret the meaning of music. These include gender studies and feminist theories; Marxist interpretations; semiotic approaches; cognitive studies; performance studies; attention to such issues as identity, post-colonialism, and the political ramifications of music; and, especially, popular music studies. The latter has risen rapidly since about 1980 under the influence of the "Manchester School" in England, and is associated with the term *cultural studies*, which denotes several postmodern theoretical approaches used to interpret popular culture. The study of popular music, however, has recently led to an apparent decrease of interest in fieldwork among ethnomusicologists and a parallel de-emphasis of the techniques appropriate to the study of "traditional" music, because popular musics are more easily studied through the media than are traditional musics.

BEFORE THE TRIP BEGINS: FUNDAMENTAL ISSUES

The Life of an Ethnomusicologist

What do ethnomusicologists actually do? How do they learn about the world's musics? We view the process as having **four basic phases**: (1) preparation; (2) fieldwork; (3) analysis; and (4) dissemination. Before going to the field, whether it be a faraway nation in Central Asia, a region of Indonesia, or a nearby town in their own country, ethnomusicologists must *prepare* themselves by learning as much as they can about the area, the kinds of music they will encounter, and the conditions under which they will do their study. This is best accomplished through the use of library, media, and Internet resources and through interaction with others who know the area, especially people who grew up there or perhaps still live there. In many cases researchers must spend years studying the language of their area, which often is one that is rarely taught. Well-prepared field researchers will need not only a good deal of expensive recording equipment but also the wits and maturity to deal with all sorts of unexpected situations, both technical and social.

> PHASES OF ETHNO-MUSICOLOGICAL RESEARCH
> (1) preparation
> (2) fieldwork
> (3) analysis
> (4) dissemination

Besides doing research in the field, ethnomusicologists must also live and eat, and these necessities may present great challenges when unfamiliar food is on the menu or living conditions are radically different. In the course of their research, scholars may seek to acquire first-hand experience through participation in various rituals, festivals, and other events, and may need to create professional documents through still photography, videography, audio recording, and interviews. A detailed journal is important, not to mention the logs that retain the details of recordings and photographs. The *fieldwork phase* can last anywhere from a few days to several years. Based on our experience, we can say that the longer one stays in the field, the more one will know but the less one will understand. This apparent irony stems from the increasing perception of complexity that accompanies prolonged exposure to any culture: the more you experience it, the more you realize how much more there is to learn. First-hand experience teaches us that all cultures are deep and complex and that understanding a music is far more demanding than simply collecting it.

What do ethnomusicologists do with the material and knowledge they acquire? It is a standing joke among ethnomusicologists that we spend thousands of dollars and months of our lives, braving tough weather and unfamiliar foods, to bring back a few videos that we look at only once. The material collected in the field is considered "raw." After it is collected, ethnomusicologists must find ways to *analyze*, *interpret*, and *disseminate* what they have collected. This is done primarily through teaching, writing and reading "papers" at professional meetings, writing chapters, journal articles, and books and, perhaps, compiling CDs or DVDs for commercial release. As researchers acquire expertise in an area, they may be called upon to referee articles submitted to journals, write reviews of books and CDs, or serve on state- or national-level panels that award grants to individuals and arts organ-

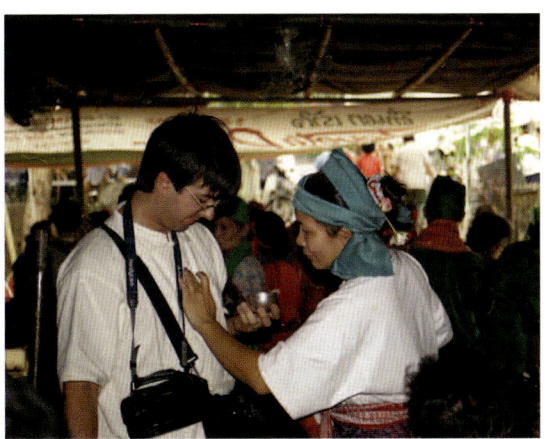

Co-author (AS) blessed by a spirit dancer in northern Thailand (Christina Shahriari)

izations. Most ethnomusicologists work as professors in colleges and universities, though some hold positions in publicly funded agencies such as the National Endowment for the Arts, while others work for museums, community programs, and art centers. A few work as freelance scholars and musicians. Few can afford to be just ethnomusicologists—that is, researchers—full time. Most must spend the majority of their time doing other kinds of work.

Representation: What Musics Does One Study?

A survey course on the musics of the world poses a challenge far different from that presented by a course covering the classical musics of Europe. In the latter case there is a rough consensus on who the "great composers" are and what the "great works" are. These make up what is called a *canon*—that is, a foundational list of core composers and works that every music student is expected to know. World music courses have no such canon, and certainly no list of great composers. The world is too large and there are too many choices for much consensus to form. Therefore, one must consider not only how to organize such a course but what to include. What should every world music student know? If the organization is geographical, what genres and particular examples should "represent" a country or culture? Our choices reveal our biases and assumptions about what constitutes the music of a given place. Some might choose to emphasize contemporary culture by including a greater proportion of urban-based popular musics than "traditional" ones. Others would argue that the essence of a culture is in its traditional music. There is no way to resolve these questions except by agreeing that any world music course is only the beginning, the first few steps of a learning journey that can last a lifetime. In a way, it does not matter *how* one begins as much as it matters that one *actually* begins.

Resources for the Study of the World's Musics

Today's students are fortunate to live in a time when resources for the study of world musics are growing exponentially. The proliferation of publications, both print and recorded, has been astounding. We suggest the following as likely the most comprehensive and readily available resources for further study.

Reference Works

Two major reference works that introduce world music include the ten-volume *Garland Encyclopedia of World Music* and *The New Grove Dictionary of Music and Musicians*. The "Garland," as ethnomusicologists label the former, includes nine volumes which cover geographically defined areas of the world, with the tenth volume being a compilation of resources. Each volume is between 1,000 and 1,500 pages and includes both general and specific articles, hundreds of photos and musical examples, a CD, and an extensive list of bibliographic and recorded resources. *The New Grove Dictionary of Music and Musicians*, second edition, in twenty-nine volumes offers extensive coverage of the world's musics, primarily through articles on specific countries. While the series emphasizes Western art music, there are numerous entries devoted to world music. The "Grove" is also available in an online form, but this will likely have to be accessed at a subscribing library. Also worth consulting is the two-volume edition of *World Music: The Rough Guide*, now in its third edition, which includes articles on musics throughout the world, often with emphasis on popular styles.

Video

The variety of world musics on video is growing rapidly. Two collections deserve special mention. First is the *JVC Anthology of the World's Music and Dance*, a series of video clips with accompanying booklets. One drawback of this collection is that it was compiled in large part from pre-existing footage, and as a result in some areas the coverage is uneven or unrepresentative. Also worth mentioning is the *Beats of the Heart* documentary series, produced by Jeremy Marre for the world music label Shanachie, which includes narrated documentaries on such varied topics as Indian *filmi* songs, Jamaican *reggae*, and music in Thailand. The Internet is now also a valuable and easily accessed place for video of an unimaginable array of world musics. While the footage found on sites such as YouTube is generally of amateur quality, it allows free access to a vast arena of world music and culture that was barely imaginable even just a decade ago.

Audio Recordings

A great variety of companies in the United States, Europe, and Japan produce commercial world music CDs that are available internationally. Unfortunately, the majority of them are produced by non-specialists, and therefore the information provided in liner notes must be approached with caution. What is perhaps the most significant series of recordings was originally released on Moses Asch's Folkways label, and is now being reissued on CD in expanded form by Smithsonian-Folkways in Washington, DC, along with new releases. Other important series have been produced by Lyrichord, Nonesuch, World Music Library, Pan, Rounder, Multicultural Media, and many other record companies around the globe. A vast amount of world music can be found online today as well. Music access applications, such as iTunes, are increasingly popular around the world and provide an ever-increasing stream of music access to our global soundscape.

Journals

Most journals are produced by scholarly societies, and therefore the articles in them tend to be specialized, and at times obscure. Serious students, however, can gain much from such material. The most significant journals to consider include *Ethnomusicology*, *Yearbook for Traditional Music*, *American Music*, *Asian Music*, *Journal of African Music*, *Ethnomusicology Forum*, *The World of Music*, *The Journal of Popular Culture*, and a variety of other journals dedicated to specific areas of the world, such as *Chime* (focused on China).

Questions to Consider

1. What do ethnomusicologists mean when they say, "Music is universal, but it is not a universal language"?
2. What are the potential problems in classifying music as "classical," "folk," or "popular"?
3. How might an ethnomusicologist approach the study of Western classical music differently from a musicologist?
4. What is "fieldwork"? What is its importance to the study of world music?
5. In what ways does world music study require an interdisciplinary approach?
6. What is ethnocentrism? Have you ever experienced it?

On Your Own Time

Visit the textbook website to find these resources for further exploration on your own.

Book: Kubik, Gerhard. *Theory of African Music, Vols. 1 & 2*. Chicago: The University of Chicago Press, 2010.
http://www.press.uchicago.edu/ucp/books/book/chicago/T/bo8648201.html

Book: Kubik, Gerhard. *Africa and the Blues*. Jackson, MS: University Press of Mississippi, 1999.
http://www.upress.state.ms.us/books/11

Book: Merriam, Alan. *The Anthropology of Music*. Evanston, IL: Northwestern University Press, 1964.
http://www.nupress.northwestern.edu/Title/tabid/68/ISBN/0-8101-0607-8/Default.aspx

Book: Blacking, John. *How Musical Is Man?* Seattle: University of Washington Press, 1973.
http://www.washington.edu/uwpress/search/books/BLAHOC.html

Book: Nettl, Bruno. *The Study of Ethnomusicology: Thirty-one Issues and Concepts*. Urbana, IL: University of Illinois Press, 2005.
http://www.press.uillinois.edu/books/catalog/56txy8mr9780252030338.html

Website: The Herb Alpert School of Music, Department of Ethnomusicology at UCLA (University of California, Los Angeles)
http://www.ethnomusic.ucla.edu/

Website: Ethnomusicology Institute, Department of Folklore and Ethnomusicology at Indiana University
http://www.indiana.edu/~folklore/ethno.shtml

Website: School of Oriental and African Studies at the University of London
http://www.soas.ac.uk/

Website: Guide to Programs, Society for Ethnomusicology
http://webdb.iu.edu/sem/scripts/guidetoprograms/guidelist.cfm

Website: International Council for Traditional Music
http://www.ictmusic.org/

Website: Musical Instrument Museum (Phoenix, Arizona, USA)
http://www.themim.org/

Website: National Music Museum at the University of South Dakota (Vermillion, South Dakota USA)
http://orgs.usd.edu/nmm/index.html

Website: Grove Music Online
http://www.oxfordmusiconline.com/public/book/omo_gmo

Website: *Garland Encyclopedia of World Music*
http://glnd.alexanderstreet.com/
http://www.routledge.com/books/search/keywords/garland_encyclopedia_of_world_music/page_1/published/

Video: JVC/Smithsonian Folkways Video Anthology of World Music
http://lyrichord.com/jvcvideoanthologyofworldmusicanddance.aspx

Journal: The Society for Ethnomusicology
http://webdb.iu.edu/sem/scripts/publications/journal/journal.cfm

Journal: Journal of the Society for Asian Music
http://asianmusic.skidmore.edu/

Journal: Journal of African Music and Popular Culture
http://www.uni-hildesheim.de/ntama/

Aural Analysis: Listening to the World's Musics

2

How to Listen to World Music	17	**Range**	27	Detail of four *khawng mon* (bossed gong circles) from Thailand
"Talking" about Music	18	**Melody**	28	
Timbre and Medium	18	*Melodic Contour*	28	
Vocal Timbre	19	*Ornamentation*	28	
Instrumental Timbre	19	*Text Setting*	29	
Aerophones: Flutes, Reeds, and Trumpets	19	**Rhythm**	29	
		Beat and Tempo	29	
Chordophones: Lutes and Zithers	21	Accent and Meter	29	
		Rhythmic Density	30	
Idiophones: Plucked, Struck, and Shaken	22	**Phonic Structure**	30	
Membranophones	24	**Dynamics**	31	
Summary	25	**Form**	32	
Pitch	25	*An Inside Look: Bruno Nettl*	32	
Tuning System	25	*Need to Know: Fundamentals of Music*	33	
Scale	27	*Questions to Consider*	33	
Interval	27	*On Your Own Time*	34	

AURAL ANALYSIS: LISTENING TO THE WORLD'S MUSIC

How to Listen to World Music

The primary objective of this book is to expose you, the reader, to a generous variety of musical traditions from cultures around the globe. Learning something about the music of other people is like gaining a window into their world and is a chance to explore the creative power of humanity. The ability to recognize various musical traditions and express some knowledge about them is a good start toward crossing the cultural boundaries that often divide us. This book is not only about world music; it is about people, cultures, geography, and history as well. Some music traditions are easy to recognize, whereas others require you to develop a systematic method for identifying what you hear. Each person's method will undoubtedly be different, but here are some initial suggestions on how to listen to unfamiliar world music.

Begin by listening to the music examples included with this text before reading any of the material. Remember your initial gut feeling. Often your first impression of a musical sound helps you remember that sound in the future. Does the music sound familiar or completely alien? Do you like it, or does it make you want to skip to the next track? Does the music seem busy, cold, happy, relaxing, heavy? Does it sound like rain, whale calls, a screeching owl, a music box? Any image you can use later to help you recognize the music could be helpful.

Make the music samples part of your daily life, even if you don't like every example. Many new musical sounds require you to develop a taste for them before they can be appreciated. Listen in your car, before you go to bed, or while exercising, walking the dog, cooking, and so on.

Use the book to help you better understand the form and intent of each example. It is necessary to read each chapter to connect what you hear with what you know. If you don't know anything about the type of music you're listening to, what you hear won't mean much. You may enjoy the music, but you can't fully appreciate it unless you understand what is happening and why.

You will know you are "familiar" with a particular musical example when you can recognize it after just a few seconds of listening, and answer "yes" to the following questions:

- Do you know which country the example comes from?
- Can you visualize the instruments, imitate the sound of the music, and anticipate changes in rhythm?
- Are you knowledgeable of the example's cultural associations? Immediately knowing in what contexts the music is performed, or with which religion it is associated, are also indicators that you are becoming familiar with the tradition it represents.

Don't limit yourself to the musical examples provided with this text. Find other recordings of the same types of music and compare them with the given ones. Identify the commonalities in musical sound so that you're able to recognize the tradition, not just the specific recordings from the book.

Remember, music is universal, but it is not a universal language. Understanding world music requires an open mind and a willingness to acknowledge that other perspectives, ideas, and attitudes are equally as valid as your own. Our world is "smaller" than it has ever been in history. You will likely have opportunities to meet people from many of the places discussed in this book. Knowing something about their music can help you communicate with them and may lead to cultural experiences you would never have anticipated. So, listen with both your mind and your emotions, as well as your ears.

"Talking" about Music

Every discipline, be it physics, economics, or art, has its own jargon, a vocabulary that must be learned. Music is no exception. Because music is conceptual, its components require names in order for discussion to occur. Music terms such as *melody* and *rhythm* are familiar to most readers, musician and non-musician alike. Other terms, such as *heterophony*, *idiophone*, or *rhythmic density* usually require some explanation. This chapter seeks to put all readers on an equal footing by explaining basic music concepts, as well as introducing certain terms peculiar to the discipline of ethnomusicology.

A musical sound has four basic components: timbre, pitch, rhythm and dynamics. **Timbre**, or the quality of a musical sound, is inherently linked to a medium—that is, to the object or person producing the sound. **Pitch** is synonymously referred to in musical terms as *tone*. It is most often expressed with a letter name equating to a frequency; for example, the standard Western concert pitch of A = 440 Hertz (Hz). **Rhythm** depends on durations of sounds, which are often organized into regular patterns. Finally, **dynamics** denotes the volume, or relative loudness or softness, of a sound, and can be measured in decibels (dBs).

Timbre and Medium

The easiest way to learn to recognize a world music tradition is to become familiar with its media—that is, the sounds of its typical instruments and vocal qualities. In order to identify a specific medium, we must first become familiar with its characteristic timbre or "color." Most terms used to describe timbre are based on analogies between musical sound and everyday physical and sensory experience. Terms such as *nasal*, *dark*, *mellow*, *strained*, *rough*, *soothing*, *grating*, and so on, are highly subjective when applied to music but are nevertheless helpful in describing "aural color."

Just as we distinguish visually among red, blue, and green, so too we distinguish between aural "colors"—that is, among the characteristic qualities that define the sounds of, say, the trumpet, the violin, or the flute. (Compare Tibetan Buddhist Ritual—CD 2.5; Cape Breton fiddling—CD 3.17; Native American flute—CD 3.28.) In the case of "visual color," determining the differences among red, yellow, and green is fairly easy. In order to differentiate among evergreen, lime, and emerald, however, one must possess a sharper and more experienced eye. Similarly, while it may be easy to hear the difference between a violin and a trumpet, learning to distinguish the similar sounds of a banjo, koto, and sitar from one another may take some time even for an attentive listener. (Compare Hindustani *Raga* (*sarod/tambura*)—CD 1.5; *Gu qin*—CD 1.16; Jali with *kora*—CD 3.1.) Fortunately, in addition to timbre there are other elements that can help you identify what you are hearing, such as pitch, rhythm, dynamics, style, and various extra-musical factors.

When listening to an example of an unfamiliar music tradition for the first time, you must determine whether you hear voices, instruments, or a combination. (Compare Steel

---

TIMBRE
The tone quality or color of a musical sound.

PITCH
A tone's specific frequency level, measured in Hertz (Hz).

RHYTHM
The lengths, or durations, of sounds as patterns in time.

DYNAMICS
The volume of a musical sound.

AURAL ANALYSIS: LISTENING TO THE WORLD'S MUSIC

band—CD 3.7; Lined Hymn—CD 3.19; Gospel Choir—CD 3.23.) The next step is to identify how many voices or instruments you hear. Either you hear a soloist or a group, also called an *ensemble*. (Compare *Gu qin*—CD 1.16; Jiangnan *sizhu*—CD 1.17.)

If what you hear is an ensemble, determine whether it is a small group, such as an instrumental trio or vocal duet, or a large ensemble, such as an orchestra or choir. (Compare *Mbira dza vadzimu*—CD 2.23; Polyrhythmic ensemble—CD 2.19.) The larger the ensemble, the more difficult it will be to distinguish specific media. However, this very difficulty may help you hear the ensemble as a whole rather than as individual performers leading you to a recognition of the tradition. In the instances where the ensemble is small enough that you can determine roughly how many performers there are, the next step is to try to identify each medium (instruments and/or voices) specifically.

Vocal Timbre

In the case of voices, you should be able to distinguish between male and female voices fairly easily, primarily based on their ranges. (Compare Bulgarian Women's Choir—CD 2.18; Amazonian Indian chant—CD 3.11.) While range is a concept related to pitch, voices can also have timbral qualities that will help you identify what you hear. Certain traditions—such as bluegrass and European opera—feature vocal timbres so distinctive that you can easily distinguish them.

Instrumental Timbre

In the case of instruments, timbre is closely related to instrument construction. The study of musical instruments is known as **organology**. Essential to organological study is the classification of instruments. In the European art music tradition, instruments are typically indentified using five basic categories: strings, winds, brass, percussion, and keyboards. This system, however, does not work well when applied to the rest of the world's musical instruments.

In the field of ethnomusicology, the **Sachs–Hornbostel system**, created by German musicologists Curt Sachs and Eric M. von Hornbostel early in the twentieth century, is the predominant system used to describe and classify instruments. The four primary categories are *aerophones*, *chordophones*, *idiophones*, and *membranophones*; *electrophones* have become a fifth category. An instrument is classified according to what part of it vibrates to produce the sound. Each of these primary categories has several subcategories. Knowledge of only the more common subcategories is usually enough to help you perceive the timbre of a musical instrument and identify it. The more specifically you can subcategorize an instrument's construction, however, the more accurately you will understand how the construction affects the unique timbre of the instrument.

Aerophones: Flutes, Reeds, and Trumpets

Aerophones are defined as instruments producing sound through the direct vibration of air, rather than through the vibration of air by another medium, such as a string or membrane. Aerophones are typically subdivided into three categories: *flutes*, *reeds*, and *trumpets*. Flutes

ORGANOLOGY
The study of musical instruments.

SACHS–HORNBOSTEL SYSTEM
Standard classication system for musical instruments created by Curt Sachs and Erik M. von Hornbostel.

AEROPHONE
Instruments that require air to produce sound—namely, flutes, reeds, trumpets, and bellows-driven instruments.

WORLD MUSIC: A GLOBAL JOURNEY

(top left)
A Japanese *noh kan* horizontal flute

(top right)
Double-reed aerophone (*pi*) from Thailand

are defined as instruments in which a column of air is set in vibration when the air is split on an edge. (Listen to Native American flute—CD 3.28.) Reed instruments have one or more small pieces of material, such as cane, bamboo, or metal, that vibrate(s) when air is blown over or through them and into a tube. (Listen to *Uilleann* bagpipes—CD 2.16.) Trumpets require the performer to vibrate the lips rather than a reed, as they blow air into the instrument. (Listen to Australian Aborigine song with *didjeridu*—CD 1.1.) Recognition of the characteristic timbres of flutes, reeds, and trumpets is an important first step toward becoming a discriminating listener. Keep in mind, however, that these terms refer to general categories, not specific instruments such as the European ("silver") flute or brass trumpet.

The *ntahera* ivory horn ensemble of the Asantehene, Kumase, Ghana (Joseph S. Kaminski)

Chordophones: Lutes and Zithers

Chordophones are defined as having one or more strings stretched between two points. Sound is produced when a string vibrates. There are many chordophones in the world of music, but two basic types, *lutes* and *zithers*, comprise the majority. The shape of the instrument is the key feature that distinguishes a lute from a zither. The strings of a zither are stretched parallel to the entire sounding board, as with a piano. Thus nearly the whole instrument acts as a resonator. (Listen to *Dastgah* for santur and voice—CD 2.8.) In addition to a resonating body, a lute has a neck, which allows a performer to vary the acoustical length of a string to produce different pitches, as with a guitar. Because its neck does not act as a resonator, a lute generally has less resonance than a zither of the same size, and its sound dissipates more quickly. (Listen to Country Blues—CD 3.24.)

The most common zithers are either hammered, as with the piano, or plucked, as with the Japanese *koto*, while lutes are generally either plucked, as with a guitar, or bowed, as with a violin. A hammered zither tends to have a more reverberant sound timbre than other types of chordophones. The resonance of a plucked lute will die away almost immediately as the vibration amplification of each note diminishes. (Listen to Arabic Taqasim (*buzuq* and *ud*)—CD 2.7.) The sounds of a plucked lute or zither are further distinguishable by whether a plectrum or a finger plucks the string. The string vibration of a bowed lute is continuous for as long as the bow hairs are pulled across the string; thus, the sound does not immediately fade until the bowing stops. (Listen to Cape Breton fiddling—CD 3.17.) In addition to being plucked or bowed, lutes are either *fretted* or *fretless*. A **fret** is a straight bar of wood, bamboo, or metal placed on the neck of a lute perpendicular to the direction of the strings, as seen on a guitar. This enables an exact pitch to be played each time the performer presses the string against the fret. A fretless lute allows the performer to slide the finger between pitches, potentially sounding all of the frequencies between two distinct tones.

CHORDOPHONE
Four types of stringed instruments: lutes, zithers, harps, lyres.

FRET
A bar or ridge found on chordophones that enables performers to produce different melodic pitches with consistent frequency levels.

(above)
The Turkish *tanbur* lute

(left)
The Finnish *kantele* zither

(Left to right) Fretless lute (*sarod*) and fretted lute (*sitar*) from India

West African spike harp (*bolon*) with strings attached to a string holder

Ethiopian lyre

IDIOPHONE Instruments that themselves vibrate to produce sound, such as rattles, bells, and various other kinds of percussion.

(Listen to Hindustani *Raga* (*sarod*)—CD 1.5.) Fretted lutes are more likely to be plucked than fretless lutes, which are more frequently bowed. This is due to the fact that plucked lutes sound tones of short duration, while bowed lutes can sustain longer tones.

Based on their construction, other major chordophones fall into the *lyre* and *harp* categories. The strings of lyres and harps are suspended by an open frame and are most often plucked. The string plane of a harp, in particular, runs perpendicular to the resonating body, rather than parallel to it as with lutes and zithers. The timbre of lyres and harps is generally difficult to distinguish from that of lutes and zithers, though visually the construction is quite distinct.

Idiophones: Plucked, Struck, and Shaken

Idiophones are defined as instruments that produce sound through the instrument itself vibrating (*idio* meaning "itself"). A strong sound can be easily produced on most idiophones. Practically anything can be considered an idiophone, from bottles to slamming doors, to change in your pocket. Bells, rattles, and a variety of other percussion instruments are common idiophones in a musical context. Most idiophones fall into one of three categories: *plucked, struck,* or *shaken.*

Small, plucked idiophones are often a type of *lamellophone,* meaning that they have a *lamella* (tongue or prong) that is flexed, and then released, causing a brief sound before the vibration of the *lamella* ceases. (Listen to *Mbira dza vadzimu*—CD 2.23.) A music box, with its comb-like metal prongs, is probably the most familiar example of a lamellophone, but

AURAL ANALYSIS: LISTENING TO THE WORLD'S MUSIC

Gourd rattle (*shekere*) from sub-Saharan Africa

Three lamellophones from sub-Saharan Africa

the next most commonly encountered is the single, plucked lamella amplified by the mouth cavity, used for surrogate speech as much as for melody. Such instruments are known by many terms, such as "mouth harp," "jaw harp," and "jews harp," the latter term probably a corruption of the French term *jeu* meaning "to play." (Note also that this type of lamellophone is not a harp, that is, chordophone, despite the colloquial references.)

Struck idiophones comprise the most varied category and include gongs, bells, wood blocks, and just about anything else that can be struck. (Listen to Vietnamese bronze gong ensemble—CD 1.9.) The great many timbres associated with such instruments are not easily generalized, though the sharp initial attack of the sound is a typical feature. Shaken idiophones are most often rattles. (Listen to *Mbira dza vadzimu* (*hosho* rattle)—CD 2.23.) Most rattles have a hollowed center filled with small objects, such as pebbles, seeds, or sand. When the instrument is shaken, the particles bounce against the outer shell of the instrument causing it to vibrate. Other rattles are constructed so that the small particles are loosely fixed to the outside of the object, such as with a netted gourd rattle (e.g., *shekere*).

Membranophones

MEMBRANOPHONE
Instruments, typically drums, that use a vibrating stretched membrane as the principal means of sound production.

Membranophones are defined as having a vibrating membrane, traditionally animal skin but often synthetic today, that is stretched over a frame. This category encompasses most drums found in the world. The different types of drums are further categorized on the basis of body shape—some, for example, are goblet-shaped, while others are barrel-shaped—and according to whether they are single- or double-headed. Most drums are struck with either the hand or some implement, usually a stick. (Compare Hindustani *Raga* (tabla)—CD 1.5; Ghanaian talking drum—CD 2.20.) There are too many kinds of drums throughout the world

Goblet drums (*djembe*) from sub-Saharan Africa

AURAL ANALYSIS: LISTENING TO THE WORLD'S MUSIC

to make generalizations about timbre; however, smaller drums usually have a higher, tighter sound, while larger membranophones are deeper and earthier in character. Some drums can be tuned to specific pitches. Becoming familiar with the unique sounds of different drums takes time and effort. The essential first step is being able to distinguish between struck membranophones and struck idiophones. Not all membranophones are struck, however; those that are not—such as friction drums and "singing membranes" (e.g. kazoos)—are less common but particularly unique in timbre. (Listen to *Samba* (cuíca)—CD 3.14.)

Summary

Learning to distinguish among aerophones, chordophones, idiophones, and membranophones is the first step in training your ear to listen attentively to world music. Being able to recognize subcategories within these instrument groups greatly enhances your appreciation of sound and helps you identify the music you hear more quickly. You will encounter many similar types of instruments, such as the Japanese *shakuhachi* and the Native American flute, that are hard to distinguish from each other based on timbre alone. Fortunately, other aspects of musical performance such as pitch, rhythm, dynamics, and style can help you identify the tradition you hear. Differences in timbre, however, are most often what distinguish the sound of two instruments, even when all other aspects are identical. Familiarize yourself with the unique "aural colors" of each recorded example supplied with this text before trying to tackle the often more complicated issues associated with musical creation.

Pitch

Every sound can be described as having either a *definite* or *indefinite* **pitch**. A definite pitch is determined by the dominance of a specific frequency level, which is expressed as Hz (Hertz or formerly, cycles per second) For example, the Euro-American "concert pitch," A above middle C, has 440 Hz as its pillar frequency. Definite pitches are necessary to produce melody and harmony. An indefinite pitch consists of a cluster of frequency levels at more or less equal volume—that is, no one level dominates. Indefinite pitches, such as those produced by handclaps or rattles, are most often used in a rhythmic capacity. (Listen to Kiribati group song (vocal—definite pitches; handclaps—indefinite pitches)—CD 1.4.) Some indefinite pitches are continuously variable, such as that of a siren. While indefinite pitches are regularly found in music traditions throughout the world, the varied uses of definite pitch are more often the primary focus of musical activity; therefore, the term *pitch* hereafter refers specifically to definite pitches.

PITCH
A tone's specific frequency level, measured in Hertz (Hz).

Tuning System

The term **tuning system** denotes the entire collection of pitch frequencies commonly used in a given music tradition. Tuning systems are culturally determined. Our ears become accustomed to the tuning system of the music we hear on a regular basis. When we hear an unfamiliar tuning system, some of its pitches may sound "out of tune" because we have been culturally conditioned to accept only certain frequency levels as "correct." Pitches with frequency levels significantly different from those in our familiar tuning system may sound strange.

TUNING SYSTEM
All the pitches common to a musical tradition.

Tuning pegs and micro-tone tuners of Turkish *kanun* zither

The basis for most tuning systems around the world is the *octave*. An octave is produced when the frequency level or Hz of a specific pitch is either doubled or halved. Using 440 Hz (A) as the example, the octave above is 880 Hz and the octave below is 220 Hz. Pitches that are an octave apart (or a series of octaves apart) are considered to be the "same" pitch (i.e., they have the same pitch name) even though they have different frequencies. An easy way to understand this concept is to listen to a man with a "low" voice and a woman with a "high" voice sing the "same" pitch. Our ears sense that the two pitches are equivalent even though the man may sing at a frequency level of 220 Hz while the woman sings at 880 Hz, two octaves higher.

In the most commonly used European tuning system (called "equal-tempered tuning"), the octave is divided into twelve equal parts. In the Thai classical music tradition, however, the same octave is divided into only seven equal parts. (Compare Thai Piphat—CD 1.11; Highland bagpipes—CD 2.15.) Consequently, some of the pitches common to the European tuning system sound different from the pitches common to the Thai tuning system, whose intervals between pitches are wider. The tuning systems common to some traditions (e.g., in the Middle East) may use more than thirty discrete pitches within a single octave. (Listen to Arabic Taqasim—CD 2.7.) After extended exposure to a different tuning system, your ear will become accustomed to its standard frequencies. Even before this, however, the very "oddness" of an unfamiliar tuning system may help you recognize the musical tradition to which it belongs.

AURAL ANALYSIS: LISTENING TO THE WORLD'S MUSIC

Scale

While a tuning system encompasses all of the pitches commonly used in a music tradition, a *scale* consists of a set of pitches (generally expressed in ascending order) used in particular performances. For example, a pentatonic scale (*penta* meaning "five," and *tonic* meaning "tone") uses only five tones from the greater tuning system. (Listen to Jiangnan *sizhu*—CD 1.17.) Different pentatonic scales can be derived from a single tuning system, as long as the number of pitches available within a tuning system is greater than five. Thus, pitches 1, 2, 3, 5, and 6 from a particular tuning system may constitute the pentatonic scale for one composition, while pitches 1, 2, 4, 6, and 7 from that same system may form the pentatonic scale in a different composition. Scales in some music compositions are limited to as few as two or three pitches, while other pieces in the same tradition may use a greater number of pitches.

Interval

An *interval* is perhaps best thought of as the "distance" between two pitches. Intervals are described as either wide or narrow. A wide interval—such as that from A ascending to G (a seventh)—is one with a large difference in frequencies, while a narrow interval—such as that between A and B (a second)—has a relatively small difference. Likewise, the interval between the bottom and top pitches of an octave is wider than the interval distance of any two pitches within the octave. The difference between narrow and wide intervals can be both seen and heard. On a piano, for example, the size of an interval can be understood visually in terms of the distance between a pair of keys and aurally in terms of the frequency levels of the keys sounded, bearing in mind that Hz are expressed proportionally. A given tradition may be partially recognizable just based on its preference for wide or narrow intervals.

Range

Range refers to the span of pitches a given instrument or voice is capable of producing. It is described as being wide or narrow as well as high or low. An instrument with a narrow range is capable of producing fewer pitches than an instrument with a wide range. Instruments with wide ranges, such as the piano, are typically, though not always, physically larger than those with narrower ranges, such as the harmonica. Vocal ranges can vary substantially: trained professionals practice to extend their range, sometimes to more than three octaves, while an average person has a narrower vocal range of roughly two octaves or less.

Ranges are also characterized in terms of where they fall on the spectrum from very low-pitched sounds to very high-pitched sounds. An instrument or voice may have a relatively high or low range in comparison to other musical media. A female, for example, generally has a higher vocal range than a male. Instruments also often have characteristic ranges; for example, a violin uses a high range, while a tuba plays in a low range. (Compare Beijing Opera—CD 1.18; Tibetan Buddhist ritual—CD 2.5.)

Melody

MELODY
An organized succession of pitches forming a musical idea.

A ***melody*** is defined as an organized succession of pitches forming a musical idea. These are the "phrases" and "tunes" that characterize a specific composition, such as "Twinkle, Twinkle Little Star." Because pitches exist in real time—that is, because each has a duration—rhythm also is always a necessary component of melody. If, for example, you play a descending C major scale on any instrument, this is generally not considered a melody. However, if you vary the duration of each pitch, that is, rhythm, to correspond to the tune "Joy to the World," those same pitches in combination with the new durations create a recognizable musical idea, or melody.

Melodic Contour

MELODIC CONTOUR
The general direction and shape of a melody.

A melody can be described in terms of its ***melodic contour***, or shape. "Joy to the World," for example, has a "descending" melodic contour as the pitches descend from high to low (see figure 1). Melodic contours are typically drawn as a graph representing the direction of the melody. It is often useful to graph the contour of a melody to identify regularly occurring features characteristic of a music tradition. For example, our graph of a Native American Plains Indian chant reveals a characteristic "cascading" melodic contour, reflecting the Plains Indian practice of holding certain pitches longer than others in the course of an overall descending melodic line (see figure 2; listen to Plains Indian Dance song—CD 3.27.)

DRONE
A continuous or repeating sound.

Drone pitches (pitches held or played continuously) can be represented as horizontal lines, while chords (several pitches played at once) are typically represented with vertical lines, as in our graph of Irish bagpipe performance (see figure 3; listen to *Uilleann* bagpipes—CD 2.16.)

Figure 1: Descending Melodic Contour

Figure 2: Cascading Melodic Contour

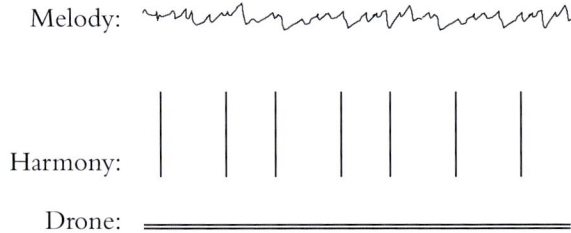

Figure 3: "Irish Bagpipe Melodic Contour"

Ornamentation

Ornamentation consists of embellishments or decorations that are applied to a melody, and thus modify the original musical idea. This is often done when performers improvise on a melody. Improvisation is the art of spontaneously creating music as it is performed. Some traditions have elaborate systematic procedures for ornamenting a melody, while others place less emphasis on ornamentation or shun it altogether. Ornamentation can consist of just a few added notes or a long series of tones meant to display a performer's skills or make the basic melody more interesting. (Listen to Kriti—CD 1.6.)

AURAL ANALYSIS: LISTENING TO THE WORLD'S MUSIC

Text Setting

Text setting, a term limited to vocal performance, is the process of combining music and words. Settings can be one of two broad types, depending on the relationship they establish between syllables of text and individual sung pitches. If each syllable of a text corresponds to one pitch, the text setting is considered *syllabic*. If, however, several pitches are sounded for a single syllable of text, the setting is considered *melismatic*. It is perhaps best, however, to think of most text setting as being on a continuum between the purely syllabic and the purely melismatic. Most vocal performance falls somewhere on this continuum, more frequently toward the syllabic side. (Compare Islamic "Call to Prayer"—CD 2.6; *Jali* with *kora*—CD 3.1.) However, some traditions strongly emphasize either syllabic settings, as with rap vocal performance in hip-hop music, or melismatic settings, as with African-American spirituals.

TEXT SETTING
The rhythmic relationship of words to melody; can be syllabic (one pitch per syllable) or melismatic (more than one pitch per syllable).

Rhythm

Rhythm is essentially the relationship of sound durations. Some rhythms fall into regular patterns while others are less predictable.

RHYTHM
The lengths, or durations, of sounds as patterns in time.

Beat and Tempo

Beat is a regular pulsation of sound. The simplest example is your heartbeat, which pulsates at a relatively fixed rate. This rate, or speed, is called *tempo*. The tempo of your heartbeat increases when you become more physically active, whereas its speed decreases when you sleep. In the same way, musical tempo can be described as relatively fast or slow in relation to a basic beat. (Listen to Hurdy gurdy—CD 2.17.)

Accent and Meter

An *accent* is an emphasized beat. Accents frequently signal a particular kind of musical activity or a specific stage in a performance or piece. For example, the louder sound of accented beats may correspond to dance steps or signal the end of a performance. Accents are often used to indicate the underlying rhythmic structure of a musical performance. In many traditions, this structure is based on a system of grouping beats into regular units. Such grouping of beats is called *meter*.

Most meters can be considered as either *duple* or *triple*. When groups of beats are divided by two, the meter is duple; when the beats are divided by three, it is triple. (Compare Russia Balalaika—CD 2.14; Mariachi—CD 3.16.) Meter may be articulated aurally by a single instrument, such as a woodblock sounding the basic beat. More typically, however, the meter is implied through the use of rhythms that elaborate on the basic beat to make the music more interesting. In some musical traditions meter can be asymmetrical (as in groupings of 2+3); in others, it is organized into closed cycles. Understanding these meters is important but hearing them is sometimes difficult. (Listen to P'ansori—CD 2.2.) In other cases, such as often occurs in Africa, musicians do not think in terms of meter but rather in terms of

Xylophones (*gyil*) from Ghana (Amy Unruh)

how rhythms relate. Ascribing a meter to music from such traditions can detract from one's appreciation of the musician's approach to music-making.

The opposite of metered music is music in *free rhythm*. (Listen to Lined hymn—CD 3.19.) Such music has no regular pulse, as is the case with speech. Without a regular beat to follow, a meter cannot be established. If you cannot easily snap your fingers to a piece of music, it may be in free rhythm. Such freely rhythmic music is usually highly ornamented and when performed vocally tends to have melismatic text settings.

Rhythmic Density

The term *rhythmic density* refers to the relative quantity of notes between periodic accents or within a specific unit of time. Rhythmic density can be described as a continuum between low and high (or thin and thick). Long sustained tones in free rhythm with little melodic activity have a low rhythmic density in contrast to music with a steady, usually quick, tempo and numerous notes of short duration. (Compare *Gu qin*—CD 1.16; *Akadinda*—CD 2.24.) If the music sounds "busy," the rhythmic density is generally high (thick); if it sounds "relaxed," the density is more likely low (thin).

Phonic Structure

PHONIC STRUCTURE
The relationship between different sounds in a given piece; it can be either monophony or some form of polyphony.

The term **phonic structure** (also *phonic music structure* and often described as *texture*) refers to the organizational relationship between or among musical sounds. A single line of music, whether performed by a soloist or in unison by an ensemble, is described as *monophonic* (adj.) or **monophony** (n.)—*mono* meaning "one"—as long as the performers play the same pitches with the same rhythms. (Listen to Ballad—CD 3.18.) Music featuring melodic lines performed an octave apart, as when male and female voices sing the same line of music in different ranges, is still considered monophonic.

For the study of world music, we have adopted the principle that multiple lines of music (or parts) performed simultaneously are considered *polyphonic* (adj.) or *polyphony* (n.) (Please note that in discussions by Western music specialists, the term polyphony is typically limited to what we have called "independent polyphony.") **Polyphony**, therefore, has three primary subsets: *homophony*, *independent polyphony*, and *heterophony*. The term **homophony** refers to multiple lines of music expressing the same musical idea in the same meter, *homo* meaning "the same." Music that is homophonic requires the use of at least two pitches played simultaneously at an interval other than an octave. In Euro-American musical traditions such music is referred to as *harmonic*, a description that generally implies the use of *chords*, or combinations of three or more tones that are blended together simultaneously to produce *harmony*. Because harmony generally supports a melody, most homophony can be described as melody with chordal accompaniment. (Listen to Bluegrass—CD 3.21.)

Independent polyphony consists of two or more lines of music expressing independent musical ideas. Each line of music is played or sung in relation to the others without any single line dominating. (Listen to Pygmy vocal ensemble—CD 2.22.) This concept covers a variety of possibilities from European counterpoint to styles in which the voice and instrumental accompaniment are melodically independent. Having several singers perform "Row, Row, Row Your Boat" starting at different times results in a kind of independent polyphony called a "round."

The term **heterophony** refers to simultaneous variations of the same line of music, *hetero* meaning "different" or "variant." As such, heterophonic music requires more than one performer—each performing the same melody, but differently, either in terms of pitch, rhythm, or both. (Listen to Jiangnan *sizhu*—CD 1.17.) Each manifestation of the melody in heterophony is shaped by the idiomatic characteristics associated with the performance style of each instrument or voice. A single melody played by two performers, only one of whom adds frequent ornaments to the melody, is considered heterophonic in structure. Complex heterophonic structures are especially common throughout much of Asia.

Dynamics

The term *dynamics* refers to the relative volume of a musical sound. The relative loudness or softness of a music can be a distinguishing characteristic of its performance. (Listen to Balinese gamelan gong kebyar—CD 1.15.) A gradual increase in volume is known as a *crescendo*, while a gradual decrease in volume is called a *decrescendo*. These and other terms related to dynamics are mostly derived from the European art music tradition, which typically uses Italian terminology. Others, such as *forte* (loud) or *pianissimo* (very quiet), are rarely used in ethnomusicological writing.

MONOPHONY
Music with a single melodic line.

POLYPHONY
The juxtaposition or overlapping of multiple lines of music; the three types of polyphony are homophony, independent polyphony, and heterophony.

HOMOPHONY
Multiple lines of music expressing the same musical idea in the same meter.

INDEPENDENT POLYPHONY
Multiple lines of music expressing independent musical ideas as a cohesive whole.

HETEROPHONY
Multiple performers playing simultaneous variations of the same line of music.

Form

Another important feature of music is *form*. This term refers to the overall pattern or structure of a piece of music as it unfolds in time. Form may be likened to architectural design in that it provides the underlying structure over time that gives a musical performance a predictable or coherent shape. Some kinds of music follow a pre-existing form with, for example, an established beginning, middle, and ending section, while others have less obvious organization. The forms used in one world music tradition may vary greatly from those used in another tradition. Becoming familiar with some of these forms will help you recognize certain traditions and will also help you understand how particular performances are conceived of by performers and audiences alike.

Bruno Nettl — AN INSIDE LOOK

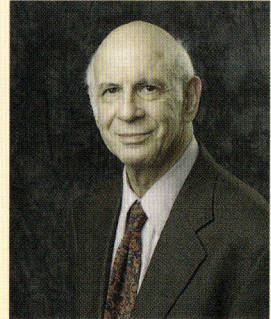

Dr. Bruno Nettl, Professor Emeritus, University of Illinois

I got into ethnomusicology in the most conventional way—by taking an elective course in 1949 at Indiana University—in one of the very few schools offering such courses. I think what turned me on to this field was the immense variety of musical sounds produced by the world's cultures; and the many different kinds of ideas about music—what it is and what it can do—that one finds in the world. I began by studying the music of Native American societies, particularly of the Northern Plains, and then went on years later to do fieldwork in Iran, and eventually found my way to India, all the while teaching undergraduates and graduates at the University of Illinois in Urbana. I've been in this profession for a half century and so have had, over the years, to change my mind about many things, and to learn new ways of studying and doing research. Today's younger students can hardly believe the kinds of technology we had (or didn't have) in the 1950s. But I think I can identify three questions that have motivated me all these years. They are related, as you'll see.

About the musics of the world, I keep wondering what it is that causes a society to have, or maybe to select, a particular kind of music for itself. Why does Native American music sound as it does? Why is the music of Iran so different from the music of Japan? When it comes to doing research, I've been concerned with understanding the differences between the ways the people in a society perceive their music, and the cultural outsider's perspective, and ways to reconcile the inevitable differences. As a teacher, I've been particularly concerned with finding ways for helping students of Western, mainly classical, music to see this music in the context of a world of musics, trying to understand why it developed the way it did, learning to value it as an expression of its culture while learning to appreciate and comprehend the world of musical sounds and musical cultures.

AURAL ANALYSIS: LISTENING TO THE WORLD'S MUSIC

Fundamentals of Music

NEED TO KNOW

TIMBRE. The tone quality or "color" of a musical sound.

MEDIUM. An object which produces a sound—a voice, instrument, or both; solo or ensemble (duet, trio, choir, orchestra, etc.); one of various instrument types (aerophone, chordophone, idiophone, membranophone).

PITCH. A specific tone determined by its frequency level. Related concepts include:

- **Tuning system.** The pitches common to a particular musical tradition.
- **Scale.** The pitches used in a particular performance arranged in order.
- **Interval.** The difference between two pitches.
- **Range.** All the pitches that a voice or instrument can potentially produce.
- **Melody.** An organized succession of pitches forming a musical idea.
- **Melodic contour.** The general direction and shape of a melody.
- **Ornamentation.** An embellishment or decoration of a melody.
- **Text setting.** The correspondence of words to melody. Text settings can be *syllabic* (one pitch per syllable) or *melismatic* (several pitches per syllable).

RHYTHM. The relationship of sound durations. Related concepts include:

- **Beat.** A regular pulsation.
- **Tempo.** The relative rate of speed of the beat.
- **Accent.** An emphasized beat.
- **Meter.** A system of grouping beats into individual units.
- **Free rhythm.** Music with no regular pulsation.
- **Rhythmic density.** The quantity of notes between periodic accents or over a specific unit of time.

PHONIC STRUCTURE. The organizational relationship between or among musical sounds. Related concepts include:

- **Monophony.** A single line of music.
- **Polyphony.** Multiple lines of music. Related concepts include:
  - **Homophony.** Multiple lines of music expressing the same musical idea.
  - **Independent polyphony.** Two or more lines of music expressing independent musical ideas.
  - **Heterophony.** Multiple performers playing simultaneous variations of the same line of music.

DYNAMICS. The volume of a musical sound.

FORM. The underlying temporal structure of a musical performance.

Questions to Consider

1. Which of the four basic components of music is most helpful in identifying a world music tradition? Why?
2. Name at least three examples from each instrument category in the Sachs–Hornbostel system. In which subcategories do these examples belong?

3. How does *pitch* differ from *tuning system*? How does *tuning system* differ from *scale*? How does *scale* differ from *range*?

4. How does *homophony* differ from *independent polyphony*? How does *independent polyphony* differ from *heterophony*?

5. What are some difficulties in using English terminology to describe the world's musics?

6. When music is represented graphically in notation, what are some of the limitations? How is Western staff notation limited in its ability to describe world music?

On Your Own Time

Book: Kartomi, Margaret. *On Concepts and Classifications of Musical Instruments.* Chicago: University of Chicago Press, 1990.
http://www.press.uchicago.edu/ucp/books/book/chicago/O/bo3774458.html

Website: Wesleyan University Virtual Instrument Museum
http://learningobjects.wesleyan.edu/vim/

Website: Comprehensive Table of Musical Instrument Classifications
http://www.music.vt.edu/musicdictionary/appendix/instruments/instrumentmain.html

Website: The American Musical Instrument Society
http://www.amis.org/

Website: The Metropolitan Museum of Art—Musical Instruments
http://www.metmuseum.org/en/about-the-museum/museum-departments/curatorial-departments/musical-instruments

Book: Sethares, William A. *Tuning, Timbre, Spectrum, Scale.* London: Springer-Verlag, 2005.
http://www.springer.com/engineering/book/978-1-85233-797-1

Website: San Francisco Symphony Kids Site (Fundamentals of Music)
http://www.sfskids.org/templates/home.asp?pageid=1

Website: Musipedia—The Open Music Encyclopedia
http://www.musipedia.org/

Book: Nettl, Bruno. *Heartland Excursions: Ethnomusicological Reflections on Schools of Music.* Urbana, IL: University of Illinois Press, 1995.
http://www.press.uillinois.edu/books/catalog/67rdq6mq9780252064685.html

Cultural Considerations: Beyond the Sounds Themselves

3

Cultural Knowledge	36	**Music and the Arts**	46
An Inside Look: Judith Becker	38	**Transmission and Pedagogy**	48
Value Systems and Hierarchies	40	**Notation Systems and the Creation of Music**	48
Music and Identity	40		
Use versus Function	42	**Exchange and Adaptation**	49
Music and Spirituality	42	**Cultural Intersections**	50
Music and Ethics	43	**A Case Study of Istanbul, Turkey: A Lesson in Geography, History, Religions, and Musical Exchange**	51
Music and the Environment	43		
New Theoretical Perspectives	45	*Questions to Consider*	59
Music Technologies and Media	45	*On Your Own Time*	59

Istanbul's "Blue Mosque," built in the sixteenth century by the Ottoman Turks

In a technical sense, music is organized sound and can be analyzed by concentrating on its elements alone, such as melody, rhythm, phonic structure, form, and so forth. But no music exists in a vacuum, free from social context, even if it primarily lives on concert stages or in recordings. All music manifests itself within a "culture," however defined, and has meanings for those who create, perform, or consume it that go far beyond the sounds themselves. This chapter briefly discusses some of the perspectives that may be brought to bear on a given musical type or style. These ideas, however incomplete, at least suggest that a full understanding of any music would require multiple approaches. Obviously, with only limited space we cannot apply all these concepts to every Site, but those that are most relevant will be discussed where appropriate.

Cultural Knowledge

Every individual absorbs a certain amount of cultural knowledge while growing up. Just being there makes you a member of a "cultural group," whether at the level of family, "tribe," community, nation, continent, or global cultural sphere (such as "the West"). Who you are depends on where you are and with whom you are living.

The experience of growing up within a given society creates a sense of normalcy; individuals develop expectations that the typical patterns they experience each day will continue. This sense that one's own culture is "normal," and that cultures which exhibit differences, both great and small, are "abnormal," "weird," or "exotic," is a natural perspective known as *ethnocentrism*.

Frederick Verney, Secretary to the Siamese (Thai) Legation in London in 1885, wrote that a great "stumbling-block" for many in the West when attempting to appreciate non-Western music is Western education, which "precludes the possibility of a full appreciation of music of a foreign and distinct school." In order for a Westerner to fully appreciate Asian music, it would be necessary "to forget all that one has experienced in the West." Ethnocentric reactions are natural and perhaps inevitable—but an awareness of ethnocentrism makes it more likely that one will come to accept and understand music that is "different." Scholars attempting to understand how music is experienced and "known" (i.e. "cognition") have developed a distinction between "outsider" and "insider" knowledge. They have dubbed the "outsider" perspective **etic** (from "phonetic"), and the "insider" perspective **emic** (from "phonemic").

ETIC
The perspective of a cultural outsider.

EMIC
The perspective of a cultural insider.

Insiders are assumed to react to their own culture's music in ways that draw on a lifetime of unconsciously absorbed cultural knowledge and attitudes. Outsiders, because they come to a given culture after their perceptions are formed, are assumed not just to inject ethnocentrisms into their interpretations but also to prefer to dwell only on those aspects of music that are observable to outsiders, such as objects and sonic structures. The major drawback to this concept of "insider" and "outsider" is that it doesn't allow for a middle ground: there's no room conceptually for the sympathetic "outsider" who has acquired "insider" knowledge. Do we value the views of an insider, simply because he or she grew up in a given culture, over those of an outsider, no matter how knowledgeable that person is? Can individuals shift identities by living among a "foreign" people? If so, for how long must they live among them? These are questions that do not have simple answers.

CULTURAL CONSIDERATIONS: BEYOND THE SOUNDS

Ivory tusk horns in Ghana are essential to the Asante court in Kumase, but African elephants are endangered, and transporting such instruments across national boundaries is forbidden (Joseph S. Kaminski)

French ethnomusicologist Alain Weber performs with "The Musicians of the Nile" from upper Egypt

Two cases in point. In 1982, when I (TM) studied the precented (lined out) psalm singing done in the Scottish Gaelic language services primarily in the Hebrides Islands but also among island ex-pats living in Edinburgh and Glasgow, the worshippers at Greyfriar's Kirk (church) in Edinburgh presented a challenge to the folklorists at the University of Edinburgh. Some years earlier, a young French woman had gone to live on the Hebridean island of North Uist, learned Gaelic, and had become exceptionally skilled in psalm singing. After moving to Edinburgh, she attended Greyfriar's and provided the strongest voice of the Gaelic-speaking congregation. Some of the folklorists contended that her singing was not "authentic" because she had come to Gael life as an adult—even though she was the group's best singer. In their view, an outsider could *never* attain insider status, even after many years of life among a new group and they did not consider her singing to be "authentic" or "valid."

In contrast to that, growing up outside a musical system's home territory is not necessarily an impediment to its mastery. Audiences worldwide have no problem in respecting orchestral conductors and musicians who grew up outside Western culture—people such as Japan's Seiji Ozawa, India's Zubin Mehta, and New Zealand's Kiri TeKanawa, the latter of the Maori ethnic minority. These artists, unlike the French psalm singer, however, were raised and trained in Western music from the beginning, even though the culture surrounding them was "non-Western."

Dr. Judith Becker

AN INSIDE LOOK

Judith Becker

My sojourn in the Shan States of Burma, from 1958 to 1961, eventually led me to the field of ethnomusicology. My husband was a Fulbright teacher in Taunggyi, Burma, and I was a newly married piano teacher. I found myself 400 miles from the nearest piano, and surrounded by music that I couldn't fathom. After studying the Burmese harp, *saung gauk*, and attending many festivals and dramas at which the Burmese percussion/gong ensemble, the *hsaing waing*, performed, I steadily grew to love Burmese traditional music. I had also come to appreciate how profound and how stimulating cultural differences and musical differences could be.

My husband and I and our three children returned to the United States in 1961 and took up residence in Ann Arbor, Michigan where my husband began studying linguistics at the University of Michigan under Kenneth Pike (the emic/etic man). I discovered then that there was a discipline called 'ethnomusicology.' William Malm had recently been hired to teach world music courses and ethnomusicological theory at the university. When I took Professor Malm's world music course, I knew that I had found my calling. Hearing for the first time the music of the Shona *mbira*, the Persian *kamanche*, the Sundanese *kacapi/suling* ensemble, not to mention Central Javanese gamelan music, left me weak-kneed. At the same time, I was taking courses in anthropology and, with a certain astonishment, read the works of Edmund Leach, Clifford Geertz, Edward Sapir, Alfred Kroeber, and Franz Boas—seminal influences all.

In 1968, during the course of my protracted graduate study, William Malm arranged for the purchase of a large gamelan ensemble and asked me to direct it. (Remember, this was the 1960s and running ethnic ensembles was still a bootstrap operation.) After many listenings to the 1967 UCLA recording, "Music of the Venerable Dark Cloud," and reading *Music in Java*, by Jaap Kunst, I taught the students to play *Bubaran Udan Mas*, in slendro and in pelog. Later in that year, we were able to invite Hardjo Susilo from UCLA to come to Michigan to teach gamelan for two weeks. When he first arrived, my students and I met with him in the gamelan room. He asked us to play for him. We played my interpretation of what I thought I heard the instruments playing on the UCLA recording. After an excruciatingly long pause, Susilo good-humoredly quipped, "Well, . . . there's Yogya style, there's Solo style, and then . . . there's Ann Arbor style." So began the beginning of my education about gamelan performance.

In 1972, I finally finished my Ph.D. and was hired as an assistant professor at the University of Michigan. For many years I directed the gamelan ensemble with help from visiting Javanese artists. Until the early 1990s, gamelan music, theory, and history were the focus of my research. This roughly twenty-year period resulted in many articles and the books, *Traditional Music in Modern Java: Gamelan in a Changing Society* (1980), *Gamelan Stories: Tantrism, Islam, and Aesthetics in Central Java* (1993/2004), and the three-volume set of translations of works on Javanese music by Javanese scholars, *Karawitan: Source Readings in Javanese Gamelan and Vocal Music* (1984, 1987, 1988).

Then, feeling that I had put into print all of the burning issues I had concerning gamelan music, I turned to a topic that had been simmering on the back burner of my mind for a long time—trance. Throughout the years in Burma and in Java I had witnessed many trance rituals, some of extraordinary beauty, all of which were compelling and mysterious. In 1996, I made a research trip specifically targeting three religious groups that included trancing as an integral part of their ceremonies, that is, Muslim Sufis in New Delhi, Buddhist *Yak-tovil* practitioners in southern Sri Lanka, and Balinese *bebuten* trancers in Indonesia. These three, plus Christian Pentecostals, formed the core of the ethnographic examples for my book on trance, *Deep Listeners: Music, Emotion, and Trancing* (2004). In that book I put forward the hypothesis that religious trancers and folks who are deeply moved by listening to music, whom I call "deep listeners," share a certain common physiology. It was clear that this intuition would remain in the realm of speculation unless I could devise an empirical methodology to test it. I was finally able to conduct a research project that involved measuring and comparing galvanic skin response of three groups, "deep listeners," Pentecostal trancers, and the control groups, while listening to music they loved. The results suggest that deep listeners and trancers do indeed share comparable lower-brain reactions to music they find moving. (See "Religious Ecstatics, 'Deep Listeners,' and Musical Emotions," *Empirical Musicology Review*, 4(2), 2009; "Ethnomusicology and Empiricism in the Twenty-First Century," *Ethnomusicology* 53(3), fall 2009.)

This venture into the realm of the science of music and the brain initiated my turn toward the biology and the neuroscience of the brain/body, an intellectual pursuit that I will not outlive, as I am now nearly 80.

I have so far written almost exclusively of my scholarly activities. But these interests were never pursued alone. Over the decades, my students, many now in leading positions all over the country in the discipline of ethnomusicology, have been both my first audience and my best critics. They have always been an integral part of my thinking-through scholarly questions about music. They have provided inspiration and, I hope, kept me honest. For me, teaching and scholarship have always been fused, and now, even in retirement, interaction with students continues to be a crucial aspect of my intellectual and musical life.

Value Systems and Hierarchies

Within any given culture, people tend to evolve value systems that dictate what kinds of music, which performers, and which instrument-makers are considered "better" than others. Although in the West many accept and others assert that "classical" music is superior to "popular" music, such a ranking begs the question of *authority*—that is, the complex question of who gets to make such judgments. What, after all, are the criteria that make one music tradition superior to another? And who decides? Is it done by some kind of consensus, by appointed critics, or by *self*-appointed critics? What are the implications of such hierarchies?

Essentially, the question is whether expressions of value are to be taken as matters of truth, opinion, or perspective. In the United States, value systems and hierarchies are now understood more in political than aesthetic terms. Many ask whether a value system can be taken seriously when it asserts that the musical heritage of a dominant group, such as European-derived peoples, is inherently superior to that of, for example, African Americans. Music is necessarily part of the current debates in our society over *canons*, *diversity*, and *hegemony*. As with the canon of "great books," the canons of "great composers" and "great works" are essentially European. Calls for "diversity" challenge not just the canons but also hitherto accepted standards of greatness. Some feel threatened by these challenges to the hegemony of European tradition, others feel liberated. Courses in "world musics" (and textbooks like this one) have been part of this partially political process. Until relatively recently, the study of "music" in education at most levels focused almost exclusively on the Western "classics."

Courses on the musics of the rest of the world, which have now become common, still do not rock the boats of established music departments as long as they are restricted to studies of musical style and "exotic" instruments. But when you add scholarly assertions that all musics are potentially valid—or, as University of Michigan Japanese specialist William Malm often said, "different but equally logical"—those devoted entirely to "Western art music" can find these contentions unsettling.

Music and Identity

A person expresses his/her identity in a variety of ways. The clothes we wear, the foods we eat, and the language we speak are all outward projections of "who we are," or more accurately, "who we *think* we are" or "want to be." Biological factors, namely race and sex, are often cited as the source of a person's identity; however, cultural factors are equally, if not more, important determinants.

For example, what makes a person "African"? Must he or she have "black" skin? That can't be the case, because Africans come in an array of skin pigmentations, including "olive" and "white." Likewise, would it make sense to consider Australian aborigines or the Trobrianders of Papua New Guinea "African" because many of them have a dark skin color? Certainly not. Rather, people are "African" because they think "African." And because they think this way, they behave as "Africans." While it is obviously naïve to think that "African" denotes any specific culture, it is equally naïve to think that "Western" is a culture as well, and yet this gigantic category of identity is often applied to anyone or anything associated with a Euro-American background.

CULTURAL CONSIDERATIONS: BEYOND THE SOUNDS

How others interpret the behaviors of an individual or group is also important to the formation of identity. If, for example, a person's behaviors are considered by others to be representative of the qualities of being "African," then that person's self-perception as an "African" is reinforced. However, if others do not agree that the person's behaviors are typical of an "African," then a conflict arises in which either the individual must modify their behaviors, thereby altering the perception of them, or the atypical behaviors must be accepted by the others as properly "African." If the conflict is not resolved, then the "African" identity of our hypothetical person would be continually questioned. Obviously, discussions of identity easily run the risk of stereotyping.

Music plays a vital role in expressions of ethnic identity. Groups and individuals often use music as a way to assert their unique ethnic qualities in relation to others. Outside perceptions of particular musical activities as normative behavior for a group or an individual reinforce the sense of ethnic identity expressed through the music. Along with other cultural elements, such as language, religion, dress, diet, and so on, music shapes how people think about themselves and their role within a society.

In many cultures, the expression of ethnic identity through music is an essential aspect of daily life, so understanding and appreciating musical activities is an important part of getting to know how people from these cultures think. Even in cultures where music is considered a specialized activity, much is expressed and revealed through the types of music common to the culture. For example, the glitz and glamour of Super Bowl halftime shows reveals the emphasis American culture places on extravagant entertainment, even though these music performances are certainly not representative of all the music found in the United States.

Japanese tourists watch a Thai Cultural Show at a Bangkok restaurant that caters strictly to tourists

Use versus Function

The anthropologist Alan Merriam spent an entire chapter of his landmark 1964 book *The Anthropology of Music* differentiating *use* from *function*. Whereas use, defined as "the ways in which music is employed in human society" (p. 210), can be easily observed, function requires much deeper inquiry into the meanings of music. Most studies of music's use are descriptive and are based on the observations of the researcher. The study of music's function, however, requires deep-level cultural knowledge and can entail much interpretation; for this reason, in answering questions of function, the perspectives of "insiders" are often privileged over those of "outsiders."

One of the most important contexts for music is its use in ritual. While the term ritual obviously encompasses religious services, it is more broadly applied to all situations in which formal patterns of behavior are repeated without question because they are seen to have meaning. Ritual behavior also occurs at sporting events, graduations, Memorial Day parades, Christmas dinners, and many other occasions when music is desired as part of the "pomp and circumstance." For example, the singing of the American national anthem occurs before virtually all sporting events in the United States. Superficially, this *use* is merely a step in a longer sequence of requisite events, but at a deeper level its *function* is to reaffirm national identity and solidarity.

When music's use in certain ritual contexts is considered, questions inevitably arise about the relationship between music and trance states. In rituals where trance occurs, such as those associated with the African-derived religious systems found in the Western hemisphere (e.g., Cuban *Santeria*), does music cause trance? Gilbert Rouget, in his seminal 1980 book *Music and Trance: A Theory of the Relations between Music and Possession*, demonstrates that seemingly trance-inducing music does not in fact cause trance, because if it did, it would automatically affect all who hear it, including the musicians and researchers. Music instead acts to stimulate, regulate, or end ritual trance states, which are not possible without training for and the expectation of altered states such as possession. Music may be *used* in a given possession ritual in order to "call the gods"—but its *function* is to regulate trance.

Music and Spirituality

The association of music with healing and spirituality goes beyond the "use" and "function" of music in ritual because it ascribes to music the power to affect beneficial change in human health, both physical and mental. In recent times, for example, many in the "New Age" movement have asserted that music can heal, directly affect the mind and its many moods, or enhance contact with the spiritual world. Some believe in the so-called "Mozart effect"—an alleged increase in intelligence among infants exposed early on to the music of Wolfgang Amadeus Mozart—while others claim that listening to specific compositions will cure certain ailments. The field of music therapy, widely accepted as having a scientific basis, uses music therapeutically to address a wide range of problems both physical and mental.

CULTURAL CONSIDERATIONS: BEYOND THE SOUNDS   3

Spiritual Baptists in the Caribbean nation of St. Vincent and the Grenadines sing a hymn in a trance state called "doption" (from the "adoption of the Holy Spirit")

Music and Ethics

Music has also been thought of in ethical terms. For Plato (428–328 B.C.E.), the ideal ruler was one shaped by an array of ethical forces, including music performed in the appropriate musical modes. Conversely, Plato also saw great ethical peril in music performed in the "wrong" modes. China's great philosopher Kong Fuzi (also known as Confucius) (551–479 B.C.E.) taught that the harmonious operation of the universe, down to the lives of individual humans, was directly affected by music. In his view, music must reflect the same order, balance, and restraint expected of human behavior. This kind of thinking persists in contemporary society where some believe that playing the music of W.A. Mozart for babies in the womb will have beneficial effect or that rock music potentially corrupts our youth.

Music and the Environment

Music, it is often said, is "everywhere." One might conclude that this "every-whereness" means that modern societies place a high value on music. For many musicians, however, music's omnipresence may be more a curse than a blessing. Music is frequently the "auditory aspirin" of modern society. Especially with the development of media capable of delivering it anytime, anyplace, anywhere, music has come to be used more and more like a drug. People use music to get themselves going, to facilitate relaxation, to enter meditative states,

Plato's student, Aristotle, founded this school near Vergina, Greece, in about 338 B.C.E. where he tutored Alexander the Great and the other children of Philip of Macedonia

to control the pace of work, or to dispel boredom. The music business has developed the means to use music as a manipulative tool. Muzak, the company, promotes its "music product" as a means of achieving increased sales, moving people in and out of rapid-turnover restaurants (or keeping them there to buy more drinks), and maintaining productivity in the workplace by responding to the natural daily cycle of human energy. Some people drown their concerns in a tidal wave of sound, indeed, loud parties and booming cars have brought about "noise" laws in many cities, in an attempt to curb what many hear as "noise pollution."

Other forms of environmental degradation have also had an effect on music-making. As numerous plant and animal species have become endangered, many long-time musical practices have been lost or permanently altered. This is because traditionally many musical instruments were made of now-rare natural materials, such as hardwoods or ivory. Dancers used feathers from now-endangered birds, or instruments were made of skins from now-endangered mammals. As a result, many old instruments cannot be brought into countries that enforce international environmental laws, and in fact may be confiscated and destroyed. New materials have been developed to substitute for restricted substances; for example, plastic or bone are now often used in place of ivory. Some instruments, though, cannot be made of substitute materials, such as the ivory elephant-tusk horns used in West Africa. In certain situations, governments permit the hunting and use of certain endangered animals that are part of the ritual tradition of a given people.

New Theoretical Perspectives

Although we cannot offer an extensive history of recent scholarship, we believe that some discussion of it is required in any essay on holistic approaches to music. The original work of the musicologist was to create authoritative musical scores based on manuscripts or prints, as close to the original as possible. Musicologists also sought to write histories of music and musicians based on "primary sources," namely first-hand documents such as letters, as did ethnomusicologists whose "primary sources" were living musicians. Documenting and describing what the musicians did was the field's original goal. This concern for "sticking to the facts" and "establishing verifiable truth" constitutes the core of what is called *modernist* scholarship.

Such work continues to be the focus of the majority of musicologists and ethnomusicologists, but a counter-trend arose as a result of new kinds of scholarship in other fields, such as literature. Whereas modernism taught that (capital T) Truth could be established, what is now called *postmodernism* teaches that "truth" is relative and has little validity beyond the person attempting to establish it. Instead of "describing facts," postmodern scholars seek to "interpret texts," a text being any manifestation of culture, including a book, painting, sculpture, or a performance of music. There are other new directions in ethnomusicological scholarship as well, including those focusing on political and economic perspectives (e.g., Marxist interpretation); gender issues, such as feminism; and non-heterosexual perspectives (e.g., "Queer Theory," which examines music-making from a gay or lesbian viewpoint). While some of this scholarship has proved to be provocative and stimulating, the specialized vocabularies common to such writing are often impenetrable to readers not familiar with the jargon or theories involved.

Music Technologies and Media

Technology has played a key role in the development of ethnomusicology. Wire recordings and the Edison wax cylinders of the late 1800s and early 1900s were important to the research of "comparative musicologists" who focused much of their attention on transcription and on the tuning systems of world music traditions. Throughout the twentieth century, technological advances enabled ethnomusicologists to record music in increasingly remote locations with greater and greater ease. While early field researchers traveled with heavy loads of equipment and numerous boxes of cylinders, later reel-to-reel tapes, and eventually cassettes and compact discs, today's ethnomusicologist can get studio-quality digital recordings with equipment that fits easily into a shirt pocket.

The media through which music is disseminated have also vastly changed over the last 100-plus years. They have evolved from radio and vinyl records to television and CDs to the Internet and MP3s—and each new development has made dissemination of the world's music easier and faster. This evolution has created greater opportunities for ethnomusicologists to disseminate their research in both academic and mass-market arenas.

The ease with which recording can be done today has resulted in a proliferation of world music recordings for sale to the general public. While many of these are well researched and come with scholarly liner notes, others are simply tourist trinkets slapped together to make a quick buck. Often what seems to be a poor-quality recording is actually an attempt to capture music in its original context, such as a crowded festival. Conversely, a studio recording with excellent sound quality may misrepresent a tradition, by, for example, leaving out instruments from an ensemble or incorporating inauthentic rhythms or melodies. It is generally best to stick to well-known labels, such as Smithsonian-Folkways or Lyrichord, although sometimes even a carelessly compiled audio collection can provide an enjoyable listening experience.

Music and the Arts

The relationships between music and other arts—including dance, theater, the visual arts, and literature—are varied and complex. While there certainly is music that stands alone for its own sake, a surprisingly great part of the world's music exists in relation to other arts.

The relationship with dance is the most obvious. Dance without music is rare. Dance music provides far more than just a beat: it must also have a character appropriate to the kind of dance it accompanies, whether the dance occurs in the world of classical ballet, folk music, opera, an Asian theater genre, or in a ballroom. A great deal of dance music may also be heard—indeed, normally is heard—separately from dance, causing us sometimes to forget that a particular song or piece was actually conceived to accompany movement.

Theater in the Western world is usually thought of as spoken drama, opera being a separate category of sung theater. The West also has theater types that include both speaking and singing such as the old German *Singspiel* of Mozart's time (the eighteenth century), the

A street performance of Chinese (Chaozhou) regional opera with percussion accompaniment in Shantou, Guangdong province, People's Republic of China

CULTURAL CONSIDERATIONS: BEYOND THE SOUNDS

The elaborate altar for a Thai *wai khru* (teacher greeting ceremony)

English ballad opera (e.g., *The Beggar's Opera*), and the American outgrowth of the latter, the Broadway musical. But throughout the rest of the world, theater without music is mostly unthinkable. This is particularly true in Asia, which has some of the world's most distinctive theatrical traditions, including Indian *Kathakali* (masked dance), Thai *Khon* (masked drama), Indonesian *Wayang* (shadow puppet theater), and Chinese *Jingju* (Beijing Opera).

Music tends to have one of two relationships with the visual arts. The first is found in the field of *musical iconography*, the study of music history and practice—and particularly musical instruments—through pictures. The second occurs when a composer, especially in the Western classical tradition, creates a work that is allegedly inspired by a work of visual art. Perhaps the most obvious example is Russian composer Modest Mussorgsky's famous *Pictures at an Exhibition*, composed in 1874 and based on a series of paintings by Viktor Hartmann.

Music can also be related to literature—primarily by association—through title, text setting, or allusion. The general term for music of this type is *programmatic music*, meaning music that alludes to something outside itself, be it a story, a great literary work, a poem, a painting, or, even more broadly, an emotion or aspect of nature. Chinese music titles commonly allude to well-known stories from novels, "Chinese opera," natural phenomena, and famous poems. Most pieces in the Chinese repertoire have titles that suggest an image, emotion, or place—such as "Meditation at the Dressing Table," "Suzhou Scenery," or "Winter Ravens Sporting over the Water."

47

Transmission and Pedagogy

Musical knowledge can be acquired in various ways: intuitively by living in a given culture, directly from a teacher, from a book, or by observation. When teaching is involved, many issues arise—such as the nature of the student–teacher relationship and the question of what educational methodologies are employed. When technologies are used in instruction, questions concerning memory, notation, and recording also arise. Some cultures have developed formal institutions that transmit music to anyone willing to learn (the conservatory, for example) and others have created institutions for preserving it within a closed system (the Japanese Imperial Household, for example). In some societies, especially those of East, South, and Southeast Asia, the music teacher is a revered individual who offers knowledge as a privilege. The Indian *guru* (and by extension, the Thai, Cambodian, and Lao *khru*) dispenses knowledge in a somewhat unsystematic fashion over a long apprenticeship; in the past, students lived with teachers and acted as their servants. The process of transmission in these instances is most often by means of *oral tradition*, in which the musical knowledge is transmitted directly to the student through performance, rather than any form of written notation. In these Asian societies, rituals that honor the teacher and the teacher's lineage are often required before learning is permitted.

In contrast, music teachers in Europe have historically sometimes been seen as odd characters deserving of ridicule, as with the exaggerated eccentricities of Don Basilio in Rossini's famous opera *The Barber of Seville* (1816). As for students, many societies offer titles or other forms of recognition, such as certificates or degrees, when students attain certain levels of skill.

Notation Systems and the Creation of Music

Students of Western music are accustomed to thinking in terms of a "composition" and a "composer." Western classical music developed a division of labor between the creator/composer and the realizer/performer. Composers are assumed to have the "genius" that leads to a work's creation. In order to maintain control over all aspects of a work, the composer represents his ideas through graphic symbols called musical notation—which must be played "as written" by subservient performers. Performers may add nuances but may not violate the composer's intentions. As a result, formal music education in the West tends to privilege "musical literacy," with the unspoken implication that cultures without notation suffer from "musical illiteracy." It is important to realize, however, that only certain aspects of music—such as pitch, melody, rhythm, meter, form, and texture—can be depicted in notation; aspects such as ornamental nuance, mood, timbre, and slight gradations of pitch and tempo cannot be written with much specificity.

Musical notation exists elsewhere in the world but most often only to preserve compositions for posterity or as a reminder to performers. Few cultures outside the West use music notation prescriptively, that is, as a guide to live performance. And even where there is notation, it is usually skeletal, because its function is to provide only what is necessary to cause performance. This type of notation is viewed as a point of departure, much as you find with jazz charts intended to include improvisation.

CULTURAL CONSIDERATIONS: BEYOND THE SOUNDS

Exchange and Adaptation

Although the existence of disparate musical categories such as *kabuki* and *bluegrass* suggests that musical systems are isolated from each other, the reality is much more complex. As distinctive as a given musical culture can be—and many are quite unique—none developed without outside influence. Some borrowed or loaned features travel better than others, however. Instruments, because they are objects, can be easily adopted by other cultures, though they are usually *adapted* as well to make them serve the aesthetic ideals of the borrower. On the other hand, even neighboring cultures can have dramatically differing musical concepts, timbre preferences, decorative styles, and tuning systems.

To give a specific example, Vietnam's musical culture is distinctive enough to be quickly recognized even by minimally experienced listeners. But it is also true that Vietnam was virtually a Chinese colony for nearly 1,000 years and adopted many aspects of Chinese music, especially its instruments. The Vietnamese transformed these Chinese instruments, however, to satisfy the requirements of their own sonic world. The most striking difference

The graphic notation for Tibetan Buddhist chant is enough to help informed practitioners remember the chants

Notice the wood is carved out from between the frets of this "Vietnamized" guitar to allow for ornamentation by pressing the strings

is the use of noticeably higher frets on the lutes, which also have loosely strung strings. While Chinese instruments were built primarily to produce fixed pitches, the Vietnamese system uses many "in-between" pitches and thus *requires* tone-bending created by pressing the strings downward between frets or sliding the fingers along the strings of fretless instruments. Though borrowed from Europe rather than China, the Vietnamese guitar, as an example, has an unusual neck with the wood between the frets scooped out to give the player the space in which to press the strings.

Cultural Intersections

To the extent that the world ever had any isolated, unique cultures, the modern world in which we live has certainly breached most of the old walls. Culture contact between and among distinctly named cultural groups is the norm. Whereas in the past this contact occurred through personal interaction as people from one group visited, encountered, traded with, fought with, or expanded into the territory of other groups, today there are also pervasive media bringing music, film, and dance to almost anyone living anywhere.

In 1991, I (TM) visited a remote village in central Laos accessible by Landrover over miles of dirt roads through other pre-modern villages. As we approached our destination, we had to disembark from our vehicle and walk the last mile, because the bridge had been destroyed during the Vietnam War some twenty years earlier and had yet to be replaced. As

A remote village house in China's Fujian Province (Shouning County) now has electricity from a nearby hydro project and—seen in the photo's center—a satellite dish bringing state television

we neared one of the larger houses, owned by the village headman, a group of traditionally dressed children, both ethnic Lao and upland minorities, emerged from the house to witness a rare visit by Westerners. After we climbed the ladder into the house, we noticed they had been watching a television powered by a car battery. On the TV were current popular music videos being broadcast from Khon Kaen, Thailand, hundreds of miles to the south. In this village seemingly 3 miles from the end of the earth, the young generation was fully aware of modern entertainments emanating from modernized Southeast Asian cities.

Throughout history, distinctive musics have resulted not from isolation but through contact. It is the unique mixing of peoples, events, and responses that generates the energy that leads to new and hybrid musical styles and instruments—and sometimes even to completely new genres. The United States offers many examples of this: jazz, blues, gospel, and salsa are four results of the energy produced when European- and African-derived peoples reacted to each other.

A Case Study of Istanbul, Turkey: A Lesson in Geography, History, Religions, and Musical Exchange

We have chosen the modern city of Istanbul, Turkey, as a case study of cultural exchange. Situated in a strategic location straddling the Bosporus (a broad river connecting the Black Sea to the Mediterranean), it marks the boundary between Europe and Asia. A remarkable amount of history and culture passed through here, profoundly affecting vast areas from Europe to Central Asia and North Africa. Indeed, travelers to Istanbul today will encounter remains and monuments from each historical layer. Although now seen as an Islamic city—albeit in a secular Turkish state—Istanbul was once a major center of Christian European civilization. How Istanbul's status changed, and the musical implications of these changes, are the subjects of this case study.

The story begins with the conquests of the Macedonian-Greek, Alexander the Great (356–323 B.C.E.), son of Philip of Macedonia (382–336 B.C.E.). Soon after being crowned in 336 B.C.E., Alexander set off to conquer a vast territory that eventually included northern Greece, much of Egypt, and lands across Western Asia into Central and South Asia, an expansion that continued until his death in 323 B.C.E. These conquests brought Macedonian-Greek (also called Hellenistic) civilization, including its architecture, language, sculpture, art, and most likely music as well, to the conquered peoples. The area around the Bosporus was well within the Greek world, and the small city founded on the European side was called Byzantium.

The Roman Empire expanded as Alexander's declined, and by the death of Emperor Trajan in C.E. 117, the Romans occupied much of western, central, and southeastern Europe, northern Africa, and most of the territory earlier conquered by Alexander. Within a few hundred years, Rome's unity would, however, crumble, and the humble village of Byzantium would grow to become one of the world's greatest cities. Because of the gradual decline of Rome and the defacto separation of the empire into western and eastern sectors, in 330 Roman Emperor Constantine I made Byzantium the capital of the [eastern] Roman Empire and renamed it Constantinople. His successor, Theodosius I, in 395 divided the empire into

The Early Islamic Empire (c.800 C.E.)

western and eastern halves, giving each of his sons dominion over one of the halves, though with the decline and fall of the western Roman Empire during the fifth century, the eastern half rose to greater prominence.

Whereas Rome was the center of what came to be called Roman Catholic Christianity, Constantinople was the center of the Eastern Rite, also called Byzantine Rite, the origin of a plethora of "Orthodox" faiths, each headed not by a pope, but a patriarch. With the fall of Rome to the Ostrogoths in 476, Constantinople assumed its place as both capital of what remained of the Roman Empire (the Eastern Empire) and center of the Eastern Church. The blending here of Greek and Middle Eastern civilizations brought about a culture, religious and otherwise, that was distinct from that of Rome. Emperor Justinian I (reigned 527–565) attempted to reform the Church, strengthened the Empire, and built one of the city's noblest churches, the Hagia (Saint) Sophia church.

The birth in 570 of Muhammad, the prophet and founder of Islam, in Mecca on the Arabian Peninsula was to change everything. By the time of his death in 632, Arabia had been converted to Islam, and by 656 parts of North Africa and most of the eastern expanses of the Eastern Roman Empire had been conquered as well. By 814 Islam had spread entirely across North Africa and into the Iberian Peninsula (Spain). At the same time, the Roman Catholic and Byzantine Churches continued to engage in disputes with each other even as

CULTURAL CONSIDERATIONS: BEYOND THE SOUNDS

The great Cathedral of St. Sophia in Istanbul, Turkey, built in the sixth century, became an Islamic mosque, with minarets added after the conquest of Constantinople by the Ottoman Turks in 1453

both were also being torn apart by internal disputes. By 1054 a formal schism between East and West completed the separation.

As Islam conquered the "Holy Lands," a succession of events led to the Crusades, organized by various European emperors and kings to reclaim Jerusalem from those who were termed the "Infidels." There were seven crusades organized in Europe and originating from various points between 1096 and 1270. The great armies raised for these crusades spent months, if not years, marching (sometimes sailing) across vast lands, rivers, and mountains intending to re-conquer Jerusalem and the Holy Land. Those that traversed the land had to fend for themselves, often resorting to raiding and destroying cities and killing their unlucky residents. Some sailed through the Mediterranean, but storms often reduced such navies to small bands of survivors. The ill-fated Fourth Crusade, organized in Venice in 1202, only reached Constantinople in 1204. Although the residents of the city were primarily Christian, the Crusaders plundered the capital of the Eastern Church, even establishing a line of weak Latin emperors, but failed to reach their goal, the Holy Land. Although there was a restoration of Eastern Emperors and a renewed flourishing of the Byzantine Church in the eleventh century, Constantinople remained under growing pressure from the Muslim Seljuq Turks, who were expanding their domain from the east.

The siege of Constantinople, begun in 1395, ended in 1453 when the city fell to the Ottoman Turks, and the city's name was changed to *Islambol* ("City of Islam"), romanized as *Istanbul*. The Turkish ruler, Mehmed II, repopulated the city with people brought from elsewhere in the rapidly expanding Ottoman Empire and converted the city's great churches into mosques. Not only were the great mosaics of these buildings covered in plaster, but towers, called *minarets*, were added around the buildings, both to indicate the importance of the mosque and to provide a tower from which a Muslim *muezzin* could call the faithful to prayer five times daily (see Chapter 8). Under Mehmed II and especially Süleyman the Magnificent (1520–1566), great mosques were constructed following the same basic cruciform (cross-like) pattern of the earlier eastern churches.

The Ottoman Empire continued to expand, especially into southeastern and central Europe, reaching its point of greatest expansion at the gates of Vienna in 1680, after which the empire began to recede and crumble. The Ottoman emperors, called caliphs, ruled from magnificent Topkap Saray Palace overlooking the Bosporus on the western side, accumulating great wealth—expressed in the arts, architecture, and music—by bleeding the subjugated areas dry of resources. Because the Ottoman Turks were exceptionally harsh masters, many rebellions arose, leading to great battles that make absorbing a full history of the Empire and southeastern Europe a daunting task.

Of special importance, because of its musical implications, is the *Janizary* (spelled *Yeniceri* in modern Turkish and *Janissary* is many Western writings), a corps of elite troops commanded by the Ottoman caliphs from the late fourteenth century until their destruction in 1826. Said to consist of Christian youths captured in the conquered Balkan provinces, these celibate (until the late sixteenth century) soldiers included bands of musicians who played martial music in parades. What made them distinctive was their use of double-reed aerophones (called *zurna*), metal trumpets, and a battery of percussion including bass drums, triangles, cymbals, and other percussion, including a pole with jingles, later called a "jingling johnny" in England. To Europeans these "exotic" instruments were later seen as quite attractive.

After 1680, as the Empire retreated from Europe, replaced by the now-growing House of Hapsburg (or at different times called the Holy Roman Empire or Austro-Hungarian Empire), the Ottoman government became increasingly corrupt and experienced various coups. After joining Germany as part of the Axis in World War I and being defeated, the Ottoman Empire was ripe for total reform. Mustafa Kemal (later given the title *Atatürk* (Father of the Turks)), disbanded the Empire in 1922 and reformed Turkey into a modern, European-oriented secular republic. Kemal also changed the writing system from Arabic to the Latin alphabet in the process. At this writing, Turkey is a member of NATO and aspires to membership in the European Union.

The modern traveler visiting Istanbul will be struck by the many layers of its history, manifested in a multitude of monuments all within walking distance of each other. There are Greek-style ruins, an Egyptian obelisk covered with hieroglyphics brought to Byzantium by conquering Romans, the incredible Roman cisterns—football field-sized chambers beneath Istanbul supported by stone columns from dismantled government buildings and designed to store water for a city notoriously short of it—great Christian churches with their magnificent mosaics, and mosques that rival the great cathedrals of Europe.

The musical results are many, too. Among the more significant of these developments we should at least briefly mention the following:

1. Greek and Arabic music theories developed in closely related ways. They in turn became the basis for Medieval European music theory, the foundation for the system used today.

CULTURAL CONSIDERATIONS: BEYOND THE SOUNDS

2. Certain procedures and melodic styles from Turkey became fundamental in southeastern Europe. Likewise, various Arabic styles penetrated Spain, Portugal, and certain Mediterranean islands.
3. When Islam expanded into Europe, it became a permanent part of many countries, including Albania, Bosnia-Herzegovina, Kosovo, Bulgaria, and Macedonia. The mosques throughout these lands practice typical Islamic forms of chant, including the Call to Prayer and the reading of the Koran, Islam's holy book.
4. Although the Byzantine Church once headquartered in Constantinople (now Istanbul) has long since disappeared, its direct descendant, the Greek Orthodox Church, even today retains many of Byzantium's musical practices.
5. Another group of people, the Romany (often called Gypsies), who came from India, migrated during the fourteenth to nineteenth centuries into northern Africa and Europe. They too brought with them much musical culture from western Asia. In some places the public music of the Romany became, or at least blended with, local traditional music, making conceptual separation nearly impossible.

Musical interchange occurred for many reasons:

1. The flow of culture from the Greek west to the conquered lands of the East (beginning with Alexander the Great), and the return flow of culture from these lands to the West as it was partially conquered by the Ottoman Turks.
2. The Crusaders, who no doubt brought aspects of European culture to the lands they crossed, and the souvenirs, mental and physical, they carried back if they were lucky enough to return home.
3. Intellectual, cultural, and material interchange within each of the great empires that successively occupied these lands. Because the Ottoman Turks were so hated in Europe, many people are still reluctant to admit the degree to which Turkish culture influenced the architecture, cuisine, dress, languages, lifestyles, and music of the conquered lands, but this influence is often quite obvious to an outsider lacking these age-old scars.

Even a casual comparison of Turkish instruments with many found in Greece, Albania, Romania, Bulgaria, and the former Yugoslav states will reveal obvious relationships. While the patterns of diffusion into both Asia and Europe are complex, we note some of the more obvious examples here:

1. *Fiddles or Bowed Lutes.* The distinctive shape of the Turkish *kemence* appears in the instruments of several southeastern European countries, including Greece (*lyra*) and Bulgaria (*gadulka*). We can speculate that these instruments are also related to such instruments as the medieval German *Scheitholt* and the French *rebec*. In some cases, the route of entry could also have been through Moorish Spain during the Muslim Arabic period.
2. *End-Blown Flutes.* The Turkish end-blown flute, called *ney,* also appears in southeastern Europe. Like the others, it is held obliquely.
3. *Dulcimer/Hammered Zither.* Among the most widespread of instrumental types is the hammered zither (also called a dulcimer), which nearly always has a box resonator of trapezoidal shape. The origin is assumed to be the Persian *santur*. This instrument

55

Turkish *kemence* (right) and Greek *lyra* (left). Note the similarities to the medieval instruments played by angels depicted in a cathedral carving

CULTURAL CONSIDERATIONS: BEYOND THE SOUNDS

(far left)
The Turkish *ney*, an end blown and obliquely held flute

Persian (Iranian) *santur* (right) with the American "hammered dulcimer" (right bottom)

traveled west throughout Europe, transforming into, for example, the Greek *sandouri*, the Rom *cimbalom*, the German *Hackbrett*, and the French *doulcemelle*. It also traveled east to East Asia (China and Korea) and Southeast Asia, and west to North America, where it is called the "hammered dulcimer."

4. *Double Reeds.* Like the dulcimer, double-reed instruments have traveled east and west, though it does not seem probable that all are related to those from western Asia. The Turkish/Arabic *zurna* instruments are the likely predecessors of the Greek *zournas*, in a chain of instruments leading all the way to the French *bombarde* and even perhaps to the capped reeds, such as the medieval and renaissance *shawm* or *Schalmei*. It is also possible that all of these instruments, including the *zurna*, descended originally from the ancient Greek *aulos*, first developed in western Asia, then transmitted back to Europe.

5. *Pear-Shaped Lute.* The name for a pear-shaped lute in Arabic and Turkish is *al-'ud*, the root of the English word "lute." As the *al-'ud* traveled west, it evolved into folk instruments such as the Greek *lauto* and Romanian *cobza*, as well as the highly refined Renaissance instrument simply called *lute*. The Renaissance lute played in France, Germany, and England most likely entered from Arabic (Moorish) Spain. The *al-'ud* also traveled east, where it became the Chinese *pipa*, the Japanese *biwa*, and the Vietnamese *dan tyba*.

6. *Round-Bodied Lute.* Round-bodied lutes abound in western Asia and southeastern Europe under a variety of names, but they also occur in Europe outside the areas occupied by the Ottoman Turks. The Turkish *tanbur* (and related instruments called *bağlama* and *saz*) is made in various sizes with movable frets, and similar instruments, usually called *tambura* or a variant of this term, are found in, for example, Bulgaria, Croatia, and

Two double-reed aerophones: Turkish *zurna* (left) and Malaysian *serunai* (right)

Turkish *ud* lute (left) with Greek *lauto* (right)

Turkish *tanbur* (also spelled *tambur*) (left) with Greek *bouzouki* (right)

Serbia. Possibly even the Italian *mandolin* derives from these prototypes. Ironically, the best-known Greek instrument, the *bouzouki*, descends from the Turkish *buzuq*, and as a result some nationalistic Greeks refuse to listen to *bouzouki* music, since they consider the instrument a survival from the culture of their Turkish oppressors.

Our study of Turkish music shows how culture ebbs and flows between and among sometimes strikingly different civilizations over time and place. These processes are always complicated and can never be sorted out precisely, but it is clear that today's world results from a series of events that have been taking place over a long period of time. Without an awareness of these interactions, it is impossible to understand why things are the way they are today.

Questions to Consider

1. How might an "insider" to a musical tradition hear it differently from an "outsider"? Are both perspectives necessary for a complete picture?
2. What music best expresses your individual identity?
3. What distinguishes "modern" from "postmodern" scholarship in music?
4. What role does music play in your spiritual life?
5. How has technology changed the kinds of music we listen to and how we hear them?
6. Why is history important to the study of world music?

On Your Own Time

Book: Becker, Judith. *Deep Listeners: Music, Emotion and Trancing*. Bloomington, IN: Indiana University Press, 2008.
http://www.iupress.indiana.edu/catalog/product_info.php?products_id=21676

Book: Stokes, Martin, ed. *Ethnicity, Identity and Music: The Musical Construction of Place*. Oxford: Berg Publishers, 1997.
http://www.bergpublishers.com/?tabid=2196

Book: Post, Jennifer, C. *Ethnomusicology: A Research and Information Guide*. New York: Routledge, 2004.
http://www.routledge.com/books/details/9780415879774/

Book: Shepherd, John and Peter Wicke. *Music and Cultural Theory*. Cambridge: Polity Press, 1997.
http://www.polity.co.uk/book.asp?ref=9780745608648

Book: Clayton, Martin, Tervor Herbert and Richard Middleton, eds. *The Cultural Study of Music: A Critical Introduction*. New York: Routledge, 2003.
http://www.routledge.com/books/details/9780415938457/

Book: Turino, Thomas. *Music as Social Life: The Politics of Participation*. Chicago: The University of Chicago Press, 2008.
http://press.uchicago.edu/ucp/books/book/chicago/M/bo5867463.html

Book: Solís, Ted, ed. *Performing Ethnomusicology: Teaching and Representation in World Music Ensembles*. Berkeley and Los Angeles: University of California Press, 2004.
http://www.ucpress.edu/book.php?isbn=9780520238312

Video: Marre, Jeremy, ed. *The Nature of Music* (3 programs: 1, Sources and Sorcery; 2, Songs and Symbols; 3, Legends and Labels). (Out of print VHS videotape but worthwhile if found in a library.)

Book: Rouget, Gilbert. *Music and Trance: A Theory of the Relations between Music and Possession*. Chicago: University of Chicago Press, 1985.
http://press.uchicago.edu/ucp/books/book/chicago/M/bo5956162.html

Oceania: Australia, Papua New Guinea, Hawaii, Kiribati

4

Background Preparation	62
Planning the Itinerary	63
Arrival: Australia	63
Site 1: Australian Aboriginal Song with *Didjeridu*	64
Arrival: Papua New Guinea	69
Site 2: *Susap* (lamellophone) from Papua New Guinea	70
***Explore More:** Singsings of Papua New Guinea*	73
Arrival: Hawaii	74
An Inside Look: Amy Ku'uleialoha Stillman	75
***Explore More:** Hawaiian Steel Guitar and Ukulele*	76
Site 3: Hawaiian Drum-Dance Chant	77
Arrival: Kiribati	80
Site 4: Group Song for *bino* (sitting dance) from Kiribati	81
Questions to Consider	85
On Your Own Time	86

Ayers Rock, known locally as Uluru, rises 2800 feet/863 meters above the central Australian plain southwest of Alice Springs (Max T. Miller)

Background Preparation

The area known as Oceania includes Australia and numerous island groups spread across a vast region in the Pacific Ocean. Whereas the land area of Australia is nearly three million square miles (more than 7.6 million square km), the total land area of the Pacific Islands is less than 500,000 square miles (just over 800,000 km), smaller than the state of Alaska. The islands of New Zealand, Papua New Guinea, and Hawaii comprise over 90 percent of this land area, while the remaining islands, numbering almost 25,000, account for fewer square miles/km of land area than the country of Belgium. The Pacific Islands are divided into three subregions: **Melanesia** (meaning "dark islands,"), **Micronesia** (meaning "small islands"), and **Polynesia** (meaning "many islands").

Most of Oceania is considered tropical or subtropical. The Pacific Islands straddle the equator, with Micronesia in the northern hemisphere and most of Melanesia and Polynesia, as well as Australia and New Zealand, being part of the southern hemisphere. While Australia and larger islands such as New Zealand and Hawaii are accessible by plane, many of the smaller islands and atolls of the Pacific are still quite isolated, with ships arriving on only a weekly or monthly basis. Tourism is a primary economic resource in the Pacific, but most indigenous groups continue to survive on subsistence farming or hunting and gathering. Australian Aboriginal communities keep their traditional practices fairly secluded, though many have adopted an urban lifestyle or rely on government support.

While European cultural influence is extensive throughout Oceania due to colonization, primarily by the British, the indigenous populations of Australia and the Pacific Islands maintain traditional cultural practices. These vary widely and are considered in many cases to be among the most ancient customs on the planet. A common denominator for all groups is a close relationship with nature. Complex animistic and totemistic spiritual systems have evolved throughout Oceania, in which practitioners call on animals and natural elements for guidance, protection, and subsistence. Rituals involving musical activity are most often associated with these beliefs, and many songs are believed to derive from ancestral spirits who are inevitably linked with spiritual forces of nature.

Along with these traditional beliefs one also finds much Christian influence, introduced by European and American missionaries during the nineteenth and twentieth centuries. Missionaries, along with colonial governments, drastically changed the cultural customs and social systems of many populations throughout Oceania. English or French are considered the "official" languages of most nations, though indigenous dialects continue to be spoken. Home to roughly 1,200 languages, Australia, Papua New Guinea, and the islands of the Pacific provide some of the world's most fertile soil for linguistic and anthropological studies.

The music of Oceania is primarily vocal, and thus effective research on music traditions often requires specialized linguistic study. With few exceptions, instruments tend to be small and portable, most being idiophones or membranophones. Slit drums are common, especially in Melanesia. The few aerophones found are primarily flutes, though the most famous instrument from the region is likely the Australian ***didjeridu***, classified as a trumpet. Chordophones—namely the guitar or derivatives of it—are largely of European origin.

Myths and belief systems, along with practical knowledge and oral histories, pass from generation to generation through song and dance. Music is often considered a link to the spiritual plane, and specialists in ritual-associated music traditions are common. Subtle

---

SUBREGIONS OF THE PACIFIC ISLANDS

Melanesia (meaning "dark islands")

Micronesia (meaning "small islands")

Polynesia (meaning "many islands")

DIDJERIDU

A long trumpet made from a hollowed tree branch and played by Aborigines from Australia. The sound is characterized by a low, rumbling drone.

4 OCEANIA

distinctions in vocal performance are considered vital to the identity of individual social groups; thus, music and dance are regarded as highly valued cultural property.

Planning the Itinerary

Our review of music traditions from Oceania begins with the mysterious sound of the *didjeridu*—an instrument found among the **Aborigines** of northern Australia, who maintain some of the planet's most intriguing and ancient cultural practices. Next we introduce an example of one of the world's most common instrument types, the mouth harp, as we travel to Papua New Guinea, an area of major anthropological interest for several decades. While ethnomusicologists have been studying this region extensively, many music traditions remain largely unexplored due to the great cultural diversity of its indigenous populations. We then arrive on more familiar ground—Hawaii—to examine indigenous vocal practices associated with the precolonial period of Polynesia, as well as more modern music, namely the Hawaiian slack-key guitar. Finally, we introduce the choral traditions of the Pacific through an example of Kiribati vocal performance, which reveals the influence of European musical creation over the last 200 years.

ABORIGINES
A generic term for an indigenous population, often used to describe native peoples of Australia.

Arrival: Australia

The Australian wilderness is home to several unique species of animals. The koala, kangaroo, and platypus, just to name a few, are among the world's most intriguing animals. While many of the coastal areas have moderate vegetation that supports such species, the interior of the continent, known as the Outback or Bush, mainly consists of vast plains and large desert regions. The major cities—Sydney, Melbourne, and Perth—are located along the coast, while the few inhabitants of the interior are mostly members of Australia's well-known indigenous population, who are referred to as Aborigines.

While most Aborigines live in urban settings today, a government reserve in the Northern Territory, known as Arnhem Land, is home to more than 30,000 Aborigines who maintain cultural practices that have existed for roughly 40,000 years. Though some of these Aborigines live in government-sponsored housing, many continue to follow a semi-nomadic

Aerial view of Sydney, Australia, and its iconic Sydney Opera House designed in 1973 (Harvey Lloyd/Getty Images)

63

An Aboriginal dance accompanied by clapsticks and a *didjeridu* (Axel Poignant, 1952)

ANIMISM
Belief systems in which natural phenomena as well as both animate and inanimate objects are considered to possess a spirit.

DREAMTIME
A term describing the Australian aboriginal spiritual belief system and concept of creation.

lifestyle. These Aborigines acquire few material possessions, mostly related either to hunting (such as spears or boomerangs), or spiritual practices (musical instruments).

The close affinity such Australian Aborigines have with their environment is revealed in their totemistic belief system. Totemism centers on the relationship of an individual or group with animals or natural objects or elements, such as specific mountains or the ocean. **Animism**—the belief that all living things as well as natural phenomena, such as wind or fire, have a spirit—also plays an important role in the Aboriginal cosmology. Known as *The Dreaming* or **Dreamtime**, this cosmology is the focus of much artistic activity within the Aboriginal communities of Australia.

Site 1: Australian Aboriginal Song with *Didjeridu*

First Impressions. The vocal exclamations in this example are accompanied by the steady pulse of wooden clapsticks and the low rumble of the *didjeridu*, an end-blown wooden trumpet that is the most distinctive feature of traditional music from Arnhem Land. The vocalist is like a storyteller shouting his words to all who would listen, including ancestral spirits, while the constant drone of the *didjeridu* may suggest to the first-time listener a cloud of hornets swirling overhead or the rumbling sound of a large waterfall.

Aural Analysis. The *didjeridu* is traditionally made from a tree branch, typically eucalyptus, hollowed out by termites. Some *didjeridu* are made of bamboo, while modern instruments used in non-traditional contexts are sometimes made of plastic or even metal. Most *didjeridu* are between 3.5 and 7 feet long (106 cm to 213 cm), with a diameter of 1–3 inches (2.5 cm

OCEANIA   4

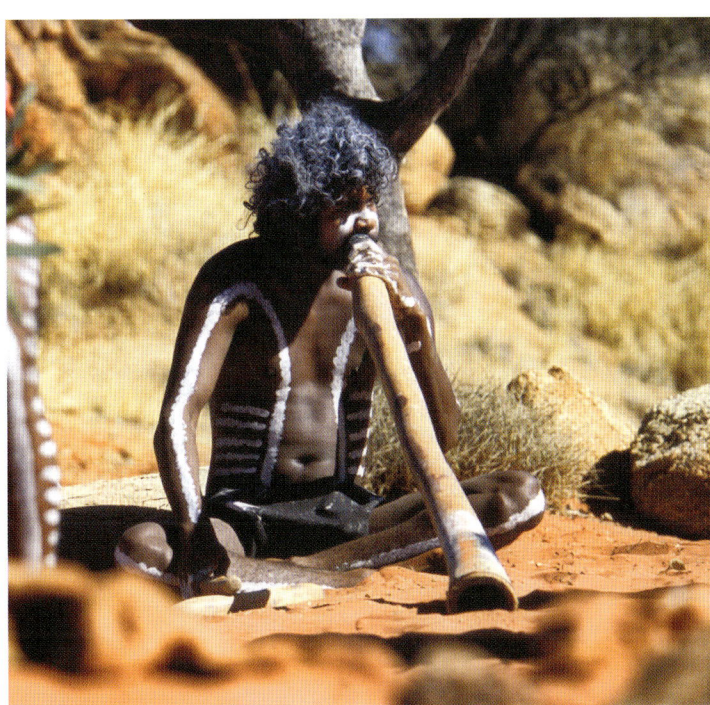

A *didjeridu* player of Australia (Grant Faint/Getty Images)

to 7.5 cm). The ring of the blowing end is covered with beeswax to protect the performer's mouth from the wood's ragged edge and to shape the blowing end to a preferred size, in order to create a secure seal for the player's mouth.

The guttural sound of the *didjeridu* is made by relaxing the lips and blowing air through the mouth to make the lips flap or buzz. This vibration echoes through the instrument producing a deep fundamental drone with a multitude of overtones. An adept performer can create different timbres and a rhythmically patterned drone by altering the airflow with his mouth and tongue. He may also force sudden bursts of air through the instrument to increase the volume or alter the pitch and timbre. Performers often add vocalizations, such as humming or growling, to change the sound of the instrument. This latter technique is especially important when performers attempt to imitate the sounds of birds or other animals.

Fundamental to playing the *didjeridu* is utilization of the **circular breathing** technique, which creates a continuous exhaled airflow, making it possible to produce a steady drone over long periods. Air is expelled through the lips by tongue and cheek muscles. As the performer exhales, he simultaneously inhales through his nose to replenish the air reserve stored in the cheeks. An easy way to try this technique is with a cup of water and a straw; a continuous airflow will maintain a steady stream of bubbles. While a beginner can soon do this with a small tube, the larger *didjeridu* is more difficult to master, because it requires much more air and pressure to produce a consistent and correct tone.

The clapsticks that are used to accompany *didjeridu* are generally made of hard woods and tend to be roughly a foot and a half (45 cm) in length and about an inch (2.5 cm) in diameter. Some Aboriginal groups use boomerangs as clapsticks, especially in ceremonies

CIRCULAR BREATHING
A technique used to maintain a continuous exhaled airflow in aerophone performance.

65

that prepare hunting parties for expeditions. The clapsticks provide a steady pulse, which the vocalist uses to frame his vocal phrases. The *didjeridu* performer may also correlate his rhythmic drone to the clapsticks by adding overtone bursts in conjunction with the pulse of the clapsticks. These bursts alter the pitch of the drone. In our example this pitch alteration, which raises the initial pitch by a semitone, occurs on roughly every other pulse shortly after the clapsticks enter. Often the clapsticks are played only during the *didjeridu* interludes and not during sung sections—though they do sound throughout both sung and instrumental sections of our example.

This performance consists of two parts: a presentation of the main text and a secondary section of vocables in which non-lexical (untranslatable) formulaic phrases are used. Though some overlapping of pitches occurs, the main text is generally sung in a higher range than the vocables section, which concludes in a comparatively lower range. Throughout the example, the melodic contour of the vocal line is typically descending. Here is a transcription of the words heard before the clapsticks enter (the main text is in boldface):

Dijan old jong, dijan iya—bushfire
(This one's an old song—bushfire)
[*Didjeridu* enters]
ga ***andegarrana andegarran(a)***
andegarrana andegarran(a)
andegarrana andegarrana *ya*
a ga na ya ya ga ga
[Clapsticks enter]
(*Bunggridj-bunggridj: Wangga Songs*, Alan Maralung; Northern Australia. SF 40430. Washington DC: Smithsonian Folkways, 1993, p. 30)

Village elders chant with accompaniment by *didjeridu* and clapsticks as well as clapping (Mark Crocombe)

The vocal timbre is nasal, and there is only one singer, which is typical among the Aborigines—though group vocal performances do occur. There is only one *didjeridu* player, as is almost always the case, because the fundamental pitches of different *didjeridu* are rarely the same. The instrumental dynamic level remains consistent throughout, while the secondary vocables section is at a slightly lower volume than the main text.

LISTENING GUIDE

CD 1.1 (1'52")

Chapter 4: Site 1
Australia: Aboriginal Song with *Didjeridu*

Voice: Single male
Instruments: *Didjeridu* (aerophone), clapsticks (idiophone)

TIME	LISTENING FOCUS
0'00"	Spoken introduction.
(0'04")	("Bushfire" said by vocalist.)
0'07"	*Didjeridu* enters playing a drone (continuous sound). Listen for the dynamic "bursts" that initiate the cycle and provide a rhythmic pulsation.
0'12"	Vocalist enters. Listen for a descending melodic contour and a tendency toward syllabic text setting in the vocal line. The vocal timbre is quite "nasal" and has a declamatory style.
0'26"	Clapsticks enter with a steady pulse.
0'31"	Vocalist, second entry.
0'51"	*Didjeridu* and clapsticks alone.
0'54"	Vocalist, third entry.
1'05"	*Didjeridu* and clapsticks alone.
1'10"	Vocalist uses partial phrases with descending melodic contours to close the sung section.
1'33"	Vocalist imitates the drone of the *didjeridu*.
1'42"	*Didjeridu* stops.
1'45"	Closing section of clapsticks and voice.

Source: "Bushfire" by Alan Maralung, from the recording entitled *Bunggridj-bunggridj Wangga Songs, Northern Australia*, SF 40430. Recorded by Allan Marett and Linda Barwick; provided courtesy of Smithsonian Folkways Recordings. © 1993. Used by permission.

ETHNO-CHALLENGE (CD 1.1): Attempt to "circular breathe" (see Aural Analysis) by blowing bubbles in a cup of water through a straw continuously throughout the performance (1'51").

Cultural Considerations. The title of this example, "Bushfire," with its animistic reference to a natural phenomenon, is indicative of the strong association between musical performance and spiritual belief characteristic of Australian Aborigines. Most traditional Aboriginal performances, whether in ritual contexts or for entertainment, have a sacred element that relates to *The Dreaming* (*Dreamtime*), the Aboriginal cosmology. *The Dreaming* tells of an ancient mythological past when the earth was merely a featureless swirl of creative energy. At that time, ancestral spirits (*wondjina*) roamed the planet creating life and shaping the topographical features of the earth. The spirits also created songs, known as "history songs," that provided the framework with which the Aborigines were able to maintain their society, the land, and totemistic relationships. Through the correct performance of these songs, the Aborigines are able to tap into this ancient and creative power left behind by the ancestral spirits. Aborigines believe that these history songs have remained unchanged since the beginning of time.

A night-time *corroboree* ritual performed by Aborigines from Goulburn Island, Arnhem Land, Australia (Axel Poignant, 1952)

While history songs are regarded as the most important, songs related to totems or social activities also exist. New songs in the latter two categories are sometimes composed, though they usually are considered to have been inspired by an ancestral spirit or taught to an individual in a dream. Women do not usually perform songs along with men, and it is taboo for women to play the *didjeridu*. The sound of the *didjeridu* is considered the most sacred of all sounds and is regarded not only as symbolic of the creative powers of the ancestral spirits but also as an actual aural manifestation of their creative energy. Female performance on the *didjeridu* is taboo primarily because Aborigines believe that exposure to the instrument's spiritual power would make a woman more fertile, causing her to give birth to too many children for the community to support.

While tourists often have access to staged performances of aboriginal music, the most common contexts for traditional Aboriginal music performances are mortuary rites and boys' circumcision ceremonies. Songs are also performed on more informal occasions, most frequently during a *corroboree*, or night-time ritual. Most of these events are considered sacred and are closed to the uninitiated; thus, there is little documentation of them. Dance plays an important role in ritual contexts. White paint is applied to the dancer's dark-skinned body according to prescribed patterns associated with a clan's totems and the specific ritual. At the night-time *corroboree*, this paint shines in the firelight. During these events, which are believed to connect participants with ancestral spirits, the hypnotic sound of the *didjeridu* helps create a feeling of disorientation from time and place.

Arrival: Papua New Guinea

While Papua New Guinea (often referred to as PNG) has a population of fewer than five million inhabitants, there are more than seven hundred languages spoken among its diverse cultural groups. Comprising the eastern half of the island of New Guinea (the western half being part of Indonesia), the region is the largest land area in Melanesia. Its precolonial history dates back roughly 50,000 years and is believed to be linked with that of the Aboriginal populations of Australia, based on several cultural and genetic similarities.

The major cities are found along the coast, while the highland interior is home to much of the population. Most indigenous groups practice subsistence farming—that is, they grow food and raise livestock for personal use rather than for commerce. While English is the official language due to years of British colonial influence, only a small portion of the population speaks it fluently. Indigenous languages predominate, along with Tok Pisin, a combination of pidgin English and Melanesian.

Christian missionaries, primarily from Europe, have had some influence on indigenous spiritual beliefs found in Papua New Guinea. Local traditions that missionaries considered pagan or erotic in nature were often prohibited by them, in particular traditional dancing that was targeted as an immoral activity thought to promote sexual promiscuity. As a result, many local customs, especially in lowland areas where missionaries have had the most influence, have been lost or modified.

Nevertheless, a wide array of traditional music and dance is still found in Papua New Guinea, and many customs have been reestablished since the country achieved independence in 1975. Tourists are visiting the island in increasing numbers, drawn by the elaborate dress and varied cultural activities of the many different ethnic groups. Probably the most

WORLD MUSIC: A GLOBAL JOURNEY

Enga men play the *kundu* goblet drum and dance in Papua New Guinea (Don Niles)

visible of instruments found among the Papuans are the large slit drums called *garamut* and the hourglass-shaped drums known as *kundu*. These are used in many ceremonial contexts and have become a staple of tourist shows and government-sponsored festivals. Less popular at these events, but perhaps the most widespread instrument in the country, is the *susap*, a bamboo mouth harp commonly played for self-entertainment.

Site 2: *Susap* (lamellophone) from Papua New Guinea

First Impressions. The *susap* has a distinctive "twangy" timbre, as if the performer were talking through an electronic voice modulator. A first-time listener not seeing the instrument might imagine the performer is striking a metal spring or taut cable with a small screwdriver, creating a wobbly "boing" effect. This unique tone quality makes our example memorable even in the absence of a singable melody or repeatable rhythm.

Aural Analysis. Mouth harps, such as the *susap*, are one of the most common instruments found throughout the world. Most are made of either wood or bamboo, but some are made from metal, such as what used to be known as a "jew's harp" common to American folk music. Such mouth harps are not actually classified as harps (chordophones) but belong, rather, to a subcategory of idiophone known as *lamellophones* (or *linguaphones*). Lamellophones in general have multiple flexible tongues (each known as a lamella) that are typically plucked to produce sound. Most mouth-resonated lamellophones have a single *lamella* that is set or cut into a frame. The performer plucks the lamella so that it vibrates within the frame, producing a distinctive "twangy" timbre, whose quiet sound is amplified

A Baruya man plays the *susap* mouth harp from the Eastern Highlands province of Papua New Guinea (Don Niles)

by the mouth cavity. The lamella must pass tightly within the frame to produce the desired effect. A small piece of wax is sometimes fixed to the end of the lamella to encourage its vibration or to change the instrument's timbre.

To play the *susap*, the performer holds its frame tightly within the lips, holding one end to maintain the proper angle while plucking an extension that is attached either to the frame or to the lamella. Often a small string is attached to the instrument and jerked to vibrate the lamella. The performer alters the sound by changing the size and shape of his oral cavity and vocal tract. While the fundamental pitch of the mouth harp does not change, the manipulation of overtones resonating in the mouth can produce recognizable melodic features, usually more closely related to speech than song.

In our example the performer maintains a steady plucking pattern but varies the rhythmic content through timbral changes. While the performance is likely improvised, the example can be segmented into four sections. The opening section includes twenty pulses without much timbral variation. This is followed by a more rhythmically active section in which the player begins to "speak" with the instrument, producing an accented low tone echoed by a faint overtone. The rhythmic emphasis shifts frequently: sometimes the fundamental tone is played twice before the echo is sounded, other times the player alternates evenly between the two timbres, producing one overtone for every low tone. This section is also marked by the frequent use of a long–short rhythmic pattern created by the performer using his tongue to silence the resonation just before plucking the instrument to produce the accented tone. One might express this rhythm as a short–long pattern, such as "du-duu, du-duu."

Close-up showing details of a bamboo lamellophone from the southern Philippines. A toothpick has been inserted to display the vibrating tongue

The third section occurs approximately ninety pulses into the performance and is characterized by a less-prominent role for the lower, accented tone and a new emphasis on varying the timbre of the higher overtones. Variations in timbre are produced through manipulations of the size of the mouth cavity and by changes in the position of the player's tongue. This section is the most speech-like of the four sections. The final section commences at approximately 150 pulses and is marked by the "boing" effect already mentioned, which is created by fluttering the tongue inside the mouth cavity to produce a wavering, "wobbly" sound. This is perhaps the most unique timbral effect of the performance.

Cultural Considerations. In Papua New Guinea, as elsewhere, the mouth harp often acts as a "speech surrogate." Performers use it to imitate speech patterns and phonemes in order to create the illusion of speech in a musical context. The sounds of the mouth harp are often considered to be speech that is "disguised," in order that it not be understood by eavesdroppers.

While mouth harps are commonly used for self-entertainment, they are also frequently found in traditional courting rituals. In Papua New Guinea the *susap* is considered to possess love-controlling magic that men can use to attract a woman's affections. By using the instrument as a speech surrogate, the man is able to "say" things to the woman that might otherwise be considered inappropriate. The instrument also provides impunity from rejection. If the woman is attracted to her suitor, then the magic has worked; if not, the magic was either ineffective or not correctly utilized by the performer. An ignored suitor either has to improve his technique or use a different instrument to attract the woman's affections. This allows the woman more freedom to act on her feelings as well, as the instrument can be blamed for affecting her action or inaction with regards to her suitor. Thus, the *susap* functions to maintain social relationships between young men and women in small communities where daily interaction is necessary for subsistence.

OCEANIA

LISTENING GUIDE

CD 1.2 (1'22")

Chapter 4: Site 2
Papua New Guinea: *Susap* (lamellophone)

Instruments: *Susap*

TIME	LISTENING FOCUS
0'00"	Opening pulse established. Timbre is consistent, with little variation.
0'07"	Second section, emphasizing a "short–long" (du-duu) rhythmic pattern.
0'24"	Section transition. High-frequency manipulation initiated.
0'28"	Third section, characterized by a "speaking" manipulation of the fundamental tone and emphasis on a single prominent overtone.
0'50"	Fourth section, characterized by "wobbly" overtone manipulation.
1'17"	Close of performance on the fundamental tone.

Source: "Badra from Buzi" ("Sounds of a *Susap*") performed by Amadu, recorded by Wolfgang Laade, Buji, Western Province, Papua New Guinea, 1964, from the recording *Music from South New Guinea*, Folkways 04216, provided courtesy of Smithsonian Folkways Recordings. © 1971. Used by permission.

ETHNO-CHALLENGE (CD 1.2): Make a "mouth harp." To do this, cut a "tongue" into a rectangular piece of plastic, metal, or wood. Experiment with different sizes and shapes.

Explore More

Singsings of Papua New Guinea

As with all of the destinations we visit, there is much more to the music of Papua New Guinea than covered in this book. While the *susap* is a common instrument, it is primarily played by children and is considered by most adults as a "toy" for those of courting age. Many other traditional forms of music have a much higher status for communities. These emphasize group vocal production, typically accompanied by communal dancing.

The most common instrument throughout PNG is the *kundu*, a small goblet-shaped drum with a face made of either lizard or snake skin. Many have anthropomorphic features, such as a crocodile shape and can exceed 9 feet (3 meters) in length. The largest drums (known as *diwaka*) are considered community property and played for important rituals and village gatherings. The smaller *kundu* are carried by the performers as they dance and sing. Other instruments include stamping tubes, a variety of flutes, and the well-known *garamut,* which are large hollow log idiophones struck with sticks that are used to communicate messages over large distances as well as accompany singing and dancing.

Singsings are among the most common contexts for musical performance among aboriginal populations in PNG. These events typically include participants from several villages, who perform clan dances and music throughout the day and often overnight. *Singsings* today are intended in part to celebrate the diverse ethnic makeup of the island communities and foster cultural exchange between groups that otherwise have little contact with each other. Participants adorn themselves in a colorful array of regalia, body paint, and sometimes face masks, attracting many outsiders to these social gatherings once considered a musical battleground between opposing clans, similar to the singing competitions found in other parts of Oceania (see Site 4: Kiribati).

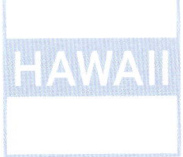

Arrival: Hawaii

The fiftieth state of the United States of America is geographically considered a part of Polynesia, a region including many other well-known islands such as Tahiti, Samoa, Easter Island, the Cook Islands, and even New Zealand. The first inhabitants of Hawaii most likely arrived from the Marquesas Islands and Tahiti, the largest of the Society Islands, sometime between the seventh and thirteenth centuries. These early settlers subsisted primarily on fish and *poi,* a pasty food made from taro root. Their social organization was essentially feudal and incorporated strict taboo systems, called *kapus.*

The first European visitor to Hawaii was the Englishman Captain James Cook, one of the most famous explorers of the late 1700s. Arriving in 1778, Cook was initially welcomed by the islanders, but relations between the British and Hawaiians soon turned sour, and in 1779 Cook died in a skirmish on a return visit to the islands. Nonetheless, within a few years the islands became an important port for European and North American trade. Increasing contact with outsiders brought many changes to indigenous ways of life. The islands were politically unified in 1810 by King Kamehameha I, who encouraged foreign trade and successfully maintained Hawaii's independence from colonial control. He also supported native cultural customs and the indigenous religion until his death in 1819.

Support for Hawaiian culture was, however, abandoned by Kamehameha's son and successor, Kamehameha II, who in less than a year destroyed the old system of *kapus* and abolished the ancient ritual practices. The temples and idols of the old religion, a complex form of animism, were ordered to be destroyed, and the king welcomed the arrival of Christian missionaries soon afterward. Visitors to the former palace in downtown Honolulu will note the strong central European influence adopted by the old monarchy. These events brought drastic changes to secular life as well, and the 1800s saw rapid changes in social organization, political power, and economic patterns. Sugarcane became a major export, and wealthy American businessmen began to acquire much power and land throughout the islands. The political power of the Hawaiian monarchy evaporated in the 1890s, and the country was eventually annexed by the United States.

The early 1900s saw an increased influx of immigrants from the United States, the Philippines, China, and Japan. Most came as laborers to work for the burgeoning pineapple and sugarcane plantations. The Japanese attack on Hawaii's Pearl Harbor on December 7, 1941, precipitated U.S. entry into the Pacific theater of World War II and made the islands of vital strategic interest to the United States. Initially, Japanese-Americans in Hawaii were distrusted, but their bravery in the ensuing war—they comprised some of the most decorated regimental military units in American history—diminished racial prejudice against them in the postwar years. Hawaii acquired statehood in 1959 and quickly became one of the most popular tourist destinations in the United States.

Amy Ku'uleialoha Stillman AN INSIDE LOOK

Hawaiian music is my birthright. My mother took me to hula lessons when I was five years old, and I had a ukulele in my hands by the time I was seven. After an adolescence hooked on Elvis and the Beatles, I returned to Hawaiian music in my high school years and have embraced it as my passion since. As an undergraduate at University of Hawai'i in the 1970s, I was shocked to read anthropological scholarship on Hawaiians that dismissed my parents' and my traditions of "modern" Hawaiian music as inauthentic because of its westernized character. I resolved then to get a Ph.D. in order to join the scholarly conversation at that level and be taken seriously.

Amy Ku'uleialoha Stillman, music researcher and scholar

A deliberate focus on research and writing precluded teaching hula performance for several decades, despite that I possessed the capacity to do so, because there were so few scholars with the aptitude for laborious archival research. My work has been devoted to exploring how contemporary Hawaiian performance retains indigenous Hawaiian aesthetics even as Hawaiian people embraced westernization and Christianity. I've reached back into archival resources and uncovered hundreds (if not thousands) of pieces of repertoire, only a fraction of which had been passed to the present in continuous performance. In the first edition of this book I wrote of my aspiration to bring the archival repertoire back to life by reuniting it with the performers who have main- tained the skills of singing and dancing. Since then, I have done exactly that, by curating three concerts and producing three CDs of contemporary settings of archival repertoire. This experience led to an opportunity to collaborate with Grammy Award-winning producer Daniel Ho on writing new songs. Our very first CD of original material, 'ikena, received the Grammy Award for Best Hawaiian Album in 2009, and our second CD, He Nani, received a nomination in 2010. My career, initially devoted to documenting Hawaiian performance, has gone full circle to creating new repertoire, by adding to the stream of tradition.

Explore More

Hawaiian Steel Guitar and Ukulele

Although *Hula* is the music and dance tradition most associated with the islands, steel guitar is also an important musical export of Hawaii. The Hawaiian steel guitar style is distinctive for its characteristic "sliding tone" (i.e., portamento) produced by sliding a metal bar along the strings without pressing them down to the fretboard. This allows the performer to sound all the frequencies between two standard pitches, thus "sliding" into many pitches of the melody. Because of the emphasis on this pitch-bending effect, melodic lines tend to have a low rhythmic density and the overall tempo is moderate to slow. Wide vibrato and harmonic overtones are common to Hawaiian steel guitar performances, particularly on electric instruments, which first became popular in the 1930s.

While the guitar is believed to have arrived in Hawaii during the 1830s, the first appearance of the "sliding" performance technique is typically attributed to Joseph Kekuku in 1885, who as a young boy experimented for several years with this sound on his guitar using various materials, string tunings to produce a variety of chords, and timbral effects, such as harmonic overtones, that were to become standard to the Hawaiian steel guitar tradition. In 1904, Kekuku traveled to the United States (Hawaii was not yet a state) and also toured Europe with his pioneering guitar style. Other performers who had adopted Kekuku's style followed, and by the mid-1920s the Hawaiian steel guitar had become popular throughout the mainland and abroad, particularly with vaudeville troupes and Country & Western musicians who incorporated the instrument into their own music, leading to the development of the *dobro* and pedal steel guitar as the instruments are known today. African-American blues artists of the 1920s–1930s also utilized a similar sliding technique, creating a "bottle-neck" style of blues music that incorporated fingerpicking as well. Hawaiian steel guitar remained popular through the 1960s, particularly in association with Hollywood movies, such as Elvis Presley's *Blue Hawaii* (1961).

Whereas the Hawaiian steel guitar tends toward a long, lilting melody, the *ukulele*, a small four-stringed Portuguese version of the guitar, often has a more rapid playing technique. Brought to the islands in the late nineteenth century, the ukulele was adopted by Hawaiians to accompany vocal performance and to be played as a solo instrument. The name translates as "flying flea," a reference to the fast plucking technique utilized by its early performers. The standard (or soprano) ukulele is roughly 18–20 inches long (46–53 cm) with twelve to seventeen frets following the Western tuning system. The strings are tuned to G–C–E–A, such that the C is the lowest pitch, with the others above in the same octave. The instrument often appears in small ensembles that also include a guitar and string bass and has become popular to accompany *hula* dances.

Another important Hawaiian style of performance is known as the "slack-key guitar," which first appeared on commercial recordings during the 1940s. This method requires the instrument strings be loosened to alter the standard guitar tuning. Instrumental performances include a rapid finger-picking style as well as hammer-on and pull-off techniques with the fretboard hand and "chime" effects produced by lightly touching a string at its harmonic node to sound an overtone. Vocalists often accompany themselves with this guitar style and pass on their songs through oral tradition. Among the most famous performers of the genre was Raymond Kane (1925–2008), a recipient of the National Heritage Fellowship in 1987, as well as Ledward Kaapana (n.d.) who is well-known today.

Site 3: Hawaiian Drum-Dance Chant

First Impressions. While chanting in most traditions is strongly speech-like, Hawaiian drum-dance chant is often more song-like. Each phrase rolls off the vocalist's tongue like the gentle lap of ocean waves on a white sand beach or the graceful, flowing arm movements of Hawaii's famous *hula* dancers. The drums add a solid, but not overbearing, undercurrent that gives the performance an earthy feel, suggestive of a spiritual connection to nature.

Aural Analysis. Hawaiian drum-dance chant consists simply of a voice, one or two drums, and accompanying dance. Other rhythmic instruments, such as stamping tubes (*ka'eke'eke*) or gourd idiophones (*ipu heke*), can be added. The preferred vocal timbre is usually full, with a deep, resonant tone quality. Vocal ornamentation is important, as with all styles of Polynesian chant. A prominent feature of Hawaiian vocal performance is the use of *vibrato* (a wavering of a tone). While vibrato is commonly used in many world traditions, it is generally applied to sustained pitches. Hawaiian vocalists, however, frequently apply vibrato to shorter tones as well. The text setting is primarily syllabic—that is, it employs only one pitch per syllable, utilizing only two tones at an interval of a minor third. The vocalist emphasizes the upper pitch but "falls" or "slides" to the lower pitch on sustained tones. This "sliding" technique is referred to as **portamento** and involves a continuous movement from one pitch to another, usually from high to low, with all of the frequencies between the two pitches being sounded. The singer in our example uses portamento occasionally at the beginning of the performance.

Another distinctive feature of Hawaiian vocal performance is inherent in the language itself. Most words end with open vowel sounds, such as *ah, oh, oo, ai*, and so on, rather than closed, hard consonants, such as *k, t*, or *p*. While hard consonants are found at the beginning of some words, they tend to be deemphasized. As such, the singing flows from one phrase to the next with smooth transitions, as in our example, which begins with the vocalist speaking the phrase *"(Ai) Kaulilua i ke anu Waì alé ale"* before singing it. The open vowel sounds facilitate the use of portamento as well as vibrato and help give the music its "flowing" feel.

The accompanying drums are known as the **pahu** and the **kilu** (also *puniu*). The *pahu* is a single-headed cylindrical membranophone that stands vertically on a carved footed base. The base and resonator are typically a single unit made from the wood of either a breadfruit or coconut tree. The *pahu* can be as short as around 9 inches (23 cm) or as tall as almost 4 feet (123 cm). Its face is traditionally made from sharkskin, or sometimes from manta ray skin, and is attached with twine made from the outer fibers of coconuts. The *kilu* is a smaller drum made from a gourd, wood, or a coconut shell and traditionally has a face made from fish skin. The *kilu* is sometimes attached to the performer's leg with a strap. It is played with a narrow strip of braided coconut fibers, creating a higher "slapping" sound relative to the *pahu*, which is played with the hand. The *pahu* is considered the more important of the two instruments, and its irregular rhythmic patterns correspond to important points in the song text and associated dance movements.

The Hawaiian ukulele (Shutterstock)

PORTAMENTO
A smooth, uninterrupted glide from one pitch to another.

PAHU
A single-headed cylindrical membranophone from Hawaii that stands vertically on a carved footed base.

KILU
A small drum from Hawaii, usually made from a coconut shell with a fish skin face.

LISTENING GUIDE

 CD 1.3 (2'02")

Chapter 4: Site 3
Hawaii: *Mele Hula Pahu* (Drum–Dance Chant)

Voice: Single female

Instruments: *Kilu* (high-pitched drum), *pahu* (low-pitched drum)

TIME	LISTENING FOCUS
0'00"	Spoken text: "(Ai) Kaulilua i ke anu Waì alé alé"
0'04"	Introductory four-pulse (duple meter) drum pattern, followed by basic pattern used throughout performance. Listen for variations in the basic drum pattern, such as at 0'28", 0'37", 0'54", etc.

Drum Introduction

Kilu (high)	-×ׄ×	-×ׄ×	-×ׄ×	×-
Pahu (low)	×	×	×	×-

Basic Pattern

Kilu (high)	-×ׄ×	×	-×ׄ×	×
Pahu (low)	×	× ×- ×		× ×-

TIME	LISTENING FOCUS
0'09"	Vocalist enters. Spoken text (at 0'00") is now chanted (0'09"–0'13").
0'37"	Both drums sound simultaneously.
0'56"	Listen for extended vibrato in voice.
1'01"	Second verse begins.
1'44"	Extended vocal vibrato closes verse.
1'49"	Closing drum pattern.
1'55"	Closing spoken verse.
1'58"	*Kilu* drum closes the chant with three strikes.

Source: "Kau ka hali'a I ka Manawa," performed by Noenoe Lewis (drum, vocal) and Hau'oli Lewis (calls, dance); from the recording entitled *Hawaiian Drum Dance Chants: Sounds of Power in Time*, SF 40015, provided courtesy of Smithsonian Folkways Recording © 1989. Used by permission.

ETHNO-CHALLENGE (CD 1.3): Write out the drum patterns for the entire example and play along with the performance.

Cultural Considerations. The best-known examples of Hawaiian music today are heavily influenced by European musical traditions. Because Christian missionaries were often strict with regard to the vocal practices of converted islanders, much of the vocal music came to be based on European hymnody and utilizes conceptions of harmony that presumably did not exist prior to contact with Europeans. Popular instruments such as the Hawaiian "slack-key" steel guitar, which uses a steel slide to stop the strings, or the *ukulele*, a small chordophone modeled after the guitar, only appeared in Hawaiian music after the colonial period began. Thus, the "traditional" ensembles that tourists often see accompanying hula dancers or hear on popular recordings reveal much Western influence.

A Hawaiian musician plays the *kilu* (left) and *pahu* (right) drums (George Bacon)

Near the edge of Hale Ma'uma'u Crater, dancers perform a *hula* in honor of Pele, the volcano goddess (Adrienne L. Kaeppler)

Hawaiian drum-dance chant, however, is considered free from outside influence and remains a vital aspect of Hawaiian musical identity. The songs play an important role in the maintenance of indigenous language, spiritual beliefs, history, and social customs. While the poetic text of these songs or chants is the primary focus, the musical delivery is also important, as it enhances the efficacy of the words. Poetry used in drum-dance chant is generally referred to as *mele*. There are several categories of *mele*, the most sacred of which, *mele pule*, consists of prayers dedicated to traditional gods, performed by ritual specialists known as *kahuna*. Lesser categories of *mele* trace genealogical histories, name and honor people, or signify specific ritual contexts, such as weddings or funerals.

Mele hula are songs specifically associated with dance. Some are purely vocal, while those called **hula pahu** are accompanied by the *pahu* drum. *Pahu* are highly valued ritual objects that hold much spiritual power (or *mana*). The sound produced is considered a voice and traditionally was believed to "speak" to the gods. Drums were typically the property of chiefs or priests and were symbolic of their authority and sacred power. As such, they were treasured items sought after by rival kingdoms. The *pahu* was used in many ritual contexts, such as important births or memorial services but today is primarily found accompanying dances and rituals promoting Hawaiian ethnic identity.

HULA PAHU
Hawaiian dance songs using drum accompaniment.

Hawaiian *hula* dancers (Shutterstock)

Arrival: Kiribati

Kiribati (pronounced "Kiribas") is a collection of islands in Micronesia situated about 2,500 miles (4,000 km) southwest of Hawaii. Its thirty-three coral islands, all but one of which are atolls (circular islands with a central lagoon), are divided into three groups: the Line Islands

OCEANIA

Uninhabited islands in the Pacific Ocean, part of the Republic of Palau in Micronesia (Shutterstock)

(east), the Phoenix Islands (central), and the Gilbert Islands (west), the latter being where most of the population resides. Kiritimati, also known as Christmas Island, is the largest coral atoll in the world and was among the many islands of the Pacific explored by Captain James Cook in 1777. Throughout the 1800s, British and American sailors visited the islands while hunting sperm whales and expanding trade routes. The British eventually claimed most of the islands of Kiribati as British protectorates; thus, English is widely spoken along with the native tongue, Gilbertese, an Austronesian language.

The first Protestant missionaries arrived in 1857, while the earliest Roman Catholics came in 1888. Much modern social life revolves around church activities. International sports, such as soccer and volleyball, are popular, along with traditional competitive activities, such as canoe racing. Many I-Kiribati, as the islanders are known, rely on fishing and subsistence farming for survival and live in traditional houses made of wood and coconut palms, though there are also a few urban areas where inhabitants live in modern houses and import much of their food and other necessities.

Site 4: Group Song for *bino* (sitting dance) from Kiribati

First Impressions. Vocal performance among Pacific islanders is often a communal activity. The choir in our example comprises both men and women and has a distinctive "childlike" tonal quality once the group begins to sing. The example may initially give the impression of a solemn occasion, but then transitions to a celebratory atmosphere with boisterous hand clapping and enthusiastic singing in a regular rhythm with harmony.

Seated dancers during a *bino* ceremony in Kiribati (Mary Lawson Burke)

Kiribati women perform in a temporary performing space at an island festival wearing a thick grass skirt and flower-and-fiber adornments, with a conductor and a seated chorus in the background (Adrenne L. Kaeppler)

Aural Analysis. Vocal choirs are common throughout Micronesia and Polynesia. Because most traditional performances are sung in unison, the use of harmony in our example reflects European musical influences, primarily introduced by Christian missionaries. Indigenous songs tend to use fewer pitches than those associated with the church—normally no more than five. The "youthful" vocal timbre of primarily the female singers is somewhat nasal and strained, in contrast to the male voices that are forceful and full.

In the Kiribati islands, vocal performances influenced by the church sometimes start with a freely rhythmic section that is closer to indigenous traditions. These are most typical of sitting dances (*te bino*), where the majority of performers are seated on the ground. More recent music/dance genres (e.g., *te buki, te kaimatoa, te kateitei*) do not have an initial freely rhythmic section. These begin with the metered section often marked by the steady pulse of handclaps. During the metered section, the voices follow a call-and-response pattern, though the call is primarily just a shout that establishes pitch and signals the choir's entrance. The text setting is mostly syllabic. A whistle is sometimes used to signal the choir to close the performance with a brief series of handclaps.

As described by Mary Lawson Burke, the ethnomusicologist who recorded the site example.

> This example of music for the bino sitting dance begins with the traditional freely rhythmic section, and then proceeds into the main body of the piece, which is characterized by a steady beat, clapping accompaniment, and alternation between "traditional" monophonic music and harmonized music. Prior to the beginning of the piece you can hear the call "akeia," which calls everyone to attention and provides the starting pitch, and then the song leader sings "au bino," or "my bino"—which is always done at the start of the sitting dance.
>
> I picked this example because the text is rather interesting in that it deals with WWII. (The famous Battle of Betio was fought on Tarawa atoll.) After the initial rather ambiguous section, the words don't discuss the local battle, but instead describe the pitiable state of Hitler (Ai kawa ra, Hitler eee), in that he thinks he will triumph in the end, but won't. America is fighting against him, with the aid of Britain. And near the end . . . the flag of victory is flying. Hurray.
>
> Except for the repeat of the last section, and some minor internal textual repeats, the text is through-composed. In performance, people would generally immediately repeat the whole thing again. The clapping patterns correspond with quick movements of the head, arms, and hands in the dance. The bino is one of over 10 dance genres, exact number depending on the island, that are distinguished by melodic style ("traditional" music genres), dance style, local vs. Polynesian-influenced, and whether the music incorporates Western harmony.
>
> (Personal Communication, 2011)

LISTENING GUIDE

 CD 1.4 (2'25")

Chapter 4: Site 4
Kiribati: Group Song for *bino* (sitting dance)

Voices: Mixed male/female ensemble

TIME	LISTENING FOCUS
0'00"	Opening section in free rhythm. Two male vocalists establish tonal center and initiate the performance.
0'14"	Choir enters singing in free rhythm with a monophonic structure.
0'35"	Main body of performance begins with regular beat and handclaps. Note that slight variations of tempo occur throughout the performance. Singing continues with monophonic structure (A section).
0'43"	Singing shifts to homophony (B section).
0'56"	Monophonic singing (A).
1'06"	Homophonic singing (B).
1'18"	Monophonic singing (A section with variation).
1'40"	Homophonic singing (B section with variation).
1'59"	Previous section (B with variation) repeats.
2'16"	Closing calls.

Source: "Kai e titirou e matie," sung with clapping by men and women of Ititin Rotorua Dance Troupe, Betio Village, Tarawa Island, Kiribati; recorded by Mary Lawson Burke, 1981. Used by permission.

ETHNO-CHALLENGE (CD 1.4): Listen repeatedly and sing along with each part of the homophonic structure (just the pitches will do). If you are able to, try to transcribe the music with Western staff notation.

MANEABA
Term for a communal meetinghouse in Kiribati.

Cultural Considerations. Choral traditions in Oceania predate the arrival of European colonialism. In Kiribati, music and dance were important symbols of social identity. All members of a performance ensemble were of the same descent group. Participation in performance was essential to community cohesion, and musical skills were regarded as valuable clan property. Song was considered a vital link to ancestral spirits and supernatural powers associated with natural elements, such as the wind or the ocean. Communities sang in communal meetinghouses called **maneaba** the night before a battle, in order to help protect warriors or weaken enemies.

In lieu of physical combat, battles between rival clans frequently took the form of music and dance contests. Contests could involve the whole community or consist of matches between individuals. Competitors drew upon their knowledge of song to empower themselves with offensive and defensive magic. A dancer might call on the wind to "knock over" his enemy or conjure up a wall of dark thunderclouds to hide himself from his opponent. Through song, powerful deities were called on for strength and disparaging insults were traded, wrapped in metaphorical phrases, intended to antagonize the rivals. For example, a deity might be called on to strike the "distant rocks" (i.e., the rival group), so that they would crumble into the ocean and be eaten by baby sharks—a request that obliquely insulted the strength of the competitors, because baby sharks were viewed as weak and harmless. Competitions could put the dancers into an ecstatic state in which the power of the spirits would seem to work through the performers. These states were marked by labored breathing, trembling, and occasional screaming, and performers generally fainted after the spiritual power had left them.

The colonial government and Christian missionaries found the dances and their associated spiritual beliefs to be irreligious, unhealthy, and unproductive. As a result, restrictions were placed on dance activity to subdue the potential for ecstatic physical states. At the same time, church-related groups and social clubs without lineal affiliation began participating in the competitions, which undermined their function as surrogate battles between lineages. The focus of the competitions shifted from an emphasis on descent groups and the supernatural powers of the participants to the artistic skills of the dancers and musicians.

Along with this shift in focus came changes in musical values. European musical practices, namely the use of harmony, became markers of superior musical performance and thus a common feature of song in Kiribati. Since achieving independence in 1979, however, Kiribati has experienced a revival of interest in traditional culture that has encouraged the performance of freely rhythmic unison singing along with the metered harmonic choral singing.

Questions to Consider

1. Why would vocal traditions predominate in Australia and Oceania?
2. How do you circular breathe? Why is this technique useful when playing certain musical instruments?
3. How do Hawaiians use music to express their unique identity within American culture?
4. Why is music important to the Australian Aborigine's cosmology, *The Dreaming*?
5. How might musical instruments be used in courting practices? Does your culture have any courting rituals? If so, does music play a role in them?
6. Name some ways in which Christian missionaries have influenced traditional music in Oceania.

On Your Own Time

Visit the textbook website to find these resources for further exploration on your own.

Australia

Book: Marret, Allan. *Songs, Dreamings, and Ghosts: The Wangga of North Australia.* Middletown, CT: Wesleyan University Press, 2005.
http://www.upne.com/0-8195-6617-9.html

Audio: Maralung, Alan, and Peter Manaberu. *Bunggridj-Bunggridj: Wangga Songs: Northern Australia.* Smithsonian Folkways: SFW40430, 1993.
http://www.folkways.si.edu/albumdetails.aspx?itemid=2318
http://itunes.apple.com/us/album/the-worlds-musical-traditions/id81978916

Audio: Seachnasaigh, Will. *Dharpa Songs of the Dreamtime.* Lyrichord: LYRCD 7442, 1998.
http://lyrichord.com/dharpasongsofthedreamtime-willseachnasaigh.aspx
http://itunes.apple.com/us/album/the-didjeridu-dharpa-songs/id56890650

Website: Music Australia
http://www.musicaustralia.org/apps/MA

Website: Australian Music Center
http://www.australianmusiccentre.com.au/

Website: Australian Government—Music
http://www.cultureandrecreation.gov.au/articles/music/

Popular Artists: Australia
Yothu Yindi   Kylie Minogue   Hoodoo Gurus   INXS

Papua New Guinea (Melanesia)

Audio: *Bosavi: Rainforest Music from Papua New Guinea.* Smithsonian Folkways: SF40487, 2001.
http://www.folkways.si.edu/albumdetails.aspx?itemid=2690
http://itunes.apple.com/us/album/bosavi-rainforest-music-from/id82375605

Book: Feld, Steven. *Sound and Sentiment: Birds, Weeping, Poetics, and Song in Kaluli Expression.* Philadelphia: University of Pennsylvania Press, 1982.
http://music.unm.edu/faculty_staff/fac_profiles/feld.htm

Website: Melanesian Music
http://www.melanesianmusic.org/

Website: National Geographic Music—Papua New Guinea
http://worldmusic.nationalgeographic.com/view/page.basic/country/content.country/papua_new_guinea_854/en_US

Internet: Popular Artists from Melanesia
George Telek   Rosiloa   The Wagi Brothers

Hawaii (Polynesia)

Audio: *Hawaiian Drum-Dance Chants: Sounds of Power in Time.* Smithsonian Folkways: SF40015, 1989.
http://www.folkways.si.edu/albumdetails.aspx?itemid=2057
http://itunes.apple.com/us/album/hawaiian-drum-dance-chants/id117733099

Video: *Holo Mai Pele: The Epic Hula Myth.* Dir. Catherine Tatge. PBS, 2004.
http://www.piccom.org/programs/holo-mai-pele

Website: Black Pearl Designs—Polynesian Culture
http://blackpearldesigns.net/index.html

Website: Hawaiian Music and Hula Archives
http://www.huapala.org/

Audio: Amy Ku'uleialoha Stillman and Daniel Ho. *Ikena*. Daniel Ho Creations: DHC 80078, 2010.
http://www.danielho.com/html/naikena.html
http://itunes.apple.com/us/album/ikena/id288690522

Book: Elbert, Samuel H., and Noelani K. Mahoe. *Na Mele O Hawai'i Nei: 101 Hawaiian Songs*. Honolulu: University of Hawaii Press, 1970.
http://www.uhpress.hawaii.edu/cart/shopcore/?db_name=uhpress&page=shop/flypage&product_id=878&category_id=b3e6237d1b1b3b8594488ed1c40d0dfb&PHPSESSID=64a98cce4139e1bb203f37073f898e6e

Book: Stillman, Amy Ku'uleialoha. *Sacred Hula: The Historical Hula 'Ala'apapa*. Honolulu: Bishop Museum Press, 1998.
http://173.201.252.229/press/web/detailed.php?ID=0-930897-73-0

Book: Kaeppler, Adrienne. *Hula Pahu: Hawaiian Drum Dances, Volume I: Ha'a and Hula Pahu, Sacred Movements*. Honolulu: Bishop Museum Press, 1993.
http://173.201.252.229/press/web/detailed.php?ID=0-930897-55-2

Website: Hawaiian Slack Key Guitar Festival
http://www.slackkeyfestival.com/

Internet: Popular Artists from Polynesia
Daniel Ho
IZ (Israel Kamakawiwo´ole)
Led Kaapana (Hawaiian Slack Key Guitar and Ukulele)

Kirbati (Micronesia)

Audio: *Spirit of Micronesia*. Saydisc: CD-SDL 414, 1995.
http://www.saydisc.com/ (Pacific)
http://itunes.apple.com/us/album/spirit-of-micronesia/id423356983

Book: Abels, Birgit. *Sounds of Articulating Identity. Tradition and Transition in the Music of Palau, Micronesia*. Berlin: Logos, 2008.
http://www.logos-verlag.de/cgi-bin/buch/isbn/1866

Book: Feinberg, Richard. *Oral Traditions of Anuta: A Polynesian Outlier in the Solomon Islands*. New York: Oxford University Press, 1998.
http://www.oup.com/us/catalog/general/subject/Linguistics/SociolinguisticsAnthropologicalL/?view=usa&ci=9780195106831

Book: Kaeppler, Adrienne. *The Pacific Arts of Polynesia and Micronesia*. New York: Oxford University Press, 2008.
http://www.oup.com/us/catalog/general/subject/ArtArchitecture/History/NonWestern/~~/dmlldz11c2EmY2k9OTc4MDE5Mjg0MjM4MQ==

Website: Jane's Oceania Home Page—Dedicated to music and culture of Oceania
http://www.janeresture.com/index.htm

Website: New Micronesian Magazine
http://newmicronesian.com/

Internet: Popular Artists from Micronesia
Ozeky
ReChuuk

Approximate divide between North (Sites 1 and 2) and South Indian (Site 3) musical regions.

Site 4

Site 2 + 3

Site

South Asia: India, Pakistan

5

Background Preparation	90	*Explore More*: Kathakali	115
An Inside Look: Shanti Raghavan	94	Site 3: Hindu *Bhajan* Devotional Song	116
An Inside Look: Aashish Khan	95	*Explore More*: Indian *Filmi Git* (Film Song)	121
Planning the Itinerary	96		
Arrival: North India	97	**Arrival: Pakistan**	122
Site 1: Hindustani (Instrumental) *Raga*	97	Site 4: *Qawwali* (Sufi Devotional Song)	123
Need to Know: Fundamentals of Indian Classical (Hindustani) Music	107	*Explore More*: Bhangra	127
Arrival: South India	108	**Questions to Consider**	128
Site 2: Carnatic Classical (Vocal) *Kriti*	108	**On Your Own Time**	128

One of many great temples on the sacred Ganges River in Varanasi (Benares), India (Max T. Miller)

Background Preparation

There are two areas of the world that can easily overwhelm someone wishing to explore their musics. The first is East Asia, where approximately one quarter of the world's people live. The second is South Asia, an area with 1.5 billion people, again nearly a quarter of the world's people. One nation—India—dominates South Asia demographically (population 1.1 billion) and in landmass, but the region also includes Bangladesh, Nepal, Bhutan, Pakistan, Sri Lanka, and even Afghanistan (in some groupings). India, Pakistan, and Bangladesh all have extensive coastlines stretching to the Arabian Sea and the Bay of Bengal, leaving the other countries landlocked—except for Sri Lanka, which is an island to the southeast of India. In addition, a few island groups, though having slight populations, are also considered part of South Asia, including the Andaman and Nicobar Islands, the Maldives, and the Seychelles. Parts of Afghanistan and Pakistan and most of Nepal and Bhutan are mountainous, but unlucky Bangladesh is not only flat but also only a little above sea level, leaving it vulnerable to numerous typhoons each year during which up to half of the country may flood.

Much of the region experiences fairly harsh climates, varying from the intense heat of India to the tropical moisture of Bangladesh and Sri Lanka to the arid winters of the northern and upland areas. Temperatures in India can reach as high as 127° Fahrenheit/53° Celsius; conversely, temperatures in India's snowy northern mountains are frigid in winter. Numerous great rivers drain the Himalayas through India and Bangladesh, including the well-known and sacred Ganges (or Ganga), along with the Indus and Brahmaputra. Parts of Pakistan and Afghanistan, however, are desert. Populations tend to be the greatest and most concentrated where water is most plentiful; most great civilizations began and flourished along rivers, and this principle holds true for South Asia.

Village in the hills near Kathmandu, Nepal, from which could be seen the tops of the Himalaya Mountains

SOUTH ASIA

A sheep herder in Afghanistan (Shutterstock)

In South Asia, India is the country no one can ignore. It is a nation of striking contrasts. India has riches in the form of palaces, treasures, and temples that are beyond imagination, but it also has great poverty. Many in the West are familiar with the plight of the underclass in places like Kolkata (formerly Calcutta), where Mother Theresa worked to alleviate suffering. India is the world's largest democracy, but struggles to maintain a balance among competing religions and ethnic groups. It is a nation where hundreds of millions of farmers work in conditions that have changed little over the centuries, but which also is home to

In Old Delhi, Jama Masjid Delhi or Masjid-i-Jahan Numa, the largest Muslim mosque in Asia (N. Scott Robinson)

the world's largest computer programming industry, clustered around high-tech Bangalore. India is home to several of the world's great religions, all having the common goal of peace—but it is also a place where tragic interethnic violence has been known to break out.

While South Asia is dominated by a small number of large countries, these monolithic political groupings belie the diversity of the region's populations. During the colonial era prior to the independence of both India and Pakistan in 1947, the British collected together some 562 small states into a single Indian colony, which originally included Pakistan and Bangladesh. While modern-day India uses only two main languages—Hindi and English—the constitution recognizes sixteen official languages. Some 25 percent of the population, mostly in the South, speak a variety of Dravidian languages. In reality there are some 1,652 languages and dialects spoken in India today. In addition to India's many languages, Persian (Farsi) and several Turkic languages are spoken in Afghanistan, Urdu and English are officially spoken in Pakistan, and Nepali in Nepal. Most of these languages are part of the vast family of Indo-European languages.

Many different religions can be found throughout South Asia. Hinduism is the major religion of India (82%). Islam is also found within India (12%), principally in the north, and is the dominant religion of Bangladesh, Pakistan, and Afghanistan. When Britain granted independence to the Raj in 1947, Pakistan was formed as a separate Muslim state and originally consisted of eastern and western portions flanking India. In 1971 Pakistan's Eastern Province seceded to become Bangladesh. Theravada Buddhism is the primary religion of Sri Lanka, though the country has a Hindu minority as well. Mahayana Buddhism predominates in Nepal and Bhutan, but some Hinduism is also found in both countries. Finally, Jainism,

The *Taj Mahal* in Agra, Uttar Pradesh, the most famous tomb in the world, built by Shah Jahan and completed in 1652 (N. Scott Robinson)

Indian street musician "charms" two cobra snakes with his *puñgī* (also called *bīn* or *murlī*), consisting of two pipes with single reeds (a drone pipe and a melody pipe with finger holes) inserted into a gourd windchest (Max T. Miller)

Sikhism, the Baha'i Faith, and Christianity, not to mention a small community of Jews, are also found in India along with small congregations of animistic practitioners.

Traditionally, social organization in South Asia was hierarchical. This was especially true in India, where the population was organized into **castes** or groupings—ranging from the highest or priestly class to the lowest or "untouchable" class—to which an individual was assigned based on their status at birth. This system, which is tenuously related to Hinduism, has now been abolished in India, though it still influences many spheres of life, such as marriages and occupational opportunities. Certain castes or sub-castes were closely associated with specific kinds of music. For example, only Brahmin priests are permitted to recite the highly sacred *Vedic* chant, while non-Brahmins normally specialize in the playing of instruments, particularly ones that involve skin (drums) or saliva (flutes and reeds). In addition, gender plays a major role in determining who can perform what kinds of music or play what kinds of instruments.

CASTE SYSTEM
A hierarchical system of social organization based on one's hereditary status at birth, found in India and associated with Hinduism.

Shanti Raghavan

AN INSIDE LOOK

I have been teaching Carnatic music for the past twenty-five years in the Cleveland area and am an exponent of the *Karaikudi* style of *Veena*. I started learning Veena at age seven and trained under Shri [honorific title] Viswanathan, a direct disciple of the legendary Shri Karaikudi Sambasiva Iyer, and then briefly under Mrs. Rajeswari Padmanabhan, granddaughter of Shri Sambasiva Iyer. From the beginning, because I displayed an innate talent for music, my teachers were delighted to see me progress quickly from one level to the next. I hail from a family of musicians. My mother, a devout lover of Carnatic music, was an excellent violinist. My sister, Mrs. Mohana Santhanam, was trained under Shri Jayarama Iyer (who was a disciple of Shri Semmangudi Srinivasa Iyer). Thus, my childhood years were inundated with these two very powerful styles of music.

Shanti Raghavan, teacher of South Indian Music

When first approached to teach music, I was hesitant and unsure if this would work out. But once I started, I have never looked back. I saw teaching Carnatic music as an opportunity to introduce Indian culture to children growing up in the United States. Therefore, I have never turned away any student for lack of apparent talent. Instead, I have taken a disciplined approach to developing talent in all students who show an interest and instilling in them an awareness of Indian culture. I have a sincere belief that music is a truly spiritual experience that brings people closer to the Almighty. I also believe that learning music brings balance to academics and enriches all facets of life. This passion and dedication has had a significant impact on the students and their parents. Not only passing on the art form has been important, but also making music part of the very being of my students has been my goal.

In 2008 my daughter, Mrs. Shruti Aring, and I founded a non-profit organization called *The Ragapriya School of Carnatic Music*. Its goal is to teach and promote Carnatic music in Northeast Ohio. The school seeks to provide a high-quality musical education by combining music theory with vocal, violin, and veena classes. Disciplined training increases my students' confidence and self-esteem, and they learn not only to appreciate music but also to perform in social and cultural events. *Bhajans* and *sloka* classes, as well as music appreciation classes, are also available for those interested. The school sponsors performances by both community members and professionals to make music a regular part of their lives. While the primary focus is on children, this school reaches out to everyone who is interested in learning music. The goal is to fill a need for structured and comprehensive musical instruction. My daughter, who is well trained in both Carnatic vocal and Carnatic violin, also gives lessons in the Cleveland area.

In keeping with the school's goals, the *Ragapriya School* has produced several thematic music programs. The inaugural program was entitled "Great Composers in Carnatic Music" and covered the lives and compositions of a dozen composers. Other programs included the "Dasavatara (the ten avataras of Vishnu)" and a fund raising program on "Devi (the life force and energy)." The school has also trained one student in music *arangetram*, which is a two-hour concert demonstrating the student's ability in all the advanced techniques of Carnatic music.

It is my hope that I have made a difference in the lives of all the children I touched through the power of music.

Aashish Khan

AN INSIDE LOOK

I was initiated into North Indian classical music at the age of five by my grandfather, the legendary Acharya Baba Allauddin Khan Sahib, exponent of the Senia Beenkar and Senia Rababiya Gharana founded in the sixteenth century by Mian Tansen, court musician to Emperor Akbar. I also learned music from my father, Ustad Ali Akbar Khan, and aunt, Smt. Annapurna Devi, both leading musicians in India. In 1953, I gave my first public performance at age thirteen with my grandfather on the All India Radio National Program in New Delhi. In 1961, I accompanied my father as a representative of the Government of India to the East–West Music Encounter in Tokyo, Japan. By 1967, I was performing the sarod internationally at such places as the Hollywood Bowl in Los Angeles (for an audience of over 20,000 people) as well as throughout India. In 1978, my brother, Pranesh Khan, and I founded the "Allauddin Academy of Music and Performing Arts" in Calgary, Alberta, Canada. In 1989, I was appointed to the prestigious post of Composer and Conductor for the National Orchestra, Vadya Vrinda of All India Radio, New Delhi, succeeding such musical stalwarts as Pandit Ravi Shankar and Pandit Pannalal Ghosh. A few years later, I traveled to South Africa on a concert tour organized by the governments of India and South Africa. I was the first Indian musician to represent India as an ambassador of Indian culture and classical music. My work can be heard in numerous films, such as Sir Richard Attenborough's *Gandhi*, John Houston's *The Man Who Would Be King*, Clint Eastwood's *Breezy*, and David Lean's

Aashish Khan, concert artist, composer, and teacher of North Indian Classical Music

A Passage to India, as well as Tapan Sinha's *Aadmi aur Aurat* and *Joturgriha*, for which I received the "Best Film Score Award" from the Bengal Film Journalist's Association. I have collaborated with such diverse Western musicians as John Barham, George Harrison, Ringo Starr, Eric Clapton, Charles Lloyd, John Handy, Alice Coltrane, George Brooks, Emil Richards, Dallas Smith, Don Pope, Jorge Strunz, Ardeshir Farah, and the Philadelphia String Quartet. I have been a music guru (teacher) for many years and have been on the faculties of the Ali Akbar College of Music, Ravi Shankar's Kinnara School of Indian Classical Music, the University of Washington, and the University of Alberta. I teach students throughout the United States, Canada, Europe, South Africa, and India while pursuing a busy career as a concert artist and composer. I am a true believer and follower of the "Guru Shishya Parampara," one of the oldest methods of teaching Indian classical music in an oral, practical, theoretical, and traditional manner. My true belief and objective is to pass on for generations to come the sixteenth-century traditions and culture from which I descend.

South Asia exhibits striking contrasts in terms of level of development. Afghanistan, a thinly populated and mountainous country with little infrastructure or internal unity, remains the least developed, while the urban areas of Pakistan and India are highly developed. Indeed, India and Pakistan have produced many of the world's greatest scientists and thinkers, and today India is a leader in the high-tech world. With its crushing population statistics, however, India must struggle to keep much of its population fed, clothed, housed, and employed. As in most developing countries, there are great contrasts between the wealth of the few and the poverty of the many. In Afghanistan and Sri Lanka, and sometimes in Pakistan as well, political instability has made modernization and development difficult to maintain. India, often described as the world's largest democracy, has remained stable even with one of the most diverse populations in the world.

Planning the Itinerary

Each of the nations that comprise South Asia offers exciting and distinctive musics, but it is the "classical" music of India that has gained most of the attention of outsiders. A visit to any large record store offering "international" releases will demonstrate this. Culturally, India is divided into a northern region and a southern region, with the former comprising two-thirds and the latter one-third of the country. Northern culture is called **Hindustani** and southern culture is called **Carnatic** (also spelled Karnatak). The north of India was deeply influenced by Indo-European invaders who brought the Aryan civilization from the northwest between 2000 and 1500 B.C.E. No one religion dominates the north, a situation not only giving rise to many coexisting faiths (Hinduism, Jainism, Sikhism, the Baha'i Faith, Islam), but also resulting in a more secular society. Hindustani music reflects this diversity and has far fewer relationships to religion than Carnatic music. Most northern languages are related to Hindi, while southern languages are mainly Dravidian, having been derived from layers of people who preceded the Aryans. The South in general has experienced less outside influence, and as a consequence Hinduism predominates—leading to a society that makes little distinction between the sacred and the secular.

Not surprisingly, Carnatic music is closely tied to Hinduism, though it has little to do with temple activities per se. Classical music in both traditions can be vocal or instrumental. The North Indian classical music with which Western audiences are much more familiar is primarily instrumental. Carnatic music, on the other hand, is primarily vocal. Indeed, much of the instrumental music of South India consists of transcriptions of vocal compositions.

Indian classical music, unlike the communal music of Africa or the ensemble music of Southeast Asia, is individual and often virtuosic. One attends a concert to hear a particular artist, rather than specific compositions or ensemble types, because most Indian classical music is composed spontaneously during performance through a process called *improvisation*. These improvisations usually unfold at a very leisurely pace: a full performance of a single improvisation can last anywhere from thirty minutes to two hours, and Indian classical concerts can easily last four or more hours.

In spite of the fact that Indian classical music is widely disseminated both in and outside India, the majority of the Indian population prefers to sing or listen to other kinds of music. Hindu lay people often sing devotional songs called *bhajans*, which can be popular in style. Music written for and transmitted by the movies is widely popular; in fact, the term for much of India's popular music is ***filmi***; and because India's film industry produces more films per year than that of any other country, the number of *filmi* songs is understandably vast. Beyond that is a great variety of popular styles collectively called "Indo-pop," while *bhangra*, a new form of popular music and dance derived from traditional Panjabi sources, first flourished among the Indian community in the United Kingdom in the 1980s and 1990s.

A musical tour of South Asia might also lead us to eastern India—known as Bengal—and to Bangladesh as well as to the west, to Pakistan. Most striking in Bengal and Bangladesh are the Bauls, free spirits who comment in their songs on topics as diverse as society, philosophy, and the joys and pains of daily life—and who can perhaps be thought of as the

HINDUSTANI
A term referring to the cultural traditions of North India.

CARNATIC (ALSO, KARNATAK)
A term referring to the cultural traditions of South India.

FILMI (ALSO, FILMI GIT)
Popular music taken from films in India.

equivalent of America's "singer-songwriters." Although Pakistan is an independent nation with a Muslim majority, no single type of music epitomizes its culture. Depending on the region, its music alternately reveals relationships with Afghanistan, Iran, or India. One kind of Pakistani music has, however, attracted a following outside Pakistan, a Sufi-Muslim devotional song genre called **qawwali** (sometimes spelled *kawwali*).

QAWWALI (ALSO, KAWWALI) Sufi-Muslim devotional songs.

Arrival: North India

India's northern cities—especially Mumbai, Pune, Delhi, Varanasi (Benares), and Lucknow—reflect the diversity of the peoples who together created modern Hindustani culture. What made North Indian culture distinctive were the many waves of people migrating or attacking from the Northwest, especially Persia. Consequently most people in the north are described as Indo-Aryan. This influx eventually brought Islam to India. Northern India offers visitors many great mosques, along with Sikh and Jain temples, the sixteenth-century palaces of the Mughal emperors, and the many governmental and celebratory edifices left by the British colonials. The region's vast cities are also home to North India's complex and sophisticated classical music tradition.

Site 1: Hindustani (Instrumental) *Raga*

First Impressions. Hindustani instrumental improvisations, called *raga*, are normally quite long. Because a piece of an hour or more would not be practical to study here, we have chosen an example that lasts less than five minutes—but that is nonetheless a "complete" *raga* performance. If you listen carefully to the very beginning, you will hear a buzzing timbre emanating from a plucked chordophone. Almost immediately, a more prominent and

North Indian (Hindustani) music played by Buddadev das Gupta, *sarod* lute; Zakir Hussain, *tabla* drums; and Elizabeth Howard, *tambura* drone lute

commanding stringed instrument asserts itself, while the first instrument continues in a slowly repetitious manner. The rather dreamy introduction music gradually grows more excited until there is a sudden deceleration, an exhale, if you will—followed by the entry of drums and return of the solo instruments. This new phase continues to the end.

Several elements stand out to the first-time listener: the "twangy" buzz of the introductory instrument, the constant ornamentation and pitch-bending of the main melodic instrument, and the steady tempo of the drums, one of which has a distinctive "scooping" sound. Noticeable changes in the level of relaxation and an increase in tension also occur as the performance proceeds.

Aural Analysis. Few other areas of the world's music require as much technical explanation as does Indian classical music. That is because an appreciation of this fascinating blend of fixed and improvised elements involves an understanding of several important musical aspects. Even as it employs a highly systematic compositional process, Indian classical music also allows for endless variation, and the genius of a performer is not in how well he or she follows established conventions but in how those conventions are manipulated for the purposes of individual expression.

The word **raga** (or *rag*, meaning "color" or "atmosphere") denotes a comprehensive system for the simultaneous composition and performance of music in both North and South India. Because the English word *improvisation* suggests a near total degree of spontaneity, it fails to capture the control, predictability, and bounded nature of *raga*. The creation of a *raga* is indeed a highly controlled compositional process, with established constructional boundaries—even if it allows for nearly unlimited individual variations within these boundaries. Western ethnomusicologists use the term **mode** to describe such systems. Think of them as *composition kits*; the elements of each *raga* provide the tools for the musician's performance. Whereas most Western music is notated on paper by "composers" before its performance, Indian classical music is unwritten, even though a *raga* unfolds in highly predictable ways. The length of a performance can vary from a few minutes to a couple of hours, depending on time constraints and the interest of the audience as sensed by the musicians.

Raga comprises several elements, the first being tonal material (what might be called a "scale"). These "scales" consist of a hierarchy of strong and weak notes, a set of typical melodic figures, and a set of extra-musical associations with such things as moods, times of the day, and magical powers. *Raga*s are sometimes represented pictorially as individual human beings or deities in miniature paintings called *ragamalas*.

The pitches of a *raga* are expressed in **solfège** syllables, a mnemonic system of names for each degree of the scale. The Indian equivalent to the West's *do-re-mi-fa-sol-la-ti-do* is *sa-re-ga-ma-pa-dha-ni-sa*, with which students of Indian *raga* can sing melody. As in the West, there are actually more pitches in the total tuning system than these seven because some pitches can be flatted or sharped; in India the total is usually said to be twenty-two, whereas only twelve pitches are used in the West. More than one *raga* may use the same set of pitches, but identical pitch sets are differentiated in practice from *raga* to *raga* due to differences in pitch hierarchy, typical melodic units, and extra-musical aspects. The two most important pitches are *sa* and *pa*, always a fifth degree apart.

The "buzzing" pitches briefly heard alone at the beginning of our audio example are played on the **tambura**, a four-stringed, long-necked lute with a large gourd body. The buzz timbre is produced due to small threads being placed under each string, causing them to

RAGA
A mode or system of rules and procedures for composition and improvisation in Indian classical music.

MODE
A set of rules and customary procedures used to compose or improvise music in a particular tradition.

SOLFÈGE
Mnemonic syllables corresponding to individual pitches in a scale.

TAMBURA
A round-bodied gourd lute used to provide the "drone" element in Indian classical music.

vibrate against the bridge when played. The person who plays this instrument, often a young disciple or a spouse of the lead instrumentalist, simply plucks the four strings successively throughout the *raga*. The four pitches reinforce the two most important pitches of the *raga*, usually the fundamental or "home" pitch (*sa*/pitch I) and another an interval of a fifth above (*pa*/pitch V), and are generally played in the order V (upper), I (upper), I (upper), I (lower). This continuous sound of the *tambura* helps solidify the tonal center of the *raga* and can be likened to incense permeating a room, except through sound rather than smell.

The main melodic instrument in our example is the **sarod**, also a long-necked lute. The *sarod* is generally around 40 inches (approximately 1 meter) long and has a large wooden body covered with goatskin. Its neck is tapering and hollow. The sarod has six main strings of metal running over a fretless metal-covered fingerboard to large tuning pegs, but there are also eleven to fifteen "sympathetic" metal strings running from within the neck (out through small, ivory-lined holes) to a series of smaller pegs on the side of the neck. These latter strings are tuned to vibrate in sympathy with the main strings, and provide a background of ethereal ringing. Sometimes the player will strum them briefly, mostly at the beginning of the piece, but otherwise they are not directly plucked in order to sound. Holding the instrument horizontally (similar to the way a guitar is held) and using a triangular pick of wax-covered coconut shell held in the right hand, the player can simply pluck the main melodic strings or pull (stretch), in the case of fretted instruments like the sitar, them to the side with the left hand to create the tone-bending and ornaments that practically define Indian *raga*.

SAROD
A fretless plucked lute from northern India.

The *tambura* lute has an untretted neck, four strings, and is played throughout a *raga* to produce drone pitches (N. Scott Robinson)

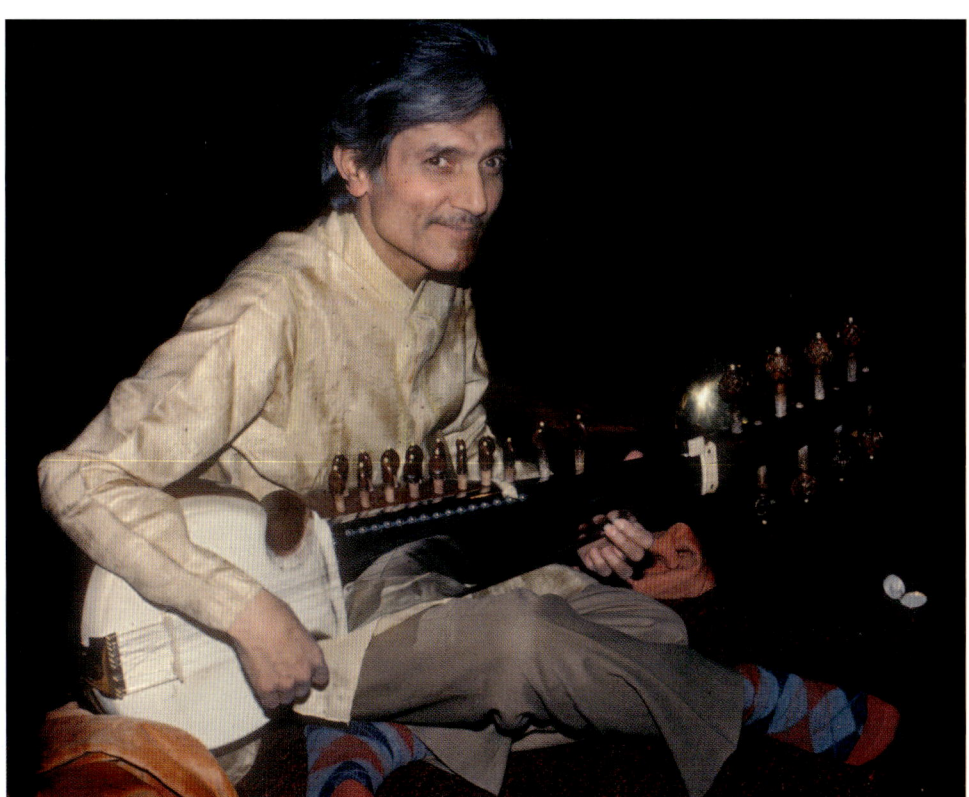

The late Indian musician Vasant Rai plays the *sarod* lute

Below the main strings of the *sitar*, and passing beneath the curved metal frets, are a large number of "sympathetic" strings that vibrate involuntarily when the main strings are played

ALAP
The opening section of a *raga* performance in which the performer "explores" the *raga*.

JOR
A regularizing of the beat in the opening section of *raga* performance in Indian classical music.

JHALA
Refers to a set of drone strings on Indian chordophones. Also, a reference to the climactic end of the *alap* section of *raga* performance in India.

TABLA
A pair of drums found in Hindustani music from India.

The first portion of a *raga* is called the **alap** and could be described as a period of exploration of the *raga* and its characteristics. The principal melodic player begins with the lower pitches, approaching them in a leisurely and experimental manner; there is no regular beat because the melody is played in free rhythm. Consequently, the drum, which is primarily responsible for the rhythmic element of a *raga* performance, is not heard during this opening section.

An *alap* can last for a mere minute or so, or be extended to an hour or more, depending on the taste of the performer and the interest of the audience. As the *alap* progresses, the player explores more pitches and melodic units, moving from the lower range of the instrument—representing relaxation or repose—into the higher ranges, which increases tension. Gradually the rhythms become somewhat steadier, though they never become totally metered; the term **jor** refers to this tenuous regularizing of beat. As the tempo and excitement increase (along with the tension), the player begins a regular alternation between melodic pitches and a set of drone strings called the **jhala**. Just as the playing reaches a feverish level of excitement, the "drive" suddenly slows as the player quickly descends through the scale back to the point of relaxation and the *alap* concludes.

At this point a pair of drums enters. These consist of a small cylindrical wooden drum with a single head called *tabla* and a larger, rounded metal drum with single head known as *baya*; together, the pair is also called **tabla**. Most players strike the smaller drum with the right hand and the larger with the left. The *tabla* (i.e., the smaller of the pair) is tuned to the *raga*'s fundamental pitch by tightening or loosening leather straps attached to the face; their tension is controlled by moving cylindrically shaped pieces of wood wedged between

5

SOUTH ASIA

Tabla refers to both the pair of Hindustani drums and to the cylindrical drum (below) in particular, while the kettle drum (above) is called *baya*

TALA
Cyclic rhythmic framework that organizes a *raga* performance in India.

the straps and the body of the drum. Each drum stroke has a name, and drummers memorize the stroke names as part of the learning process. Indeed, most drummers can *speak* the strokes, in a kind of "verbal drumming"—and many listeners are able to keep track of the cycle of strokes through patterns of handclaps and waves (see below).

The drummer plays a cycle of strokes called the **tala**. A *tala* is considered a closed cycle, because it has a fixed number of beats; these are subdivided into three or four sections. In Hindustani music there are hundreds of possible *talas*, each with its own name and specific number of beats, theoretically ranging from 3 to 128. In practice far fewer are used, and *talas* using seven to sixteen beats predominate. Of these, the best known and most often encountered is *tintal*, a *tala* having sixteen beats divided into four groupings of four pulses each. While *talas* are played beginning on beat 1, they do not end on the last beat, that is, 16, but rather end on beat 1 of what would have been the next cycle. The audience can hear where they are in the cycle by listening for the deep tones of the *baya* drum; in *tintal*, the *baya* either drops out or is played quietly during the third group (beats 9–12), allowing listeners to anticipate the restatement of beat 1.

Each drum stroke—whether played on a single drum or on a combination of drums—has a name, such as *dha*. Totally there are more than a dozen named strokes, some involving one drum, some both, some closed, that is, dampened (the fingers stay on the head, deadening the tone), some open (the fingers spring away allowing the head to vibrate). Drum stroke names are called **bols**. The entire pattern or set of words for a given *tala* is called the **theka**. The most basic *theka* for *tintal* is: *dha, dhin, dhin, dha/ dha, dhin, dhin, dha/ dha, tin, tin, ta/ ta, dhin, dhin, dha. Talas* can be recited in syllables as well. Skilled drummers play patterns that go far beyond this basic set, including a great many elaborate "compositions," each based on the *tala*'s cycle of beats.

BOLS
Mnemonic syllables corresponding to drum strokes in Indian drumming traditions.

THEKA
(pronounced *teh-kah*) The entire pattern or set of words (*bols*) for a given *tala* in classical Indian music.

During the *tabla*'s performance, disciples and audience members may "keep the *tala*" in a pattern involving claps, counts, and waves. As mentioned, tintal has four sections with four beats each. For sections 1, 2, and 4, you clap on beat 1 and silently count beats 2, 3, and 4. In section 3, you turn one hand over, giving a mini-wave (instead of clap) and then silently count the remaining three beats. When silently counting, you can either touch your right hand to the left or touch your thumb to three successive fingers.

GAT
The skeletal melody used as a basis for improvisation in a *raga* performance of classical Indian instrumental music.

When the drum enters, it often starts in the middle of the *tala* cycle (beats 9–16), but exceptions occur frequently. In our example, the **gat** begins on beat 1 and the drum enters on beat 11. The *sitar* or *sarod*, now relaxed and calm, plays a short composition—a kind of tune—called the *gat* (in vocal music this is called *chiz*). The *gat* is the skeletal melody around which the player will improvise. When improvising, the player may fragment the *gat*, restate

Schematic of the North Indian *tala* in a sixteen-beat cycle called *tintal*.

it in whole, or depart from it entirely. Some longer *raga* performances have more than one *gat*, perhaps a slow *gat* (*vilambit*) first that is longer in duration, a medium *gat* (*madhya*), then a fast *gat* (*drut*) that takes the shortest time to complete. The rhythmic density of the slow *gat* is the lowest, whereas the fast *gat* has the highest rhythmic density, contributing to the increasing tension of the music. The name of the *raga* remains the same regardless of the *gat* chosen, and although the *gat* is a composition, it does not usually have a "title" and the identity of its composer is regarded as insignificant.

The length of the *gat* matches the length of the *tala*; therefore, the use of *tintal* requires a 16-beat *gat*. In a sense, anything can happen during the overall *gat* section, which can last anywhere from a few minutes to an hour. As with the *alap*, the length of the *gat* depends on the audience's reaction, the performers' skill level and ability to cooperate or challenge each other in positive ways, and the context of the performance.

The instruments of India are numerous, and quite a few of them can be used as the lead melodic instrument in *ragas*. In the West, the instrument that has become most famous is the *sitar*, which for Westerners is virtually synonymous with Indian music. The *sitar* is a long-necked plucked lute, with a body made from a gourd and with seventeen arched metal frets running up the neck. Over these frets four main melodic strings and three *jhala* (rhythm/drone) strings and beneath them pass around twelve sympathetic strings. *Ragas* can also be performed on many other stringed instruments, such as the *sarod*, the *santur* (hammered zither), or the *sarangi* (bowed lute), as well as on non-stringed instruments such as the *bansri* (flute) and several reed instruments, such as the *shehnai*. Among the most curious of instruments used in *ragas* is the *jal tarang*, a semicircular series of small china bowls each filled/tuned with different levels of water and struck with a small beater. *Ragas* are also sung. Vocal *ragas* are structured according to one of two formal patterns, both of which differ from patterns used in instrumental *ragas*. These patterns, called *Dhrupad* and *Khyal*, both require great endurance on the part of performers. Full appreciation of vocal *ragas* naturally requires knowledge of Indic languages, which is perhaps why instrumental performers tend to be more internationally recognized.

Now that we have run through some of the basic principles and characteristics of the *raga*, we will return to our musical example. It is *Raga ahir bhairav*, a type of *raga* appropriately performed at daybreak. The ascending and descending scale used in this performance consists of the pitches C♭, D♭, E, F, G, A, B♭, c—though in the ascending form the G is often avoided. The *tala* used is a fast *tintal* (16 beats).

Cultural Considerations. If you were to attend a *raga* performance, you would probably be amazed at the musicians' dexterity, creativity, and stage presence, and at the way that their music can involve an audience. These are some of the aspects that have long made Indian *raga* attractive to Western audiences and to a number of Western popular performers, such as George Harrison and John McLaughlin.

While a *raga* performance may be relatively easy to follow on an aural and visual level, there is, however, much more involved than mere sound and sight. Important extra-musical cultural and philosophical matters come into play as well, encompassing the *raga*'s relationship to, and effect on, both the individual listeners and broadly on the smooth working of the universe.

The extra-musical aspects of *raga*, which may seem merely curious to outsiders, are essential to Indians. Each *raga* has an articulated mood, called **rasa**, which creates in

RASA
A mood or sentiment associated with artistic activity, such as *raga* performance, in India.

LISTENING GUIDE

 CD 1.5 (4'38")

Chapter 5: Site 1

India: Hindustani (Instrumental) *Raga*

Instruments: *Sarod* (fretless plucked lute), *tambura* (plucked lute), *tabla* (pair of hand drums)

TIME   **LISTENING FOCUS**

The duration of the initial *alap* section—the exploratory opening section of the overall form—is much shorter than normal in this performance, due to the recording's time limitations. Note the use of free rhythm and the absence of drum during the *alap* section.

0'00"   *Tambura* enters. Plays four pulses before melody begins on *sarod*. Listen for the characteristic "twang" of the *tambura* drone at 0'04", 0'14", 0'18", 0'25", 0'35", etc.

0'03"   *Sarod* enters. Note that the melodic pitches that are emphasized begin in the lower range of the instrument and gradually work toward the upper range. Listen for the "sliding" between distant intervals (rather than "bending"), which is characteristic of a fretless chordophone.

Also listen for the gradual increase in rhythmic density of the melodic content. These two aspects (range and rhythmic density) encourage an increasing feeling of tension in the music, though the shortened *alap* encourages the performer to build the tension continuously into the composed section of the performance.

2'10"   The *gat*, or composed section of the overall form, begins. Note the transition into a rhythmic meter and the appearance of the drum (*tabla*). Listen for the characteristic "boing" timbre of the lower-pitched drum (*baya*).

2'13"   Listen for the "melodic hook," repeated again at 2'17" just before the *tabla* enters. This short four-note motif appears many times throughout the *gat* and often signals the end of the *tala* cycle, such as at 2'34" and 2'58".

2'18"   *Tabla* enters. The *tala* is a sixteen-beat cycle. Listen for the "one" pulse on the third strike of the drum. (Begin the "Ethno-Challenge" here.)

4'19"   Final use of the "melodic hook" to signal the end of the piece. The performers likely made prior visual contact to signal the approaching ending.

4'23"   *Tabla* stops.

4'27"   *Sarod* stops. The *tambura* (drone) closes the performance.

Source: "*Raga* Ahir bhairav," played by Buddhadev DasGupta, *sarod*. From *The Raga Guide: A Survey of 74 Hindustani Ragas*, Nimbus NI 5536/9 (4 CDs and 196-page book), 1999. Used by permission.

ETHNO-CHALLENGE (CD 1.5): "Keep the *tal*" (sixteen beats) during the *gat* section of the performance (clap on beats 1 and 5; wave on beat 9; clap on beat 13). Listen especially for how your "1" pulse corresponds to the melodic hook throughout the performance. Anticipate the final pulse of the performance and stop counting.

performer and listener alike a state of mind, such as love, heroism, or anger. The *rasa* can become so pervasive that listeners begin to conceive of the *rasa* as a person. Personified *ragas* are frequently depicted in miniature paintings called *ragamala*, often showing humans performing music. Some *ragas* are believed to have magical powers. A *raga* performed correctly can heal, influence personality, and even bring the divine into both performer and listener. *Raga Dipak* is said to create fire when performed well, and the *Mallar ragas* can create rain. *Kedar ragas* will cure diseases and melt stones. Indian jailers, always ready to earn some extra money, were said to have taught *Raga Kedar* to prisoners who hoped to melt the stones of the prison and escape.

Each *raga* is to be performed at a proper time of day, and consequently there are *ragas* appropriate for specific times, from before dawn to after sunset. For Indians this is important because they believe there is a reciprocal relationship between the sound of music and a smoothly functioning universe. Walter Kaufmann, who researched *ragas* in India prior to World War II, reported that one great musician predicted the coming of that terrible war, which he claimed would result from the Western habit of playing music at the wrong times (as when funeral music is played when there is no funeral). He shouted to Kaufmann, "How long will the universe tolerate this abuse of music, music, mind you, a most sacred thing?"

An Indian minature painting, or *ragamala*, entitled "Krishna and Radha watching rain clouds," from India's Punjab Hills, *c.*1790 (Cleveland Museum of Art)

As a result of this negligence a great calamity would befall the West, he said—and indeed it did.

During the 1960s, many Westerners turned to the East—India in particular—in search of spiritual enlightenment. Because Indian music is overtly spiritual, it soon became popular with Western audiences. Ravi Shankar, the Hindustani sitar specialist, who has also composed many film scores, toured the United States as early as 1964 and soon became a cultural icon. George Harrison of The Beatles studied sitar with Shankar, and Harrison's use of the sitar in several Beatles' songs, including "Love You Too" from *Revolver* (1966) and "Within You Without You" from *Sgt. Pepper's Lonely Hearts Club Band* (1967), brought about a rising interest in Indian music. Around the same time England's John McLaughlin, leader of both Shakti and the Mahavishnu Orchestra, also invoked Indian sounds and spirituality. These groups, and many others, added Indian drummers and sitarists, making the distinctive dry timbre of the tabla and the twangy sitar familiar to many Westerners. Today the sounds of the tabla and sitar can be easily imitated on synthesizers and have become commonly accepted in mainstream Western popular music.

Ravi Shankar, India's most famous musician, plays the *sitar*, a fretted North Indian lute with sympathetic strings (Jack Vartoogian/FrontRowPhotos)

Because Indian music is played by soloists, one finds both virtuosos and a "star" system associated with its performance. Ironically, Indian musicians can make more money touring in Europe and North America than in India. Ravi Shankar made a great success for himself doing this, and his daughter, Anoushka Shankar, has followed in his footsteps. A few Americans, such as Ken Zuckerman, have completely mastered Indian instruments and styles and have become professional Indian musicians, touring both here and in India. Even though Indian music no longer holds Western popular culture in its thrall, Indian concerts in the West continue to attract large audiences of both Indian expatriates and Westerners.

Fundamentals of Indian (Hindustani) Classical Music

NEED TO KNOW

Modal System. *Raga* denotes a comprehensive system governing the creation of melody—improvised or composed. Its elements include:

- Tone material (a limited number of pitches presented in both ascending and descending forms)
- Pitch hierarchy (strong and weak pitches that define the tonal center of the mode. The *vadi* is the strongest—and central—pitch followed by the *samvadi*; these are reinforced by the sounds of the drone instrument)
- Solfège (a system of syllables used to articulate pitches, called *sargam* and expressed in ascending order as *sa, re, ga, ma, pa, dha, ni, sa*)
- Magical powers (Indian musicians ascribe magical powers to some individual *ragas*)
- Mood or character (each *raga* has a *rasa* or mood/feeling/personality that can be personified in small paintings called *ragamala*).

Rhythmic/Metric System. *Tala* denotes a comprehensive system governing the organization of the music in time. Its elements include:

- Fixed number of beats organized into a closed cycle
- Grouping of beats into units
- Visible means of "keeping the *tala*" with a clap followed by counts or a wave followed by counts
- Words to represent drum strokes (known as *bols*) used by drummers during learning or in demonstrations of drumming.

Form. Although partly improvised, *raga* performance follows expected patterns. These include:

- *Alap*, the beginning section of melody (vocal or instrumental) accompanied only by the drone instrument
- *Jor*, as the alap proceeds, it becomes faster and emphasizes the higher pitches of the *raga*. In the *jor* the music becomes somewhat steady, but not yet in tala
- *Jhala*, coming at the end of the *alap*, the music reaches maximum tempo and rhythmic density. It is mostly steady in beat, while the player repeatedly use drone strings (called *jhala* string) in alternation with the melodic pitch
- *Gat*, the section that coincides with the entry of the drum(s). The *gat* is a relatively short composition that becomes the basis for further improvisation. *Gat* refers to instrumental *ragas*; the vocal equivalent is called the *chiz*.

Arrival: South India

South India has been less influenced by outside cultures over the centuries than the northern region, which was more affected by foreign peoples who invaded or established trade routes through the area. Primarily Hindu, southern India is thought to preserve what remains of India's earliest civilization, that of the Dravidians. The sophisticated music of South India, called Carnatic (also Karnatak) music, is closely associated with Hinduism, though not specifically with temple rituals. There is a greater emphasis on vocal performance, though many instruments, such as the Sarasvati vina, are distinctive to the region. Many Carnatic music enthusiasts claim that the music of the south is more "pure" than that of northern India due to its historical insulation from outside influence.

Site 2: Carnatic Classical (Vocal) *Kriti*

First Impressions. Our example begins with a sustained drone, after which a rich toned male vocalist begins to sing in free rhythm, as a drum is briefly heard warming up in the background. The opening section seems also to be a "warm-up" for the singer as he improvises on a few non-lexical syllables. As he improvises his phrases, another instrument—a bowed instrument that sounds like a violin—shadows him. After a brief pause, the vocalist initiates a metered section, that prompts the drummer to join the performance with accented pulses and short flourishes of rhythmic vibrancy. Listening closely, it is evident that the singer is repeating the same lyric with each vocal phrase, decorating his performance with a fascinating display of ornamentation and seeming improvisation. Compared to the previous track (Hindustani *raga*), the rhythm and meter are clearly articulated by strong drum beats, giving it an almost march-like feeling.

Aural Analysis. The most important difference between the classical music of North and South India is that whereas Hindustani music is mostly improvised, Carnatic music is based on fixed compositions. Improvisation occurs only after the composition has been fully presented, and even the highly patterned ornamentation performed by the singer is part of the composition. Carnatic music's most important compositional form is a type of devotional song called **kriti**, which is based on a genre of devotional Hindu poetry of the same name. While the lyrics could speak of devotion to God, they can also be religious, love, or historical stories. The composer of a *kriti* normally writes both the poetry and the melody, the former being written in one of several South Indian languages, each with its own script (e.g., Telugu, Kannada, Malayalam, and Tamil). Pitches are written in one of the many local notational systems; only the main pitches are indicated, ornamentation being determined by oral tradition, highly patterned, but not freely improvised. Vocalists usually perform an improvised introduction called *alapana* before launching into the *kriti* itself, though these can be extremely brief in some cases. This serves to ready the vocalist for the more demanding vocal feats of the ensuing performance and helps to prepare the audience as well.

The enclosed example is "Manasā! Etulorttune" ("O unworthy Mind!"), a *kriti* by Sri (usually translated as "saint") Tyāgarāja (1767–1847), South India's most famous composer. The language is Telegu but the title is Sanskrit. *Kriti* texts are typically in three sections. The first, called *pallavi*, consists of one or two lines of text which reappear throughout a

KRITI
A South Indian genre of devotional songs using Hindu poetry.

A Carnatic (South Indian) classical singer performs a *kriti* devotional song, accompanied (left to right) by a *mridangam* drum, *kanjira* hand drum, *tambura* lute, and violin (N. Scott Robinson)

performance, a kind of refrain. This *kriti*'s text begins with the words "O unworthy Mind! How long can I put up with you, if you do not listen to my counsel!" (translation by T.K. Govinda Rao, *Compositions of Tyāgarāja*. Chennai, Tamil Nadu: Gānamandir Publications, 2009, p. 136). The *pallavi* is followed by a second section, called *anupallavi*, which begins "Follow my advice. Spend your time in singing the glory of Srī Rāma, the jewel of the solar race with humility and devotion." The final section of the text, called *charanam*, is longer than the others and is followed by the *pallavi* text, giving it a "rounded form." Improvisation, if present, follows the *charanam*, but the work will always conclude with a restatement of the *pallavi*. Regarding the overall form, where improvisation loosely based on the *pallavi* melody occurs, some describe the form as resembling "theme and variations." The enclosed track only goes through the beginning of the *anupallavi*, but the complete *raga* performance is included in the website that accompanies this book.

South Indian *ragas*, whether they are *kritis* or other musical forms, operate on principles similar to the *ragas* of North India—but the specifics are quite different. The Carnatic system is, at least on the surface, unusually extensive because there are so many theoretically possible scales. If you allow for all possible arrangements of the seven pitches (some pitches are available in two variants as well), there are seventy-two possible scale forms. When you factor in other variables, such as ornamentation and pillar pitches, there are theoretically some 36,000 possible *ragas*. In practice, only a small number of *ragas* are commonly used. Our example is *Raga Malayamārutam*, whose pitches in ascending order are C♯, D, F, G♯, A♯, and B (if sounded on a Western instrument such as piano). Expressed in solfège, the *raga* is Sa, Ri, Ga, Pa Dha, Ni, Sa; the *raga* then has six tones, the fourth pitch (Ma) being omitted.

South Indian drum cycles, like those in the North, are also called *tala* but follow a different set of operating principles. As with the *raga* system, the Carnatic *tala* system also allows for far more cycles than are actually used. In practice, the system is actually fairly simple, but like so much of Indian music, it can be confusing to beginners because of its extensive terminology.

A Carnatic *tala* consists of three variable elements, called *anudrutam, drutam*, and *laghu*. As in the North, South Indian music uses a system of hand gestures to symbolize *tala* patterns. The *anudrutam* is signed as a one-beat clap; the *drutam* is a clap followed by a wave gesture of the right hand; the *laghu*, which consists of a variable number of beats, is signed as a clap followed by right-hand finger counts. South Indian audience members often "keep the *tala*" on their hands during a performance, and sometimes a singer will also use the gestures as s/he performs. Each *tala* has a name that combines two elements: a *tala* name and a *jati* name, with the latter representing a variable number of beats in the *laghu*. The most commonly used *tala* in Carnatic music is properly called *triputa* (*tala* name) *chaturasra* (*jati* name), consisting of a four-beat *laghu* (clap and three counts) and two *drutam* (each a clap and wave). The full cycle of eight beats, then, is "clap, count, count, count, clap, wave, clap, wave." Because the name *triputa caturasra* does not roll off the tongue so easily, the nickname *adi tala* ("ancient" tala) is commonly used. It is unlikely that you could ever attend a Carnatic music concert and not hear *adi tala*. The selected track, however, is an exception, using a much shorter *tala* called *rūpakam*, which consists of only three beats, consisting of an *anudrutam* and a *drutam*, with no *laghu*; it is signed as "clap, clap, wave." But because the cycle is so short, the performers have combined four repetitions into an overarching twelve beat cycle (3+3+3+3).

South Indian *mridangam* drummer plays during a concert surrounded by six more drums (N. Scott Robinson)

The most commonly used drum in Carnatic music is called *mridangam*; it is a two-headed barrel drum with leather strap lacing, and heads that are weighted (tuned) with a mixture of cooked rice mixed with iron filings and perhaps ash; this pasty mixture adds weight to the drum head, thereby lowering the pitch. Players use their hands to strike each head. Many players also wrap the body of the drum in cloth. The recording also includes a *kanjira*, a small frame drum consisting of a jackfruit frame, a single head usually of monitor (lizard) skin, and a single hole in the frame into which three or four thin metal discs or old coins are placed to rattle when the drum is struck by the player's hand. The *kanjira* is essentially the same as what Westerners know as the "tambourine." This instrument only became common in classical playing in the 1930s.

The first sounds heard in our example, those of the drone, could be the *tambura*, the same drone chordophone found in Hindustani music, but in this performance the musicians employ a small "black box" called a *sruti box* that emits continuous drone pitches electronically. As in the North, the drone reinforces the basic pitches of the *raga*. The bowed instrument that shadows the singer is a European violin—but one that is held in a way that no Western violinist would ever employ: it is placed between the chest and right foot of a player seated on the floor. The violin, like the harmonium, was introduced into India by British colonialists but completely transformed into an Indian instrument. Its function in Carnatic music is to closely follow and imitate the singer. Thanks to the way that the instrument is held, players can easily slide their left hand along the neck to create any of the twenty-three named ornaments found in both the instrumental and the vocal music of South India.

LISTENING GUIDE

CD 1.6 (4'14")

Chapter 5: Site 2
India: Carnatic Classical (Vocal) *Kriti*

Voice: Single male
Instruments: Violin (bowed lute), *sruti* box (electronic drone), *mridangam* (barrel-shaped drum)

TIME	LISTENING FOCUS
0'00"	*Sruti* box (drone) begins. (Tonal center = C♯). Note the violin tuning and *mridangam* (drum) warming up in background.
0'09"	[*Alapana*] Voice begins with highly melismatic improvisation in free rhythm.
0'14"	Listen for the violin "imitating" the melodic contour of the vocalist. Note this exchange of voice followed by violin throughout the opening section of the performance.
2'59"	Applause signals the end of the opening section.
3'04"	[*Pallavi* section] Vocalist begins the "composed" section of the performance. Note that the violin (3'06") no longer "imitates," but plays along with the same melody as the vocalist.

	Line 1 (first half): *Manasa! Etulorttune*
	("O Unworthy Mind! How long can I put up with you,")
	Repeats a total of five times before the second half of the line begins.
3'10"	*Mridangam* enters.
3'24"	Line 1 (second half): *Manavi Cekonave*
	("if you do not listen to my counsel.")
3'28	Return to beginning of line 1 and sung three times.
3'51"	Return to first half of line 1.
3'56"	Vocalist sings on syllable "O!"
4'04"	Drums signal end of the *pallavi* section.
4'07"	Second section [*anupallavi*] begins just before the excerpt fades. Though brief, listen for the change in text.
	Line 2: *Dinakarakula Bhushununi*
	("Follow my advice.")

Source: "Manasā! Etulörttunë" *Raga Malayamārutam, Rūpakam Tala*, composed by Sri Tyāgarāja and performed by Sri V. Ramachandran, vocal; Sri S. Varadharajan, violin; Ramnad Sri Raghavan, *mridangam*; Sri R. Balasubramaniam, *kanjira*; recorded at the 2002 St. Thyagaraja Festival by the Thyagaraja Aradhana Committee, Cleveland, Ohio, 2002. Used by permission.

ETHNO-CHALLENGE (CD 1.6): Mimic the vocal melody, along with the violin part, during the introduction (*alapana*). Also, sing along and memorize the melody of the composed section (*pallavi*) as if you were a student of this musician.

ARADHANA
A South Indian festival.

Cultural Considerations. Whereas Hindustani music is primarily improvised, albeit with a pre-composed *gat* or *chiz* serving as a skeletal framework in the metrical portion of the performance, Carnatic music is primarily composed in song form, though with the expectation that the performer will add typical (and codified) ornaments to the main notes. Consequently, South India has, like Europe, a small pantheon of saint-like composers, of whom Tyāgarāja (1767–1847) is the most famous. Other renowned composers include Muttusvami Diksitar (1776–1835), Syama Sastri (1762–1827), and Svati Tirunal (1813–1846), all contemporaries of Beethoven, Schubert, Chopin, and others from early nineteenth-century Europe. Tyāgarāja, a man who prophesied his own death and is therefore called "Saint" in English, is celebrated in an annual **aradhana** (festival), originally held in Tamil Nadu state but now observed in many parts of the world, including the United States. Since 1907 the festival has included, in addition to *puja* (worship), performances of Tyāgarāja's compositions by both amateurs and professionals. One of the largest festivals is held each year in Cleveland, Ohio, when the local community brings in major singers and instrumentalists from India.

A South Indian violinist plays during a St. (Sri) Tyāgarāja Festival in Cleveland, Ohio. Note how he holds the instrument between his chest and right foot, making it easier to play the ornamentation required in this music

While they predominate, *kriti* are not the only vocal form found in South Indian classical music. Vocalists sometimes improvise extensive *alapana*, together with a violinist who imitates entire phrases following the main performer's rendition. Carnatic repertory also includes other song genres, including the *varnam, ragamtanam-pallavi*, and *tillana*. Some are secular, even erotic, and may include extended melismatic passages in which the performer shows off his or her mastery of improvisatory techniques. Carnatic dance is typically accompanied by vocal performance, especially the widespread *Bharata Naatyam* dance tradition.

WORLD MUSIC: A GLOBAL JOURNEY

Sri Tyāgarāja (1767–1847) is South India's most famous composer, whose music is still celebrated in festivals throughout the world (Aradhana Committee, Cleveland, Ohio)

SARASVATI VINA
A plucked lute from South India, often associated with the Hindu goddess Sarasvati.

NAGASVARAM
A double-reed aerophone from South India.

TAVIL
A pair of drums from South India, often used to accompany the *nagasvaram*.

    The instruments of South India are fewer than those of North India, but several are worthy of mention. The most important is a plucked lute called **sarasvati vina** (or *veena*). Held horizontally or even placed on the floor, this instrument has up to nine strings for playing melody and rhythm but generally no sympathetic strings. Players may use plectra or their bare fingertips. The most memorable South Indian instrument is a long, black double-reed called **nagasvaram**, usually played in pairs and enthusiastically accompanied by a pair of short barrel drums called **tavil**. One may also encounter performers using the *venu* (flute) or the *dilruba* (fretted bowed lute). In recent years, several new Western instruments have been adapted into Carnatic music, most prominently the mandolin, made famous by one player, the youthful U. Srinivas. Other Western imports include the violoncello (or 'cello), the viola, the alto saxophone, and the clarinet; the latter's reeds and mouthpiece have been altered to allow for greater ornamentation and tone-bending. In South India, instrumental music consists primarily of vocal compositions performed without words, though the original melody is generally elaborated on through improvised passages requiring great virtuosity.

SOUTH ASIA

The *sarasvati vina* lute of South India

Explore More

Kathakali

Attending a performance of Indian *Kathakali* dance drama, whether in India or a touring group, is an unforgettable experience. Perhaps you will not recall the musical accompaniment (drums, percussion, singing), but you cannot have ignored the actors' make-up or costumes. Going beyond the fascinating visual aspects, however, requires the detailed study of all the aspects appreciated by connoisseurs: gestures, make-up codes, facial expressions, dance movements, and the accompanying music, including the meaning of the sung words and their role in telling the story. Although it originated in the extreme southern state of Kerala, *Kathakali* is considered particular to that state alone but has come to the notice of audiences not just throughout India but worldwide. But understanding the words, which are in a southern language called Malayalam, sometimes mixed with Sanskrit, is near impossible for people living elsewhere. Fortunately, most of the clips of *Kathakali* available on the Internet include subtitles. None of the actors, whose facial colors indicate

Kathakali performance: two drums on left, two actors in middle, two gong players on right

115

character (e.g., green indicates a noble character), speaks or sings, this being done by off-stage performers, because the actors' gestures, expressions, and dance are so complicated. But the musicians are clearly seen on stage: one or two drummers (a horizontal drum played with the hands (*maddalam*) and one vertical played with sticks (*chenda*)) on the viewer's left, and two players who strike small gongs with wooden beaters on the right.

Traditionally sacred in character, though never part of Hindu temple rituals, the 101 classical stories derive from many sources, especially the epic tale called the *Mahabharata*. In earlier times a performance lasted the entire night, but today's performances are shortened to three or four hours (although on-tour performances are much shorter). In addition to the old stories, writers have created new stories, such as from the Bible, from Shakespeare's dramas, and even from Goethe's *Faust*. Learning to perform *Kathakali* requires up to ten years just to appear on stage followed by a lifetime of continuing effort, including the study of Kerala-style martial arts. Because arts such as *Kathakali* are so "deep," serious connoisseurs also grow over time, coming to see and hear more with every new performance. This inherent allure to appeal to both novice and veteran audiences makes the *Kathakali* one of the most memorable of Indian theatrical genres.

Kathakali dancer (Wikimedia Commons)

BHAJAN
Hindu devotional songs from India.

Site 3: Hindu *Bhajan* Devotional Song

First Impressions. Along with a reed instrument and pair of drums, a male vocalist sings a short line, which is answered by a group of singers, both male and female, who sound more like a congregation of ordinary people at worship than professional singers. The melody they sing is rather simple, repetitive, and easy to imitate with the melodic instrument providing the pitch outline of the vocal phrases. A metallic instrument joins the group, adding a steady rhythmic element like the sound of a model train chugging along to the beat.

Aural Analysis. The reedy sound of the melodic instrument is a *harmonium*, a free-reed pump organ originally from France. Full-sized harmoniums became popular parlor instruments in "better" American and European homes during the nineteenth century, and many families today still preserve one as a treasured heirloom. These domestic instruments were fairly large, often had extensive wood carvings as decorations, had a keyboard, a bank of pull stops, and were pumped by two pedals.

Portable versions of the harmonium became popular by mid-century and were quite compact with a small keyboard and a hand-pumped bellows at the rear of the case. This type of harmonium was originally designed for missionaries and other traveling religious leaders, who used them to accompany hymn singing. Many British missionaries went to India, taking the harmonium with them—though they certainly did not anticipate that Indians would embrace the instrument so enthusiastically and blend it into their traditional music. In *bhajans* today the harmonium player often provides just a steady drone, but can also play the lead melody to support the vocal line, as with our audio example.

In addition to a harmonium, a drum (or, more properly, two drums) is often heard in *bhajan* performance. The sound should seem familiar, as it is a *tabla*, an instrument heard earlier in the Hindustani *raga* (see above). Unlike the *tala* patterns heard in classical performances of Hindustani *raga*, the one rhythm here is simple and regular, alternating between a four- and an eight-beat cycle. The metallic instrument that is also heard is peculiar to the overseas Indian community in Trinidad and Tobago, called a *dandtal* (or *dental*), and consists of a steel rod struck from within a horseshoe-shaped beater. In this example, it plays a short–short–long pattern throughout.

Bhajan singing typically follows a call-and-response format in which a leader (in this case male) sings a phrase that is then sung by the group. This pattern differs from call-and-response performance in most traditions, because normally a group completes a vocal line

A man sings while playing a hand-pumped harmonium at a temple in Kathmandu, Nepal

sung by its leader, rather than simply repeating it. Therefore, *bhajan* practice is closer to antiphonal singing, in which leader and group alternate. Practically speaking, the leader in *bhajan* performances is also prompting the singers, who might not know the words otherwise. The vocal lines are very simple melodically and are repeated. In our example, there are basically two phrases, both of which use a pentatonic scale. The five tones could be described as 5, 6, 1, 2, 3, with 5 and 1 as the most important and 1 as the fundamental pitch. Because the term *bhajan* denotes a great range of devotional songs sung by members of virtually any of India's faiths (though they are most prominent in Hinduism), and because they are normally sung by lay people, the texts can be in whatever local or national language is preferred.

The text of our example was written for the Hindu sect that follows the great **guru** (teacher) Sai Baba, and begins (in translation) with these exhortations: "Lord Ganesha, son of mother Parvati and Lord Shiva. You are ever pure. Protect me O Blissful Lord. You confer auspiciousness."

GURU
A teacher or spiritual guide, primarily associated with Hindu traditions from India.

LISTENING GUIDE

CD 1.7 (1'36")

Chapter 5: Site 3

India: Hindu *Bhajan* Devotional Song

Voice: Male vocal lead and mixed-group response
Instruments: Harmonium (keyed aerophone), *tabla* (pair of hand drums), *dandtal* (idiophone)

TIME	LISTENING FOCUS
0'00"	*Tabla* and harmonium enter.
0'02"	Lead vocal enters with first verse.
	Line 1: *Parvati Nandana Gajanana*
	(Translation: Lord Ganesha, son of mother Parvati and Lord Shiva.)
0'07"	Congregation responds with repetition of the first line.
0'13"	Lead vocal, then congregation, repeats first line.
0'18"	*Dandtal* enters with a consistent short–short–long rhythm.
0'25"	Lead vocal enters with second verse.
	Line 2: *Pashupati Nandana Niranjana*
	(Translation: You are ever pure.)
0'31"	Congregation responds with repetition of the second line.
0'37"	Lead vocal, then congregation, repeats second line.

0'48"	Lead vocal, then congregation, sings first line again. (Repeated.)
1'11"	Lead vocal enters with third line.
	Line 3: *Pahi Prabho Mam Pahi Prasanna*
	(Translation: Protect me O Blissful Lord. You confer auspiciousness.)
1'16"	Congregation responds with repetition of the third line.
1'22"	Lead vocal, then congregation, repeats third line.

Source: "Parvati Nandana Gajanana," recorded by Terry E. Miller at the Sai Baba Temple, Longdenville, Trinidad, 1985. Used by permission.

ETHNO-CHALLENGE (CD 1.7): Sing along, as if you were a member of the congregation. Additionally, clap the *dandtal* rhythmic pattern throughout the example. For an additional experience, watch one or more *bhajans* on YouTube and ascertain as much as you can about the visuals that accompany it.

Swaminarayan Akshardham Temple in Delhi, the world's largest Hindu temple (N. Scott Robinson)

Bhajan performance at Hindu temple near Chaguanas, Trinidad, West Indies. Accompaniment is provided by drum, harmonium, and *dandtal*

The *dandtal* is a metal rod struck with a horseshoe-shaped metal beater used to accompany *bhajans*

Cultural Considerations. *Bhajans* are devotional songs sung by lay people for many occasions, both formal and informal, at home or in a temple, accompanied or unaccompanied. They can be traditional songs, homemade ones, or a blend of traditional and popular music styles. In a sense they parallel Protestant hymns in the Christian tradition. Indeed, some Indian Christians have adopted *bhajans* to their own faith. *Bhajan* meetings, predominantly associated with Hindus, are often held during the week, and anyone in the congregation can lead a song.

If Hindu, services usually begin with the chanting of *om*, the fundamental sacred sound of Hinduism. *Bhajan* texts can be sung in any language and may consist of nothing more than a repetition of the names of God, because God is believed to have many incarnations. Other texts express the devotees' love for God, and offer praise and devotion.

Bhajans can be heard throughout India, Nepal, the Tamil parts of Sri Lanka, and anywhere else where there are Indian or Hindu communities, such as South America and the Caribbean, particularly Guyana and Trinidad and Tobago. Among the Hindu spiritual teachers who have attracted followings outside India is Sai Baba, originally from the Indian states of Andhra Pradesh and Karnataka. *Bhajan* singing typically takes place in Sai Baba temples on Thursday or Sunday. The *bhajan* selected for inclusion here was recorded in a Sai Baba temple in Chaguanas, a town in central Trinidad, where there is a concentration of Hindus. (Around 40 percent of Trinidadians are descendents of Indians brought to the country as indentured workers after slavery ended.) *Bhajan* singing is a major aspect of Sai Baba worship but is also found among Hare Krishna devotees, another sect that has also established congregations and temples worldwide.

BOLLYWOOD
An informal name for India's film industry, combining "Bombay" and "Hollywood."

Explore More

Indian *Filmi Git* (Film Song)

While Indian film songs, or *filmi*, are clearly not part of the classical *raga* tradition, many film directors and performers were trained in Indian classical music, and as a result *filmi* retains some classical characteristics. Most films are laden with musical productions that break away from the basic plot and encourage an escapist experience for the audience. Though atypical in modern cinema, historical film buffs will recall that many American films from the 1930s to the 1960s also included numerous songs. Just as *The Sound of Music* (1965) or *Singin' in the Rain* (1952) would be unremarkable without musical performance, so, too, would the hundreds of similarly produced film-musicals found in Indian cinemas and abroad today. While the song-film format fell out of favor in the West long ago, it has not in India, a country where millions toil every day in the heat for little reward. Movies that help to transport people from the grinding poverty of their own lives into fantasies of love, adventure, or exceptional religious devotion is clearly valued by its primary audience.

A dance scene typical of Indian film with actress singing a *filmi* song (Shutterstock)

The Indian film industry, colloquially referred to as "**Bollywood**" (a combination of the words "Bombay" and "Hollywood"), has become the world's number-one producer of films, releasing more than 2000 films per year. Hindustani artists traditionally dominated the Indian film industry, and as a result for many years mainstream *filmi git* were also generally Hindustani. Eventually, the South developed its own style of film songs, and in recent years these have gained popularity throughout India and abroad.

The first Indian "talkie" was released in 1931. Early films required the actors themselves to sing songs derived from "light classical" Indian music into a "single-system" camera. By the 1940s, however, when sound and image could be recorded separately, producers began using "playback singers," individuals who recorded the songs in a studio; the songs were then played back to the actors who lip-synched the words on the film set. Because of India's diverse population and languages, songs were frequently recorded in more than one of India's major languages. Film producers hired music directors who, with a team of writers and musicians, created, performed, and recorded all the music for a given film. To this end, studios had to retain a great many musicians playing primarily Western orchestral instruments plus a few Indian instruments, especially for "traditional" scenes.

Today's film music, however, makes greater use of synthesizers. Certain of the film music producers became major figures in their own right, and most of them were musicians themselves. The "playback" singers who have performed most songs since the late 1930s are far fewer in number than the actors and actresses they sing for, meaning that audiences often hear the same voices doing the songs in film after film, regardless of who is being seen on-screen.

Two figures have tended to dominate the genre, either personally or by setting the style. Male actor-singer Kundan Lal Saigal set the standard early on with his warm voice, which recorded well with the early microphones. But a single female singer, Lata Mangeshkar, dominated the industry for six decades, since 1942; her light, "little girl" voice being virtually the signature sound of Indian *filmi*. Cited by the *Guinness Book of World Records* as having produced more recordings than any other singer, she has recorded thousands of film songs in numerous languages. Her younger sister, Asha Bhosle, is similarly an iconic figure of the *filmi* music industry. In recent years, the Indian film industry has become increasingly prominent on the global market with many films achieving critical acclaim and financial success rivaling the Hollywood film industry. The recent success of British production, *Slumdog Millionaire* (2008), which was filmed and set in India, has done much to heighten global attention to South Asian cinema. While the musical format is often absent from these newly released films, *filmi* remains a popular music style of the majority of Bollywood films.

Arrival: Pakistan

Pakistan, like many other nations formed out of colonial empires, took its form more as a result of external forces than around common culture or language. Unified geographically by the Indus River basin and by its religion, Islam, Pakistan was home to some of the world's earliest civilizations and a crossroads of numerous cultures arriving both through trade—it was on the "Silk Route"—and because of invasions. By the nineteenth century, Pakistan had become the western portion of the British Raj encompassing most of South Asia. Soon after the British granted independence to its Indian empire in 1947, disputes broke out between the Hindu majority and the Muslim minority which were resolved in the agony of one of history's greatest human migrations; millions of Hindus left the provinces of both the east and west for what became India and millions of Muslims left India for either the eastern or

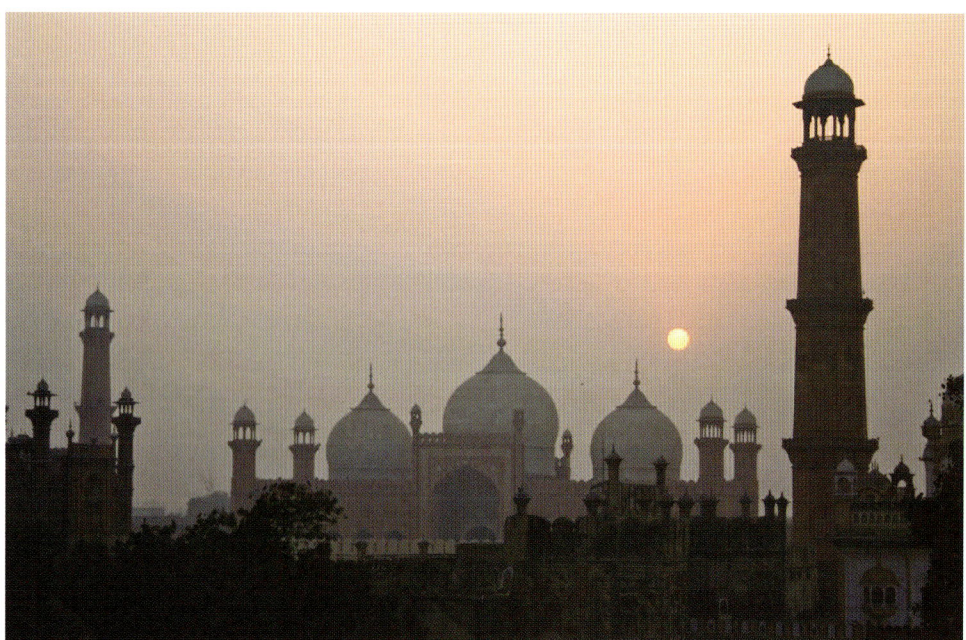

Lahore, Pakistan, at sunset with minarets silhouetted in the fading sunlight (Shutterstock)

western provinces, which together became Pakistan later that year. Following numerous disputes with India over Kashmir and internally with East Pakistan, in 1971 the eastern province of Bengal broke away and became the nation of Bangladesh.

Pakistan, whose area is slightly smaller than Texas, has a population of 187 million, making it the second most populous Muslim country after Indonesia. In addition to its two official languages—English and Urdu—there are more than sixty other languages spoken among the country's numerous ethnic groups, Punjabis being the largest (44 percent). The country's capital, Islamabad, with a population of only 700,000, is dwarfed by its largest city, Karachi, with a population of around fourteen million. Because of its ethnic diversity, Pakistan has long been stressed by ethnic division, and although the military has traditionally been the glue that held the country together, its territories along the Afghanistan border have remained notoriously difficult to govern.

Visitors to Pakistan would rightly ask, "what is 'Pakistani music'?" There is no easy answer because each of Pakistan's cultural regions has more in common with neighboring countries (Iran, Afghanistan, India) than with a national culture. Further, when the great migration occurred in 1947, a great number of people from India settled in West Pakistan, and yet the country's new identity was founded on being distinct from India. As a result, the most sophisticated form of Pakistani music (what some call its *raga*-based "classical music") is virtually the same as Hindustani (Indian) *raga*. After that there are nearly endless forms of regional and local music associated with particular ethnic groups. In the 1960s Pakistan's national radio attempted to use *qawwali* songs to represent the national culture. Unofficially this continues to hold true in that *qawwali* is Pakistan's most prominent music in the eyes of the rest of the world.

Site 4: *Qawwali* (Sufi Devotional Song)

Qawwali performance by Rizwan-Muazzam Qawwali during the WOMAD Festival, 2010 in Wiltshire, United Kingdom (David Corio/Getty Images)

First Impressions. The clustered tones of a reed instrument are immediately joined by one—or sometimes two—voice(s) in a seemingly improvisatory melody. Three quick raps on a drum allude to the coming main section in which drums help define the meter. Sometimes sounding subdued, sometimes not, the singers reach sudden points of intensity, suggesting this is more than mere poetry but perhaps a personal declaration.

Aural Analysis. Two elements constitute the sound of *qawwali* song: instruments and voices. The melodic instrument heard immediately is the harmonium, a small hand bellows-powered keyboard instrument whose sounds emanate from small cane free-reeds. This instrument was discussed more fully in the *bhajan* site (see above). The player, who is usually also the singer, parallels the sung melody. Typically, two kinds of drums participate: first, a pair of drums called *tabla* (see Chapter 5, Site 1), and second, a small two-headed barrel drum called *dholak*, better known for its widespread use in Indian film music, *bhajan* singing, and other "light" forms of South Asian music. *Dholak* can be tuned using metal turnbuckles or traditional rope lacing; the left head is "loaded" with a pasty mixture to tune it.

The lead singer or singers dominate the vocal element. In this case there are two: the world-famous Sabri Brothers, who sometimes alternate and sometimes sing together. Joining them now and then is a chorus of four or five men, who also provide clapping sounds on the strong beats. The chorus also repeats some of the lines sung by the soloists to emphasize their importance.

The song heard here makes use of a simple diatonic scale of seven tones, approximating the Western C major scale but theorized by *qawwali* musicians as a *raga* (see Chapter 5, Site 1). When the drums enter, the metrical pattern is a three-beat *tala* (rhythmic cycle),

Two kinds of Pakistani drums: *naal* (left) and *dholak* (right), the latter the mainstay of *qawwali* singing (N. Scott Robinson)

creating the feeling of triple meter. The sung text of this section, part of a much longer composition, begins "*Jamale kibriya main hoon*," meaning "Man is the light of God. Adam modeled in clay is made of divine transparence. Adam, the first of men, opens the way." Originally sung in Persia's main language, Farsi, most *qawwali* today are sung in Punjabi or Urdu, though songs exist in many other languages as well.

Qawwali songs typically last between fifteen and thirty minutes, too long to be reproduced here in full. Some, however, last more than an hour. During that time period the song changes mood, from the restrained emotion of the beginning—heard here—to increasing power and emotion.

LISTENING GUIDE

CD 1.8 (4'09")

Chapter 5: Site 4

Pakistan: *Qawwali* (Sufi Devotional Song)

Voices: Two male leads, male vocal group of four to five singers.
Instruments: Two harmoniums, *tabla*, *dholak*

TIME	LISTENING FOCUS
0'00"	Harmoniums enter in free rhythm, followed by lead vocalists and then vocal group in brief. The text setting is strongly melismatic, paralleling the ornamented melodic line of the harmoniums.
0'44"	*Tabla* and *dholak* (drums) sound briefly.
0'53"	Melodic performers pause, followed by a gutteral vocal utterance, "Allah."
0'54"	Male vocalists continue, exchanging the lead. Note that the text setting is less melismatic than the opening section.
1'18"	Both male vocalists sing together.
1'46"	Vocal group enters along with drums. The text setting tends toward syllabic singing.
2'06"	Lead vocalists return briefly.
2'12"	Vocal group returns with repeated refrain.
2'31"	Dynamic level diminishes as only a couple of male background vocalists continue.
2'37"	Audio example is edited to transition to next section.
2'39"	Example fades in during antiphonal chanted section between lead vocalists and vocal group. The text setting is strongly syllabic. A steady beat is emphasized with hand claps.
3'11"	Drums stop as the music shifts to free rhythm. Lead vocalists and harmonium continue in upper melodic range.
3'39"	Steady beat returns as drums and vocal group enter at a faster tempo.

4'03"	Music shifts again to free rhythm as vocal group and drums drop out.
4'04"	Gutteral vocal utterance, "Allah," is heard as example fades.

Source: "Jamale kibriya main hoon" performed by the Sabri Brothers, from *Musiciens Kawwali du Pakistan/Les Frères Sabri/Musique Soufli, vol. 3*, Arion ARN 64147, 1991. Used by permission.

ETHNO-CHALLENGE (CD 1.8): Accompany the vocal group throughout the performance. For a more difficult challenge, sing along with the lead vocalists.

Cultural Considerations. Associating *qawwali* music with Islam seems counter intuitive at first, because of Islam's traditional distrust of the sensuous art of music. *Qawwali*, however, is not part of mainstream Sunni or Shia Islam, rather it is expressive of the mystical Sufi sects of both Pakistan and India. Sufis are indeed Muslims but are considered heretical by many for their pursuit of spiritual and mystical experiences that bring them into communion with God. Music is an important element in most Sufi religious meetings (see Chapter 8, Site 5). The musicians (called *qawwal*) heard in this example traditionally performed at shrines for Sufi saints on their anniversaries, but sometimes weekly on Thursday or Friday as well for audiences of devotees. Revered for having achieved exceptional nearness to God, the saints are celebrated by modern Sufis wishing to achieve such spiritual elevation, which can be enhanced by hearing *qawwal* sing. As the song progresses from calm to agitation and exclamation, the listeners, too, can experience heightened spirituality to the point of achieving a trance state. As the song winds down, then, the participants are guided in gradually withdrawing from their trance back to normalcy.

For devotees, the most important element in *qawwali* is the poetry, for, although the music can reach great intensity, it is the text that affects their minds and arouses their spirituality up to and including a trance state. Much *qawwali* poetry, however, is strikingly earthy, speaking directly of human love. But this is the surface meaning, and devotees understand that all is metaphorical for the love and connection between humans and the divine. For this to happen, listeners must understand the language of the singer, suggesting that traditional performance was assumed to take place within a small community. This being so, it is somewhat surprising how *qawwali* has managed to become one of the most sought after of "world musics," for audiences who are neither Muslim nor speakers of the singer's language.

Qawwali came to the notice of the non-Muslim world primarily as a result of the career of one of its greatest exponents, Nusrat Fateh Ali Khan (1948–1997), who became head of his family's *qawwali* group in 1971 at the age of 23. By the early 1980s he began touring in Europe and later participated in several of Peter Gabriel's WOMAD world music concerts in the early 1980s and appeared on numerous RealWorld label releases. From 1992 to 1993 he was a visiting artist at the University of Washington. Nusrat's untimely death in 1997 cut short a career that had nevertheless put *qawwali* on the world's stages. Our example was recorded by the Sabri Brothers, a family group headed by lead singers Haji Ghulam Farid

SOUTH ASIA

Qawwali ensemble led by Farid Ayaz (Jack Vartoogian/FrontRowPhotos)

Sabri and younger brother Maqbool Ahmed Sabri. Ghulam died in 1994 at the age of only 64. Both the Sabris and Nusrat went beyond traditional *qawwali*, participating in the sound tracks of numerous Pakistani films. In addition Nusrat (or his songs) were featured in two American films: *The Last Temptation of Christ* (1985) and *Dead Man Walking* (1995).

Explore More

Bhangra

Bhangra is a music style originally associated with the Punjabi populations of northern India and southern Pakistan. The music is common to group celebratory dances, particularly in association with harvest festivals and weddings. The major instruments heard in *bhangra* are the *dhol*, a large barrel drum played with two sticks on both ends, and the *tumbi*, a single-stringed plucked lute. Other instruments, such as the harmonium, are also common, but the *dhol* and *tumbi* provide the basic rhythm and tonal center for performances. A lead male vocalist with accompanying group response is typical in both folk and popular contexts.

During the late 1960s and 1970s, large numbers of Punjabis, primarily Sikhs, migrated to Great Britain and elsewhere around the world in search of economic prosperity. *Bhangra* accompanied them and remained an important cultural activity to remind these populations of their homeland. By the 1980s, however, Punjabi youth in London, England, began blending *bhangra* rhythms and vocal performance with modern music styles to create a new "pop" genre of *bhangra* that reflected their cultural identity in a diaspora community. The sound quickly spread throughout Punjabi populations around the world, making its way back to India and Pakistan where the music is commonplace alongside Bollywood *filmi* music and other forms of Indian popular music. *Bhangra* superstars, such as Malkit Singh and Daler Mehndi, perform internationally to huge audiences and frequently record for Hindi film soundtracks that have helped to promote *bhangra* to global audiences as well.

Questions to Consider

1. Why does the Indian classical tradition dominate the musical image of South Asia in the West?
2. Discuss the following terms important to a Hindustani classical music performance: *Raga, Alap, Gat, Tala, Rasa*.
3. Compare and contrast Hindustani and Carnatic music traditions.
4. How do *filmi* songs differ from *Qawwali* songs?
5. In what ways is Indian music spiritual?
6. What made India and Indian music attractive to the "world traveler" or "hippy" generation of the 1960s and 1970s?

On Your Own Time

Visit the textbook website to find these resources for further exploration on your own.

India

Book: *The Oxford Encyclopedia of the Music of India.* New York: Oxford University Press, 2011.
http://www.oup.com/us/catalog/general/subject/Music/Reference/?view=usa&ci=9780195650983

Website: Official website of Ravi Shankar
http://www.ravishankar.org/

Audio: *The Raga Guide: A Survey of 74 Hindustani Ragas.* Nimbus Records, NI 5536/9, 1999.
http://www.wyastone.co.uk/the-raga-guide-an-illustrated-survey-of-74-hindustani-ragas.html
http://itunes.apple.com/us/album/the-raga-guide-a-survey-74/id220037848

Website: Bhangra
http://www.bhangra.org/

Website: Chhandayan (Indian Classical Music)
http://www.tabla.org/

Website: Ali Akbar—College of Music
http://www.aacm.org/

Book: Lavezzoli, Peter. *The Dawn of Indian Music in the West.* New York: Continuum International Publishing Group, Inc., 2007.
http://www.continuumbooks.com/Books/detail.aspx?ReturnURL=/Search/default.aspx&CountryID=2&ImprintID=2&BookID=125074

Book: Nelson, David P. *Solkattu Manual: An Introduction to the Rhythmic Language of South Indian Music.* Middletown, CT: Wesleyan University Press, 2008.
http://www.dartmouth.edu/~upne/0-8195-6871-6.html

Book: Ganti, Tejaswini. *Bollywood: A Guidebook to Popular Hindi Cinema.* New York: Routledge, 2004 (2nd edition, 2012).
http://www.routledge.com/books/details/9780415583886/

Internet: Popular Artists from India
　A.R. Rahman
　Lata Mangeshkar
　Asha Bhosle
　Sukhwinder Singh
　Alka Yagnik
　Udit Narayan
　Malkit Singh
　Daler Mehndi

Pakistan

Book: Qureshi, Regula Burckhardt. *Sufi Music of India and Pakistan: Sound, Context, and Meaning.* New York: Oxford University Press, 2006.
　http://www.oup.com/us/catalog/general/subject/Music/WorldMusicEthnomusicology/?view=usa&ci=9780195979107

Website: Pakistani Music
　http://www.pakistanimusic.com/

Audio: Nusrat Fateh Ali Khan. *Shahen Shah.* Real World Records, 1989.
　http://realworldrecords.com/catalogue/shahen-shah
　http://itunes.apple.com/us/album/shahen-shah/id270807704

Internet: Popular Artists from Pakistan
　Ahmed Rushdi
　Nazia Hassan
　Nusrat Fateh Ali Khan
　Hadiqa Kiyani

Southeast Asia: Vietnam, Thailand, Laos and Northeast Thailand, Indonesia (Java and Bali)

6

Background Preparation	132
Planning the Itinerary	134
An Inside Look: Priwan Nanongkham	135
Arrival: Vietnam	137
Site 1: Vietnamese Central Highlands Bronze Gong Ensemble	138
Site 2: *Nhac Tai Tu* Amateur Chamber Music	141
Arrival: Thailand	145
Site 3: Classical *Piphat* Music	146
Arrival: Laos and Northeast Thailand	152
Explore More: The Ramayana	153
Site 4: *Lam Klawn* Repartee Singing	155
Site 5: *Luk Thung* Popular Song	159
Arrival: Indonesia (Java and Bali)	164
Site 6: Javanese Court Gamelan	166
Site 7: Balinese *Gamelan Gong Kebyar*	171
Explore More: Kecak: *The Balinese "Monkey Chant"*	177
Questions to Consider	178
On Your Own Time	178

Bangkok's Wat Arun (Temple of Dawn), a Buddhist complex next to the Chao Phraya River, attracts thousands of visitors each month drawn to its architectural design and brilliant colors

Background Preparation

It is difficult to imagine a more colorful region of the world than Southeast Asia, a vast area split between the Asian mainland and some of the largest islands in the world. As a result of both internal histories and colonization, the region has developed into eleven independent states, seven on the mainland and four among the islands, of which all but Thailand were earlier colonized by European powers before gaining independence during the twentieth century. Prior to the colonial period, Southeast Asia consisted of both large and small kingdoms, the borders of which constantly expanded or retreated depending on a given power center's projection of influence. The names of some countries may be familiar, but others are understandably little known, including that of the region's newest nation, Timor-Leste (East Timor), which only gained independence from Indonesia in 1999. The nations on the mainland include Myanmar (formerly Burma), Cambodia, Laos, Malaysia, Singapore, Thailand, and Vietnam, while the island nations are Brunei, Indonesia, the Philippines, and Timor-Leste.

There are many more ethnic groups than there are states, however—mainland Southeast Asia alone is home to more than 140 named ethnic groups and the islands another sixty or more. Population densities throughout the region vary widely: both Vietnam and Indonesia (especially the main island, Java) have high-density and rapidly growing populations, while the populations of Burma and especially Laos are scattered and sparse. The largest urban areas grew rapidly during the last half of the twentieth century, especially as rural populations migrated to the cities seeking safety (during periods of war) or economic opportunities. The region's largest cities include Jakarta in Indonesia, Bangkok in Thailand, Ho Chi Minh City in Vietnam, Manila in the Philippines, and the city-state of Singapore at the tip of the Malaysian Peninsula. Some capital cities, however, remain relatively small and undeveloped; these include Vientiane in Laos and Phnom Penh in Cambodia. Myanmar, however, recently built an entirely new capital in an isolated area 500 miles/800 km north

Typical of modern Southeast Asian cities, Bangkok's endless traffic and general congestion can be both exhilarating and exhausting

A typically timeless village near the banks of the mighty Maekhong River in southern Laos near the Khong waterfalls

SOUTHEAST ASIA

The terraced rice paddies of Bali, Indonesia, effectively utilize every inch of available space (Amy Unruh)

of the old capital in Rangoon (Yangon) called Nay Pyi Taw. Because Southeast Asian cities exhibit the most modern aspects of life in each country, it is in the small towns and villages, where rice-growing and animal husbandry are the chief occupations, that "traditional" culture thrives.

Many aspects of Southeast Asian life—agricultural, ritual, and festive—are shaped by broad weather patterns called *monsoons* (winds). Life on the mainland is governed by alternating wet and dry monsoons; the former come from the sea and bring on the rainy season, and the latter come from the Asian continent and bring dry weather, either cool or hot. During a given season, the weather tends to vary little. Island climates are generally more even throughout the year, because the humidity that produces rain is nearly always present. Overall, equator-straddling Southeast Asia is tropical and rather humid, but upland areas, especially on the mainland, can become quite cold during the cool, dry monsoon. Temperatures in northern Thailand and upland Laos can drop to freezing, and snow has been known to fall in the highlands of central Laos. Because most rice is grown in flooded paddy fields, rice agriculture is restricted to the rainy season except where irrigation systems have been constructed. Countries experiencing a dry monsoon period otherwise have only one harvest, while those with rain year-round may have two or more.

Poverty remains a major issue in many Southeast Asian countries. Economically, most of Southeast Asia is still considered "developing," though Malaysia, Thailand, and Singapore have achieved rapid growth and modernization in recent decades. In economically advanced countries such as these, one finds fully developed communication and sanitation infrastructures, but in the less developed areas, such as Laos, there are still few paved roads, no railroads, and little modern communication.

Planning the Itinerary

Because around 200 distinct, named ethnic groups are found throughout Southeast Asia, an exploration of the region's cornucopia of musics is as daunting as it is exciting. Each of the larger nations, with the exception of the Philippines, has or had aristocratic courts that were longtime patrons of the arts. Wherever these court systems thrived, highly sophisticated "classical" music developed, performed by relatively large instrumental ensembles in a variety of contexts, including dance, theater, and ritual. In one case, that of Bali in Indonesia, these ensembles were primarily associated with Hindu temples rather than with the royal court. Outside courts and temples, music largely flourishes in the rural areas, primarily in villages, because Southeast Asian farmers prefer to live in clusters. In these areas, music-making is necessarily simpler because few musicians are able to devote themselves to it full-time or afford expensive kinds of instruments. Many Southeast Asian nations also have large minority groups, usually living in remote uplands. Their music is often unrelated to that of the dominant lowland cultures. In addition, most cities have large segments of Chinese or Chinese-descended people who are either well integrated, like those of Thailand, or remain more separate, as in Indonesia or Malaysia. Throughout Southeast Asia, though especially in urban areas, there is also a great variety of modernized popular music. In countries with developed media, this type of music reaches into the most remote areas, even if the televisions have to be powered by car batteries.

Southeast Asia is especially known for two materials used to make instruments—bronze and bamboo. Bronze is an alloy of the naturally occurring metals copper and tin. Bronze metallurgy is extremely old, going back to around 2000 B.C.E. For this reason, a great variety of bronze instruments are found throughout the region. Being rigid and heavy, bronze instruments are invariably idiophones. Most ensembles that feature bronze instruments also include non-idiophones, especially drums. A second key feature of this region's music is the widespread use of bamboo, although bamboo instruments are also commonly found in East Asia. In Southeast Asia's tropical climate, bamboo grows rapidly and easily, providing material not just for musical instruments but also for numerous everyday objects, such as bowls, knives, building materials, even textiles from the interior fibers.

Demographics must be considered when categorizing the music of the region. One basic division is between lowland and upland peoples. Lowlanders mostly live in villages and are generally wet rice farmers, though the people of the great lowland cities, who vary from wealthy businessmen and high-ranking government officials to unskilled laborers, live quite differently. Uplanders everywhere remain rural, with some practicing swidden agriculture, in which nomadic communities clear hillsides or mountaintops for temporary agricultural use by slashing and burning the trees and planting dry crops such as rice or maize. Besides its indigenous peoples, Southeast Asia also hosts great numbers of Chinese immigrants, most of whom came to the cities to engage in commerce during the nineteenth and early twentieth centuries, often retaining their distinct temple traditions, instrumental music, and opera. On a smaller scale, the same is true of immigrants from India.

Southeast Asia is a subcontinent known more for instrumental ensembles than for soloists. Vocal music also plays a strong role, because many traditional forms articulate narratives of great warriors, royalty, and religious men, as well as great women, comic characters, and superhuman heroes. Theater is exceptionally important as well, and virtually all Southeast Asian theater types combine instrumental music, song, and dance. Additionally,

Priwan Nanongkham

AN INSIDE LOOK

I grew up in a rice-farming village in Northeast Thailand, a region that is culturally Lao and known locally as Isan. When I was in the seventh grade at the local secondary school, I joined a Thai music club. At that time people said that playing Thai classical music was not just for enjoyment but it also influenced people to be good human beings. There I began my first music lesson on the *ranat thum* (lower xylophone) and later *saw u* (two-stringed coconut fiddle), the first two instruments that brought music into my life. I really enjoyed playing music in our school's music club ensemble. We practiced and rehearsed after school and weekends and had chances to perform locally.

At the end of that academic year, I came to the conclusion that music was what I wanted to do for the rest of my life. Thus, I decided to switch schools and restarted seventh grade in Roi-et city at the local *Natasin*, a kind of high school for the arts that includes the first two years of college. There I majored in *piphat* ensemble, one of the classical genres from central Thailand. Classical was the only genre offered as a major program in academia in the mid-1980s.

As an Isan native, however, I felt that I should also know the music of my home region. My school also offered the study of local music as elective courses, but only for the fourth year-students and beyond, and I could not wait that long. In my second year, I began informally taking lessons on Isan music with an older friend at school. The first Isan instrument I studied was the *khaen*, a free-reed mouth organ that is the primary instrument in Lao culture. By the third year I was ready to join our school's "Isan traditional music" troupe (consisting of musicians and dancers) known today as *wong ponglang*. It was so named after the *ponglang*, a vertical log xylophone, the main instrument of an ensemble created during the 1980s to help preserve our tradition in the face of influences from modernization and globalization. Our school troupe rehearsed after school and during vacation periods.

Priwan Nanongkham, Thai musician and teacher

We were invited to perform throughout Thailand and even went to Germany and the Netherlands in the summer of 1989.

After having six years of intensive training as a performer at Natasin Roi-et, I decided to expand my work in music through the study of pedagogy at Chulalongkorn University in Bangkok, where I earned a Bachelor of Music Education degree in 1992. The following year I entered the masters program in Cultural Studies at Mahidol University near Bangkok where I began my graduate music study. Before finishing, however, I decided to pursue an opportunity to go to the United States to teach Thai music in 1994. Soon after I moved to New York where I taught Thai music in a Thai Buddhist temple. Following that I entered the graduate program in Musicology-Ethnomusicology at Kent State University and wrote an MA thesis on *ponglang* music from Isan. My dream, after completing my Ph.D, is to become a music professor, field researcher, scholar, and musician focused on the study of the music of my own regional culture, Thailand as a whole, and of the rest of Southeast Asia, if not the world.

The famous triple *chedi* in fourteenth-century Wat Sri Samphet in Thailand's former capital, Ayuthaya, which was destroyed by Burmese armies in 1767

theater employing puppets of various sorts—especially flat, leather "shadow" puppets—is a major art form throughout the region. Vietnam's unique water-puppet theater, which takes place in a pond with the puppeteers behind a screen standing waist-deep in water, features amazingly agile wooden puppets placed at the ends of long, complex mechanical arms.

All musics, whether traditional or modern, require a system of patronage in order to survive. While the courts and royal families of Vietnam, Laos, and Burma have long since disappeared, royal arts in those countries continue to a degree thanks to modest state support. Even in Thailand, Malaysia, and Cambodia, which retain kings and royal families, patronage has also been taken over by the state, which encourages the arts in various ways, especially through the educational system. Only in Indonesia, where Javanese sultans still hold court, does royalty actually help sustain the traditional arts. But even there, government-supported music conservatories can be found. Traditional music, theater, and dance at the local and regional levels, however, are mostly left to their own devices. Many music traditions have had a tough time surviving due to increased modernization and the spread of popular culture through globalization. Some forms have retained widespread support by modernizing, but many have simply become rare or extinct as people turn increasingly to various popular musics, both of local and of foreign origin. All Southeast Asian countries now have their own popular music, much of it originally stimulated by the importation of Anglo-British ballroom dance music from the 1930s and continuing to today with the latest releases from European, American, and Asian pop stars.

SOUTHEAST ASIA

Arrival: Vietnam

Vietnam stretches dragon-like along the South China Sea for some 1,500 miles (2,400 km). Two major rivers create vast sandy deltas before they empty into the sea: the Red River in the north, which flows past the capital city, Hanoi, and the Maekhong River (sometimes spelled Mekong), which splits into nine branches—the "Nine Dragons" (*Cuu Long* in Vietnamese)—and flows through the endless rice fields of the southern delta. Vietnam's backbone is a chain of mountains that runs from south to north, spilling into neighboring Cambodia, Laos, and China. Vietnam's vast population of more than eighty-seven million people is predominantly Viet (or Kinh), a wet rice-growing people who live in the lowland plains between the mountains and the sea. In central Vietnam, the coastal plains are sometimes no more than a few miles or even a few hundred feet wide. Indeed, between Danang and the old imperial capital of Hue, "Sea and Cloud Pass" brings the mountains into the sea itself. The majority of Vietnam's people live in the lowlands, while some fifty-four minority groups, most unrelated to the Viet, live in the interior hills and mountains that border Cambodia and Laos to the west and China to the north.

Culturally speaking, Vietnam has three distinct regions: the north, the center, and the south. Each has a different history, a distinct accent, and different preferences for instruments and genres of music or theater. The north includes Hanoi, the country's ancient capital and the locale for several important kinds of music, including the music of the distinctive water-puppet theater. The center's heart is the old imperial city of Hue, seat of the Nguyen dynasty from the early nineteenth century until 1945, when Vietnam's last emperor, Bao Dai, abdicated. The south, centered on Ho Chi Minh City (formerly Saigon) and several major cities in the delta, has the youngest culture and is the least formal in behavior.

An upland Bahnar village near Kontum, Vietnam. Note the lightly framed houses with stucco walls and the steps carved into a log

137

WORLD MUSIC: A GLOBAL JOURNEY

Members of the Jarai ethnic group, the same ones heard in the track, perform on a set of flat bronze gongs and a drum in Vietnam's Central Highlands (Phong Nguyen)

The people who live in the mountains are mostly different from the Viet and speak a variety of Austro-asiatic and Malayo-Polynesian languages. Living in isolated villages and often practicing "slash-and-burn" or "swidden" agriculture on the mountainsides, they relocate from time to time when the fields are depleted. Their musical cultures encompass both songs and instrumental music. Most instruments in the uplands are made of bamboo and other organic materials, but they are nonetheless incredibly varied. Perhaps most surprising are the large bronze gong sets played during year-round rituals and festivals.

For many in the West, "Vietnam" is a war, but, of course, it is actually a country—and *one* country, not two as during that war. The capital, Hanoi, formerly only known as a forbidding Communist city and the prime target of American bombers in "North Vietnam," is located along the broad Red River, whose delta forms a vast plain in the north. Hanoi's architecture reflects three eras: fascinating temples dating back to the eleventh century, French colonial architecture created during the later nineteenth and twentieth centuries, and the modern buildings of a capitalist-leaning and increasingly cosmopolitan Vietnam reborn in the 1990s.

Site 1: Vietnamese Central Highlands Bronze Gong Ensemble

First Impressions. The clanging sound of the gongs may remind you of church bells, albeit a very large set of them, in a small country church. This hypnotic music seems simple, using mainly metal gongs with somewhat "fuzzy" pitches for the short-repetitive melody. A careful listen reveals a mix of sound changes because the musicians are walking in a circle past a stationary microphone.

Aural Analysis. The ensemble heard in our example consists of approximately thirty members, all from the Jarai ethnic group, and was recorded in Pleiku in Vietnam's Central Highlands. Led by young female dancers, the male musicians walk counter-clockwise in a circle, each striking a single bronze gong. These vary in diameter from about 24 inches (61 cm) to around 12 inches (30 cm). Some have bosses (raised knobs), and others are flat; all are struck by padded beaters. In addition, the ensemble includes two horizontally played barrel drums and metal cymbals. A careful listen reveals six pitches in the octave, expressed as 1, 2, 3, 4, 5, and 7—but because the Jarai do not theorize about their music, this scale has no name. The range of the melody is relatively narrow, and the intervals between adjacent melodic pitches are no more than a fifth.

Because each musician has only one gong, each capable of producing only a single pitch, the sounds of the different gongs are "strung together" to produce melody. This is an example of *interlocking construction*, in which a succession of individual pitches played by different people creates the effect of a continuous melody. A Western music tradition that parallels this idea is a bell choir, often heard during the winter holiday season. Considering that each musician only strikes one gong, it is not surprising that there is no ornamentation, as this would disrupt the continuity of the melodic line.

The rhythm follows a clear duple meter and sounds fairly simple except for a certain freedom displayed in the pitches' non-simultaneity. One senses that these performers cooperate but do not feel obligated to play in lockstep. The melodic units are relatively short and have a narrow range that falls toward the lowest pitch (1). This pitch is the tonal center, or "home" note that creates an aural feeling of rest and resolution. Although the music consists primarily of a single melodic line, making it monophonic, accompanying gong-players sound the "pillar" pitches of 1 and 5 from time to time, giving the music a strong tonal framework. Its form is iterative in that the melody is repeated for as long as necessary. There are no intentional dynamic shadings.

LISTENING GUIDE

CD 1.9 (1'11")

Chapter 6: Site 1
Vietnam: Central Highlands Bronze Gong Ensemble

Instruments: Bronze gongs of various pitches, small cymbals, low- and high-pitched drums

TIME	LISTENING FOCUS
0'00"	Cymbals signal beginning of performance.
0'02"	Opening gong establishes the duple meter and central pitch. The cymbals also mark this regular pulsation, initially at half the rhythmic density of the opening gong and then with the same density (at 0'09").
0'05"	Melodic gongs enter and repeat the melody every sixteen beats. Listen for the primary melodic pitches of 1 and 5 in contrast to the interlocking melodic gongs. The drum also enters, but is not easily distinguished until roughly 0'10".
0'13"	The melodic line repeats.
0'14"	A low-pitched drum enters, adding a recurring "roll" throughout the performance.

0'21"	The melodic line repeats. Listen for further repetitions at 0'28", 0'36", etc.
0'48"	A syncopated "inner" melody is added to the performance.
1'01"	A very high-pitched gong adds an additional syncopated rhythm.

Source: Gong ensemble of the Jarai, Pleiku City, Pleiku province, recorded by Terry E. Miller and Phong Nguyen; from *Vietnam: Mother Mountain and Father Sea*, White Cliffs Media WCM 9991 (6 CDs and 47 pp. book), 2003. Used by permission.

ETHNO-CHALLENGE (CD 1.9): Walk along with the basic beat and then choose a prominent pitched gong heard in the recording (such as 1) and clap at the points in the melody where it sounds.

Cultural Considerations. Ensembles of gongs are typical among upland Vietnam's ethnic groups. They are associated with both festivals and religious rituals, including funerals and the annual buffalo sacrifice. Because they require a large number of musicians, no one of whom dominates, these ensembles reflect the communal nature of upland village life. In this music, as in the society, each person has a specific role to play: some reiterate the pillar-like pitches, some play melody, and some dance; overall, there is no apparent distinction between "musician" and "non-musician." Anyone in the community could expect to participate, if so inclined.

Gong ensembles typically play for funerals and thus have a strong association with the afterlife. But visitors are more likely to encounter them during public upland festivals now promoted by the government. Perhaps the most difficult event to witness is the buffalo sacrifice, during which several young men seem to become nearly hypnotized as they begin piercing the hide of a buffalo tied to a tree. Accompanied by the gongs, whose music lends itself to this hypnotic state, they continue stabbing the buffalo until it finally dies. For most visitors, this is not a pleasant experience—but for central highlanders the sacrifice is an important ritual that honors the spirits in order to assure the continuity of human life and successful harvests.

Many unanswered questions remain about the relationship between upland and lowland cultures. While bronze metallurgy has been dated to around 2000 B.C.E., it is unclear which culture developed it first. Are the upland peoples the remnants of the original inhabitants of Southeast Asia, whose ancestors were pushed from their lowland homes by advancing peoples (the early ancestors of the Viet) coming from the north? Because the lowland Viet make little use of bronze and play instruments that reflect Chinese influence, it is tempting to conclude that the upland peoples reflect the earliest layer of musical culture in Vietnam. Others argue, however, that upland cultures have always been at the margins of Vietnamese society and have absorbed and preserved aspects of lowland culture no longer prominent there. That would suggest that upland cultures reflect what is called "marginal survival," in which aspects of mainstream culture now lost are preserved in outlying areas, where culture changes more slowly. At present, however, there is no way to prove either theory. In 2005 the Central Highlands were designated as "The Space of Gong Culture" in the Third

SOUTHEAST ASIA

Proclamation of UNESCO's "Masterpieces of Oral and Intangible Heritage of Humanity" program.

Site 2: *Nhac Tai Tu* Amateur Chamber Music

First Impressions. **Nhac tai tu** has a free and improvisatory feel in both melody and rhythm that includes much tone-bending and syncopation. While a prominent fiddle cuts through with a busy melodic line, lower stringed instruments complement with a cornucopia of timbres and rhythmic riffs. The music well reflects the casual setting where a group of friends meet to play favorite compositions, be it in a private village home or in a music club room in the market area of a town.

NHAC TAI TU
(pronounced *ni-yak tai tuh*) A type of chamber music ensemble from southern Vietnam.

Aural Analysis. While many Vietnamese instruments were derived from Chinese instruments, they nearly always have been modified to allow for the tone-bending so preferred by Vietnamese musicians. Thus, to accommodate this fundamental aspect, Vietnamese stringed instruments have higher frets and looser strings than their Chinese equivalents. The decoration on Vietnamese instruments also tends to be unlike that found on Chinese instruments—generally, it features much intricate mother-of-pearl inlay. These refined decorations are in some ways analogous to the ornamentation that is so crucial in Vietnamese music.

A southern instrumental chamber genre, *nhac tai tu* is a gathering of amateur instrumentalists who play more for their own enjoyment than for others. In this way it is similar to the Chinese *sizhu* "silk and bamboo" chamber music from Shanghai (see Chapter 7). The recording features three melodic instruments—the *dan kim* lute, the *dan tranh* zither, and the *dan co* fiddle—plus the **song lang** "slit-drum" clapper. While this is a typical ensemble for this type of music, on some occasions other instruments may also join in such as a Vietnamese guitar (*dan ghi-ta*), a horizontal flute (*sao*), or a pear-shaped lute (*dan tyba*).

SONG LANG
(pronounced *shong long*) A "slit-drum" clapper idiophone from Vietnam.

At My Tho, along one branch of Vietnam's *Cuu Long* ("Nine Dragons") making up the delta of the Maekhong (Mekong) River, the area where *nhac tai tu* flourishes

WORLD MUSIC: A GLOBAL JOURNEY

A southern Vietnamese *nhac tai thu* group performs at a festival in Ho Chi Minh City. From left to right: *dan nhi* (fiddle), *dan nguyet* (lute), singer with guitar behind, and *dan tranh* (zither) (Phong Nguyen)

A Vietnamese *song lang* clapper/slit drum. The small beater strikes the slit wooden gong to produce the "clicks" that articulate the rhythmic cycle in Vietnamese music (Phong Nguyen)

    Vietnamese music is generated from a complex modal system. Each mode has its own set of pitches (basically five), a hierarchy of strong and weak tones, required ornamentation, and associated extra-musical meanings. In this way, the Vietnamese system resembles the *raga* system of South Asia more than music processes found in East Asia, even though East Asia is the source of Vietnamese instruments. Certain pitches in each of the Vietnamese modes are outside the Western tempered tuning system, giving Vietnamese music a piquant feeling for those accustomed to Western tuning.

SOUTHEAST ASIA

Another aspect of Vietnamese music that relates to India is the use of a closed cycle of beats similar to the Indian *tala*; in Vietnam, the clicks of the *song lang* clapper articulate points in these cycles. Unlike the Indian cycle, however, but similar to the Thai cycle, the *final* beat is the most accented. Our example is organized in a four-beat cycle called *nhip tu*, and the *song lang* is struck on beats 3 and 4. It may be easier to feel and hear this cycle in sixteen beats instead of four, counting the clapper strikes on beats 12 and 16. Another distinctive feature of Vietnamese rhythm is its tendency toward rhythmic syncopation (i.e., toward shifting the accent to a weak beat in a measure).

The musicians in a *tai tu* ensemble all play the same fundamental melody but add different kinds of ornamentation typical of their instrument, resulting in the phonic structure called *heterophony*. Before the group begins playing the tune, it is customary for each musician, in succession, to improvise a short introduction in free rhythm. Improvisation of this sort is atypical of the rest of Southeast or East Asia, lending further credence to the view that Vietnamese culture, while deeply influenced by East Asia, sometimes exhibits traits more typical of South Asia where a freely rhythmic introduction is common in classical music performance.

LISTENING GUIDE

CD 1.10 (1'37")

Chapter 6: Site 2

Vietnam: *Nhac Tai Tu* Amateur Chamber Music

Instruments: *Dan Kim* (plucked lute), *dan tranh* (plucked zither), *dan co* (bowed lute, i.e., fiddle), *song lang* (clapper idiophone)

TIME	LISTENING FOCUS
0'00"	*Dan tranh* (zither) enters with a freely rhythmic improvisation.
0'05"	*Dan kim* (lute) enters.
0'09	*Dan co* (fiddle) enters.
0'23"	*Song lang* (clapper) sounds to mark the transition to the composed/metered section of the performance.
0'24"	*Dan tranh* initiates composed section with a gradual increase in tempo.
0'26"	The *dan kim* and then the *dan co* reenter to affirm the basic pulse, but listen for the heavy use of syncopation.
0'28"	*Song lang* sounds on the third beat of the rhythmic cycle. Breaking the cycle down into sixteen subdivisions, the instrument marks the twelfth subdivision.
0'31"	*Song lang* sounds again on the fourth beat (sixteenth subdivision) to close the rhythmic cycle.
0'42"	Melodic instruments "close" the melody (i.e., reach a cadence) on the sixteenth beat of the cycle as the *song lang* sounds.

0'50"	*Song lang* sounds on the third beat (twelfth subdivision).
0'53"	*Song lang* sounds on the fourth beat (sixteenth subdivision).
1'03"	Melodic line reaches a closing cadence again.
1'25"	Closing cadence.
1'47"	Closing cadence.
1'55"	The example fades.

Source: "Xuan tinh (Spring Love)" performed by Nam Vinh, *dan kim*; Sau Xiu, *dan tranh*; and Muoi Phu, *dan co*; recorded by Terry E. Miller and Phong Nguyen. From *Vietnam: Mother Mountain and Father Sea*. White Cliffs Media WCM 1991 (6 CDs and 47 pp. book), 2003. Used by permission.

ETHNO-CHALLENGE (CD 1.10): Keep track of the *song lang* rhythmic cycle and clap on the beats where it sounds.

Cultural Considerations. Vietnam is, musically, an extremely complex country. The example used here, *tai tu*, is but one of many kinds of music that are essentially songs accompanied by a small instrumental ensemble. Some types of music were originally associated with court ceremonies in the former imperial capital, Hue; some are associated with rituals such as possession rites or funerals; and some, like *tai tu*, are still used simply for entertainment. Sophisticated poetry is much appreciated in Vietnam, and even though *tai tu* songs are "amateur," they are also refined.

It is difficult to divide Vietnamese music into categories such as "classical" and "folk," because the same repertory of tunes can be played in many different ways. A learned musician will most likely approach a given piece differently than a farmer would—but in fact many farmers are highly refined and skilled musicians. Within the span of a few days, the same musicians might be hired to play for a religious rite and a theater performance—and might also perform together for their own enjoyment. In fact, *tai tu* music was the basis for the music that accompanied the *cai luong* theater, a "popular" (i.e., commercial) genre created and cultivated in the south from around 1917 until its gradual decline in the 1990s in the face of competition from film and television.

The challenge for visitors to Vietnam today is finding genuine "traditional" music as opposed to what is normally offered as such, what the Vietnamese call *cai bien* music and which can be translated as "neo-traditional." During the communist period from the 1950s until the 1990s, many northern Vietnamese studied in eastern Europe where they learned about the propaganda value of "folkloric" state troupes that presented modernized forms of old music, fully composed and rehearsed, that conveyed ideas of national solidarity and identity. Most returned as professors at the Hanoi Conservatory of Music, and there they created Vietnam's response to these ideas. They combined "improved" (i.e., modernized) versions of lowland Viet instruments with similarly altered versions of instruments from the Central Highlands and composed elaborate compositions making use of harmony, full orchestration, and having politically loaded titles. Although the promoters claimed the music came from "the people," in fact it came from European ideas of "socialist realism," an aesthetic philosophy that uses music to influence people's political thinking. Conservatories came to teach this style almost exclusively, and the current generation of students tends to believe that this is indeed Vietnam's "traditional music."

Arrival: Thailand

Thailand has long been one of Southeast Asia's favorite tourist destinations. For many years travelers entered the country through Bangkok's Suvarnabhumi (pronounced *Suwannaphum*) Airport, but with the development of southern Thailand's beaches and island resorts, quite a few fly directly to Phuket (pronounced Poo-ket) Island and skip Bangkok altogether. As beautiful as these islands are, they provide visitors with little of the country's musical and artistic culture. Although going to Bangkok is obligatory for anyone wishing to experience Thai music, many visitors also travel to the northern region and its principal city, Chiangmai, where many tourist-oriented regional musical performances can be heard. Few travelers, however, make it to the northeast region, called Isan. Isan maintains a vibrant traditional culture, which, if somewhat modernized at times, remains an integral part of society and is not geared toward outsiders.

Bangkok is a busy, sprawling city famous for its gorgeous Buddhist temples, palaces, shopping, and, alas, world-class traffic jams. Tourists are still enticed to Thailand by colorful posters of small boats laden with produce and crafts on the *khlong* (canals), but if you want to see this "floating market" phenomenon, you must now travel southwest of Bangkok, where it is maintained both for tourists and for Thai. While old neighborhood open markets can still be found in many areas, the outlying and newer parts of Bangkok are served by gigantic

Old-fashioned *khlong* (canal) at Bang Khen east of Bangkok in 1972. The same area now is fully developed with high rises, the small boats replaced by fast, modern boats

malls and megastores that dwarf American Wal-Marts and attract throngs of shoppers, many from Japan and China who fly to the country specifically for this purpose.

The tourism authorities have in recent years promoted the slogan "Amazing Thailand." What we find most amazing about Thailand is that, no matter how modern it seems, beneath the apparent development, commercialization, and Westernization is a "Thainess" that triumphs over all things imported or imposed. As you walk through one of Central Corporation's many gigantic malls and observe thousands of ordinary Thai walking, shopping, eating, and generally relaxing in the air conditioning, understand that hidden within remains a Thai worldview that makes room for spirits alongside Toyotas, magic alongside the stock market, a faith in Buddhism alongside a job running computers, and a complex form of traditional "classical" Thai music alongside every imaginable form of popular music, both domestic and imported. Sometimes this clash can be maddening to a foreigner trying to figure out just what Thai culture is. While there is the appearance of modernization, democratization, and globalization through the Internet, there are also factors such as the monarchy, Buddhism, village life, and age-old rituals (such as the "teacher greeting ceremony"), which connect even the most forward-looking Thai to the past and his/her culture.

Traditionally, Thailand (or Siam, as it used to be called) was an absolute monarchy. Following the revolution in 1932, the monarchy lost political power, though it retains tremendous moral authority to this day. Thailand is now a constitutional monarchy with a revered royal family headed by King Bhumibol Adulyadej, Rama IX—who, incidentally, earlier aspired to become a jazz musician. Traditional music requires a context in which to thrive, and as much of that context (age-old rituals, old-style farming, close-knit villages, a slow pace of life, etc.) has diminished, some of the music and dance associated with it has disappeared or survived by moving to the stage. One thing that remains, however, is "classical" music. Though classical music was never popular with the masses, there is a general tendency to think of classical traditions, such as the *piphat*, as representing the essence of Thainess through music.

Site 3: Classical *Piphat Music*

PIPHAT
(pronounced *bee-paht*) A type of classical ensemble from Thailand characterized by the use of melodic and rhythmic percussion and a double-reed aerophone.

First Impressions. For many listeners new to world music, **piphat**, considered the main Thai classical court ensemble, may have to be appreciated as an acquired taste. The percussive timbre of the melodic instruments overlaid with a nasal aerophone play what seems to be a clamor of notes only held together by drums and some minimal percussion. After an initial listening, some elements will stand out, such as the regular ring of a small pair of cymbals and the predominance of a very active high-pitched xylophone. Several different melodies seem to overlap continuously in a sort of "organized chaos."

Aural Analysis. Called *piphat mai khaeng* ("hard-mallet *piphat*"), this ensemble produces what is perhaps the most characteristic sound of Thai traditional music. Central Thai instruments are quite varied. They may include prominent wooden- or bamboo-keyed instruments played with mallets (higher and lower xylophones), circular frames of tuned metal gongs, bowed and plucked strings, flutes, double reeds, drums, and small rhythmic percussion. Although some of these have solo repertories, Central Thai instruments are more characteristically found in ensembles. Three ensemble types predominate: (1) *piphat,* made

A *piphat* ensemble performs for a *wai khru* (teacher greeting ritual) at Bangkok's Thammasat University. From left clockwise: *pi* (double reed), *khawng wong yai* (large gong circle), *klawng that* (barrel drums), *ranat thum* (lower xylophone), *ranat ek* (higher xylophone), and *taphon* (horizontal drum)

up of melodic and rhythmic percussion and the double reed (heard in this track); (2) *mahori*, consisting of melodic and rhythmic percussion, strings, and flute; and (3) *khruang sai*, consisting of strings and flute with minimal rhythmic percussion. Whereas the *piphat* primarily plays theater, dance drama, and ritual music, the other ensembles ordinarily play lighter, more entertaining and tuneful music.

Piphat ensembles require at least three melodic instruments and two rhythmic instruments but usually add to these. The lead instrument is a high-range xylophone (*ranat ek*) with twenty-one bars of either hardwood or bamboo suspended over a boat-shaped resonator. Although this instrument's performance is the most rhythmically dense, the lower circle of tuned gongs (*khawng wong yai*)—whose player sits in the middle of its round rattan frame—plays the fundamental form of the composition. In addition a full ensemble includes a lower-ranged xylophone (*ranat thum*) that plays a highly syncopated, even playful, version of the composition, plus a higher-ranged gong circle (*khawng wong lek*) that plays a highly embellished version of the main melody. The aerophone used in hard-mallet ensembles is a quadruple-reed oboe (aerophone) called **pi**, and its duty is to play a flexible, seemingly distinct, version of the same main melody. Although it works as a double reed, each half is folded, making it actually quadruple.

The Thai tuning system has seven equidistant tones in an octave in contrast to the European system of twelve equidistant pitches, meaning that some of its pitches can sound "out of tune" to non-Thai ears. This is not always obvious since within a given passage a melody will mostly employ a pentatonic scale of only five tones, in the form of 1, 2, 3, 5, 6. Because this kind of music sometimes shifts from one tonal center to another, it is possible to hear a total of six or even seven pitches used in a given composition, including those heard here.

Virtually all Thai music is in duple meter, which means it operates with groupings of two, four, or eight beats. Certain strong beats are articulated by a pair of small cup-shaped

PI
(pronounced *bee*)
A double reed aerophone found in the piphat classical ensemble of Thailand.

WORLD MUSIC: A GLOBAL JOURNEY

(top left) *Khawng wong yai* (large gong circle) and *ranat ek* (higher xylophone)

(left) Left to right: two sizes of *pi* (double-reed aerophones), three sizes of *khlui* (vertical flutes)

(top right) Left to right, rear: *thon* (goblet drum), *rammana* (frame drum). Left to right, front: *chap lek* (larger cymbals), *ching* (small cymbals), and *krap sepah* (wood clappers)

CHING

A pair of cup-shaped cymbals from Thailand.

bronze cymbals, called *ching*, that are attached to each other with a string. The **ching** plays two strokes, the undamped (open) "ching" and the damped (closed) "chap." Thai meter is organized cyclically, somewhat like an analog clock. The cycles of much of the repertory have four *ching* strokes ("ching-chap-ching-chap"), with the final stroke ("chap") being accented. This means that Thai music is actually *end*-accented, making it the opposite of Western music generally, which accents beat 1. There are three relative rates of ching strokes, the slowest (called "third level" or *sam chan*), a medium rate twice as fast (called "second level" or *sawng chan*), and a fast rate twice as fast again (called "first level" or *chan dio*). These relationships are relative to the rhythmic density and not the absolute tempo. The track included here consists of three separate compositions: the first (*Sathukan*) uses only "ching" strokes, the second (*Sathukan klawng*) alternates "ching" and "chap," and the final one (*Rua*) returns to "ching" alone. There are two drums: 1) the *taphon*, a two-headed drum mounted horizontally on a stand, and 2) the *klawng that*, a pair of large barrel drums tilted at an angle toward the player.

The lower gong circle (*khawng wong yai*) is key to the organization of *piphat* music. It plays the simplest and least dense form of a given composition; its part has fewer notes—a lower rhythmic density—than the other instruments. Although it can be hard to hear, all of the other melodic instruments play idiomatic variants of the lower gong circle's version. Thus, the phonic structure of Thai *piphat* music is best described as a kind of layered heterophony often referred to as *polyphonic stratification*—that is, a layering of simultaneous variants of the same melody.

All Thai music is composed, and the names of the composers are known for most compositions created after about 1800. Unlike Western composition, however, the composer writes nothing, for until the mid-twentieth century there was no notation system used in Thai music. The composer was also a musician and transmitted his creations to fellow ensemble members (or students) by playing the large gong circle version. The others then "realized" that structure into the particular idioms of their own instruments; all memorized the composition.

The track included here presents the first two compositions of a much longer suite played during the "Teacher Greeting Ritual" (*Pithi wai* **khru**) explained below. All are classified as "action tunes" (*phleng naphat*) because in addition to appearing in several different ritual suites they also accompany the masked drama (*khon*), dance drama (*lakhon*), and the large shadow puppet theater (*nang yai*). The first piece, "Sathukan" (meaning "Greeting" and referring to the Thai custom of greeting each other with hands in "prayer position"), like most "action tunes" is too old to have a known composer but is the opening piece played for all ritual suites and for many theatrical performances. Motivic rather than melodic, this work flows continuously without obvious phrasing, and its rhythmic structure is marked by continuous "ching" strokes. "Sathukan klawng" (meaning "Greeting the drum") immediately follows. It is more clearly phrased, and the *ching* plays alternating "ching" and "chap" strokes. Completing the track is a short coda called "Rua" (referring to the tremolo technique used by the instruments to sustain pitches) which can be attached to many parts of the suite. It is non-metered, uses only "ching" strokes, and requires players to rapidly alternate the beaters to produce "tremolo."

KHRU
A Thai teacher; the term is linguistically associated with the word *guru* in the Hindi language.

LISTENING GUIDE

 CD 1.11 (4'48")

Chapter 6: Site 3
Thailand: Classical *Piphat* Music

Instruments: *Pi* (reed aerophone), *ranat ek* (high xylophone), *ranat thum* (low xylophone), *khawng wong yai* (gong circle), *daphon* (barrel drum)

TIME	LISTENING FOCUS
0'00"	*Daphon* (drum) initiates the performance. Listen for the contrasting high and low pitches of each drum face. Although it follows a cycle, the patterns played do not regularly repeat.
0'02"	*Ranat ek* (high xylophone) initiates the melodic content followed by the *pi* (reed aerophone) and remaining instruments. Listen for the higher range of pitches on the lead xylophone played in octaves and its busier rhythmic density in comparison to the other instruments. Also, note the "duck call" timbre of the *pi* that is quite prominent.
0'05"	Listen for the *ching* (small hand cymbals) entrance. Note there are no "chop" strokes during this section of the performance.
0'13"–0'14"	The heterophonic structure of Thai classical music makes it difficult to follow the melodic content. A good thing to focus on is the point at which the *khawng wong yai* reaches a cadence (closing phrase). Listen for the "ringing" timbre and thinner rhythmic density of this instrument, which provides the fundamental melody.
0'49"–0'55"	Listen for the *ranat thum* (low xylophone). This instrument is most difficult to hear, having a mellower timbre than the lead xylophone. Listen for its characteristic syncopations, broken octaves, and quick three-note ornamentations. Its melodic line frequently moves in a direction contrary to the other instruments.
1'16"–1'29"	Listen for the brief decrease in rhythmic density of the *pi* for twelve *ching* strokes as the ensemble moves toward a cadence point that quickly passes. Note how the *pi* (and other instruments) matches the ending pitch of the phrase at 1'29".
2'30"	Contrast the tempo at this point in the performance with the opening material. The tempo has increased significantly. (From roughly 84 beats per minute to about 104 by this point in the music.)
2'49"	Tempo slows dramatically at closing of opening section.
2'59"	Second section begins. Note the use of both "ching" and "chop" strokes with the *ching*. Also, note the increased activity of the *daphon* and clearer synchronization of the melodic instruments.
3'24"	Melody repeats.
3'45"	Tempo slows as ensemble reaches end of section.
3'51"	Third section begins. Note the ensemble plays in free rhythm to the end of the performance. Listen for the contrasting timbre and melodic style of each instrument.

Source: "Sathukan" and "Sathukan Klawng." Produced by The Committee of the College of Music Project, Mahidol University, Bangkok, Thailand, 1994.

ETHNO-CHALLENGE (CD 1.11): Match the basic rhythmic density of the *khawng wong yai* by tapping your hands on your book at each pitch. Listen again and match the rhythmic density of the *ranat ek* (lead xylophone), using both hands simultaneously from start to finish (as is the performance technique of the musician). An easier challenge is to listen to the example repeatedly following each instrument through the performance to note its unique realization of the fundamental melody.

Cultural Considerations. During the heyday of the Thai monarchy in the nineteenth and early twentieth centuries, classical music was generously patronized and played a major role in court ceremonies, both secular and Buddhist-related. As a consequence, Thai classical music is closely associated with the society's most important state occasions, festivals, and sacred rites of passage, such as ceremonies to honor teachers, ordinations, funerals, and certain Buddhist rituals. Perhaps we can say that Thai classical music as a sonic structure is mainly of interest to musicians; for others, it serves to engender positive feelings and to reaffirm Thai cultural identity. Although relatively few Thai choose classical music for general listening, there is a broad consensus that classical music best represents the country and its traditional culture.

In Thai society, the acts of teaching and learning, of passing on and receiving knowledge, are considered near sacred, and one honors not just the present-day living teacher, but that person's entire lineage leading back to the ultimate sources of knowledge, the pantheon of gods drawn from animism, Hinduism, and Buddhism. Before a master can begin transmitting knowledge to a student, the latter must perform a ritual "teacher greeting ceremony" or *phithi* (pronounced *pee-tee*) *wai khru*, the last word being the Thai pronunciation of the well-known Indian term *guru*. Simple *wai khru* ceremonies are performed at schools in which students simply reaffirm their allegiance to all their teachers, but for classical musicians and other such artists the teacher greeting ceremony is one of the most important rituals of their life.

A *piphat* ensemble using a pair of *klawng khaek* drums (in front) performs at a festival to honor a great teacher near Bangkok, Thailand

A teacher initiates new students of Thai music at the annual *wai khru* "teacher greeting" ceremony at Bangkok's Chulalongkorn University (Andrew Shahriari)

A *wai khru* ceremony requires an elaborate altar area containing tables covered with many kinds of food, finely crafted objects, theatrical masks of the deities, and a full set of musical instruments, many being newly made in order to receive blessing during the ritual. A male ritualist intones sacred words in a mix of Thai and Pali, the latter being the sacred language of Thai Buddhism. The *piphat* ensemble performs several pieces throughout the ceremony—which concludes when the ritualist marks the forehead of each student and musician with ashes and places a small cone made of banana leaf behind one of their ears. If a student has not studied before, they are given a ritual first lesson on the large gong circle or, for young children, a lesson on playing the small *ching* cymbals.

Although few non-musicians normally experience Thai classical music except in passing or as background to rituals and ceremonies, such as the *wai khru*, general attention to serious *piphat* music became widespread after the release in 2004 of Itthisoontorn Vichailak's hit film titled *Homrong* (The Overture), now available with English subtitles. A partially fictional life story of Luang Phradit Phairoh (1881–1954), Thailand's most famous composer, the film includes extended footage of classical music performed both solo and in ensemble, climaxing with a dramatic contest between the protagonist and his chief rival, Khun In, the latter played by an actual master musician. Musically, it is accurate in most details and recommended as an introduction to Thai music and culture.

Arrival: Laos and Northeast Thailand

Various historical events, including the European colonization of much of Southeast Asia, led to the Lao people being separated into two areas. Currently, only about five million live in sparsely populated Laos north and east of the mighty Maekhong River, while approximately thirteen million live in the northeast region of Thailand. The people of both countries

SOUTHEAST ASIA 6

Explore More

The *Ramayana*: An Indian Epic from a Southeast Asian Perspective

One of the great epics of world literature is the *Ramayana*, a story based on Hindu mythology and believed to be more than 3,000 years old. Originating in India, this tale spread throughout much of South and Southeast Asia and is fundamental to understanding many elements of the cultures of the region. The *Ramayana*'s influence has been profound. Social and moral codes exemplified in the stories and characters of the *Ramayana* shaped political structures, city planning, marriage customs, and basic human interaction for centuries. Indeed, the present king of Thailand is known as Rama IX, after the *Ramayana*'s main character.

Scenes found in the *Ramayana* inspire much artistic activity in Burma, Cambodia, Laos, and Indonesia, as well as Thailand, in the visual arts, dance, and music. In Thailand, where the story is called *Ramakian*, the most important classical genre of entertainment, known as *Khon*, is based on this work.

Scene from a *khon* masked dance performance of the *Ramakian*, Thailand's version of the Indian epic *Ramayana*, at the Siam Society. Rama (right) with the "good" demon Pipek (rear), Rama's brother, Lakshmana (left), and fallen monkey warrior, Sukreep.

Mural scene from the epic *Ramakian* at the Temple of the Emerald Buddha in Bangkok. The performance scene shows a *piphat* ensemble and the large shadow puppets that actually depict the *Ramakian* story

Performed monthly at the National Theater in Bangkok, *Khon* features masked dancers who enact a different scene from the epic with each performance to the accompaniment of a *piphat* ensemble. The dancers do not speak while on stage; rather, a vocalist chants/sings the story as the actors mime the epic's best-known scenes. *Khon* has become symbolic of the arts in Thailand; it is performed by students and professional performers in tourist shows, school plays, and television broadcasts, as well as in festivals and other cultural programs overseas.

Although countless variations exist, the basic storyline of the *Ramayana* is as follows: Prince Rama, an incarnation of the Hindu god Vishnu, retreats to the forest at his father's request for several years accompanied by his wife, Sita, and brother, Lakshmana. During his exile, Sita is kidnapped by the evil demon Ravana (Totsakan in the Thai version) after the two brothers are lured from her protection by a golden deer. Ravana takes Sita to his island fortress, Lanka, where he tries to persuade her to marry him, but she refuses as she is loyal to her husband and confident in her rescue. During her capture, Sita drops a clue for a watching band of monkeys

> who aid Rama in rescuing his wife. Key among these characters is Hanuman, the white monkey god who has many supernatural powers. Hanuman's adventures are numerous as he searches for Sita. He eventually discovers where Sita is imprisoned and returns to Rama to aid in a great battle with Ravana's demons. Allied with the monkeys and bears of the forest, Rama defeats Ravana's demon army, kills Ravana, and rescues the princess.
>
> The conclusion of the story varies depending on the region. In the Indian version, Rama and Sita return to his kingdom together, but rumors casting doubt on Sita's fidelity while imprisoned force her to undergo a trial by fire to prove her loyalty. Although she passes the test, Rama still exiles her to prevent his rule from being undermined by rumors that continue to persist. In the Thai version, Rama and Sita are reunited after the trial by fire and live happily ever after.

share a common language, cuisine, literature, and traditional way of life, but the two populations are also now quite different due to their political separation. Until the 1970s both areas where the Lao people are concentrated were equally undeveloped: Laos was a French colony until 1949 with no modern infrastructure while the northeast of Thailand was that country's most neglected region. After 1975, when the Royal Lao government fell to the communist Pathet Lao, Laos went backward economically and is only now beginning to recover, whereas Northeast Thailand's level of development was raised dramatically by Thailand's booming economy and the government's new attention to the region after the 1970s. Indeed, the northeast now includes two of Thailand's largest cities—Khon Kaen and Nakhon Ratchasima (known also as Khorat).

Of the six million plus people in Laos, a significant number live in the uplands—which account for much of the country's terrain—and speak non-Lao languages. The ethnic Lao live in the lowland areas, primarily along the Maekhong and its tributaries. Because the Lao are primarily farmers, growing glutinous (also called sticky) rice in wet paddy fields, the cities are small and economically dominated by Vietnamese and Chinese. Vientiane, the capital, has only about 700,000 residents. With infrastructure being so underdeveloped, Lao culture has developed regionally, giving rise to more than a dozen local musical styles. Northeast Thailand, commonly known as **Isan**, is primarily a flat plateau, and although subject to dramatic variations in weather—drought to flood—facilitates easier travel. With modern development has come the growth of the media and the rise of a vibrant popular music culture drawn from its traditional music. While the people of both Isan and Laos share the same cultural roots, those of Isan are strongly oriented toward Bangkok and the dominant culture. Since World War II great numbers of young Isan people have migrated to Bangkok seeking employment in factories, in construction, as maids, and as taxi drivers, bringing with them their vibrant culture. Earlier looked down upon as inferior and rustic, Isan culture is now viewed positively, and its attractive music (along with its food) was a principal reason.

Music in Isan includes both old-fashioned forms and many newer ones—including pop songs featuring troupes of dancing women, a rock combo, and bright lights. Even the modern types often appear in a traditional context, however, such as a Buddhist or New Year's festival. Our audio example exemplifies an older form of traditional singing that was popular until the 1990s, when it was eclipsed by more modern styles, but people today continue to honor this style by showcasing it at cultural events.

ISAN
(pronounced *ee-sahn*) A term referring to Northeast Thailand and its regional culture, including music.

SOUTHEAST ASIA   6

Mr. Ken Somjindah plays the northeastern Thai *khaen* with sixteen pipes in See-Kaeo village, Roi-et province

Site 4: *Lam Klawn* Repartee Singing

First Impressions. Many first-time listeners will find the sound of the instrument heard in *lam klawn*, known as the *khaen*, relatively familiar, likening it to a harmonica or an organ. The instrument seems to play harmony, a musical concept usually reserved for European-inspired traditions. The two vocalists—one male, one female—have a slightly nasal quality and often seem to be speaking their lyrics between extended melismatic phrases. As the music moves into a more regular rhythm, their performance seems like a Southeast Asian "freestyle rap" more than melodic singing.

Aural Analysis. Musically, what defines a Lao is playing the **khaen**, the culture's most significant instrument. The *khaen* is a free-reed bamboo mouth organ ranging in length from about 23 inches (0.6 meter) to more than 3 feet (one meter). It has sixteen thin bamboo tubes fitted into a carved, hardwood windchest with the pipes wrapped at three points with a kind of wide, dried grass. Each bamboo tube has a small, rectangular hole cut into its wall fitted with a thin plate of copper-silver alloy into which is cut a three-sided tongue, the "reed" (technically, a "free reed") that produces the sound as it vibrates. With the reeds sealed inside the windchest by a black insect wax, the reed tongue vibrates up and down when the player either inhales or exhales through the windchest. Each tube has a finger hole, and its reed only sounds when the finger hole is covered. Since many finger holes can be covered at once, the *khaen* is capable of clusters of pitches which form sounds analogous to Western chords, that is, harmony.

KHAEN
A bamboo free-reed mouth organ from Northeast Thailand and Laos.

155

The *khaen* shown in side view and front view with parts labeled.

LAM KLAWN (pronounced *lum glawn*) Vocal repartee with *khaen* accompaniment from Northeast Thailand.

Isan singers perform *lam*, a kind of singing in which the melody is generated according to a basic pattern coordinated with the lexical tones of the words. (Lao and Thai are tonal languages, meaning that each syllable has, in addition to consonants and vowels, a tonal inflection. Without this inflection, the word's meaning may be unclear or erroneous.) The language is Lao as spoken in Northeast Thailand, which has six tones. The term *maw* denotes someone with a skill, and thus a singer is a *mawlam* and a *khaen* player is a *mawkhaen*. There are numerous genres of *lam* among the Lao; the one heard here is performed by a pair of singers—one male and one female—and is called **lam klawn** (poetry singing) or *lam khu* (pair singing). Although *lam klawn* has lost much of its popularity in the last twenty years as several modernized genres of *lam* have become the rage among the younger generation, it is still performed for special events and embodies Isan–Lao traditions better than any other form.

An old-fashioned traditional performance of *lam* begins around 9.00 p.m. and continues to nearly 6.00 a.m. The performance takes place on a temporary stage, and the singers and *khaen*-players stand to perform. When the male is singing, the female usually performs a simple but graceful dance, and vice versa. The performance proceeds in three sections, the first lasting most of the night. Called *lam thang san* (literally "short-way singing"), this first

SOUTHEAST ASIA   6

A female *mawlam* singer, accompanied by *khaen*, performs on a small temporary stage at a Northeast Thai Buddhist temple in Mahasarakham, Thailand. Her male counterpart dances next to her

section consists of the male and female vocalists singing in alternation (known as a "repartee"), each beginning a section with an unmeasured introduction, usually on the phrase, "*O la naw*," followed by the main poem in meter. The scale is pentatonic and could be described as C, D, E, G, A (or 1, 2, 3, 5, 6), with C (1) as the "home" pitch. The meter is always duple. Singers memorize vast amounts of poetry, all written in four-line stanzas with a rhyme scheme peculiar to Lao poetry. The example here represents the beginning of *lam thang san* for both male and female singers.

LISTENING GUIDE

 CD 1.12 (3'07")

Chapter 6: Site 4

Thailand: *Lam Klawn* Repartee Singing

Vocals: Single male, single female
Instruments: *Khaen* (free-reed aerophone, i.e., mouth organ)

TIME	LISTENING FOCUS
0'00"	*Khaen* enters with improvisatory free rhythm. Listen for the three musical elements of drone, chord accompaniment (polyphony), and melody.
0'04"	Male vocalist enters with improvisatory free rhythm on a single non-lexical syllable ("O"), using a three-pitch melodic line to establish the tonal center.
0'14"	Vocalist continues improvisation with extended melismatic phrase, "*O la naw.*"
0'30"	Vocalist introduces some poetic verse while the *khaen* continues to play in free rhythm.
0'55"	Melismatic improvisation on the phrase "*O la naw,*" again with a brief verse to close the phrase.
1'14"	Vocalist transitions to the metered section with poetic verse.
1'19"	*Khaen* follows the vocalist with duple-metered performance and regular melodic content.
1'46"	Example briefly fades. Normally, the male vocalist sings for several minutes before the female vocalist enters.
1'48"	*Khaen* enters with improvisatory free rhythm. Listen for the change in mode (i.e., the pitches utilized).
1'53"	Female vocalist enters with melismatic improvisation on the phrase "*O la naw,*" sung in free rhythm.
2'07"	Vocalist introduces some poetic verse while the *khaen* continues to play in free rhythm.
2'27"	Melismatic improvisation on the words "*O la naw,*" again with a brief verse to close the phrase.
2'44"	Vocalist transitions to the metered section with poetic verse.
2'48"	*Khaen* follows the vocalist with duple-metered performance and regular melodic content.
3'00"	Example fades, though the female vocal section would normally continue for several minutes.

Source: "Lam thang san" (excerpts), sung by Saman Hongsa (male) and Ubon Hongsa (female), and played by Thawi Sidamni, *khaen*; recorded by Terry E. Miller in Mahasarakham, Thailand, 1988.

ETHNO-CHALLENGE (CD 1.12): Learn the melismatic style of the vocalists by matching the introductory phrases ("*O la naw*"). Clap the beat during the metered sections of the performance.

SOUTHEAST ASIA

Cultural Considerations. There is a saying about the Lao people: if a man lives in a house on stilts, eats sticky rice, and plays the *khaen*, he is a Lao. Traditionally, the Thai, Lao, Khmer, Burmese, and even Malay lived in houses built on stilts, partly for protection, partly to provide a shelter for their animals beneath. Sticky, or glutinous, rice, however, is peculiar to the Lao; the rest of Asia eats ordinary rice.

Lam klawn is not merely entertainment, even though it can be highly enjoyable. While a performance often takes the form of an imaginary courtship between the singers, and can involve earthy double entendres, it also addresses many essential aspects of Lao life. The vocalists often "discuss" or debate (in sung verse) matters of history, religion, literature, politics, geography, etiquette, and excerpts of famous stories, sometimes, but not always, offering listeners a model of approved thinking and behavior. Here is a typical example of love poetry, sung by a female:

> *O la naw* [introductory words without meaning] You are a handsome one. Please divorce your wife and then marry me. I will also divorce my husband and we will marry each other; can you? *O la naw*, you are a handsome man. One day I looked at the stars in the clear night and found the moon and many stars. But for myself, I could find no one.
>
> (Translation by Jarernchai Chonpairot)

As recently as the 1980s, *lam* was enjoyed by people of all ages throughout Northeast Thailand. Before Northeast Thai villages acquired electricity, entertainment was scarce, and everyone availed themselves of the chance to hear live music. In Laos the old days remain because there has been less development; the situation there remains much as it was in Isan thirty years ago. In Northeast Thailand, *lam* was most often heard during the cool or warm dry seasons (November to April), in conjunction with various events including monk ordinations, Buddhist festivals, the New Year (Western, Chinese, and Thai), an annual temple fair, and even funerals. People gathered and sat on the ground around the stage, which was open on four sides and the grounds were flanked by vendors selling snacks. As the *lam* performance progressed without breaks, audience members ate, slept, snacked, wandered off, flirted, or gossiped.

This form of *lam* lost popularity in the later 1980s as electricity—and thus radio and television—became widespread, and as a type of popular song called *luk thung* (see Site 5) became the rage. *Lam* singers fought back, creating a new fast-paced, popularized, brightly lit genre called **lam sing** (*sing* meaning "racing" or anything that is fast). *Lam sing* and other modernized genres have since swept Northeast Thailand, although they have barely penetrated Laos. Because there are so many Isan people living and working in Bangkok, *lam sing* and its related genres have also become well known there and throughout Thailand. As a result, Isan music in particular and Isan culture (and food) in general have become popular. Even McDonalds in Thailand for a period offered the now famous Isan green papaya salad called *somtam*.

LAM SING
(pronounced *lum sing*) A popular music form from Northeast Thailand.

Site 5: *Luk Thung* popular song

First Impressions. As the song starts, it sounds vaguely like the *lam* poetic verse heard in the previous track. But with the addition of drums, other instruments, and harmony this

The three most common musical instruments of Northeast Thailand, left to right: *saw pip* (fiddle), *phin* (lute), and *khaen* (free-reed mouth organ)

suggests popular song with an attractive, danceable beat. Those who are accustomed to current forms of American popular music may find this style old-fashioned and folky, but it is among the most attractive of current pop styles in Thailand, especially among people living in or from the northeast region.

Aural Analysis. Melodically, the accompaniment stays close to the traditional style of the *khaen* mouth organ heard in the previous track but here it is played by an electric guitar. During the later 1980s, when this song first appeared, musicians had not yet adapted the traditional plucked lute of the northeast, the **phin**, into a useable electric form, but the guitar heard in this track clearly imitates the style of the *phin*. Accompaniment is provided by a basic rock combo that includes a keyboard synthesizer, electric bass, and drum set. The scale form heard is pentatonic but unlike that of the *lam* in the previous track. Here it sounds minor, having the pitches A, C, D, E, and G, with A as the "home" pitch; sometimes it also uses pitch B in passing.

The song's title, "Sao Jan Kang Kop," translates as "Miss Chan's Broken Heart." It was released in 1986 by male singer Phawnsak Sawng-saeng (b. 1960) who was born and raised in Isan's Khon Kaen province. Beginning in 1981 with three albums of *luk thung isan* songs—country songs that used the Isan language but little of any local style—he switched to the new *mawlam* style for this album. Because *luk thung mawlam* remains immensely popular, Phawnsak's popularity has held over a long period as well, and this song retains its popularity today. While the title suggests a broken heart, *kangkop* literally means "to shade one's eyes," referring to the female protagonist constantly looking into the distance for her

PHIN

(pronounced *pin*)
A fretted, plucked lute from Northeast Thailand.

SOUTHEAST ASIA

Two "classic" *luk thung* covers: (left) Four *luk thung* artists, one holding the *khaen* mouth organ as a reminder of *luk thung*'s connections to traditional northeast Thai music; (right) scene of traditionally dressed singer with drawing of old fashioned village and water buffalos

Luk thung pop songs are part of the performance of *lam sing*, a modernized form of the traditional *lam klawn* repartee. This performance took place on a temporary village stage on New Year's Eve southwest of Mahasarakham, Thailand

Bangkok lover, who broke his promises to follow her back to Isan. The lyrics imply that she was too easy in giving in to the demands of her selfish boyfriend who left her without saying "good bye" after exploiting her. She constantly looks into the distance, searching for him. The singer, however, speaks as a local village boy who did his best to warn her of the dangers of Bangkok, of city people, and especially of central Thai. He says "I warned you but you never listened to me. Instead you got mad at me. Now, see! You deserve what happened."

161

Most of the lyrics are in Isan dialect (actually Lao) and set to a flexible version of a traditional melody called *lam toei phama*, literally "Burmese toei." About halfway through, however, the style changes abruptly to a typical *luk thung* melody similar to such tunes found throughout Thailand. Even within the *toei* sections, however, the singer switches between central Thai and northeast Thai several times. After the pop melody, he returns to the *toei* melody before repeating both sections.

LISTENING GUIDE

CD 1.13 (3'17")

Chapter 6: Site 5

Thailand (Northeast): *Luk Thung* Popular Song

Voice: Single male
Instruments: Electric *phin* (plucked lute), keyboard synthesizer, electric bass, rock drum set with *klawng fifa* (electric drums), *chab lek* (cymbals)

TIME	LISTENING FOCUS
0'00"	(Intro section) Drum set, electric bass, and synthesizer begin with a steady beat in common meter. Listen for the melodic shift of the synthesizer (0'10").
0'17"	(A section, "*toei*") Electric *phin* enters followed by the vocalist who sings in the Central Thai language. The text setting is syllabic and the rhythmic density of the voice in this section is thick in comparison to the B section (below). Note also that the synthesizer sustains a single pitch to provide a strong tonal center.
0'40"	(A section) Section repeats with different lyrics sung in the Isan language.
1'12"	(B section, "*luk thung*") The rhythmic density of the voice lessens and is more melodic. The lyrics are again sung in the Central Thai language. Note the synthesizer plays a complementary melodic line.
1'40"	A section returns with the lyrics sung in the Isan language.
2'05"	B section returns with the lyrics sung in the Central Thai language.
2'32"	A section returns with the lyrics sung in the Isan language.
2'59"	(Outro section) Opening content returns to finish the performance.

Source: "Sao Jan Kang Kop" sung by Phawnsak Sawng-saeng, from *Sao Jan Kang Kop*, JKC Marketing Co., Ltd, JKC-CD 157 (nd), used with permission.

ETHNO-CHALLENGE (CD 1.13): Investigate *Luk Thung* artists and popular music from Thailand via the Internet to find the karaoke video associated with this example.

SOUTHEAST ASIA

Cultural Considerations. Thai popular music developed out of the ballroom dance music that began to be created in the 1940s by the Suntaraphon Band. With their sophisticated poetic texts, these songs came to be called *luk krung*, literally "children of the city." During the 1950s some composers began creating songs with poetry that commented on the lives of the working people, both farmers and city people, using more direct and casual words. These were first called *phleng talat* ("market songs") but later came to be called *phleng luk thung* ("children of the fields"). Today outsiders call these "country songs," and in many ways the suggestion of Nashville is justified. But while country songs originated in central Thailand, especially in Bangkok, the present track comes from the northeast, culturally Lao but now referred to as Isan. Because this song shows a clear relationship with traditional *mawlam*, it is a *luk thung mawlam*, the current favorite among both immigrants from Isan living in Bangkok and back home in the villages and towns of the northeast. Some of the artists singing these started in traditional *lam* but crossed over into *luk thung*.

Luk thung songs have no clear point of origin, but their predecessors, found from the 1940s onward, were those Thai popular songs (called *phleng sakon*, "modern songs") that had less-sophisticated texts and often commented on the lives of common working people, including farmers. Like the "city songs" with their sophisticated poetry, many were in ballroom dance tempo, especially cha-cha-cha and rumba. Others derived from the music for a Thai couple dance called *ramwong* ("circle dance"), which had its origins in the 1940s. They differed in that *ramwong* songs were accompanied by small percussion only—principally a small clay drum—while *luk thung* used melodic instruments as well.

During the later 1960s and early 1970s singers took traditional regional styles from the north, south, and northeast and began infusing them with local elements. Besides the usual combo instruments—drums, electric guitar, and, later, keyboard—some added regional instruments; whether present or not, composers imitated the styles of local instruments. Many *luk thung* singers had a background in traditional genres and crossed over when it became apparent there was money to be made. *Luk thung* from the north and south, however, declined in popularity, while those from the northeast became increasingly favored, eventually coming to dominate the Thai media in the 1980s. This process snowballed because tens of thousands of northeasterners had been migrating to Bangkok over the years as Thailand developed into an "Asian Tiger" economy. These economic refugees, many of whom became relatively prosperous, became a natural market for all manner of *luk thung*-related media products and events. These included *luk thung* movies, live *luk thung* shows, and, of course, *luk thung* cassettes, CDs and VCDs. Get into most any taxi in Bangkok and you will hear northeast *luk thung* songs on the radio or on cassette, because most taxi drivers come from the northeast. Go into the servant's quarters of an upper-class house or into factories and you will encounter them as well.

Each stanza of the song includes a switch from the Lao language of the Northeast (called *Isan*) to Central Thai. When this song first appeared, the Central Thai still looked down on Northeasterners, seeing them as country bumpkins. By singing part of the song in Central Thai, the singer demonstrates that he is bilingual and therefore "respectable." By the advent of the twenty-first century attitudes had changed, and it is now "respectable" to sing in the Isan language alone.

Luk thung has given rise to star singers who, in spite of the sparseness in which they grew up, have become quite wealthy singing songs that express the feelings and lives of their compatriots. Early favorites who solidified the style in central Thailand include the late female singer Pompuang Duangjan and the late male singer Suraphon Sombatjalern. Today there are too many *luk thung* singers to mention, some making recordings and being heard throughout the land, others singing their songs in local restaurants and clubs in gritty upcountry towns. *Luk thung* shows nearly superseded traditional *mawlam* by the late 1980s, and traditional performers, because they receive little government support even as honored "culture carriers," had to change in order to stay in business. The traditional theater genres of Isan adopted *luk thung* songs into their format, as did the *lam klawn* form, with its alternating male and female singers. Because Isan was producing the most popular type of music in Thailand, many people in the other regions modified their thinking of Isan as a backwater full of poor rice farmers and came to see it instead as a hotbed of stylish young musicians.

Arrival: Indonesia (Java and Bali)

Map of Indonesia. Note locale of Java and Bali

Indonesia, the largest archipelago in the world, consists of more than 13,000 islands created by centuries of volcanic activity, which continues to this day, sometimes resulting in devastating tsunamis that engulf coastal areas. Though many of these islands are uninhabited, the larger islands, especially Sumatra and Java, are densely populated, making Indonesia the world's largest Muslim nation with 240 million people. The first-time visitor will be struck immediately by the extreme heat and humidity, due to Indonesia's position on the equator and its sea-level elevation. Tropical rainforests, which have suffered extensive deforestation, are found in many of the areas, along with mist-shrouded mountains and volcanoes, white sand beaches with spectacular offshore underwater reefs, colorful flowers, and unique wildlife on less-populated islands, such as orangutans. The heavy annual rainfall helps support an agricultural system largely based on wet rice cultivation, which together with seafaring activity provides the mainstays of Indonesian cuisine.

SOUTHEAST ASIA

Dancers at the Akademi Seni Tari Indonesia (College of Indonesian Dance) in Yogyakarta, Java, Indonesia, perform a refined court dance (R. Anderson Sutton)

Indonesia recognizes several religions: Islam, Hinduism, Buddhism, Christianity, and a variety of animistic traditions, each with their own varied cultural activities. Throughout the main islands of Java and Sumatra, Islam gave rise to the courts of the sultans who were the traditional patrons of the arts. Bali, however, preserves an even richer tradition of music, dance, and theater associated with the Hinduism that makes the tiny island so distinctive. Though there are over 300 languages spoken throughout the islands, the national language is Bahasa Indonesia, an Austronesian language common throughout the region and Malay peninsula. English is widely spoken as well in areas frequented by tourists, but the colonial language, Dutch, has virtually disappeared.

The music of Indonesia, which is dominated by ensembles of bronze instruments, is perhaps the most studied and best known in academia of all world music traditions. Many pioneer ethnomusicologists, such as Jaap Kunst, Colin McPhee, and Mantle Hood, took an interest in the music of Indonesia and spread knowledge of it through writings, teaching, and their own musical compositions. Various composers, including Claude Debussy, Benjamin Britten, Francis Poulenc, Philip Glass, and Steve Reich, have also acknowledged the influence of Indonesian music on their works. Indonesian music has therefore greatly affected the development of modern music in Europe and America, and its influence can still be heard in everything from orchestral music to television commercials.

Although there are hundreds of distinct musical traditions found throughout the numerous islands of Indonesia, the most recognized music is that of the **gamelan** ensemble. We will focus on two traditions, Javanese court gamelan and Balinese *gamelan gong kebyar*, in order to introduce this intricate and entrancing music.

GAMELAN
An ensemble from Indonesia comprised primarily of membranophones and metallophones.

Site 6: Javanese Court Gamelan

Gamelans are normally made of bronze, but this full Javanese gamelan at Northern Illinois University, DeKalb is actually made of iron, a less expensive, yet satisfactory, substitute for bronze

First Impressions. A gamelan is an ensemble that primarily comprises idiophones made of either bronze or iron, including a variety of hanging gongs, rack gongs, and metal-keyed instruments. The ethereal sound of the instruments is hypnotic, as is the music's repeating cyclical structure. Other instruments, such as flutes, zithers, various drums, and a fiddle called the *rebab*, may also be present along with vocalists, both male and female. The voices, too, contribute an elegant air to the overall feel of the performance. The music of the Javanese

A Javanese gamelan at the *kraton* (palace) of the Sultan in Yogyakarta with a court musician seated at the *gender*, an instrument with bronze keys and tube resonators (Jack Vartoogian/ FrontRowPhotos)

court gamelan is divided into two basic styles, *soft* and *strong*. The soft style has a "misty" quality that is mellow and tranquil, reminiscent of an early morning fog lifting as the sun rises from the ocean. In contrast, the strong style is bold and loud; more reflective of the midday sun watching over hard-working rice farmers during a harvest.

Aural Analysis. Javanese court gamelan is based on a *colotomic structure*, meaning that its music is organized into cycles defined by periodic punctuation played by a specific instrument—in its case, hanging gongs. The principal melody is typically provided by either voices and/or melodic instruments, such as the rack gongs, metal-keyed instruments called metallophones, wooden-keyed instruments called xylophones, or non-idiophones such as the fiddle or bamboo flute. Other rack gongs, metallophones, and xylophones embellish this melody by filling in the aural space, giving the music its "misty" quality.

Javanese gamelan must be built and tuned as a unit; interchanging instruments from one ensemble to another is not permitted due in large part to the individuality of the tuning. There are two primary tuning systems: *sléndro* (comprising five relatively equidistant pitches to an octave) and *pélog* (comprising seven pitches to an octave at non-equidistant intervals). Gamelan instruments tuned in one system cannot be played with a set tuned in the other. Furthermore, the fundamental frequencies of two different gamelan using the same system, for example, *pélog*, do not always match, so interchanging instruments even in this case is not possible. Indeed, individual gamelan sets have specific names (the one housed at UCLA in Los Angeles is "The Venerable Dark Cloud"), suggesting the instruments are to be thought of as part of one family. A complete ensemble includes a subset of instruments in both *sléndro* and *pélog* tunings, which can be thought of as siblings in the same gamelan "family." The example here is in *sléndro* tuning—that is, it uses a five-tone pentatonic tuning/scale.

Our example includes two styles of Javanese court gamelan performance, described as *strong* and *soft*. Strong-style gamelan emphasizes the metallophones and bossed rack gongs, which carry the principal melody at a faster tempo and are struck powerfully. Although the soft-style gamelan, when the metal bars or gongs are struck with less force, often includes a female vocal soloist and a male chorus, this example does not. The non-idiophone instruments, namely the fiddle, zither, and bamboo flute, support the principal melody, and the tempo is slower than in the strong style.

After a brief introduction by a *bonang* (rack gong), the principal melody is loudly proclaimed. This melody can be simply notated using numbers to represent pitch. The full ensemble enters on the last pitch of the introduction, which is also the start/stop point of the cycle marked by the largest and deepest pitched hanging gong (*gong ageng*).

Principal Melody of Javanese Gamelan Audio Example

Introduction	- 1 1 1	5 6 1 2	2 1 6 5	6 1 6 5
A	6 5 3 2	6 5 3 2	2 3 5 3	6 5 3 2 (repeat)
punctuation		- * - -	- * - -	- * - +
B	1 5 6 1	5 6 1 2	2 1 6 5	6 1 6 5 (repeat)
punctuation		- * - -	- * - -	- * - +

* = upper hanging gong + = lower hanging gong

Each melodic line is repeated once before the entire melody is repeated (AA-BB-AA-BB-AA, etc.). Notice that the phrasing of the melody is symmetrical (there are two groups of four phrases with four beats each), exemplifying an emphasis on balance typical of Javanese music. Underlying this melody is the periodic punctuation provided by the hanging gongs (marked by * and +). These instruments punctuate specific points in the cycle to articulate the underlying aural framework of the piece. Falling between the pitches of the principal melody at twice the rhythmic density are the quiet embellishments of other metallophones and rack gongs. These three parts are most easily heard in the strong-style gamelan performance.

The soft-style section is signaled by the drums. The tempo slows and the quieter instruments become the aural focus, providing the principal melody along with the subdued sounds of the gongs. The colotomic structure and embellishing instruments are still present, but the shift in mood gives the music a haunting quality. The dynamic level diminishes with the slowed tempo and both increase again when the strong-style gamelan returns.

LISTENING GUIDE

CD 1.14 (5'34")

Chapter 6: Site 6

Indonesia: Javanese Court Gamelan

Instruments: Full instrumental *gamelan* ensemble (metallophones, flutes/chordophones, drums)

TIME	LISTENING FOCUS
0'00"	*Bonang* (rack gongs) enter with a brief introduction.
0'05"	Full ensemble enters with principal melody (A), embellishments, and periodic punctuation. Listen for each of these musical elements during repeated listening. Use the table included in the Aural Analysis to follow the principal melody and periodic punctuation.
0'13"	Melodic phrase (A) repeats.
0'21"	Second phrase of principal melody (B).
0'28"	Melodic phrase (B) repeats.
0'35"	Melodic phrase (A) returns.
0'43"	Melody phrase (A) repeats.
0'51"	Melodic phrase (B) returns.
0'58"	Melodic phrase (B) repeats.
1'06"	Melodic phrase (A) returns
1'14"	Melodic phrase (A) repeats. The tempo gradually slows in anticipation of the "soft-style" interlude.

1'27"	Melodic phrase (B) returns at a slower tempo.
1'31"	"Quieter" instruments, namely the *rebab* (fiddle), *celimpung* (plucked zither), and *suling* (flute), become the aural focus. The principal melody (B) continues, most easily identified by the low-pitched metallophones heard in the background. Listen for the *gong ageng* (lowest-pitched hanging gong) sounding the end of each phrase.
1'49"	Melodic phrase (B) repeats.
2'10"	Melodic phrase (A) returns.
2'32"	Melodic phrase (A) repeats.
2'54"	Melodic phrase (B) returns.
3'15"	Melodic phrase (B) repeats.
3'36"	Melodic phrase (A) returns.
3'56"	Melodic phrase (A) repeats. Drums quietly signal the reentrance of the louder metallophones.
4'02"	Drums play at a louder volume and the tempo increases as the metallophones gradually return as the aural focus (4'06").
4'11"	Melodic phrase (B) returns.
4'20"	Melodic phrase (B) repeats.
4'28"	Melodic phrase (A) returns.
4'36"	Melodic phrase (A) repeats.
4'45"	Melodic phrase (B) returns.
4'53"	Melodic phrase (B) repeats.
5'01"	Melodic phrase (A) returns.
5'09"	Melodic phrase (A) repeats at a lower dynamic level and slowing tempo to close the performance.

Source: "Udan Mas" ("Golden Rain"), from the recording titled *Music of the Venerable Dark Cloud: The Javanese Gamelan Khjai Mendung*. Institute of Ethnomusicology, UCLA, IER 7501, 1973. Used by permission.

ETHNO-CHALLENGE (CD 1.14): Imitate the upper and lower gongs utilized during the "periodic punctuation" heard throughout the example.

Cultural Considerations. Although the gamelan music of both Java and Bali uses similar instrumentation and is organized in structures governed by colotomic periods, the sharp contrast of musical characteristics between Javanese Court Gamelan and Balinese *gamelan gong kebyar* (see below) reveals strong differences in musical values. These values are in large part due to differences in the function and contextual associations of the two musics.

The population of Java is predominantly Muslim, though the Islam here is peculiar to Java. Javanese gamelan music is frequently associated with court ritual functions, usually presided over by a sultan. The sultan is regarded as a secular authority with divine powers, and his palace grounds are imbued with spiritual significance. The slow, stately sound of the court gamelan reflects the regal atmosphere of this environment, and the music is characteristically calm, to avoid distracting attention from the sultan or the ceremonial activity. The music serves the occasion rather than being the primary focus of the event.

Dancers at the Sultan's Kraton (palace) in Yogyakarta perform *bedhaya*, considered the "crown jewel" of Javanese court dances (Jack Vargoogian/FrontRowPhotos)

A Javanese gamelan at the Sultan's palace in Yogyakarta with a musician seated at a large *bonang*, a set of bronze pot-shaped gongs in two rows (Jack Vartoogian/FrontRowPhotos)

Most often, gamelan performance accompanies dance and/or theatre. The *bedhaya* dance is among the most sacred, symbolizing the mythical union between a historical sultan and the goddess of the sea, an indication of pre-Islamic spiritual beliefs helping to legitimize Islamic secular authority. The slow-moving choreography and subtle gestures of the dancers express serenity and refinement, just as the gamelan itself demonstrates the tranquility and balance valued so highly in Javanese culture. Gamelan also accompanies shadow-puppet theatre, known as *wayang kulit*. The storylines for these productions often draw from the ancient Indian epics of the *Ramayana* and the *Mahabharata*, similarly revealing the underlying Hindu influence on Javanese culture that pre-dates Islamic rule, which first appeared in Indonesia during the twelfth century.

Site 7: Balinese *Gamelan Gong Kebyar*

First Impressions. Whereas the music of Java conveys a sense of tranquility, the music of Bali is filled with dynamic energy. Similar instruments are used, including bronze gongs, metallophones, flutes, and drums, but the character of the music continually shifts, with sudden bursts of brilliant virtuosity contrasting with airy melodic phrases. A feeling of continual agitation pervades the music as it accelerates, slows, crescendos, and relaxes. Then just when you think you have it figured out, the music again turns in an unanticipated direction.

Aural Analysis. Balinese **gamelan gong kebyar**, like the Javanese court gamelan, is organized according to a colotomic structure. However, this structure is not always as evident as with its Javanese counterpart. Many compositions are through-composed, meaning that

GAMELAN GONG KEBYAR

An ensemble type from Bali, Indonesia, primarily comprising metallophones and characterized by rhythmically dense performance technique

Balinese gamelan at the "Full Moon Festival" in Bedulu village, Bali (Shutterstock)

A portion of Bowling Green State University's *gong kebyar* (gamelan) showing flutes and fiddle (front row) with keyed instruments and drum behind. Gamelan, both Javanese and Balinese, have been common since the 1960s in universities worldwide

the melody does not repeat in a series of continuous cycles. Also, *gamelan gong kebyar* frequently uses sectional solos in which different instruments, such as the drums and cymbals, flutes, metallophones, or rack gongs, are highlighted. This shifting orchestration emphasis, along with dynamic variation and sudden tempo changes, contributes to the sudden shifts of mood that characterize the Balinese gamelan style.

The high rhythmic density of Balinese *gamelan gong kebyar* is also a distinguishing characteristic. In many sections of a performance the musicians interlock their parts, so that multiple musicians playing identical instruments are required to produce a complete melodic line. For example, if Player X plays the odd-numbered pitches (1, 3, 5, 7) and Player Y plays the even-numbered pitches (2, 4, 6, 8), the players must interlock their pitches to play them in consecutive order from one to eight. This interlocking of melodic pitches, known as *kotekan*, enables the performers to create a high rhythmic density, so that the music sounds as if the melody is being played at a "superhuman speed"; indeed, it is often faster than a single player could perform. While this technique is used in Javanese gamelan as well, the super-thick rhythmic density is associated primarily with the Balinese style.

Another noticeable distinction of the Balinese *gamelan gong kebyar* is what might be described as the "shimmer effect." This shimmering sound is most evident in the wavering tones of the small metallophones on long sustained pitches. The effect is produced by the use of pairs of identical instruments tuned slightly apart. When the instruments are played simultaneously on the same pitch, the slight tuning difference in frequency produces a perceptible pulsation due to the minimal increase in volume as the pitch frequencies overlap. Therefore, a complete Balinese gamelan must include identical pairs of metallophones, with

SOUTHEAST ASIA

A pair of *gendèr wayang* bronze-keyed idiophones with tube resonators used, with an identical pair (not shown) tuned slightly differently to produce shimmering sounds, to accompany the shadow play (*wayang kulit*). The larger, lower one is called *gedé* or *pemade*, and the smaller, higher one is *barangan*

Danced by two males, the *barong* is a Hindu-derived mythological beast that represents "good" in Balinese theater (Amy Unruh)

173

separate players on each instrument playing the same notes but with slightly different tuning. When coupled with the need for interlocking pitches, four or more musicians may be required to produce a complete melodic line.

LISTENING GUIDE

CD 1.15 (4'01")

Chapter 6: Site 7

Indonesia: Balinese *Gamelan Gong Kebyar*

Instruments: *Gender* (metallophones), *bonang* (rack gongs), *gong ageng* (pair of hanging gongs), *kempli* ("timekeeper" gong), *suling* (flute), and *kendang* (barrel-shaped drums)

TIME	LISTENING FOCUS
0'00"	*Gender* initiate performance.
0'04"	Double-interlocking technique (known as *kotekan*) on the *gender* first appears. A "timekeeper" gong is also heard providing a steady beat as lower-pitched metallophones enter.
0'10"	The largest of the *gong ageng* sounds, and the melodic instruments pause. Listen for the "shimmering" sustain of the metallophones.
0'14"	Melodic activity resumes.
0'20"	Another melodic pause and "shimmering" sustain. The *gender* become the aural focus, continuing with "start/stop" melodic activity.
0'53"	Lower metallophones and "timekeeper" gong return. The example continues, with frequent melodic pauses followed by "bursts" of melodic passages introduced by the *gender* and followed by the "timekeeper" gong and others.
2'00"	A new melodic section begins to anticipate entrance of full ensemble. A dancer often performs during this section of the music.
2'26"	Full ensemble enters, including *bonang* and drums.
2'38"	*Bonang* performs solo, utilizing the double-interlocking technique to achieve a thick rhythmic density.
2'58"	*Gong ageng* sounds briefly in the background.
3'00"	*Gender* return as aural focus. Tempo is slower.
3'07"	Drums sound to introduce return of full ensemble.
3'15"	Listen for the *suling* (flute) playing as the metal instruments play more quietly.
3'42"	Listen for the *gender*'s more frequent use of syncopated rhythms, which generally corresponds to a dancer's movements.

Source: "Hudjan Mas," recorded in south Bali by a *gamelan gong kebyar* ensemble; from the recording titled *Gamelan Music of Bali*, Lyrichord CD 7179, n.d. Used by permission, Lyrichord Discs Inc.

> **ETHNO-CHALLENGE (CD 1.15):** Try to perform the "superhuman" double-interlocking technique (*kotekan*) along with a friend by tapping your hands on a flat surface or by using a musical instrument, such as a piano or xylophone. Once successful, add another matching pair of performers.

Cultural Considerations. While Java's population is chiefly Muslim, the island of Bali is predominantly Hindu. Temples are found throughout the island, each devoted to a particular Hindu deity. Most temples have a gamelan ensemble that is expected to perform for festivals or other events associated with the temple's deity or the Hindu faith. Frequently performances function as a musical offering, and the music is therefore intended to attract and entertain the deity as well as participants. The dynamic character and bright timbre of the Balinese *gamelan gong kebyar*, with its "superhuman speed" and bright, boisterous metallophones, becomes the center of attention. Dances are often vigorous and characteristically "angular," with quick movements of the head, arms, and legs. These performances, too, are typically related to Hindu mythology and often involve spirit possession and demonstrations of supernatural power, particularly in masked drama performances, such as the *barong* dance.

Gamelan gong kebyar, which often accompanies such performances, is a relatively recent musical style that first appeared in the early twentieth century. While numerous styles of gamelan exist on Bali, *kebyar*, translated as "to flare up" or "to flower," is by far the most

A young boy dances *Baris*, a warrior dance, to the accompaniment of a Balinese gamelan (Amy Unruh)

WORLD MUSIC: A GLOBAL JOURNEY

Young dancers perform a Welcome Dance at the Full Moon Festival in Bedulu village, Bali (Shutterstock)

A Balinese puppeteer brings the story of the *Ramayana* to life through his skillful manipulation of leather shadow puppets (Amy Unruh)

SOUTHEAST ASIA

prominent. The explosive character of the music and astounding displays of virtuosity by its musicians require hours and hours of practice to achieve precise performance. The music is carefully composed, though musical notation is not generally used, and rehearsals are intense, particularly in preparation for the frequent contests that attract ensembles from throughout the island. The high demand for this music encourages experimentation and continual creation of new music to the delight of tourists, locals, and academics alike. Many ensembles have found success touring internationally, presenting spectacular shows to audiences worldwide. The popularity of the *gamelan gong kebyar* has spread to academic institutions around the world as well, where student ensembles perform the music often with the assistance of a guest artist/composer direct from Bali who teaches the ensemble.

The respective styles of gamelan music from the islands of Java and Bali give listeners a strongly differing musical experience. Indeed, the contrast between the hypnotic serenity of the Javanese court gamelan and the entrancing dynamism of the Balinese *gamelan gong kebyar* is a testament to the creative power of Indonesian musicians, who have managed to create two very different musics out of similar resources.

KECAK
A Balinese theatrical performance of *The Ramayana*

Explore More

Kecak: The Balinese "Monkey Chant"

The "Monkey Chant" has become one of the most popular tourist attractions on the island of Bali. Its performers, who are considered a kind of "human gamelan," act out scenes from the Indian epic the *Ramayana* (see p. 153) with minimal stage props and costumes. The name of the genre, **kecak**, is derived from the interlocking "cak" sounds of the performers as they imitate armies of monkey soldiers in a mythological battle of good versus evil. Other performers sound out the colotomic structure by imitating gongs of the gamelan ensemble. In addition to the monkey armies, whose performers are dressed merely with a black-and-white checkered sarong, there are costumed dancers who portray the major figures of the story. Such performances were originally intended as musical offerings to the Hindu deity

In Bali, a circle of men sway in unison during a *kecak* dance, a modern variation of an ancient *sang hyang* trance dance (Ernst Haas/GettyImages)

Rama, a major character in the epic. This association, however, as well as the storyline, is typically unfamiliar to Bali's many visitors.

Questions to Consider

1. To what extent are the terms *classical*, *folk*, and *popular* appropriate labels for describing Southeast Asian musics?
2. What are some factors that help maintain traditional Southeast Asian music in the face of modernization?
3. Metrical cycles are characteristic of many Southeast Asian musics. How do they work in the sites reviewed?
4. How do the types of "heterophony" found in Vietnamese *Tai Thu*, *Thai Piphat*, and Javanese Gamelan differ?
5. Though Thailand and Vietnam are both part of Southeast Asia, what historical and cultural factors have determined the present musical differences?
6. Compare Javanese and Balinese Gamelan in terms of their function and use. How do their differing functions affect their respective musical styles?

On Your Own Time

Visit the textbook website to find these resources for further exploration on your own.

Vietnam

Audio: Ngyuen, Phong T. and Terry E. Miller. *Music from the Lost Kingdom Vietnam: The Perfume River Traditional Ensemble*. Lyrichord, LYRCD 7440, 1998.
http://lyrichord.com/musicfromthelostkingdomvietnam-theperfumerivertraditionalensemble.aspx
http://itunes.apple.com/us/album/music-from-lost-kingdom-vietnam/id78666859

Book: Reyes, Adelaida. *Songs of the Caged, Songs of the Free: Music and the Vietnamese Refugee Experience*. Philadelphia: Temple University Press, 1999.
http://www.temple.edu/tempress/titles/1426_reg.html

Internet: Popular Artists from Vietnam
My Tam
Quang Dung
Lam Truong

Thailand

Film: Homrong (The Overture). Directed by Ittisoontorn Vichailak. Sahamongkol Film International, 2004.
http://en.wikipedia.org/wiki/The_Overture
http://www.imdb.com/video/screenplay/vi418906393/

Audio: *Royal Court Music of Thailand*. Smithsonian-Folkways, SF 40413, 1994.
http://www.folkways.si.edu/albumdetails.aspx?itemid=2330
http://itunes.apple.com/us/album/royal-court-music-of-thailand/id83572118

Audio: *Silk, Spirits, and Songs: Music from North Thailand*. Lyrichord, LYRCD 7451, 2006.

http://lyrichord.com/silkspiritsandsongmusicfromnorththailand.aspx
http://itunes.apple.com/us/album/silk-spirits-song-music-from/id258470887

Book: Shahriari, Andrew. *Khon Muang Music and Dance Traditions of North Thailand.* Bangkok: White Lotus Press, 2006.
http://www.whitelotuspress.com/bookdetail.php?id=E22486

Book: Wong, Deborah. *Sounding the Center: History and Aesthetics in Thai Buddhist Performance.* Chicago: The University of Chicago Press, 2001.
http://www.press.uchicago.edu/ucp/books/book/chicago/S/bo3629073.html

Audio: Fanshawe, David. *Music from Thailand and Laos.* ARC, 1997.
http://itunes.apple.com/us/album/music-from-thailand-and-laos/id285183310

Internet: Popular Artists from Thailand
Keyword: Loso
Keyword: Tay Orathai
Keyword: Katreeya English

Indonesia

Audio: *Gamelan Music of Bali—Gamelan Angklung, and Gamelan Gong Kebjar.* Lyrichord, LYRCD 7179, 1997.
http://lyrichord.com/gamelanmusicofbali-gamelanangklungandgamelangongkebjar.aspx
http://itunes.apple.com/us/album/gamelan-music-of-bali/id49332149

Audio: *Java Court Gamelan.* Nonesuch: 79719, 1971.
http://www.nonesuch.com/albums/java-court-gamelan
http://itunes.apple.com/us/album/java-court-gamelan/id128049636

Book: Spiller, Henry. *Gamelan Music of Indonesia.* Abingdon, Oxford: Routledge, 2008.
http://routledge.customgateway.com/routledge-music/ethnomusicology/gamelan-music-of-indonesia.html

Book: Tenzer, Michael. *Gamelan Gong Kebyar: The Art of Twentieth Century Balinese Music.* Chicago: University of Chicago Press, 2000.
http://www.press.uchicago.edu/presssite/metadata.epl?mode=synopsis&bookkey=3630827

Audio: *Indonesian Popular Music: Kroncong, Dangdut, and Langgam Jawa.* Smithsonian-Folkways, SF 40056, 1991.
http://www.folkways.si.edu/albumdetails.aspx?itemid=2298
http://itunes.apple.com/us/album/music-indonesia-vol-2-indonesian/id151045292

Internet: Popular Artists from Indonesia
Rhoma Irama
Dangdut (music genre)
Jeni Anjani

East Asia: China, Mongolia, Korea, Japan, Tibet

7

Background Preparation	182	
An Inside Look: Luo Qin	185	
An Inside Look: Masayo Ishigure	186	
Planning the Itinerary	187	
Arrival: China	189	
Site 1: The *Guqin* (Seven-String "Ancient" Zither)	192	
Site 2: *Jiangnan Sizhu* ("Silk and Bamboo") Ensemble from Shanghai	195	
Site 3: Beijing Opera (*Jingju*)	203	
Site 4: Revolutionary Beijing Opera (*Yangbanxi*)	208	
Explore More: Popular Music in East Asia	212	
Arrival: Mongolia	213	
Site 5: Mongolian *Urtïn Duu* (Long Song) with *Khöömei* (Overtone or Throat Singing)	214	
Arrival: Korea	217	
Site 6: *P'ansori* Narrative	218	
Arrival: Japan	223	
Site 7: *Sankyoku* Instrumental Chamber Music	224	
Explore More: Komuso	227	
Site 8: *Kabuki* Theater	228	
Explore More: Taiko	232	
Arrival: Tibet	233	
Site 9: Tibetan Buddhist Ritual	234	
Questions to Consider	238	
On Your Own Time	239	

The Great Wall of China north of Beijing (Max T. Miller)

Background Preparation

Culturally, East Asia incorporates not just the immense nation of China but also North and South Korea, Japan, and Mongolia. Although disputed, Tibet and Taiwan are also parts of China, the latter remaining independent as the Republic of China. Geographically, East Asia also encompasses the eastern half of Russia, including Siberia, which constitutes Northeast Asia. East Asia is home to roughly one quarter of the earth's population: China has 1.38 billion people, the Koreas 71 million, Taiwan 23 million, and Japan 127 million, for a total of 1.56 billion. The other areas, including Mongolia and eastern Russia, have very slight populations spread over a vast territory. Tibet, an autonomous region of China, is often viewed by outsiders as a distinct nation under Chinese occupation while the Chinese government views it as an integral part of China.

The term *Chinese*, broadly speaking, can be applied to cultural activity found not only in the People's Republic of China and the Republic of China (Taiwan) but also in the self-governing city of Hong Kong and in other places where "Overseas Chinese" comprise important segments of the population. These places include Malaysia, where nearly one-third of the population is of Chinese ancestry, and the city-state of Singapore. Throughout the world there are cities with large Chinese populations, including Bangkok, Thailand; Manila, Philippines; Jakarta, Indonesia; Ho Chi Minh City, Vietnam; Toronto, Canada; New York, USA; London, UK, and in smaller concentrations throughout the world. Roughly ninety million people out of China's total population belong to some fifty-five non-Chinese minority groups, which are as diverse as the Hmong and Dai of the southwest and the Koreans of the northeast.

潮州弦诗全集

국제민속음악학회 회의 및
국제민속음악제

一つとや

ひと夜あくれば賑かで　賑かで、

おかざり立てたる松飾り　松飾り。

From top to bottom, the scripts are from China (top), Korea (middle), and Japan (bottom)

In spite of its immense size, East Asia is unified in numerous ways. Foremost among the factors that bind East Asian cultures together is an ideographic writing system developed by the Chinese millennia ago, in which icon-like "characters" have meaning rather than phonetic sound. At various times in history, each East Asian culture has adopted the Chinese writing system, allowing literate people in all areas to communicate even though the spoken languages (e.g., Japanese, Korean, Vietnamese, or Mongolian) were otherwise unrelated and mutually unintelligible. Over time, however, distinctive writing systems also developed in Japan, Korea, and Mongolia, while Vietnam romanized its writing system because of the influence of French and Portuguese missionaries.

Geography has played a major role in the development of East Asian culture. The original Chinese civilization, that of the "Han" Chinese, arose along the Yellow River in northern China forty centuries ago (*c.*2000 B.C.E.) and over time spread through the vast territory of East Asia, even into Southeast Asia. At the same time, Chinese civilization was profoundly influenced by outside cultures, especially those coming from Western and Central Asia along the "silk road." Many foreign elements, such as Buddhism, came to the Chinese first, were transformed into a Chinese form (a process called *sinicization*), and then absorbed and further modified by neighboring cultures. Within China, Han Chinese civilization spread mostly to the south and southeast, because much of eastern China is relatively flat, while the rest of the country consists of mountains, deserts, and high plateaus. Even today, in fact, the vast majority of China's billion-plus people live in the eastern third of the country. The Korean civilization developed on a peninsula to the northeast of China, and although Korea was profoundly influenced by China, its culture is otherwise distinct. Because the Korean peninsula is to the north and rather mountainous, Korea has limited arable land and harsh winters, and the Korean people have often had to struggle to survive. After the division of Korea into South and North Korea in 1945, the South has prospered and developed its own form of democracy, while the North has suffered immense ecological damage from industrialization and deforestation, which has brought cycles of droughts and floods. In addition, its autocratic government has brought isolation to North Korea. The result is that many people in the North are starving and much of their culture has been completely politicized.

Japan's culture is also deeply affected by its geography. Japan is a chain of islands, stretching from cold and bleak Hokkaido in the north to the warm and lush Ryukyu Islands trailing southwest from Kyushu, Japan's southernmost major island. Although influenced by Chinese civilization, Japan was relatively isolated until the nineteenth century, which allowed it to develop a distinct culture. With most of Japan's population, nearly half that of the United States, crowded into the main islands of Honshu, Shikoku, and Kyushu—together smaller than the state of California—efficient land use is critical. The Japanese have developed an amazingly homogenous culture, though ethnic diversity certainly does exist, particularly in rural areas. The country's historical isolation from outside political and cultural influences until the mid-nineteenth century supports this mindset of the Japanese as a strongly nationalistic and unified entity.

	CHINA	KOREA	JAPAN
B.C.E. 1200	**ANTIQUITY** Xia 21st to 16th century Shang c. 1600–1045		
1100	Zhou 1045–256		
1000			
900			
800			**ANTIQUITY**
700	Spring and Autumn 770–476		Zyômon to c. 200
600			
500			
400	Warring States 475–221		
300	**DYNASTIES OF IMPERIAL CHINA**		Yayoi c. 200 B.C.E.–250 C.E.
200	Qin 221–206 Han 202 B.C.E.–220 C.E.		
100			
C.E. 0			
100			
200	Three Kingdoms 220–280	**THREE KINGDOMS**	
300	Jin 265–420	Koguryŏ ?–668	Kohun Culture c. 300–400
400	Northern and Southern Dynasties 420–589	Paekche ?–660 Silla ?–668	**IMPERIAL PERIOD**
500	Sui 581–618	**DYNASTIES OF ROYAL KOREA**	Asuka c. 550–710
600	Tang 618–907	Unified Silla 668–935	
700			Nara 710–794
800			Heian 794–1192
900	Five Dynasties and Ten Kingdoms 902–979 Liao (Qidan [Khitan]) 916–1125	Koryŏ 918–1392	
1000	Song 960–1279		**MEDIEVAL PERIOD**
1100	Northern Song 960–1127 Southern Song 1127–1279		Kamakura 1192–1333
1200	Jin (Nüzhen [Jurchen]) 1115–1234		
1300	Yuan (Mongol) 1279–1368		Muromati 1334–1573
1400	Ming 1368–1644	Chosŏn 1392–1910	
1500			**PREMODERN PERIOD**
1600			Azuti–Momoyama 1573–1610
1700	Qing (Manchu) 1644–1911		Edo 1600–1867
1800		**MODERN KOREA**	**MODERN JAPAN**
1900	**MODERN CHINA** Republic of China 1911–	Japanese colonial period 1910–1945 Republic of Korea (South) 1948–	Meizi 1868–1912 Taisyô 1912–1926
2000	People's Republic of China 1949–	Democratic People's Republic of Korea (North) 1948–	Syôwa 1926–1989 Heisei 1989–

Luo Qin

AN INSIDE LOOK

As a professional violinist (concert-master), amateur composer, and occasional conductor, I had learned how to lead an orchestra and to create musical works for an ensemble. I was basically a Western-centered person at this time, although I was familiar with Chinese music and instruments as well. However, the graduate program at the Shanghai Conservatory of Music, where I majored in the history of Chinese music, changed my thoughts. After teaching at the Conservatory for several years, in 1991, as a young scholar and graduate student, I entered the Ethnomusicology program at the University of Washington and then went on for doctoral study in ethnomusicology at Kent State University. During my time in the States, I not only learned various musics from around the world but also came to understand the peoples, societies, and cultures related to these musics.

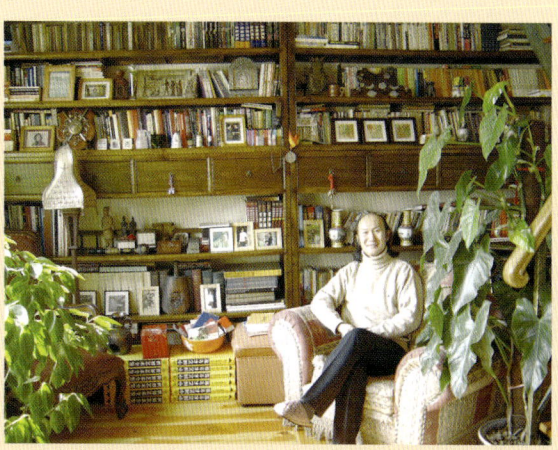

Dr. Luo Qin, Professor of Musicology, Shanghai Conservatory of Music; president and editor-in chief of Shanghai Conservatory Press

Through the study of the theories and practices of Ethnomusicology, I feel I became a true musician, scholar, and person who loves music, culture, people, and their lives. I specialize in two fields: the history of Chinese music and the urban ethno-orientated study of Shanghai City and its people. I have done much fieldwork and published several works, such as *History of Chinese Musical Instruments*; *Kunju, a Chinese Classical Theater and Its Revival in Social, Economic, Political and Cultural Contexts*; *Street Music: An Epitome of American Society and Culture*; *Heart & Music.com: World Music and Its Narration*, and others. I also love to create music for people who intend to communicate with each other by playing music. For example, while directing Kent State's Chinese Ensemble, I revised a violin concerto called *The Butterfly Lovers* into a work combining violin solo and Chinese ensemble.

After receiving my Ph.D. degree I came back to China. At present, I am a Professor of Musicology at the Shanghai Conservatory of Music, one of China's premier music institutions. In addition I am in charge of the Research Department. Through several years teaching, I have learned that I could and should do more if I want people to understand more musics and their cultures. Therefore, I entered the publishing business. Right now, I am the president and editor-in-chief of the Shanghai Conservatory Press. Nonetheless, I still teach. I hope to continue making contributions to the society in which I live and work and help more and more people to love music.

AN INSIDE LOOK

Masayo Ishigure

While growing up in Japan I started to learn the *koto* under the influence of my mother at the age of five. Because there was no child-sized *koto*, I had to use a full-size instrument from the beginning. For reasons unknown I loved to play the *koto* and never thought of quitting lessons. I first thought of the *koto* as a possible profession when I met Tadao Sawai, who was one of the greatest virtuosos and composers of *koto* music in the twentieth century. After studying under him at a music college, I became a special research student at the Sawai Koto Academy of Music. As a result of coming into contact with his outstanding music while improving my own performance skills every day, I was so fascinated with the depth of the *koto* music that I decided to become a professional *koto* player and teacher.

Mr. and Ms. Sawai had progressive ideas regarding the education of *koto* players. They actively accepted international students and sent high-level disciples to many countries such as the United States, Australia, and The Netherlands to promote the *koto* as well as Japanese culture generally. After moving to the United States in 1992 to teach *koto* to students at Wesleyan University in Connecticut, I participated in innovative performances involving classical orchestra, jazz musicians, and also made recordings for films and computer games. Participating in the recording for the sound track of *The Memoirs of a Geisha* with world-class musicians was an unusually fulfilling experience. At the same time I spend much of my time teaching the *koto*, currently involving about fifty students—half of them are Americans who are interested in Japan, and the rest are Japanese residing in the United States. I haven't changed my mind or beliefs when I'm teaching outside Japan, but I find that the students in the United States are quite free from the formal conventions usually associated with the traditional (conservative) art world in which I grew up. In my academy I give them chances to perform in front of large audiences as much as possible. I believe this is a joy for all the performers.

Masayo Ishigure professional *Koto* musician

In Japan the number of people playing traditional musical instruments is fewer than those playing Western music. In spite of this situation, traditional music has not been abandoned as an old-fashioned art but is still very much alive in the present time along with our famous theaters, "Noh" and "Kabuki". Why? You may think it strange that in Japan, a country known for its high-tech industry, there is also careful conservation of the traditional culture handed down from our ancestors. We love to participate in our culture's many seasonal events throughout the year. I think the sound of Japanese traditional musical instruments symbolizes a consciousness that lies deep both in our culture and in our individual psyches. Within this meaning, we can say that our musical instruments are devices to convey not only sound or

> melody but also a metaphysical sense of who we are. Perhaps this type of sense exists within all Japanese people and the musical instruments merely reawaken such consciousness. The Japanese people will feel a "communal satisfaction" from it. It would be interesting to study whether foreign people develop the same sense as Japanese people, or if they can create a new culture beyond their own tradition without having that sense.
>
> The *koto* is the essence of my life. I have been fortunate to continue concentrating on the *koto* while living in a competitive music world for years without questioning my choice.

Whereas Western histories are conceived in terms of centuries, Chinese history—and by extension Korean and Japanese history—are conceived in terms of dynasties, a **dynasty** being a succession of related rulers, such as the Sung or the Ming. The Chinese dynastic chart reveals a fairly consistent pattern of change. First, an energetic new Chinese dynasty forms and quickly unifies the country under newly effective rule; then, over time the dynasty's effectiveness erodes, enemies begin nibbling at China's borders, and public services and safety break down; finally, the dynasty crumbles, and following a period of instability, a new dynasty establishes itself. Between China's greatest, most stable, and longest-lasting dynasties were periods of disunity and chaos, such as the "Warring States" period (403–221 B.C.E.) and the "Six Dynasties" (222–581 C.E.). During certain dynasties, such as the Yuan (1260–1370) and Qing (1636–1911), foreign invaders—in these cases, the Mongols and Manchurians respectively—dominated China. Even though the rulers were foreigners, the vast Chinese bureaucracy maintained a control over Chinese institutions that insulated them from foreign cultural influence. Indeed, some foreign conquerors such as the Mongolians and Manchurians ended up being Sinicized to the extent that their own cultural distinctiveness eroded or disappeared.

DYNASTY
In China, a ruling family, like the Ming, and the era characterized by that family's dominance.

The arts have long been elements of the political process in China. Seeing the arts as far more than mere entertainment, the government has often harnessed music and theater for their ability to influence the thinking and behavior of the general population. Underlying this is a belief that music can have an influence on a person's ethical character. In ancient China—and by extension elsewhere in East Asia—the views of philosopher Kong Fuzi (551–479 B.C.E.; romanized as Confucius) had a profound influence on the role of music in the lives of the scholar class. In more recent times, Chairman Mao Zedong (1893–1976), China's communist leader from 1949 to 1976, not only believed that music and theater could influence people, but insisted the arts be harnessed by the state to create correct political thinking. Similarly, the government of North Korea has used music and related arts to influence its population.

Planning the Itinerary

Our musical tour will encompass China, Mongolia, Korea, Japan, and Tibet. The music of each country is quite distinct in overall sound, timbre, character, and process. Yet all share certain traits that bind them together, making the concept of "East Asian" music a reasonable one. One way to explain this is through an analogy with food. If you have had opportunities to visit both Chinese and Japanese restaurants outside Asia (Korean, Mongolian, and Tibetan restaurants are rarer), you have probably noticed striking differences. Those differences in the way food is prepared and presented and in overall atmosphere are analogous to some of the differences between the various countries' musics. Consider the décor: Chinese restaurants are usually highly decorated with colorful lanterns, dragons, and phoenixes (mythological birds) in strong shades of red, gold, blue, and green, whereas Japanese restaurants tend more toward plain white walls and natural wood, especially blond varieties. Whereas Chinese dishes, which feature colorful mixtures of many ingredients, are randomly placed on the table and shared by everyone, Japanese meals are usually served individually on lacquered trays with many compartments for well-separated delicacies. The space separating the food in Japanese restaurants is analogous to the silence separating sounds in Japanese music. Whereas the behavior of both patrons and staff in a Chinese restaurant—especially in Chinese cities—is informal, enthusiastically loud and busy, behavior encountered in a Japanese restaurant is much more formal, quiet, and subtle. Once again, many of these distinctions also apply to Chinese and Japanese music.

A second analogy may perhaps help explain some of the major differences in East Asian attitudes toward "tradition," preservation, and change. Consider the following metaphor: a wonderful, ancient bridge (akin to traditional music) occupies a key position in a city. Because it is no longer adequate to handle modern traffic, the government calls for engineers to study the situation—one Chinese, one Korean, and one Japanese. After a thorough consideration, the Chinese engineer announces that the bridge will be "preserved" by bringing it up to modern standards. Workers will replace and widen the deck, put on new railings, add modern lampposts, rebuild the support system, and level the approaches. Thus,

The statue of China's greatest philosopher and teacher, Kong Fuzi (Confucius), in the Kong temple of Quanzhou, China

they claim, the old bridge will remain, but it will have been "improved" and "modernized." The Korean and Japanese engineers, however, conclude that the bridge is wonderful in its present form and should be preserved as it is. Recognizing the demands of modern travel, however, the engineers recommend both keeping the old bridge open for those who prefer to use it and building a new one nearby for those who need it.

Thus, in China most "traditional" music struggles to survive as best it can, while newly arranged and orchestrated music, considered "improved" and "modernized" by many Chinese officials, is commonly used to represent Chinese music to the outside world. In Korea and Japan, however, institutions both public and private preserve all surviving forms of traditional music and theater as living anachronisms in an otherwise modern world. As a result there is little difficulty in defining "tradition" in Korea and Japan. Within China there are differing views of what is traditional and what music should represent China, while foreign researchers often have views that contradict those of the Chinese. The state of traditional music in Mongolia resembles the Chinese situation, whereas traditional Tibetan music survives intact, including among exiles living in countries such as India, Nepal, and Bhutan.

Arrival: China

As with all major civilizations, the Chinese developed their great cities and agricultural centers along rivers and around great lakes. Indeed, the names of many Chinese provinces reflect geographical features. For example, the name of Shandong province means "east of the mountains," while Shanxi means "west of the mountains." Similarly, Hubei is "north of the lake" and Hunan is "south of the lake." China's greatest threats in earlier times came from the northern border areas where non-Chinese invaders, including the Jürched, the Mongols (of Chinggis (also spelled Genghis) Khan fame), and the Manchu originated. China's Great Wall, stretching 1,400 miles over the northern mountains, was built to keep out the northern "barbarians."

Being a vast land, China has more than one gateway city. These include Beijing (the capital), Shanghai (China's largest city and commercial center), and Guangzhou (its most internationalized city). Beijing, a sprawling city of thirteen million built around the spacious Forbidden City (the former palace of the emperors), is the center of government and culture, whereas Shanghai and Guangzhou are centers of industry, commerce, and banking. The majority of the Chinese population lives in eastern China, an area with a remarkable number of surprisingly large cities unknown to most foreigners. Though little known to outsiders, Shandong province in central China nonetheless produces products that are much appreciated. Owing to Shandong's earlier "colonization" by Germany, it is the center of Chinese beer-making, with Qingdao being the home of "Tsingtao" beer. But to the Chinese, Shandong is more important as the ancestral home of Kong Fuzi (Confucius) in the small city of Qufu near the sacred mountain called Tai Shan.

China has undergone an extreme makeover since the 1990s, and the construction crane is far more prominent than temples or red-tiled roofs. Skyscrapers, department stores, vast restaurants, and wide, traffic-clogged roads represent China today, and one cannot go far without stumbling on a McDonalds ("Mai dang lao"), Pizza Hut ("Pi shang ke"), KFC ("Ken de ji"), or Wal-Mart ("wo er ma"). In this din of modernity, traditional music is only one small voice.

In terms of culture, it is customary to make a distinction between northern and southern China. One essential difference is that the northern Chinese prefer wheat (in the form of flatbreads, dumplings, and noodles), because it grows more readily in the relatively dry and temperate north, whereas in southern China, which is subtropical, rice is the fundamental carbohydrate. Even within northern or southern China, there are numerous regional distinctions, often identified with specific provinces. As is widely known, there are regional styles of Chinese cuisine, such as Sichuan (Szechuan), Hunan, Guangdong (Cantonese), Shanghai, Beijing, and so forth. Language is also regional, because Chinese civilization developed in relatively isolated pockets. While all Chinese languages are related (as all the European Romance languages are), many are also mutually unintelligible, even though the writing system is the same for all. Even within a single province there are several languages; in Guangdong, for example, these include Cantonese, Hakka, and Chaozhou. At the provincial level, languages may differ markedly from village to village because the mountainous terrain imposes such isolation. Today's national language, called *Mandarin* in English and *pu tong hua* in Chinese, originated in the north. Regional distinctions are also extremely important in Chinese music, especially in the narrative and theatrical genres.

Until the latter part of the twentieth century, most writing on Chinese music focused on ancient instruments, rituals, and aesthetic principles. The great Chinese music documents often took into account the living music of the time, but when Westerners began writing about Chinese music, they tended to omit living music. European scholars from the early twentieth century often viewed living music as unsophisticated and insignificant remnants of the glorious past. Ethnomusicological research into Chinese music only blossomed during the last three decades of the twentieth century, because, in earlier years, China had been off limits to most foreign researchers because of near continuous war from the 1920s until 1949 and the country's later political convulsions. This was particularly so during the **Cultural Revolution** (1966–1976), a top-down upheaval initiated by Chairman Mao Zedong and his influential wife, Jiang Qing, a former actress. After the end of the Cultural Revolution, a few foreign researchers came to China at a time when most Chinese scholars were still collecting "folk music" for use in compositions by conservatory-trained professionals. Much of the new research, however, was confined to urban phenomena because the government for some time rarely permitted research in rural areas and favored sending conservatory ensembles on foreign tours. Today the government no longer views music as a tool of propaganda and has allowed all kinds of music to flourish as best they can. But the question of what music best represents Chinese culture to the outside world remains a topic for discussion even today.

China has an incredibly diverse array of instruments, many of which had origins outside China but were Sinicized over time. Traditionally, the Chinese classified musical instruments into eight categories, known collectively as the ***bayin*** (or "eight materials")—namely, wood, bamboo, metal, stone, clay, skin, silk, and gourd. For the Chinese, the number "8" had a philosophical and aesthetic significance, and a philosophically complete ensemble would necessarily include instruments from all eight categories. Many ensemble types have names that refer to these material categories, including one studied here, the "silk and bamboo" ensemble (***sizhu***).

Chinese music is fundamentally vocal music. Besides a vast quantity of regional folk songs, there are many regional forms of narrative song and theater, the latter always having music. Because of the language problem, however, Western recording companies have preferred to release instrumental music, giving a skewed impression of the reality in China.

CULTURAL REVOLUTION
A ten-year period in China's history, from 1966–1976, marked by severe social and political upheaval.

BAYIN
The Chinese organological system based on eight materials.

SIZHU
A "silk and bamboo" music ensemble, comprising Chinese stringed ("silk") instruments and flutes ("bamboo").

Chinese music is primarily based on melodies that can exist in any number of guises and contexts, be they vocal or instrumental, solo or ensemble. Most have programmatic titles that allude to nature (e.g., "Autumn Moon and Lake Scenery"), literature or myth (e.g., "Su Wu the Shepherd"), a mood (e.g., "Joyous Feelings"), or even musical structure (e.g., "Old Six Beats"). Whether a composer's name is known or not—most are anonymous—the tune exists at an almost conceptual level, ready to be performed as an unaccompanied or accompanied instrumental solo, an ensemble piece, a song with or without accompaniment, an orchestral piece arranged for modern ensemble, or even as an operatic aria or modern popular song.

Besides this vast body of instrumental and vocal music, there is also the now rarely heard but once vibrant narrative tradition in which singers combined speaking and singing to tell long tales, accompanied by one or more instruments. More prevalent today are the nearly countless regional forms of theater, all of which have music and singing as integral parts. Beyond these one could also explore a variety of forms of instrumental and vocal music associated with Daoism and Buddhism, as well as the now revived music of Confucian ritual. The twentieth century also saw the development of many new forms of Chinese music reflecting "international" (read, "Western") influence, from violin-inspired *erhu* fiddle playing, to fully orchestrated arrangements of Chinese traditional melodies played by Western-style orchestras using "traditional" instruments, to all manner of Western-style classical music and popular song. Now experiencing a surprising revival is the politically influenced Revolutionary Operas and Revolutionary Ballets created during the Cultural Revolution (1966–1976) and imposed on the population to the exclusion of all else during that difficult time.

Inner court of the Kong Temple (Confucian) temple in Quanzhou, China

WORLD MUSIC: A GLOBAL JOURNEY

Site 1: The *Guqin* (Seven-String "Ancient" Zither)

QIN/GUQIN
A bridgeless, plucked zither with seven strings.

First Impressions. The **guqin** represents Chinese culture at its most historical and refined. Many first-time listeners are struck by its sparseness, its lack of a clear beat, and its variety of odd timbres, including scraping sounds and ringing overtones. The character of the music is intimate and meditative, as if the performer were just playing for himself. Indeed, this quiet contemplation was for centuries a music particular to Chinese scholars and philosophers.

Aural Analysis. The *guqin* (also spelled (*gu*) *ch'in*—pronounced "chin") is one of the most ancient instruments in the world to have remained in continuous use. The instrument is a roughly 51 inch (130 cm)-long rectangular board zither made of paulownia wood (top only) painted black, and has seven strings, traditionally of twisted silk, running lengthwise from end to end, without frets or bridges. There is also a series of eleven inlaid mother-of-pearl circles along one side marking the acoustical nodes or vibration points for each string. To the player's left, the strings pass over the end and are tied underneath to two small peg-like feet attached to the instrument's lower board. At the right end the strings run over a slight ridge that acts as a bridge, then pass through holes to the underside where each is tied to a small wooden peg. The instrument is tuned by twisting these pegs to loosen or tighten the string's tension. The player, seated on a chair with the instrument on a table or frame, plucks the strings with the fingers of the right hand and stops the strings with the fingers of the left hand.

The Chinese *guqin* (seven-string bridgeless zither), one of China's most ancient instruments

The characteristic timbres of the *guqin* are many, as a typical performance includes plucked sounds produced either by the nail or the flesh of the finger, tone-bending created by the sliding movements of the left hand, and the use of harmonics (clear, hollow sounds produced by gently touching the string at a node). Scraping sounds are produced when the player slides the left hand along the rough textured strings. Sometimes these sliding movements continue even after the string has stopped vibrating, expressing the view that music does not have to be heard to exist. Each string is tuned differently, but many of the same pitches can be produced at various nodes on different strings. Sometimes a pitch is repeated not on one string but on different strings or stopping points, which creates a series of slightly different timbres. While *guqin* music is fundamentally pentatonic (comprising five tones), other pitches may come into play, though all sound familiar enough to ears accustomed to the Western tuning system, because the Chinese system is similarly constructed.

Rhythmically, *guqin* music sounds fluid, improvisational, alternately halting or rushing, especially because often there is no clear beat to define a steady meter. *Guqin* notation is in a form called **tablature**; more precisely, it consists of a chart that indicates how to pluck, stop, or touch each string, with minimal indications of pitch or rhythm. Thus, it is left up to each individual performer to express the meaning of a piece in his or her own idiosyncratic rendition.

Guqin music, like most traditional Chinese music, is basically monophonic, but is more often built of short motives rather than extended melodic lines. For this reason, *guqin* compositions may sound inconsistent at times because they can suddenly change style or mood. Perhaps this explains why the *guqin* is a connoisseur's instrument and its sound something of an acquired taste.

Our example, titled "Yangguan Sandie" (Parting at Yangguan—a mountain pass used as an outpost in ancient China), illustrates the most common *guqin* traits: a contemplative atmosphere, a rather changeable form, and a great variety of subtly different timbres. Much of the beginning is played with stopped tones, but there are brief passages of harmonics at 1'30." During some of the higher-range passages you can clearly hear the scraping sounds, produced as a finger or thumb of the left hand slides up or down to reach the next pitch.

TABLATURE
Notation that indicates how to pluck, stop, or touch each string rather than indicating pitch.

Guqin tablature notation

LISTENING GUIDE

 CD 1.16 (2'04")

Chapter 7: Site 1
China: *Guqin* ("Ancient Zither")

Instruments: *Guqin* (bridgeless plucked zither)

TIME	LISTENING FOCUS
0'00"	Melodic theme begins performance.
0'12"	Listen for tone-bending as the performer slides between pitches.
0'21"	Listen for "scratching" sounds that add timbral variation.
0'35"	Listen for subtle variations in timbre as the performer plays the same pitch on two different strings.
0'37"	Melodic variation of the opening theme.
1'29"	Melodic variation of the opening theme using harmonic overtones until 1'35".

Source: "Yangguang sandie," performed and recorded by Bell Yung, Pittsburgh, PA, 2002. Used by permission.

ETHNO-CHALLENGE (CD 1.16): Find a chordophone—for example, a guitar—and sound the overtones on a single string by lightly touching various harmonic nodes (at the mid-point, or a quarter or an eighth along the length of the string, for example) while plucking with your other hand.

Cultural Considerations. From ancient times and continuing at least into the nineteenth century, the *guqin* was closely associated with the *literati* or scholar class, from which the Chinese government chose its officials. Scholars were required to be knowledgeable in Confucian Chinese literature, poetry, calligraphy, divination, history, philosophy, and music. Music, rather than being a pleasurable or sensuous art, was a way of inculcating and expressing the ethical values of Confucianism, which include restraint, order, balance, subtlety, and hierarchy. Nonetheless, much *guqin* music is indeed quite sensuous. When scholars played a *guqin* composition, they had to flesh out and interpret the minimalist score by taking into account the meaning of the piece, its mood, and their own feelings in relation to it. In short, *guqin* music was a form of personal expression that aided in self-development and brought the player closer to China's highest ideals through a kind of sonic meditation.

Because *guqin* playing was part of a scholar's general cultivation of learning and of sensitivity to the arts, it is not surprising that "Parting at Yangguan" was inspired by a poem—specifically, a Tang Dynasty poem by Wang Wei (701–761) titled "Seeing Yuan Er Off to Anxi." Sometimes performers will sing this poem as they play "Parting at Yangguan" on the *guqin*, because the form of the composition closely parallels the poem's verse structure. The earliest tablature notation of "Parting at Yangguan" appeared in 1491 in a collection titled *Zhiyin Shizi Qinpu*, although the version performed here is from an 1864 publication.

Guqin playing, because it was cultivated by a small elite, was probably always rare and little known to the general public. Today it is similarly rare, and the scholar class of bureaucrats who once practiced *guqin* playing along with their calligraphy and poetry has long been abandoned by Communist Party functionaries. Nonetheless, *guqin* players of many nationalities are still found throughout the world in small numbers, and in recent years, these scattered groups of musicians have been linked together by the Internet. In 2003, UNESCO designated *guqin* playing as an "Oral and Intangible Heritage of Humanity."

Site 2: *Jiangnan Sizhu* ("Silk and Bamboo") Ensemble from Shanghai

First Impressions. Most listeners find China's "silk and bamboo" ensemble music readily accessible. Compared to *guqin* music, one can more easily hear a tune, clear phrases, consistent rhythm, and repetition of certain musical ideas. The music is quite busy, as each instrument plays continuously throughout and makes frequent use of ornamentation. But, because most instruments play in a high range, the overall sound is "thin," due to the lack of low range instruments and absence of harmony.

Aural Analysis. Why the name *silk and bamboo* (*sizhu*)? Recall that the Chinese classified instruments according to eight materials. "Silk" instruments are those with strings, both plucked and bowed, because the original material used for strings was twisted silk. "Bamboo" instruments are flutes, both vertical and horizontal. Thus a "silk and bamboo" ensemble consists of fiddles, lutes, and flutes, with or without a few small percussion instruments. These ensembles play named compositions or tunes from a limited repertory, especially the "eight great compositions" that every musician must know.

Some *Jiangnan* compositions, like much Chinese music generally, have titles that suggest an emotion, allude to a poem, describe a scene, or reference something historical. Our example's title, "Huan Le Ge," means "Song of Joy" and suggests its character as a "happy" piece. But *Jiangnan* music also has a great many pieces whose titles suggest musical structure, such as "Lao Liu Ban" meaning "old six beats" and referring to the structure of the original notation. Another well-known piece in the repertory is "Zhong Hua Liu Ban," literally, "middle flowers, six beats," also describes technical aspects of the music's organization. The Chinese term *fangman jiahua* means "slowing down and adding flowers" (i.e., ornaments), and thus *zhonghua* refers to a "middle" degree of ornamentation (*zhong* is "middle" and *hua* is "flower"). This process of "adding flowers" suggests a traditional approach to embellishing melodies spontaneously but according to the idiomatic characteristics of each instrument.

The "silk" category includes a wide variety of bowed and plucked stringed instruments, including certain lower-range versions introduced during the twentieth century as part of China's drive to modernize. Four instruments, however, are essential: the *erhu* (fiddle), *yangqin* (hammered zither), *pipa* (pear-shaped lute), and *dizi* (horizontal bamboo flute). Other instruments can be used as well. Our track adds the *xiao* (vertical notch flute), *ruan*

This amateur *Jiangnan sizhu* "silk and bamboo" music group meets each Sunday afternoon in a neighborhood school in Shanghai to play through favorite compositions

The Chinese *erhu* (two-stringed fiddle)

(round bodied long-neck lute), *san xian* (three-stringed lute), plus two small percussion instruments, a *ban* woodblock struck with a small beater in the right hand and a *gu-ban* clapper held by the left hand.

The *erhu* fiddle consists of a round or hexagonal wooden resonator with python skin covering one face. The scales of the snakeskin influence the timbre of the instrument: larger scales produce a deeper sound, while smaller scales encourage the preferred thin and grittier timbre of the *erhu*. A long stick serving as the neck pierces the body and has two rear tuning pegs at the top. Two strings, traditionally of silk but now often nylon, run the length of the instrument, although their acoustic length is limited to the section between the string loop along the neck and the bridge in the middle of the resonator. The horsehairs of the bow pass between the two strings, and the player pulls or pushes the bow hairs against the appropriate string while touching the strings with the left hand to create specific pitches; unlike the violin, the strings are not pressed so as to touch the neck.

The *yangqin* dulcimer, formerly a small trapezoidal-shaped instrument with two rows of bridges, was modified during the twentieth century to increase its range and power, first to three bridge sets, then four, and most recently to five or six. Each "string" is actually a course of two or three strings, which the player strikes with two small bamboo beaters, one in each hand. The *yangqin* is often used as an accompanying instrument, much like the piano in Western music.

The *pipa* lute is one of China's quintessential instruments, as it has an extensive solo repertory in addition to appearing in ensembles. It has a hollow wooden pear-shaped body with four strings that pass over raised bamboo frets that allow for the use of all twelve tones

The Chinese *yang qin* (hammered zither)

WORLD MUSIC: A GLOBAL JOURNEY

The Chinese *pipa*
(pear-shaped lute)

The Chinese *dizi*
(bamboo flute)

of the Chinese tuning system. Earlier instruments had fewer frets because older Chinese music used only seven tones. The player, using fingernails or plectra covering the nails of the right hand, plucks the strings in an *outward* fashion (unlike finger-picking a guitar). The use of all five fingers in rapid-fire motion to sustain a pitch during some passages is a particularly distinctive stylistic feature of *pipa* performance.

The *dizi* is a bamboo tube ranging in length from about 16 inches (41 cm) to 2 feet (51 cm), with a blowing hole at the left end, a membrane hole, and six finger holes. The membrane hole must be covered with a thin membrane taken from the inside of a piece of bamboo. When properly attached and stretched, this skin vibrates to create a buzz that gives the *dizi* its particular timbre, somewhat like a subtle kazoo.

While some regional styles of Chinese music make use of pitches that sound out of tune to Western ears, "silk and bamboo" styles originating in the Shanghai region, such as our example, use pitches that sound quite familiar. Players need only instruments capable of playing the seven regular pitches of the D major scale. Seven pitches are required even though the music is essentially pentatonic, because the melodies expand to more than five pitches through shifts in tonal center or conjunct passages. The two most common keys—called *diao* in Chinese—are D and G, especially in the Shanghai area. Unlike *guqin* music, the meter of which is often vague, "silk and bamboo" music has a clear duple meter, with obvious downbeats and upbeats. Rhythms tend to be relatively simple, with nothing more complex being found than a few syncopations and many dotted values.

What might strike you about our example, though, is that all the musicians are playing the same tune—but differently, resulting in a heterophonic structure. Heterophony is a fundamental phonic structure of most east and southeast Asian traditional music ensembles. Virtually all instruments in *sizhu* have a high range, giving the music a bright, busy quality. If you listen carefully, you can hear the timbres of individual instruments and differences in the way each plays a phrase. The *erhu* "slides" into some notes, the *dizi* "flutters," the *pipa* utilizes its tone-bending and "rapid-fire" plucking techniques, while the *yangqin* "bounces" along adding occasional ornamentations, primarily at the octave. Also notice that the instruments play all the time and that there is little or no shading of dynamics. This type of music is quite tuneful, so you may find yourself humming the catchier melodies, some of which are quite well known and are part of the foundational repertory of Chinese music. Even though such compositions are tuneful, the more advanced repertory—of which "Huan Le Ge" is an example—tends to be through-composed or continuously unfolding. What binds a piece together is the use of a number of short musical motives that reappear often, as well as the use of a single key and a consistent heterophonic structure. For the most part, this music is played at one dynamic level and with little more subtlety as far as tempo is concerned than a slowing down at the end. What makes the music fascinating, however, is the ever-evolving interplay of the different instruments, which makes each performance unique in its details.

LISTENING GUIDE

CD 1.17 (5'32")

Chapter 7: Site 2
China: *Jiangnan Sizhu* ("Silk and Bamboo") Ensemble

Instruments: *Erhu* (bowed lute), *gaohu* (bowed lute), *pipa* (plucked lute), *dizi* (flute), *yangqin* (hammered zither), *zhong ruan* (mid-range plucked lute), *ban* (woodblock idiophone) and *gu ban* (hand-held clapper).

TIME	LISTENING FOCUS
0'00"	Wood block (*ban*) initiates the piece.
0'06"	All instruments enter following a heterophonic structure. Listen attentively for the timbre of each instrument and note the individual interpretations of the melodic line. The initial five pitches are noted as 3, 2 3, 5, 1.
0'29"	Listen for the brief sustain on the sixth scale degree (6) of the pentatonic scale (1, 2, 3, 5, 6). Note that an additional pitch (7) appears as a passing tone periodically throughout the performance (e.g., 0'33", 1'18", 1'54", etc.).
0'48"	Melodic resolution on first scale degree (1).
1'07"	Brief sustain on sixth scale degree (6). Listen for such sustains on this pitch throughout the performance (e.g., 1'44", 3'04", etc.).
1'27"	Melodic resolution on the first scale degree and again at 2'03".
2'44"	Brief sustain on third scale degree (3). Listen for such sustains on this pitch throughout the performance (e.g., 3'13", 3'32", etc.).
2'50"	Brief tonal shift to second scale degree (2).
3'39"	Melodic resolution on the first scale degree and again at 4'25".
4'28"	Musicians pause and then transition to faster tempo section.
5'16"	Tempo slows to final resolution on the first scale degree (1).

Source: "Huan Le Ge" recorded in Shanghai, PR China by Terry E. Miller, 2007.

ETHNO-CHALLENGE (CD 1.17): Using the pitches indicated in the Listening Guide, notate the basic outline of the melody using cipher (numeral) notation.

Cultural Considerations. As with Chinese cuisine, "silk and bamboo" music is regional, and there are at least four distinct traditions. Our example, as we have already noted, represents the tradition found in and around Shanghai. Because the mile-wide Yangtze River, the more southern of China's two major rivers, reaches the ocean at Shanghai, it forms a major

Jiangnan sizhu meeting: three lutes (from left to right) small *san xian* (three-stringed lute), *ruan* (round lute), and *pipa* (pear-shaped lute)

geographical marker for the region. For this reason, the region is known as *Jiangnan* ("south of the river"), and the "silk and bamboo" music from the area is called *Jiangnan sizhu* or the "silk and bamboo music south of the river." Other distinct regional types include *Cantonese* (from Guangdong province in the south), *Chaozhou* (from eastern Guangdong province), and *Nanguan* (from Xiamen and Quanzhou in southern Fujian province).

"Silk and bamboo" music is best described as an amateur music because it is typically played by non-professionals in a casual clubhouse setting for their own pleasure, rather than on a stage for an audience. Originally, however, Jiangnan music was more widely heard in other settings, including weddings, and was also used to accompany one of the operatic genres of Shanghai as well as a local narrative singing tradition. As in many Asian cultures, professional musicians in China traditionally had a low social status, especially those who played for opera performances, weddings, and above all funerals. "Silk and bamboo" ensembles allowed ordinary working people the opportunity to be artistic without being tainted as "professional musicians." While all regional styles are typically played in a private clubhouse or meeting room situations, the *Jiangnan* style can be heard by visitors to the Mid-Lake Pavilion Teahouse in Shanghai's historical district, where the sounds of the music mingle with the chatter of patrons and the clatter of dishes. In addition, music conservatories now teach students to play this music but from refined, fully written-out arrangements.

Experienced Chinese musicians play without notation from a knowledge of the tune's basic structure plus the idiomatic characteristics of the instrument. Less experienced musicians may prefer to read notation using *jianpu*, a form of Chinese notation using Arabic numerals (referred to as cipher notation in English). Probably adopted originally from Western missionaries, most likely from France, who brought hymnals printed in numeral

Measures 1-3 of "Huan Le Ge" in *jianpu* (numeral) notation. Pitch 1 is Western pitch D or do. Order of instruments from top to bottom: *dizi* (horizontal flute), *sheng* (mouth organ), *pipa* (lute), *san xian* (three-stringed lute), *yangqin* (dulcimer), *erhu* (fiddle), *zhong hu* (middle-range fiddle), and *ban/gu* (clapper and drum). Ed. Ma Sheng-Long and published in Shanghai in 1986/2000

A *Jiangnan sizhu* ("silk and bamboo") ensemble playing informally in its meeting room, Shanghai, China (Phong Nguyen)

notation, *jianpu* is quite practical and easy to read. Regardless of key, the "home" pitch (tonic or keynote) is 1. In "D diao" (key of D), 1 is D, 3 is F♯, and 5 is A, but in "G diao" pitch 1 is G, 3 is B, and 5 is D.

Though Chinese melodies are mostly diatonic and remain in a single key, this notation can also be used to notate more complex compositions using additional signs from Western staff notation, such as sharps (♯) or flats (♭) and other graphic signs. Much traditional music is played in D and G *diao*, though other keys are possible. Dots above or below a number indicate octaves above and below the main octave, respectively. Rhythm/duration is indicated with horizontal lines below the numbers, while measures are marked with vertical lines.

Site 3: Beijing Opera (*Jingju*)

First Impressions. On listening to our recorded example, you probably cannot help but notice the clangor of the percussion, particularly the "rising" and "falling" sound of the gongs. The prominent fiddle is quite nasal-sounding and some of the pitches it plays probably strike you as out of tune. The vocal quality is piercing compared to most world music traditions, particularly in comparison to opera traditions from the West. The music of the Beijing Opera is often challenging for first-time listeners to appreciate, although the chance to see a live performance would no doubt win some new fans with its visual spectacle: the vivid costumes, the striking painted faces of some of the performers, and the stage action—especially the acrobatics, which are inspired by Chinese martial arts.

Aural Analysis. With many musics from around the world, timbre is the aspect that most challenges the first-time listener due to unfamiliarity with the instrument sounds and vocal styles. This is certainly true of Beijing Opera, called **jingju** (meaning "capital city opera") in Chinese. For most listeners, even in China, the vocal quality of *jingju* is decidedly different from what is normally encountered. All roles are sung with little or no vibrato, and many sound rather nasal and quite high in range. Men playing female roles, a common practice

JINGJU
Literally "capital city opera," known as "Beijing" or "Peking" Opera.

Jingxi (Beijing Opera) performance: a red-faced general is flanked by a painted face (*jing*) to his left and a young man (*xiao sheng*) to his right

The *jing hu* (fiddle), the main instrument of the *jingju* opera

Student musicians accompany a rehearsal performance of *jingxi* (Beijing Opera) at the Shandong Opera School, Jinan, China

in *jingju,* use the falsetto (or "head") voice. The *jing* (painted-face characters) tend to sing in a rough, declamatory style.

The instrumental accompaniment is a combination of melodic and percussion instruments that play as two groups. The melodic group is divided into "civil" and "military" sections, the former led by the genre's distinctive short, two-stringed bamboo fiddle, called *jinghu,* the latter by the loud double-reed called *suona.* Other melodic instruments include an *erhu* fiddle, the moon-shaped *yue qin* lute, and sometimes other lutes, such as the *pipa.* The military group, comprised entirely of percussion, is led by a "conductor" who plays a clapper (*guban*) held in the left hand, and uses a stick held in the right hand to beat on a distinctive small drum (*bangu*). He is accompanied by musicians playing both large and small gongs and cymbals. The conductor's drum has a dry, hollow timbre, while the tone of the large gong (*daluo*) decays downward (i.e., its pitch drops as its volume falls), and that of the small gong (*xiaoluo*) decays upward (its pitch rises as the volume falls). Besides marking beats, these percussion instruments also provide sound effects that symbolize actions, emotions, or objects.

Singers have to work closely with both the "conductor" and the *jinghu* player, because singing is improvised according to a host of variables, which comprise what is called a "modal system." This practice is quite unlike that of many other regional opera traditions, which require lyricists simply to write poetry to fit pre-existing, named tunes. Simply put, the "modal system" that governs the creation of melody here consists of several variables that allow for a kind of composition simultaneous with performance. Among these are: (1) role type; (2) melodic mode; (3) metrical/rhythmic pattern; and (4) linguistic tone.

Our example features an aria from the opera *Mu Kezhai* (named after the main character), which is sung by a female warrior, Mu Guiying, the daughter of an infamous outlaw from the Sung Dynasty. After an introductory section performed by the percussion, during which she performs militaristic stage actions, the female warrior begins singing in speech-like rhythms, accompanied by the melodic instruments. After another percussion interlude, she begins a section in a regular duple meter during which the conductor's clapper is clearly heard.

LISTENING GUIDE

CD 1.18 (3'24")

Chapter 7: Site 3

China: Beijing Opera (*Jingju*)

Vocal: Single female (*Dan*)
Instruments: *Ban gu* (wood clapper/drum), *xiao luo* (small, high-pitched gong), *da luo* (large, low-pitched gong), cymbals, *jinghu* (high-range bowed lute), *erhu* (middle-range bowed lute), *yue qin* (plucked lute)

TIME	LISTENING FOCUS
0'00"	Percussion introduction begins with the *ban gu*, followed by the gongs and cymbals.
0'01"	Listen for the "rising" pitch of the small gong compared with the "falling" pitch of the larger gong.

0'21"	Short percussion break. Instruments resume in anticipation of the vocal solo.
0'32"	Melodic ensemble enters. Note that the music is in free rhythm.
0'55"	Vocalist enters. Listen for the *jinghu* (high-range bowed lute) supporting the vocal line. The music continues in free rhythm.
1'57"	Percussion returns.
2'23"	Melodic ensemble returns. Note that the music follows a regular beat.
2'47"	Vocalist returns as music continues with a regular beat.
2'57"	The tempo gradually decreases.
3'14"	Vocalist drops out and the melodic ensemble returns to a faster tempo with a regular beat.

Source: "Tao Ma Tan (role), aria from *Mu Kezhai* (opera)," from the recording titled *The Chinese Opera: Arias from Eight Peking Opera*, Lyrichord LLST 7212, n.d. Used by permission, Lyrichord Discs Inc.

ETHNO-CHALLENGE (CD 1.18): For theatrical performance such as this example, it is important to see the on stage activity. Watch a video recording of a Beijing Opera (*Mu Kezhai*, if possible) in its entirety.

Cultural Considerations. Typically, Asian theater traditions strive for symbolic rather than realistic action, depict individual characters as universal types, make music an integral part of the performance, and generally stylize all aspects of performance. *Jingju* perhaps develops these tendencies to a greater degree than any of the other local theater traditions found throughout China. Most of those use realistic, if stylized, scenery, but *jingju* does not. The props are minimal, normally only a table and two chairs. As in most Chinese theater traditions, *jingju* actors use a special stage language, though the comedians speak in Beijing dialect to indicate their low class status. Although many of the local types of theater were—and continue to be—performed in a ritual context on a temporary stage within a temple facing the main god's altar, *jingju* is mostly performed in formal theaters, the other context for Chinese opera. In most local operas, players receive informal training within a troupe, but *jingju* can be studied formally in government-supported schools. Indeed, *jingju* has come to be the preferred way to represent traditional Chinese culture to the outside world; other kinds of Chinese theater are rarely encountered outside of China except within the confines of an overseas Chinese community.

The typical *jingju* performance places the music ensemble on stage left (the audience's right). Actors and actresses enter and exit from and to the left or right, using the table and two chairs to represent everything from a throne scene to a mountain battle site. An actor holding a stick with a simulated mane is understood to be riding a horse, and an official flanked by young actors holding cloth flags with wheels painted on them is understood to be riding in a chariot. For many years, men had to play women's roles, singing in falsetto (head) voice, because women were often banned from the stage as theater was seen as morally corrupting. Today, with such bans long gone, women not only play female roles but some-

EAST ASIA

A performance of a military style play in Taipei's Military Theater as seen from the lighting booth

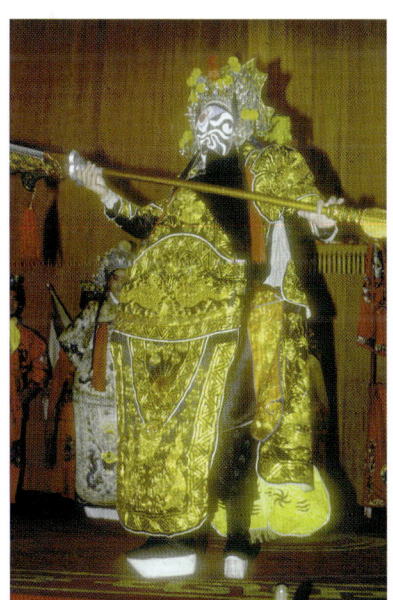

Military *jing* painted face character

Imprisoned *dan* (female) character with *chou* (comedian) keeper

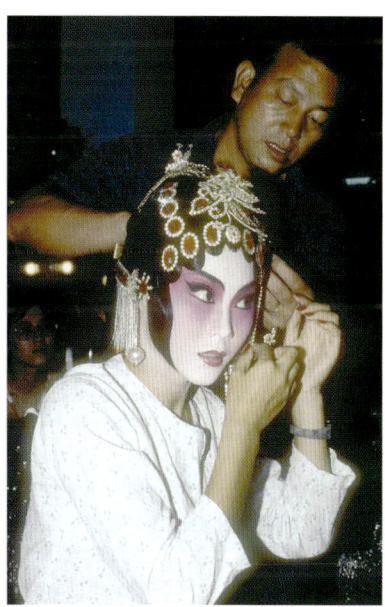

Dan (female) preparing make-up in dressing room

Military scene with numerous generals

times play men's roles as well, while some men continue to impersonate women. Regardless of his or her gender, each performer specializes in a role type. There are four major role types with numerous subdivisions: (1) *sheng* (male roles), subdivided into young man, old man, and military male; (2) *dan* (female roles), which are similarly subdivided; (3) *jing* (painted face roles), which feature a facial pattern that symbolizes the person's character; and (4) *chou* (comedians), who are easily identified by the white patch in the middle of their faces.

If you see a performance given in North America by a visiting troupe, chances are the singing portions will be shortened and the acrobatic sections lengthened, because it is commonly believed that Western audiences cannot tolerate the musical aspects of *jingju* well. But within North America there are also *jingju* clubs that give performances for connoisseurs who do not need rapid stage action to maintain interest.

YANGBANXI
Literally, "model revolutionary [Beijing] Opera," the Chinese term for Beijing Operas infused with communist and nationalist political messages during the Cultural Revolution (1966–1976).

Site 4: Revolutionary Beijing Opera (*Yangbanxi*)

First Impressions. Were you able to see a live performance of what is translated as "Revolutionary Peking (Beijing) Opera," (or **yangbanxi** in Chinese), you would be struck by a host of differences between this form and traditional *jingju* (Beijing Opera). First, in *yangbanxi* the actors and actresses wear modern costumes, including military uniforms. Second, the stage is much more realistic looking, because it features props and background scenery. Third, frequently some or even all of the instruments used are Western, and even when the instruments are all or mostly Chinese, the music is arranged and often uses Western harmony. Some of the elements of *yangbanxi* may be reminiscent of *jingju*, especially the use of percussion and the sound of most voices, but unlike the fanciful stories found in *jingju*, in *yangbanxi* the story clearly has political ramifications. Indeed, even without knowing Chinese you can easily differentiate the "good guys" from the "bad guys." The former stand nobly tall, have determined looks, and are well lighted with healthy-looking skin, while the latter are often hunched, even cowering, have unhealthy greenish-looking skin, and are dimly lit. Invariably, the "good guys" are the followers of Chairman Mao, while the "bad guys" are variously the nationalist Chinese led by General Chiang Kai-Shek, the Japanese, evil Chinese landowners, or even, in one opera, American soldiers.

Scene from the Revolutionary Beijing Opera *Taking Tiger Mountain by Strategy* (Peking: Foreign Languages Press)

The hero character in the Revolutionary Beijing Opera *Taking Tiger Mountain by Strategy* challenges his oppressor (Peking: Foreign Languages Press)

Aural Analysis. During the ten years of the Cultural Revolution (1966–1976), a number of "modernized" Peking Operas were made into political (i.e., "revolutionary") works. Some of them, including our example, the 1967 work *On the Docks*, were held up as models to represent communist ideals. Although *On the Docks* was not the most satisfactory revolutionary opera in terms of its dramatic effectiveness, it was considered the most politically progressive of all. Mao's wife insisted on a revision of the work in 1972, and this revised version is heard on the recording we have selected. Originally recorded by the "On the Docks" Group of the Peking Opera Troupe of Shanghai, the opera combines Western orchestral instruments with certain traditional Chinese instruments, including the *jinghu* fiddle and the percussion section.

The music of revolutionary opera, depending on the version, may preserve many or just a few sounds of traditional *jingju*; whatever the case, it is played from a completely written-out score. More like film music than old-style Chinese music, it creates dramatic shifts of mood. Those versions that were most modernized also use many Western orchestral instruments, and the scores include other Western features such as harmony, counterpoint, and orchestration. Excerpts from the one-page English synopsis included with the Chinese-language libretto give an idea of the opera's political goals:

> "On the Docks" depicts the spirit of patriotism and internationalism of the Chinese working class. The time is early summer in 1963. The place, a dock in Shanghai. FH, secretary of the Communist Party branch of a dockers' brigade, and KC, are communist team leaders, who are leading the dockers in a rush job before the coming of a typhoon. They have to finish the loading of a big batch of rice seeds for shipment to Africa so as to support the anti-imperialist struggle of the Asian, African and Latin American peoples. [Wheat sacks left out must also be moved.]
>
> During the rush young docker HH, who looks down on his work and is absent-minded, accidentally spills a sack of wheat. . . . Pretending to help sweep up the spilled wheat, C seizes the chance to pour the fiberglass in his dustbin into the wheat sack [and mixes it with the other sacks meant for export.]
>
> FH, working closely with her mates, discovers the incident of the spilled sack. What happened? With this problem in mind, she re-reads the Communiqué of the Tenth Plenary Session of the Eighth Central Committee of the Chinese Communist Party. [Eventually] H awakens to his mistake and exposes C's criminal activities. The enemy is completely revealed and the dockers fulfill their aid mission with flying colors.
>
> Red flags fly over the rippling waters and in the morning sun the Shanghai dockers march on with revolutionary militancy toward the great goal of communism."

Cultural Considerations. Music and politics have long been intertwined in China as they have sometimes been in the West as well. From the time of Kong Fuzi (Confucius, d. 479 B.C.E.), music was viewed as having ethical power—that is, the ability to influence people's thinking. Right music led to right thinking and right behavior. Confucianism has continued to underlie much of Chinese culture to the present, requiring restraint, balance, and non-individuality. But China underwent severe disruption to its traditional society in the twentieth century. In the 1920s a civil war broke out between the communists under Mao Zedong and the nationalists under Chiang Kai-Shek, which led, after the defeat of Chiang

LISTENING GUIDE

CD 1.19 (2'35")

Chapter 7: Site 4
China: Revolutionary Beijing Opera (*Yangbanxi*)

Vocal: Male lead and supporting male vocal ensemble
Instruments: *Jinghu* (high-range bowed lute), *erhu* (mid-range bowed lute), Beijing opera percussion (cymbals, gongs, etc.). European-style orchestra (strings, woodwinds, brass, percussion)

TIME	LISTENING FOCUS
0'00"	Orchestral opening. Listen for the variety of "Western" instruments, such as violins, trumpets, flutes, harp, and so on.
0'09"	Whistle sounds in correspondence with on stage actor's activities.
0'25"	Actors shout.
0'32"	Chinese melodic instruments enter along with the orchestra.
0'42"	Spoken text followed by the vocal lead solo. Notice the full-bodied vocal timbre in contrast to the "pinched" nasal quality of the Beijing Opera vocal timbre.
1'14"	Orchestral break.
1'19"	Voice returns. Listen for the *jinghu* supporting the vocal line.
1'36"	Orchestral break.
1'42"	Voice returns.
1'51"	Tempo slows and the orchestra follows the rhythmic phrasing of the vocal lead.
2'20"	Actors shout again and Chinese percussion is heard prominently.
2'24"	Spoken dialogue as example fades.

Source: Scene 1, "A Rush Shipment," from the recording titled *On the Docks: Modern Revolutionary Peking Opera*, performed by the "On the Docks" Group of the Peking Opera Troupe of Shanghai. China Record Company, M-958, n.d. Used by permission.

ETHNO-CHALLENGE (CD 1.19): As locating video recordings of complete Revolutionary Opera performances is difficult, do some library or Internet research to find photos and video excerpts from *On the Docks* and other *Yangbanxi* performances.

in 1949, to the founding of the People's Republic of China, while the nationalists fled to Taiwan where the Republic of China continues to this day.

Chairman Mao Zedong, leader of China's Communist Party from 1920 to 1976, understood the power of music and theater and used them as his most potent weapons both to fight his enemies and to influence and control his subjects. It was actually one of Mao's wives, former actress Jiang Qing, who supervised the politicization of *jingju*, primarily during the Cultural Revolution, a period of top-down revolution and chaos in China during which "traditional" culture, including Beijing Opera, was prohibited.

During the years from 1966 to 1976 the Chinese people were subjected to non-stop propaganda, much of it in the form of artistic productions (including music, dance, spoken theater, opera, art, and literature). Jiang Qing oversaw the creation of the "Eight Model Works": five Revolutionary Beijing Operas, two Revolutionary Ballets, and one Revolutionary Symphony. When President Richard Nixon surprised the world with his visit to China in 1972 at the height of the Cultural Revolution, he witnessed a performance of *The Red Detachment of Women*, one of the Revolutionary Ballets, an event that is central to John Adams's 1987 opera *Nixon in China*.

Besides the Revolutionary stage works, there was an abundance of new music written with socialist themes, mostly played by new sorts of ensembles (with or without vocalists), which used full orchestrations and harmony. These works varied from settings of Chairman Mao's words to music (e.g., the song "A Revolution Is Not a Dinner Party"), to music praising Chairman Mao (e.g., "Chairman Mao's Love for Us Is Deeper Than the Ocean"), to music calling for revolutionary action (e.g., "The People in Taiwan Long for Liberation") or extolling the communist work ethic (e.g., "Driving Tractors in Dazhai-Type Fields").

Because Chinese people heard so much revolutionary music and opera during the Cultural Revolution, you might be surprised to learn that record companies have released karaoke versions of the operas, and new VCD (video compact disc) versions of the films have been reissued to feed a nostalgic appreciation for the music of that period. The younger generations of Chinese, however, were nearly all born after the Cultural Revolution and only know the economically liberalized nation of today. For them, popular music is virtually the only music that they are exposed to, and as the government releases its grip on culture, there is more and more of it. Forty years ago Chinese traditional artists had to struggle against government controls to be heard, but now they struggle against the near total dominance of popular music, both local and imported from the West as well as from nearby countries.

Explore More

Popular Music in East Asia

Popular music in East Asia is steadily growing in its influence around the world. While few specific artists are known to most people outside the region, pop culture generally has embraced many innovations from the region, such as Karaoke, Japanese *anime*, and martial arts films from Hong Kong, which have inspired modern-day action films in the United States and abroad. Teenagers and young adults from this region are as familiar with the icons of Western mainstream pop, such as Lady Gaga, as their Western counterparts, but add to their iPods music from indigenous superstars, such as Hikaru Utada, Namie Amuro, Gackt, Ayu, Anita Mui, Faye Wong, and Jackie Chan, the latter being best known as an international movie star but also a pop music icon in East Asia. The majority of pop stars from East Asia are from Japan and Hong Kong, though others from Taiwan and Korea find regional fame as well.

Mainland China, however, has produced very few popular music stars due primarily to the communist political climate of the last half century, which largely discouraged popular styles as having a negative influence on society. The irony is that popular music throughout much of East Asia is considered to have originated in Shanghai during the 1920s as a mix of Chinese traditional music and American jazz called *shidaiqu* ("contemporary songs"). The most famous figure associated with this early style was Zhou Xuan (1918–1957), a singer and movie actress who became popular during the late 1930s. After the Chinese Civil War (1945–1949), however, the new communist government restricted this music as well as other outside influences coming from the West. Famous popular artists, such as Elvis Presley and The Beatles, were largely unknown on mainland China until the end of the Cultural Revolution (1966–1976). Elsewhere, however, the popularity of American and European music idols thrived, inspiring the various modern music styles of J-Pop (Japanese Pop), K-Pop (Korean Pop), M-Pop (Mando (Mandarin)-Pop), and C-Pop (Canto-Pop), as well as other East and Southeast Asian styles, including *Luk Thung* (Thailand) and *Dangdut* (Indonesia).

Arrival: Mongolia

If there's a place that deserves the title "Big Sky Country," it would be landlocked Mongolia, tucked between China to the south and Russia to the north. Its open grassland landscapes—called *steppe*—and the great Gobi Desert, plus most days being cloudless, give visitors a feeling of great openness. With little arable land, sparse rainfall, and a short growing season, the Mongolians long ago learned to co-exist with their harsh climate, hot in the summer and extremely cold and windy in the winter. Originally a nomadic people dependent on their beloved horses, today only 30 per cent of the population of only 2.9 million maintain this life style. In spite of this tiny population, Mongolia is a country of great diversity, of numerous if little-known ethnic groups, and of religious complexity. While many Mongolians continue to practice their ancient form of shamanism—shamans being specialists in "traveling" to the land of the spirits—they long ago also embraced the Tibetan form of Buddhism, as seen in magnificent temples in urban areas.

A first-time visitor will be struck by Mongolia's apparent emptiness. Although the capital city, Ulaanbaatar (also spelled Ulan Bator), appears large, its population is only slightly more than half a million—nonetheless, the city is home to nearly 40 per cent of the country's population. With a land area nearly four times that of California and equal to that of Iran, Mongolia has one of the lowest density populations in the world. Mongolia's neighbors include Chinese Turks to the southwest, Russia to the northeast, and the Republic of Tuva (properly, Tyva) to the northwest; the latter, a member of the Russian Federation, is home to thriving musical traditions similar to those found in Mongolia. Despite Mongolia's historically small population, in the twelfth century the Mongol civilization became extremely powerful, and the armies of the Khans (emperors), particularly Chinggis (Genghis) Khan (d. 1227), subdued not only China during the Yuan Dynasty (1260–1227), but a vast area stretching from Korea to the Black Sea and including parts of Southeast Asia. When

WORLD MUSIC: A GLOBAL JOURNEY

Mongolian round canvas homes (*yurt*) (Shutterstock)

Italian adventurer Marco Polo visited China in the late thirteenth century, his host was the Mongol emperor Kublai Khan, grandson of Chinggis.

The capital city of Mongolia is hardly a haven for traditional culture; instead, it reflects the Soviet influence Mongolia came under after achieving independence from China in 1921. The city's architecture looks far more Soviet than Mongolian, and it was under Soviet influence that Mongolians developed their "folkloric troupes" to represent Mongolian culture to the outside world, as well as visitors.

Originally, much of Mongolia's music had spiritual and religious significance, because music was often considered a form of communication between the worlds of humans and spirits. Under communism, however, most musical traditions were secularized and put on the stage. Music that had been—and mostly continues to be—passed down orally has also been harnessed by the European-style music conservatories. It is "**overtone** singing" that has brought Mongolian music to world attention. While overtone singing is both important and distinctive, the country's most typical form of music is actually the *urtïn duu*, the "long songs" accompanied by Mongolia's most distinctive instrument, a trapezoid-bodied, long-necked bowed lute called the *morin khuur*. Where the overtone singing lacks lyrics, the long songs retell the culture's great stories and history as well as describe the natural environment; some say that these "sing the landscape."

OVERTONE
One of the ascending group of tones that form the harmonic series derived from the fundamental pitch.

Site 5: Mongolian *Urtïn Duu* (Long Song) with *Khöömei* (Overtone or "Throat" Singing)

First Impressions. It is not the instrument that attracts our attention—that is clearly a bowed lute—or the female's singing but rather the other performer's singing, if that is the right term.

Some listeners describe these sounds as unearthly and find them "haunting." Some observers say it resembles whistling and wonder how such sounds are produced. Additionally many ask what might have inspired a culture to produce such sounds.

Aural Analysis. Traditional Mongolian life was and, for many, continues to be lived in nature and among one's flocks of sheep and goats. Without horses, Mongolians would have no way to travel or herd their flocks, and thus it is not surprising that they would enshrine the horse on their principal bowed lute, the *morin khuur* which, because of the carved horse-head at the top is translated as "horse-head fiddle." This long-necked fiddle, with two silk strings and a separate bow, is normally played by a seated male, with the body of the instrument resting on his knee and the neck resting against his shoulder. The song they are performing, *Sünder Agula* (Sünder Mountain), alludes to the sacred nature of mountains in old Mongolian society. It comes from a song genre called *Urtïn duu* or "long songs" and originated in western Mongolia. In addition to the "normal" singing by a female, a male performs regular singing while another sings with what sounds like a whistle. It is this kind of vocal production that has attracted so much attention to Mongolia over the past thirty or so years.

Mongolian "throat" singer, Ts. Sengedorj, performs in full costume (Jack Vartoogian/ FrontRowPhotos)

Two Mongolian musicians play the *morin khuur* (two-stringed, "horse-head" fiddle) (Shutterstock)

KHÖÖMEI
Throat or overtone singing from Mongolia.

The Mongolian term for this type of singing is **khöömei** (also romanized as *höömii*), while in English it is called *throat-singing* (a somewhat odd label, because all singing takes place in the throat) or *overtone singing*. What makes this singing so distinctive is the way in which the singer manipulates what are called *overtones*. Any tone or pitch, except perhaps one generated electronically, consists of a fundamental and a series of harmonics, called *overtones* or *partials*. The timbre of a given tone is determined by which overtones are emphasized—a function of how the fundamental was produced (e.g., by a double reed, a vibrating string, buzzing lips, etc.)—and by the relative weakness or strength of the various overtones. A tone in which the lower overtones are emphasized will likely sound "warm," whereas one in which the upper overtones are more prominent will sound "bright," "harsh," or perhaps "hollow."

In overtone singing, the performer—formerly only male, now female as well—produces, usually with significant pressure on the glottis (a part of the vocal cords), a fundamental and, by shaping the mouth cavity, brings out different patterns of overtones. A series of well-controlled, changing overtones produces an actual melody over a drone. Highly skilled singers can even produce both the lower melody and the overtone melody simultaneously, as heard in this track.

LISTENING GUIDE

 CD 2.1 (2'39")

Chapter 7: Site 5

Mongolia: *Urtïn duu* (Long song) with *khöömei* (overtone or throat singing)

Voices: Single female, single male, male also performing overtone singing
Instrument: *Morin khuur* (horse-head fiddle)

TIME	LISTENING FOCUS
0'00"	*Morin khuur* begins.
0'07"	*Khöömei* vocalist enters. Listen for the deep fundamental drone tone along with the overtone singing. Note that the overtone melody follows the melodic line of the fiddle.
0'20"	Female vocalist enters as *khöömei* vocalist stops. Note that the singer and instrumentalist follow the same melodic line.
1'16"	*Khöömei* vocalist joins the singer and instrumentalist.
1'30"	Male vocalist enters as the *khöömei* and female vocalists stop. Note again the singer and instrumentalist follow the same melodic line.
2'27"	*Khöömei* vocalist joins the singer and instrumentalist.

Source: "Urtin duu Sınder Mountain" from *Mongolia: Living Music of the Steppes/ Instrumental Music and Song of Mongolia*, Multicultural Media, MCM 3001 (1997). Used with permission.

EAST ASIA

ETHNO-CHALLENGE (CD 2.1): Sing a deep drone pitch and change the shape of your mouth to create different timbres. Listen for the subtle changes in overtones and try to amplify these over the fundamental sung pitch.

Cultural Considerations. Among "world music" enthusiasts little has garnered as much attention in recent years as "throat-singing," also called "overtone singing." While a similar form of singing found in the nearby Republic of Tuva has perhaps attracted a greater following in the West in recent years, Mongolian overtone singing is certainly just as striking. Singers in other areas of the world, including Altai, Khakassia, the Chukchi Peninsula, Tibet, Japan's Hokkaido (now extinct), Sardinia in the Mediterranean as well as the Inuit of Alaska, practice various forms of overtone singing, but less prominently than in Mongolia. Few outsiders will have the opportunity to hear Mongolian overtone singing in its original context—performed in a *yurt* (round tent) with singers surrounded by family and friends. Nonetheless, many recordings of overtone singing exist, sometimes even combining it with various forms of art and popular music. American musician Bela Fleck, for example, has collaborated with Mongolian throat singer Kongar-Ol Ondar, and under the indirect influence of German avant-garde composer Karlheinz Stockhausen, created an extended work titled *Stimmung* in 1968, which features overtone singing.

In Mongolia this unique style of singing is closely tied to the shamanistic/animistic beliefs still held by many Mongolians. The voice is meant to imitate the sounds of nature, attempting to duplicate the rich timbres of natural phenomena such as the swirling wind or rushing water. Mountains, rivers, and animals are believed to contain a spiritual energy that is manifested not only physically but sonically as well. Echoes reflected from a cliff, for example, are said to be infused with spiritual power. Overtone singers believe they can assimilate this power by recreating such sounds. Some speculate that overtone singing originated from the efforts of herders to imitate animal sounds when trying to rescue newborn animals when unable to nurse or when rejected by the mother. Sometimes herders soothed or coaxed their animals with their overtone singing. From these functions it is believed that herders honed their abilities until this form of singing became part of the musical traditions of Mongolia.

Arrival: Korea

Although the Korean language is unrelated to the languages of its closest neighbors, China and Japan, the fact that it is partially written in Chinese characters shows that early in its history Korea absorbed many aspects of China's civilization. Korea also accepted Confucian teachings and philosophy, the emperor system, Chinese Buddhism and Daoism, and many of China's instruments and musical types.

Sandwiched between China and Japan, Korea has suffered repeatedly as each of these kingdoms expanded. From 1910 to 1945 Korea was a colony of Japan. Following World War II, Korea found itself as the battleground in a struggle between China and the West; this led to a kind of internationalized civil war, which ended with an armistice in 1952. Today, the Korean peninsula remains divided into two countries—North Korea and South Korea.

Altogether, the Korean peninsula is only the size of the United Kingdom. While North Korea is the larger of the two countries, it has less than half of South Korea's population. The two nations are unequal in many other ways as well: the South is a modern, developed, democratic nation that manufactures goods for the entire world, whereas in the North, currently under the strict control of a quixotic ruler Kim Jong-Il, malnutrition and starvation stemming both from government policies and natural disasters are common. Culturally speaking, both countries have departed from the old Korean traditions, the North because of its peculiar form of communism, the South because of modernization. Nonetheless, in some major cities, such as Seoul, the capital of South Korea, "traditional" culture continues to flourish in the "museums" of certain government-sponsored institutions.

Just as Korean cuisine has attained little prominence in the West, Korean music has also struggled to be appreciated, even within Korea; for many Westerners both the food and the music can be described as "acquired tastes," the spiciness of Korean food being likened to the sonic spiciness of Korean music. From the first century onward Korea absorbed much Chinese musical culture, especially court and ritual musics, much of which was essentially preserved through the centuries, even as music in China continued to change. As a consequence, Korea maintains one of the oldest continuously living music traditions in the world, the Confucian ritual music called *a-ak*. These hymns to the ancient Chinese philosopher, Confucius, are still sung once a year on his birthday (September 27). The Chinese originals first had to undergo change to accommodate Korean tastes. Similarly, Korean court music, preserved today by several cultural institutions, remains extremely archaic.

In the face of the politically induced stresses of the last century, particularly the Japanese occupation (1910–1945), World War II, the Korean War, and the Korean Peninsula's division into north and south, traditional forms of music have struggled to survive. South Korea has preserved some forms in educational and cultural institutions, where they are still taught and performed as museum pieces, while North Korea has discarded most vestiges of tradition in favor of newly created and highly politicized forms of music inspired by the old Soviet "Socialist Realism," an approach that requires all art to have political ramifications and inspire the people to uphold state policies.

South Korea nonetheless retains a rich repertory consisting of solo, semi-improvised instrumental music (called *sanjo*), ensemble music, narrative and lyrical song, theatrical music, "farmer's band music," and the now widely known folk-derived percussion music called *samul-nori*. Although there are exceptions, China's instrumental timbres tend to be bright and clear, while those of Korea might be described as "rough," "fuzzy," and "wavering" because of the strong use of vibrato. While China's music is clearly based on tunes, Korea's does not generally sound tuneful to foreign ears; indeed, when Korean ensembles play together, some listener's have trouble hearing the instrumental parts as even being related to each other. Finally, ornamentation in Korean music tends to come unevenly in sudden spurts.

Site 6: *P'ansori* Narrative

P'ANSORI
Korean narrative vocal performance style, featuring epic-length stories.

First Impressions. ***P'ansori*** is a passionate music. The vocalist begins with a cathartic wail, so powerful that it strains the limits of the recording equipment. Accompanied by seemingly random drumbeats, she employs a great variety of vocal techniques, from near whispers to

EAST ASIA 7

Korean *p'ansori* (narrative) performers, the singer on the left, the *puk* barrel drummer on the right (Embassy of Korea)

speaking to singing and raspy shouting. A noticeable wide vibrato heightens the emotion, encouraging a highly evocative and dramatic performance. Even while the language is a barrier to non-native speakers, the fierceness with which *p'ansori* performers display their craft attracts loyal followers around the world.

Aural Analysis. *P'ansori* is one of Asia's greatest narrative forms and certainly among the most dramatic. Although considered a form of "folk" music, *p'ansori* requires extensive training, a prodigious memory, and incredible physical strength and vocal endurance. Today singers perform only five stories, each potentially lasting several hours, but in the distant past there were as many as twelve. Our example provides an excerpt from one of the five, *Ch'un-Hyang-Ka*, the story of a young woman whose name means "Spring Fragrance." As with many classical stories from East Asia, the plot revolves around a young student and his lover; in this case, the student is named Li Mongnyong and his lover is called Ch'un-Hyang. Ch'un-Hyang's mother is a *kisaeng*—that is, a professional singer and entertainer—but does not want her daughter to follow in her footsteps. The two lovers are secretly married before Li Mongnyong departs for Seoul to begin the classical studies that will hopefully lead to a position of authority in the government. After many years as an official, he returns to his hometown disguised as a beggar to check on his wife and discovers that she and her mother have suffered greatly during his absence. He then reveals his true identity. Some have interpreted the story as a critique of feudalism and its abuses.

The story is realized by two performers, a vocalist—in this case a respected and elderly female master—and a drummer. The drum used is the *puk*, a shallow barrel drum with two tacked heads. Held vertically by the drummer, he strikes the right head with a stick and the

Drummer playing *puk* drum to accompany *p'ansori* (narrative) (Embassy of Korea)

left head with his hand, occasionally calling out praise or encouragement to the singer. Both performers have a degree of freedom to improvise, limited within strict conventions. The vocalist's performance is governed by a modal system that provides an appropriate scale, melodic motives, and conventional ways to express emotions. The drummer's part is based on fixed cyclic patterns of drumbeats, but because the cycle is rather long in duration and the drumbeats are not continuous, the cycle may have a random feel to non-connoisseurs.

The range of vocal timbres is exceptionally rich, as the vocalist varies from speaking to declamation to song, to raspy, tense bursts of sound. The vocal range is unusually wide. Different pitches (depending on the particular scale/mode) have different degrees and kinds of vibrato, a distinctive feature of *p'ansori* performance. Connoisseurs of this music recognize the distinctions in vibrato, which gives them a greater appreciation of the performer's ability. The intensity of expression throughout a performance parallels the emotional intensity of the story. Indeed, emotional intensity is characteristic of *p'ansori* and of Korean music in general, despite the restraint and balance otherwise demanded by Confucian aesthetics.

LISTENING GUIDE

CD 2.2 (2'11")

Chapter 7: Site 6
Korea: *P'ansori* Narrative

Vocal: Single female
Instruments: *Puk* (shallow barrel drum)

TIME	LISTENING FOCUS
0'00"	Example fades in with vocalist and accompanying drum.
0'08"	Listen for the quiet declamations of the percussionist.
0'16"	Note how the descending melodic contour of the vocalist includes little vibrato in this phrase.
0'22"	Now listen for the heavy use of vibrato in the voice to contrast with the preceding phrase. Pay attention to such variations in the vibrato throughout the performance.
0'39"	Listen for the strong, raspy quality of the vocal timbre at the start of this phrase.
0'49"	Listen for the timbre heard when the stick strikes the drum's face, and compare this with the sound made when it strikes the drum's side (0'55") or strikes simultaneously with the hand (1'04").
1'08"	Vocalist sings with falsetto.
1'27"	Vocalist shifts to spoken dialogue.
1'57"	Vocalist transitions back to sung text.

Source: "P'ansori, Ch'un-Hyang-Ka, Song of Spring Fragrance," sung by Mme. Pak Chowol with drum accompaniment by Han Ilsup, and recorded by John Levy; from the recording titled *Korean Social and Folk Music*, Lyrichord LLST 7211, n.d. Used by permission, Lyrichord Discs Inc.

ETHNO-CHALLENGE (CD 2.2): Sing a comfortable pitch and attempt to vary the level of vibrato from none to very wide and back again.

Cultural Considerations. Before 1910, when Korea was still a kingdom, certain music traditions were maintained by the court while others were practiced by ordinary people of the villages. A tremendous variety of instrumental and vocal music existed, performed in ritual contexts, on official occasions, during calendric festivals, and for entertainment. Many traditions were prohibited or lost during the twentieth century, because of the Japanese occupation and especially because of the Korean War and the consequent division of Korea. After 1952, as South Korea modernized into one of the "Asian Tigers" and North Korea slid into despair under Kim Il-Sung's "cult of personality"-style rule, traditional music struggled to survive. In the North, music was harnessed for state purposes under the banner of "socialist realism," and was both "modernized" and turned into propaganda. In the South, the government made the decision to preserve rapidly dying cultural traditions by keeping them living aural museums. Traditional ways of life were "preserved"—really reconstructed—in designated "ethnographic" villages where time stands still both politically and technologically. Music, dance, and theater are similarly preserved in rather rigid forms within certain government-sponsored cultural institutions and the educational system. Independently, however, modern Korean artists have created completely new forms of expression derived from tradition, but for the most part, the traditional and the modern are kept separated.

P'ansori is one of the types of music that has been preserved through government support. Its storytellers were once found amidst festival events, where their voices had to compete with other activities. These wandering bards traveled the countryside telling their tales. Some found favor with aristocratic audiences, who continually debated over the artistic value of these talented but lower-class performers. *P'ansori* performers were an "endangered species" by the middle years of the twentieth century, until 1964, when the Ministry of Culture and Information designated several performers as "holders of artistry of intangible cultural assets." Since that time *p'ansori* has been found primarily on concert stages in an institutionalized setting along with other traditional Korean arts, such as *sanjo*.

A visitor to South Korea can still hear and see the most formal of ritual musics, the most refined of vocal and instrumental genres, and even "folk song," all alive but now unchanging. These are studied in many cases with designated masters—living national treasures—the nation's most valued culture-bearers. Unusual as this practice of keeping archaic forms of music alive artificially may seem from a Western viewpoint, it reflects a decision that traditional Korean music is worth preserving as an expression of what is most essential and defining in the Korean soul.

While much of Korean musical culture came originally from China, most of this imported Chinese culture was modified to suit the nature and personality of Korea. For example, the Chinese zither (*zheng*), formerly having sixteen strings but now expanded to twenty-one, is played with plectra (originally finger nails), giving it a crisp, clean timbre. The Korean equivalent, the *kayagum*, has only twelve strings, but they are thicker and played with the fleshy part of the fingers, giving the music a more diffused timbre. There are also, however, aspects of Korean musical practice that are not derived from China, such as the Korean preference for 6/8 and 9/8 meters, this being exceptional not just in East Asia but in all of Asia. These meters give Korean music a lilting rhythmic quality not heard elsewhere.

Korean musicians have built new kinds of music while keeping the old alive. Today one finds orchestras of traditional instruments, the mixing of Korean and Western instruments, and various kinds of popular music that sound more or less Korean. Most striking of all, however, is a new genre that has received worldwide attention, *samul-nori*. Derived from the old-time "farmer's band music," *samul-nori*, which means "four instruments playing," was created in 1978 by four musicians in Seoul who played large and small gongs (*ching* and *kwaenggwari*), an hourglass-shaped drum (*changgo*), and a barrel drum (*puk*), performing mostly fixed compositions with amazing agility and passion. During the 1980s and especially the 1990s, other groups expanded *samul-nori* to include more and larger drums, creating one of the most dramatic, energetic, and appealing new genres in the world. Because *samul-nori* has grabbed the attention of foreigners as no other Korean music had before, even the government is now promoting it as an expression of Korean identity in spite of the music's newness.

Arrival: Japan

Because Japan is an island nation, consisting of four main islands (from north to south, Hokkaido, Honshu, Shikoku, and Kyushu), plus the Ryukyu chain, land and resources are severely limited. With nearly 80 percent of the land being too steep for housing and difficult for farming, the Japanese have been forced to use their land to extreme efficiency. In a country slightly smaller than California but with a population nearly four times as large, the Japanese also have to be tolerant of each other due to such crowded conditions. Additionally, Japan's position on major geological faults brings devastating earthquakes. These the Japanese have learned to defeat structurally, but as the 9.0 earthquake of March 2011 showed, any resulting tsunamis can be far more devastating. Although profoundly influenced by Chinese civilization, Japan (like Korea) modified the culture imported from China to suit its own needs and to express its individualism. Also like Korea, Japan has tended to preserve its traditional music, theater, and dance separately from new developments, offering visitors the opportunity to experience archaic forms much as they were hundreds of years ago.

Just as Japan itself is compact, its traditional arts are few and well defined. Japan's court music and court dance, called **gagaku** and *bugaku* respectively, are among the oldest continuously living musical genres on the earth; to be appreciated properly, they are best experienced live and in their original context. Three forms of traditional theater are particularly striking: the ancient *noh*, the more recent *kabuki*, and the incredible puppet theater known as *bunraku* with each puppet's three human manipulators in plain sight. Three instruments—the *koto* (zither), the *shakuhachi* (flute), and *shamisen* (plucked lute)—are essential in Japanese music. When they play together with a vocalist, they comprise Japan's best-known chamber music, called **sankyoku**, meaning "three instruments." Other essential types of traditional music include folksong, festival and dance music, and Buddhist chant, as well as the globally popular *taiko* drum ensembles originally associated with Shinto ritual practices.

Japan's music, like its arts generally, is best understood in terms of Japanese specialist William Malm's well-known aphorism, "maximum effect from minimum means." Whereas much Chinese and some Korean musics can sound continuously "busy," Japanese music prefers minimal activity and makes silence an integral part of the soundscape. This sparseness, together with the use of strongly articulated notes, requires calm and attentive listening on the listener's part. In Japan, musical instruments are treated as extremely refined, artistic objects and remain unusually expensive, even student models. Indeed, most kinds of Japanese performance, including performances of folksongs or music for *bon* (festive) dancing, are quite formal, even ritualized.

Whereas Chinese tunes are continually rearranged and are embellished freely, Japanese music tends to be played with greater consistency. Musical spontaneity is not characteristic; in fact, some Japanese instrumental music is notated exactly, even down to the ornamentation. In short, whereas flexibility and casualness are characteristic of Chinese music, Japanese music is characterized more by fixedness and great refinement of detail.

GAGAKU

A Confucian-derived ritual court ensemble from Japan; literally, "elegant music."

SANKYOKU

A Japanese chamber ensemble, consisting of voice, *koto* (zither), *shakuhachi* (flute), and *shamisen* (lute).

(left) The Japanese *koto* zither with thirteen strings

(right) The Japanese *shamisen* lute

Site 7: *Sankyoku* Instrumental Chamber Music

First Impressions. A small group of instruments—two plucked and sounding percussive, one blown and sounding sustained—begins in a deliberate tempo which expresses a calmness in contrast to modern urban lives, particularly those of crowded and bustling Tokyo, where the underground trains can become so overwhelmed as to require "pushers" to get all the people inside and allow the doors to close. This music has an even temperament and restraint that seems almost without emotion. While the instruments are clearly together, their relationships are anything but simple, one of them sometimes seeming to wander off the main path for brief periods.

Aural Analysis. *Sankyoku*, which means "three instruments," elegantly embodies everything that Japanese musicians value in their music. Each instrument is primary in Japanese culture: *koto* (zither), *shamisen* (lute), and *shakuhachi* (vertical flute). The *shakuhachi*, whose name expresses its length in a Japanese measurement system, is a vertically held bamboo flute of varying length—21 inches/54 cm being average. Traditional models have four topside finger holes and one rear thumb hole, but some models have seven or nine holes now. The upper end is cut at an angle, creating a sharp edge over which the player splits the air and sets the air column in vibration. Players can produce vibrato by moving their head. The *koto* is a board zither of paulownia wood 70 inches (178 cm) long with ivory or plastic moveable

The Japanese *shakuhachi* with notation spread before him (Jack Vartoogian/FrontRowPhotos)

bridges suppporting thirteen strings, formerly of twisted silk but now usually of nylon. Players pluck the strings using large ivory or plastic picks attached to the right hand's thumb and first and second fingers with a leather band, and use the left hand to press strings to create pitches in addition to the pentatonic scale to which the strings are tuned. The *shamisen* is a plucked lute with a relatively long neck of varying length and a square wooden body covered with white catskin. A broad plastic or ivory bridge supports three strings of silk or nylon. The player holds the instrument at an angle (similar to a guitar) and plucks the strings with a large plastic or ivory plectrum resembling an ice scraper called a *bachi*. When these three instruments play together as an ensemble, with or without singing provided by either the *koto* or *shamisen* player, the result is *sankyoku*. During the earlier period of *sankyoku* history, the seventeeth and eighteenth centuries, the ensemble used a four-stringed bowed lute called *kokyu* that resembles a *shamisen* played with a bow, but during the nineteenth century the *shakuhachi* replaced the now-rare *kokyu*.

Although *sankyoku* music may sound somewhat free, there is virtually no improvisation in Japanese music, and most music is fully notated in various systems peculiar to each instrument. All three players (and voice when present—which it is not in this example) perform the same basic melody, but each instrument's idiomatic version is distinct, based on the characteristics of the instrument's style. While the *koto* and *shamisen* are plucked and their sounds decay quickly, requiring many reiterations in order to sustain a pitch, the *shakuhachi*'s style is continuous and flowing. Although the two plucked instruments have similar timbres, you can hear the differences clearly in the "call-and-response" passages.

The track's title is *Keshi no Hana* meaning "The Poppy Flower," a song originally composed in the early nineteenth century for *shamisen* by Kikuoka Kengyo (1792–1847), with the *koto* part added by Matsuzaki Kengyo (1824–1871), and the third part for *shakuhachi* by an unknown composer. The title alludes to the poetry associated with this instrumental version, which describes a poppy flower but as a simile for a beautiful courtesan: "How pretty is the poppy flower here in my hand. When plucked its fragrance is unworldly. But how pitiful once the petals have fallen."

LISTENING GUIDE

CD 2.3 (4'32")

Chapter 7: Site 7
Japan: *Sankyoku* (Instrumental Chamber Music)

Instrument: *Shakuhachi* (vertical flute), *koto* (plucked zither), *shamisen* (plucked lute)

TIME	LISTENING FOCUS
0'00"	*Shakuhachi*, *koto* then *shamisen* enter. Listen to alternation between *koto* (left channel) and *shamisen* (right channel) using stereo headphones. Note the relative slow tempo and use of a pentatonic scale.
0'07"	Note the *shamisen* timbre playing a lower melodic range.
0'21"	Melodic line alternates between the *shakuhachi/koto* pair and *shamisen*.
0'27"	Note the increase in tempo.
0'50"	*Shamisen* is highlighted followed by the melodic line alternating between *shakuhachi/koto* pair and *shamisen*.
1'14"	Note a brief increase in rhythmic density to build tension.
1'53"	Listen for the *koto* glissando (*kararin*).
2'01"	Tempo slows briefly as form transitions to next section at previous tempo with increased rhythmic density. Listen for variations of melodic content heard in the previous section.
4'03"	Tempo slows briefly as form transitions to final section.
4'09"	Closing section begins with new melodic material at higher rhythmic density and faster tempo.
4'23"	Tempo slows for final phrase.

Source: "Keshi no hana" from *Japanese Shamisen/Chamber Music (Jiuta) with Koto and Shakuhachi*, Lyrichord Archive Series, LAS 7209, 2010.

ETHNO-CHALLENGE (CD 2.3): Determine the pitches of the scale used in this example using a keyboard/piano. Transcribe the melodic line of each instrument using either numeral or staff notation.

EAST ASIA

Cultural Considerations. China's "silk and bamboo" chamber ensembles are notable for their casual but "busy" sounding melodic decoration, but the obvious differences between, for example, *Jiangnan* "silk and bamboo" music (Chapter 7, Site 2) and this example of Japanese *sankyoku* chamber music demonstrates most of the fundamental differences between the Chinese and Japanese aesthetics. In contrast to dense number of notes in Chinese music, Japanese music minimizes the notes, but making each one count, an example of William Malm's maxim quoted above. Where most Chinese ensemble music presents the melody in lock-step among the instruments, here the relationships are much less obvious, made complex by both differences in idiom and timing; it would be much more difficult here than in China to extract a "generic" form of the melody. Instead, it is better to think of each instrument's part as a distinct manifestation of the same melody.

Japanese chamber music is an art celebrated and enjoyed by small groups of connoisseurs in small spaces rather than by crowds in a large hall. *Sankyoku* could perhaps be compared to other well-known Japanese arts such as calligraphy, *bonsai* (the art of growing trees in miniature form), *kirigami* (paper cutting and folding), and the wearing of the *kimono* (formal dress). Where Chinese chamber music is played casually by amateurs in a clublike setting, with friends sitting around smoking, drinking tea, and talking, Japanese chamber music performance is highly formal, even ritualistic in behavior, and the audience is equally formal. Where Chinese instruments are relatively inexpensive and handled casually, Japanese instruments are highly refined in form and finish, expensive, and handled as revered art objects.

Explore More

Komuso

Even in Japan the sight of someone wandering around town dressed in robes, wearing a basket over his head, and playing *shakuhachi* flute had to attract notice. That this person was a *spy* justifiably gives rise to an obvious question: how secret can a spy be with a basket over his head? Delving into the history of the *komuso* only deepens the mystery, starting with their oxymoronic descriptor as "lay-priest." Far from being religious men, they were former *samurai* warriors who had lost their masters during the upheavals and civil wars of the late sixteenth century. Their duty was to roam the streets to observe what the citizens were doing and saying and report back to the authorities, but because their headquarters was at a former Buddhist temple, many believed they were somehow priests; hence, the idea of the "lay-priest." The *shakuhachi* was not just a large tube of sturdy bamboo but

A Japanese *Komuso* playing the *shakuhachi* (Thomas Holton/Getty Images)

227

its lower end was thick and rough from being part of the bamboo root. If need be, the *komuso* could defend themselves by striking opponents with the instrument's lower end. When not having to fight however—most of the time—they actually played the *shakuhachi*, developing a growing body of compositions. After being disbanded in the mid-nineteenth century, when the stigma of violence was separated from the instrument, the *komuso* promoted what came to be one of Japan's most treasured repertories. After that it was embraced by *sankyoku* musicians and came to replace the *kokyu* bowed lute.

One of the non-musical influences on *sankyoku*, as well as – most Japanese music, is *Zen* Buddhism, a form of Buddhism derived from the Chinese *Chan* and brought to Japan in the twelfth century. Where some Buddhist sects emphasized the study of the scriptures, resulting in much intellectualizing, Chan/Zen emphasized clearing one's mind through meditation in order to reach enlightenment. Thus, in the Zen aesthetic, emptiness is valued over busyness, plain white space over decorated space, and in music, silence over continuous sound. Zen Buddhism and the music influenced by it were the inspirations for the so-called "Minimalist" movement in Western art, which rose to prominence during the late 1960s and early 1970s. During that time many European and American artists had a fascination for Japanese art and music, one aspect of a period filled with a broad range of interests in the non-Western world.

Site 8: *Kabuki* Theater

KABUKI
Popular music theater form developed for Japan's middle class in the seventeenth and eighteenth century.

First Impressions. In comparison to Western theatrical genres, the sound of *kabuki* is much more subdued. Twangy plucked lutes, a single flute, and a collection of small drums accompany a solitary storyteller as the action unfolds on stage. No fiddles or brash trumpets or reeds, no crashing cymbals or heavy drums—this music is refined and deliberate. Perhaps most easy to recognize are the "yo" and "ho" calls of the drummers at the transition from vocal to instrumental sections, a distinctive feature of *kabuki* and Japanese *noh* drama.

Fight scene in a Japanese *kabuki* performance

EAST ASIA | 7

(left) *Kabuki* star Shoroki displaying his "mie" glance in the role of "The Spirit of the Earth Spider" in the *kabuki* play *Tsuchigumo* at the Metropolitan Opera House (Jack Vartoogian/FrontRowPhotos)

(right) Famed *onnagata kabuki* star Bando Tamasaburo V dancing "Kanegamisaki" ("The Cape of the Temple Bell") during a solo performance at the Japan Society, New York City (Jack Vartoogian/FrontRowPhotos)

Two leading actors in a Japanese *kabuki* play

229

WORLD MUSIC: A GLOBAL JOURNEY

Kabuki musicians who accompany *nagauta* songs: (back row left to right) singers, *shamisen* (lute) players; (front row) *taiko* (drum), *o-tsuzumi* (side-held drum), *ko-tsuzumi* (shoulder-held drum), and *nokan* (transverse flute) (Jack Vartoogian/ FrontRowPhotos)

Chobo narrators (left) and *shamisen* players accompany the story in a Japanese *kabuki* performance (Jack Vartoogian/ FrontRowPhotos)

Aural Analysis. When listening to an audio recording of a music theater work, it can be difficult to make sense of the music because one cannot see how it relates to the dramatic action. **Kabuki**, a theater type developed in Japan during the late seventeenth and early eighteenth centuries as a newly rising middle class of business people coalesced in the city of Edo (now called Tokyo), has considerably more action and visual interest than Japan's earlier and more reserved theater, *noh*. *Noh* features slow-moving actors behind masks playing eternal human types to the minimalist accompaniment of three drums and a horizontal flute. *Kabuki* kept the instruments used in *noh* but added plucked lutes, sound-effects instruments (such as wood blocks, cymbols, and scrapers), and a greater variety of vocal sounds.

Our example features various forms of theatrical speech, and several types of instruments. First among the instruments heard is a group of long-necked plucked lutes called *shamisen*. The *shamisen*'s square resonator body is covered with catskin that supports a bridge carrying three strings from the bottom up the fretless neck to the top end. Because players use a large ivory (or plastic) pick, the resonator skin has an additional patch around the area where strings are plucked for its protection. The large picks give the instrument its strongly percussive timbre. Three drums then begin to punctuate the *shamisens*' sound: an hourglass-shaped drum called *o-tuzumi*, which is held at the hip; a smaller version of the same drum, called *ko-tuzumi*, which is held on the shoulder; and a small barrel-shaped drum called *taiko*, which is played with two sticks. Next, a horizontal bamboo flute called *nokan* joins the ensemble. Lastly, one of the sound-effects instruments, a small metal gong, joins in. Throughout you hear occasional calls of "yo" and "ho." These surprising elements are drummers' calls and are considered part of the audible pattern of drumming. The total effect is one of diverse, unblended sounds that together make *kabuki* a unique sonic world.

As with much Japanese music, tonal subtleties abound, especially because of the frequent tone-bending heard in the *shamisen* and *nokan* to a lesser degree. Although each part seems to operate in its own world, all work together to achieve a continually changing flow of tension, relaxation, movement, and meaning. Underpinning this are the standard drum patterns, but their minimal number of beats makes perception of a regular downbeat or meter a challenge.

LISTENING GUIDE

CD 2.4 (1'42")

Chapter 7: Site 8
Japan: *Kabuki* Theater

Vocals: Single male vocal lead, briefly heard male vocal ensemble
Instruments: *Shamisen* (plucked lute), *nokan* (flute), *o-tuzumi* (hourglass-shaped drum), *ko-tuzumi* (smaller hourglass-shaped shoulder drum), *taiko* (barrel-shaped drum), *atari-gane* (small gong)

TIME	LISTENING FOCUS
0'00"	*Shamisen* (plucked lute) begins performance, followed by male vocalist.
0'19"	Vocal group utters non-lexical declamation to anticipate instrumental section.
0'21"	Remaining instruments enter. The *nokan* (flute) is the aural focus as the other instruments play supporting melody and rhythm.
1'02"	*Shamisen* briefly becomes the aural focus.
1'12"	*Nokan* reappears.
1'20"	Vocalist returns. Note how the *shamisen* and voice follow the same melodic line.
1'22"	Small gong enters.

Source: "Excerpt from *Dozyozi [Dojoji]*," performed by the Kyoto Kabuki Orchestra and recorded by Jacob Feuerring; from the recording titled *Japanese Kabuki Nagauta Music*, Lyrichord LLST 7134, n.d. Used by permission, Lyrichord Discs Inc.

ETHNO-CHALLENGE (CD 2.4): With theatrical performances such as this, it is important to see the on stage activity. Locate and watch a video recording of a Kabuki performance in its entirety (*Dozyozi*, if possible).

Cultural Considerations. Kabuki theater, like Japan's other "classic" arts, is preserved in a living, but museum-like setting. In the heart of Tokyo's fashionable shopping district, the Ginza, sits a major theater, the Kabuki-za, which is dedicated entirely to twice-daily performances of *kabuki*. Inside this otherwise modern building is a wide proscenium stage. Two aspects are exceptional, however. First, there is a long walkway leading through the audience to the front of the stage area over which actors enter and exit when required. Second, most of the musicians are plainly visible on stage (positioned at stage left). Most of the singing and all of the narration are performed by a single vocalist accompanied by a *shamisen* player; this pair is known as *chobo*. Unlike the *noh* stage, which has no props and only a painted pine tree as a backdrop, the *kabuki* stage has realistic scenery and props, including building facades.

Performances begin in the morning and continue in the afternoon following a lunch break, which may be taken within the theater itself (patrons may bring box lunches and eat them in their seats). Because of this schedule, there tend to be more women, some drawn to their favorite actors, than men in attendance, because most men work during the day. Women actresses have been banned from public *kabuki* performance for centuries, and some of *kabuki*'s most famous actors actually specialize in women's roles. In private contexts, geisha (female traditional artists) will sometimes perform *kabuki* for their exclusive patrons. The stories depict the lives of imaginary people from Japan's feudal age, the age of the *samurai* warrior. The example here is taken from a play titled *Dozyozi* or *Dojoji*, about a Buddhist monk who refuses the advances of a beautiful woman who later turns herself into a monster. As with virtually all Asian theater traditions, the goal is not realism but a highly stylized depiction of archetypical human scenarios, behaviors, characters, and emotions.

Explore More

Taiko

Taiko (meaning "big drum" in Japanese) references one of the most popular world music genres to draw international audiences in the past several decades. More correctly referred to as *kumi-daiko*, the first taiko drum ensemble was created in 1951 by Daihachi Oguchi (1924–2008), a Japanese musician with a love for American jazz. He gathered a variety of taiko drums associated individually with other traditions and combined them into a single ensemble. His early compositions were rooted in the drumming patterns of *Shinto* ritual music, but the organization was inspired by the structure of a jazz drum kit. Large, low-pitched taiko (e.g., *odaiko*) emulated the kick drum, while high-pitched taiko (e.g., *shime-daiko*) played more complex rhythms as would a snare drum.

Other taiko (e.g., *nagado-daiko*) along with cymbals and other percussion paralleled the remainder of the kit. The result was an ensemble with a strongly traditional sound but a distinctly modern style.

Oguchi's idea was quickly appealing, and soon other *kumi-daiko* troupes formed. New compositions and performance techniques were incorporated, inspired by Japanese traditional arts. Choreography, drawn from martial arts movements, became an essential feature of performance. By 1964, this new style of taiko performance was popular enough to be featured in the opening ceremonies of the Summer Olympics in Tokyo. By the end of the decade, *taiko* troupes were traveling and performing for audiences throughout Europe and the United States. The San Francisco

EAST ASIA

Taiko Dojo (est. 1968) helped spawn amateur and professional ensembles throughout the United States, which have flourished since the 1980s. *Kumi-daiko* ensembles are now a fixture of many music education programs in Japan and are commonly found throughout the world in association with Cherry Blossom Festivals, an annual Japanese celebration of flowers and the coming of Spring. Professional troupes, such as Kodo, are heralded by international audiences and have performed at many prestigious venues, such as Carnegie Hall (New York City, USA) and the Greek Acropolis. Taiko music is also often featured in Hollywood films and television commercials, as the style continues to thrive as part of a growing public interest in world music traditions.

Japanese *taiko* drummer (Shutterstock)

Arrival: Tibet

Tibet is often referred to as "The Rooftop of the World" because it has the highest elevation of any inhabited region on the planet. The southern border of Tibet is formed by the Himalayas, which includes Mount Everest, the tallest mountain in the world at over 29,000 feet (8,800 meters). The northern and western borders are also surrounded by mountains, making the Tibetan plateau one of the world's most isolated areas.

Most Tibetans live between 4,000 and 17,000 feet (1,200 and 5,100 meters) above sea level. Generally, they live in rural areas practicing subsistence farming or raising small herds of Tibetan yaks, which provide milk and meat for nourishment as well as fur and leather for clothing and shelter. While nights in Tibet are typically bitter cold, daily temperatures vary widely. Early morning hours are often below freezing, while by midday the temperature can rise to more than 80 degrees Fahrenheit (26.6 Celsius).

Sudden storms are common, and travelers must always be prepared to find shelter should a sudden dust or snow storm occur. The high elevation and lack of vegetation result in low oxygen levels. While outsiders visiting Tibet may find it difficult to breathe, centuries of living in the region have enabled Tibetans to develop increased lung capacity. Still, Tibetans are cautious not to sleep at high elevations while traveling for fear of death from lack of oxygen. Tibetans cope with such survival difficulties through a strong spiritual life.

233

Tibetan Buddhism is practiced by the majority of the population, despite the region being considered a part of the People's Republic of China. While Tibet's relationship with China has ebbed and flowed for many centuries, Tibetans lived with relative autonomy under a theocratic government until 1959, when the communist Chinese government asserted its authority over the region and invaded. The Chinese placed severe restrictions on religious practice and in general attempted to Sinicize the region. The Dalai Lama, considered by most Tibetans to be a "living Buddha" as well as their secular and spiritual leader, fled to India to escape capture. Many monasteries were pillaged and numerous monks and other Tibetans were killed defending sacred sites and the Tibetan way of life.

Relations remain strained between Tibetans and the Chinese authorities. The Dalai Lama remains in exile but has helped to establish many Tibetan communities in India, Nepal, Bhutan, and even in the United States. While restrictions against religious practices in Tibet have eased, many of the monasteries are today considered museums and are more frequented by visiting tourists than occupied by monks. Tibetan secular culture continues to survive, but the centuries-old spiritual practices of the Tibetans are best examined in monasteries and Tibetan communities outside of the region.

Site 9: Tibetan Buddhist Ritual

First Impressions. For most outsiders, Tibetan ritual music has a mysterious and eerie sound. Alternately blaring and foghorn-like sounds produced by trumpets come in slow waves, supported by the rumble of drums and punctuated by the sound of a single cymbal. The guttural chants of Buddhist monks seem to summon centuries of sacred spirits, pressing listeners in the modern era to expand our definitions of music.

Aural Analysis. The music of Tibetan Buddhist ritual involves a limited number of instruments. The *kang dung* trumpet, traditionally made from a human thighbone but today made of metal, is most prominent with its widely wavering blare. *Dung kar* conch shell trumpets are played with a similar technique and are difficult to distinguish from the *kang dung* based on timbre alone. The *kang dung* and *dung kar* are played in pairs, with one performer overlapping his sound with the other so that a continuous sound is produced. In our example the *kang dung* sounds first with a slightly brighter timbre and a higher pitch, while the *dung kar* echoes at almost a semitone lower. The other distinctive instrument is the **dung chen**, a metal trumpet that is usually between 5 and 12 feet (1.5 and 3.5 meters) long; the longer of these are usually played outdoors. *Dung chen* produce very low pitches and are also frequently played in pairs.

DUNG CHEN
A long metal trumpet with low tones blown during Tibetan ritual.

The percussion instruments found in Tibetan Buddhist rituals usually include drums and cymbals. The most common drums, *nga bom*, are double-faced frame membranophones that hang vertically in a stand and are struck by a hook-shaped stick. They have a deep timbre and are struck with slow, solitary pulses that usually correspond to either the trumpets or chanting. Large cymbals, called *rom*, are common as well and are most often played to accompany chant. While our example includes only one cymbal, which is struck lightly with a wooden stick, the *rom* are usually quite loud and are used to punctuate the ends of chanted phrases.

Throughout our example, the upper trumpets waver on their respective pitches a mere semitone apart, creating a very dissonant, unsettling sound. The *dung chen* begins with a low straight tone before rising to the pitch produced by the *kang dung*, which is the interval of a tritone (flatted fifth) above—an interval that Western theorists historically considered "uncomfortable." The percussion instruments are heard as well, seemingly in free rhythm, but actually following a long metric cycle articulated primarily by the drum. After the opening instrumental section, the drum provides a steady pulsation that accompanies the chanting monks, who dwell on a single low pitch. The instruments then interrupt before the *dung chen* sounds with percussion accompaniment.

Tibetan Buddhist monks of the Gyuto sect performing the *dung-chen* (long trumpets) (Jack Vartoogian/FrontRowPhotos)

Tibetan Buddhist monk plays the *gyaling* (double reed aerophone)

WORLD MUSIC: A GLOBAL JOURNEY

Tibetan Buddhist monks play a *rom* (pair of large cymbals)

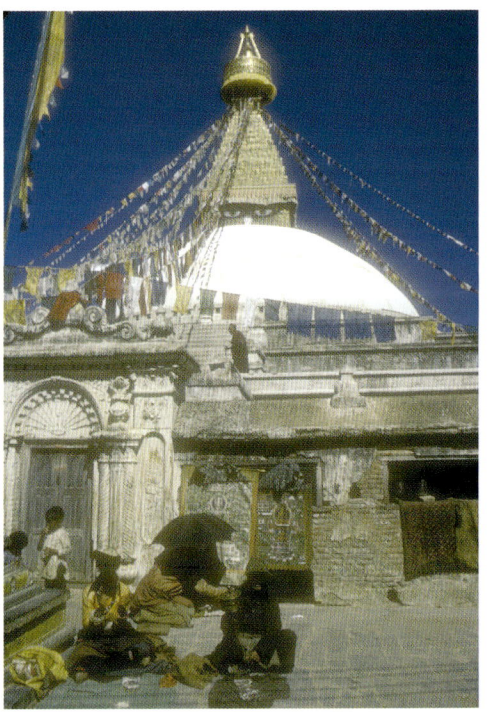

Bodhnath Stupa, a temple frequented by Tibetans living in exile near Kathmandu, Nepal. A man chants on the left while another turns a prayer wheel on the right

LISTENING GUIDE

 CD 2.5 (2'03")

Chapter 7: Site 9

Tibet: Buddhist Ritual

Vocals: Male vocal ensemble
Instruments: *Dribu* (bell), *dung chen* (low-range trumpets), *kang dung* (mid-range trumpets), *nga bom* (drum), *rom* (cymbals) and woodblock

TIME	LISTENING FOCUS
0'00"	*Dribu* (bell) sounds at start of example, followed by a *kang dung* (trumpet) and then a second *kang dung*. Listen for the "wavering" timbre and overlapping technique of the two trumpets.
0'02"	*Rom* (cymbals), which play throughout the performance, enter.
0'04"	*Dung chen* (long trumpets) enter.

236

0'07"	*Nga bom* (drum) enters.
0'10"	The *dung chen* sounds a higher pitch.
0'31"	Brief pause in the trumpet performance.
0'48"	*Kang dung* stop.
0'50"	Congregation of male vocalists chants along with more active performance on the *nga bom* and a woodblock.
0'55"	*Dung chen* stop.
1'07"	*Dribu* sounds again, followed by the *kang dung*, *rom*, and *dung chen*.
1'35"	The *kang dung* stop and the *dung chen* play a series of low bursts along with the *rom* and *nga bom*.
1'54"	Congregation of vocalists returns, accompanied by the *nga bom* and woodblock as the example fades.

Source: "Genyen gi topa ('In praise of Ge-nyen')," performed by the monks of Thimphu and nuns of Punakha and recorded by John Levy; from the recording titled *Tibetan Buddhist Rites from the Monasteries of Bhutan, Volume 1: Rituals of the Drukpa Order*, Lyrichord LYRCD 7255, n.d. Used by permission, Lyrichord Discs Inc.

ETHNO-CHALLENGE (CD 2.5): Make a necklace of prayer beads—that is, a rosary (known as *mâla*) of 108 beads. Chant the sacred mantra, "*Om Mani Peme Hung*" (Om, Jewel of the Lotus) 108 times or, for a real challenge, one million times, as many Tibetans do for purification and to acquire spiritual merit.

Cultural Considerations. In Tibet, the chants and instrumental performances that appear in Buddhist ritual are regarded more as spiritual sounds than as music. The primary intended audience for such performances is the various deities and spirits associated with Tibetan Buddhism.

Buddhism is thought to have come to Tibet during the mid-eighth century with the arrival of Padmasambhava (717–762 C.E.), a legendary monk who was believed to have great magical powers that could drive away demons. Padmasambhava practiced a unique form of Buddhism known as Tantrism, which emphasized the use of symbols, ritual objects, and yoga practices in the quest for enlightenment. A primary goal of Tantric Buddhism, as Tibetan Buddhism is often called, is to overcome the fear of death and thus make death powerless to prevent a person from attaining enlightenment.

Tibetans have long been preoccupied with death. The fragility of life in the harsh environment of the Tibetan plateau led, before the arrival of Buddhism, to the development of a spiritual belief system known as *Bonism*, which was centered on a group of dangerous and fearful demons. Because these demons could control the elements and take life unexpectedly, Bonist priests performed rituals and gave offerings in order to appease them. Many of these priests were feared, as human sacrifices were among the methods used to win the demons' favor. When Padmasambhava arrived with the assurance that Buddhism could overcome death and drive away such demons, most Tibetans embraced the new religion and its non-sacrificial rites.

One of the more interesting customs found in Tibetan Buddhism is the use of prayer wheels. While the ultimate goal of all Buddhists is to attain enlightenment, most accept that attaining a higher rebirth in the next life is a more practical spiritual goal. Chanting prayers is considered a way to earn spiritual merit, which in turn helps boost one's chances of a higher rebirth. Prayer wheels can help with this accumulation of merit. Each wheel has a prayer written on the outside, as well as a prayer written on parchment inside. Tibetan Buddhists believe that each time the wheel is spun, the words are "written on the wind."

Musical performances are most important to rituals involving groups rather than individuals. The blaring sounds of the trumpets are meant either to drive away evil deities or to call benevolent ones. The deep sound of the *dung chen* is said to imitate the trumpeting of the elephant, which is considered a powerful animal. The *dung kar*, which are highly valued instruments because conch shells are rarely found so far from the sea, can call spirits as well but are also frequently used to make announcements or to sound warnings. The *kang dung* is ideally made from a human thighbone, to remind believers that physical life is impermanent. These trumpets often play a prominent role in calling the faithful, be they living or ancestral spirits. The percussion instruments function primarily to emphasize structural points, by marking the ends of both instrumental and chanted phrases.

Chanting the *sutras*, or Buddhist prayers, is a primary activity among Tibetan Buddhist monks. The deep guttural utterances are said to represent the fundamental sound of the human body when all else is in complete silence. Complete awareness of one's physical self is an important aspect of preparing for the body's eventual demise. The body is, however, merely the cup that holds the spiritual nectar. When the body dies, the spirit is released and is housed in a new form. This consciousness of the impermanence of all things is fundamental to Tibetan theology.

Certain Tibetan Buddhist sects practice a unique form of chant in which they sound two tones at once, a low fundamental tone and a high frequency overtone. This technique is believed to enable a monk's spirit to travel to the spiritual plane. By visiting the spiritual plane, the monk is able to achieve "death without dying," and he thereby gains knowledge of the afterlife, thus robbing death of some of its fearful sting. During this chanting, a monk's heartbeat can slow dramatically and his breathing may become almost imperceptible. While only Tibetan monks perform these spiritual practices, the spiritual life of all Tibetan Buddhists is focused on overcoming death.

Questions to Consider

1. How do attitudes toward traditionality and modernization affect music differently in China than they do in Japan and South Korea?
2. In China, how did the Cultural Revolution affect the development of music and theater?
3. How are the aesthetics of music in Japan shaped by both Confucianism and Buddhism?

EAST ASIA

4. How are the types of East Asian theater different from theater and opera in the West?

5. What spiritual role does music play in Tibetan Buddhist ritual?

6. Discuss East Asian attitudes toward professional musicians and actors and explain why amateur music-making was held in such high esteem.

On Your Own Time

Visit the textbook website to find these resources for further exploration on your own.

China

Book: Yung, Bell. *The Last of China's Literati: The Music, Poetry and Life of Tsar Teh-yun*. Seattle, WA: University of Washington Press, 2008.
http://www.washington.edu/uwpress/search/books/YUNBEL.html

Website: North American Guqin Association
http://www.guqin.org/

Website: Chinese Guqin Playing and Notation
http://www.peiyouqin.com/

Website: Instruments of Sizhu Music
http://www.cfmw.com.tw/eng/instruments.html

Book: Thrasher, Alan. *Chinese Musical Instruments*. New York: Oxford University Press, 2001.
http://www.oup.com/us/catalog/general/subject/Music/WorldMusicEthnomusicology/?view=usa&ci=9780195907773

Book: Joshua Goldstein. *Drama Kings Players and Publics in the Re-creation of Peking Opera, 1870-1937*. Los Angeles: University of California Press, 2007.
http://www.ucpress.edu/book.php?isbn=9780520247529

DVD: *Farewell My Concubine*. Dir. Kaige, Chen. Miramax, 1993.
http://www.illuminatedlantern.com/cinema/review/archives/farewell_my_concubine.php

Book: Lu, Xing. *Rhetoric of the Chinese Cultural Revolution: The Impact on Chinese Thought, Culture, and Communication*. Columbia, SC: The University of South Carolina Press, 2004.
http://www.sc.edu/uscpress/books/2004/3543.html

Internet: Popular Artists from China, Hong Kong, and Taiwan
Jackie Chan
Teresa Teng
Faye Wong
Anita Mui
Cui Jian

Mongolia (and Tuva)

Book: Pegg, Carole. *Mongolian Music, Dance and Oral Narrative: Performing Diverse Identities*. Seattle, WA: University of Washington Press, 2001.
http://www.washington.edu/uwpress/search/books/PEGMOC.html

Book: Levin, Theodore. *Where Rivers and Mountains Sing: Sound, Music, and Nomadism is Tuva and Beyond.* Bloomington, IN: Indiana University Press, 2006.
http://www.iupress.indiana.edu/catalog/product_info.php?cPath=1037_1160_1408&products_id=625621

Audio: *Tuva: Voices from the Center of Asia.* Smithsonian-Folkways, SF40017, 1990.
http://www.folkways.si.edu/albumdetails.aspx?itemid=2058
http://itunes.apple.com/us/album/tuva-voices-from-center-asia/id95703572

DVD: *Genghis Blues.* Dir. Belic, Roko. Wadi Rum Productions, 1999.
http://www.genghisblues.com/

Website: Mongolian Music Blog
http://mongolianmusic.blogspot.com/

Internet: Popular Artists from Mongolia
Kongar-ol Ondar
Nominjin

Korea

DVD: *Chunhyang.* Dir. Im Kwon-taek. CJ Entertainment, 2000.
http://en.wikipedia.org/wiki/Chunhyang_(2000_film)

Book: Park, Chan E. *Voices from the Straw Mat: Toward an Ethnography of Korean Story Singing.* Honolulu: University of Hawaii Press, 2003.
http://www.uhpress.hawaii.edu/p-3195-9780824825119.aspx

Audio: *Korean Folk Music—Four Thousand Years.* (Digitally Remastered.) Essential Media, 2009.
http://itunes.apple.com/us/album/korean-folk-music-four-thousand/id292787678

Internet: Popular Music Artists from Korea
Seo Taiji
Shinwa
SHINee
Rain
Girls' Generation

Japan

Audio: Nonesuch Explorer Series: Japan
http://www.nonesuch.com/store/explorer-series-east-asia/world-music

Book: Malm, William. *Traditional Japanese Music and Musical Instruments.* Tokyo: Kodansha International, 2000 (original, 1959).
http://www.kodansha-intl.com/books/9784770023957/

Website: The International Shakuhachi Society
http://komuso.com/top/index.pl

Book: Blasdel, Christopher. *The Shakuhachi: A Manual for Learning.* Tokyo: Printed Matter Press (reprint), 2008.
http://www.shakuhachi.com/PG-Blasdel.html

Website: Shochiku Kabuki Official Website
http://www.kabuki-bito.jp/eng/top.html

Book: Brandon, James R., and Samuel L. Leiter. *Masterpieces of Kabuki: Eighteen Plays on Stage.* Honolulu: University of Hawaii Press, 2004.
http://www.uhpress.hawaii.edu/p-3195-9780824827885.aspx

Book: Foreman, Kelly M. *The Gei of Geisha: Music, Identity and Meaning.* London: Ashgate, 2008.
http://www.ashgate.com/default.aspx?page=637&calcTitle=1&title_id=6974&edition_id=9918

Website: Discovery Channel—Japan: Geisha Culture
http://dsc.discovery.com/videos/discovery-atlas-japan-geisha-culture.html

Website: San Francisco Taiko Dojo
http://www.sftaiko.com/

Website: Kodo (Taiko Ensemble) Official Website
http://www.kodo.or.jp/news/index_en.html

Internet: Popular Artists from Japan
Mr. Children
Hikaru Utada
Namie Amuro
Gackt
Ayumi Hamasaki (Ayu)

Tibet

Audio: *Tibet Buddhist Rites from the Monasteries of Bhutan.* (Four Volume Series) Lyrichord, LYR 7255, 1993.
http://lyrichord.com/tibetanbuddhistritesfromthemonasteriesofbhutanvolumeiritualsofthedrukpaorderfromthimpuandpunakha-variousartists.aspx

Book: Jansen, Eva Rudy. *Singing Bowls, A Practical Handbook of Instruction and Use.* Havelte, Holland: Binkey Kok Publications, 1992.
http://www.altamira.nl/index.php?action=boek_detail&bid=352&cid=81

Website: International Tibet Network
http://www.tibetnetwork.org/

Website: Gyuto Monasteries and Centers
http://www.gyuto.org/

The Middle East: Islam and the Arab World, Iran, Egypt, Sufism, Judaism

8

Background Preparation	244	**Arrival: Egypt**	262	Egypt's great temple of Ramses II at Abu Simbel moved to its present location when the Aswan High Dam was built in 1970 (Max T. Miller)
An Inside Look: George Dimitri Sawa	246	Site 4: *Takht* Instrumental Ensemble	263	
Planning the Itinerary	247	**Arrival: Sufism**	268	
Arrival: Islam and the Arabic World	247	Site 5: Sufi *Dhikr* Ceremony	269	
Site 1: Islamic *Adhan*, "Call to Prayer"	248	**Arrival: Judaism**	272	
Site 2: Arabic *Taqasim* for *Ud* and *Buzuq*	253	Site 6: Jewish *Shofar* and Liturgical Cantillation	274	
Arrival: Iran	257	**Questions to Consider**	278	
Site 3: *Dastgah* for *Santur* and Voice	258	**On Your Own Time**	278	

Background Preparation

Geographically, the area covered in this chapter defies easy description. The designation *Middle East* is conventional and convenient—but it is also ethnocentric, as are *Near East* and *Far East*. After all, the regions these terms describe are only "near" or "far" from the perspective of the West. On the other hand, referring to the "Middle East" as "West Asia and North Africa" is clumsy. For this reason, we have chosen to adhere to the conventional term, whatever its drawbacks.

A second problem is that the boundaries of this region are less clear cut than those of most other areas: potentially, they encompass everything from Morocco in the west (directly south of Europe) to China's westernmost province, Xinjiang. The nations that can be said to comprise this area straddle three continents: part of Turkey is in Europe; five of the Middle Eastern nations are in Africa; and the rest are in Asia. However, some consider the former republics of the Soviet Union, such as Turkmenistan, Uzbekistan, and Kazakhstan, to be part of "Central Asia" rather than of the Middle East, but few books, including this one, can afford the luxury of a Central Asian chapter.

It has been customary to subdivide the Middle East into sectors. The major units are: (1) the **Maghrib** or North Africa, consisting of Morocco, Algeria, Tunisia, and Libya; (2) the **Mashriq**, consisting of Egypt, Israel, Jordan, Lebanon, Syria, and Iraq; and (3) the Arabian Peninsula, consisting of Saudi Arabia, Yemen, Oman, and the various smaller nations on the Persian Gulf. Turkey, Iran, and Central Asia are usually treated as separate areas, and culturally speaking Israel and Armenia are considered as special cases.

It is tempting to describe this vast region as the "world of Islam" because its nations and peoples are predominantly Muslim, but there are important exceptions such as Christian Armenia and Georgia, and Jewish Israel. Islam, while certainly the predominant faith, is no more a unified monolith than, say, Christianity is in the West, or Buddhism is in Asia. Linguistically, while several mutually unintelligible language families are present, a certain unity has been created through the use of classical written **Arabic**, allowing learned people over a vast area to communicate, much as Latin once unified Europe and Sanskrit (or Pali) parts of Asia. Arabic belongs to the Afro-Asiatic family of languages, which includes all Semitic languages, Hebrew and Egyptian among them. The Indo-European languages are represented in the region by the Indo-Iranian subfamily, which includes Persian and Kurdish. Armenian is a stand-alone language, while Turkic languages, which stretch from Turkey to China's Xinjiang, are part of the Altaic family and are related both to Mongolian in the east and to Hungarian in the west. While language similarity might be expected to create greater unity, that is not always the case; for example, Arabs and Hebrew-speaking Jews have related languages but have been at odds for decades. Similarly, while Islam would seem to unify the region, it also can be the basis for division, because Islam has numerous factions that can be as different from one another as Christianity's multitude of sects.

When the Middle East is mentioned, many outside the region likely envision deserts, camels, nomads, pyramids, and simple villages where people are surviving at a subsistence level. While it is true that much of the Middle East is desert, other parts are quite lush, especially along the Nile, Tigris, and Euphrates rivers. and there are even regions filled with green fields, forests, and mountain streams. Parts of the Middle East also get quite cold and experience snow in the winter. While some Middle Eastern nations have major oil deposits, others have none and must import all the oil they use.

MAGHRIB
Literally, "the time or place of the sunset." The Arabic name designating the region from present-day Libya west through Morocco.

MASHRIQ
Literally, "the time or place of sunrise—the east." The Arabic name designating the parts of Asia (and Egypt) conquered and populated by the Arabs.

ARABIC
A Semitic language originating with the Arab ethnic group; also, the holy language of Islam, and a musical tradition whose history is intricately linked with the spread of the language.

THE MIDDLE EAST

The exquisite Patio de los Leones (Courtyard of the Lions) is the most famous place in Granada's fourteenth-century Moorish palace, the Alhambra

The Middle East is home to some of the world's earliest and most important civilizations. Indeed, the valley of the Tigris and Euphrates rivers, once called Mesopotamia and now largely within Iraq, is sometimes called the "Cradle of Civilization." The ancient Egyptians developed a great civilization along the Nile, leaving the world with incredible monuments, the pyramids among them. And Alexander the Great, a Greek-Macedonian, conquered much of the Middle East, leaving a strong imprint of his civilization throughout the region. The Middle East is dotted with extensive Greek and Roman ruins, testaments to the early spread of Greek learning and culture and the development of sophisticated urban areas.

During Europe's Middle Ages following the dissolution of the Western Roman Empire and the splintering of Europe into small, disorganized entities, classical learning flourished among the Arabs. Alexandria, Egypt, was home to what was perhaps the world's greatest library until 642, when its contents were burned on the orders of the city's conqueror, Omar, Caliph of Baghdad. Arabic scholars, such as al-Kindi (790–874) and al-Farabi (872–950), preserved and developed Ancient Greek music theory, which later influenced European theory. Today's Middle East continues to produce highly sophisticated music, often in combination with some of the world's most fluid and sensuous poetry. In the midst of war and internecine violence, the Middle East remains home to unusually attractive music in spite of much of Islam's traditional distaste for such a sensuous art.

George Dimitri Sawa

AN INSIDE LOOK

I was born in Alexandria, Egypt. For socio-economic and political reasons, my music career began with Western rather than Arabic music. Before European colonization, an *ud* (lute) was often part of an Egyptian bridal dowry, but afterward middle-class wealth combined with the Arab inferiority complex toward the West caused us to replace it with the more expensive and "technologically advanced" piano. My father, who provided for his yet unmarried sister, and who always planned ahead, bought a piano as part of her dowry. My aunt never married, and lived with us, so the piano became part of our household.

I began my musical career by playing Egyptian popular songs by ear on the piano. My father, eager for me to develop good technical habits, took me at the age of ten to a private teacher, the eccentric and highly talented violinist and pianist Madame Irene Drakides. She had been a student of Alfred Cortot and had many stories to tell about her acquaintances with famous French composers Maurice Ravel and Gabriel Fauré, some of whose works she had premiered. She trained me well, and I later contemplated a career as a concert pianist. However, when I was in Sweden as an exchange student in electrical engineering, and played both Arabic and Western music on the piano to my hosts, they asked me the obvious question that I had never asked myself: "Why don't you play an Arabic instrument?" So I resolved to learn the *qanun* (zither), an instrument that had fascinated me from early childhood.

At the Higher Institute for Arabic Music in Alexandria, the teachers were all touched that an Egyptian skilled at the piano would turn to the *qanun*! I had a lot to learn, such as oral learning and the art of improvisation, but more to unlearn, because Arabic pre-composed pieces were not frozen entities, but instead improvised ornaments, tastefully executed, that made every performance unique.

George Dimitri Sawa, Egyptian musician and historian

After completing degrees in piano, *qanun*, and yes, electrical engineering, I emigrated to Canada to study musicology and ethnomusicology. Arabic music was to be my career, and there was no turning away from it. I was most interested in its performance history, which led me to research the medieval sources on theory and ethnography. No music program in North America could provide the training for this type of work, so I created my own program by doing a Ph.D. in two departments, Music and Middle Eastern studies. The latter gave me the necessary training in socio-cultural history and the bibliographical tools to research my subject. The medieval Arabic world that unraveled before my eyes was stunning. There was a fusion of musical styles, Arabic, Persian, and Byzantine; court patronage that generously maintained practitioners and scholars; a scholarship that combined the writings of the practitioners with Greek music theory and Middle Eastern humanities. In short, it was a discipline that predates modern ethnomusicology by a thousand years. I was hooked for life.

THE MIDDLE EAST

Arabic influence on Europe goes far beyond the ancient Greco-Arabic music theory that formed the theoretical systems of Europe's first millennium. The city known consecutively as Byzantium, Constantinople, and Istanbul served a historic role as a bridge between Asia and Europe over which culture passed in both directions. The vast **Ottoman Empire** that incorporated much of Southeast Europe for hundreds of years—in some places even into the early twentieth century—left those areas with many Turkish instruments and musical influences. In fact, most of Europe's instruments can ultimately be traced to Arab sources. These instruments entered Europe both through Turkey and from North Africa, especially via Spain. For a thousand years or more before the expulsion of the Moors and Jews from Spain in 1492, both North Africa and Southern Europe were part of a unified Mediterranean culture. Europe—and European music in particular—would be unthinkable without Arab influence.

OTTOMAN EMPIRE
A powerful Turkish dynasty that ruled over various parts of West Asia, Eastern Europe, and northern Africa from the thirteenth to the early twentieth century.

Planning the Itinerary

For readers whose curiosity remains unsatisfied by this necessarily brief survey, there are still more areas to explore. This is especially so of the Central Asian nations, whose music remains little known in the West. Beyond that is distant Xinjiang, the westernmost province of China, where Turkic peoples create music with close ties to the music of Turkey itself. At the other end of the Middle East, there is Morocco, where the remnants of Moorish-Andalusian music survive from Spain's Middle Ages.

While three major language groups are found in the Middle East—Arabic, Turkic, and Persian—Turkic and Arabic musical traditions are similar enough that we can combine them and discuss Middle Eastern music through two broad traditions: Arabic and Persian music.

Because Islam is of central importance throughout the entire region, we must of necessity give some consideration to the relationship between music and mosque. But because Israel is the world center of Judaism, we must also consider the role of music in the synagogue. In fact, because of the significance of religion in the region, we have departed somewhat from the structure of the book's other chapters: our last two "Arrivals" are not centered on places per se but on religious faiths, namely Sufism and Judaism.

Arrival: Islam and the Arabic World

With more than 1.5 billion adherents, or 23 percent of the world's population, Islam is not just a major religion but a profound influence on culture—both generally and musically—around the globe. Though there is a close connection between the Middle East and Islam, both historically and demographically, Islam is also a major force in numerous countries beyond the Middle East, especially in Africa, South Asia, and Southeast Asia. Looking eastward, northern India is predominantly Muslim along with Pakistan and Bangladesh. Afghanistan, straddling both South Asia and the Middle East, is Muslim. In Southeast Asia two countries are predominantly Muslim: Malaysia and Indonesia, the latter being the most populous Muslim country in the world. In addition, the southern Philippines is Muslim. Muslims are also found in Thailand, Vietnam, and in smaller numbers in most countries of Southeast Asia. Western China, especially Xinjiang province, is Muslim, and most nations of Central Asia (Azerbaijan, Kazakhstan, Kyrgyzstan, Tajikistan, Turkmenistan, and Uzbekistan) are predominantly Muslim. In Africa, besides the northern tier countries—considered part of the Middle East at least culturally—Islam is prevalent in many countries, especially Nigeria. Because of the earlier expansion of the Ottoman Empire into Europe, much of Southeast Europe includes Muslim communities, while three nations—Kosovo, Albania, and Bosnia-Herzegovina—are predominantly Muslim. In the rest of Europe there are increasing numbers of Muslims stemming from the many "guest workers" brought to places such as the United Kingdom, France, and Germany, as well as from refugees and political dissidents. Islam also flourishes in the United States, with the greatest concentration found in Dearborn, Michigan.

Most Muslims—estimated at 80–90 percent—belong to the Sunni branch. What sets Sunnis apart is their adherence to the *Qur'an* (also Koran), Islam's most sacred writings, and the *Sunnah*, which is the record of Muhammad's life. Sunni believe that Muhammad specified no particular leaders to follow after him, and therefore Sunni Muslims have no hierarchy of ecclesiastical leaders. The Shia, however, believe that Muhammad's cousin and son-in-law, Ali ibn Abi Talib, was his designated successor, and they consider Ali to have been the first *imam*, who are the religious leaders of Shia Islam. The Shia constitute only about 10–20 percent of the world's Muslims, but they have been exceptionally prominent politically because of conflicts in Iraq with Sunnis and because Iran is primarily Shia. Beyond these two major branches, there are numerous smaller branches, the most prominent being the Sufis, who are discussed in detail in Site 5.

Site 1: Islamic *Adhan*, "Call to Prayer"

First Impressions. In our example, which features a man calling the faithful to prayer, the vocalist performs a single melodic line, adding fairly extensive and technically demanding ornamentation. This performance seems to meet most definitions of "music," as it has definite pitch, rhythm, and contour. Yet, in an Islamic context, this would not be considered as "singing"; it would be thought of, rather, as heightened speech or "holy" speech, delivered in a style requiring both declamation and the spinning out of syllables.

Aural Analysis. Anyone who has visited a Muslim nation has likely heard the "Call to Prayer"—in Arabic, the **adhan**—which is uttered five times daily. In most places today, considering the size of modern cities and the amount of noise from traffic, *adhan* are now transmitted through loudspeakers mounted on a tower at a local mosque. Because the purpose of the call is to communicate a specific message and because Islam discourages the use of the sensual arts, the call consists essentially of spoken words, but the manner of delivery takes on characteristics of melody. Indeed, some versions of the *adhan* are highly virtuosic and melismatic. The set of pitches used is normally characteristic of a musical *mode*, a term denoting not just a scale but typical melodic patterns as well. *Adhhan* are melodically improvised to a certain degree and are also in free rhythm, being a series of declaimed phrases each separated by a pause. The words used are declaimed in classical Arabic and are virtually the same throughout Islam—the only exceptions being that the line "Prayer is better than sleep" is only chanted during the predawn call, and that Shia Muslims add the line "Ali is his successor" after affirming that **Muhammad** is the prophet of God:

ADHAN
The Islamic Call to Prayer.

MUHAMMAD
Muslim prophet and Arab leader who during his lifetime (570–632 C.E.) spread the religion of Islam and unified a great deal of the Arabian Peninsula.

Allahu akbar, Allahu akbar	God is great, God is great,
Ashhadu an lail aha illa ll ah	I testify that there is no god but God.
Ashhadu anna Muhammadan ras ul Allah	I testify that Muhammad is the prophet of God.
Hayya 'al a'l-sal at	Come to prayer.
Hayya 'al a 'l-fal ah	Come to salvation.
(Al-Salat khayr min al-nawn)	(Prayer is better than sleep.)
Allahu akbar, Allahu akbar	God is great, God is great.
Lail aha ill all ah	There is no god but God.

LISTENING GUIDE

 CD 2.6 (1'49")

Chapter 8: Site 1
Islam: "Call to Prayer"

Vocals: Single male (*muezzin*)

TIME	LISTENING FOCUS
0'00"	Vocalist calls in free rhythm. The text setting is syllabic. Note that throughout the example, each initial line is primarily syllabic and then repeated with increased melisma. Line 1: *Allahu akbar, Allahu akbar* ("God is great, God is great").
0'07"	Line 1 is repeated with increased melisma.
0'17"	Line 2: *Ashhadu an lail aha illa ll ah* ("I testify that there is no god but God").
0'25"	Line 2 repeated with increased melisma.
0'35"	Line 3: *Ashhadu anna Muhammadan ras ul Allah* ("I testify that Muhammad is the prophet of God").
0'45"	Line 3 repeated with increased melisma.
0'58"	Line 4: *Hayya 'al a'l-sal at* ("Come to prayer").
1'05"	Line 4 repeated with increased melisma.
1'14"	Line 5: *Hayya 'al a 'l-fal ah* ("Come to salvation").
1'22"	Line 5 repeated with increased melisma. Note line 6 (see above) is not heard in this example.
1'30"	Line 7: *Allahu akbar, Allahu akbar* ("God is great, God is great").
1'40"	Line 8: *Lail aha ill all ah* ("There is no god but God").

Source: Islamic "Azan" ("Call to Prayer") by Saifullajan Musaev from the recording *Bukhara, Musical Crossroads of Asia*/Recorded, compiled and annotated by Ted Levin and Otanazar Matykubov, provided courtesy of Smithsonian Folkways Recordings, Smithsonian/Folkways CD SF40050, © 1991. Used with permission.

WORLD MUSIC: A GLOBAL JOURNEY

> **ETHNO-CHALLENGE (CD 2.6):** Visit a local mosque (with permission) and observe a service such as Friday prayers.

Cultural Considerations. Islam has a great deal in common with Judaism and Christianity, despite the misunderstandings and conflicts that have arisen among adherents of these three religions. All three are monotheistic—in fact, they worship the same god, who is called Allah by Muslims, Yahweh or Jehovah (also known as Adonai, meaning "Lord") by Jews, and God by (English-speaking) Christians. All trace their lineage to Abraham and recognize the biblical prophets. While Jesus of Nazareth, the man who is the basis of Christianity, is considered by many to have been a prophet as well as messiah, most Jews see Jesus as a "false messiah" or pay little heed to his presence, since Judaism does not place individual humans at the center of their faith.

For Muslims, Muhammad (570–632) was not just a prophet, but the central prophet. Born in the Arabian Peninsula, Muhammad lived in Mecca and Medina and founded Islam there. While all Muslims accept the teaching of Muhammad, divisions arose after Muhammad's death. As a consequence, there are "denominational" differences in Islam, especially between the more dominant **Sunni** and the minority **Shia** branches of the religion. (Note, however, that Shia Muslims are the majority in Iran and Iraq.) Shia Muslims differ from Sunni because of their belief that Muhammad's cousin and son-in-law, Ali, was the rightful successor, in contrast to the Sunni who do not accept Ali's legitimacy. Also, Shia designate spiritual leaders as *imam*, Ali having been the first of them. In addition to these main sects, there are many smaller sects, including the **Sufi**. Because Sufis seek union with

SUNNI
The mainstream or majority branch of Islam.

SHIA
The minority branch of Islam that follows Muhammad's cousin, Ali.

SUFI
The mystical branch of Islam.

The Beyazit Camii (Mosque), built in 1504, is Istanbul's oldest standing mosque

God through trance, often induced through a whirling dance accompanied by music, some Muslims view Sufis as being so unorthodox that they are not considered mainstream Muslims.

Muhammad designated Mecca as Islam's holy city and built a great mosque there containing Islam's holiest shrine, the *Ka'ba*. Since that time, every Muslim capable of doing so is expected to make a pilgrimage (*hajj*) to Mecca; pilgrims are honored as *hajji* upon their return home. Muslims are also expected to pray five times a day, facing in the direction of Mecca. The Call to Prayer developed as a reminder to the faithful to fulfill this obligation. In English the term *mosque* denotes any building used for Islamic worship but the Arabic term is *masjid*. There is no typical architectural form associated with mosques; indeed, many early mosques were converted Christian churches. In Istanbul the oldest mosques, those built in the sixteenth century, follow the same basic design as the city's much older Byzantine churches: both feature a central dome surrounded by smaller half-domes. Each mosque, however, has a *mihrab*, a semi-circular niche in a wall that helps orient worshippers toward Mecca for their daily prayers. Mosques are relatively empty compared to churches, because worshippers pray on the (usually carpeted) floor. While Friday is the day for hearing sermons in the mosque, Muslims are expected to pray seven days a week.

Two minarets of Istanbul's famous Sultanahmet Camii, better known as the "Blue Mosque," built in 1616. A *muezzin* calls the faithful to prayer from the *minaret* five times a day

Worshippers praying at Imam Mosque, Isfahan, Iran (Shutterstock)

One architectural feature that distinguishes all but the earliest mosques from churches is the presence of one or more tall, thin towers called *minarets*. An essential function of the minaret is to provide a place from which to sound the Call to Prayer. The person who gives the call is commonly called a *muezzin* (properly a *mu'adhdhin* in Arabic). When Muslims hear the call, they are expected to stop what they are doing and either pray or be still and silent. This applies to traffic as well as to television programs in many countries, although this degree of observance occurs more frequently in Islam-dominated states, such as Yemen, than in secular states such as Turkey.

Although Islam is primarily associated with the Middle East, it is a major religion in other areas as well, including much of the central third of Africa, northern India, parts of southeastern Europe (especially Albania and Bosnia), and parts of Southeast Asia, especially Malaysia, Indonesia, and the southern Philippines; indeed, Indonesia has a greater population of Muslims than any other country. Consequently, one hears the Call to Prayer in places outside the Middle East such as Singapore; Bangkok, Thailand; Manila, The Philippines; New Delhi, India; and Lagos, Nigeria, not to mention the United States. For overseas Muslims out of hearing range of a mosque, two substitute methods have been devised. Some believers tune into a radio station that broadcasts the Call to Prayer, while others rely on computer applications and clocks programmed to emit a recorded Call to Prayer five times a day.

Most branches of Islam are suspicious of music, which they view as overly sensual. In Islamic aesthetic theory, expressions that combine pitch and rhythm—all of which would usually be classified as "music" in Western culture—are divided into a higher-level category called *non-musiqa* (non-music) and a lower-level category called *musiqa* (music). All categories of *non-musiqa*, including the Call to Prayer, are considered "legitimate." These include readings from Islam's holy book, the Qur'an (or Koran), which are delivered in heightened speech, as well as chanted poetry. Some *musiqa* is also legitimate, including familial and celebratory songs, occupational music, and military band music, but the classical genres of *musiqa* as well as local types of "folk music" are considered "controversial," meaning that more fundamentalist Muslims generally discourage these traditions. At the bottom of this hierarchical scale is "sensuous music," such as American popular music, which is branded "illegitimate." However melodic, musical, or sensuous you may find the Call to Prayer, it is considered by Muslims to be "non-music" and unsensuous, and therefore legitimate. These views clearly illustrate that definitions of "music" are culture-based and not universal.

Site 2: Arabic *Taqasim* for *Ud* and *Buzuq*

First Impressions. The timbre of the opening instrument sounds very much like a guitar. The timbre of the following lute has a much brighter quality, the two together suggesting perhaps "belly dance" music, though with a much dreamier atmosphere. The melodic line seems spontaneous without a regular rhythm, the two instruments alternating the lead role. This kind of music is heard throughout the Arab world, including Turkey. We could be in Beirut (Lebanon), Damascus (Syria), Baghdad (Iraq), Cairo (Egypt), Tripoli (Libya), Amman (Jordan), Istanbul (Turkey) or any number of other places throughout the Middle East.

Aural Analysis. The deeper sounding instrument first heard in the example is the **ud**, a large pear-shaped lute with a short fretless neck. The *ud* is found throughout much of the Middle East and is associated mostly with the "classical" tradition rather than village styles. With a history going back to the eighth century C.E., the *ud* has undergone numerous changes over time in terms of size and number of strings. Today the instrument most typically has five

UD (Also, AL 'UD) A fretless, plucked pear-shaped lute that is found in Arabic music traditions and is the origin of certain lutes of Africa, Asia, and Europe.

Ali Jihad Racy, originally from Lebanon and now of the United States, plays the Arab *buzuq* (lute) (Linda Vartoogian/FrontRowPhotos)

Close-up of the face of an *ud* (lute) (see full picture Chapter 3, page 58).

"courses" of strings, a course being a pair tuned in unison, but *ud* with four, six, or even seven courses exist today. The musician can stop the strings anywhere on the neck, because there are no frets; this allows for fine gradations of intonation. The player uses a plectrum, or sometimes the fingers or fingernails of the right hand, to pluck the strings over the middle of the instrument's body. The Middle Eastern *ud* is considered the original form of an instrument that traveled to Asia—where it became the Chinese *pipa*, the Japanese *biwa*, and the Vietnamese *tyba*—and to Europe, where it became the European *lute*, which reached its greatest popularity during the Renaissance, then gradually fell from favor during the eighteenth century. Indeed, the word lute derives from the word *ud*, typically referred to as "*al'ud*," that is, the *ud*.

The brighter sounding instrument that appears second in the example is called the *buzuq* and is different in many ways from the *ud*. It is used in both classical and non-classical music and has a rounded body, nylon frets wrapped around its neck, and three double courses of strings played with a plectrum. One of the three double courses plays the melody, while the other two are primarily strummed to create intermittent drones. The *buzuq* probably derives from a similar instrument that the Turks call *saz*, and a form of it is found in Greece where it is known as the *bouzouki*.

MAQAM (Also, MAKAM)
Arabic/Turkish mode or system of rules and expectations for composition and improvisation.

The music in our example may sound improvised, because it is unmetered and the melodic line seems to spin out spontaneously. Middle Eastern "improvisation," however, should not be understood as a license for the players to do whatever they want. Rather, it provides an opportunity for the performer to compose, within strict boundaries, while playing. The usual Arabic term for the system within which improvisation occurs is **maqam** (*makam* in Turkish), a word loosely translated as "mode." As with the broad sense of the term *mode* (e.g., as when it is applied to the Indian *raga*), each *maqam* (pl., *maqamat*) consists not only of a scale but also of specific melodic forms, moods, and other non-musical associations; they are perhaps best viewed as "composition kits." In fact, there are many fully written ensemble compositions that include no improvisation but still follow the conventions of *maqam*.

Each *maqam* has a name and is characterized by a specific starting and ending note—as well as a set of specific pitches organized into two groups of four pitches, each called a *tetrachord* in English. Describing these pitches is difficult, however, because many differ in intonation from all twelve pitches of the Western equal-tempered chromatic scale. Arabic theorists have devised a system—which may vary slightly in actual practice—of twenty-four pitches in an octave, with each measuring fifty **cents** (i.e., a half semitone or quartertone). The basic seven steps of individual scales consist of combinations of two, three, four, or six quartertones. Two of these quartertones equal one Western semitone and four equal a Western whole tone, but three comprise an interval that is between a Western semitone and whole tone and six form an augmented (raised) second interval. If that sounds complex, indeed, it is.

To add to the complexity, a given performance may shift from one *maqam* to another. The complete track from which our excerpt comes begins in *maqam kurd*, with the pitches D, E♭, F, G, A♭, B♭ and octave C, but then shifts to *maqam rast* (F, G, A♭, B♭, C, D, E♭), to *maqam 'ajam* (F, G, A, B♭, C, D, E), to *maqam nahawand* (F, G, A♭, B♭, C, D♭, E♭), and, finally, to *maqam bayyati* (C, D♭, E♭, F, G, A♭, B♭). Theorists disagree on the number of *maqamat*: some claim there are up to seventy or more. There is also disagreement on the categorization of *maqamat*, which are divided into three families by some theorists. In our excerpted example, two musicians realize the *maqam* through improvisation—that is, they explore the characteristic intervals and melodic fragments gradually and spontaneously, alternating between *ud* and *buzuq*. When one musician is prominent, the other strums lightly, playing drone effects or modestly mimicking the phrases of the other. Any resulting simultaneity of notes is incidental and does not constitute harmony of any sort because the music is conceived monophonically. These improvisations may occur alone or as part of a longer suite that also includes fixed compositions in meter. An unmetered movement featuring improvisation is called a *taqasim* (or *taqsim*) when performed by instrumentalists, and *layali* or *mawwal* when performed by vocalists. Whereas musicians of nearly any skill level can play metered compositions, only the most skilled can play *taqasim* with any authority.

Cultural Considerations. In addition to being suspicious of the sensual aspects of music, Islamic aesthetics frowns on realistic representation in art, especially of the human form, to avoid the temptation toward idol worship. But as with sound, it may not always be obvious to outsiders what is considered art and what is not. Important mosques boast interiors covered with beautiful ceramic tiles, which certainly appear "artistic" to the Western eye, even if their designs are non-representational. Indeed, even Arabic calligraphy lends itself to incorporation into decorative design and can be considered artistic. Such designs are appreciated as expressions of spirituality and respect toward Allah, rather than secular indulgences in artistic splendor.

Within various cultures, an apparent correlation often exists between the degree of decoration found in art and architecture on the one hand and music on the other. In the case of Arabic music, this correlation is fairly compelling. Mosques characteristically have little

CENTS
A way to measure sound intervals with 1200 cents in an octave and a semitone measuring 100 cents.

LISTENING GUIDE

 CD 2.7 (1'57")

Chapter 8: Site 2
Arabic *Taqasim* Improvisation for *Ud* and *Buzuq*

Instruments: *Ud* (fretless plucked lute), *buzuq* (fretted plucked lute)

TIME	LISTENING FOCUS
0'00"	The *ud* begins the performance. Listen for the mellower timbre and lower range of this instrument compared with the brighter timbre of the *buzuq*. Also, note that the performance is in free rhythm throughout.
0'02"	The tonality of the improvisation is established with this sustained pitch.
0'31"	*Buzuq* enters, overlapping with the concluding phrases of the *ud*. Listen for the *ud* returning to the tonal center, but an octave lower than what was originally established. Note also that the *ud* does not drop out entirely, but just lowers its volume and melodic activity as the aural focus shifts to the *buzuq*.
0'51"	The aural focus shifts again to the *ud*. Note that the *buzuq* continues to play at a quieter volume and with less melodic activity.
1'15"	The aural focus shifts yet again to the *buzuq*. New tonalities are briefly established, but the phrase returns to the original tonal center at its conclusion.

Source: "Maqam Kurd," performed by Ali Jihad Racy, *buzuq*, and Simon Shaheen, *ud*, from *Taqasim: Improvisation in Arab Music*, Lyrichord LYRCD 7374, n.d. Used by permission, Lyrichord Discs Inc.

ETHNO-CHALLENGE (CD 2.7): The first phrase of this example (played on the *ud*) makes heavy use of a *tremolo* plucking technique (very fast on a single string). If not a musician yourself, locate a guitarist to show you the plucking technique and match the rhythmic density of this tremolo. Note how Western-trained musicians tend to pluck lutes by moving their forearm up and down, while Asian musicians pluck the instrument by rotating their forearm with a bent wrist.

undecorated space within them, and this is paralleled by the busy character of much Arabic music, in which the distinction between main notes and ornamentation is frequently blurred. Interestingly, whereas the ornamentation of classical *musiqa* is clearly categorized as "controversial," the same thing in a Call to Prayer is "legitimate" because the *adhan* is non-*musiqa*.

From the eighteenth century onward, Arabic decoration made a strong impression on Europeans. The French term *arabesque* came to denote European architectural embellishments featuring floral or curling patterns. In music the term denotes elaborately embellished melodies or countermelodies, such as Claude Debussy's *Deux arabesques* for piano. Few of these compositions, however, have any further relationship to Arabic music per se. Some

THE MIDDLE EAST

Though not considered to be artwork, the intense decoration of a mosque is analogous to the ornamentation of Arabic music. The recess in the center (*mihrab*) orients worshippers toward Mecca, Saudi Arabia, as seen in Istanbul's Beyazit Cammii (Mosque) of 1504

composers and musicians, particularly pianists, at Middle Eastern conservatories otherwise devoted to European music have sought to assert something of their roots by composing or improvising their own "arabesques" as well.

Arrival: Iran

Little visited these days by Western travelers, Iran, a country the size of Alaska or Quebec, is home to nearly seventy million people. Because much of the country is mountainous and rainfall is scanty except along the Gulf of Oman coast, Iran's large population often has to cope with difficult and dangerous conditions. Earthquakes are a constant concern in many areas, and when one occurs, typically large numbers of people die.

Iran, known as Persia until the twentieth century, is different from most of its neighbors on several accounts. The vast majority of its inhabitants share a non-Arab origin and speak Farsi, an Indo-European language related to that of the Kurds, who live at the juncture of Iran, Turkey, and Iraq. Most of Iran's population is Shia Muslim, Shia being the division of Islam that in many places is associated with the lower economic classes and that tends

257

to express itself more emotionally and militantly than Sunni Islam, which has become the mainstream form of Islam in most Middle Eastern countries. Shia Islam has a more developed clergy, the lower-ranking members being called *mullahs* and the higher-ranking ones *ayatollahs*. At various times, the more radical manifestations of the group's fundamentalist tendencies, such as the 1979 Iranian hostage crisis, have strained political relations between people and governments not only in the West but also among non-Shia Muslims and neighboring countries as well.

Persia has a long history, from its first flourishing in the sixth century B.C.E. under Cyrus the Great, through its periods of subjugation by Alexander the Great, the Parthians, the Turks, and the Mongols, to independence in the eighteenth century. Some consider its greatest period to have been during the rule of the Sasanian dynasty (third to seventh centuries C.E.). Modern Iran was created in the early twentieth century, along with a hereditary line of rulers called *shahs*, the last being Shah Muhammad Reza Pahlevi, who ruled until deposed by a revolution in 1979. Since 1979 Iran has been a theocratic democracy, ruled by an uneasy union of semi-official *ayatollahs* and official secular leaders.

Site 3: *Dastgah* for *Santur* and Voice

First Impressions. Iranian classical music often has a melancholy mood. Both the instrumentalist and vocalist in this example express this quality through pitch, rhythm, and dynamics. Even the vocal timbre is heartfelt, encouraging an intimate atmosphere that is typical of Persian classical performance. On first hearing, this Iranian example may sound rather similar to the Arabic example heard earlier. It begins with a stringed instrument

Dome of mosque and two minarets in Isfahan, Iran, one of the country's centers of Islam (Rex Shahriari)

playing a rhythmically free melody in an improvisatory manner. This section then gives way to a section featuring an unaccompanied female singer, who continues the rhythmically free approach. Despite the apparent similarities between Arabic and Iranian music (or, more properly, Persian music), however, the two systems are conceptually quite different.

Aural Analysis. Although the instrument that introduces our example is a chordophone, a careful listener will detect a percussiveness that distinguishes it from the plucked instruments heard earlier in the Arabic *ud* and *buzuq* duet. Indeed, the player is using two small wooden hammers to strike the strings. Organologically, such an instrument is called a "dulcimer" or a "hammered zither," because the strings are parallel to a soundboard without a neck, and struck by mallets. The instrument is a Persian **santur**, Iran's most distinctive and centrally important instrument. It is also considered by academics as the predecessor of the rest of the world's dulcimers, which are distributed as far as China and Korea in the east, Thailand and Vietnam in Southeast Asia, and Europe and the United States in the West. Indeed, some scholars even consider the European piano to be inspired in part by the *santur*, because pianos work on the same principle of sound production, except that keys flip the hammers against the strings.

SANTUR
A hammered zither from the Persian classical tradition.

The *santur* is constructed of a hardwood, trapezoidal-shaped body with a lower side around 3 feet (91 cm) in length and an upper side only around 14 inches (35 cm) across. Courses—groups—of four strings each stretch from tuning pins on the right over two rows of moveable bridges, in rows of thirteen and twelve respectively, to tunable anchor pins on the left. Players hammer the strings near the bridges on either side of the left row and on the left side only of the right row of bridges. If plain wooden hammers are used, the tone is more percussive than when players cover the mallet tips with felt or cloth, as is the case in our example. The *santur*, in slightly different forms, is also played in other Middle Eastern countries, though elsewhere it is not the centrally important instrument it is in Iran. Iconographical evidence dates the *santur* at least to the Babylonian period (1600–911 B.C.E.).

The vocal soloist who enters following the introductory section sings verses from the *Masnavi*, a book of mystical poetry written by the thirteenth-century poet Jalal al-Din Muhammad Rumi, who also founded the Mevlevi order of Sufi Islam, famed for its "whirling dervishes" (see Chapter 8, Site 5). Written in rhythmically free verse, the sung text begins with the following lines: "The grieving of the heart announces the state of love / And there is no illness like that of the heart." Persian music, like Arabic music, is based on an elaborate modal system (recall that the term *mode* refers to a "composition kit" used in improvisation), which in Persian music is called **dastgah** (plural, *dastgah-ha*). Officially there are twelve *dastgah*, each having seven pitches, plus a number of sub-modes called *avaz*. The track heard here is in *Dastgah shur* (also spelled *shour*), which uses the pitches C, D♭ (flat one quarter step), E♭, F, G, A♭, B♭, and C.

DASTGAH
Persian mode or system of rules and expectations for composition and improvisation.

There are, however, essential differences between the Arabic *maqam* and Persian *dastgah* systems. Unlike Arab musicians, who rely on an oral tradition of melodic phrases appropriate to a specific mode, Persian musicians have created a vast body of "composed" melodic phrases that amount to short compositions; these are called *gusheh*. Each *dastgah*, then, is learned by memorizing a variable number of these short *gusheh* compositions that can then be strung together to create a longer and more complete performance/composition. Groups of *gusheh* are organized around specific pitches of the *dastgah*, allowing the player to progress from the lowest (or home) note, called the *ist*, to higher pitches, where the musical

The Persian *santur* (dulcimer)

tension becomes greater. The number of *gusheh* employed in any particular performance depends on the performer's knowledge and needs, while the specifics of the *gusheh* used vary according to the player's "school" (or tradition). For pedagogical purposes, as well as to set a kind of national standard, scholars have collected and printed all the *gusheh* for all the *dastgah* in a book called the *radif*. Therefore, a student can memorize as many *gusheh* as might be needed for performance, but the *radif* itself differs from "school" to "school" ("school" being the tradition of a single master).

A complete performance of a *dastgah* typically unfolds in several sections and requires a substantial amount of time, because the sections can be quite different from each other. A typical performance's opening movement, called the *daramad*, is rhythmically free and emphasizes the lower-pitched *gusheh*. Following this is the *tahrir*, another section in free rhythm emphasizing melismatic melodic work. Then follow two metered pieces called *kereshmeh* and *chahar-mezrab* respectively, which are followed in turn by a repetition of the rhythmically free *daramad*. The track included here features only the first two of these sections.

Cultural Considerations. The classical *dastgah-ha* of Iran form a vast and flexible system, which allows musicians to create both fixed compositions and improvisations by stringing together numerous short compositional blocks. Naturally, this system also calls for an element of individual creativity, because Persian music-making is about far more than building Lego-like performances. The art comes in how the *gusheh* are joined to each other and in how they are subtly changed and elaborated. Because musicians belong to various "schools" and

THE MIDDLE EAST

LISTENING GUIDE

 CD 2.8 (2'55")

Chapter 8: Site 3
Iran: *Dastgah* for *Santur* and Voice

Vocals: Single female
Instruments: *Santur* (hammered zither)

TIME	LISTENING FOCUS
0'00"	*Santur* begins in free rhythm. Listen for the creative use of variations in volume. Also, note the free-flowing tonality, challenging the listener to hear a tonal center, which is only finally solidified on the last pitch in octaves heard just before the voice enters (0'59").
0'04"	Tonality focuses on G (fourth scale degree).
0'13"	Tonality focuses on F (third scale degree).
0'24"	Tonality focuses on D (tonal center).
0'50"	Tonality focuses on C (seventh scale degree).
0'59"	Tonality centers on D (tonal center) to anticipate the entrance of the vocalist.
1'02"	Vocalist enters, confirming the tonal center. Listen for her melismatic ornamentations that diverge from the tonal center briefly and then return.
1'38"	*Santur* plays solo break.
2'11"	Vocalist returns. Listen for the *santur* reinforcing the basic pitches of the melodic line.

Source: "Dastgah of Shour" by Mohamed Heydari, *santour*, and Khatereh Parvaneh, voice, from the recording entitled *Classical Music of Iran: The Dastgah Systems*, SF 40039, provided courtesy of Smithsonian Folkways Recordings. © 1991. Used by permission.

ETHNO-CHALLENGE (CD 2.8): Use an electronic tuner to determine how many cents "flat" the named scale degrees (C, D, F and G) are in this example compared with standard Western tuning (A = 440 Hz). Sing the fundamental pitch (D—quarter tone) throughout the vocal section to hear how the singer ornaments around this pitch.

consequently have learned different approaches to the *dastgah*, specific *gusheh* generally sound different from one performance to another. The use of measured rhythm in metrical cycles is no longer as significant in Persian music as it once was, and the metered pieces found in suites, such as the *chahar-mezrab*, employ fairly simple rhythmic patterns. While foreign audiences generally prefer the metered compositions because of their use of one or more drums and their steady beat, Persian musicians and connoisseurs value rhythmically free improvisations most highly for the display of refined musicianship they allow.

The Persian *tar*, a distinctively shaped lute with six strings

Although the *santur* is probably Iran's most distinctive instrument, other kinds of instruments are important as well. These include two plucked lutes, the *sehtar* and the *tar*. The latter's skin-covered body has a distinctive shape, resembling the number "8." Also important is the round-bodied bowed lute called *kemancheh*. One aerophone, the *ney*, an end-blown notch flute found throughout the Middle East, is commonly heard. The main percussion instrument is a goblet-shaped, single-headed drum called the *dombak* or *zarb*, which resembles the Arabic *darabuka*.

Arrival: Egypt

If any nation typifies the Middle East, it is Egypt. Her ancient civilization, nearly as old as civilization itself, seems to live on through incredible relics—the pyramids, the Sphinx, great temples, hieroglyphics, wall paintings, and mummies—and is symbolized by the River Nile, which flows thousands of miles northward out of Africa to the Mediterranean Sea. This nation, which constitutes the northeast corner of Africa, is smaller than Canada's Ontario province, but has a population of eighty-three million. That the land can support so many is surprising considering how much of Egypt is desert. Most of the fertile land is found along the Nile, where many crops, including great quantities of cotton, are grown. The Suez Canal, opened in 1869, connects the Red Sea to the Mediterranean Sea and separates the main part of Egypt from the Sinai Peninsula.

Although ancient paintings depict musicians playing harps, lyres, lutes, flutes, double reeds, and other kinds of instruments, little is known about the sound of Egyptian music

THE MIDDLE EAST

Egypt's Great Sphinx of Giza, which along with the pyramids, is a symbol of ancient Egypt (Denise A. Seachrist)

until long after contact with Islam. However, coastal Egypt, particularly Alexandria, was part of the ancient Mediterranean civilization, where Islamic-period Arab music theory was brought to an intellectual zenith during the first millennium of the Christian era. Music in modern-day Egypt reflects a welter of more recent influences, including European art music, which has made Egypt—at least urban Egypt—a center of European musical culture outside Europe. For example, Italian composer Giuseppe Verdi's opera *Aida*, whose music is European but whose locale is set in Egypt, was commissioned by Khedive Ismail of Egypt in 1869 for the opening of the Cairo Opera House.

Site 4: *Takht* Instrumental Ensemble

First Impressions. With its catchy beat and sinuous melody, this piece may bring to mind the image of a veiled belly dancer swaying gracefully before an audience. Some of the instruments might seem familiar, including one that sounds like a tambourine, but the tuning of a number of the intervals heard sound "off," one in particular.

Aural Analysis. Songs accompanied by instrumental ensembles pervade Egyptian musical life. They run the gamut from religious songs—as heard in this case—to folk songs, wedding songs, and love songs. Egyptian instrumental ensembles may also, however, perform on their own, without a vocalist. The musical systems found among Egyptians generally contrast slower-paced and unmetered music played by a single musician with clearly metered music played by a group, with or without a vocal part. In contrast to the improvisatory approach that is such an important part of solo performance, instrumental groups play fixed compositions. In Egypt the typical ensemble is called a **takht** and consists of three to five players, though more are possible. In modern times these ensembles have often been enlarged through the addition of new instruments, some borrowed from Europe, what some Middle Easterners jokingly call the "Near North".

Most of the melodic instruments found in *takht* ensembles are chordophones, such as bowed lutes, plucked lutes, and zithers, but at least one aerophone, the end-blown cane flute (*ney*), is nearly always present as well. Among the most prominent of the plucked lutes is a pear-shaped *ud* lute. Of the bowed lutes, the *kemanja*, an unfretted spike fiddle, is most prevalent, but today *takht* ensembles may also incorporate violins, 'cellos, and even string

TAKHT
An Arabic music ensemble including zithers, bowed and plucked lutes, drums, aerophones, and sometimes non-traditional instruments.

263

WORLD MUSIC: A GLOBAL JOURNEY

A small *takht* ensemble. Front row: Ebrahim Eleish: *ud*, lute; George Sawa: *qanun*, zither; Suzanne Meyers Sawa: *darabuka*, drum. Back row: Dahlia Obadia: Middle Eastern dancer, and Sonia Belkacem, singer. (George Sawa)

QANUN (ALSO, KANUN)

A plucked zither used in Turkish and Arabic music traditions, prominent in *takht* ensembles.

basses. The most important zither is the **qanun**, an unusually shaped, four-sided instrument resembling an autoharp that has an amazing number of tuning mechanisms to allow for various tunings (see photo on page 26). Our recorded example features *ud* (plucked lute), violin (bowed lute), *ney* (end-blown flute), *qanun* (plucked zither), *riqq* (tambourine), and *tablah* (goblet drum). The melodic instruments perform the same melody but with slight variations, resulting in a slightly heterophonic structure.

Three types of drums may be found in *takht* ensembles: the *duff*, the *riqq*, and the *tabla*. The *duff* is a small, single-headed drum sometimes having snares; the *riqq* is similar but has pairs of small cymbals inserted into the frame that jingle when the head is struck (i.e., it is a tambourine). The *tabla* is a small, goblet-shaped single-headed drum similar to others with different names found throughout the Middle East but is not related to the Indian pair of drums of the same name.

Arabic drumming is highly organized, and much of it is conceived as being in closed cycles of beats. The standard, named patterns realized by drummers are known in Arabic as *iqa* (plural, *iqa-at*), best translated as *rhythmic modes* in English. Using named drum strokes, drummers continuously play a given mode or cycle, with greater or lesser degrees of elaboration and ornamentation, to reinforce the metrical organization of a composition's melodic parts.

Even when Egyptian composers create fixed pieces, they work within the Arab modal system called *maqam*, which governs the choice of pitches and intervals and offers standard

8 THE MIDDLE EAST

Collection of Middle Eastern hand drums: (clockwise from left) Moroccan *bendir* with snares inside, Persian *daf* with internal ring chains, Nubian *tar* from southern Egypt and northern Sudan, and Arab *riqq* or *def*; (center) Egyptian *tabla* goblet drum, called *darbuka* in Turkey (N. Scott Robinson)

melodic patterns as well. Compositions are also divided into certain well-known set forms, with names such as *dulab*, *tahmlla*, and *bashraf*. Our recording is an example of the last form, which originated during the Turkish Ottoman Empire, and features the alternation of a recurring theme *(tasllm)*—called a "rondo" or "ritornello" in European music—and new melodic material. This form is often used, as in this case, for light music. In a *bashraf* composition, the change from one section to the next is sometimes signaled by a change in the mode being used. The main mode used in this *bashraf* has a prominent augmented second interval right above the home pitch and could be expressed as C, D, E, F, G, A♭, B, C. Certain of the pitches, especially the F, sound out of tune to Western ears, as their intonation differs from the Western equal-tempered scale. A second scale could be expressed as C, D, E, F, G, A, B, C and sounds more familiar as far as tuning goes.

During the mid-twentieth century, an orchestra-sized variant of the *takht* ensemble appeared. Known as *firqa*, these larger ensembles sometimes include a chorus in addition to the principal vocalist. As with the smaller ensembles, the instruments used are mostly chordophones and aerophones, the former including most Arab possibilities plus members of the Western violin family, and the latter being mostly end-blown flutes of the *ney* variety. While traditional ensembles play heterophonically, performances by modernized *firqa* ensembles are usually highly arranged, with varied orchestration and occasional harmony.

LISTENING GUIDE

 CD 2.9 (9'41")

Chapter 8: Site 4

Egypt: *Takht* Instrumental Ensemble

Note: The below description was contributed by Scott Marcus, the lead member of the ensemble in this recording.

Instruments: *ud* (plucked lute), violin (bowed lute), *ney* (end-blown flute), *qanun* (plucked zither), *riqq* (tambourine), and *tablah* (goblet drum)

TIME	LISTENING FOCUS
0'00"	The set starts (with *ud*) in *maqam nahawand* on G, similar to the Western minor (G A B♭ c d e♭ f♯ g) except that the minor third is significantly lower in pitch than the piano's equal-tempered minor third. Many (theorists) understand this third to be a Pythagorean minor third (294 cents as opposed to 300 cents), although performers do not think in terms of cents.
0'58"	Next, we play a *dulab* in *maqam nahawand* on G. *Dulab* is an instrumental genre. The compositions are very short. *Dulab*s serve to set the *maqam* of the following pieces; in this sense, they serve the function of a prelude, although note that 'prelude' is a Western term that is not used in Arab music. *Dulabs* are generally older compositions, understood to come from an unknown past: no known composer, they were part of the tradition in the late nineteenth century, but we do not know when the genre or these specific compositions appeared. As in our example, *dulabs* commonly move between two different rhythmic modes, the first called *wahdah*, and the second called *maqsum*.
	The pattern for *wahdah* is D – MT – KT – (i.e., dum – ma tak – ka takk –).
	The pattern for *maqsum* is DT – TD – T – (dumm takk – takk dumm – takk –). Both of these patterns take the same amount of time. In staff notation, they are written as 4/4. In our *dulab*, there are six repetitions (six measures) of *wahdah*, then seven repetitions of *maqsum*, then a return to *wahdah*.
1'40	Next we have a violin *taqasim* on a *wahdah* ostinato in *maqam nahawand* on G.
2'42"	Full ensemble returns.
3'23"	Next a *ney* (end-blown reed flute) *taqasim* in *maqam nahawand* on G on a G drone (no ostinato).
4'28"	Then a *qanun* (plucked zither) *taqasim* on a ciftetelli ostinato. This ostinato is twice as long as the *wahdah* or *maqsum* rhythms, and thus could be understood as an 8/4: (D – MT – K T – D – D – T –). The first half is similar to the *wahdah* pattern. The *qanun* includes a modulation to *maqam nawa athar* on G: G A B♭ c♯ d e♭ f♯ g.
5'37"	(Pause) Then we play a high energy instrumental composition composed by Muhammad 'Abd al-Wahhab (*c*.1900–1991). This composition occurs in the middle of a lengthy song that 'Abd al-Wahhab composed for the singer Umm Kulthum (*c*.1900–1975). The song is called "Fakkaruni." (Note each instrument is highlighted with brief solo passages.)

THE MIDDLE EAST

7'38" In the middle of this instrumental piece, we feature a drum solo. The drum, called tablah, in Egypt, is metal with a plastic head (the norm since the old-style clay drums with skin heads lost out in the mid- to late 1980s).

8'36" We conclude after the drum solo by returning briefly to the Fakkaruni composition.

Source: A short *waslah* performance in *maqam nahawand* and *maqam nawa athar*, performed by members of the University of California, Santa Barbara Middle East Ensemble, Dr. Scott Marcus, director, 2011. Used by permission.

ETHNO-CHALLENGE (CD 2.9): Find and record a song by a local musician or group. Play the recording back to them and ask for a description of the piece from an "insider" view. Create a Listening Guide, such as that above, based on their commentary.

Cultural Considerations. In addition to accompanying singers, *takht* ensembles also accompany dance. From the perspective of most Westerners, Middle Eastern dance is synonymous with "belly dance," which is often assumed to be erotic because of the undulating pelvic movements that are so stereotypical. In fact, this dancing is a highly skilled activity that is often appreciated for its technical merits. Traditionally, the dancers who mastered the most rapid hip movements were called *ghawazi*, a term derived from the name of the Ottoman coins that adorned their costumes. The nearest equivalent to the Western conception of belly dance is the **raqs sharqi**, which varies from performances by fully clothed artistic dancers to stripteases. Interestingly, the latter were historically performed by foreigners rather than Arab women, because Arab women could never hope to be married if they had been associated with erotic displays. Another distinctive form is the *sham'idan* (candelabrum dance), so called because the dancer performs with a large, heavy candelabrum with lighted candles balanced on her head. Some theorize that these dances once symbolized fertility for Egyptians, but others claim that they came from the Halab and the Ghajar, two Rom tribes from India who entered Egypt most likely with the Ottoman Turkish armies in 1517.

Dance in Egypt is also closely associated with religious expression, particularly among members of the more mystically inclined sects. Dance in a religious context can bring participants to great spiritual heights, including states of ecstasy and even possession.

Ali Jihad Racy, a noted scholar and performer of Arabic music heard on CD 2.7—Arabic Taqasim, asserts that the essential difference between European music and Middle Eastern music is that the former strives for the representation of images and concepts (including structural patterns), and the latter strives to evoke intense emotions in both the performers and the listeners. These emotions can affect people in both positive and negative ways, a concept known as *ethos* to the Greeks and *ta'thir* to the Arabs. Indeed, for Arabs, music has the power to heal and to bring people closer to union with God. As Racy remarks in his book *Making Music in the Arab World*, "In Arab culture, the merger between music and emotional transformation is epitomized by the Arab concept of **tarab**" (p. 5). Although much Arabic music can be described in purely technical terms (e.g., the modal system), the goal of Arab music-making is not so much to create clever structures as to bring listeners into a state of ecstasy. Although this ecstasy can have a religious dimension—by bringing the hearer

RAQS SHARQI
The Arabic name for what is commonly referred to by outsiders as "belly dance."

TARAB
Arabic word for a state of emotional transformation or ecstasy achieved through music.

WORLD MUSIC: A GLOBAL JOURNEY

Belly dance performance accompanied only by violin and *darabuka* (behind dancer) (Andrew Shahriari)

into spiritually heightened states—music's sensual aspect is still viewed as suspicious by Islamic theologians, and consequently, as we have read, *musiqa* is proscribed from the mosque.

Arrival: Sufism

Sufism is frequently described as the "mystical" branch of Islam. While Sufis regard themselves as being part of the Sunni tradition and as having the same core religious values as all branches of Islam—namely, belief in Muhammad as the last prophet of Allah—their interpretation of the Qur'an allows for activities, especially with regards to music, that are discouraged or prohibited by most other Muslims. A fundamental philosophy of Sufism is that a person can become one with Allah through the elimination of the ego, a belief rejected by orthodox Islam. This controversial belief results in varied opinions of Sufi practices. Many Muslims consider Sufis devoted followers of Allah, but others view them as heretics whose ritual practices are sacrilegious. In Turkey, Sufis have been held in high esteem for centuries. The Mevlevi sect, one of the best-known Sufi orders, was founded there in the thirteenth century and exerted great influence on rulers of the region for several centuries.

The term *Sufi* is derived from the Arabic word *suf*, meaning "wool," in reference to the woolen robes worn by devotees. Sufi brotherhoods are numerous, each having its own rules and rituals. Many Sufis seclude themselves in monasteries, called *tekke* or *khanegah*, in order to focus exclusively on their spiritual quest to know Allah. Others practice trades in the secular world and perform the sacred rites of their brotherhood only on specific occasions. Still others commit themselves to an itinerant existence. This latter lifestyle earned Sufis a secondary title, *dervish*, which loosely translates as "beggar," as the wandering clerics rely on alms from the general public for their survival. *Dervish* is the term most frequently used in the Western world for those Sufi orders that present public performances of sacred music and dance as a means of disseminating knowledge about their religion.

Site 5: Sufi *Dhikr* Ceremony

DHIKR (Also, ZIKR)
A Sufi devotional act in which believers chant the name of God with the goal of entering an ecstatic state.

First Impressions. Unlike most Islamic worship, with its solemn mood, Sufi music is often upbeat, though with an undertone of seriousness. This performance, a hymn recorded in Turkey, is almost like a spinning top: it seems repeatedly to slip and then straighten itself, until it finally slows and comes to rest. Accompanied by several instruments, the voices swirl round and round and up and down. This exuberant celebration of love for Allah then gives way to a more solemn mood as a single voice cries out over the hearty chant of fellow worshippers.

Aural Analysis. Sufi hymns, known as *ilahi*, vary in mood and instrumentation. The *ud*, *qanun*, *kamance* (also spelled *kemanja* and *kamence*; a spiked bowed fiddle), *ney*, and *bandir* (a frame drum) are the most common instruments, although the *tanbur* (a fretted plucked lute), *riqq* (tambourine), and occasionally the *kudum* (a kettle drum) and *halile* (cymbals) are sometimes included as well. The *ney* is particularly important in Sufi ceremonies and is often used for extended solos.

Vocal performance in Sufi music belongs to one of three categories. The most prominent type is associated with the male vocal specialists known as *zakirler*, who perform metered passages in unison. This type of singing is heard in the first section of the track. The melodic contour of this vocal performance continually rises and falls, supported by the melodic instruments, while the *bandir* provides a steady duple-metered pulse. The tonal center shifts frequently, keeping the music always slightly off-balance. While the text setting is primarily syllabic, melismatic descents occur at the peaks of concluding phrases.

After this "swirling" singing, the tempo slows and the other two vocal categories are heard simultaneously. In the foreground, the vocal soloist chants rhythmically free melismatic passages akin to the *muezzin*'s Call to Prayer. This style of singing is known as *kaside*. Some instruments accompany the voice, providing key melodic pitches for the vocalist's reference rather than complete melodic passages. This allows the vocalist to improvise his melodic phrases without being bound to a specific melody or rhythm. Other instruments do, however, follow a pulse, which is articulated by the remaining *dervishes*, whose performance is an example of the third vocal category. The chorus sings a deep, raspy chant, consisting of repetitions of the phrase "*Hu, hu*," meaning "It is He" ("He" being Allah).

LISTENING GUIDE

CD 2.10 (1'54")

Chapter 8: Site 5
Turkey: Sufi *Dhikr* Ceremony

Vocals: Male vocal ensemble. Single male vocal with male group chant.
Instruments: *Ney* (end-blown flute), *kemanja* (bowed lute), *ud* (plucked lute), *kanun* (plucked zither), *bandir* (frame drum).

TIME	LISTENING FOCUS
0'00"	Listen for the "swirling" ascending–descending vocal line and matching melodic instruments following a steady duple meter. Note the reference to "Allah" in the text that corresponds to an ascending melodic contour.
0'06"	Text changes and several voices drop out.
0'21"	Tonality shifts, but note the continued use of a "swirling" melodic line that now emphasizes a descending contour.
0'35"	Tonality shifts again, but continues with the descending melodic phrases.
0'50"	"Allah, Allah" refrain returns.
1'05"	Vocal ensemble drops out and tempo slows.
1'09"	Listen for the regular pulsation of the ensemble's hearty chanting. The instruments continue to be heard, but the melodic instruments are minimally active.
1'16"	A single male vocalist chants a freely rhythmic and melismatic text setting.
1'28"	The *ney* (flute) can be heard briefly, supporting the lead vocalist's melodic line.

Source: "Sufi Hymn (Turkish)," performed by the Jarrahi Dervishes and recorded by J. During, Konya, Turkey, 1982, from the recording entitled *The Silk Road: A Musical Caravan*, SF 40438, provided courtesy of Smithsonian Folkways Recordings. © 2002. Used by permission.

ETHNO-CHALLENGE (CD 2.10): Perform the "whirling" dance of the Sufis by spinning continuously throughout this example. As you spin, experiment with moving your hands away from your body and tilting your head to the side. Note what body positions encourage a "disconnected" feeling more quickly.

Cultural Considerations. For Sufis, chants provide the believer with the opportunity to attain union with Allah. Indeed, they believe that music is a primary way of reaching this ultimate goal. Sound is thought to be a vital link between the spiritual and physical realms. Whereas orthodox Islam, as we have seen, generally discourages musical performance, especially in the context of worship, Sufis emphasize its use as a means of heightening spirituality. Rather than believing that music tempts the soul away from Allah, Sufis assert that music merely strengthens a person's inclinations and temperament. Thus, music performed in religious contexts with the intention of uplifting the soul is acceptable and often necessary, whereas music played in the context of sensual indulgence only reinforces the sinful nature of the flesh.

One of the most important contexts for Sufi musical performances is the *sema* ritual, where the devotional act known as *dhikr* (also called *zikr*), a name that translates as "remembrance" is performed. The practice of *dhikr* differs among Sufi orders, but the best-known form of the ceremony is associated with the Mevlevi sect founded by **Jalal al-Din Muhammad Rumi** (1207–1273 C.E.). In this version of the ceremony—which is particularly associated with the December 17 memorial celebrations held in Rumi's honor in Konya, Turkey—music and dance are often performed for the public. The Western notion of Sufis as "Whirling Dervishes" is derived from this and similar ceremonies because the dances require performers to spin in a circle on one foot for an extended period at varying speeds. When a dancer is spinning at his fastest, his white robes become a blur, much like an ice skater doing a final spin at the Olympics.

A Sufi devotee uses music and dance in these ceremonies to progress through the evolutionary stages of the soul toward the ultimate goal of experiencing the absolute reality of Allah. By chanting the names of the ninety-nine divine attributes of Allah while performing specific ritualistic movements, Sufis enter a trance-like state in which they become spiritually ecstatic. Sufis describe this feeling as "soaring." Many Sufi ritual performances are hidden from the public and involve such amazing feats as piercing the body with swords, chewing on glass, or walking on hot coals to demonstrate the power of Allah working through the individual believer. Our recorded example is typical of the music found in private ceremonies.

The "whirling" dances of the Mevlevi sect are also intended to help believers achieve a spiritually ecstatic state. As the musicians play, the dancer rises and removes his black

JALAL AL-DIN MUHAMMAD RUMI
Sufi saint of Islamic mysticism known for his poems and as the founder of the Mevlevi religious order.

Sufi Muslims of the Mevlevi ('Whirling') sect, perform the *sema* ritual on stage in New York (Jack Vartoogian/ FrontRowPhotos)

outer garment, which symbolizes the darkness of the secular world. Beneath this outer garment are inner white robes that symbolize the purity of Allah. As the dancer spins, he raises his right hand toward the sky and lowers his left hand toward the earth. This action represents Allah handing down his divine grace to all humanity. The spinning motion symbolizes the movement of the heavenly bodies—that is, the earth and moon—and helps the dancer to detach himself from the material plane and achieve a heightened sense of spiritual awareness.

Arrival: Judaism

While Judaism is practiced by more than fifteen million adherents throughout North Africa, Western Asia, Europe, and the Americas, its "homeland," the state of Israel, is in the Middle East. A nation half the size of Switzerland, Israel was created on May 14, 1948, from an area formerly known as Palestine. Sometimes called "The Holy Land," Israel is of great religious significance for Jews, Christians, and Muslims, as it has what are perhaps the most revered historical sites or monuments for each group: the Wailing Wall for the Jews, the Church of the Nativity for Christians, and the Dome of the Rock mosque for Muslims and Jews. As a result this land has been fought over for more than one thousand years, going back to the time before the medieval Crusades. Traditionally, people of all three religions lived together in the region—and they still do—but since 1948 there has been continuous tension over land, water, and religious and political rights and privileges.

Israel is a nation with both "traditional" (i.e., Asian/North African) and immigrant populations (European, American, Asian, and African). Historically, most Jews lived in the

The Temple Mount in Jerusalem, including the Western Wall and the Dome of the Rock (Shutterstock)

THE MIDDLE EAST

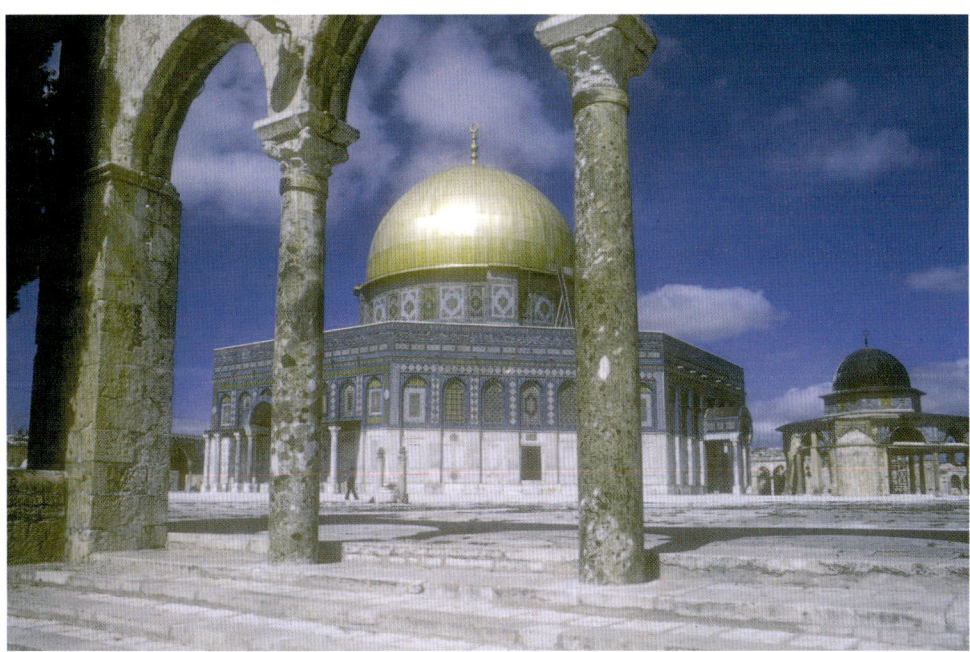

Jerusalem's Dome of the Rock, called *Qubbat As-Sakhrah* in Arabic and built between 687 and 691, is a revered shrine (*mashhad*) for Muslims

"Diaspora"—that is, the countries outside the Middle East to which they spread—often suffering discrimination and marginalization. In Europe, Jews were long kept at arm's length from the mainstream populations but allowed to establish themselves in certain occupations, music being one of them. Over the centuries, in many times and places, Jews were made scapegoats for Europe's problems. Following the rise of Adolf Hitler in the 1930s, the Nazi Germans began a policy designed to exterminate the Jewish population, not just in Germany but also throughout Europe, and during the 1940s, before the liberation in 1945 by the Allies, the Nazis murdered some six million Jews in what came to be called The Holocaust. In reaction to this history of oppression, Zionism, a Jewish political movement begun in central Europe in 1897, advocated the founding of a Jewish state that would be a refuge for Jews worldwide. The establishment of Israel in 1948 realized that goal, though European Jews had already been migrating to Palestine for many years.

Jews in the Diaspora belong to several distinct communities. The term *Sephardic* originally referred to Jews forced out of Spain by King Ferdinand and Queen Isabella at the end of the fifteenth century but has come to be applied to any Jew of North African or Asian origin. Jews from Europe are called Ashkenazi Jews, and because they were the primary advocates for the establishment of Israel, they tend to dominate modern Israeli politics. The musical traditions of the two communities are quite different, and among Sephardic Jews there are many distinct local traditions, such as that of Jews from Yemen.

The terms *Jewish music* and *Israeli music* are difficult to define. The former refers not only to music (both chanting and singing) heard in tabernacle ritual but also to non-liturgical songs of many sorts having Jewish content. Israeli music can only be defined as the sum of its parts, because Israeli society is partially secular and comprises people from all over the world. Perhaps the best-known representative of "Israeli music" is **klezmer**, a kind of European-derived dance music mostly developed in the United States and influenced by

KLEZMER
A European-derived dance music commonly associated with Jewish celebrations, influenced by jazz and other non-Jewish styles.

jazz and other non-Jewish styles. We have chosen to represent the religious side of Jewish identity through a genre from the synagogue, liturgical cantillation.

Site 6: Jewish *Shofar* and Liturgical Cantillation

First Impressions. This unaccompanied male singing seems rather random and hardly tuneful, suggesting that the text itself might be more important than the performance's musical qualities. Not being able to understand the words is a serious obstacle in this case. There is one scale interval in particular that sounds Middle Eastern.

Aural Analysis. The musical elements present in our example are mostly functional, that is, they serve primarily to give the text prominence. If you listen carefully, you'll detect eight pitches spanning slightly more than one octave. In notation, from low to high, they are D, E, F, G♯, A, B, C, E. Two of them seem more important than the others, the A and lower E. These are the reciting pitches, with E being the resting point that gives a feeling of finality. The G♯ is what gives the chant its Middle Eastern flavor, because G♯ down to F natural is an augmented second. Descending from G♯ to F also produces an incomplete feeling only relieved by hitting the lower E. There is no regular meter; rather, the words are delivered in "speech rhythm." While the text setting is generally syllabic, there are also some melismas present.

Toledo, Spain, once the home for a large Jewish community, preserves the Synagogue of Santa Maria la Blanca, a twelfth-century building with Moorish arches. It was later converted into a church in 1411 when the Jews were driven from Toledo

THE MIDDLE EAST

Jewish cantillation, called *nusach*, is an oral tradition, though some scholars have attempted to notate the chants of particular singers. We say "attempted" because notating a freely sung text is an inexact science. The version performed here is attributed to a European singer named Zev Weinman and has been notated in a collection of service music in transcription. Tabernacle singers (called *cantors*) construct melodies from a body of traditional modes and melodic formulas that can be freely interpreted. The text chanted in the audio example is "L'dor vador nagid godlecha" and is sung in Hebrew, the sacred language of Judaism as well as the national language of Israel. The words, taken from a Sabbath morning service, are:

L'dor vador nagid godlecha	From generation to generation we will declare Thy greatness,
u l'neitzach n'tzachim	and to all eternity
k'dushatcha nakdish.	we will proclaim Thy holiness.
V'shivchacha, eloheinu,	And Thy praise, O our God,
mipinu lo yamush l'olam va'ed,	shall never depart from our mouths,
Ki el melekh gadol v'kadosh ata.	Because Thou art a great and holy God and King.
Baruch atah adonai,	Blessed art Thou, O Lord,
ha-el hakadosh.	our holy God.

While the above text is exactly as printed in the prayer book, the performer, Peter Laki, added the following comments:

1. I sang using an Ashkenazi pronunciation, which is like an Eastern European dialect. The transliteration follows official Israeli Hebrew, which is the Sephardic pronunciation.
2. Twice I sang "kel" instead of "el" (third line from bottom and last line). This is because "El" is the name of G-d, which the Orthodox don't pronounce unless they are actually at the synagogue. They add a "K" to "disguise" the name.

LISTENING GUIDE

CD 2.11 (1'01")

Chapter 8: Site 6
Judaism: Jewish *Shofar* and Liturgical Cantillation

Vocal: Single male
Instrument: *Shofar* (trumpet)

TIME	LISTENING FOCUS
0'00"	*Shofar* sounds on two pitches followed by cantor.
0'27"	*L'dor vador nagid godlecha* ("From generation to generation we will declare Thy greatness,")
0'31"	*u l'neitzach n'tzachim k'dushatcha nakdish* ("and to all eternity we will proclaim Thy holiness").

0'36"	*V'shivchacha, eloheinu, mipinu lo yamush l'olam va'ed* ("And Thy praise, O our God, shall never depart from our mouths,")
0'42"	*Ki el melekh gadol v'kadosh ata.* ("Because Thou art a great and holy God and King").
0'46"	*Baruch atah adonai,* ("Blessed art Thou, O Lord,")
0'51"	*ha-el hakadosh.* ("our holy God").

Source: "Cycle of 10 Calls During Additional Service" by David Hausdorff, from the recording entitled *Kol Háshofar (Call of the Shofar)*, Folkways Records FW8922, provided courtesy of Smithsonian Folkways Recordings, 1957. Used by permission. "L'dor vador" sung by Dr. Peter Laki, recorded by Terry E. Miller, Kent, Ohio, 2005. Used by permission.

ETHNO-CHALLENGE (CD 2.11): Visit a local synagogue and observe a service.

TORAH
In Judaism the first five books (*Pentateuch*) of the Bible or more generally, all sacred literature.

SHOFAR
A Jewish ritual trumpet made of a ram's horn.

Cultural Considerations. The term *cantillation* is used to denote a kind of heightened speech that is between speaking and singing. Most religions of the world employ some kind of cantillation, because full-fledged singing is often forbidden or discouraged for various reasons, its sensuality being the common objection. In some cases, religious ritualists are forbidden to sing; thus, even if the cantillation they perform is quite melodic, it is still not referred to as "singing." It appears to be true throughout the world that sacred texts or holy words are thought to have more authority and mystery, and to be more clearly understood, if delivered in some form of heightened speech. The human relationship with the spirit or spiritual world requires an extraordinary form of dialogue, one that takes it outside the realm of ordinary speech or song.

Jews worship the same god as Christians and Muslims, but Judaism traces continuous communication with that god during their more than 4,000-year history through a line of prophets beginning with Abraham. Judaism is especially distinguished by its careful attention to sacred law, which requires Jews to observe greater or lesser numbers of specific requirements depending on their position in the continuum from Ultra-Orthodox to Reformed. The audio example comes from the Orthodox tradition, though Conservative and Reformed Jews may also chant in this style.

The sacred texts of Judaism, written in Hebrew, constitute what is called the Old Testament by Christians. Of these books, the first five, called the **Torah** or *Pentateuch*, are most important. Sacred writings, both biblical and non-biblical (as in the present example) are read in heightened speech, or cantillation. Such readings may occur either in a synagogue or in a home. The term *service* describes liturgical rituals that can be held several times each day, though those held at the beginning of the Sabbath (also called Shabbat, Friday evening after sundown) and during the Sabbath (Saturday, before sundown) are most important. Jews also celebrate their religion through an annual cycle of festivals, as well as through more private rites of passage such as circumcision, *bar mitzvah* or *bat mitzvah* (held when, respectively, a young man or woman comes of age), and marriage. In Orthodox Judaism only males may recite the scriptures and liturgy. The use of musical instruments is generally avoided, but there are exceptions. Jews traditionally have used a ram's horn, called a **shofar**, as a ritual trumpet blown to mark divisions in a service.

THE MIDDLE EAST

A Jewish ram's horn trumpet or *shofar* played by a rabbi in Yemen (Shutterstock)

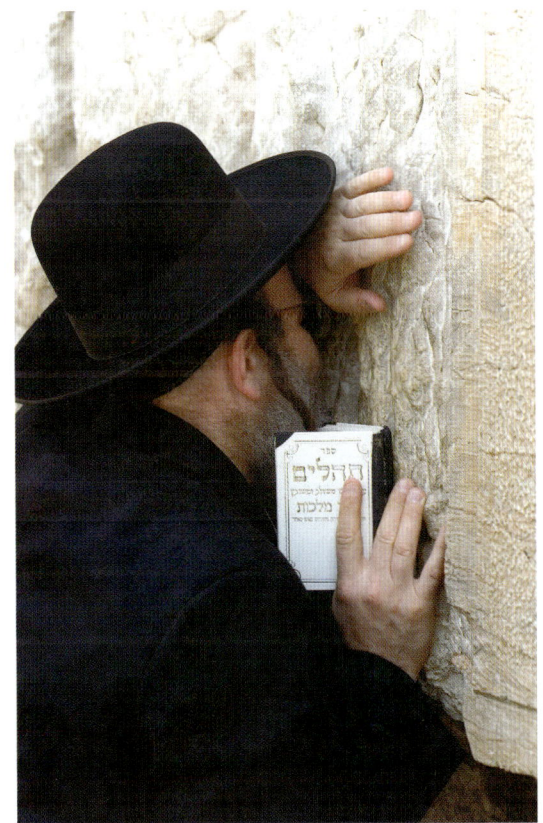

An Orthodox Jew praying at the Western (or Wailing) Wall in Jerusalem (Shutterstock)

After the Jews failed in their revolt against their Roman conquerors in 70 C.E., the great temple at Jerusalem was destroyed, leaving only the "Wailing Wall," and the Jews were dispersed to many parts of the world. Jewish congregations today tend to be either Sephardic or Ashkenazi, though mixed tabernacles exist. Sephardic congregations preserve musical practices derived from the *maqamat* tradition of Arabic modal music. Ashkenazi congregations practice what is called the "Jerusalem-Lithuanian" style characteristic of Eastern European Jews. The audio example represents the tradition common to Eastern Europe, especially Poland, German, and Hungary. In Ashkenazi tabernacles the main ritualist who intones the sacred texts—the cantor—sings in a European style and may be accompanied by an organ in contexts where instruments are permitted, especially in Reformed congregations. While cantors in both traditions are not considered singers per se because what they do is technically "cantillation," many cantors are in fact fine singers and have turned their cantillation into a performance art rather than merely a way to declaim texts. Indeed, some, such as Robert Merrill, were also renowned opera virtuosi.

Questions to Consider

1. How has Islam shaped conceptions of music for the peoples of the Middle East?

2. What is modal improvisation? Is it primarily a compositional or a freely expressive form of performance?

3. Because the Islamic Call to Prayer and Jewish biblical cantillation clearly have musical characteristics, why are they not considered "music" or "singing"?

4. What are the key factors that make Persian classical music different from Arabic music?

5. How do Sufi attitudes toward music differ from attitudes found in the other branches of Islam?

6. Taking into consideration the material discussed in Chapters 3 and 10, what are some of the musical relationships between the Middle East and Europe, especially in terms of instruments and musical styles?

On Your Own Time

Visit the textbook website to find these resources for further exploration on your own.

Middle East

DVD/Website: *Empire of Faith.* Dir. Robert H. Gardner. PBS Documentary, 2005.
http://www.pbs.org/empires/islam/

Book: Regev, Motti, and Edwin Seroussi. *Popular Music and National Culture in Israel.* Berkeley: University of California Press, 2004.
http://www.ucpress.edu/ebook.php?isbn=9780520936881

Iran

Book: Farhat, Hormoz. *The Dastgah Concept in Persian Music*. Cambridge: Cambridge University Press, 2004.
http://www.cambridge.org/gb/knowledge/isbn/item1151289/?site_locale=en_GB

Audio: *Classical Music of Iran: The Dastgah Systems*. Smithsonian-Folkways: SF40039, 1991.
http://www.folkways.si.edu/albumdetails.aspx?itemid=2294

Website: Iran Music
http://www.iranmusic.eu/

Arabic Music

Book: Touma, Habib Hassan. *The Music of the Arabs*. Milwaukee, WI: Amadeus Press, 2003.
http://www.halleonardbooks.com/product/viewproduct.do?itemid=331635&lid=0&keywords=arabs&menuid=10303&subsiteid=165&

Book: Racy, A.J. *Making Music in the Arab World: The Culture and Artistry of Tarab*. Cambridge: Cambridge University Press, 2004.
http://www.cambridge.org/gb/knowledge/isbn/item1132943/?site_locale=en_GB

DVD: *Umm Kulthum: A Voice Like Egypt*. Dir. Goldman, Michal. Arab Film Distribution, 1996.
http://www.npr.org/templates/story/story.php?storyId=90326836

Sufism

Book: Shah, Idries. *The Sufis*. New York: Anchor Books, 1964.
http://www.randomhouse.com/book/164623/the-sufis-by-idries-shah

Website: The Threshold Society
http://www.sufism.org/

DVD: *Sufi Soul: The Mystic Music of Islam*. Dir. Simon Broughton. Riverboat, 2008.
http://movies.netflix.com/WiMovie/Sufi_Soul_The_Mystic_Music_of_Islam/70105236?trkid=2361637#height1547

Book: Olsson, Tord, Elisabeth Ozdalga, and Anders Hammarlund, eds. *Sufism, Music and Society in Turkey and the Middle East*. New York: Routledge, 2005.
http://www.amazon.com/Society-Research-Institute-Istanbul-Transactions/dp/07007/1481

Judaism

Website: Jewish Music Research Center
http://www.jewish-music.huji.ac.il/

Book: Horowitz, Amy. *Mediterranean Israeli Music and the Politics of the Aesthetic*. Detroit, MI: Wayne State University Press, 2010.
http://wsupress.wayne.edu/books/1149/Mediterranean-Israeli-Music-and-the-Politics-of-the-Aesthetic

Website: Jewish Music.com
http://www.jewishmusic.com/

Internet: Popular Artists from Middle East
Umm Kulthum   Cheb Mami   Amr Diab
Googoosh   Ofra Haza   Soap Kills
Khaled

Europe: Greece, Spain, Russia, Scotland, Ireland, Hungary, Bulgaria

9

Background Preparation	282	*An Inside Look:* Morag MacLeod	302	Lübeck, center of the fourteenth century Hanseatic League, is traditionally entered through the *Holstentor*, a mid-fifteenth century double tower
"Classical" versus "Folk"	285	Site 4: Highland Bagpipes	303	
Planning the Itinerary	287	Arrival: Ireland	308	
Arrival: Greece	287	Site 5: *Uilleann* Bagpipes	309	
Site 1: Greek Orthodox (Byzantine) Chant	288	Arrival: Hungary	314	
Arrival: Spain	291	Site 6: *Tekerölant* (Hurdy Gurdy)	314	
Site 2: *Flamenco*	292	Arrival: Bulgaria	318	
Arrival: Russia	297	Site 7: Bulgarian Women's Chorus	319	
Site 3: *Balalaika* Ensemble	298	Questions to Consider	322	
Arrival: Scotland	301	On Your Own Time	323	

Background Preparation

Exactly what do we mean when we say "Europe"? If a friend were to tell you, "I'm going to Europe this summer," he or she would probably mean "Western" Europe, especially the United Kingdom (casually called Britain), France, Germany, Italy, Spain, and perhaps Switzerland and Austria. When a news reporter uses the term *European Union*, he or she refers not to all European nations but to a specific group of countries (which might come to include Turkey, a country not considered geographically part of Europe). In music history courses, when we refer to "European music," we mostly mean the "classical" tradition of "Western Europe." What, then, is Europe: a political entity, a geographical unit, a cultural area, or all of these things?

There are today some forty-one nation-states that constitute Europe, ranging from Russia, the world's largest country, to miniature city-states such as Monaco and Luxembourg. While forty-one may seem like a high number, before many of the modern nations such as Germany and Italy were created in the nineteenth century, Europe consisted of scores, if not hundreds, of tiny states headed variously by kings, princes, dukes, and so forth. Many of the territories that are now part of nation-states were also successively part of the Roman, Holy Roman, and Austro-Hungarian Empires—though the "unity" of these empires was tenuous at best. During the nineteenth and early twentieth centuries, many nation-states were cobbled together out of linguistically, culturally, and ethnically distinct regions, some following a war (e.g., World War I). This process has recently begun to reverse itself: over the past twenty years or so, many small nations, particularly in central and southeast Europe, have formed after breaking away from larger ones. Even so, there are numerous other ethnic groups that would claim their own nations if they could, including the Basque, the Russyns, and the Vlachs.

In Telgart, Slovakia, the musicians are of Gypsy (Rom) descent, but they continue to play local music similar to that collected by Béla Bartók in the early twentieth century

Europe is also home to several groups who are not associated with any one region but are spread throughout the continent. One such group is the Rom—also called "Gypsies"—a traditionally migrant people who originated in India. In those countries where the Rom have settled, whether they live in their own communities or are integrated into the mainstream, they have become an important part of the indigenous musical culture. Historically at least, the position of Jews in European society was similar; like the Rom, they were simultaneously insiders and outsiders but were nonetheless important to Europe's musical life.

Both Roman and Orthodox Christianity along with Islam co-existed in Mostar, Bosnia and Herzegovina, once part of unified Yugoslavia, until the Balkan Wars of the early 1990s, when the famous Turkish bridge (*Stari Most*) over the Neretva River was destroyed; now it is rebuilt

WORLD MUSIC: A GLOBAL JOURNEY

A Croat musician in the historic walled city of Dubrovnik plays the *lirica* (fiddle), an instrument type found throughout the former Ottoman Empire in southeastern Europe as well as in modern Turkey

Sorting out Europe's peoples is challenging, but one possible way to group them is by language family. While most Europeans speak languages that belong to the overarching Indo-European family, some, such as the Finns, Hungarians, and Estonians (members of the Altaic family) and the Basque as well, speak non-Indo-European languages. Most Indo-European languages are members of one of four families: Germanic, Italic (or Romance), Balto-Slavic, and Celtic. In addition, there are at least three Indo-European languages that do not belong to any of these families: Greek, Albanian, and Rom. The table opposite classifies nations according to their primary language; some nations, such as Switzerland and Belgium, have more than one official language, however.

While Ireland is listed in the Celtic category, relatively few Irish people still speak Gaelic. Celtic languages are also spoken (or were until recently) in the highlands and islands of Scotland, French Brittany, Wales, Cornwall in England, and in small pockets elsewhere.

While categorizing European peoples into language groups does help us to understand certain broad strands in European music, it is also essential to understand that none of these strands is isolated. As Hungarian composer and ethnomusicologist Béla Bartók (1881–1945) discovered early in the twentieth century, national musics cannot realistically be considered

Table 9.1 European Countries by Language Group

Germanic	Italic (Romance)	Slavic	Slavic (continued)	Celtic	Independent
Germany	France	Russia	Macedonia	Ireland	Greece
Austria	Belgium	Latvia	Serbia	(in part)	Albania
Switzerland	Italy	Lithuania	Montenegro	Wales (UK)	
Denmark	Spain	Belarus	Slovenia	Scotland (UK,	
Sweden	Portugal	Poland	Croatia	in part)	
Norway	Romania	Czech Republic	Bosnia-	Cornwall (UK)	
United Kingdom	Andorra	Slovakia	Herzegovina		
Netherlands	Monaco	Moldova	Georgia		
Iceland		Ukraine			
Luxembourg		Bulgaria			

self-contained and unique unto themselves. Bartók, an ethnomusicologist before he became a composer, came to understand that Hungarian music, though distinctive, only existed in relationship to the musics of rival neighbors such as the Serbs, Romanians, Bulgarians, and even the Turks, with whom Hungary had long-standing hostilities. National boundaries within Europe have changed so many times over the years that it is all but impossible to think of any area as culturally "pure." On the other hand, it is also difficult to think of all these overlapping regions as comprising one "culture." Bearing this in mind, is it ever reasonable to use the term "European music"? The short answer is, probably not.

"Classical" versus "Folk"

As with music everywhere else in the world, music in Europe is closely connected with notions of nation, region, ethnicity, and social class. The all-too-freely used terms *classical*, *folk*, and *popular* derive from European conceptions of how music exists in society. It is important to realize that these categories exist only in peoples' minds and imply value judgments and hierarchical ways of thinking. The term *classical* refers to what is considered the highest class of music. This music is judged by standards that privilege complexity and "sophistication," and that usually rate a long composition for a large ensemble as a "greater" achievement than a short piece for a small ensemble. Because music scholarship has primarily focused on "classical" music, and music scholars primarily work in universities, music students in universities, colleges, and conservatories worldwide study "classical" music almost exclusively. Consequently, for them "classical music" *is* European music—and, by the same token, European music *is* "classical music." Because classical music only flourished where there were wealthy patrons, courts, and aristocracies, much less originated in southeastern Europe or much of eastern Europe or in other places where such support systems and contexts were often missing, such as Ireland, Finland, Portugal, and Greece. The areas formerly under Ottoman Turkish control, some until the early twentieth century, naturally could not develop a "classical" music in the European tradition until they had established their independence.

What the field of ethnomusicology adds to the study of European music is a focus on what is usually designated "folk music," as well as an "outside" perspective on classical music. *Folk* is a demographic concept based on the assumption that there are "folk" and "non-folk." What is implicit is an evaluative hierarchy that places "folk music" in a humble position relative to "classical music." The notion of a "folk"—and by extension of "folk music"—is an outgrowth of Romanticism, an aesthetic orientation that flourished in the latter part of the eighteenth century and throughout much of the nineteenth century. Romanticism originated in the northern sectors of Europe, especially German-speaking areas, and was viewed as an antidote to the domination of "classical" French and Italian culture. Most spoken drama at the time, for example, was in French and most opera was in Italian, even in places such as England and "Germany" (in quotes because Germany as a unified nation did not yet exist). Germanic peoples were made to feel that their culture and languages were inferior to Mediterranean culture and languages—but with the rise of Romanticism they began to assert their cultural independence.

The term *folksong* (*Volkslied* in the original German) was coined by the philosopher Johann Gottfried Herder (1744–1803), who believed that the essence of a culture was in its peasants—whose pure souls were uncorrupted by the Industrial Revolution that had created poverty, pollution, and the destruction of traditional patterns of life. The "folk" were the antidote to the ills of the modern world. This notion stimulated a great deal of field research into northern roots, especially seen in the collecting of folk tales and folk songs. Many of these tales and songs were published in influential collections, such as *Grimm's Fairy Tales* and *Des Knaben Wunderhorn* (The Youth's Magic Horn), the latter a compilation of songs collected from the "folk" by Arnim von Achim and Clemens Brentano early in the nineteenth century. *Folk*, then, is a category that existed only in the minds of "non-folk" advocates such as Herder.

France's Chartres Cathedral, built by an unknown architect between 1194 and 1260, has mismatched towers

Our view, however, is that European music cannot really be divided into discrete "folk" and "non-folk" categories—there is, rather, a continuum from the music of the "lowliest" villager in Slovakia, for example, to the most sophisticated music of the aristocracy in Paris. Indeed, some of the historical music studied in music history classes as part of the "classical" evolution was originally the music of non-aristocrats. Likewise, in Europe much "classical music" was everyone's music: reed bands organized by factory workers played excerpts from symphonies, amateur choruses sang excerpts from operas, and player pianos and other automated musical instruments included classical excerpts on their rolls and barrels.

When its regions are considered together and all layers of its music are explored, the musics of Europe are revealed to be incredibly rich. Extensive as the classical orchestral instruments are, their number pales in comparison to the variety of instruments seen at the village level, from medieval survivals to the many exotic instruments that came to Europe from the Middle East via the Ottoman Empire and Moorish Spain. Collectively, the various vocal styles found throughout Europe feature most of the sounds humans are capable of uttering. "European music," then, encompasses everything from lullabies to operas, and its sounds range from the plaintive melody of a shepherd's flute to the power of a massed orchestra or pipe organ.

Planning the Itinerary

Europe consists of so many individual nations—many of which are home to several distinct peoples—that it is impossible in this brief survey to explore more than a few examples of European music. Of necessity, our itinerary must be highly selective.

Though Judaism exists in parts of Europe and Islam is important in the southeast, particularly Bosnia and Albania, and is increasingly significant in France and Germany, Europe is otherwise predominantly Christian—thus, we include some music that is related to Christianity—Greek Orthodox (Byzantine) chant. From Europe's vast array of attractive and sometimes unique instruments, we have chosen two that allow exploration of several broad issues: the Russian *balalaika* and a representative of the *hurdy gurdy* family. Because bagpipes are pervasive throughout Europe—and not just a Scottish phenomenon—including bagpipes is a must. We have chosen two types—Irish and Scottish—in order to contrast two methods of operation. Bulgarian choirs, particularly women's choirs, have been widely noticed outside Bulgaria, as has the Flamenco tradition from Spain, so we have chosen to include discussions of these as well

Arrival: Greece

Greece can be considered in two ways: (1) as one of the classical cultures that forms the foundation of Europe; and (2) as a modern nation that shows much influence from its centuries under Ottoman Turkish rule. Classical Greek civilization centered on Athens from about 800 to 300 B.C.E., then spread throughout the Macedonian-Greek Empire of Philip of Macedonia and his son, Alexander the Great, the latter having been responsible for spreading "Hellenistic" culture over a vast area of Central Asia and North Africa. When the succeeding Roman Empire divided into West and East, Greece became part of the latter. After 1453, when it came under Ottoman Turkish rule, Greece was profoundly influenced by its conqueror, and modern Greece, especially in the north; this is displayed in its cuisine, architecture, and musical instruments. While urban Greece is clearly European, the countryside preserves distinctive patterns of architecture, cuisine, life style, animal husbandry, and music-making that reflects a complex history and much earlier traditions.

Site 1: Greek Orthodox (Byzantine) Chant

First Impressions. If you were expecting something like the music from movies such as *Zorba the Greek* or *My Big Fat Greek Wedding*, then Byzantine Chant, an austere form of Eastern religious music, might come as a surprise. It is typical of the religious singing of the Greek Orthodox Church, also called the Byzantine Rite, as practiced in Greece. In all voices, the low drone underscores the higher melodic line that carries the text. Together they call up visions of bearded, robed men solemnly singing in an ancient church bathed in the colored light of stained glass windows.

Aural Analysis. In churches where a formal order of service is observed—what is called the *liturgy*—the spoken and sung texts are regulated year round according to church season and feast. Among the most important seasons is Christmas, celebrating the birth of Jesus of Nazareth. The present example is a Greek Orthodox Christmas hymn, the text of which begins "Come, faithful, let us see where Christ was born" and continues saying (paraphrased) "Let us see the manger, let us regard the three wise men who came to honor Him, the shepherds who came to pay homage to the one born of a virgin." In church perhaps as few

Modeled after early Christian churches in the Eastern Roman Empire, this modern Greek Orthodox church is in downtown Athens

High above the sea on a sheer cliff, the fourteenth-century Monastery of Simonopetra (Simon and Peter) is one of dozens scattered throughout the mountainous Athos peninsula, technically the Monastic Republic of Athos—a roadless enclave belonging to the Greek Orthodox Church

as two men perform the hymn. Our track was recorded by a small choir supported by the Society for the Dissemination of National Music in Athens consisting of males, the upper octave being performed, not by women (who customarily do not sing in a religious service) but by boys.

The first sound heard—let's call it E for simplicity's sake—continues to be held as the second (and upper) part begins the melody. The lower held part is called a drone. While drones can sound above or below the melody, low drones such as this are a typical feature of Byzantine chant. The melodic part ascends using pitches E, F, G♯, A, B, C, D, and the upper octave, E, thus restricting the melodic range of the chant to one octave. Rhythmically, the chant is simple, with only two durations, the longer one being twice the length of the shorter one, creating an overall feeling of duple time, though not rigidly so. About three-quarters of the way through there is a brief passage in which the C becomes a C♯, giving the chant a "major" feel—but almost immediately C♯ begins alternating with C natural, and in the last part of the chant the scale returns to its original form.

The scale heard here does not conform to any standard scale form known elsewhere in Europe. It is neither major nor minor, nor any variant of them. Byzantine chant theory centers around a complex system of modes that provides both scales and a broader basis for melodic composition, a system somewhat like that of the Indian *raga* or Arabic *maqam*. These modes are called *echoi* (singular, *echos*). The scale of the present example is described as *kathisma*, chromatic fourth mode. It is believed that over time the chant became more and more complex melodically, to the point that church goers could not understand the words. At some point the chant was reformed through simplification, which the reformers assert is more like its early form.

LISTENING GUIDE

CD 2.12 (1'43")

Chapter 9: Site 1
Greece: Greek Orthodox (Byzantine) Chant

Vocals: Mixed male/female ensemble

TIME	LISTENING FOCUS
0'00"	Vocal drone is established on a pitch slightly below E♭. The upper voices rise to A♭.
0'08"	First verse begins. Listen for the continuous drone on E♭. Note that the melodic line establishes a regular pulsation at a tempo of roughly 104 beats per minute. Observe that the number of pulses for each line is inconsistent. The first phrase consists of ten pulses.
0'13"	Observe that the number of pulses for this phrase consists of nine pulses.
0'18"	Observe that the number of pulses for this phrase consists of eleven pulses. Continue to monitor the number of pulses for each phrase of the text.
1'02"	Listen for the unstable shift to a "major" sounding pitch (B), which then quickly returns to the original mode.
1'16"	The drone pitch drops to an A♭. Listen for the change in melodic pitches as well.
1'28"	The drone pitch returns to an E♭.
1'38"	Chant concludes with the drone pitch and melodic voices on A♭ (an octave apart).

Source: "Come, Faithful," from the recording entitled *Byzantine Hymns of Christmas*. Society for the Dissemination of National Music SDNM 101, n.d. Used by permission.

ETHNO-CHALLENGE (CD 2.12): Keep track of the number of pulses used for each line of text. Also, try singing the drone pitches throughout the performance.

Cultural Considerations. Note that only male voices are heard. Following a strict interpretation of Paul's admonition to the Corinthians, "Let your women keep silence in the churches; for it is not permitted unto them to speak" (I Corinthians, 14:34), the early churches forbade women from speaking, singing, or preaching; this is still true in some denominations today. In the Greek Orthodox Church, the leadership is exclusively male.

Today's Greek Orthodox Church represents the survival of the old Byzantine Church, originally centered in Byzantium (later called Constantinople), in modern Turkey. For centuries, the Byzantine (or Eastern) Church was more or less unified with the Western Church under the leadership of the Pope in Rome. In 1054, however, the Eastern Church split off, and from then on a Patriarch based in Constantinople oversaw it. After the fall of

Constantinople to the Ottoman Turks in 1453, Eastern Christianity retreated back into Europe, and as the Turks expanded into southeastern Europe bringing Islam with them, the center of the Eastern Church retreated further to a mountainous peninsula off northern Greece called Mount Athos. Isolated from the Turks and Islam, thousands of monks built marvelous monasteries, many high above the sea and accessible only by dangerous mountain trails. Today the Athos peninsula remains a technically independent religious entity, the Monastic Republic of Athos, administered by the Greek Church; it is mostly lacking roads and other forms of development and is strictly off limits to women. There, a much-diminished number of monks preserve the Church's oldest traditions, including its chant.

This chant is also heard throughout Greece in numerous "Greek Orthodox" churches and in some overseas churches. Byzantine chant, therefore, is one of the oldest continuously living song traditions in the world, linking us directly to the splendor of the old Byzantine churches still seen in modern Istanbul and in other areas of Turkey. The church buildings in which it is heard may be of great interest too. In the northern city of Thessaloniki (to whom the Apostle Paul addressed his epistles to the Thessalonians in the Greek Bible's New Testament), chant is still heard in mosaic-filled churches that date back to the fifth and sixth centuries, as well as in exotic-looking churches from the thirteenth century built in Byzantine style. During services, a small male choir stands near the front around a large wooden lectern reading from a large chant book. The congregation takes no part in the chanting, because in this ancient tradition, mass is said *for* the congregants, not by them.

Arrival: Spain

The beaches and bullfights of sunny Spain attract more than forty million visitors per year. The many holy days of the Roman Catholic calendar present numerous opportunities for *fiestas* throughout the country. Perhaps the best known of these includes the "Running of the Bulls" during the Feast of San Fermín celebrations in July in the northern city of Pamplona, reflecting the zest for life that permeates Spanish culture. Olive groves and vineyards are plentiful, especially in Andalusia in the south, where *cantaoras* sing late into the night to the accompaniment of a flamenco guitarist, and *tapas* bars serve wine and piquant delicacies until dawn.

Separated from the rest of Western Europe by the Pyrenees Mountains that form the border between the Iberian Peninsula and France, Spain exhibits a unique blend of European and North African cultural characteristics. The Romans occupied the peninsula for roughly seven hundred years (second century B.C.E. until the sixth century C.E.) before the Christian Visigoths (Germanic peoples) spread into the region, reducing it to a nominal vassal state of Rome. In addition, most cities had a Jewish quarter after the destruction of the great Temple in Jerusalem in 70 C.E. The Moors (Muslims) invaded from North Africa in the eighth century C.E. and occupied much of the peninsula for more than seven hundred years (711–1492), diminishing Roman Catholic influence in Spain and establishing the western front of the Islamic realm.

Arabic dominance began to recede in the eleventh century as the few remaining Christian rulers, encouraged by the Crusades, began to reestablish control of the peninsula. While Muslims, Christians, and Jews had lived in relative peace under Moorish rule, religious fervor came with the re-conquest of Spain, resulting in the infamous Inquisitions

WORLD MUSIC: A GLOBAL JOURNEY

An architectural gem in World Heritage city Toledo, Spain, the thirteenth-century Church of Santiago del Arrabal is described as Mudejar, a blend of Visigothic Christian (Mozarabic) architecture and Arabic decoration

Flamenco dancers and guitarists perform in a club in Cadiz, Spain (Robert Garfias)

(1478), the expulsion of the Jews and Moors (1492), and the aggressive conversion practices of the Roman Catholic missionaries who followed Spanish Conquistadors to the Americas beginning in the sixteenth century. The Spanish kings soon established Spain as a colonial world power dominating much of the "newly discovered" Western hemisphere.

Until recently Spain, along with Portugal, was the most isolated region of Western Europe. Long years of internal conflict and dictatorial leadership slowed its modernization and political development. Only after the death of General Francisco Franco in 1975 did Spain begin to catch up with the rest of Western Europe, a process hastened by the country's gradual integration into the European Union. As a result, Spain still retains a strong "Old World" sensibility that is felt less and less in other parts of the continent.

Site 2: *Flamenco*

First Impressions. **Flamenco** is a vibrant music. The powerful voice of the singer, the percussive performance of the guitarist, and the rhythmic clapping and heel-stomping of the dancers as onlookers shout "olé!" create a synergetic experience that propels the participants to heights and depths of emotion that can bring tears of both sadness and joy within the span of a single song. To feel this passion is to understand flamenco, no matter if you hail from Spain or elsewhere.

EUROPE 9

FLAMENCO
A Spanish musical tradition featuring vocals with guitar accompaniment, characterized by passionate singing and vibrant rhythm.

Young Spanish *flamenco* dancer playing the castanets (Shutterstock)

Close-up photo of a single pair of castanets (Shutterstock)

Aural Analysis. *Flamenco* includes one of the world's most virtuosic of guitar styles. Guitarists must have incredible dexterity with both hands in order to convey the power and delicacy the style demands. Performers use the fleshy part of the fingers for some sounds, while the characteristic strummed "flourishes" of flamenco and much of the solo work are produced using the fingernails. Percussive accents are commonly added by slapping the face of the guitar to emphasize a melodic passage or articulate a specific rhythm.

The guitar accompanies the *cantaora* (vocalist). The singer can be either male or female, though male performers predominate. The singer frequently sings in the higher reaches of his vocal range. This creates a strained timbre that encourages the sense that he is "giving it his all" by singing to the point where his voice nearly breaks. The heavy use of melisma is also a key feature of the flamenco singing style. The intricately ornamented melismas are intended to have an emotional effect, by making the singer sound as if he is crying, almost wailing, as he empties his soul into song. The lyrical content of flamenco is deeply personal, with death and devotional love, either accepted or rejected, being common themes.

Handclapping (*palmas*) as well as finger-snapping (*palillos* or *pitos*) are common in traditional flamenco performance. These gestures articulate the basic beat, though frequently the onlookers interlock their claps to create a thick rhythmic density that heightens the tension of the music. The dancers also add a rhythmic vibrancy through their toe- and heel-stamping choreography and/or use of castanets, a wooden clapper held in each hand.

Flamenco music generally emphasizes minor keys, and triple meters are more common. Our example follows a twelve-beat pattern divided into two six-beat phrases, which can be heard from the opening guitar chords. The home chord changes on beat 3 and returns on beat 9. The handclaps add syncopation before slipping into an interlocking pattern. The vocalist enters on the ninth repetition of the twelve-beat pattern and sings through three measures. Soon the tempo picks up dramatically as the dancers infuse their own energy into the music. While this particular example does not do so, many *flamenco* performances shift the meter from triple to duple and back to triple frequently within a single song. Rhythmically free passages may be interspersed within a performance.

Improvisation is a key element of *flamenco*, on the part of the guitarist, vocalist, and dancers. While the vocalist generally leads a performance, any of these three elements—voice, guitar, or dance—can change the mood of a performance through shifts in meter, tempo, dynamics, or rhythmic complexity. This stark change in mood is best illustrated in our example by a passage that occurs shortly after the dancers increase their tempo and rhythmic density. In this section, the guitarist plays alone, with the dancers adding occasional foot-stomps and finger-snaps to accent the rhythm. This quieter passage uses a different harmonic progression with a slightly fluctuating tempo. After a solo dance interlude, the performance then slips back to its initial energy level as the tempo increases, the original guitar accompaniment returns, the *cantaora* sings, and the dancers increase their intensity.

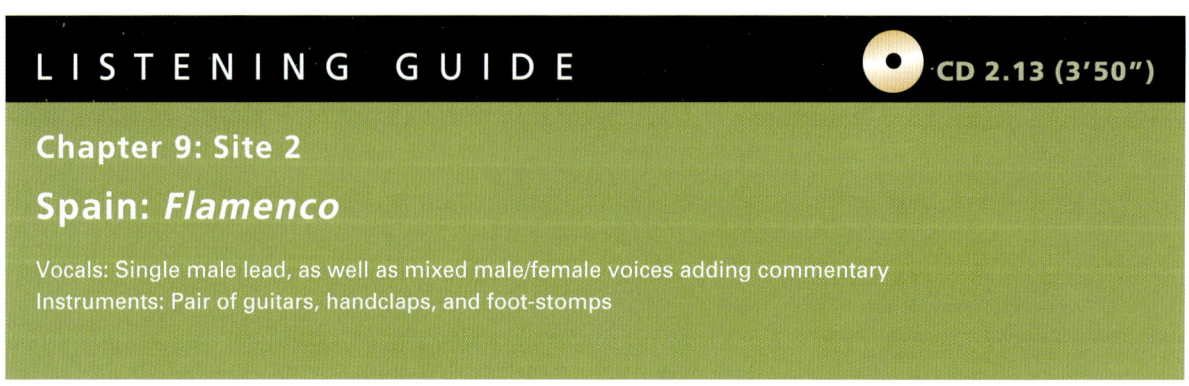

LISTENING GUIDE

CD 2.13 (3'50")

Chapter 9: Site 2
Spain: *Flamenco*

Vocals: Single male lead, as well as mixed male/female voices adding commentary
Instruments: Pair of guitars, handclaps, and foot-stomps

TIME	LISTENING FOCUS
0'00"	Listen for the exhortations of the onlookers and participants.
0'01"	Guitars enter using chords (i.e., harmony). Listen with headphones to hear the clear separation of the two instruments (lead guitar in the left channel and the supporting guitar in the right channel). Note that they begin with a loose adherence to a triple meter with six pulses.
0'06"	Listen for the handclaps, presumably contributed by one of the dancers, and the continued encouragement of the onlookers.
0'13"	Listen for the lead guitar playing a melodic line while the supporting guitar continues to play chords.
0'17"	Listen for the interlocking handclaps as other participants join the performance. Note that the guitarists now play with a more consistent attention to the meter.
0'39"	Vocalist enters. Listen for the extended use of a melismatic text setting.
0'54"	Focus returns to the guitars (and the dancers) as the handclaps continue.
1'02"	Listen for the vocalists' shout, "*Arriba*!" ("Take it up!" i.e., "faster").
1'04"	The tempo accelerates. Also, listen for the inclusion of foot-stomping by the dancers and the return of interlocking handclaps.
1'24"	Music pauses. Listen for the encouragement of the onlookers and the lead vocalist's praise of the dancers.
1'26"	The tempo slows as the lead guitar performs a solo passage emphasizing a single melodic line in a triple meter. Listen also for the declamations of the onlookers, indicating a new dancer is featured.
1'38"	Finger-snaps are briefly heard.
1'43"	Listen for the foot-stomps, finger-snaps, and handclaps of the featured dancer.
2'05"	Tempo accelerates as the rhythmic density of the dancer's foot stamping increases.
2'11"	Second guitar returns. Guitars now emphasize chords over melodic lines.
2'12"	Vocalist returns.
2'33"	Guitarists stop. Listen for the onlookers' declamations.
2'35"	Listen for the foot-stomping and occasional finger-snaps of the featured dancer.
2'37"	Note the vocalist's announcement of a "solo" section for the dancers.
3'00"	Lead guitars returns. Listen for the acceleration of tempo.
3'04"	Supporting guitar returns.
3'06"	Listen for the increase in the rhythmic density of the interlocking foot-stomping as more dancers appear.

3'15"	Listen for the climactic "wailing" of the vocalist and shouts of encouragement from the onlookers.
3'43"	Performance concludes, followed by applause and cheers from the onlookers.

Source: "Alegrias," performed by Carlos Lomas and Pepe De Malaga, from the recording entitled *Andalusian Flamenco Song and Dance*, Lyrichord LYRCD 7388, n.d. Used by permission, Lyrichord Discs Inc.

ETHNO-CHALLENGE (CD 2.13): Perform the interlocking handclapping and foot-stomping with a friend. If possible, find a flamenco dance class in your local area and take a few lessons.

DUENDE

A Spanish word meaning "passion," which refers to an emotional quality considered essential in performances by Spanish *Flamenco* singers.

Cultural Considerations. Many Spanish musicians would likely assert that flamenco is the most passionate music on the planet. While a high degree of musicianship is essential, successful performances are judged according to the level of emotional intensity, or **duende**. Vocalists are expected to pour every bit of their emotion into a performance, whether the intent is to express extreme sorrow or exultation, and the goal is to achieve a state of catharsis for themselves and their listeners.

Flamenco was born in Andalusia, the southern region of Spain. Originally, flamenco featured the voice alone, in a song form known as *cante*. This traditional Spanish style of singing incorporates the strained timbre and heavy use of melisma typical of Arabic vocal traditions, reflecting the more than seven hundred years of Arabic influence in the region. Arabic influence is also reflected in the style's generally vibrant rhythmic activity. *Cante* is typically divided into three forms—deep, intermediate, and light—determined by the subject matter and rhythmic structure. *Cante* performances frequently feature audience participation in the form of handclapping, dance, and vocal interjections.

The earliest evidence of *flamenco* in its modern form dates from the early nineteenth century, when Gypsy (*gitano*) musicians were observed singing the *cante* forms with instrumental accompaniment. The private "jam sessions" of the Gypsy musicians in the bars and brothels of some of the larger cities, such as Seville and Madrid, caught the attention of upper-class clientele. By the 1840s *Cafés cantantes*, clubs devoted specifically to *flamenco* performance, became popular throughout the country. The guitar became the standard accompanying instrument, a choice reflecting both the Arabic emphasis on intricate melodic passages and the European taste for harmony.

While modern *flamenco* is frequently performed on a concert stage, traditional contexts for *flamenco* are much more intimate. The ideal setting is a *juerga*, an informal event in which the separation between musicians and audience is blurred. Everyone participates, if only with clapping and shouts of encouragement known as *jaleo*. These gatherings can happen almost anywhere, on a side street, in a *tapas* bar, at a musician's home, and so on. They usually last late into the night, often until dawn, and are characterized by much laughter and a family feeling.

Flamenco has continued to develop in new ways. Theatrical productions of *flamenco* dance and song are common, and *flamenco* troupes are frequently found on international tours. Since the 1960s some artists have fused *flamenco* with other music forms, such as jazz and rock, to create popular sounds with a global appeal. Artists such as Paco de Lucía and the Gipsy Kings have helped to widen the audience of flamenco through their innovative compositions, while remaining true to the roots of the music and the spirit of *duende*.

Arrival: Russia

Russia is the largest country on the planet. While more than 80 percent of its territory is in Asia, it is European Russia, the part west of the Ural Mountains, that represents Russia's political and cultural identity to the outside world. The two largest cities, Moscow and St. Petersburg, are the destinations for most tourists, who discover a unique juxtaposition of the architecture of Czarist Russia, with its pastel-colored Baroque-like palaces and onion-domed Russian Orthodox churches, and Soviet Russia (1917–1991), which exchanged color for monumental concrete buildings and statues of steel. Since the dissolution of the Soviet Union in 1991, Russia, still a world power, has striven to transform itself from a totalitarian communist regime to a democratic free market society. This transition has not been easy, but the Russian people are resilient, having dealt with many dramatic political changes in their history.

During the nineteenth and twentieth centuries, Russian nationalism inspired much artistic development, especially in music. Many Russian "art music" composers, such as Nikolai Rimsky-Korsakov (1844–1908), Pyotr Ilich Tchaikovsky (1840–1893), and Igor Stravinsky (1882–1971), are counted among the greatest composers of the last two centuries. While many urbanites of modern Russia would rather consider these composers and their

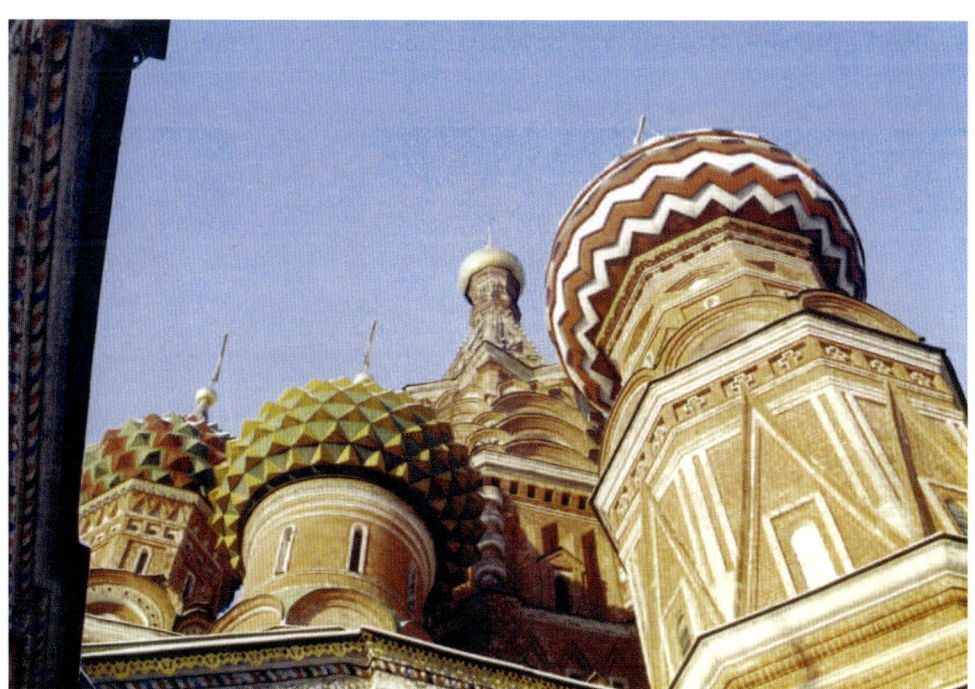

In Moscow, Russia, St. Basil's Cathedral, built by Czar Ivan the Terrible between 1555 and 1561, sits at the edge of Red Square (Andrew Shahriari)

music as the essence of Russian musical identity, the work songs, *chastushki* (playful songs), and dance tunes of the Russian countryside inspired many of the most revered Russian composers and are in fact more indicative of Russia's distinctive musical culture.

Site 3: *Balalaika* Ensemble

BALALAIKA
A triangle-shaped, fretted plucked-lute from Russia.

First Impressions. The "chattering," high-pitched sound of the *prima balalaika* is apparent even in a full **balalaika** orchestra, as is heard in our example. This music may remind you of a German Oktoberfest as it has a "polka" feel, but it is distinctly Russian. Though the instrumentation is certainly different, such dance genres are also a staple of Russian folk music.

Aural Analysis. As is typical of musical performance in Europe, harmony is the key musical element. In this case, the major instrument heard is the *balalaika*, the most popular folk instrument in Russia. The *balalaika*'s most distinctive feature is its triangular-shaped resonating body. The instrument can be found in varying sizes, but the most common type is the *prima balalaika*, which has a wooden sound box a little more than 1 foot (30 centimeters) long on each side and a fretted neck that extends the instrument to nearly 3 feet (91 cm). Most *balalaika* have just three strings. Two strings are tuned to the same pitch or an octave apart, while the third string is tuned to a fourth above the root. The strings are usually made of steel, nylon, or gut and are played with the fingers, though sometimes a leather plectrum may be used.

The *balalaika* was most commonly used as a courting instrument, but also was found among court musicians. Its popularity waned during the early nineteenth century with the introduction of the harmonica, until its cause was picked up by a Russian nobleman, Vasily Vasilyevich Andreyev (1861–1918), who is today nicknamed the "Father of the Balalaika."

Members of the St. Nicholas Russian Orthodox Church Balalaika Orchestra of Mogadore, Ohio, use instruments in several sizes. In the front row are seen the typical *prima balalaika* in triangular shape and the *domra* with a round body

The bass *balalaika* performed by a Russian street musician (Rex Shahriari)

Andreyev first became intrigued by the instrument after hearing one of his workers play it. In the spirit of Russian nationalism, he promoted the *balalaika* as the distinctive musical instrument of Russia and succeeded in modernizing the instrument so that it could play a classical repertoire. Andreyev had five different-sized *balalaika* created, the largest being the size of a double bass. His ensemble had its debut in 1888 to great acclaim and by 1892 had won the support of the Russian royalty. Afterward his Russian Balalaika Orchestra toured Europe and even visited America.

As is typical of European folk music, the melody is relatively short and repetitive. The double bass *balalaika* plods along with the basic harmonic structure as smaller-sized *balalaika* and *domra* "chatter" out the melody. An accordion helps to fill in the harmony and adds another timbre to the overall sound. Of note is the near absence of "percussion" instruments other than the occasional rattling of a tambourine.

LISTENING GUIDE

CD 2.14 (2'01")

Chapter 9: Site 3
Russia: *Balalaika* Ensemble

Instruments: *Balalaika* (high- and mid-range plucked lute), *bass balalaika* (low-range plucked lute), *domra* (high-range plucked lute), accordion (reed aerophone), tambourine, gourd rattle

TIME	LISTENING FOCUS
0'00"	Listen for the steady duple meter and absence of percussion instruments. Note that the bass *balalaika* is primarily responsible for articulating the basic pulse as well as the harmonic root.
0'06"	First melodic phrase repeats.
0'12"	Second melodic phrase with repetition.
0'25"	Accordion enters. Listen for a third melodic phrase.
0'38"	First melodic phrase returns.
0'52"	Second melodic phrase returns. Listen for the syncopated "upbeat" rhythm of some of the chordophones as the performers dampen strings to add an additional timbre.
1'04"	Third melodic phrase returns.
1'17"	First melodic phrase returns. Listen for the tambourine adding an additional rhythmic element.
1'30"	Second melodic phrase returns. Note that the tambourine stops.
1'43"	Third melodic phrase returns.
1'55"	Note the gourd rattle entering to emphasize the end of the piece.

Source: "Yablochka," from the recording entitled *Eastern European Folk Heritage Concert: St. Nicholas Balalaika Orchestra*, private issue, 2003. Used by permission.

ETHNO-CHALLENGE (CD 2.14): Using numeral or staff notation, write out the pitches and rhythm of the three melodic phrases.

Cultural Considerations. Though polyphonic vocal ensembles are more characteristic of Russian folk music, the *balalaika* has become the distinctive visual symbol of Russian musical identity. The predecessor of the *balalaika* is a similar lute, known as a *domra*, which has a round resonator. The earliest records of the *domra* date to the seventeenth century. The primary performers on the instrument were wandering minstrels and jugglers who performed for weddings, festivals, and other celebratory activities. These entertainers, known as *skomorokhi* ("jesters"), commonly appeared in costume, dressed up as, for example, an animal or a witch, in order to attract an audience.

Unfortunately, the ruling powers of the time issued decrees that put strict restraints on various peasant activities, including the performance of music. In 1648 the czar ordered that all music instruments be burned and decreed that anyone who dared to play music would be flogged and exiled to the outer reaches of the kingdom. The *balalaika* likely developed as a consequence: because it was easier to make a triangular-shaped body than a round one, it could be more quickly made if a musician had been forced to abandon his original instrument for fear of persecution. After the harassment of Russian musicians subsided in the eighteenth century, the instrument became quite popular for its distinctive look and characteristic "chatter-like" sound. The *balalaika*'s name is derived from the Russian word meaning "to chat," and its sound is intended to contrast with the violin, which is considered to "sing."

Andreyev encouraged the dissemination of the *balalaika* among the populace by teaching soldiers and common folk to play the instruments, often giving them free instruments. Under Soviet rule, the *balalaika* continued to play a vital role in promoting Russian nationalism, and by the end of the twentieth century, it had regained its prominence as the most popular instrument in the country. Today it is frequently sought after by tourists and is used by *balalaika* "combos," which are popular in major cities throughout Europe. The film *Dr. Zhivago* (1965), which featured the *balalaika* in its soundtrack, helped to familiarize Western audiences with the instrument.

Our example is performed by an ensemble based in the United States, the Balalaika Orchestra of St. Nicholas Church in Mogadore, Ohio, just east of Akron. Founded in 1985, this group of skilled amateurs performs a variety of folk music from Russia. Russian communities can be found throughout the United States, but that of northeast Ohio is one of the oldest. Indeed, Cleveland is also home to St. Theodosius Cathedral, the oldest Russian Orthodox church in the United States and the church featured in the 1978 film *The Deer Hunter*, which examined the experience of the Vietnam War in the lives of small town Americans. Balalaika orchestras, such as the St. Nicholas Balalaika Orchestra, have become an important means of expressing Russian identity for people in the Russian Diaspora, especially in the United States.

Arrival: Scotland

Although Scotland is often thought of as a country, in reality it has not been one since 1707; rather, it is a constituent part of the United Kingdom (or Great Britain), along with England, Wales, and Ulster (Northern Ireland). During the Roman occupation of Britain—from the mid-first century until the fourth century—what is now Scotland was inhabited by the much-feared but little-known Picts and was considered a fearsome land. To keep the Picts at bay, the Romans built a stone wall from sea to sea across northern England during the 120s C.E.; remnants of this construction, known as Hadrian's Wall, can still be seen today, though it barely keeps sheep from crossing now.

Scotland was a hardscrabble land for most of its inhabitants, especially those trying to eke out a living in the rocky highlands or the bleak, peat-covered plains of the Hebrides Islands, the areas of "traditional" Scottish Gaelic-speaking highland culture to the west and northwest. People working the land for a subsistence living were sheltered in "blackhouses"—sod or stone huts with thatched roofs and little light but much smoke. At the end of the eighteenth century, the English gentry, who owned most land in Scotland, decided that raising sheep was more profitable than renting land to small farmers and forced the Scots from their land in what is called The Clearances (1790–1845). Some of the Scots removed from their land died, while many others were forced to migrate. A segment of these Scottish immigrants settled permanently in northern Ireland, while others remained in Ireland for a time, then went on to North America to start a new life. Indeed, the "Scots-Irish" provided much of the backbone of Appalachian culture in the United States, while other waves of migration brought Scottish culture to Canada as well.

Modern Scotland, home of two great cities—industrial Glasgow and learned Edinburgh—is now as prosperous as England. Thanks to "devolution," the political process by which the United Kingdom's four regions have obtained local governance, Scotland has been able to redefine itself to a far greater degree than it could in the eighteenth century while under the English yoke. Though many assume that Scots speak Gaelic (pronounced "gao-lick"), a Celtic language, today few do—mostly in the Outer Hebrides—the rest speak English or remnants of an earlier form of Scottish English seen in the poems of Robert Burns.

Morag MacLeod

AN INSIDE LOOK

Morag MacLeod, transcriber and editor of Gaelic song

I was on the staff of the School of Scottish Studies at the University of Edinburgh, Scotland, from 1964 to 2001. I was appointed as a transcriber of Scottish Gaelic texts and later of music attached to Gaelic song texts, and gradually moved up to the status of Senior Lecturer in Gaelic Song, my position on retirement. During my time at the school, I became very much involved in its series of publications of cassettes and CDs, becoming responsible to a large extent for selection and annotation of items, but especially in the transcription and translation of song texts.

The School's audio publications have been produced by Greentrax Limited, and the productions with which I was particularly involved were: *Gaelic Bards and Minstrels*, a double CD of William Matheson's vocal illustrations of two types of poetic meter in Gaelic, seventeen of one, eighteen of the other; *Seonag NicCoinnich* (Joan MacKenzie), a CD of twenty-one songs sung by one of Gaeldom's favorite singers; and *Clò Dubh Clò Donn*, a collection of popular songs by a variety of singers. I am, however, particularly interested in the unique way of singing the metrical Psalms of David using precenting, or "putting out the line," which is practiced in Gaelic-speaking congregations of the Presbyterian church in Scotland.

Another of my special interests is *waulking* songs, which were used to accompany the finishing process in the production of Harris Tweed, a cloth made from the wool of black-faced sheep in the Scottish Highlands. The cloth is rubbed and thumped onto a wooden board by the hands of a team of women who use the songs as a way of coordinating the rhythms. These items appear on *Gaelic Psalms from Lewis* (Greentrax, 2000) and *Waulking Songs from Barra* (Greentrax, 1993) respectively. A few years before retirement, I became editor of *Tocher*, a magazine for publishing items from the archives, with each issue usually focusing on a theme, in Scots, Gaelic, or English. The magazine started life as a quarterly, but teaching and other commitments have made it difficult to get one out in a year. At the same time it is a much more substantial production now.

I now live in Scalpay, a small island that is part of the Hebrides where lovely, varied views of hills, rivers, and the sea compensate for difficulty of access to colleagues, libraries, and other facilities to be enjoyed in Edinburgh. Fortunately, we now have the Internet bringing the world to us.

Site 4: Highland Bagpipes

First Impressions. Most North Americans have heard the Scottish highland **bagpipes** (called "pipes" for short), perhaps at a funeral, or at a festival, and certainly on television. Scotland's highland pipes have become commonplace for public funerals in the United States, especially those for police and other public officials. If you've ever been around someone playing these pipes, you know they are more appropriately played outdoors, because their strident tones can be deafening indoors. As with most bagpipe performances, our example features a highly ornamented melody together with sustained drone pitches. For American events, pipers customarily play "Scotland the Brave" or "Amazing Grace." Singly or as a band, they stand or march proudly, dressed in colorful kilts, with a *skean dhu* (knife) in their sock and greater or lesser amounts of regalia, depending on whether or not they are connected with the military or police.

BAGPIPES
A reed aerophone consisting of an airbag (bellows), *chanter* (melody pipe), and drone pipes.

The medieval stronghold of the Macraes, Eilean Donan Castle in Dornie, Scotland, was reduced to rubble in 1719 by the English and only restored in the twentieth century to become Scotland's most photographed castle

WORLD MUSIC: A GLOBAL JOURNEY

Aural Analysis. The Scottish highland pipes, called *a' phìob-mhór* (pronounced "Uh feep vore") in Gaelic, are just one of dozens of types of bagpipes found throughout Europe, North Africa, and Turkey, though they are the most widely known. European bagpipes can be of two kinds: lung-driven or bellows-driven. The highland pipes are the former and the Irish *uilleann* pipes (see Chapter 9, Site 5) are the latter.

Bagpipes illustrate well the concept of a "folk instrument," in that all their parts (melodic chanter, drone pipes, and bag windchest) can be made or obtained in both urban and rural areas. The melody line is created on a *chanter*, a wooden pipe with finger holes given voice by a double reed made of cane, which is set in vibration when air passes through it. European double reeds, unlike many of those found in Asia, are not particularly loud,

An "exploded" display of Scottish bagpipe parts in the Pipe Museum on the Isle of Skye off the northwest coast of Scotland

making them difficult to hear in outdoor situations. The pressure necessary to increase volume requires a good bit of lung power. The bagpipe solves these problems with a reservoir of air that is driven through the double-reed pipe and through additional drone pipes with single reeds by arm pressure. The air is stored in a bag traditionally made from the skin, stomach, or bladder of various common farm animals, especially goats and sheep. Cloth—usually a tartan—covers the animal-skin bag to hide its "unpleasant," if natural, appearance. The apertures—that is, the leg holes—into which the chanter and the three drone pipes are placed were natural to the animal. To fill the bag with air, the player blows into a fifth pipe, which incorporates a non-return valve to prevent the air from escaping when the piper is drawing more breath. When the player inflates the bag through the blowing pipe and squeezes the bag with his left arm, air is driven through the drone pipes and *chanter*, producing the exciting din of highland bagpipe music.

To operate the bagpipes, the player must first fill the bag with air and begin pressing on it. The three drone pipes—one bass and two tenors—are the first part of the instrument to sound, often coming to life with a grumpy-sounding groan. These use single reeds comparable to those used with the clarinet or saxophone, and the pipes are built in sections, allowing the player to tune by lengthening or shortening them (lengthening lowers the pitch, shortening raises the pitch). Once a full, steady drone is achieved, the performer begins playing melody on the chanter, which is a double reed, giving it a different and more penetrating timbre.

The most familiar bagpipe music consists of tunes, such as "Scotland the Brave," "Mull of Kintyre," and "Amazing Grace" (which is not known to be Scottish). There is also much dance music for bagpipes, including jigs, reels, marches, waltzes, and even polkas, as well as the famous "sword dance." Little known but highly developed is the **pibroch** (*piobaireachd* in Gaelic), an elaborate form of theme and variations, in which the "theme" is actually a "ground" (a sort of bass line) rather than a tune. In all cases, the piper embellishes the melody extensively with quick ornamental notes made possible by the motions of the fingers on the chanter. This suggests that ornamenting a melody is as much a physical act as it is a melodic one, since the typical ornaments are remembered more in the muscles than in the brain. Our track includes two polkas, both duple meter dance-like tunes. "The Royal Scots Polka," heard first, was composed by Pipe Major Willie Denholm of the First Battalion, The Royal Scots, a military pipe band. The second one, called "The Black Watch Polka," is considered "traditional," meaning the composer is unknown. The pipe band heard is the multiple world championship City of Glasgow Police Pipe Band, which was formed in 1912 by combining bands from nearby Govan Burgh with that of Glasgow. After 1975 this band was reorganized as the Strathclyde Police Pipe Band, which remains active today.

Virtually all Scottish bagpipe music, including that heard here, is in meter. In some *pibroch* compositions, the tempo may be so slow with such extensive ornamentation that ascertaining the basic pulse is difficult. Individual pipers or, more likely, marching pipe bands are usually accompanied by bass and snare drums. Nearly all highland piping is done outdoors because it is associated with outdoor events, not to mention being quite loud. Some have called the highland pipes the "war pipes," and claim that pipers led clan troops into battle. Whether this is true or not, the term "war pipes" comes from a misunderstanding of *mhór* (pronounced "vore"), a Gaelic word that sounds like war but means "great."

PIBROCH (pronounced *pee-brohk*) A form of Scottish bagpipe music with an extended theme-and-variations structure.

LISTENING GUIDE

CD 2.15 (2'58")

Chapter 9: Site 4
Scotland: Highland Pipes

Instruments: Highland (Scottish) bagpipes, snare drums, bass drums

TIME	LISTENING FOCUS
0'00"	Snare drum rolls begin the performance.
0'03"	Drones sound just before the main melody begins.
0'06"	Opening theme ("Royal Scots Polka") begins (A). Each melodic phrase is four beats with four full measures for the complete melodic line (sixteen beats total).
0'16"	Opening theme repeats (A).
0'27"	Second line begins and repeats (B).
0'37"	Second line repeats with minimal variation (B).
0'48"	Variation of main theme begins (A').
0'58"	Variation of main theme repeats (A').
1'08"	Second line with variation begins (B').
1'19"	Second line with variation repeats (B').
1'30"	New theme begins (C). ("The Black Watch Polka")
1'41"	New theme repeats (C).
1'52"	Second line of new theme begins (D).
2'02"	Second line repeats (D).
2'13"	Third line of new theme begins (E).
2'24"	Second half of third line (E cont.)
2'34"	Final line begins (F).
2'45"	Final line repeats (F).

Source: Highland bagpipes by the City of Glasgow Police Pipe Band, "The Royal Scots Polka" and "The Black Watch Polka" from *All the Best from Scotland/ 35 Great Favorites*, vol.2, CLUC CD 77, n.d.

ETHNO-CHALLENGE (CD 2.15): Research and observe bagpipe performers in your local area. For a real challenge, try constructing your own bagpipe.

Cultural Considerations. The old Gaelic language and culture, part of the larger Celtic culture and family of languages, is typically used to represent Scotland to the outside world. But Scotland also includes the lowlands where a form of English has always been spoken, the English of poet Robert Burns that is so difficult for outsiders to understand. Gaelic culture, to the extent that it survives today, is found in the north and northwest of the "mainland" and in the Hebrides Islands off the northwest coast, including Skye, Lewis, Harris, North and South Uist, and Barra. The health of Gaelic culture depends on the survival of the language, and in recent years, despite efforts to reverse the trend, there has been a steady decline in the number of native speakers. Much of the classic Gaelic culture is now seen only on special ceremonial occasions and in tourist shows.

Inextricably linked to Scotland, the highland pipes serve as a symbol of Scottish identity, both visually and aurally. While it is true that piping was associated with clans and with both martial and festive occasions, the original Scottish musical instrument was not the pipes but the Celtic harp. In early times Scottish culture was an extension of Irish culture, and the harp was the basic instrument of both. Bagpipes are no more intrinsically Scottish than Scotland's other major instrument, the fiddle (or violin). Indeed, the highland pipes can be dated back only to the sixteenth century.

As much as pipes, tartans, and kilts are markers of Scottish identity, it was not always so. Hugh Trevor-Roper has written a fascinating study of the "invention" of Scottish cultural icons published in *The Invention of Tradition*, a collection of chapters edited by Eric Hobsbawm (Cambridge University Press, 1983). There Trevor-Roper traces the history of how all of these now deeply embedded "traditions" came about, including the outright creation of Ossian, allegedly Scotland's greatest poet of the past. While this scholarship challenges deeply held notions of Scottish identity—and there's no doubt this *is* Scotland's identity now—it also suggests that similar processes have happened elsewhere in the world as well.

Scottish highland pipers march for visitors in Portree, Skye, in the Hebrides Islands off the northwest coast of Scotland

In North America the highland pipes have come to be linked with funerals, particularly those of public officials and policemen killed in the line of duty. Pipers and pipe bands routinely play "Amazing Grace," a melody that originated in North America and is not known to be Scottish. Highland pipes have also become associated in North America with St. Patrick's Day, a celebration of Ireland's patron saint. While it is true that Irish police bands have used the highland pipes since the nineteenth century, this association is a stretch. Contemporary popular culture in the United States prefers to blend all Celtic areas together, so that pipes from Scotland can now symbolize Ireland as well. In fact, Ireland has its own pipes, but they are less commonly encountered and cannot be used for marching.

Arrival: Ireland

Ireland, often called the "Emerald Isle," is a mostly rural island generously speckled with castles, monasteries, and great houses, many in ruins. It also boasts the rugged beauty of the western seacoast, including the unforgettable Cliffs of Moher. One of Ireland's most enduring cultural attractions is its music, spanning everything from that played in local pubs by amateurs to sophisticated versions of traditional tunes presented by groups such as The Chieftains who are internationally renowned. Indeed, there has been an explosion of new types of Irish-based music generally labeled "Celtic."

But Ireland was not always a placid locale for music and sheep herding. Over the centuries Ireland endured successive waves of invasions, as the many ruined "round

Celebrated in song as well as visited by thousands of tourists each year, the Cliffs of Moher in western Ireland are among Europe's most dramatic sites (Sean Williams)

towers," roofless, ruined priories, and other fortifications attest. In spite of this fate, Ireland was long one of the most developed and cultured places in medieval Europe, with many great centers of learning, religion, and the arts.

While the Republic of Ireland has been independent from the United Kingdom since 1922 (technically, it was actually formed in 1949), one of its original four counties, Ulster (or Northern Ireland), remains a constituent part of the United Kingdom, a testament to an incomplete revolution. It is nonetheless important to recall that until the twentieth century Ireland itself was not independent and that English speakers far outnumber the fabled Gaelic speakers, who are mostly found in the west of the country. The population of Ireland, around four million today, suffered many sudden declines over its history, caused by disease, war, and famine, to mass migrations, especially to the United States, where there are far more people of Irish ancestry than in Ireland itself.

Site 5: *Uilleann* Bagpipes

UILLEANN BAGPIPES
The bellows-driven pipes of Ireland.

First Impressions. Compared to the Scottish bagpipes, the Irish pipes sound mellower and much fuller with a warmer tone quality. Along with the expected melody and drone, one hears occasional "chords," groups of consonant notes sounded together. If this instrument sounds less martial, it is because the Irish pipes are played indoors for domestic occasions. In fact, you are just as likely to encounter these pipes playing with other instruments, such as the fiddle, banjo, wooden transverse flute, and perhaps even spoons, as to hear them solo.

(left) Eliot Grasso (the piper heard in the music track) playing the Irish *uilleann* pipes (Ivor Vong)

(right) Close-up of *uilleann* pipes showing chanter (right) and drone pipes with regulator levers

Aural Analysis. The Irish pipes, known in Gaelic as **uilleann** (pronounced *ill*-en) and erroneously in English as "union," are bellows-driven, meaning they have less power than mouth-driven pipes and as a result are played indoors. After the Siege of Limerick (1689–1691), the Irish *Piob Mor*, or warpipe, fell out of practical use. Historically, it was no longer heard of after the Battle of Fontenoy (May 11, 1745) in which the French army dispensed with the Anglo-Dutch-Hanoverian army in the War of Austrian succession. It is possible that the decline of the warpipes in Ireland in the eighteenth century caused a rise in popularity of the non-martial, quieter *uilleann* pipes. The *uilleann* pipes are thought to have originated in Ireland in the mid-eighteenth century and have been played by both men and women. *Uilleann* piping was widespread in Ireland during the years prior to the Great Potato Famine of the 1840s. Pipers stricken with disease and starvation either perished or emigrated, thus causing a decline in *uilleann* piping in Ireland.

An *uilleann* pipe player sits with the bellows on the right hip secured with a belt, the drone pipes lying across his lap. The word *uilleann* is the genitive singular/plural form of the Irish-Gaelic word *uillinn*, meaning elbow, corner, or angle, and was perhaps named so because of the use of both elbows in the playing of the instrument. In pre-Famine contexts, the *uilleann* pipes were not built to any standardized pitch. However, the kind of concert pitch 'D' instrument heard in the audio example was first pioneered in Philadelphia around 1875 by the Drogheda-born Taylor brothers, William and Charles, to accommodate the instrument's use with pianos, accordions, and other fixed-pitch instruments. In 1893, the Gaelic League was founded and strove to revive and "promote values of the Irish folk" by reinstituting the Gaelic language and other aspects of indigenous culture including the playing of the *uilleann* pipes. The heated enthusiasm of this movement slowly cooled until the founding of Na Píobairí Uilleann ("The Uilleann Pipers") in Dublin in 1968, an organization whose primary goal is the promotion of the instrument and its music.

Disassembled for storage, the *uilleann* pipes consist of the bag, the bellows and strap, a chanter pipe, three drone pipes, and—in full sets—an additional three pipes fitted with a series of large metal keys. These additional pipes, called "regulators," allow the player to produce the chords that are the *uilleann* pipes' most distinctive feature. There can be anywhere from one to four regulators on a set of *uilleann* pipes. The chanter, drones, and regulators are powered by air sucked in through a bellows under the piper's right arm, forced through a tube across the piper's waist, and into a leather bag under the piper's left arm. Thus, a player must be exceptionally coordinated, having to pump the bellows with the right arm, press the bag with the left arm, play the melody on the chanter with the fingers of both hands, and sometimes press the regulator keys with the side of the right hand. Without doubt, the *uilleann* pipes in their fully developed form are the most complex bagpipes in the world.

Irish music is one of the world's most developed melodic traditions. The repertory is vast, though numerous individual tunes may be variants of other tunes. Sometimes the same tune is known by different names depending on the region, and sometimes tunes with the same name are musically distinct. Those that are not lyric songs with texts are likely to be one of the several types of dances tunes found in Ireland: namely, the jig (quick 6/8 or 12/8 time), the reel (quick 2/4), the hornpipe (6/8 or 12/8 time), and the polka (quick 2/4 time). Some tunes fall into the major–minor tonality system, but there is a tendency for them to be structurally pentatonic (i.e., to employ a five-tone scale) with the possibility of additional passing notes.

Because Irish traditional instrumental music is often played for dancers, it is typical to play two or more tunes consecutively. The two tunes played on this track, titled "Lilies of the Field" and "Fairhaired Boy," are *reels*. A reel is a dance tune genre in duple meter with two parts of equal length, each part typically consisting of eight measures. Each of the reels on this track, however, is a *single reel*, meaning that there are only four instead of eight measures per A and B part. Because the Irish instrumental tradition is largely an oral one in which tune authorship is not always known, these two reels remain anonymous.

In Irish traditional music, there is both a downbeat (where your foot would normally tap) and an upbeat (subtler and not necessarily acknowledged by all instrumentalists with the same attention). When playing the *uilleann* pipes, grace notes are often incorporated before eighth notes on beats 1, 3, 5, and 7 to communicate the dance rhythm clearly, indicating to a dancer when his or her foot ought to hit the floor.

LISTENING GUIDE

CD 2.16 (1'58")

Chapter 9: Site 5
Ireland: *Uilleann* Bagpipes

Instruments: *Uilleann* Bagpipes

TIME	LISTENING FOCUS
0'00"	Chanter sounds two introductory pitches followed by the main melody of Reel 1 ("Lillies of the Field") and entrance of the drone pitches (A1).
0'06"	Main melody repeats with variation (A2).
0'11"	Second melodic line begins and repeats with variation (B1, B2).
0'20"	Main melody returns and repeats with variation (A1, A2). Listen for the "tapping" versus "sustain" sound of the regulators, as well as changes in chords.
0'30"	Second melodic line returns and repeats with variation (B1, B2).
0'39"	Main melody returns and repeats with variation (A1, A2).
0'48"	Second melodic line returns and repeats with variation (B1, B2). Note the regulators stop during this section.
0'58"	Main melody of Reel 2 ("The Fairhaired Boy") begins and repeats with variation (C1, C2). Note the regulators return.
1'07"	Second line of Reel 2 enters and repeats with variation (D1, D2).
1'17"	Main melody of Reel 2 returns and repeats with variation (C1, C2).
1'26"	Second line of Reel 2 enters and repeats with variation (D1, D2).

> **1'36"**   Main melody of Reel 2 returns and repeats with variation (C1, C2). Note the regulators stop during this section.
>
> **1'45"**   Second line of Reel 2 enters and repeats with variation (D1, D2). Note the regulators return. Example ends on sustained chord.
>
> Source: "The Lilies of the Field" and "The Fairhaired Boy," private studio recording by Eliot Grasso, 2011. Used by permission.

> **ETHNO-CHALLENGE (CD 2.16):** Listen through the example and note the timecode reference for each of the "variation" melodic phrases (A2, B2, C2, D2).

Cultural Considerations. If much Irish music seems sad or sentimental, Irish history has provided many reasons for such emotions. Although blessed with natural beauty and generous rainfall, Ireland has experienced more than its share of violence over the course of history, from the Anglo-Norman invasions of the twelfth century, to English Protestant Oliver Cromwell's scorched-earth policy of the seventeenth century. Between invasions there were numerous intertribal battles, as various peoples and clans tried to gain dominance over one another and fought over land and religion. All of this has provided Irish songwriters with more than ample subject matter. The Great Famine that lasted through much of the 1840s not only starved many to death but also drove much of the population—reduced from 8.5 million to around four million in less than five years—from the island to the New World. The Irish population in North America, particularly in places such as Boston, New York, and Chicago, then struggled as a Roman Catholic underclass in a predominantly Protestant nation before eventually rising to prominence and power. While the Irish are widely associated with police work, many of them had to labor in the most menial of jobs before harvesting the fruits of upward mobility. Nonetheless, they were luckier than their compatriots overseas, because Ireland remained impoverished until the late twentieth century, when it became a fast-growing, technologically savvy success story in the European Union.

As already mentioned, the original Irish instrument was the courtly harp, but this fell into oblivion by around 1800. In the twentieth century, there has been a revival of the harp, which was reconstructed on the basis of pictures and written descriptions and inaccurately portrayed as a folk instrument. Besides this and the *uilleann* pipes, there are several other prominent Irish instruments: the fiddle (really just an inexpensive violin), the vertical tin whistle (a kind of metal recorder), the "timber" flute (a wooden transverse flute), and a variety of bellows-driven free reed instruments with keyboards such as the melodeon, concertina, and accordion. Over time several foreign instruments have been adopted, including the Italian mandolin, the American tenor banjo, the guitar, and a hybrid lute derived from the mandolin called *bouzouki* after the Greco-Turkish lute. Percussion is limited to the well-known but recently introduced *bodhran*, a goatskin-covered frame drum played by the right hand using a wooden beater, and a pair of wooden "bones" (possibly borrowed from America along with the banjo), or spoons.

Traditionally, Irish music was played communally for family and friends in various settings, many private. Visitors are most likely to encounter Irish music in a public house (pub), where local musicians gather in their reserved corner in the evening to play for each other, the rest of the pub patrons being casual listeners rather than a formal audience. These gatherings are called "sessions" (*seisiún ceoil*). Because they are informal and ad hoc, the instrumental makeup varies greatly. The Irish pipes are one of the possible instruments found and blend well with the quieter sounds of other indoor type instruments. When an evening event features dancing and a named band, the group is called a *céilí* band; these events are also the most likely context for Irish music in North America today.

Music has become an important element of Ireland's tourist industry, and in areas where tourists tend to congregate, especially in the west, there is a conscious effort to have music every evening during the summer. Nowhere is this more so than in the village of Doolin in County Clare, where enormous, standing-room crowds gather nightly. Visiting musicians may join a session, though there are unwritten rules for participating. Outside the tourist pubs, visitors should request permission before taping or photographing musicians.

With the rise in popularity of all things "Celtic," another kind of music has also arisen that is better described as "pan-Celtic," meaning it sounds vaguely Irish but in fact reflects a variety of influences. This includes such phenomena as varied as Michael Flately's popular "River Dance" shows and the *cha-cha-cha* version of "Sleepy Maggie."

Donegal musicians gathered outside for a late afternoon session. From left to right: pennywhistle, *bodhran*, accordion, guitar (Sean Williams)

Arrival: Hungary

Like Hungary itself, the Hungarian people stand astride both West and East. Descended from the semi-nomadic Magyars who originated in the Ural Mountains of present-day central Russia, the Hungarians arrived in the Danube Valley and the Great Plain in the late ninth century. Over time they mixed with Germanic and Slavic peoples, and during the late tenth century they settled into a stable agricultural life under their first king, Stephen. But their location at the crossroads of Europe left them vulnerable to competing armies and subject to invasions. These invaders included the Mongols in the thirteenth century, the Ottoman Turks in the fifteenth, and finally, through marriage and other alliances, the Hapsburgs of Austria in the sixteenth. As a consequence, Hungary remained more oriented toward Central and Western Europe than to the East. Independence was achieved in 1919, but for much of the twentieth century Hungary was dominated first by Nazi Germany and then the Soviet Union. Rural Hungary preserves a lively folk music culture. Budapest is also home to a mature, European classical music establishment, and throughout the country the **Rom** (Gypsies) practice their own forms of music.

ROM (ALSO, ROMANI)
An ethnic group originating in India characterized by a semi-nomadic lifestyle; popularly known as Gypsies.

HURDY GURDY
A chordophone common in France and Hungary that uses a wheel turned by a crank to vibrate the strings.

Site 6: *Tekerölant* (Hurdy Gurdy)

First Impressions. With its nasal tone and constant drones, the *tekerölant* (or **hurdy gurdy**) might strike some as sounding like bagpipes. If you saw a hurdy gurdy player—perhaps one of the well-known but little understood "organ grinders"—you would note that he was turning a crank with the right hand and pushing keys with the left. The sheer volume of sound can be deceiving; only one player is required to play this seeming "symphony in a box." Indeed, a medieval name for the instrument was *symphonia*.

A typical Hungarian village house in Oskü, north of Lake Balaton in central Hungary (left) Sean Folsom, plays the Hungarian *tekerölant* (hurdy gurdy), a cranked chordophone

(right) With the cover lifted, you can clearly see the parts of the Hungarian *tekerölant* (hurdy gurdy)

Aural Analysis. The *hurdy gurdy* is classified as a chordophone because its sound emanates from three or four strings. Specifically it is a lute, with a slightly differentiated body and neck, the latter being very short and thick. The *hurdy gurdy*'s continuous tone suggests that it is a bowed, rather than plucked, lute. Indeed, it is, but its creators have also solved the two biggest problems associated with playing such instruments: bowing smoothly and accurately stopping the strings. The result is the ultimate "user-friendly" instrument, a foolproof fiddle with the added bonus of drones to eliminate the need for an ensemble. Such instruments have a long history in Europe dating back to medieval times, when they were even used in church, but by the eighteenth century they had begun to die out, except for two prominent forms: the French and the Hungarian versions. To some extent both forms have been in continuous use as traditional instruments right up to the present time, and both also played a prominent part in twentieth-century folk music revivals in their respective countries.

To allow for smooth and continuous bowing, the makers of the *hurdy gurdy* installed a resin-coated wheel turned by a crank held in the right hand. The strings are tensioned against the wheel and sound continuously, though some models allow for the disengagement of the drone strings. The melody string is stopped, not by the player's fingers, but by a series of wooden *tangents* (or keys) placed along the bottom side of the instrument so that gravity causes them to fall back after being pressed against the string. Consequently, the *hurdy gurdy* produces both melody and drone as a continuous sound. In addition the player can produce accents by moving into place a "buzzing bridge" that lifts one drone string enough for a buzzing sound to be created when the crank is "jogged" (jerked) as it is turned.

Much of the traditional instrumental music of the Hungarian Great Plain is intended to accompany dance, but players often begin by playing a section that lacks a regular beat before beginning the metrical dance section. The Hungarian ethnomusicologist and composer Béla Bartók referred to the unmeasured section as being *parlando-rubato*, that is, "in speech rhythm," and to the measured or metrical section as being in *tempo giusto*, meaning "precise tempo," a phrase suggesting that a regular beat is present.

The track heard here consists of a series of tunes played on an instrument with one melody string and three drone strings, with the drones tuned A, e, a (the A being the tonic). Most of the melodies heard use the scale A, B, c♯, d, e, f♯, g, a, which is equivalent to the medieval Mixolydian "church mode," but in some passages the c♯ changes to c, producing the scale A, B, c, d, e, f♯, g, a, which has no church mode equivalent.

The track consists of five short melodies played without break, beginning with a *parlando-rubato* "song air." A second "song air" begins when the "buzzing bridge" is activated at 0'25." As the tempo picks up, you hear three "jumping dances" (at 0'58," 1'13," and 1'27"), with the repeat of the last one slowing down slightly. Completing the set is a "fast *czardas*" beginning at 1'59." The *czardas*, with its simple side steps, is Hungary's best-known "popular" dance. The meter is duple, but the phrasing of the fast *czardas* breaks the monotony of 4/4 time. The initial descending phrase, played twice, has four beats. Then follow three phrases of two beats each, producing a phrase with six beats. Thus, the dance shifts phrase groupings from four to six and back.

LISTENING GUIDE

CD 2.17 (2'13")

Chapter 9: Site 6

Hungary: *Tekerölant* (Hurdy Gurdy)

Instruments: *Hurdy gurdy*

TIME	LISTENING FOCUS
0'00"	Drone pitches begin on pitches A–E–a. Listen for the melodic pitches establishing the basic harmony (an A chord, A–C♯–E–a) as they move into the melody, using a fluctuating tempo (i.e., *parlando-rubato*). Also, note the brief sounding of the "buzz" timbre that will be used later to add a rhythmic element.
0'13"	Opening melody repeats.
0'25"	Listen for the change in melody, increased rhythmic density, and faster tempo at a steady rate of pulsation. Also, note the addition of the "buzzing bridge."
0'36"	Second melody repeats.
0'46"	Second melody repeats a third time.
0'57"	Listen for the change in melody, increased rhythmic density, and faster tempo.
1'13"	Third melody is repeated with variation.
1'27"	Third melody is repeated with variation. Listen for the introduction of new pitches in the scale at 1'31."
1'57"	Final section. Listen for the change in melody, increased rhythmic density, and faster tempo.
2'06"	Example fades. Note that the drone pitches have sounded throughout the entire example.

Source: Medley of traditional tunes performed by Sean Folsom, 2003 (private studio recording)

> **ETHNO-CHALLENGE (CD 2.17):** Clap the basic meter throughout to note the use of *parlando-rubato* and changes in tempo.

Cultural Considerations. Although traditional Hungarian music possesses certain distinct instruments and styles, it is better understood as part of a larger central and southeast European cultural sphere. When Béla Bartók began serious field research into Hungarian folk music in 1907, his goal was to isolate those elements that were quintessentially Hungarian. Inspired by Hungarian nationalism, his research was colored by the Hungarian antipathy toward non-Hungarian neighbors, especially the Romanians and Slovaks. To his surprise, however, Bartók discovered that Hungarian music had to be seen in a context that encompassed not only the music of Hungary's immediate neighbors but also the music of central and southeastern Europe as a whole. Owing to the Ottoman Turk influence on Hungarian music, he also conducted further work in Turkey and North Africa.

Bartók's research into "true" Hungarian village music did, however, reveal a side of Hungary that had been hitherto ignored; namely, traditional Hungarian folk music that was distinct from the music of the Rom (Gypsies). During the nineteenth century a number of composers, especially those working in Vienna, had a certain fascination with exotic sounds and styles they considered "Hungarian"; most turned out to be of Rom origin. Franz Liszt, for example, sometimes wrote music in "Hungarian style," such as the *Mélodies hongroises* (1838–1839) and *Ungarische Rhapsodien* (1846–1847)—but most of the sounds he understood to be "Hungarian" were actually Rom. Likewise, German composer Johannes Brahms's "Hungarian Dances" (1880) were really Rom in style. The same was true for most other "Hungarian" compositions of the time, because their encounters with the Rom were entirely in the sphere of urban public music-making where "Gypsies" predominated.

Collecting songs in the village of Darázs (now Dražovce), Slovakia, in 1907, Hungarian ethnomusicologist-composer Béla Bartók has the singers project directly into the horn of a cylinder recording device (De Agostini Picture Library/Getty Images)

9

WORLD MUSIC: A GLOBAL JOURNEY

Local musicians playing the *citera* zither (left) and *köcsög* friction drum (right) in Bugac, Hungary, a village near Kecskemet on the Great Plain (*Puszta*)

CIMBALOM

A hammered zither from Eastern Europe, commonly associated with Rom (Gypsy) music. Also, the national instrument of Hungary.

The old "folk" world that Bartók revealed has largely disappeared because of the tremendous disruption and displacements of World Wars I and II, changes in national borders, the rise and fall of communism, and, more recently, the modernization that has resulted from Hungary's joining the European Union. While there are undoubtedly rural areas where ordinary local people continue to play folk music, much of Hungary's "traditional" music is now revivalist in nature. Young musicians have sought to reenact the old culture of their grandparents by forming strictly old-fashioned ensembles specializing in music that might have been transcribed from Bartók's field recordings. These ensembles may employ a number of fascinating instruments—some of which are otherwise obsolete—including bagpipes (*duda*), friction drums played by vibrating a wet stick that passes through the membrane (*köcsög*), a zither (*citera*), a large hammered dulcimer (**cimbalom**) played both by Hungarians and by Rom, a struck lute (*gardon*), and long end-blown flutes (*hosszú furulya*).

Arrival: Bulgaria

Bordering Turkey and the Black Sea on the southeast and east, Bulgaria is about as far "southeast" as you can go in Southeast Europe. Modern-day Bulgaria is about the size of Ohio or the country of Guatemala. A part of the Roman Empire from around 50 C.E., the region came to be inhabited by Slavs during the 500s, then was conquered by the Bulgars from the north shore of the Black Sea in the 600s. The Bulgars converted to Christianity and established the Bulgarian Orthodox Church, an independent body within the greater family of Byzantine (Eastern) churches. After reaching its peak in the 800s, the Bulgarian Empire was conquered by the Ottoman Turks in the 900s and was not free from them until 1878, some 900 years later. Bulgaria's history during the two world wars is too complicated to relate here, but after World War II the country came under communist rule, which lasted until the collapse of the Soviet Union in 1991. Originally an agricultural nation where colorful regional cultures created some of Europe's most attractive and vibrant music, Bulgaria industrialized during the twentieth century, and aspects of its musical culture were reformulated for the stage to serve state purposes during the communist period.

Site 7: Bulgarian Women's Chorus

First Impressions. The singing of a Bulgarian women's chorus is quite striking to first-time listeners because it sounds so forceful and has an unusual tonal quality: it is open-throated and yet pinched, almost reed-like. As different as these characteristics are from the usual warm tones and vibrato of Western European and American voices, this singing is strangely attractive to many people. Perhaps you are already familiar with these sounds from a television commercial or a recording of a performance of arranged folksongs by the group *Le mystère des voix bulgares*. Singing by Bulgarian master Valya Balkanska, accompanied by two bagpipes (*gaidas*) recorded in the Rhodope region was included in the recording sent into space with the Voyager space-probe in 1977.

The Bulgarian *gayda* bagpipes clearly show the origin of the bag from a goat or similar animal (Shutterstock)

WORLD MUSIC: A GLOBAL JOURNEY

Colorfully dressed members of the Bulgarian State Women's Choir perform onstage (Jack Vartoogian/FrontRowPhotos)

Aural Analysis. Work songs are found throughout the world. In some places their rhythm helps coordinate a group activity, in order to make the work more efficient, to sustain it, or to discourage uncoordinated movements that might result in injury. In other places, work songs are simply commentary on the task at hand, as is the case here. This harvest song is from the Shop (rhymes with "hope") region in western Bulgaria, which lies not far from Sofia. Its singers comment on how the sun is coming up earlier and earlier, scorching the fields and making the farmers miserable in the heat. Other songs might focus on any part of the workday, from going to the fields in the morning, to the fatigue experienced at the end of the day.

The singers, all female, divide into two groups. Each group performs a low drone and melody. The drone is established with a quick rising glide at the beginning; the singers call this "following" or "bellowing." The other singers perform the melody, rising as high as an octave, but often dwelling on the seventh scale degree, which the singers call "crying out." Throughout our example, there are sudden glides down from the seventh on the sound "eee," a typical trait in Bulgarian singing. Two other characteristics contribute to an intriguing, admittedly "mysterious" quality: the music's non-metrical flow and its use of both the minor second and major second intervals, which create an exhilarating tension with the drone/tonic. When singers perform these close intervals, they seek to "ring like a bell," as the sound is described. You also hear sounds that resemble *ululation* (high pitched and trill like), but they are actually a series of quick glottal stops on a single pitch.

LISTENING GUIDE

CD 2.18 (1'34")

Chapter 9: Site 7
Bulgaria: Women's Chorus

Voices: Female ensemble

TIME	LISTENING FOCUS
0'00"	Listen for the "slide" into the drone pitch (E) by the first group of vocalists.
0'02"	Listen for the melodic voice as it moves away from the drone pitch with melismatic text setting.
0'05"	Listen for the melodic voice returning to the fundamental drone pitch.
0'07"	The melodic voice moves away from the drone pitch again to increase tension and "ring like a bell." Listen for this tension-release process throughout the performance.
0'10"	Listen for the return to the drone pitch.
0'12"	Note that a new group of vocalists have taken over performance of the drone pitch. This occurs throughout the performance. Listen with stereo headphones to note which group of vocalists is performing.
0'14"	Melodic voice moves away from the drone pitch again.
0'20"	Listen for the melodic voice's return to the drone pitch and subsequent departure.
0'22"	First group of vocalists return.
0'34"	Second group of vocalists return.
0'44"	First group of vocalists return.
0'56"	Second group of vocalists return, etc.

Source: "Harvest Song" (originally published on Balkanton BHA 1293), from the CD accompanying Timothy Rice's *Music in Bulgaria: Experiencing Music, Expressing Culture*. New York: Oxford University Press, 2004. Used by permission.

ETHNO-CHALLENGE (CD 2.18): Listen for the release of tension when the vocalists sing the same pitch. Create a graphic notation indicating the times when this occurs, as well as when the different groups of vocalist perform.

Cultural Considerations. Bulgaria, because of its specific history and geopolitical location, offers some of Europe's most attractive and colorful music. Long embedded in the Turkish Ottoman Empire, Bulgaria absorbed instruments and stylistic influences from Western Asia, both from the Turks and from the Rom, the latter of whom still provide many of the musicians heard in Bulgarian villages today. In addition to the close harmonies of its vocal music,

Bulgaria is known for its lively and driving instrumental music, often played on the bagpipes called *gaida*. Much of the dance music, especially that of the southwest, matches intricate step patterns to melodies based on "asymmetrical" time units. Instead of using phrases that are evenly divided or consistently in two or four beats, these melodies use a meter in which there is an uneven or asymmetrical grouping of beats, such as $5 = 2 + 3$; $7 = 2 + 2 + 3$; and even $11 = 2 + 2 + 3 + 2 + 2$. Some refer to these meters as "additive," because the meter is created by adding together two, three, or four short groupings of beats. This instrumental music forms quite a contrast to vocal music of the type we have heard, which is usually slower and unmetered.

Bulgarian music made a strong impression on Béla Bartók, who did extensive collecting in Bulgaria, especially the southwest region, the area that borders Macedonia, a newly independent nation that was formerly part of Yugoslavia. The complex asymmetrical meters he encountered, recorded, analyzed, and transcribed were usually labeled "Bulgarian meter." They are especially prominent in such works as his String Quartet Number 5, movement 3; the "Six Dances in Bulgarian Rhythm" from his pedagogical work for piano, the *Mikrokosmos*; and in many of his works with a title including the word "dance."

In Eastern Europe under communism, music became a potent tool for state expression and control. Because the masses ("peasants") were privileged under Marxism, their music was sometimes used to symbolize the power and unity of the state. As a consequence most communist regimes in Eastern Europe founded and supported "folkoric" ensembles that represented the nation's culture both to the internal population and to the world at large. Though staffed by people who in many cases had learned folk music in a "traditional" way, these state troupes were designed to perform arranged music on stage or for television and radio. The intent of their performances was to reinforce state philosophy in some manner, be it subtle or obvious. Many types of Bulgarian music were so treated, including the music of the women's choruses. Some performers, such as the group known as *Le mystère des voix bulgares*, achieved international recognition through tours and recordings. Because Bulgarian women's choral singing is so attractive to many non-Bulgarians, it has become one of most prevalent facets of "world music." Consequently, Bulgarian singing is now performed by many non-Bulgarian groups, used in advertisements to sell goods, and sometimes combined with other kinds of music to create multiethnic "world beat" recordings.

Questions to Consider

1. How is the history of European and Arabic cultural contact revealed through musical characteristics in places such as Spain and Bulgaria?

2. What defines a music as "classical" as opposed to "folk" in the European context? How has "classical" music influenced "folk" music style and performance and vice versa?

3. Drone is especially prominent in many European music traditions. What are some specific manifestations and how does drone relate to the overall sound?

4. Some "folk" instruments are designed to be easy to play but others require advanced

techniques. Discuss examples of European instruments that typify both ends of the spectrum.

5. How are music and musical instruments used to express national identity in Europe?
6. Is language a reliable demarcation of musical style in Europe? Why or why not?

On Your Own Time

Visit the textbook website to find these resources for further exploration on your own.

Greece

Website: The Divine Music Project
http://www.stanthonysmonastery.org/music/Index.html

Website: Learn Byzantine Chant
http://chant.hchc.edu/

Book: Jeffery, Peter. *The Study of Medieval Chant: Paths & Bridges, East & West.* Rochester, NY: Boydell Press, 2002.
http://www.boydellandbrewer.com/store/viewItem.asp?idProduct=12131

Spain

Website: Flamenco World
http://www.flamenco-world.com/flamenco.htm

Book: Leblon, Bernard (trans. Sinéad ní Shuinéar). *Gypsies and Flamenco: The emergence of the art of flamenco in Andalusia.* Hatfield, UK: University of Hertfordshire, 2003.
http://www.herts.ac.uk/about-us/our-structure/subsidiary-companies/uh-press/romani-studies/gypsies-and-flamenco.cfm

Website: Centro Flamenco
http://www.centroflamenco.com/about.html

Website: Paco Peña
http://www.pacopena.com/

Internet: Popular Artists from Spain
Gipsy Kings (France)
Paco de Lucia
Camaron de Isla
Ojos de Brujo

Russia

Website: The Washington Balalaika Society
http://www.balalaika.org/index.htm

Book: Prokhorov, Vadim. *Russian Folk Songs: Musical Genres and History.* Lanham, MD: Scarecrow Press, 2002.
http://www.scarecrowpress.com/Catalog/SingleBook.shtml?command=Search&db=^DB/CATALOG.db&eqSKUdata=0810841274

Website: Los Angeles Balalaika Orchestra
http://www.russianstrings.com/

Internet: Popular Artists from Russia
Dmitri Hvorostovsky
Dima Bilan
Alla Pugacheva
Mikhail Shufutinsky

Scotland and Ireland

Website: Celtic Instruments
http://www.celtic-instruments.com/

Book: Donaldson, William. *The Highland Pipe and Scottish Society, 1750-1950*. Edinburgh: Tuckwell Press, 2008.
http://www.birlinn.co.uk/book/details/Highland-Pipe-and-Scottish-Society—The—1750-1950-9781904607762/

Book: Hobsbawm, Eric. *The Invention of Tradition.* Cambridge, UK: Cambridge University Press, 1992.
http://www.cambridge.org/us/knowledge/isbn/item1143303/The%20Invention%20of%20Tradition/?site_locale=en_US

Audio: *The Bagpipe*. Lyrichord: LRYCD 7327, 1994.
http://lyrichord.com/thebagpipe-variousartists.aspx
http://itunes.apple.com/us/album/the-bagpipe/id49307197

Book: Cannon, Roderick. *The Highland Bagpipe and its Music*. Edinburgh: Birlinn Press, 2008.
http://www.birlinn.co.uk/book/details/Highland-Bagpipe-and-its-Music—The-9781841586663/

Book: Spillane, Davy, and Tommy Walsh. *Uilleann Pipe Tutor*. Pacific, MO: Walton's Mfg., 1997.
http://www.melbay.com/product.asp?ProductID=WM2183

Audio: Ennis, Seamus. *Forty Years of Irish Piping*. Green Linnet: GLI 1000, 2000.
http://greenlinnet.com/album.php?id=375
http://itunes.apple.com/us/album/forty-years-of-irish-piping/id265131126

Website: *Uilleann* Obsession
http://www.*uilleann*obsession.com/

Website: Hotpipes.com
http://hotpipes.com

Internet: Popular Artists from Scotland and Ireland
The Chieftans
Clannad
Altan
Gaelic Storm
The Pogues
Flogging Molly (American)

Hungary

Website: Gurypedia
http://www.gurdypedia.com

Book: Muskett, Doreen. *The Hudry Gurdy Method*. Muskett Music, 1998.
http://www.hurdygurdymethod.co.uk/

Website: Hungarian Hurdy Gurdy Maker
http://www.musicart.hu/balazs/index_en.htm

Website: Drehleier Musik (German-language site)
http://www.drehleier-musik.de

Audio: Vasson, Henri. *Hurdy Gurdy Music*. Smithsonian-Folkways: FW08747, 1976. (French Hurdy Gurdy)
http://www.folkways.si.edu/albumdetails.aspx?itemid=1502
http://itunes.apple.com/us/album/hurdy-gurdy-music/id279016462

Internet: Popular Artists from Hungary
P. Mobil
Bikini
Dopeman

Bulgaria

Book: Rice, Timothy. *May It Fill Your Soul: Experiencing Bulgarian Music*. Chicago: University of Chicago Press, 1994.
http://press.uchicago.edu/ucp/books/book/chicago/M/bo3633856.html

Book: Buchanan, Donna. *Performing Democracy: Bulgarian Music and Musicians in Transition*. Chicago: University of Chicago Press, 2005.
http://press.uchicago.edu/ucp/books/book/chicago/P/bo3641153.html

Audio: *Le Mystére des Voix Bulgares*. Nonesuch: 79165, 1987.
http://www.nonesuch.com/artists/le-mystere-des-voix-bulgares
http://itunes.apple.com/us/album/id151627271

Website: The Mystery of the Bulgarian Voices
http://themysteryofthebulgarianvoices.com/

Internet: Popular Artists from Bulgaria
Elitsa Todorova
Emil Dimitrov
Miro (Miroslav Kostadinov)
Esem

Sub-Saharan Africa: Ghana, Nigeria, Central Africa, Zimbabwe, Uganda, Senegal, The Republic of South Africa

10

Background Preparation	328
An Inside Look: Adesanya Adeyeye	331
An Inside Look: Habib Iddrisu	332
Planning the Itinerary	334
Arrival: Ghana	334
Site 1: Polyrhythmic Instrumental Ensemble	335
Site 2: "Talking Drums"	340
Arrival: Nigeria	345
Site 3: *Jùjú* Popular Music	345
Arrival: Central Africa	349
Site 4: Mbuti Pygmy Music from the Democratic Republic of the Congo	350
Arrival: Zimbabwe	353
Site 5: *Mbira Dza Vadzimu*	354
Arrival: Uganda	358
Site 6: *Akadinda*	359
Arrival: Senegal–Gambia	362
Site 7: *Jali* with *Kora*	362
Arrival: The Republic of South Africa	366
Site 8: *Mbube*	369
Explore More: Ladysmith Black Mambazo	371
Questions to Consider	372
On Your Own Time	373

Kete drummers in a funeral procession in Kumase, Ghana (Joseph S. Kaminski)

Background Preparation

Africa, the world's second-largest continent, is home to nearly 3,000 separate ethnic groups spread across 11.7 million square miles (30.3 million square km). While Africa boasts many densely populated urban areas, most other areas remain rural with limited infrastructure. Farming is the primary occupation of most Africans, although many people living in areas rich in natural resources, such as diamonds and coal, are employed by large mining companies and related industries.

The continent is customarily divided into three cultural zones: the pan-Arabic zone in the north, including the countries bordering the Mediterranean Sea; the Sahel zone, including those areas dominated by the vast Sahara desert; and sub-Saharan Africa, the rest of the continent south of the Sahara desert; the latter is the focus of this chapter. Western, eastern, and central Africa are equatorial and therefore quite hot and humid. Rainforests dominate the central interior, whereas the red-soiled Kalahari Desert typifies the arid landscape of southern Africa. Few mountain ranges exist, though several dormant volcanoes, the most famous being snow-capped Mount Kilimanjaro in northeastern Tanzania, provide a contrast to the vast rolling plains seen throughout most of sub-Saharan Africa. Wildlife preserves are scattered throughout much of the continent, which are home to such well-known animals as the African elephant, lion, zebra, giraffe, and rhinoceros.

While the ancient Egyptian pharaohs ruled the most famous kingdoms of North Africa, the kings of sub-Saharan Africa also held dominion over vast territories for numerous generations. In western Africa, the earliest known kingdom was the Kingdom of Ghana, which controlled the trade routes of West Africa from roughly the fifth to the eleventh century C.E., when Muslim militants from present-day Mauritania overtook it. Other important empires prior to the colonial era included the Mali kingdom (mid-thirteenth to late fourteenth century), and the Songhai kingdom (fifteenth to late sixteenth century), both

Zebras in a South African game reserve, one of Africa's visual icons (Max T. Miller)

Islamic. In southern Africa, the Zulu King Shaka (1787–1828) is best known, having organized a powerful military machine that conquered many peoples throughout South Africa and as far north as Tanzania. Historical warriors and royal lineages continue to play a vital role in the cultural identity of modern Africa.

The political borders of present-day Africa, however, resulted from European colonial occupation. Throughout much of the nineteenth century and into the early twentieth century, vast regions of Africa were claimed as colonies by several European powers. The 1884–1885 Berlin Conference is often cited as a decisive moment in Africa's political history, particularly for the Congo region. At this meeting, German, Belgian, French, British, and Portuguese officials, along with representatives of governments that had no colonial stake in the region, such as the United States, allocated territorial rights to most of central and southern Africa without the presence of a single African. Thereafter, based on these colonial entities, newly independent African nations were later formed with little regard for the cultural differences of the various peoples living within their borders. Consequently, many different ethnic populations, with diverse cultural traditions, often live in close proximity within a single country, while their brethren also live in neighboring countries.

Decades of European colonial rule left strong marks on African religious life, governmental structures, and languages. Travelers to Africa will encounter multilingual speakers who may speak multiple indigenous languages (of which there are nearly 800 in sub-Saharan Africa alone), as well as one or two European languages, the most common being English, French, and Portuguese. Though colonialism affected many of the cultural activities of African peoples, often oppressively, traditional practices still thrive throughout the continent, especially in rural areas. Islam and Christianity have long co-existed in sub-Saharan

Kete dancer at an Asante funeral in Kumase, Ghana (Joseph S. Kaminski)

Africa, though aspects of earlier animistic traditions have often been reinterpreted into the ritual activities of the mainstream institutionalized religions.

An emphasis on the collective community remains an overarching principle essential to the social organization and cultural identity of many African populations. Social identity is valued over individual identity, as expressed by the common proverb, "I am because we are." Each person serves a function within the overall group. In smaller villages, everyone is considered part of the same family, whether or not they are related by blood. A person's possessions are frequently "shared" with other members of the community, as if everyone lived in the same house. Furthermore, these "extended families" comprise not only living members of the community but also the spirits of ancestors. Even when a person is physically "alone," he is accompanied by one or more ancestor spirits who act as guardians and confidants.

Music is a vital aspect of the daily lives of people throughout sub-Saharan Africa. Even the most mundane tasks, such as canceling stamps at the post office, pounding millet, or walking are made enjoyable by putting them into the rhythms of music. Dance and singing are equally essential; indeed, music, dance, and singing, conceptualized as distinct from one another in the West, are described in many places with the same terminology, because they are considered inseparable. The importance of the collective community that characterizes traditional African life is reflected in three main activities associated with music: communal dance, call-and-response singing, and the use of **polyrhythm** in instrumental performance. Informal dance activity often takes place when large groups of people are gathered. An individual may spontaneously step out from the crowd to dance in conjunction with a musical performance. The crowd may respond with cheers, and others may be inspired to dance as well. Spontaneous dance participation, however, is generally brief, and the dancer will fall back into the group to make way for others. The individual thereby demonstrates deference to the community by only briefly asserting an individual identity within the context of a larger social scheme. Formal dance activity also tends to emphasize group participation, though dance in ritual contexts, such as trance dancing, often involves only a few specialized performers. In these instances, the performance requires a specific knowledge of tradition or that the individual dancers are of a specific social status, such as performers with royal patronage. The set choreography of these dances differs from dancing in informal contexts and may not include opportunities for individual expression. Formal dance activities are performed with some social function in mind, such as honoring royalty or inviting ancestral spirits to participate in community events.

Vocal performance can occur as part of religious ceremonies or other ritual activities, in the context of storytelling, dance, or royal functions, or merely as entertainment. Though many solo vocal traditions can be found, the majority of vocal performances involve group singing, generally with a call-and-response organization. In call-and-response, an individual sings a "call" and the group "responds" appropriately. (A familiar American example: *Call*: Give me a G . . ., *Response:* G!; *Call*: Give me an 'O . . .', *Response:* 'O!'; *Call*: What's that spell?!, *Response*: Go!!!) This organization may also be thought of as a "question" by the caller and an "answer" by the group and is therefore clearly different from "prompting," in which the leader cues the group, which responds with the same words (as, for example, in the lined hymn to be studied in Chapter 13).

POLYRHYTHM

A term meaning "multiple rhythms"; the organizational basis for most sub-Saharan African music traditions.

Adesanya Adeyeye

AN INSIDE LOOK

My maternal grandmother was an Osun priestess (Osun is the Yoruba goddess of the river). During the usual Osun ceremonies at Ilesa, Osun State, normally held three or four times a year, children like myself were encouraged to partake in the ceremonies especially in dancing and playing musical instruments. I was about five years then, in 1957. Elders play the Lukorigi drums, an ensemble comprising three cylindrical double headed drums of varying sizes with two *agogo* (iron bells) of different sizes to accompany chants and songs in praise of Osun, who is believed to cure barrenness in women. The overwhelming atmosphere created by the festivities had a greater influence on my musical perception and interest and later served as an impetus in my taking up music and music technology as a profession. But even as a child I was part of the usual village children's use of pawpaw stems and bamboo pallets in making musical toy whistles. That was in my father's village, via Ilesa.

My exposure to formal musical learning only began when I left secondary school, after 1971 through 1981 in Lagos. After enrolling at the Nigeria Institute of Music headed by Taiwo Ogunade and Chris Ajilo in 1978, I passed the Grade 8 Associated Board of the Royal Schools of Music theory examination. During these ten years in Lagos I also got musical training by playing guitar in *jùjú* and *highlife* bands. As a choir member of the Regina Mundi Catholic Church, Mushin, Lagos, I discovered that I was naturally gifted in playing the *sekere* (gourd shaker). Even though I had a keen interest in playing the *konga* drums (*agbamole* and *ogido*), choir master Mr. Joseph Osho was so much fascinated by the way I played the *sekere* that he would not allow me to play the drum but only the *sekere*. Thus seven years as a church choir member playing only sekere had a very strong influence in my musical life including later as a *sekere* maker. In 1981 I began undergraduate music studies at Kent State University, Ohio, United States.

Adesanya Adeyeye, professional musician

After graduation from Kent State I went to Los Angeles for nine months (January to September 1986) and became involved in instrument making. I turned to *sekere* making, and this was my starting point into music technology. I became financially secure and gained cultural recognition in Los Angeles and the suburbs, like Pasadena and Hollywood. I went on to exhibit my *sekere* in various black cultural festivals in Los Angeles where they were highly admired. I lived very comfortably on sales of *sekere* in Los Angeles during the last six months of my stay. After that I returned to Nigeria in June 1987.

In Nigeria I embarked into research on the construction of musical instruments. Since my knowledge of the construction of *sekere* was limited to the *sekere ikanyere* (the type using plastic beads), I decided to learn the art of making *sekere aje*, which use cowrie shells.

That same year my father-in-law, a traditional Chief of Kajola in the Atakumosa local government of Osun state, introduced me and my wife to Pa Jimoh Omoleke, the leader of the *sekere aje* players in Osogbo, and he taught us the art of constructing *sekere aje*. Pa Omoleke also provided us with the historical origin of *aje*, which he linked with the Iba Ologbo compound in Oyo Alaafin.

Between 1989 and 1992 while I was also researching the *Ifa eerindinlogun* divination corpus in the cult of Osun in Ijebu-Jesa, I was able to learn how to construct *Lukorigi* and *Ukoko* drums. As noted earlier, *Lukorigi* are ritual drums in the worship of Osun. *Ukoko* is a set of clay pot drums used socially in various Ijesa traditional festivals. The art of making *Lukorigi* and *Ukoko* drums was passed on to me by Pa Sunday Akunmudan, a close relation on my mother's side at Ijebu-Jesa.

I have also learned the construction of other musical instruments by disassembling and then re-assembling them. They include the Western classical guitar, the *bata, sakara, samba, konga, oja, atenteben*, and many more. I have also carried out innovative construction of instruments through inspiration from fellow music technologists. Such instruments include the Western descant recorder and flageolets. Between 1988 and 2000 while I was a lecturer and researcher at the Music Technology department of the Polytechnic, I was also able to learn the construction of yet more instruments from traditional instrument makers who came to instruct my students. Such instruments include *agogo ide* (brass gong) and *saworo ide* (brass bell). In addition I have been able over the years to carry out my own original design of tools and machines used in the fabrication of innovative musical instruments, including circular saws, turning machines, and wood rolling machines.

Habib Iddrisu — AN INSIDE LOOK

I was born into the Dagomba/Dagbamba family of court historians and musicians in Gukpegu/Tamale in northern Ghana. There I was brought up under the tutelage of my grandfather, Manguli-Lana Adam Alhassan, chief drummer in Tamale, and was inspired by my great uncles, many of whom were famous Dagbon musicians, especially Jabling (Fuseini Alhassan).

Like many of my cousins, I started playing both the *lung-a* (talking drum) and *gungong* (supporting drum) at age six. By age eight, I was renowned throughout the region for my dancing and drumming in styles such as Takai, Bamaya, and Atikatika. As a young man I studied traditional Dagbamba music and dance as well as other genres from across Ghana and West Africa. The wealth of expressive styles that I encountered sparked my interest in sharing and teaching this material to as broad an audience as possible. Soon I was coaching in Ghana's largest cities, especially in Accra where I taught and performed with some of the city's finest cultural groups. Then I traveled extensively around the world to perform, and I won Ghana's Best Dancer Award in 1992.

Between 1999 and 2004, I studied at Bowling Green State University where I received undergraduate and graduate degrees in African Studies and History respectively. I also coached a variety of African music and dance classes. In 2002, my choreography was selected and presented at the National American Dance College Festival at the Kennedy Center in Washington, DC. My studies have significantly enriched and broadened my artistic and analytical thinking. The music of Dagbamba *Lung-si* (drummers) is completely filled with language. Its rhythmic nature may lead an outsider to think the music is entirely improvised, but the reality is that almost every drum phrase represents Dagbamba spoken language (Dagbanli).

The music of my tradition is very intricate, yet easy to understand. It is intricate in that performance depends entirely on a person's ability to listen and memorize all the drum language that accompanies each occasion. Because drummers are storytellers, they must be able to talk (on their drums, of course) about the history, politics, and economic lives of the people. The drum language dictates the mood of not only the listeners but also the musician. When we drum in weddings, naming ceremonies, for the enskinment of a new chief, or just for a commoner in the marketplace, the atmosphere at the time is quickly absorbed by the *Lung-si*. For instance, when we drum during funerals, we react to the mood around, not like actors or actresses taking roles but as those whose heartbeats are attached to the messages the *lung-a* is sending at the time. The *Lung-si* role is quite versatile within the context of the community's needs. At any occasion when we drum, someone may fall into trance. When this happens, we assume the role of the "healer" who controls the mediums responsible for trance, thereby subduing the spirits and leading the person out of the trance at the appropriate time. Our main role in the community is to keep the history of our people alive and exciting, and this is what makes us *Lung-si*.

Habib Iddrisu, Dagbon drummer and dancer

Polyrhythm is the predominant structure for organizing instrumental (as well as some vocal) musical performance in sub-Saharan Africa. For centuries, the polyrhythmic music traditions of sub-Saharan Africa were largely incomprehensible to outsiders. Missionaries and foreign explorers often characterized the rhythmically dense drumming traditions of western Africa as "chaotic." Colonial governments suppressed these musical practices and often labeled the "wild" playing associated with "pagan" rituals as evil music that corrupted the soul. Ignorance of how the complex polyrhythmic music organization worked was a primary factor behind these negative attitudes. Since the 1950s, however, ethnomusicologists, both foreign and African, have developed a better understanding of the inner musical workings of these traditions, which are some of the most complex on the planet, and helped to disseminate this knowledge to others. The old ethnocentric discrimination of African music has given way to great enthusiasm for these many vibrant musical traditions.

While drumming is assumed by many Westerners to be the primary African musical activity, much other music occurs involving aerophones and chordophones, either with or without accompanying idiophones and membranophones. Unique vocal traditions, many of them polyphonic, are common, and both storytelling and recounting the histories and genealogies of many of Africa's ethnic groups are passed from generation to generation via oral tradition.

Planning the Itinerary

Our survey of musical performance in sub-Saharan Africa is of necessity brief and highly selective but seeks to illuminate some of the key elements of African music-making. An examination of drumming traditions from Ghana, the type of African music perhaps most familiar to the outside world, begins our tour. We then make a stop in Nigeria to hear the popular music genre known as *juju*. Our visit to Senegal–Gambia will introduce the renowned poet/praise-singers/oral historians of the Mandinka, called *jali*. We will then consider the music of the Mbuti Pygmies of Central Africa, a xylophone tradition from Uganda, and lamellophone performance in Zimbabwe. Finally, we will examine a Zulu choral tradition from South Africa known as *mbube*, which has a musical organization that contrasts with that of much music found in the rest of sub-Saharan Africa.

Arrival: Ghana

The Western world is perhaps most familiar with the cultural activities of West African populations because this region is geographically closer to both Europe and the Americas than is any other area of sub-Saharan Africa. The bulk of Africans forced into slavery by Europeans and sent to the Americas during the colonial period (roughly early 1500s to late 1800s) were taken from this region, and as a result the cultural traditions of West Africa were disseminated throughout the Caribbean and the Americas. The spiritual traditions of the Dahomey people from Benin and of the Yoruba from Nigeria, for example, are found throughout the "New World" in various permutations, namely as *vodou* (voodoo) in Haiti, *candomblé* in Brazil, and *santeria* in the United States and Cuba. Textiles and clothing used by African Americans to represent their African heritage frequently draw on the stylistic features of West African formal attire, and characteristics particular to music traditions from western Africa, especially the prominent use of drumming, have come to represent—incorrectly—all music from the sub-Saharan region. The reductive Euro-American characterization of African music as "drumming," while not accurate for the continent as a whole, is thus understandable, as drumming is so prominent in West Africa. Ghana, a former British colony (with English as its official language) and nearly equal to the United Kingdom in size, was one of several colonies—most others being French—on Africa's "Gold Coast." Its twenty-four million people speak around seventy-five different African languages along with English.

Site 1: Polyrhythmic Instrumental Ensemble

First Impressions. Polyrhythmic music can seem bewildering on first listening. The music does not follow "a beat" in the Western sense of the term; that is, no consistent pulsation seems to articulate an easily identifiable meter. The complexity of the interwoven rhythmic patterns creates a dense sound that agitates some listeners while hypnotizing others. High-pitched and low-pitched drums, rattles, bells, and voices all combine to create a multifaceted kaleidoscope of sound that continuously spins the same musical elements into an energetic torrent of "rhythmic melody." While these polyrhythms are difficult to grasp analytically, their effect can be powerful and immediate. Even many novice listeners will be inspired to dance along with this vibrant music.

Aural Analysis. Polyrhythm is a system of musical organization that may be challenging to those steeped only in European harmonic musical creation, where rhythm is organized into simple units of 2, 3, 4, or 6 beats most of the time. In the African polyrhythmic tradition no conductor articulates the basic beat for everyone to follow, and there is no need for notation telling the musician what to play. Each participant plays a rhythmic pattern that in and of

The Nsuase *kete* drum group performing at an Asante funeral in Kumase, Ghana (Joseph S. Kaminski)

itself is generally not difficult. Each pattern follows its own time—or what some scholars refer to as a timeline—without respect to the kind of underlying meter found in Western music.

The simplest example of polyrhythm is the "two against three" cross-rhythm. In this example, one pattern follows a timeline pattern of two pulses while another pattern provides three pulses within the same time span. You can try this yourself or with a friend. Pat your left hand on your knee with an even duple pulse, "1-2-, 1-2-, 1-2-. . . ." Now, tap on a book with your right hand to an even triple pulse, "1-2-3-, 1-2-3-, 1-2-3- . . .," making sure to sound the "1" beats of both pulses simultaneously. As you will quickly discover, while each pattern is simple in and of itself, combining the two becomes a significant challenge.

When these two patterns are combined, they form a *rhythmic melody* that can be articulated as one idea, namely as a "1–2&3–, 1–2&3–, 1–2&3- . . ." pattern, in which the "&" falls between the last two pulses of the triplet. Try the cross-rhythm again by starting with the right-hand triple meter tap, and just pat your left hand on the "&." This should be easier. Once you've gotten that down, add a pat on the "1" beat as well. The resulting rhythm is the same as the "two against three" pattern you initially tried, but the difference is that you are no longer thinking in terms of separate rhythms (duple vs. triple), but in terms of a unified whole (see Table 10.1). This latter conception is more in line with the way African musicians approach performance: for them, each individual musical element is part of the collective whole. Of course, however Africans themselves perceive of polyrhythmic music, understanding the intricacies of individual timeline patterns leads to a greater appreciation of the music's complexity.

Oftentimes it is easier to recognize the individual timeline patterns when the musicians can be seen. In our cross-rhythm example, you can say the phrase "Look to the left" in rhythm as you play. Seeing your left hand play the duple pattern will help you to hear it more clearly. Now say, "Look to the right" in rhythm and watch your right hand sound the triple pattern. Your ears will focus on that pattern more clearly. The absence of visual references requires that you listen for different timbres—for example, drums versus bells.

Our example of an Akan recreational band from Ghana features voices and several instruments: the **donno**, a double-headed hourglass variable-pressure drum played with a hooked stick and capable of producing more than one pitch; the *tom-tom*, a pair of tall, single-headed hand drums; the *afirikyiwa*, an iron clapper bell; and the *axatse* (pronounced "a-ha-che"), a gourd rattle with external beaded netting. Together, the musicians create complex polyrhythms, far more difficult to perform than our cross-rhythm example. In order for the musicians to collectively play the correct rhythmic melody, each individual musician must interlock his particular pattern very precisely with the other musicians' patterns.

A helpful analogy can be made to a bicycle wheel. One rhythm typically functions as a density referent, a pattern that is like the center of a bicycle wheel. Because drumming ensembles tend to be loud, a louder instrument with a distinctive timbre, such as a bell or a rattle, usually plays this part. Once the central rhythm is established, the other musicians

DONNO
A double-headed hourglass-shaped drum found in Ghana and elsewhere in West Africa.

Table 10.1 Two against Three Cross-Rhythm

Left Hand	1			&	
Right Hand	1		2		3	

play their parts in relation to it; held together by this central reference point, these other parts are like the spokes of the wheel. (Complicating our analogy, however, is the fact that musicians often use more than one reference rhythm to play their part, and thus interlock their pattern with multiple instruments at once.)

Once all the patterns are added together, forming the collective analogous to the rim of the wheel, the music spins along without trouble. If, however, one of the patterns falls out of sync, then the wheel might start to wobble. The music starts to feel unbalanced, and if the troublesome part does not drop out and reenter correctly, the entire ensemble is in danger of "crashing." This frequently happens when amateur ensembles in the United States attempt to play African music. The music may spin easily for a while, but a slight distraction may cause one musician to lose concentration and fail to play his or her simple pattern in sync with the complex whole. As a result, the music falls apart like a house of cards, and the musicians must start over, typically by reestablishing the density referent and then gradually adding the other patterns until the music flows again.

The musicians in our recorded example are obviously quite skilled. The vocal parts follow a call-and-response pattern, while the instruments perform polyrhythm. It is not necessary to know what the specific rhythms are to appreciate the music as a whole. Representing all the parts of the music in metrical notation, as is frequently done by Western musicians, will mask the way African musicians generally perceive a rhythm as a timeline pattern. Nonetheless, focusing on specific instruments and parts can be a helpful way of explaining how polyrhythm works in a complex example such as this.

Turning to the bell (*afirikyiwa*) part first, we hear a rhythm that could be written as "1–2–3–(4), 1–2–3–(4), 1–2–3–(4). . . ." This three-pulse pattern with a silent fourth pulse can be heard as a reference point for the handclaps, which sound only once in the course of the bell pattern. When is the clap heard? The clap follows its own timeline, which is just one clap per cycle. If you think in terms of meter, then the clap in isolation can be considered to follow a duple meter, "1–(2)–, 1–(2)–, 1–(2)–. . . .," in which the second pulse is silent.

Alternatively, you can consider the clapping as falling slightly ahead of the "&" after the third bell pulse. But the tempo of the music is moving very quickly. Trying to count "1&2&3&4&, 1&2&3&4&, 1&2&3&4& . . ." in order to clap in the correct place is difficult and quite unnecessary. If you forget counting and just listen to the bell, you can "fit" your part in much more easily. Sometimes it also helps if you think of a phrase that suggests the rhythm as a whole. For example, try thinking of the rhythm as the phrase, "What do you think?" with the bell part sounding on "What do you" and the clap falling on "think." Easier? It should be, because when you do this you are hearing the rhythmic melody created by the combination of bell and handclaps.

While this discussion places the bell pattern as the reference point in order to more easily hear how the handclaps work in relation to it, the central density referent in our audio example is *actually* the handclaps themselves. The bell pattern, as well as the rattle's three-note pattern, anticipates the claps, leaving space for them to sound and thus be heard clearly. The call-and-response form of the voices also references the handclaps to fit their "timeline" into the performance correctly, by emphasizing the third syllable of the vocal phrase in conjunction with the handclaps. The drums (*donno* and *tom tom*) alternate between high-pitched and low-pitched sounds in a duple pattern, with the lower drum corresponding to the handclaps. The alternating drum sounds may either be created by a single drummer, or by two drummers in tandem. Without seeing the performers, it's hard to know which is the case in our example.

Throughout the performance, the drummers slightly alter their patterns to make the performance more dynamic but then return to their initial pattern. The music spins like a bicycle wheel, or perhaps the aural equivalent of a kaleidoscope: it uses the same "pieces" but changes them just enough to make the music different each time the cycle repeats. Once you can identify each part individually, try listening to the whole ensemble again as a collective performance.

LISTENING GUIDE

CD 2.19 (1'45")

Chapter 10: Site 1

Ghana: Polyrhythmic Instrumental Ensemble

Vocals: A single male lead and a single female lead. Also, a mixed male/female ensemble response
Instruments: Drums (*donno*, *apenteng*, *pate*), metal bells (*afirikyiwa*, *dawuruta*, *aggre*), rattle (*akasaa*). Also, handclaps

TIME	LISTENING FOCUS
0'00"	Example fades in with instrumental activity. Listen for the varying timbre of the drums, rattles, and bells. Refer to above discussion for more complete discussion of individual rhythms.
0'02"	Male lead vocalist enters.
0'19"	Group response, repeating the verse of the lead vocalist.
0'36"	Female lead vocalist enters.
0'41"	Male lead vocalist returns.
0'46"	Female lead vocalist returns.
0'52"	Group response.
1'08"	Male lead vocalist returns.
1'25"	Group response.

Source: "Fante Area: Vocal Band" performed by the Odo ye few korye kuw Vocal Band, recorded by Roger Vetter, Abura Tuakwa, Ghana, 1984, from the recording entitled *Rhythms of Life, Songs of Wisdom: Akan Music from Ghana, West Africa*, SF 40463, provided courtesy of Smithsonian Folkways Recordings. © 1996. Used by permission.

ETHNO-CHALLENGE (CD 2.19): Choose a rhythmic pattern, such as that made by the bell or the handclaps, and play it throughout, singing along with the group response.

Cultural Considerations. Polyrhythm is the basis for musical creation throughout much of sub-Saharan Africa. For those who grow up in cultures where polyrhythmic music is common, understanding comes "naturally" because these insiders are surrounded by it in various contexts, such as festivals, funerals, marketplaces, and so on. For outsiders, however, polyrhythm is one of the least penetrable forms of musical organization found anywhere in the world.

Our example is typical of music performance among the Akan—whose language is part of a family of languages that includes such ethnic groups as the Asante (Ashanti), Fante, and Denkyira—as well as among non-Akan speaking peoples of Ghana, such as the Ewe and the Igbo. Even though the performers are ordinary villagers from a small farming community, the musicians nonetheless display a high degree of musical skill. Such "recreational bands," as they are often called, play at wakes, funerals, and for annual festivals, as well as for social clubs, special community events such as weddings, and purely for entertainment.

Polyrhythmic ensembles often have a master drummer who oversees all aspects of a performance, including vocal performance and dance. The master drummer knows a multitude of rhythms that work within the performance and is responsible for helping each musician to "fit" within the group. He may briefly play specific "timeline" patterns that correspond to those of other instruments, establish a new pattern that someone will then follow, or play within the overall polyrhythmic activity, frequently "speaking" with his drum to communicate with the other musicians, dancers, or audience.

The majority of musicians who play in polyrhythmic ensembles learn their craft in an informal manner. Continual exposure to polyrhythmic music throughout childhood gives most an intuitive sense of rhythm and timing, though only a few become specialists capable of leading an ensemble.

Adzewa group performing at a funeral at the Asante court in Kumase, Ghana (Joseph S. Kaminski)

Site 2: "Talking Drums"

First Impressions. This example alternates short sections of a text spoken by a young woman with drum passages that seem to mimic the girl's words, both tonally and rhythmically. What we are hearing are the famous "talking drums" (which usually are not coupled with spoken word passages; we have chosen this example because it makes the drumming's relationship to speech particularly clear). This is not music for dancing but for listening. In fact, it is not considered music at all but is rather a speech-substitute (also called "surrogate speech") in the context of a music performance.

Aural Analysis. Language is an integral part of music performance in Africa. Many African languages are "tonal," meaning that the intonation of the voice (for example, high/low tones or rising/falling tones) is as important to the meaning as the phonemes used.

Although tonal languages are encountered in many cultures, such as China and Nigeria, no European languages are tonal. One way to understand how intonation can change the meaning of a word is to listen to the different ways the word "yes" is pronounced, depending on whether it is used as a question or an answer. When it is used as a question, the speaker's inflection has a rising tone, whereas when it is used as an answer the tone is level or slightly falling. Unlike inflected languages, however, tonal languages make the contoured or level inflection an integral part of the word regardless of context.

In Ghana, a drum capable of tone-bending is used to imitate the rising and falling inflections of the voice, in order to communicate words through music. Double-headed hourglass pressure drums, such as the *donno*, are especially equipped to accomplish tonal variation, as squeezing the strings that secure the faces and thus changing the tension of the drum can alter the pitch. When the drum only produces a single fixed pitch, two drums of differing pitches can be used to imitate the direction in inflection; for example, a low pitch followed by a high pitch would convey a rising tone. Additionally, drummers replicate the "speech rhythm" of the words they imitate. By coupling the tones and rhythms of specific phrases, drummers can create surrogate speech comprehensible to native speakers of the language who are additionally familiar with the conventions of drum language.

A non-native speaker will not always recognize when linguistic meaning is being conveyed through musical performance. Musicians may do this in a variety of contexts: while praise-singing a chief or king, announcing the passing of a royal family member, recounting historical events, and so on. These performances may be solo or occur in the context of ensemble playing.

The "talking drums" played in this example are *atumpan*, a pair of large, goblet-shaped hollow logs with heads of tightly stretched animal skin, typically antelope. The particular piece praises a king and may be performed with or without the vocalist. In this case, the musician speaks in Twi, a common tonal language found throughout Ghana, before playing each phrase on the drums. The novice listener may perhaps be better able to appreciate the musical relationship between the language and music by first listening for the drummer's imitation of the speech's tonal aspect. Keep in mind that rising and falling pitches require two consecutive drum strokes, going from low to high or high to low, respectively.

SUB-SAHARAN AFRICA

The *mpintin* drum group of the Asantehene, Kumase, Ghana. The *mpintin* consists of several *donno* (hourglass pressure drums) (left), *mpintintoa* (membranophone with gourd resonator) (right), and other drums (not pictured) (Joseph S. Kaminski)

LISTENING GUIDE

 CD 2.20 (1'54")

Chapter 10: Site 2
Ghana: "Talking Drums"

Vocals: Single female
Instruments: *Atumpan* (pair of drums played with wooden angled-sticks)

TIME   **LISTENING FOCUS**

The complete translation for this example is found on pages 343–345. This guide refers to some key points to note.

0'00"   Example begins with the vocalist speaking the text, followed by the mimicking *atumpan*.

0'26"   Start of the section featuring drum language glorifying the king of Denkyira. Listen for the drum's manifestation of the spoken phrase "Adawu, Adawu."

0'34"   The phrase "*Ma wo ho me ne so*" ("Come forth in thy light") is used several times throughout this example. Listen for the manifestation of this phrase on the drum at 0'38" and try to identify it each time without referencing the text.

WORLD MUSIC: A GLOBAL JOURNEY

Atumpan drums from Ghana, often used as a speech surrogate (Amy Unruh)

0'38"	Drum manifestation of the phrase "*Ma wo ho me ne so.*"
0'44"	Listen for the drum's manifestation of the spoken phrase "*Kronkron, kronkron, kronkron.*" Note that the drum sounds four times per word, indicating that the speech rhythm in performance is determined by more than merely the syllables of a word. (Two syllables, yet four drum strokes.)
1'47"	Final drum manifestation of the phrase "*Ma wo ho me ne so.*"

Source: "Talking Drum" by Elizabeth Kumi, and Joseph Manu from the recording entitled *Rhythms of Life, Songs of Wisdom: Akan Music from Ghana*, SF 40463, provided courtesy of Smithsonian Folkways Recordings. ©1996. Used by Permission.

ETHNO-CHALLENGE (CD 2.20): Imitate your own speech rhythm and tonal inflections using a drum or other instrument that has a high or low sound.

Cultural Considerations. In Ghana drums are used as a surrogate for speech to give the words more power and to enable the praise-singing to be heard by ancestral spirits as well as the living. "Talking drum" performances often occur to honor someone of royal lineage or to praise a powerful ancestral spirit. Because royalty may be considered descendents of powerful spirits, praise-singing or praise-drumming frequently accomplishes both objectives simultaneously. Prior to the colonial period, chiefs customarily included in their entourage musicians capable of rendering poetic performances in honor of the chiefs and their lineage. This practice has diminished considerably but is still found among some groups, especially the Asante.

Here is a transcription and translation of the words in our example, first recited in honor of the king of the Denkyira people and then echoed by the *atumpan*:

Greetings to Those Present

Me ma mo atena ase, Nana ne ne mpaninfoo	I welcome you, Nana and his elders
Owura dwamtenani, *Enanom ne agyanom* *ne anuanom a yeahyia ha,* *yegye me asona*	Mr. Chairman, mothers, fathers and brethren here gathered, the response to my greeting is "asona"
Saa atweneka yi fa Odeefoo Boa Amponsem, Denkyira hene ho	This drum language is about Odeefuo Boa Amponsem, King of Denkyir
Odomankoma kyerema, ma no nko!	Creator's drummer, let it go!

Actual Drum Language Glorifying the King of Denkyira

Adawu, Adawu, Denkyira mene sono.	Adawu, Adawu, Denkyira the devourer of the elephant.
Adawu, Adawu, Denkyira pentenprem, Omene sono, ma wo ho mene so	Adawu, Adawu, Denkyira the quicksand, devourer of the elephant, come forth in thy light, exert yourself
Pentenprem, ma wo homene so,	Quicksand, come forth in thy light,
Ma wo ho me ne so	Exert yourself, in glory
Kronkron, Kronkron, Kronkron;	Your holiness, holiness, holiness;
Amponsem Koyirifa, ma wo ho me ne so	Amponsem Koyirifa, come forth in thy light in glory
Ako nana ma wo ho mene so	Grandsons of the Parrot, come forth in thy light
Ako nana a ho a ne mframa mene boo, ma wo ho me ne so	Grandsons of the Parrot whose winds sweep and devour even the stones, come forth in thy light
Wo a wofiri dodoo mu,	you who came from many,
Wo a wutu a ewiemu den se asamando, ma wo ho me ne so	You who fly and the skies become still like the cemetery come forth in thy light
Amponsem nana a "odi sika to," atomprada, ma wo ho me ne so	Amponsem's grandson who "eats mashed gold dust," and uses only freshly mined gold in his daily transactions, come forth in thy light
Agona adegyekan nana *Wo a wode osee ye oyo*	First grandson of the Agona line, You promise and you fulfill it
De nkoden akyekyere Denkyiraman, de ape no sibre, ma wo ho me ne so	Having fought hard to establish the Denkyira state, and having found it a place among the nations, come forth in thy light
Ayekra Adebo nana	Grandson of Ayekra Adebo [first ruler, fetish priestess of Denkyira]
Ahihi Ahaha nono	Grandson of Ahihi Ahaha
Wirempi Ampem nana a owo ntam na yenka, ma wo ho me ne so	Grandson of Wirempi Ampem whose oath is not to be sworn, come forth in thy light
Otibu Kwadwo nana	Grandson of great King Kwadwo Otibu, [accompanying audio ends here]
Wo a wode Denkyiraman firii Abankesieso baa Jukwaa, ma wo ho me ne so	who led the Denkyira people in their great migration from Abankesieso to settle in Jukwa, come forth in thy light

Odeefoo, ma wo ho me ne so	Benefactor, come forth in thy light
Ma wo ho me ne so Agona,	The Agona clan,
Denkyiraman da wo ase,	The Denkyira state,
Yeda wo ase a ensa,	Expresses its endless,
Esie ne kagya nni aseda	Gratitude to you

(Text and translation from *Rhythms of Life, Songs of Wisdom: Akan Music from Ghana, West Africa*. Smithsonian Folkways SF 40463, 1996, pp. 17–18.)

This translation provides the literal meaning of the message conveyed by the "talking drum"—but these words also have a deeper level of symbolic meaning that is unintelligible to cultural outsiders. Understanding the extra-musical aspects of musical performance is one of the most fascinating challenges of ethnomusicology, and of linguistics and anthropology as well.

Arrival: Nigeria

Nigeria, smaller than Egypt, is Africa's most populous country with nearly 160 million inhabitants, twice that of Egypt. Nearly half of this population lives in urban areas such as Lagos, the nation's largest city. With massive deposits of oil, the country has been a promising prospect for investors at the start of the twenty-first century despite the political challenges faced by its budding democracy over the past decade. Nigeria has more than 250 ethnic groups with the dominant ones being the Fulani, Hausa, Yoruba, and Igbo. Nigeria's linguistic and musical tapestry is therefore quite diverse, leading to an incredible array of vocal and instrumental music traditions. The "talking drum" is also a common feature of music from this region where there are many types of hourglass pressure drums, such as *gan gan*, *dun dun*, and *kalangu*. These drums are heard in a variety of rural and urban contexts, particularly in association with festive and royal events, as well as the popular music style known as *jùjú*.

Site 3: *Jùjú* Popular Music

First Impressions. *Jùjú* blends the traditional foundation of polyrhythmic percussion and storytelling with modern elements of instrumentation and concert performance. The music has immediate appeal for its easily discernable "beat" but also an undercurrent of complex rhythm that requires a deeper appreciation of the music's Yoruba roots.

Aural Analysis. *Jùjú* music flows like a river with many ripples and eddies to attract the attention of even the novice listener for several minutes and beyond. Holding interest in an unfamiliar music is often a challenge when exploring world music. Modern audiences are accustomed to three-minute pop songs, a supra-cultural conditioning due to the early limits of recording technology that have continued to dominate the popular music soundscape. Music outside the popular music sphere, however, is typically not bound by such time limitations; for example, an Indian *raga* performance or a Western symphony. By and large, however, popular music around the world still follows this expectation of short performance. Not so with *jùjú* music, where a single song performance can easily last several hours.

Jùjú music first appeared during the 1920s and is considered to be an innovation of Tunde King (Abdulrafiu Babatunde King). This early style utilized an acoustic guitar or banjo with a drum, gourd rattle, and tambourine as rhythmic accompaniment. Vocals were presented in a call-and-response pattern with a repetitive refrain and vocal harmony. Short instrumental solos were interspersed between verses, which included lyrics typically rooted in Yoruba proverbs and poetry, as well as praise-singing. This basic structure continues to be the primary form for modern *jùjú* music, even though the use of polyrhythmic percussion has become a more essential element.

Rhythm, as with most music from sub-Saharan Africa, is fundamental to *jùjú* and a primary reason a performance can hold the listener's attention for so long. While melody and harmony are more central in popular music in other parts of the world, the continuous undercurrent of complex polyrhythms drives this music. The duple meter provides a central, almost hypnotic, pulse surrounded with complex and subtle variations of rhythm and a multitude of percussive timbres.

Atop this polyrhythmic canvas are the vocal and melodic instruments, which punctuate, rather than dominate the *jùjú* sound: electric guitars, synthesizers, pedal steel guitars, sometimes saxophones or other melodic instruments mixing with local instruments, such as "talking drums," known as *gan gan* (hourglass pressure drums), *sakara* (frame drums), and *shekere* (gourd rattles) as well as a plethora of other percussion common to Western popular music idioms. The vocal parts similarly enhance the atmosphere with short phrases rather than extended melodic lines. Weaving its way through these musical elements is the lead electric guitar, or sometimes the *gan gan* or *iya ilu* (also an hourglass pressure drum), again sounding succinct passages that accentuate, rather than distract from the focus of the underlying rhythmic foundation.

LISTENING GUIDE

 CD 2.21 (3'58")

Chapter 10: Site 3
Nigeria: *Jùjú* Popular Music

Vocals: Single male lead (King Sunny Adé, aka KSA), male vocal group
Instruments: Electric guitars, electric bass, Hammond B-3 organ, drum set, *gan gan* ("talking" drum), *sakara* (frame drum), *shekere* (shaken idiophone)

TIME	LISTENING FOCUS
0'00"	KSA establishes tempo with a four beat count, followed by instrumental introduction. Note the undercurrent of polyrhythmic percussion sounding throughout the example.

0'20"	KSA then male chorus enter on title refrain, "Oro Yi Bale." Melody instruments stop during this opening phrase. *Gan gan* is also heard leading into vamp phrase.
0'27"	Organ and guitars play the primary "vamp" phrase.
0'36"	Vocal refrain.
0'43"	Instrumental vamp. The *gan gan* features more prominently in this section.
0'51"	Vocal refrain.
0'58"	Instrumental vamp. The lead electric guitar features more prominently in this section.
1'07"	Vocal refrain.
1'14"	Instrumental vamp.
1'25"	*Gan gan* leads into new vocal lyric.
1'34"	Instrumental vamp.
1'43"	Extended vocal verse.
2'09"	Instrumental vamp. The *gan gan* features prominently before crossfade.
2'20"	Example edited to crossfade into organ solo. Lead electric guitar plays in background.
2'56"	Lead guitar becomes aural focus. Organ plays in background.
3'50"	*Gan gan* sounds just before the example fades.

Source: "Oro Yi Bale" from *Bábá mo Túndé*, composed and arranged by King Sunny Adé and his African Beats. © 2010 Mesa/Blue Moon Recordings/IndigeDisc. Used by permission.

ETHNO-CHALLENGE (CD 2.21): Listen to King Sunny Adé's recordings via the Internet (iTunes) to hear how his style develops over time. Compare his music to that of other popular artists from West Africa.

Cultural Considerations. After World War II, musicians in Nigeria began incorporating electric instruments into their *jùjú* recordings. Innovators such as Ebenzer Obey and I.K. Dairo expanded the musical elements further by adding other instruments, such as the accordion, and introducing a greater variety of Yoruba percussion, the "talking drum" in particular. Nationalism was at its peak during the late 1950s and early 1960s when Nigeria achieved independence from the United Kingdom. *Jùjú* was an important musical means of expressing Nigerian cultural identity, especially for the Yoruba population.

As rock music became increasingly popular around the globe throughout the 1960s, *jùjú* incorporated musical elements from various Western genres. By the 1970s, funk and reggae were also important musical influences on *jùjú* musicians, such as King Sunny Adé (b. 1946), the reigning monarch of modern *jùjú* music. Modeling his early performances on those of I.K. Dairo, KSA (as he is known in Nigeria) made his first local recording of *jùjú* in 1967. By the mid-1970s, he had become one of the primary figures in the style's development, highlighting the use of the "talking drum" as a soloist, dropping the accordion in the instrument line-up, and featuring the pedal steel guitar, synthesizers, and electronic effects, such as "wah-wah" pedals. KSA was highly acclaimed for his guitar skills and on stage performances.

KSA also achieved prominence in part due to his royal lineage, which created some controversy due to his career path as a professional musician, traditionally regarded as a low status occupation. In many ways, this enhanced his popularity among the masses, who admired his willingness to resist social convention in order to pursue his passion for music. His fans also lauded the moral themes prevalent in his music, which encouraged people to live with high ideals and respect their cultural roots. Many of his lyrics are based on traditional Yoruba poetry and storytelling, as with our listening example, which deals with the subject of female infidelity, a "heavy topic" (*Oro Yi Bale*) in Yoruba culture.

KSA achieved international recognition with his seminal recording, *Jùjú Music*, released in 1982 on Island Records, founded by Chris Blackwell in Jamaica. Blackwell was betting on KSA to become a successor to the deceased Bob Marley (1945–1981), who had elevated Jamaican reggae music into a fixture of the mainstream music market. KSA toured the United States and Europe, fueling interest in Afropop, which until then had achieved limited interest. While this exposure established KSA as a world music icon, *jùjú* music itself did not achieve the popularity Blackwell had hoped for, and he was soon dropped from the label. Nevertheless, KSA continued to record for local and other international labels, producing more than 100 albums over the course of his career. The listening example, "Oro Yi Bale" is from his recent release, the highly acclaimed *Bábá mo Túndé* (2010), an homage

Nigerian musician and singer King Sunny Adé and his band (Al Pereira/WireImage/GettyImages)

SUB-SAHARAN AFRICA

King Sunny Adé
(Jack Vartoogian/
FrontRowPhotos)

to the founder of *jùjú* music. KSA continues to be the watermark for *jùjú* musicians from Nigeria and is rivaled in stature only by Fela Kuti, the founder of *Afrobeat*, another of Nigeria's most successful popular music styles.

Arrival: Central Africa

Modernization's spread to Central Africa beginning in the twentieth century has led to the destruction of much wildlife, most notably the endangered silver-backed gorilla, probably the best-known animal inhabiting the Congo basin rainforests. Even so, this region still maintains some of the most pristine areas of tropical vegetation on the planet and is home to one of the most intriguing and talked-about peoples of Africa, the Pygmies.

The total Pygmy population is unknown. Whatever their true numbers—estimates range from as few as 40,000 to nearly 600,000—they are spread across several countries in Central Africa, including The Congo, the Democratic Republic of the Congo (DRC), Gabon, Cameroon, and the Central African Republic (CAR). *Pygmy* is a generic term for a diverse population of forest-dwellers who are short by Western standards, being on average less than 5 feet tall. Contrary to popular belief, many Pygmies live in villages and farms, interacting with surrounding ethnic groups on a daily basis. Other **Pygmy** cultural groups, however, still live within the forest and maintain a nomadic lifestyle. Our focus is on a specific cultural group known as Mbuti.

Some Western anthropologists, including Colin Turnbull, have been intensely interested in the typical social structure of nomadic Pygmy groups, which provides one of the few examples of an egalitarian society. An egalitarian society is one in which every member of the community is considered equal. Certain individuals may take a leadership role depending on the context—for example, a strong young man may lead a hunting party—but there is no formal hierarchy. Cooperation rather than competition guides the social interaction within a Pygmy community, because each person is dependent on the others for his or her survival.

PYGMIES
A general term describing the many ethnic groups of forest-dwellers in the rain forests of Central Africa.

Site 4: Mbuti Pygmy Music from the Democratic Republic of the Congo

First Impressions. The aspect of Mbuti Pygmy music that generally strikes the listener first is the intricacy of the vocal performance. The "hoots and hollers" swirl around the listener

Performance of the Wunga dance by Pygmies of the Bangombe ethnic group in the forests of southwestern Central African Republic (Gerhard Kubik)

SUB-SAHARAN AFRICA

Batwa Pygmy dancers perform for visitors to Bwindi National Park, Uganda (Shutterstock)

as the vocalists sing, yodel, and clap. Few instruments are heard in Mbuti music, usually only flutes, an occasional rattle, a pair of clapsticks, or small drums.

Aural Analysis. Mbuti Pygmy music is dominated by vocal performance. Although Mbuti singing frequently employs a call-and-response organization like many other African traditions, it also features a unique polyrhythmic vocal style that makes it quite distinctive. As with other African traditions, polyrhythm is central to the structure and creation of Mbuti music. Since few instruments are used, the voice creates the basic timeline patterns that would otherwise be produced instrumentally among non-Pygmy ethnic groups in sub-Saharan Africa.

In our example, performed by a group of Mbuti Pygmies from the Democratic Republic of the Congo (DRC), a set of clapsticks plays a repetitive rhythm with minor variation that acts as the aural referent. If you consider it to be in a duple meter (though the musicians by no means think in terms of meter) with eight pulses, the basic clapsticks rhythm would be 1 2-4-6 7-. A lead vocalist provides the essential lyrical content necessary for the ritual, while the rest of the singers interweave their voices to create a complex polyrhythmic structure. As with instrumental performance elsewhere in Africa, each person performs a short repeating melodic pattern. Some performers may sing a basic theme, while others sing variations. Each pattern interlocks with and overlaps those of the other performers, resulting in the unique rhythmically dense layering of melodic lines typical of Mbuti vocal performance. Handclaps or instruments may function as a density referent, as in our example, but often the basic theme acts as the aural center for the performers. Though soloists are not always set apart, call-and-response singing often occurs in addition to the polyrhythmic singing.

LISTENING GUIDE

 CD 2.22 (1'39")

Chapter 10: Site 4

Democratic Republic of the Congo: Pygmy Music

Vocals: Single male lead and mixed male/female ensemble
Instruments: Clapsticks

TIME	LISTENING FOCUS
0'00"	Listen for the "duple meter" with eight-pulse subdivisions of the clapsticks. Note the varying accented rhythms, loosely emphasizing a 1 2-4-6 7- pattern.
0'04"	Note the rumbling thunder in the background. This performance is part of an animistic ritual intended to bring rain.
0'06"	Listen for the lead male vocal declamation.
0'11"	Lead male vocal returns. Listen for his reappearance throughout the performance.
0'14"	Listen carefully to the varying parts of the vocal melodic–polyrhythm. A prominent upper female voice is briefly heard at this point.
0'22"	Note the return of the upper female voice.
0'33"	Lead male transitions to speaking.
1'03"	Clapsticks rhythm noticeably shifts to a new rhythmic pattern loosely emphasizing a 1-3 4-6- rhythmic pattern.
1'32"	Loud thunderclap ends the musical activity. Exclamations by the performers are heard as the example fades.

Source: "Elephant Song" performed by Mbuti Pygmies from the recording entitled *Music of the Rain Forest Pygmies: The Historic Recordings Made by Colin M. Turnbull*, Lyrichord LYRCD 7157 (original recording, 1961). Used by permission, Lyrichord Discs Inc.

ETHNO-CHALLENGE (CD 2.22): Choose a recognizable vocal timbre and sing their part throughout the performance.

Cultural Considerations. The nomadic lifestyle and egalitarian social structure characteristic of Mbuti Pygmies are reflected in their musical performances, which are considered community activities. Each person plays an "equal" role, contributing his or her individual talents to the collective performance. The creation of complete melodic lines and thick rhythmic density requires the interlocking of parts and thus a dependency on other performers. The Mbuti's nomadic lifestyle is also reflected in the music's emphasis on the voice; after all, large instruments are not easily transported, but the voice can travel anywhere.

Communal performances among the Mbuti usually include dance as well as music, especially circle dances. These dances may be performed for ritual occasions, such as puberty ceremonies, or in anticipation of an important event, such as a hunt. Because animism predominates in the Mbuti spiritual belief system, music is often sung in conjunction with related ritual activity.

Arrival: Zimbabwe

Much of Zimbabwe, located in east Africa and being the size of Japan, consists of vast grasslands inhabited by a variety of animals, such as impalas, hippopotamuses, crocodiles, hyenas, and baboons. The rainy season occurs from November to March, creating an average annual rainfall of between 23 and 33 inches (58 and 84 cm). Mining is a major industry, though most people earn a living as farmers, growing tobacco and various foodstuffs. The great Victoria Falls is found in Zimbabwe's western region bordering Zambia and is one of the most attractive tourist destinations anywhere in Africa.

Victoria Falls on the border between Zambia and Zimbabwe (Max T. Miller)

Known as Rhodesia until achieving independence in 1980, Zimbabwe had been a colony of the British. Consequently, the official language is English, though many native languages are spoken as well. The predominant indigenous languages include Ndebele and Shona. The Shona ethnic group, who constitute more than 80 percent, has been of particular interest to ethnomusicologists due to a distinctive musical instrument they play known as the *mbira dza vadzimu*.

Site 5: *Mbira Dza Vadzimu*

MBIRA
A general reference to lamellophones found throughout Africa, in particular those common to the Shona and other ethnic groups from Zimbabwe.

First Impressions. The gentle sound of the *mbira dza vadzimu* (often simply referred to as **mbira**) is much like that of a child's music box. The music seems to float in an endless cycle, punctuated by an occasional somber cry from the performer. The sound of a small rattle helps maintain a steady pulse, while a distinctive "buzzing" sounds throughout the performance. This is hypnotically soothing music that might make you feel as if you were rocking in a chair on the front porch watching and listening to heavy raindrops fall from the eaves to puddles of water below.

Aural Analysis. It is accurate to describe the *mbira dza vadzimu* as a music box. As with a Western music box, tones are produced through the plucking of flat metal strips of various lengths. Such instruments are known as lamellophones, a subclassification of the idiophone

Mbira dza vadzimu (lamellophone) from Zimbabwe

Close up of lamellae (springy metal tongues) (Shutterstock)

family. Similar instruments are found among many other ethnic groups throughout sub-Saharan Africa and are called by various names, such as *likembe* or *kalimba*. The term *mbira* has become generalized in the Western world to denote all African lamellophones.

Performers pluck the long, narrow tongs of the *mbira dza vadzimu* with their thumbs and forefingers. A large, resonating gourd with one portion removed amplifies the quiet tones, making them audible to a small circle of listeners. Small seashells or pieces of metal, such as bottle caps, are usually affixed to the resonator to create the "buzzing" timbre, a characteristic sound of many instruments found throughout the continent. Often bottle caps are also found on a metal bridge attached to the keyboard of the *mbira*. The percussion instrument that enters shortly after our example begins is the *hosho*, a gourd rattle with internal beads. Usually, two *hosho* are used to maintain a steady cross-rhythm (two against three) throughout a performance.

Mbira dza vadzimu music has a minimum of two parts. The lead part, known as the *kushaura*, is most often played in the higher range of the instrument and is more easily heard. The *kutsinhira*, or "following" part, is typically played on the lower-pitched keys of the instrument. These two parts interlock and overlap to create polyrhythm. In our example, the higher *kushaura* pattern plays with a triple pulse, while the lower *kutsinhira* pattern follows a duple pulse. The accents of the *hosho* fall on the duple pulse with a deemphasized interlocking pulse.

The *hosho* reinforces the "following" part, and thus helps clarify the underlying harmonic rhythm of the piece. Harmony is a term most commonly associated with European music traditions (see Chapter 9), but a kind of African harmonic movement can be perceived in *mbira dza vadzimu* music as well. A *mbira dza vadzimu* piece often has four harmonic segments that repeat with seemingly endless variations. In our example, each segment has four beats articulated by the lower *kutsinhira* pattern and the *hosho* accents.

Three types of lamellophones (top, left to right) *mbira dza vadzimu* and *karimba*, (lower) *matepe* (N. Scott Robinson)

Try to hear the four four-beat segments of this *mbira dza vadzimu* song. Tap the duple pulse of the *hosho* with your right hand. Once you have established this reference point, listen closely to the upper *kushaura* melodic pattern. The melodic pattern starts in the high end of the instrument's range and then switches to slightly lower pitches. When you hear the melodic line of the lead part lower in pitch, start counting to four with your right-hand fingers. This change in the melody of the *kushaura* part marks the middle point of the four segments. The theme begins when the melodic line rises again. When you hear the melody return to higher pitches, use your left hand to count each segment as your right hand counts the "1" pulse again. The first two four-beat segments of the song use higher notes, while the second two segments use lower notes before the entire theme is repeated.

The *kushaura* and *kutsinhira* parts provide the basic structure of the music. Variations are often added, especially to the lead part. A single musician may even add a third "middle" part to increase the rhythmic density of the music. The ability to add variations and rhythms is the sign of a skilled performer. A second *mbira dza vadzimu* performer may also add variations and interlocking rhythmic patterns to the basic theme, as is heard in the background of this example.

The musicians may also sing. In our example, the musicians' voices enter just after the second pulse of the first harmonic segment and drop out at the end of the four-segment theme. In most *mbira dza vadzimu* performance contexts, the singer, not the *mbira*, is the primary focus. Call-and-response is common in group singing, but solo vocal performances are frequent as well.

LISTENING GUIDE

CD 2.23 (1'41")

Chapter 10: Site 5
Zimbabwe: *Mbira Dza Vadzimu*

Vocals: Single male. Secondary vocalizations also appear
Instruments: Pair of *mbira dza vadzimu* (lamellophone), pair of *hosho* (gourd rattle)

TIME	LISTENING FOCUS
0'00"	A single *mbira* enters to establish the referent melodic–rhythmic pattern. Listen for the contrasting range of high pitches interlocking with the lower pitches. Also note the buzzing timbre that accompanies each plucked tone.
0'04"	A single *hosho* (rattle) enters, marking the basic pulse twice before the second *hosho* is added to complete the rhythm (0'06"). A second *mbira* enters at this point as well. Note that the melody is halfway through its content and that the tempo increases.
0'09"	The overall melodic content repeats at this point. Listen for the division of the melodic content into four equal sections of four pulses each.
0'10"	Listen for the high-range descending melodic scale of the second *mbira*.
0'16"	Overall melodic content repeats again.
0'20"	Vocalist enters.
0'24"	Overall melodic content repeats again. Listen for this repetition with subtle variations throughout the performance.
0'36"	Secondary vocal declamation.
1'09"	Ululation is heard in the distance.
1'20"	A faint percussive timbre (wood tapping) is heard in the background, contributing to the polyrhythmic structure.
1'24"	Listen for the high-range descending melodic contour of the second *mbira*.

Source: Shona ancestral spirit song, "*Nyama musango*," performed by Elias Kunaka and Kidwell Mudzimirema (Mharadzirwa); recorded by John E. Kaemmer, Jirira, Zimbabwe, 1973. Used by permission.

ETHNO-CHALLENGE (CD 2.23): Play the *hosho* pattern heard throughout this example using a pair of gourd rattles or similar-sounding idiophones. For a real challenge, construct your own *mbira*.

BIRA
A spirit possession ceremony of the Shona ethnic group from Zimbabwe.

Cultural Considerations. The Shona use the *mbira dza vadzimu* in a variety of contexts, such as storytelling, entertainment, and rituals. The most important ritual context is the Shona spirit possession ceremony known as **bira**. The example heard here is from a *bira* ceremony in which ancestral sprits are invited to appear to the community through the body of a spirit medium. These spirits are believed to guide and protect the community members in their day-to-day activities.

Perhaps because of this association with spirit possession, the Shona consider the *mbira dza vadzimu* a specialists' instrument, one that requires a high level of skill for performance in ritual contexts. Many *mbira dza vadzimu* musicians are "called" to learn the instrument by an ancestral spirit and thus feel obligated to become proficient at performance to help facilitate possession during these rituals. Certain pieces are only to be played for these ceremonies and are prohibited from performance in other contexts.

Arrival: Uganda

Uganda, along with Kenya and Tanzania, borders Lake Victoria, the second-largest freshwater lake in the world. The country has an exceptionally diverse population, with numerous languages spoken in addition to English. Chimpanzees roam through its jungles,

Karamojong women dancing in northeastern Uganda (Shutterstock)

and leopards hunt in its grassland regions. Most inhabitants are agriculturists, though fishing provides a significant income for those along the lake. Thatched huts can still be found in rural areas, though as the country develops they are becoming increasingly rare.

Uganda's known history dates to the fourth century C.E., when it was a major crossroads connecting northern Nilotic cattle herders and southern Bantu agriculturists via the Nile River, which flows from Lake Victoria through the region. The kingdom of Bunyoro became a powerful unifying force in the late fifteenth century but was eventually overshadowed by the kingdom of Buganda, which became the region's major power in the early nineteenth century. The kings of Buganda (known as *kabaka*) soon confronted British colonialists, who arrived on the heels of the Christian missionaries who had begun proselytizing throughout the region during the middle of the nineteenth century. By 1890 the kingdom and the areas around it had become a British protectorate, and Uganda's present boundaries were set.

After achieving independence in 1962, the country survived some rather notorious political and economic misdirection. Idi Amin, a brutal ruler, seized control of the government in 1971 and orchestrated a reign of terror that abolished the former kingdoms, ousted more than 70,000 "Asians," and massacred more than 300,000 Ugandan citizens. By the end of the decade, he was at war with neighboring Tanzania, whose forces, allied with Ugandan rebels, drove him from power. Since then, Uganda has struggled to regain stability and its footing as a regional power and trade partner.

Site 6: *Akadinda*

First Impressions. This music is like a sped-up film of a busy New York City street corner during rush hour. Looking for "space" in this continuous welter of sounds is futile. It is crowded and unrelenting. This is, perhaps ironically, one of the types of music that inspired "minimalist" composers such as Steve Reich, Philip Glass, and Terry Riley, who in the 1970s and 1980s created music that wove simple, repetitive phrases into intricate, interlocking, densely textured patterns of sound.

Aural Analysis. The **akadinda** is a large, heavy log xylophone with between seventeen and twenty-two bars. The wooden bars are arranged over banana tree trunks that rest on the ground set at a 90-degree angle to the logs. Long sticks driven into the ground separate the bars and keep them from shifting sideways during performance. The largest bars can be more than 2 feet (61 cm) long, and the instrument itself is nearly 7 feet (2.13 meters) long. *Akadinda* are also found in sets, in which case each instrument produces pitches in different ranges, so that altogether they cover between four and five octaves. The lowest ranged *akadinda* is often placed in a shallow pit, which serves as a resonator and gives the instrument a deeper sound.

While most xylophones in sub-Saharan Africa have bars with a flat surface, *akadinda* bars frequently have a carved "dip" in the center, and *akadinda* performers may strike the center of the bar at the "dip," which gives the instrument its unique "hollow" timbre. Mallets are either made of straight pieces of soft wood or have a "hook" shape to better strike the center of the bars. *Akadinda* performance requires substantial interlocking of parts. Two groups of three men each sit opposite each other with the xylophone between them. The first group plays a repetitive rhythmic pattern, typically in octaves, while the second group

AKADINDA

A large, heavy log xylophone from Uganda that uses interlocking patterns that can approach nearly 600 beats per minute.

Performers on the *akadinda* xylophone of Uganda (Moya A. Malamusi)

fills in an interlocking pattern to create a thick polyrhythmic structure. *Akadinda* performance usually also involves a third group of performers playing yet another interlocking pattern, and consequently the resultant tempos of such music can approach nearly 600 strikes per minute. This triple-interlocking technique is unique to *akadinda* performance; other African xylophone traditions have fewer performers and are limited to double-interlocking of rhythmic patterns.

It is nearly impossible to decipher this fast-moving music merely by listening to it. To unravel the intricacies of the interlocking parts would require seeing the performers in action. Nevertheless, as with all polyrhythmic music, just by listening you can begin to hear some of the subtleties. The music may initially strike you as chaotic, but if you focus on just one or two distinct sounds, you can start to hear how they work within the whole.

In our example, the highest-pitch strand is played with a steady pulsation on just one pitch in what can be thought of as a duple meter. While this pulse is part of a larger pattern, following it is a first step toward hearing individual parts. In the low-pitched patterns, a longer cycle can be heard that can be articulated as a pattern of high (H), center (C), and low (L) pitches, and can be rendered as: HC-HC-HL-HC-HCCC-. To put it in "Western" terms, the high pitch anticipates the main beat, which corresponds to the earlier single-pitch pattern in duple meter. This "beat" falls on the center pitches of the first two pairs, the low pitch of the next, the center of the following pair, and the first and third center pitches of the four-beat finish. You might sound this out as "&1-&1-&Low-&1-&123," with the main beat on the ones and three.

Again, keep in mind that this way of singling out particular patterns is not how the African musician thinks about musical creation. A Ugandan musician is concerned with how the patterns fit together rather than with how they can be pulled apart.

LISTENING GUIDE

CD 2.24 (1'52")

Chapter 10: Site 6
Uganda: *Akadinda*

Instruments: *Akadinda* (log xylophone)

TIME	LISTENING FOCUS
0'00"	As mentioned in the reading, the triple-interlocking technique of *akadinda* performance is especially challenging to follow using your ears only. To begin, listen for the different ranges of pitch rhythms: high, middle, and low.
0'16"	Listen for the low-range melodic–rhythmic pattern. This is described in the reading as: HC-HC-HL-HC-HCCC- (H = high pitch, C = center pitch, L = low pitch).

	Expressing the rhythm with minimal reference to pitch level helps to indicate where the basic pulse is: &1-&1-&Low-&1-&123-. The 1, Low, and 3 mark the basic pulse, indicating a six-beat cycle at a tempo of approximately 126 beats per minute.
0'19"	The cycle at 0'16" repeats. Listen throughout the performance for this melodic–rhythmic pattern, which repeats after roughly every three seconds.
0'30"	Listen for the high-range pitches played between two alternating pitches. You might express the basic pattern as "Up/Up-Down, Up-Down, Up-Down, Up-Down. Up-Down, Up-Down." The double "Up" falls on the first pulse of the melodic–rhythmic pattern described above. The remaining "Up" strokes reinforce the basic pulse.

Source: Buganda *akadinda* song "*Gganga aluwa*" ("Gganga escaped with his life"), performed by Sheikh Burukan Kiwuuwa and his group of royal *akadinda* musicians; recorded by Peter Cooke, Kidinda Village. Mpigi, Buganda, Uganda, 1987. Used by permission.

ETHNO-CHALLENGE (CD 2.24): Attempt the triple-interlocking pattern with two friends, labeling each person A, B, and C. Start slowly, alternating hands as you play. Each person should play on the following beats respectively: A (1, 4), B (2, 5), C (3, 6). Gradually increase your tempo and maintain the numerical order between players.

Cultural Considerations. Xylophones are among the instruments most common to sub-Saharan Africa. Many, such as the *balafon* found in West Africa, are small enough to be carried and played as solo instruments. Others, such as the *timbila* of Mozambique, exist in a variety of sizes and are typically played in larger ensembles. The polyrhythmic nature of xylophone performance combines with the use of melodic pitches to create exceptionally complex music.

Uganda is home to many xylophone traditions, but the *akadinda* is perhaps the most challenging and highly respected of them. Before the colonial period, *akadinda* musicians were part of the musical entourage that accompanied the *kabaka* (king) of Buganda. Their music was considered "royal" and was not played outside courtly functions. The melodies played on the *akadinda* are believed to be derived from vocal music; thus, through their association with specific texts, *akadinda* performances could convey a story or offer praise to the *kabaka* without needing a singer. Our example would be understood by Ugandans to have a specific meaning, despite being purely instrumental; according to the Africa volume of the *Garland Encyclopedia of World Music*, it "celebrates the rough justice meted out to Gganga, a young page of the palace who was caught sexually molesting the Princess Nassolo" (p. 824). The *akadinda* is closely related, both physically and in its performance practices, to the *amadinda,* another xylophone found in Uganda and other nearby regions, though usually in less formal contexts. Whereas the *akadinda* has seventeen or twenty-two individual keys, usually played with three distinct interlocking parts, the *amadinda* has only twelve individual keys and is played with two interlocking parts and a third resultant pattern that includes elements of the first two parts.

WORLD MUSIC: A GLOBAL JOURNEY

Arrival: Senegal–Gambia

The Gambia, about the size of Connecticut or Jamaica, is a sliver of a country embedded into the southern portion of the much larger Senegal at the western edge of the African mainland. Approximately 200 miles (320 km) from east to west and only 30 miles (50 km) wide from north to south, the country runs along the mouth of the Gambia River, which flows into the Atlantic Ocean. Most Gambians are agriculturists, the primary crop being peanuts. Because the country was formerly a British protectorate, English is common, as is French, the national language of Senegal, the nation that surrounds The Gambia on three sides. Indigenous languages are commonly spoken as well, especially Wolof, Jola, and Mandinka, the languages of the predominant ethnic groups of the Senegal–Gambia region.

Of particular musical interest in this region is the tradition of the *jali* (or *jeli*), a specialized musician associated with the Mandinka populations. In Mandinka society, the *jali* (pl., *jalolu*) serves as an oral historian, a role held by similar artisans throughout many parts of Western Africa. The history of most African populations is passed from generation to generation through oral tradition rather than through writing or other forms of empirical evidence. Though members of the community are usually familiar with the major events of their ethnic group's history, the responsibility of maintaining both this history and individual family genealogies is hereditary, usually falling on one particular family. In some societies, such as the Mandinkas, this activity is considered a family trade involving skills and knowledge passed down just as a blacksmith might pass on his skills to the next generation.

Site 7: *Jali* with *Kora*

JALI (Also, JELI; pl. JALOLU)
A poet/praise-singer and oral historian from the Mandinka of Western Africa.

First Impressions. The music of the **jali** offers proof of the diversity of African music, which is frequently stereotyped by outsiders as revolving around drumming. No percussion is heard, merely a vocalist and his instrument, a plucked chordophone known as the **kora**. The opening flourishes on this instrument lead to a steadily repetitive melodic "groove." This churning, repeated pattern underlies the rapid-fire delivery of the vocalist. He has something important to tell you and displays his virtuosity with words rather than melody. His shouted praises for the group's VIPs are meant for everyone to hear.

KORA
A harp-lute or bridge harp played by a *jali* during his poetic recitation.

Aural Analysis. *Jalolu* play a variety of other instruments as well, especially the *balafon,* a small xylophone, or the *koni,* a lute, depending on their geographic location and preference. The *kora*, the most distinctive of *jali* instruments, is a type of bridge harp unique to West Africa. The *kora* is constructed of a large resonating calabash (a type of gourd), which is cut so that the face of the instrument can be covered with cowhide. The neck pierces the body and forms the tailpiece at the base of the instrument. The strings, now made of nylon fishing line but formerly from thin strips of twisted antelope hide, are stretched between rawhide collars on the neck and an iron ring in the tailpiece. Instead of ending in the string holder, they pass over a tall bridge standing upright in its place on the resonator.

As on all harps, the strings of the *kora* lie in a plane perpendicular to the face of the instrument, but on the *kora* there is an additional feature. Since the strings pass over notches on either side of the bridge, there are two planes, both perpendicular to the face or sound

SUB-SAHARAN AFRICA

(left) Malick Pathe Sow of Senegal plays the *kora* (Shutterstock)

(right) *Kora* bridge

table (and approximately parallel to each other). A typical *kora* has twenty-one strings, ten on the right, eleven on the left, though players today often add others. The player holds the instrument upright, grasping two tall handgrips embedded into the calabash and flanking the neck, and plucks with forefingers and thumbs. At first glance, it appears that the playing technique would involve a right-hand part and a left-hand part, but this is not the case, for the ascending scale is distributed alternately on the right and left sides of the bridge, meaning that scalar passages are played by alternate plucking of right and left. This allows for rapid virtuoso passages. Some pieces include an additional sound—a flick of the forefinger against the right-hand grip, and if a second person is available, he may tap the back of the *kora* in a rhythm tied to the piece being played. An accessory consisting of a thin metal plate with wire loops threaded around the edge is sometimes mounted atop the bridge. Known as *nyenyemo*, this leaf-life plate vibrates in sympathy with the strings, adding a buzzing or sizzling-like sound, something typical of many African instruments. Today it has largely been replaced with an amplifier pickup instead.

    The performer ideally sits on the ground to play, with the instrument resting on the ground for increased resonance. A performance has two distinct sections—referred to as *birimintingo* and *kumbengo*—that allow the performer to show his skills both as a musician and as a praise-singer. The *birimintingo* sections are marked by flourishing solo runs on the *kora*. A performer may solo for an extended period of time in order to collect his thoughts, to survey the audience, or merely for his own enjoyment.

During the *kumbengo* sections, the performer plays a steady repeated pattern on the *kora* while singing praises that relate the history of the Mandinka or of individual family lineages. The steady rhythm of the *kumbengo* is maintained throughout the performance and underlies both the *birimintingo* solos and the vocalist's melodic passages. The *kumbengo* rhythm is yet another demonstration of the tendency of African musicians to use polyrhythm in performance.

In our example, the *kumbengo* is established after a short introductory *birimintingo* "flourish." A low and high part can be heard. The lower part provides a root rhythmic pattern while the upper part interlocks with it to produce a cross-rhythm. The repetitive nature of the *kumbengo* allows the performer to focus on his singing without thinking much about his *kora* performance. During *birimintingo* sections, the *kumbengo* is usually maintained in the lower part by the thumbs while the fingers play the upper melodic runs.

Kora (bridge-harp) performed by the late *jali* (praise singer) Bai Konte, from Brikama, The Gambia (Roderic Knight)

The melodic contour of the vocal part can generally be described as descending. The *jali*'s praises start high and fall to a long sustained tone at the end of the phrase. The performer does not sing continuously; rather, the vocal phrases are separated by instrumental sections that allow the musician to collect his thoughts before the next bout of praise-singing. The text setting tends to be syllabic with little or no melisma. A performance usually ends with a final *birimintingo* section.

LISTENING GUIDE

CD 3.1 (2'57")

Chapter 10: Site 7
Senegal: *Jali* with *Kora*

Vocals: Single male
Instruments: *Kora* (bridge harp)

TIME	LISTENING FOCUS
0'00"	Opening starts with *birimintingo*, a freely rhythmic improvisation. Note the absence of the underlying *kumbengo* rhythm.
0'32"	Vocalist quietly hums along with his instrumental melody until the *kumbengo* begins.
0'38"	*Kumbengo* rhythm begins. Listen for the contrasting low, middle, and high pitch ranges and the interweaving rhythmic patterns these produce. The low melodic–rhythm has a three-pitch

	ascending melodic contour, while the middle and high melodic–rhythms provide complementary motives.
1'06"	Vocalist enters. Note the declamatory singing style that utilizes a syllabic text setting, as well as the overall descending melodic contour.
1'19"	Second phrase of opening verse.
1'32"	Extended instrumental *kumbengo* break.
1'50"	Vocalist returns, connecting two melodic phrases (the second at 1'59") with a generally descending melodic contour.
2'12"	Text setting becomes more strongly syllabic, nearing speech, until the example fades.

Source: "Kuruntu Kallafa," performed by Salieu Suso with *kora*; from the recording entitled *Griot: Salieu Suso*, Lyrichord LYRCD 7418, n.d. Used by permission, Lyrichord Discs Inc.

ETHNO-CHALLENGE (CD 3.1): Write a "praise" poem/song about an ancestor of your own. Trace your family history as far back as possible and note how many generations separate you from your most distant ancestor.

Cultural Considerations. Among the Mandinka, a person's surname will often indicate the nature of his family trade; Kouyate or Suso are well-known names for *jali*. Even if a person chooses another occupation, his family name indicates a link to ancestors who at one time practiced that trade. Once a *jali* learns the name of an individual, he can extemporize a musical performance that praises the contributions to the community of that individual, his family, and his ancestors. For example, Smith is a common surname in the United States. The name is derived from the word "Blacksmith," a common occupation among English-speaking settlers in North America. As a result, many of these early settlers from England, whether still in this trade or not, had the original name of Blacksmith shortened to Smith. A present-day "Smith" is not likely to be a blacksmith, but it is likely that his or her ancestors pursued such an occupation.

The texts of praise-songs are extemporaneously drawn from a pool of generic poetic verses learned over the course of a lifetime that can be customized for particular families and individuals. Praise-songs are most often reserved for members of royal lineages or, in modern times, for wealthy patrons, though almost anyone can be praised in this fashion. The person praised responds with gifts, usually money, which enables a *jali* to earn a living.

As already mentioned, the texts of *jali* praise-songs may relate to a specific individual, but frequently they deal more generally with the great deeds of the Mandinka people and with Mandinka history. In our example, Salieu Suso, the *jali*, sings of a Mandinka warrior who battled against the Fulani, another ethnic group in West Africa. The warrior, Kallafa (or Kelefa), captures many prisoners, who refuse to return to the Mandinka stronghold. Kallafa ties the prisoners together and has to "pull" them back home, and in so doing causes great dust clouds on his approach to the kingdom. The people mistake the dust clouds for smoke from fire until Kallafa is within sight. After recounting this episode, the *jali* then sings of the great deeds Kallafa performs as he enters the city. While the *jali*'s praises are improvised, they are based on a stock set of phrases and images known as "Kuruntu Kallafa" (or "Kelefa") ("Kallafa Pulling"), passed down through generations.

Through such stories, the *jali* is able to pass on knowledge of historical events to future generations and enhance community pride in the accomplishments of the Mandinka peoples. More specifically, however, since it is the descendents of Kallafa who are especially honored in this song, the song's performance obligates those descendents to reward the musician for his gracious praises. This is done by "spraying" him, either by placing money on his forehead, usually after a performance, or by putting money in his instrument through the resonator hole.

"Spraying" is important not only for the economic subsistence of the musician but also for the well-being of the community. A common belief throughout sub-Saharan Africa is that ancestral spirits can be brought into the presence of the community by invoking their names. These spirits have the power to help the community by keeping people healthy, maintaining good crops, warding off natural disasters, and so on. If, however, the spirits are not respected properly, they may become malevolent and cause disease, drought, or harmful accidents. The *jali*'s ability to praise the names of so many hundreds of ancestors is viewed by the Mandinka populations as a kind of supernatural power. A great warrior spirit, such as Kallafa, can protect the community from outside evils, or, if not respected properly, reveal his anger by, for example, making community members sick or causing a fire to spread throughout the village. Thus, the *jali* must be appropriately compensated for his services as a praise-singer in order to help ensure the security of the community.

Arrival: The Republic of South Africa

The Republic of South Africa is the southernmost country on the African continent. Equal in size to Texas, New Mexico, and Arizona combined, and larger than Egypt in north Africa and having a population of fifty million, the country has a diverse landscape marked by tall mountain ranges that separate its high interior plateaus from its extensive shoreline. As with much of sub-Saharan Africa, wildlife, including unique small black rhinoceroses, ostriches, and baboons, are found in several large game reserves, such as the more than 7,500 square mile (2,900 square km) Kruger National Park along the Mozambique border. Parts of the Western Cape (north and northeast of Cape Town) so resemble the wine country of Europe that visitors often cannot believe they are in Africa. Indeed, much of South Africa belies any stereotypes anyone might have about Africa, including its temperate climate.

South Africa is home to diverse ethnic groups representing a variety of racial families. The main ethnic groups that comprise more than three-quarters of the population include the Zulu, Xhosa, Sotho (North and South), Tswana, Tsonga, Venda, and Ndebele. White South Africans are primarily of British and Dutch descent. In addition, the country is home to more than a million people of Asian-Indian ancestry.

Archaeological evidence dates South Africa's earliest inhabitants, *Australopithecus africanus*, one of mankind's earliest ancestors, back more than three million years. More recent historical evidence indicates that hunter-and-gatherer groups, such as the San and Khoikhoi, inhabited the region along with Bantu-speaking peoples from West Central Africa, who settled as agriculturists and are believed to be the ancestors of the modern Nguni

Traditional round house as seen in South Africa and elsewhere in Africa (Shutterstock)

peoples, who include the Zulu, Xhosa, and other ethnic groups. Though explorers passed through the region in the late fifteenth century, the first colonialists to settle there arrived only in 1652. These settlers were Dutch and are known as the Boers, meaning "farmers." They landed at the Cape of Good Hope where they established a fort and a provision station for the many trading ships on their way to and from Asia. In 1814 the British bought the Dutch territories, and within a decade thousands of British colonialists arrived, soon demanding that English law govern the region's affairs. Many of the descendants of the Boers, known as **Afrikaners**, refused to accept the new government's authority and began migrating north during the 1830s, shortly after the British abolition of slavery in 1833, with plans to reestablish their own colony. By this time, indigenous peoples had asserted their dominion over the northern territories, and thus the migrating Afrikaners became embroiled in conflicts with various African groups.

The best known of the African kings who held sway in the northern regions was the Zulu warrior **Shaka** (1787–1828), who had uprooted many indigenous groups in the process of establishing one of the area's most powerful kingdoms. Shaka's repressive ruling tactics and impressive war machine have made him one of the most important historical figures in South Africa's history. Though viewed as a cultural hero by many, for others he is a tyrant whose remembered brutality still influences spiritual and social matters. The Afrikaners, who soon established their own independent territory where they maintained strict segregation of blacks and whites, defeated his successors.

Following the discovery of diamonds in 1867 and of gold deposits by 1886, the Afrikaner and British communities were continually at odds. By 1902 the British had overwhelmed the Afrikaner armies by pursuing a "scorched-earth" policy that destroyed Afrikaner farms and forced many women and children into concentration camps, where an estimated 20,000

AFRIKANERS
The descendents of Dutch colonialists in South Africa.

SHAKA ZULU
Zulu warrior king of the late eighteenth and early nineteenth centuries who reigned over much of South Africa.

Soweto Township near Johannesburg, South Africa, a place of great contrasts

APARTHEID
A policy of racial segregation and political and economic discrimination against non-Europeans in South Africa.

Afrikaners and roughly 14,000 indigenous Africans died. To help end the war with the Afrikaners, the British agreed to allow the Afrikaners to continue their practice of strict segregation. By the middle of the twentieth century, this social separation had been instituted as a set of laws, referred to as **Apartheid** (Afrikaans for "separation"), which resulted in the segregation not only of blacks and whites, but also of "Asians" (i.e., East Indians) and "Coloureds" (people of mixed racial descent). Many Afrikaners attained positions of political power and succeeded in promoting governmental support of apartheid legislation.

Apartheid policies were maintained for the next few decades in the face of increasing disapproval from the international community. During this time, several anti-apartheid organizations struggled to find ways to end the oppression by South Africa's white minority of the rest of its population. The African National Congress (ANC), in particular, began seeking non-violent means for ending racial and social discrimination in South Africa after its inception in 1912. Opposition to the apartheid government finally reached its peak in the mid-1980s after half-hearted reforms resulted in numerous riots and hundreds of deaths. The government found itself in a perpetual state of emergency as it tried to maintain order and eventually lost the support of nearly all its foreign investors.

Nearly bankrupt, unable to maintain civil order, and finding itself increasingly isolated from the international community, the apartheid government finally became untenable. In 1989 Frederick Willem De Klerk, soon after accepting the South African presidency, began serious reforms that eventually led to an end of apartheid in 1992. He and newly freed ANC leader Nelson Mandela received a joint Nobel Peace Prize in 1993 for their cooperation in ending racial segregation and apartheid rule. Mandela became the first truly democratically elected president of South Africa the following year.

Site 8: *Mbube*

First Impressions. The lush harmonies of Zulu choral singing are immediately attractive to most Western audiences. No instruments are heard, just an all-male choir with a dominant lead vocalist and bass-heavy backing vocals. The performance is obviously well-rehearsed, with precise attention paid to tone, timbre, and rhythm. Though these are amateur vocalists, they have a professional sound. This is music for the stage, not an informal communal event.

Aural Analysis. Though some female vocal groups exist, most *mbube* is performed by all-male vocal groups. A solo voice (referred to as the "controller") leads the group (called the "chord"), following the call-and-response organization typical of sub-Saharan African vocal performance. In this case, however, the responding group may also sing backing harmonies as the lead singer "tells his story." This is heard throughout this example, in which the lead vocalist laments the suffering of black people in apartheid South Africa.

By varying the interaction between the lead vocalist and the group, the performers are able to create definite changes in mood. In our example, the opening verse follows a call-and-response format, with the group responding to the leader's call in harmony. This section is then repeated. In the next section, the lead vocalist is featured, as supporting group harmonies establish a beat behind him. The third section models the first: the group responds to the lead vocalist, then blends with his voice in the concluding harmonies. This section is also repeated. In the final section, the lead vocalist makes his final declaration before the "bombing" harmonies of the group carry the music to its conclusion.

While Zulu choral singing existed prior to the colonial period, its harmonies and strong cadences (closing phrases) as currently heard reveal European musical influence. A distinctive feature of the *mbube* sound, however, is an emphasis on the lower vocal range. (The vocal ranges are described using European musical terminology; namely, *soprano*, *alto*, *tenor*, and *bass*.) The lead vocalist generally sings in a middle or upper register, though bass leads are found as well. One or two voices in the choir will represent the other upper parts, while the rest of the performers sing bass. For every one of the upper parts, there are often five or six bass voices giving the music its rich harmonic foundation. This distinctive emphasis on the lower range of voices is considered to be a characteristic of Zulu choral performance that predates the colonial period.

The *mbube* style is also distinctive for its frequent changes in tempo. The lead singer commonly begins his phrases in a "loose" manner approximating speech, that is, he does not emphasize a definite beat. The ends of vocal phrases often feature a slight slowing of the tempo and a short pause afterward that does not follow the established beat. The closing repeated refrain follows a tempo different than the rest of the performance, especially in competition pieces when the performers walk off stage (the footsteps of the exiting vocalists can be heard toward the end of our example).

LISTENING GUIDE

 CD 3.2 (2'53")

Chapter 10: Site 8
Republic of South Africa: *Mbube*

Vocals: Single male lead with supporting male ensemble

TIME	LISTENING FOCUS
0'00"	Lead vocal ("Controller") enters and the group responds, followed by a second line with a call-and-response form and a closing call-and-response line. Listen for the use of harmony in the group responses and the emphasis on a low range of pitches.
0'09"	Listen for the harmonic tension–resolution of the closing cadence. Also, note that the tempo (approximately 104 beats per minute) slows at the end of the phrase.
0'13"	Opening verse is repeated, continuing in free-rhythm.
0'27"	Lead vocal is featured.
0'31"	Backing vocals return, articulating a regular beat (approximately 104 beats per minute).
0'41"	Closing harmonic cadence returns.
0'48"	Repetition of featured lead vocal part, supported by rhythmically regular backing vocals and followed by closing harmonic cadence.
1'10"	Return to call-and-response ("Controller" and "Chord") organization. Listen for the increased emphasis on the lower range of the group response at 1'20".
1'31"	Call-and-response section repeats.
1'51"	Lead vocal solo is featured in free rhythm.
2'00"	Lead vocal initiates the "bombing" section characterized by the "swooping" harmonies of the group response. Listen for the decrease in tempo (to approximately 84 beats per minute). Note that a second high voice adds another vocal line to contrast with the lead vocal and ensemble parts.
2'16"	Group harmony moves back to consistent pitch levels. Listen for the lead vocal initiating each repetition of the group response.
2'29"	Listen for the footsteps of the performers as the example fades.

Source: "Phesheya Mama" ("Mama, they are overseas") sung by the Utrecht Zulu Singing Competition and recorded by Gary Gardner and Helen Kivnick, 1984; from the recording entitled *Let Their Voices Be Heard: Traditional Singing in South Africa*, Rounder 5024, 1987. Used by permission.

ETHNO-CHALLENGE (CD 3.2): Research the music of South Africa in relation to the politics of the apartheid period. Search for music in your own culture that addresses political circumstances related to your own nation's history—for example, American music about the Vietnam War.

SUB-SAHARAN AFRICA

Cultural Considerations. As with much of Zulu traditional culture, the roots of *mbube* are thought to have originated during the lifetime of Shaka. Whether this belief is accurate, it is an indication of the degree to which Zulu people identify themselves with this great king. Shaka was regarded not only as a powerful warrior but also as a great dancer and strong singer. Much of the Zulu traditional repertoire is attributed to him, as he was said to have composed many songs to help keep morale high among his soldiers.

More recent influences on the sound of *mbube* are traceable to the 1920s, when migrant workers began holding evening singing competitions as a form of entertainment after long arduous days of hard labor in the gold and diamond mines found throughout South Africa. Many unique music traditions came from the labor camps, known as townships, in which most blacks were forced to live during the years of apartheid. The segregation was so strict that armed guards were often found at the gates leading to the townships. The townships were also divided into black and "coloured" (Indian or mixed descent) encampments. Soweto, meaning "Southwestern Townships," is a vast area near Johannesburg where millions of people still live in housing that varies from cardboard shacks to mansions. This area was home to Nelson Mandela before his imprisonment in 1962, as it still is to Archbishop Desmond Tutu.

By the late 1930s, nighttime *mbube* singing competitions had become characteristic of the Zulu encampments and hostels. One of the earliest recordings of this style of singing, "Mbube," was made by Solomon Linda and his Evening Birds vocal group. The single became very popular and later inspired two American hits, "Wimoweh" by the Weavers (1951) and "The Lion Sleeps Tonight" by the Tokens (1961). The song's title became the name for the "bombing" vocal style (so-called for its frequent descending melodic contour) exemplified by Solomon's group, with its deep four-part harmonies and soprano lead voice.

The best-known derivative of the *mbube* style is *isicathamiya* (a tongue "click" occurs on the romanized *c*, ISI-"click"-A-THA-MEE-YA), popularized by Ladysmith Black Mambazo, a vocal group from Ladysmith, South Africa, which gained international prominence after their collaboration with American artist Paul Simon on his highly successful *Graceland* album (1986), and soon after they won a Grammy for their own album, *Shaka Zulu* (1988). The name *isicathamiya* means "to walk like a cat" (i.e., stealthily), and is derived from a description of the dance that accompanies the singing. This style of dancing uses "tiptoeing" choreography and flowing gestures, in contrast to traditional Zulu dancing which frequently features hard stamping and vigorous "warrior" movements. The *isicathamiya* sound reflects this subdued dance style and tends to be "softer" and "smoother" than *mbube*.

Explore More

Ladysmith Black Mambazo

BONUS TRACK: CD 3.3, Source: Ladysmith Black Mambazo, "Because I Love You" from *Raise Your Spirits Higher*, Heads Up International, 2004.

Ladysmith Black Mambazo (LSBM), South Africa's iconic choral group, has remained one of the most popular of world music artists around the world. While their members often change, Joseph Shabalala (b.1941), the group's founder, has remained the driving force behind the group's success.

Shabalala formed his first group of *mbube* singers in 1960, following the conventions of the genre as exemplified in the audio site example. While successful, their performance was not otherwise unique among their contemporaries. In 1964, he writes that he had a dream that prompted him to create a new vocal group that would "cut down" his rivals in the local *mbube* "nightsong" competitions. At the time, *mbube* groups emphasized loud dynamic levels as a show of their strength and power over the other groups. Shabalala, however, took the opposite approach, creating the quiet *isicathamiya* style. His new group, Ladysmith (the name of his hometown) Black (a reference to the black ox—a symbol of strength) Mambazo (meaning "axe" with the implication of "cutting down" the competition) found rapid success throughout Durban and Johannesburg. Soon the group was able to travel as professional musicians and was frequently featured at nightsong events as non-competitors to help draw audiences; they had become so dominant in winning the competitions the other groups would refuse to participate.

In 1973, LSBM made their first recording on Gallo Africa, the nation's largest record and broadcasting company. The recording, *Amabutho*, was historic as it was the first gold record (selling more than 25,000 copies) made by all-black musicians in South Africa to earn this award. The group continued to record throughout the decade and became particularly popular with religious community groups after their conversion to Christianity in 1976. Many of their songs then came to emphasize this spiritual orientation or have a moralistic theme. By the early 1980s, LSBM had accepted invitations to perform in Europe, and their recordings made their way overseas to the American world music market as well. By the time they appeared on Paul Simon's *Graceland* (1986) album, they were already one of the best-known artists in world music circles. The tremendous success of that album, however, catapulted them into the mainstream for several years. They have since earned numerous awards and performed for many famous international figures, such as Pope John Paul II (1920–2005), Queen Elizabeth II (b.1926), and fellow-South African, Nelson Mandela (b.1918), a Nobel Peace Prize laureate. LSBM continues to record and perform internationally. We have included a "bonus" track of their music, "Because I Love You" from their grammy-winning release, *Raise Your Spirit Higher* (2004), to present the contrasting styles of *isicathamiya* and *mbube*.

The well-known South African vocal group, Ladysmith Black Mambazo, performing on stage in New York City (Jack Vartoogian/FrontRowPhotos)

Questions to Consider

1. How do the principal musical manifestations found in sub-Saharan Africa reflect the collective community and encourage group participation?
2. How is polyrhythmic music created in sub-Saharan Africa?
3. What linguistic elements are required to make a drum "talk"?

4. In what ways do *Jùjú* and other types of popular music in sub-Saharan Africa draw on traditional music for inspiration?

5. What role does music play in maintaining oral histories and legitimizing royalty?

6. In what ways has music in South Africa reflected the particular history of the country?

On Your Own Time

Visit the textbook website to find these resources for further exploration on your own.

Africa

Book: Stone, Ruth. *The Garland Handbook of African Music.* New York: Routledge, 2008.
http://www.routledge.com/books/details/9780415961028/

Book: Chernoff, John Miller. *African Rhythm and African Sensibility: Aesthetics and Social Action in African Musical Idioms.* Chicago: University of Chicago Press, 1981.
http://press.uchicago.edu/ucp/books/book/chicago/A/bo3638026.html

Website: The African Music Encyclopedia
http://africanmusic.org/

Website: Afropop Worldwide
http://www.afropop.org/

Ghana

Audio: *Asante Kete Drumming—Music of Ghana.* Lyrichord: LYRCD 7454, 2007.
http://lyrichord.com/asanteketedrumming-musicofghana.aspx
http://itunes.apple.com/us/album/asante-kete-drumming-music/id268781221

Audio: *Rhythm of Life, Songs of Wisdom—Akan Music from Ghana, West Africa.* Smithsonian-Folkways: SFW 40463, 1996.
http://www.folkways.si.edu/albumdetails.aspx?itemid=2377
http://itunes.apple.com/us/album/rhythms-life-songs-wisdom/id82056000

Website: Ghana Nation
http://www.ghananation.com

Book: Younge, Paschal Yao. *Music and Dance Traditions of Ghana: History, Performance and Teaching.* Jefferson, NC: McFarland & Co., Inc., 2011.
http://www.mcfarlandpub.com/book-2.php?id=978-0-7864-4992-7

Internet: Popular Artists from Ghana
E.T. Mensah   Koo Nimo   George Darko

Nigeria

Book: Waterman, Christopher. *Juju: A Social History and Ethnography of an African Popular Music.* Chicago: University of Chicago Press, 1990.
http://press.uchicago.edu/ucp/books/book/chicago/J/bo3774389.html

Website/Audio: King Sunny Ade—*Juju Music*
http://www.island50.com/albums/detail/juju_music
http://itunes.apple.com/us/album/juju-music/id340558

Audio: King Sunny Ade. *Baba Mo Tunde*. Mesa/Bluemoon Recordings, 2010.
http://itunes.apple.com/us/album/baba-mo-tunde/id393248160

Website: King Sunny Ade—Mesa Blue Moon (Record Label)
http://mesabluemoon.com/all-artists/mbm-artists/king-sunny-ade

Website: Iyailu ("Mother Drum")
http://www.iyailu.com/

Website: Fela.net (Dedicated to Fela Kuti, Founder of Afrobeat music)
http://www.fela.net/

Internet: Popular Artists from Nigeria and Benin
- Angélique Kidjo
- Fela Kuti
- Sir Shina Peters
- King Sunny Adé
- Segun Adewale
- Sir Victor Uwaifo

Central Africa

Website: African Pygmies.org
http://www.pygmies.org/

Audio: *Music of the Rainforest Pygmies* (recorded in 1960 by Colin M. Turnbull). Lyrichord: LYRCD 7157, 1991.
http://lyrichord.com/musicoftherainforestpygmies.aspx

Book: Duffy, Kevin. *Children of the Forest: Africa's Mbuti Pygmies*. Long Grove, IL: Waveland Press, 1995.
http://www.waveland.com/browse.php?t=1248r=s/forest

Internet: Popular Artists from Central Africa
- Franco & OK Jazz
- Papa Wemba
- Awilo Longomba

Zimbabwe

Book: Berliner, Paul. *The Soul of the Mbira: Music and Traditions of the Shona People of Zimbabwe*. Chicago: University of Chicago Press, 1978.
http://press.uchicago.edu/ucp/books/book/chicago/S/bo3644709.html

Audio: *Shona Mbira Music*. Nonesuch Records: H-72077, 1977.
http://www.nonesuch.com/albums/zimbabwe-shona-mbira-music
http://itunes.apple.com/us/album/zimbabwe-shona-mbira-music/id40582109

Website: Mbira.org
http://www.mbira.org/

Internet: Popular Artists from Zimbabwe
- Dumisani Maraire
- Khiama Boys
- Ephat Mujuru
- Oliver "Tuku" Mtukudzi

Uganda

Website: Uganda Tourism Board
http://www.visituganda.com/

Website: African Music Safari
http://www.african-music-safari.com/african-xylophone.html

Audio: *Royal Court Music from Uganda.* SWP Records: SWP008, 1998.
http://www.swp-records.com/Products/Catalogue%20list/8.html
http://itunes.apple.com/us/album/royal-court-music-from-uganda/id111915695

Internet: Popular Artists from Uganda
Samite   Geoffrey Oryema   Bebe Cool

Senegal–Gambia

Audio: *Griot—Salieu Suso.* Lyrichord Discs: LYRCD 7418, 1991.
http://lyrichord.com/griot-salieususo.aspx
http://itunes.apple.com/us/album/griot/id49360204

Book: Hale, Thomas A. *Griots and Griottes: Masters of Words and Music.* Bloomington, IN: Indiana University Press, 2007.
http://www.iupress.indiana.edu/catalog/product_info.php?products_id=68409

Book: Charry, Eric. *Mande Music: Traditional and Modern Music of the Maninka and Mandinka of Western Africa.* Chicago: University of Chicago Press, 2000.
http://press.uchicago.edu/ucp/books/book/chicago/M/bo3629899.html

Website: Cora Connection
http://www.coraconnection.com/

Website: The Kora Workshop
http://www.thekoraworkshop.co.uk/

Website: The Art of the Kora
http://www.kora-music.com/e/frame.htm

Internet: Popular Artist from Senegal and surrounding regions
Youssou N'Dour   Salif Keita   Baaba Maal   Cheikh Lo

The Republic of South Africa

Book: Erlmann, Veit. *Nightsong: Performance, Power, and Practice in South Africa.* Chicago: University of Chicago Press, 1996.
http://press.uchicago.edu/ucp/books/book/chicago/N/bo3632138.html

Website: South Africa Info—Mbube
http://www.southafrica.info/about/arts/mbube-210206.htm

Website: Ladysmith Black Mambazo—Official Site
http://www.mambazo.com/

DVD: *Ladysmith Black Mambazo: On Tip Toe.* Dir. Eric Simonson. Docurama Films, 2000.
http://www.docurama.com/docurama/ladysmith-black-mambazo-on-tip-toe/

DVD: *Amandla!: A Revolution in Four-Part Harmony.* Dir. Lee Hirsch. Artisan Home Entertainment, 2003.
http://itunes.apple.com/us/movie/amandla-a-revolution-in-four/id252225815

Internet: Popular Artists from South Africa
Miriam Makeba   Zola
Hugh Masekela   Vusi Mahlasela
Arthur Mafokate

11

The Caribbean: Haiti, Jamaica, Trinidad and Tobago, The Bahamas, Cuba, The Dominican Republic

A typical fishing village on the Caribbean island of St. Vincent, the main island of St. Vincent and the Grenadines

Background Preparation	378
Planning the Itinerary	379
Arrival: Haiti	379
Site 1: *Vodou* Ritual from Haiti	380
Arrival: Jamaica	385
Site 2: Reggae	385
Arrival: Trinidad and Tobago	390
Site 3: Calypso	391
Explore More: Soca	397
An Inside Look: Olivia Ahyoung	398
An Inside Look: Ellie Mannette	399
Site 4: Steel Band (Pan)	400
Arrival: The Bahamas	404
Site 5: Rhyming Spiritual	404
Arrival: Cuba	407
Site 6: Cuban *Son*	408
Arrival: The Dominican Republic	414
Site 7: *Merengue*	414
Questions to Consider	418
On Your Own Time	418

Background Preparation

The Caribbean represents many things to different people: white sandy beaches with clear blue water, dreadlocks and reggae music, cruise ships, Cuban communism and Fidel Castro, sugarcane, steel bands, or perhaps even offshore financial havens. For Americans, none of it is geographically very far away and yet most of it remains little known. There is much material poverty, but the region is a cornucopia of colorful and dynamic cultures. Despite a history of colonial brutality against the native population and of slaves being forcibly brought from Africa, the mixing of different peoples occurs more easily there today than practically anywhere else in the world, and this mixing has produced tremendous cultural and artistic energy. Tiny islands have developed stentorian cultural voices, producing music appreciated worldwide. Most readers likely will have heard steel band music, calypso, soca, reggae, and some form of Afro-Cuban music.

A map of the Caribbean shows a curving string of islands running from the Bahamas off the coast of Florida down to Venezuela. The largest islands—Cuba, Jamaica, Hispaniola (comprising Haiti and the Dominican Republic), and Puerto Rico—are in the center. The pre-contact population consisted of several indigenous groups, including the Arawak and Carib, but attempts to enslave them only led to their deaths or deportation. Today there are still black Caribs—a mixture resulting from contact with Africans—in a few places such as Honduras and St. Vincent. Contact with Europeans resulted first from the four voyages of Christopher Columbus, who between 1492 and 1503 "discovered" not "America" (meaning North America) but the Caribbean islands, Central America, and a bit of South America. After that, Spain claimed virtually all of the New World, though over time its rivals, the English, Dutch, and French, took possession of certain islands. Today, the Caribbean remains one of the world's last bastion of colonialism; Martinique and Guadeloupe remain French possessions and the Dutch **Antilles** (Curacao, Aruba, and Bonaire) belong to the Netherlands.

ANTILLES
Two chains of islands in the Caribbean, the Lesser and Greater Antilles.

The diversity of languages spoken in the Caribbean reflects the region's complex and colorful history. The main language currently spoken in any given place is the language of that country's most recent colonial master, but in many places a layering of languages can be heard; for example, in Trinidad and Tobago everyone speaks English normally, but one finds many Spanish place names and some Spanish terms have infiltrated the English spoken there. Spanish predominates in Cuba, Puerto Rico, and the Dominican Republic, whereas French predominates in Haiti, Martinique, and Guadeloupe. English is the main language of most of the remaining islands, including the Bahamas, Jamaica, the Virgin Islands, Dominica, St. Lucia, Barbados, Grenada, St. Vincent and the Grenadines, and Trinidad and Tobago, to name only the better known ones. Dutch and English predominate in the Dutch Antilles. In many islands one also finds linguistic blends, often called Creole or Patois, or old forms of English or French impenetrable to outsiders. Anyone who has listened to reggae "dub" or "dancehall" will know how difficult it can be to understand some forms of island English.

Most Caribbean islands have predominately African-derived populations. After their failure to enslave the Arawak and Carib, Spanish colonialists attempting to continue tobacco and sugar plantations and goldmines began importing African slaves in the early sixteenth century. This practice became pervasive by around 1650, as part of a trading triangle. Europeans exported manufactured goods to Africa in exchange for human cargo that was shipped primarily to South America and the Caribbean, after which sugar and rum produced by slave labor were exported back to Europe. Slave trading reached its peak during the eighteenth century. Periodically there were violent slave rebellions, and many Caribbean slaves escaped into the hills, mountains, or other remote areas; escaped slaves were called by the Spanish term *cimarron*, anglicized as *maroon*.

The English abolished slave trading in 1807, the French in 1818, and the Spanish in 1820, but Brazil allowed it until 1852 and the United States until 1862. The English abolished slavery in 1834 in their colonies and the French in 1848 in their possessions, but it lingered until 1865 in the United States, 1873 in Puerto Rico, 1886 in Cuba, and 1888 in Brazil. Amazingly, the number of slaves emancipated in the United States (some four million) was greater than the combined total for the rest of the Americas. Following the end of slavery, the English brought indentured laborers from other parts of the world, especially India and China, while the Dutch brought them from Java. Indentured workers were only a step above slaves but could work their way to freedom. As a result, there are significant populations of people from India in Trinidad and Guyana (in South America), from China in Trinidad and Jamaica, and from Java in Suriname.

The Caribbean, with its incredible mix of peoples, also retains aspects of old cultures from Europe, Africa, and India. In the Bahamas and other nearby English-speaking islands, people of African descent sing old English traditional ballads and perform English **mummer** plays during Christmas. In Trinidad, also during Christmas, people still sing *parang* songs from Spain and Portugal. African traditional religions, surviving intact or in part, flourish in such places as Trinidad, Grenada, Jamaica, Haiti, the Dominican Republic, and Cuba. Aspects of eighteenth-century English hymn singing and some early "Negro spirituals" survive in the Bahamas, because during the Revolutionary War British loyalists left the rebellious colonies and settled in the Bahamas, taking their slaves with them. Many kinds of Spanish-derived music survived in Cuba, the Dominican Republic, and Puerto Rico.

MUMMER
A type of street theater actor, usually in English-derived performances staged during the Christmas season.

Planning the Itinerary

While the Caribbean is home to numerous little-known, though fascinating, kinds of music, it is also a wellspring of some of the world's best-known music genres. Steel band music, calypso, soca, reggae, and merengue all originated there and exemplify the idea that small countries can have big voices. Latin-based ballroom dance music fashionable around the world—*cha-cha-cha, mambo, rumba* (or *rhumba*), *merengue, bolero,* and *salsa*—derives from Cuban, Puerto Rican, and Dominican styles. Granted, some of these musics are better described as "popular" rather than "traditional," but reggae and calypso, to name only two, are thoroughly embedded in the cultures of their homelands, Jamaica and Trinidad respectively. We therefore survey most of these well-known musics, along with the Bahamian rhyming spiritual, which is especially interesting because of its roots in the United States.

Arrival: Haiti

Haiti, a nation of around seven million people, occupies the western end of Hispaniola. Originally Spanish, it was ceded to France in 1697. Following a slave-led revolution that lasted more than ten years, Haiti became the first independent nation in the Caribbean in

1804. While the official language is French, most Haitians speak Creole, a blend of French, Spanish, Portuguese, English, and various African languages that is incomprehensible to outsiders. Today Haiti remains one of the world's most impoverished nations, in part because of frequent natural disasters, such as earthquakes, floods, and hurricanes, and the low value of its main crop, sugarcane; its population has also suffered through a series of brutal or ineffective political regimes. The 7.0 magnitude earthquake of January 12, 2010, resulted in the deaths of possibly 316,000 people and the destruction of much of the capital, Port-au-Prince. Virtually all Haitians are of African descent, but class differences based on skin color remain, and as a result Haitians with lighter skin (from mixing with Europeans) tend to hold more wealth and power than the rest of the population. Nonetheless, Haiti is alive with music and dance.

Site 1: *Vodou* Ritual from Haiti

First Impressions. *Vodou* (or *Voodoo*) is often stereotyped by outsiders as a dark religion with malevolent "black magic" rituals where pins are placed in dolls to hurt someone, or a mysterious powder is sprinkled on someone's doorstep to turn them into zombies. These characterizations are unfortunate and highly inaccurate. As for our recorded example, if you listen to it superficially, you will no doubt be struck by its similarity to West African music—which it essentially is—emphasizing polyrhythmic percussion and call-and-response singing.

Aural Analysis. The audio example consists of two sections: the first includes vocal with drums, the second vocal with bamboo wind instruments. There are two main musical elements in the first part of the example: the rhythmic accompaniment played on drums and other percussion, and the vocal parts, which in this case contrast a male soloist and a group made up mostly of women. The structure of the vocal parts is responsorial—that is, it is based on a call-and-response pattern in which the soloist begins a sentence or thought that the group then completes. These songs are passed on through oral tradition, making them

Haitians dance, offer food and ask the *vodou* saints for help in the Day of the Dead in November, a festival devoted to the god Gede (Dario Mitdieri/Getty Images)

A display of various drums used in Haitian *Vodou* ritual

vary somewhat from one group to another, even as certain elements that maintain the song's identity are preserved.

The language is a combination of Creole and *langaj*, the latter being a ceremonial language derived from several West African and Central African religions. The accompaniment in *Vodou* rituals typically consists of three *rada* drums, sometimes along with an African iron bell or similar object, and some kind of shaken rattle, usually with the shells or seeds fastened to an external net; for example, shekere. The largest drum is the leader, the middle drum provides additional rhythms, and the smallest provides a steady reference beat for the other instruments. As with other types of West African music, these polyrhythmic patterns result from short units known to scholars as "timeline patterns," rather than being thought as a continuous meter (see Chapter 10). Individual accompaniments and songs are specific to particular deities, and are played to invite those deities to a ritual. In a typical *Vodou* ritual, a succession of deities will be invited, each with its own music. Participants seek to be possessed by the deity they are invoking, and when this happens their dancing incorporates gestures and actions that express the character of that deity. The audio example features a song for Legba and part of a dance for Ogoun (see below).

The second part of the audio track again has responsorial voices, but there are no drums. Instead a group of bamboo "trumpets" called *banbou* (also, *vaksin*) is heard, each instrument playing just a single note. However, because each instrument has a different pitch, a melody results from the interlocking patterns of these single pitches when played together as a group. The performance occasion is called *Rara*; processions of singers and players who go from one sacred spot (e.g., a cemetery) to another during the period between Carnival (the period preceding Ash Wednesday, the beginning of Lent) and the onset of Easter.

LISTENING GUIDE

 CD 3.4 (1'37")

Chapter 11: Site 1
Haiti: *Vodou* Ritual

Voices: Parts 1 and 2—single male lead and mixed male/female ensemble
Instruments: Part 1—*Rada* drums, *bas* (frame drum), *klòch* (bell), *ason* (gourd rattle); Part 2—*banbou* (bamboo trumpet aerophones, also called *vaksin*), shakers and wooden sticks (idiophones)

TIME	LISTENING FOCUS
0'00"	Part 1: Listen for the lead male vocalist followed by the group response throughout the performance.
0'01"	Listen for the tapping beat on the lead drum, which establishes the basic pulse.
0'05"	Listen for the rattle matching the basic pulse. Note that the tempo gradually increases throughout the performance.
0'07"	Listen for the first entrance of the *rada* drum, which is followed by the bell and the remaining instruments.
0'21"	Listen for the lead drum improvisations within the overall polyrhythmic organization of the ensemble.
0'43"	Part 1 fades out.
0'45"	Part 2 fades in. Listen for the continued use of call-and-response vocal organization, but the difference in lyrical content.
	Note the absence of drums. Listen for a steady pulse provided by a low shaker (idiophone), along with a pair of wooden sticks that contributes additional rhythms.
	Listen for the interlocking melodic pattern of the *banbou* (aerophones).
1'08"	Listen for the appearance of a high-pitched trumpet.
1'12"	Listen for the lead vocal's change in text and the consequent change in group response at 1'17".
1'31"	Example fades out.

Source: Excerpts from "Bosou Djo Eya (Mayi rhythm)" performed by Sociètè Jour M'alongè Fòc Nan Point Dieu Devant, recorded by David Yih, Carrefour, Haiti, 1987, and "Guantanamo Song (Rara Rhythm, Southern Style)," recorded by Elizabeth McAlister, Port-au-Prince, Haiti, 1993. From the recording entitled *Rhythms of Rapture: Sacred Musics of Haitian Vodou*. SF 40464, provided courtesy of Smithsonian Folkways Recordings. © 1995. Used by permission.

ETHNO-CHALLENGE (CD 3.4): Find musical examples from other African-derived traditions similar to *Vodou* (e.g., *Santeria, Candomblé*, etc.) and compare ritual musical performance dedicated to the same deities.

Cultural Considerations. *Vodou* is an African-derived religious system incorporating newly encountered and adapted influences from Roman Catholicism. Although at least 10 percent of the Africans brought to the New World were originally Muslims, the vast majority practiced traditional African religions. Some of these systems involved interaction with the spirits of ancestors, whereas others focused on a pantheon of personified natural forces, called *orisha* in the more widely known Yoruba language but called *loa* in Haiti. For example, in the Yoruba tradition found in present-day Nigeria, thunder and lightning are personified into a single god, **Shango**. In predominantly Roman Catholic colonies (which comprised most of South and Central America and much of the Caribbean), African slaves vastly outnumbered their European masters, because great numbers of workers were required to farm the sugar plantations. As a result, the Africans in these colonies were able to retain a fair amount of their African heritage, including their religions. More precisely, while many Africans appeared to profess Catholic Christianity, most saw Christ, the Virgin, and the Saints and Apostles as equivalents to African gods—an example of a process called *syncretism*. For instance, in some traditions Shango is equivalent to John the Baptist. Thus, the *Vodou* practitioners considered there to be no contradiction between attending Mass in a church and participating in African rituals at an African temple.

Haitian *Vodou*, which blends the spiritual tradition focusing on ancestors with the one focusing on a pantheon of nature gods, derives mostly from Benin (formerly Dahomey) and nearby areas of West Africa. The two gods invoked in our example, both *loa* in the *Vodou* tradition, are Legba and Ogoun. Both are well-known Yoruba-derived deities classified into the "Rada" group in *Vodou*. Legba, the guardian of crossroads and barriers, is artistically depicted as a handsome old man with a flowing beard who limps while walking with a cane and likes meat and alcoholic drinks.

Ogoun, the god of iron, is often depicted with a sword, and can be quite fierce and active. While it is true that most African religions include some aspect of destructive power, they are actually predominately positive in focus, as the principal goals are good health and healing, social cohesion, successful harvests, and the like. Participants reaffirm the power of the gods in rituals that involve dancing, singing, drumming, and possession. During possession a person's essence temporarily leaves the body, allowing the *loa* (deity) to "mount" the believer, who is considered to be the "horse." The possessed person acts out the personality of the god and demonstrates the god's traits in dance and gesture. At the conclusion of a possession, the "horse" may suddenly fall to the ground, after which s/he is given time to reunite with his/her human essence.

Each deity is associated with a particular drumming pattern and song. Performing that

SHANGO

A Yoruba name for the god of thunder and lightning in the West African pantheon. Consequently, also the name for a West African-derived religion found primarily in Trinidad.

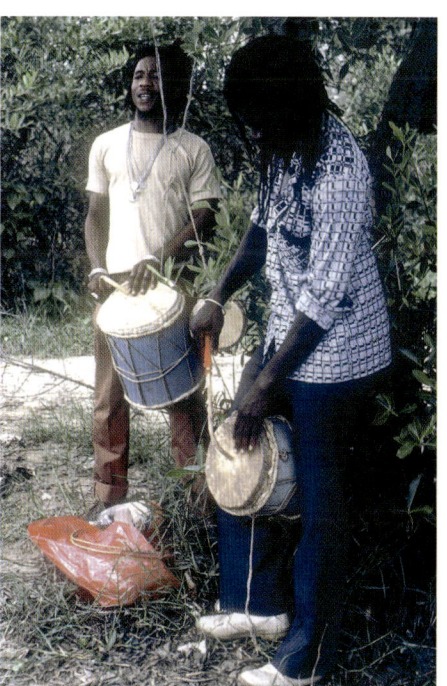

In Trinidad, two musicians play African-derived drums and sing for a Shango ceremony, a syncretistic religious tradition related to Haiti's *Vodou*

At the seacoast of Trinidad, six leaders of the African-derived Shango religion bow before ritual offerings about to be floated into the sea for Oshun, the goddess of the sea

music invites a named god to appear and hopefully to possess one or more lucky "horses." Despite myths to the contrary, *Vodou* music itself does not cause possession, because, if it did, anyone hearing it would be possessed. Indeed, the percussionists—almost always male—stay outside the ritual circle and are not subject to possession. *Vodou* ritual music *regulates* possession—that is, it makes the process of possession more even and efficient. Before a person can be possessed, he or she must learn how to become possessed; otherwise the experience of a *Vodou* ritual can be useless or even dangerous. A full ritual must begin with a song to Legba, the guardian of crossroads and gatekeeper to the spirit world. This is followed by a series of songs for other deities, presented in a prescribed order. These deities can be either nature gods or ancestors; some are violent or energetic, while others are calm. During possession, the "horse" may receive healing energy. Others nearby may also benefit or may ask the deity questions about life and the future. Extraordinary ritual acts, such as walking through fire, can occur at such a ritual, but these feats are intended to demonstrate the power of the deity and verify his/her presence. Such rituals are often sensationalized by outsiders, particularly in the movie industry, without understanding or conveying the purpose behind the actions. For followers of *Vodou*, however, they are recognized as a confirmation of their faith and considered an essential element of their spiritual belief system.

There are a great many African-derived religions in the New World, though admittedly *Vodou* is the best known and most notorious because of negative stereotyping. Other African-derived religions include *Santeria* and *Abakwa* in Cuba, *Batuque, Umbanda,* and *Candomblé* in Brazil, *Shango* in Trinidad, and *Cumina* in Jamaica. Caribbean immigrants have transplanted some of these, including Vodou, to the United States, Canada, and England. Although not advertised, rituals associated with these religions may be found in cities such as New York, Miami, Toronto, and Los Angeles, as well as in many smaller cities.

Arrival: Jamaica

Jamaica is widely known for its white sand beaches along the north coast at Montego Bay, Ocho Rios, or Negril, classy resort hotels, and welcoming local musicians playing gentle calypsos and limbo dance music. For many Jamaicans, however, life is a different reality, one of hardscrabble poverty and crime. The population of this Connecticut-sized island is 2.5 million, of which fully one-third live in the greater Kingston area. In Jamaica, as in Haiti, there is a stark contrast between the very wealthy and the very poor. The country's colonial past, the low prices fetched by its principal exports (sugarcane and bauxite), and overpopulation in the Kingston area are all partly responsible for this situation and together comprise a recipe for tension and violence. Kingston can, unfortunately, be a dangerous city for foreign visitors. Nonetheless, it was in Kingston's slums that Jamaica's most vibrant music—reggae—originated.

The majority of Jamaica's population is of African descent, their forebears having come shackled in slavery. Spanish colonialists controlled Jamaica until the mid-seventeenth century, when English pirates drove them away. The country then became a British colony in 1670. Throughout Jamaica's history there were occasional slave rebellions, and many slaves escaped into the Blue Mountains in the east and into the uncharted "Cockpit Country" in Trelawny Parish in the west. In these regions, they were able to re-establish an African way of life, including what remained of their ancestral religion, called *Cumina*. Since achieving independence in 1962, Jamaica has struggled politically, going through—among other things—a disastrous experiment with socialism under Michael Manley. Not surprisingly, a great number of Jamaicans have left the island seeking a better life, principally in Miami, New York, Toronto, and London.

Site 2: Reggae

REGGAE
A popular music from Jamaica characterized by a rhythmic emphasis on the offbeat and by politically and socially conscious lyrics.

First Impressions. Many world music enthusiasts enjoy the easygoing "walking" feel of **reggae** music. Its characteristic "offbeat" emphasis (beats 2 and 4, instead of 1 and 3) help distinguish it for even the novice listener. Several major reggae artists, such as Bob Marley and Jimmy Cliff, have achieved international recognition in the mainstream music business, bringing attention with it to some of the island's other musical creations, such as *ska* and *rock steady*. But while the sound of reggae may be familiar, the cultural context out of which the music was born and the meaning its lyrics hold for many Jamaicans are less well known.

Reggae is much more than a form of pop music. Those who enjoy the music purely as entertainment often overlook the politically and socially conscious lyrics that are the essence of the genre. The long, twisted hair (called *dreadlocks*) often worn by reggae musicians, the prevalence of the colors red, green, and gold, the frequent references to "Jah," even the celebration of *ganja* (marijuana), are not merely fashion statements or fads—they are part of a spiritual system of beliefs and way of life that infuses much reggae music.

Aural Analysis. While the majority of instruments introduced throughout our study are unfamiliar to students new to world music, reggae music typically includes routine rock/pop instruments, such as electric guitars and bass, drum set, and electric keyboards. Some aspects of timbre distinguish their use in reggae performance. The tone quality of the electric guitar,

Reggae's most famous artist, Bob Marley, as seen on the cover of his album, *Legend*

for example, is usually set to emphasize the "treble" or high-end frequencies in order to contrast with the deep, low-end frequencies of the electric bass. The snare drum is often "tight" with the snare wires disengaged. European trumpets and saxophones are often heard, and the use of "back-up" singers is common for emphasizing the lyric refrain. Most important, however, is the lead vocalist, whose lyrics are intended to convey a message to the audience, whether of peace or protest. While much music with a "reggae sound" today lacks the socially conscious lyrics of classic reggae artists such as Bob Marley, these themes are expected of musicians who identify themselves with the genre.

A street market in Kingston, Jamaica, the breeding grounds for reggae music

Cultural Considerations. Reggae is different from most other types of music featured in this book, first because it has been commercially successful, and second because songs usually come from known, individual creators who infuse their life experiences into their work. Reggae musicians often view their music as having the power to prompt people into action against political and social injustice on behalf of those who are oppressed or marginalized in society. Reggae artists regularly regard their position on stage as an opportunity to educate their audience about these issues or other important associations with their music and culture. Our example, "Torchbearer," is such a song; written by Carlos Jones, a reggae musician from Cleveland, Ohio, the song pays homage to Bob Marley, the most famous figure associated with reggae music.

LISTENING GUIDE

CD 3.5 (3'42")

Chapter 11: Site 2
Jamaica: Reggae

Voices: Single male lead, backing female ensemble
Instruments: Electric guitars, electric bass, electric keyboard, drum set (snare, toms, bass, cymbals, etc.), bongo drums, shaker

TIME	LISTENING FOCUS
0'00"	Electric guitar begins the performance.
0'02"	Listen for the focus on snare drum, leading into the start of a regular pulsation and the entrance of the remaining instruments at 0'06".
0'06"	Listen for the "upbeat" emphasis on the second and fourth pulses of the four-beat phrase.
0'08"	Lead vocalist enters with spoken dialogue. Listen for the reference to Bob Marley. Note the use of electronic "echo" on the voice at 0'10," 0'14," and 0'19."
0'24"	Listen for the lead vocalist transitioning to a singing voice.
0'27"	Listen for the backing vocals and first appearance of the "Torchbearer" refrain.
0'39"	Listen for the reference to "Jah."
0'58"	Listen for the reference to "I and I."
1'06"	First verse begins. Note the various examples of *rasta* terminology, references to Bob Marley's influence on the lead vocalist, and the review of Marley's personal history.
2'17"	Listen for the *Nyabinghi* reference.
2'26"	Listen for the "Yeah, yeah, yeah" lyric, used to close the first verse.
2'33"	Listen for a melodic–harmonic change as the lead vocalist continues the verse, with female vocalists singing in the background.
3'00"	"Torchbearer" refrain returns.
3'37"	Example fades.

Source: "Torchbearer," performed by Carlos Jones and the PLUS Band; from the recording entitled *Roots with Culture*, Little Fish Records LF02912, 2004. Used by permission.

ETHNO-CHALLENGE (CD 3.5): Transcribe the lyrical content of this example. Research the various references to Rastafarianism and Bob Marley's personal history.

Bob Marley (a.k.a. Tuff Gong), born Robert Nesta Marley on February 6, 1945, is considered the most important of reggae's many stars, especially for the quality of his lyrics and his articulation of fundamental Rastafarian concepts (see below). His career began in 1960 after he joined with a childhood friend, Bunny Wailer (born Neville O'Riley Livingston), to form The Wailers. Later joined by Peter Tosh (born Winston Hubert McIntosh), they recorded songs that encapsulated their life experiences in Kingston's most notorious slum, Trench Town. Through international tours, including one to North America called "Babylon By Bus," they spread their music to non-Jamaican audiences. Marley's 1981 death from cancer at the age of thirty-six was a devastating blow to both reggae and Jamaica, because, although establishment Jamaica shunned the Rastafarian "rude boys," the public had embraced Marley. Eventually a statue in honor of him was placed outside the National Stadium in Kingston.

Although some might view reggae as simply a Jamaican popular music, it is steeped in very particular aspects of Jamaican history and culture. Reggae is often challenging on several fronts, including the spiritual and the political. Many lyrics combine elements of Jamaican vernacular English with the peculiar vocabulary of the Rastafari religion that informs reggae. Reggae's roots are complex and tangled, as it draws on many contradictory styles, including American rock and rhythm & blues, evangelistic hymns and choruses, and African drumming and singing.

A full understanding of reggae should include a discussion of Marcus Garvey and the roots of the Rastafari spiritual tradition. Garvey (1887–1940), a major force for West Indian nationalism and a promoter of black social pride, founded the Universal Negro Improvement Association (U.N.I.A.) in Kingston in 1914. In 1916 he traveled to New York City where he founded a branch of the U.N.I.A. and started a number of businesses (such as the Black Star Shipping Company), a newspaper (*Negro World*), and a church (the African Orthodox Church). His arrest in 1925 on fraud charges led to his being deported back to Jamaica in 1927. It is reported that after returning home he proclaimed, "Look to Africa, where a black king shall be crowned." Indeed, Garvey's teachings led to the beginning of a "back to Africa" movement in Jamaica and beyond.

Many in Jamaica thought Garvey's words had been fulfilled when, in 1930, they read that an Ethiopian tribal chieftain named Ras Tafari Mekonnen had been crowned **Haile Selassie I**, the King of Kings, the Lord of Lords, Conquering Lion of the Tribe of Judah, the Emperor of Ethiopia. Many came to believe that Haile Selassie (meaning "Power of the Holy Trinity") was the black reincarnated Christ and that the black peoples of the Diaspora were the lost children of Israel held captive in Babylon, awaiting deliverance by Jah (God) and their return back to Zion—in this case Ethiopia, the spiritual home of all black African-descended populations. The colors red, green, and gold became associated with Zion, because they are Ethiopia's national colors.

Those who embraced this loosely organized faith were called Rastafarians. In addition to their core beliefs, they adopted a lifestyle that included the wearing of dreadlocks and the smoking of *ganja* (the Hindi term for marijuana). *Ganja*, or "herb," was already a traditional medicine in Jamaica but was brewed as a tea or eaten with food. Rastafarians believed, however, that smoking "herb" would put adherents into a more prayerful state and bring them closer to Jah. Rastas justify their use of *ganja* with passages from the Bible, such as Revelation 22:2, which states "The leaves of the tree were for the healing of the nation."

HAILE SELASSIE
An Ethiopian emperor considered by Jamaican Rastafarians to be a black incarnation of Jesus Christ.

The audio example uses several instances of the language peculiar to Rastafarians, or *Rastas* as they are called for short. The phrase 'I and I' serves as both a singular and a plural pronoun, its use signifying that Jah (the Rastafarian term for God) is always present with the speaker. In plural form it refers to the mystical relationships within a group and between the group and Jah. A *Nyabinghi* (referred to in the line "Nyabinghi shakes the ground") is a Rasta ritual convention at which chanting and drumming occur. The term, which is derived from the name of an earlier anti-colonial movement in Rwanda, also refers to dreadlocked Rastas and may be shortened to "Nya-man," as heard in the example. References to "vibration" in the song highlight the metaphysical goals of peace, brotherhood, and love espoused by Rastas generally. Jones also mentions Marley's bi-racial background (Marley had a white father and a black mother), and refers to Peter Tosh using his original surname, McIntosh.

In Jamaica, Rastas are often scorned by the establishment. Their close association with reggae, due in large part to Marley's adherence to the spiritual tradition, has prompted much of the music to express challenges to the social order. Because Rastas consider the white world to be "Babylon" (referring to the captivity of God's chosen people) and Africa their true home, reggae lyrics also often challenge white hegemony. While not every reggae musician is necessarily a practicing Rastafarian, virtually all are sympathetic to this spiritual system.

Ethiopian Emperor Haile Selassie I, "Lion of Judah," born Lij Tafari in 1892, crowned emperor in 1930 until his death in 1970 (Rastafari Archive and Ras Adam Simeon)

Reggae artist Carlos Jones, composer and performer of "Torchbearer," of Cleveland, Ohio (Larry Koval)

Because live performances of reggae were long prohibited in Jamaica, the music was a phenomenon of Kingston's many small recording studios. There the musicians, using both acoustic and electric instruments, laid down tracks that were mixed to the liking of the audio engineer. Reggae music was then disseminated on vinyl recordings. Many party venues and dancehalls hired soundmen to bring sound trucks to provide reggae music for dancing. By the 1980s these DJs had discovered that by turning down the melody track and boosting the bass and rhythm track, they could "talk" over the music through a microphone. Eventually recordings without the vocals—or so-called "dub" versions—were made specifically for such improvised speech. This led to the creation of "dub" poetry, later evolving into a style called "dancehall." Some DJs became virtual reggae poets, creating long, complex poems that commented on life. Reggae "**dub**" also has a close relationship with the origin and rise of African-American rap and "toasting."

DUB (ALSO, DANCEHALL) Recorded music that emphasizes the bass and rhythm tracks so that a DJ can "talk" over the music through a microphone.

Reggae music derives in part from a number of earlier styles that were not associated with Rastafarians and rarely had political lyrics. The oldest style was *mento*, a creolized form of ballroom dance music that was popular in the 1940s. With independence in 1962 and the increasing concentration of the population in Kingston's burgeoning slums came *ska*, a Jamaican response to American rhythm and blues and rock and roll. By the mid-1960s *ska* was slowing down and incorporating more politically charged lyrics; these changes led to a new style called *rock steady*. Reggae, the name of which is attributed to Toots Hibbert, emerged around 1968. It incorporated not only these older styles but also new forms of blues, Latin American music, and Jamaican religious music. Reggae was also influenced by the music of Rastafarian religious gatherings, which blended the choral style of Christian revival meetings with *Cumina*, African-derived drumming and singing.

Arrival: Trinidad and Tobago

Trinidad and Tobago, five times smaller than the state of Hawaii and with only 1.3 million inhabitants, has more than made up for its small size by contributing three of the world's favorite musics—steel band, calypso, and soca. The nation consists of two islands: Trinidad, the larger, is only about 50 miles by 30 miles (80 by 50 km), and Tobago is a mere 25 miles by 8 miles (40 by 13 km). The name of the capital, Port-of-Spain, suggests something of the island's history. "Discovered" by Christopher Columbus during his third voyage in 1498, Trinidad was held by Spain until the English wrested it away in 1797, holding it as a colony until 1962. The native population, the Carib, disappeared after the first Spanish colonists brought their slaves to Trinidad to establish sugar plantations. Even after the end of slave trading, Britain brought more than 134,000 East Indians, 8,000 Africans, and 1,000 Chinese as indentured laborers to work the land. As a result, today's population is around 40 percent East Indian. The range of religions found is quite varied as well: the country boasts a colorful landscape of Christian churches, Muslim mosques, and Hindu temples, along with many African ritual centers.

Most visitors to Trinidad come for Carnival, a festival preceding Lent, when Port-of-Spain comes alive with near non-stop music and dancing. Because the beautiful beaches on the north coast of Trinidad remain little known and undeveloped, Tobago's easy to reach beaches have been the main destination for swimmers and surf lovers. Trinidad's Great Pitch Lake is perhaps the world's largest pitch (tar) deposit and has been the source of material for paving roads in both Europe and the Americas.

Site 3: Calypso

First Impressions. Our example of **calypso** opens with the sounds of a small dance band dominated by winds. Soon a male vocalist is introduced, who speaks as much as he sings; in a simple but direct manner, he gives his personal view of money and its corrosive influence on people. The repetitious music behind him sounds almost incidental, more a vehicle for the singer to convey the words than an attempt to charm the listener with a sophisticated melody.

Aural Analysis. Studio-recorded in New York City in 1979, using an eclectic group of pan-Caribbean musicians, our example opens with a simple melodic line consisting of four short instrumental phrases; this melody returns periodically during brief interludes and also serves as a coda to the song. While the trumpet and clarinet dominate the purely instrumental sections, quieter instruments, including violin, piano, guitar, and electric bass, are heard accompanying the singing. Throughout, a **conga** drum reinforces the beat.

The singer's stage name is The Growling Tiger, but he was born Neville Marcano in Siparia in southern Trinidad. A prizefighter and sugarcane worker in the early 1930s, he was inspired to become a calypso singer ("calypsonian") in 1934 during a trip to San Fernando, the largest city in the south. Within a short time, his talents as a lyricist and singer had become apparent, and in 1935 he and other singers were sent to New York City to record for Decca Records. Among these early recordings, now considered classics, is Tiger's calypso "Money is King." The present track is a re-recording of this song done some forty-four years later when Tiger was at least in his sixties.

"Money is King" is a Depression-era commentary on the lives of the haves and the have-nots, with the calypsonian, of course, speaking for the latter. Organized into five stanzas,

CALYPSO
A popular music from Trinidad characterized by improvised lyrics on topical and broadly humorous subject matter.

CONGA
A tall, barrel-shaped, single-headed drum used often in Latin American music.

Viewed from Fort George, houses in the hills above Trinidad's capital, Port of Spain, where both *pan* and *calypso* began

the lines of the song are not consistent in length or in rhyme pattern, and do not fit neatly with the music; the singer forces some lines into the allotted time by rushing the words in speech rhythm. Each stanza has eight lines, and thus the melody consists of eight phrases. The first four melodic phrases, however, are the same, whereas each of the second four is different, leading to a melodic structure that can be expressed as A, A, A, A, B, C, D, E.

In the first stanza Tiger declares that if you have money, you can get away with murder, and people will not even care if you have the disease *kokobe* (yaws)—but if you are poor, you are little more than a dog. The latter theme reappears in the third, fourth, and fifth stanzas. In stanza two Tiger asserts that if you have money, the storeowner will treat you like a king and will even go as far as sending your goods to your house on a motorbike. The third stanza declares that even a college-educated man with no money will not be given credit at a Chinese restaurant ("'Me no trust-am,' bawl out the Chinee [sic] man"). In the fourth stanza Tiger says that even a dog can find scraps of food around, and if it's a good breed, people will take it in as a pet—but a "hungry man" will be treated worse than a dog. Finally, without money a man cannot attract a woman, buy her gifts, or show affection. His conclusion: "If you haven't money, dog is better than you." (These lyrics are quoted in Hill 1993, pp. 259–260.)

LISTENING GUIDE

CD 3.6 (2'08")

Chapter 11: Site 3

Trinidad: Calypso

Voices: Single male
Instruments: Guitar, bass guitar, piano, clarinet, trumpet, violin, conga drums

TIME	LISTENING FOCUS
0'00"	Listen for the instrumental "hook," a refrain that highlights the trumpet, violin, and clarinet parts. Note that the bass, guitar, piano, and drums play a supporting role throughout the performance.
0'03"	Vocalist enters. Listen for the violin imitating the melodic contour of the vocalist and adding supporting harmony.
0'14"	Listen for the change in melody and supporting harmony.
0'23"	Listen for the lyrics "dog is better than you," which conclude the verse.
0'24"	Listen for the instrumental refrain.
0'35"	Second verse.
0'55"	Listen for the lyrics "money is king," which conclude the verse.
0'57"	Instrumental refrain.

1'08"	Third verse.
1'27"	Listen for the lyrics "dog is better than me," which conclude the verse.
1'29"	Instrumental refrain.
1'39"	Fourth verse. Listen for the explanation of why a "dog" is better than a poor man.
1'58"	Listen for the phrase "dog is better than you," which concludes the verse.
2'00"	Instrumental refrain as the example fades.

Source: "Money is King," performed by Growling Tiger and the Trans-Caribbean All-Star Orchestra; from the recording entitled *Growling Tiger: High Priest of Mi Minor—Knockdown Calypsos*, Rounder 5006, 1979. Used by permission.

ETHNO-CHALLENGE (CD 3.6): Transcribe the lyrical content of this example. Write your own "calypso" verse to add to the present song.

Cultural Considerations. Trinidad's particular history of "kinder and gentler" colonialism helped create the more relaxed attitude reflected in its arts, quite unlike Jamaica, where an oppressed underclass continues to seethe with anger against the wrongs of both today and the past. Although Spain originally claimed the islands of Trinidad and Tobago, few Spanish actually settled there. After the English drove the French out of certain islands of the Lesser Antilles group during the mid-eighteenth century, some French and their slaves resettled

Calypso monarch The Mighty Sparrow (aka Slinger Francisco) performing at the Lincoln Center Out of Doors "Caribbean Cultural Center: 30 Years of Carnival" concert in New York City (Jack Vartoogian/FrontRowPhotos)

WORLD MUSIC: A GLOBAL JOURNEY

His costume more than 12 feet high and 10 feet wide, Anthony Paul portrayed the "Splendour of Moonlight" during Trinidad's annual Carnival parade (Unknown)

CARNIVAL

A pre-Lent festival celebrated in predominantly Roman Catholic cultures, primarily in Europe and the Caribbean. Known as Mardi Gras in the United States.

in Trinidad, bringing Roman Catholicism with them. The French had a relatively laissez-faire attitude toward their slaves, but tolerance of slave customs declined after the Protestant English took control of the island in 1797. Slavery was abolished in Trinidad in 1843, after which great numbers of indentured laborers, especially from British India, were brought to the country. Thus, the population of nineteenth-century Trinidad consisted of freed slaves, indentured workers (free or still under contract), and a small number of French and English colonials.

Carnival, the period of celebration before Lent begins—called Mardi Gras in New Orleans—is widely celebrated in Roman Catholic countries, and although Trinidad became

Calypso Rose, Trinidad's most famous female calypsonian

Lord Kitchener (né Aldwyn Roberts, 1922–2000) from Trinidad performing at the Caribbean All-Star Calypso Festival at Radio City Music Hall, New York City (Jack Vartoogian/FrontRowPhotos)

English, its Spanish-French heritage remained strong. Early Carnivals were polite affairs celebrated publicly by the upper classes, while the working classes were left to their own devices. By the mid-nineteenth century, however, the "rowdy" classes had taken over Carnival, now celebrated through street dancing, the singing of songs that often mocked the upper classes, stick fighting, and a great parade of costumed revelers. The British authorities attempted to bring this growing chaos under control by passing and enforcing laws against excessive noise. In 1883 the government passed a "music bill" that permitted "drums, tambours, and chac-chacs [rattles]" to be played only under license and forbade all such music at night. The prohibitions on drumming led to protests, riots, and the singing of increasingly critical songs. Not to be outwitted by the British, Trinidadians denied drums began beating or stamping on bamboo tubes, creating the "tamboo bamboo" band—the term *tamboo* being derived from the word *tambor*, meaning drum.

During the latter part of the nineteenth century, government officials, especially Norman Le Blanc, began a process of both co-opting and civilizing Carnival activities. By creating competitions among singers (called *chantwells*) and bands, held in tents during Carnival, he simultaneously harnessed what came to be called calypso song and provided an acceptable place for its expression. At the same time, the language of the songs was changed from *patois* to English. Eventually, these now tamed topical songs became one of Trinidad's national musics.

Thus, a "calypso" is a topical song or musical commentary on current events, the foibles of the upper classes, recent scandals, or odd fashions. As such they have a short shelf life, but during their brief existence they often sting. Yet calypso is rarely an angry music like reggae; parody, satire, and ridicule are its methods, though, as is often pointed out in the lyrics, these are used *sans humanité* ("without mercy"). Because calypso songs were created in response to particular events close to home, they also did not export well, and calypso recordings have not had the wide distribution that recordings of steel band have. However, when the Andrews Sisters rerecorded Lord Invader's "Rum and Coca Cola" in the United States in 1945 and sold millions of copies, they showed that some songs could appeal to a broad market. (Lord Invader, who had not received any royalties, later sued and won a settlement.) Jamaican-born Harry Belafonte has also made a career of singing watered-down calypso music for a mass audience in North America.

Many calypsonians took on bombastic names, to match their sometimes bombastic lyrics. Major figures have included Attila the Hun (Raymond Quevedo, a labor leader and politician), The Mighty Sparrow (Slinger Francisco), Lord Protector (Patrick Jones), The Mighty Chalkdust (Hollis Liverpool, a school teacher), Lord Kitchener (famous for his "Pan in A"), and others with names such as Roaring Lion, Cro Cro, Lord Superior, Lord Executioner, Houdini, Calypso Rose (a rare female singer), and Immortal Spoiler. Because they were considered thoughtful commentators rather than popular stars, many continued to perform into old age. Among the new generation of calypsonians are Brian London, Kizzie Ruiz, and Superblue.

Trinidad, however, has not been immune to other musical currents, and calypso has faced stiff competition from North American rock, soul, and jazz, as well as reggae, Afro-Cuban music, and *zouk* (from the French Lesser Antilles). In the late 1970s some singers began blending calypso with aspects of rock and reggae, creating *soca* (soul-calypso), a more danceable style with less consequential words. New blends of calypso and other genres continue to be produced, but because the calypsonians retain a significant place in

Trinidadian society as commentators, the pure calypso tradition continues. However, since calypso is mostly performed during Carnival, the singers can rarely make a year-round living through their art. Many work in other sectors the rest of the year, and some live abroad, returning to Trinidad only for Carnival.

Explore More

Soca

While calypso is considered a popular music, its success in recent years has been limited mainly to local audiences. The tremendous international interest in Caribbean folk and popular music during the 1950s and early 1960s subsided as rock music and its many strands of styles took over the radio airwaves throughout the world. Calypso, as with so many other local popular world music traditions, absorbed some of these influences in order to maintain its popular appeal. By the 1970s, these influences were taking calypso farther and farther away from its traditional roots as an outlet for social commentary. Many calypso artists and fans criticized the new developments, stating that the music had lost its "soul."

Among these critics was calypsonian Lord Shorty (born Garfield Blackman (1941–2000)), who is today regarded as the Father of Soca music. His style fused calypso with rock music, as well as Indian *filmi*, which was hugely popular among Trinidad's large Indian population. Though these musical elements broadened the music's appeal, Shorty maintained the social commentary of his lyrics, describing this as the "soul of calypso," which was abbreviated to "soca" as a way of describing the new style. The peppy new sound did indeed appeal to audiences and musicians alike, but Shorty's hope to maintain the focus on the lyrics came to be overshadowed by an increasing number of soca dance hits emphasizing more universal "party" themes; for example, drinking, dancing, and casual love affairs, particularly in association with the Carnival festivities that attract thousands of tourists to the island each year.

Soca received huge international recognition with the global success of "Hot, Hot, Hot" recorded by Arrow (Alphonsus Cassel) in 1982 and later, in 1987, as a cover version by American artist, David Johansen. The song has become an unofficial anthem for the Carnival celebrations today, at least with those visiting the islands. Natives to Trinidad and Tobago, as well as surrounding islands, are more interested in modern artists, such as Destra Garcia and Bunji Garlin, who have more modest international appeal. Though soca dominates the Carnival soundscape today, calypso still maintains local interest with popular artists, such as David Rudder, as well as many older generation calypsonians, such as Mighty Sparrow. Chutney-soca is also a popular local music, leaning more heavily on Indian popular music influences with artists such as Rikki Jai.

Olivia Ahyoung

AN INSIDE LOOK

I consider myself fortunate to have been born in the country of Guyana (the former British Guiana) a land of six ethnic races each with its own interesting cultural background, co-existing and blending with each other to make a uniquely Guyanese culture. Being the only English-speaking country on the South American continent, Guyana shares cultural similarities with the English-speaking Caribbean rather than those of Latin America, and it was in this atmosphere that my appreciation and love of Caribbean music with its infectious rhythms grew and flourished.

Growing up in a musical household, at an early age I was exposed to classical music through private piano and string lessons, competitions at music festivals and annual examinations. Yet I had always been captivated by the performances of folk songs and dances by local groups and the fascinating array of drumming rhythms I heard in local African, Indian and Chinese ceremonies. But it was the sweet sound of pan emanating from the "pan yards" as the all-male steel bands played intricate melodies and arrangements without music that intrigued me the most.

In Guyana during my tenure teaching music at a boys' high school, I got the opportunity to learn more about the instrument by visiting pan yards to talk and learn from the players, and subsequently taught pan, and wrote arrangements of folk and other local music for the school's steel band. I was helped in this process by the shift in emphasis from classical to indigenous music that came about after the country's independence, and working with the pan alongside other classical instruments was a very rewarding experience for me and the students.

Olivia Ahyoung

Some years later here in the USA, I again got the opportunity to teach and lead a college steel band that was started by my late husband, an ethnomusicology student who hailed from Trinidad. It was a fun and challenging experience introducing die hard classically trained musicians on the path to a music degree, to the infectious beat of Caribbean music and a different concept of rhythm. Challenge turned into excitement as the repertoire grew to include many styles of music including classical, even as the band spawned other groups.

It has been decades since I first heard and fell in love with the steel pan, and since playing the pan was not socially acceptable for females when first introduced in Guyana from Trinidad, I was delighted to find that my musical journey led me to it both at home and in the United States. As the twentieth century's only new instrument, I use every opportunity to talk to music teachers, students and other interested persons about the role pan has played in my musical life and my rich cultural heritage in general.

Ellie Mannette

AN INSIDE LOOK

In 1937, when I began participating in the steel drum art form, I had no idea how it would impact the world of music. I was little more than an adolescent who had, along with my brothers and other young men in our working-class neighborhood of Trinidad, West Indies, wanted to simply express the music that was inside us. Between the years of 1941 and 1946 I created several key innovations in the realm of pan (also called steel drums), such as inverting the playing surface from convex to concave, wrapping sticks with rubber for the first time, and building the first instrument from a 55-gallon drum. Little did I know these advancements would usher in the era of the modern steel drum instrument. When I was offered a scholarship to study music at the Birmingham School of Music in England in 1946, I turned it down so that I could devote my life to furthering the steel drum art form. However, I did make it to London a few years later, in 1951, along with eleven other panmen as members of the Trinidadian All-Star Percussion Orchestra (TASPO), which represented Trinidad in the Festival of Britain. As my reputation spread across the island, I was asked to provide music for audiences at the Little Carib Theater and for the first radio program to include steel band music. I also crafted a band for the U.S. Navy upon their request.

My career has led me all around the world where I have received countless awards and recognitions including from the Queen of England (in the 1960s), the National Endowment for the Arts (in 1999), an Honorary Doctorate from the University of the West Indies (2000), and my induction into the Percussive Arts Society Hall of Fame (2003). That desire to express the music within me led to my creating seven of the ten voices in the modern steel band, and when I moved to the United States in 1967 that passion fueled my desire to spread the art form in the public education systems across the United States. In 1982, I formed a partnership known as the Mannette Touch with then-freelance journalist Kaethe George that enabled me to

Dr. Ellie Mannette, former artist-in-residence, West Virginia University; founder and emeritus CEO, Mannette Steel Drums

continue being at the forefront of the steel band movement in this country for thirty-five years.

In 1992 my appointment as an artist-in-residence at West Virginia University's Creative Arts Center allowed me to form an innovative apprentice program known as the University Tuning Project, and through it realize my dream of training future tuners and builders. And now following my recent retirement I can see the fruits of my teaching and training in the scores of steel band programs across the world and in the handful of gifted builders and tuners that have been fully trained at Mannette Steel Drums, a for-profit company that works in partnership with West Virginia University's Research Corporation. I would feel proudest if my legacy indicates that I passed along my skills to young people so that our art form was able to progress and that I created instruments that made people happy by enabling them to express the music within them.

Site 4: Steel Band (Pan)

PAN
A musical instrument from Trinidad made from a steel oil drum.

First Impressions. Uninitiated listeners could easily mistake the sounds of a steel band for a steam calliope, a theater organ, or some sort of automatic pipe organ contraption. In fact, the steel band is an unlikely orchestra, made up, in part or entirely, of 55-gallon oil drums, whose heads have been beaten into a series of circular concave dents or depressions. Steel band music is usually energetic, highly rhythmic, and pop music flavored—but it can also be serene, even "classical." In existence now for more than fifty years, steel band has soared in popularity in North America recently, resulting in an increasing number of schools, colleges, and universities that sponsor steel band ensembles. This music is tiny Trinidad's most famous gift to the rest of the world.

Aural Analysis. All but the rhythm instruments of the steel band began life as 55-gallon oil drums. A steel band ensemble consists of multiple steel drums, called pan (pronounced like "pawn"), plus a rhythm section known as the "engine room," which comprises a conventional drum set, conga drum, automobile brake drums, and possibly other kinds of percussion such as **maracas** (rattles), *claves* (sticks beaten together), the *güiro* (scraped gourd), and the cowbell (an echo of the African iron bell). There is no fixed number of pan, nor are their names used consistently. The higher-pitched pan are cut from the full drum, leaving a short "skirt" (side of the drum), whereas the lowest pans use the full skirt. Notes of definite pitch are produced by striking tuned dents that have been carefully hammered into the head of each pan; the higher-pitched instruments are capable of producing many more pitches than lower-pitched ones, because the area required for a high pitch is small and for a bass pitch large. Some pitch ranges require multiple pan, because bass pans often can produce only four pitches each. The leading melodic pan are known variously as the *tenor*, *ping-pong*, *lead*, *soprano*, and *melody* pan. Those creating harmony or "strumming" effects in imitation of guitars are called variously *guitar*, *double second*, *double guitar*, *quadraphonic*, *triple guitar*, and *cello*. The bass line is provided by the *bass* pan. Because the tuning process is most critical, and the ensemble's overall sound depends on good tuning, skilled tuners are highly sought after.

MARACAS
A pair of small Caribbean gourd rattles with interior beads.

Steelbands arrive for the National Small and Medium Preliminaries competition at Victoria Square, Port of Spain (Sean Drakes /LatinContent/ Getty Images)

11
THE CARIBBEAN

Full steelband with bass pans in front

A lead or melody pan showing many sunken "note areas," each representing a pitch

   The title of our example, "Jump Up," refers to the kind of dancing also known as "breakaway," performed in the streets during Trinidad's Carnival. This is the joyful, outdoor kind of music that really epitomizes Carnival: fast, rhythmic, full of syncopation. Because performances are typically extended and because players have to learn all compositions by memory, repetition is naturally a part of most pieces. "Jump Up" is no exception. Listen carefully and you'll be able to follow its progression.
   The piece begins with an eight-measure introduction with much syncopation, played four times. Then follows the main tune, also eight measures in length, which is played twice. Following this, a third section of eight measures, perhaps best called an interlude, is played four times, after which the melody is repeated twice and the interlude four more times. The main melody then returns before fading out in our excerpted example.

LISTENING GUIDE

 CD 3.7 (2'02")

Chapter 11: Site 4
Trinidad: Steel Band

Instruments: Steel drums (melodic idiophones), electric bass, drum set (membranophones and cymbals), brake drum (idiophone)

TIME	LISTENING FOCUS
0'00"	Listen for the drum set introduction, and the following introductory melodic section. Note the consistent rhythmic pattern of the idiophone and frequent use of syncopation in the melody and snare drums in particular.
0'07"	Listen for the contrasting descending melodic contour of the lower-ranged steel drums which sound to close the melodic phrase.
0'08"	Introductory melody repeats, and repeats again at 0'15" and 0'23."
0'30"	Listen for the short pause and drum accent that initiate the first melodic section.
0'39"	First melodic section repeats.
0'47"	Listen for new melodic material.
1'01"	First melodic section returns.
1'18"	Second melodic section returns.
1'32"	Listen for an ascending melodic contour in the main melody.
1'40"	First melodic section repeats. Listen for the addition of a secondary contrasting melody in the upper-range steel drums.
1'55"	Example fades.

Source: "Jump Up," performed by the Miami (Ohio) University Steel Band; from the recording entitled *One More Soca*. Ramajay Records. Used by permission.

ETHNO-CHALLENGE (CD 3.7): Using a cookie tin or some other shapeable "steel drum," make your own pan by creating various pitches.

Cultural Considerations. The steel band, locally called pan, is doubtless the best-known and most widely distributed kind of ensemble invented in the New World. Pan were originally made from the thousands of oil drums left behind in Trinidad, first by the British, then during World War II by Americans, who had built a forward base west of Port of Spain for flights to Africa. Like the *tamboo bamboo* instruments, their invention was due to the British ban

A "panyard" where steel bands in Trinidad assemble to practice (M.Tyler Rounds)

on drum playing during Carnival. In the 1930s revelers began picking up various discarded metal cans such as "biscuit tins" and beating rhythms on them; these groups became known as "dustbin bands." Creative Trinidadians soon discovered that by pounding (or "sinking") circles into the tops of oil drums abandoned as junk, it was possible to produce multiple pitches on a single surface. Obviously, these instruments were not portable like the dustbin instruments. Over the next few years, however, the makers developed *pan* of various sizes to allow for a full range of pitches and to enable performers to produce full chords. Little did the British or Americans know that their refuse would be recycled into the voice of a nation: in 1992 *pan* became the official national instrument of Trinidad.

In its early years, however, *pan* was not so respectable, for, like the *tamboo bamboo* and dustbin bands, it was associated with the shantytowns in the hills above Port of Spain and with gang violence. As with calypso, the authorities gradually tamed pan by integrating it into the country's social fabric, especially by arranging competitions. The earlier "Pan Is Beautiful" competition has given way to the current "Panorama" competitions. These are held near the end of Carnival, when dozens of bands, both amateur and near professional, compete by playing three currently required numbers: a Western classical composition of their choice, a mandatory test piece specific to that year, and a calypso of their choice.

Most players are amateurs who learn their parts by rote. Important to the process, then, is an arranger who creates the piece (more often than not in notation) and painstakingly teaches it one measure at a time to the ensemble. Many bands can play (from memory) extended and sophisticated European compositions as long as symphony and concerto movements, and some now play entirely original compositions in a relatively modern style.

Steel bands have spread throughout the Caribbean, and some other islands, such as Antigua, have had them since the late 1940s. The use of a single tenor (melody) pan as part of an unrelated ensemble is now common too, sometimes just to invoke the idea of the "West Indies." Steel bands also flourish wherever West Indians have settled, especially in New York, Toronto, and London. Additionally, in recent years ensembles directed by non-West Indians and featuring non-West Indian players have sprung up in high schools, colleges, and universities throughout the United States. Steel bands are becoming prevalent in Europe as well, especially Sweden and Switzerland, and they have also been seen on the streets of Paris.

Arrival: The Bahamas

The Bahamas were the first islands of the "New World" visited by Christopher Columbus in 1492. At that time, the region was inhabited by the Arawak people, who after contact with Europeans were quickly wiped out by European diseases. The Spanish, despite having funded Columbus's voyage, did not lay claim to the islands, and it was the British who eventually settled Eleuthera and New Providence Islands during the mid-seventeenth century. The region became a stronghold for marauders, most notably the British-born pirate Edward Teach, better known as Blackbeard.

By the eighteenth century, the British government had asserted its control over the entire region and claimed the Bahamas as a colony. The islands became an important refuge for loyalists to the British crown after the American revolutionary war in 1776. Many Carolinians fled to the islands with their African-descended slaves. Baptist missionaries accompanied them as well, establishing churches throughout the islands. After slavery was abolished in 1833, many British-descended residents left as economic prosperity declined. As a result, more than 90 percent of today's population in the Bahamas is of African descent.

Today, the Bahamas, with its roughly 700 islands, is one of the most popular tourist destinations in the Western hemisphere. More than three million tourists visit the country each year to enjoy the white sand beaches, spectacular coral reefs, and the splendors of Caribbean cuisine. Grand hotels and luxury cruise ships contrast with chalky stucco houses and solitary sailboats drifting offshore. Seafaring activity has long faded as the primary economic activity of the country as tourism brings in revenue of more than 1.3 billion dollars annually.

The huge emphasis on tourism has greatly affected cultural activities throughout the Bahamas. Most musicians seek employment at hotels or with tourist shows, resulting in a disinterest in music that does not "sell" to the predominantly American audience. Thus, reggae, calypso, and popular music from the United States and Europe dominate the musical landscape of the Bahamas, whereas the "quaint" rhyming spirituals, *goombay* ensembles, and "rake and scrape" bands of the locals usually remain unheard by the average tourist.

Site 5: Rhyming Spiritual

First Impressions. Enthusiasm characterizes this performance. The reverent opening quickly moves into a rousing rendition of "The Lord's Prayer" from the Christian tradition. Sounding

THE CARIBBEAN

A woman dances in spectacular costume in Nassau, The Bahamas, during Junkanoo, an African-derived festival that resembles Carnival (Shutterstock)

either slightly inebriated or "caught in the spirit," this male vocal trio performs a rhythmically vibrant rhyming spiritual that is raw rather than sanitized for tourist consumption.

Aural Analysis. The focus of a rhyming spiritual is on the lead tenor voice, known as the *rhymer*. While the music does not strictly follow a call-and-response form, the rhymer starts each phrase and guides the changing tempo. Though each rhyming spiritual has an established melody and basic narrative, the rhymer is free to extemporize the lyrical and melodic content of a performance. In this case, the rhymer begins with the expected lyrics of the spiritual and then uses "The Lord's Prayer" as the basis for his improvisations after the sixth refrain. He also extends his vocal phrases to make them overlap the refrain provided by the accompanying voices.

As the rhymer "bobs" along, the supporting cast adds unique vocal timbres: a deep growling lower voice and a near-falsetto upper voice repeating the refrain, "My Lord help me to pray." Rhyming spirituals are expected to have at least the rhymer and the lower voice, known as the *basser* but are frequently enhanced by the addition of one or more upper voices. The inclusion of the upper voices helps clarify the vocal harmony rooted in the lower voice and allows the rhymer more freedom to elaborate his melodic content.

LISTENING GUIDE

CD 3.8 (1'25")

Chapter 11: Site 5
Bahamas: Rhyming Spiritual

Voices: Male ensemble, featuring *rhymer* (lead), *basser* (low voice), plus a middle "refrain" voice

TIME	LISTENING FOCUS
0'00"	Lead voice begins the performance. Note that the example follows a free rhythm with a loose sense of a duple meter.
	Line 1: *Oh Lord, What a faithful soul.*
0'03"	Listen for the lead and low voices singing the refrain, while the middle voice hums to find a contrasting harmony pitch.
	Refrain: *My Lord, help me to pray.*
0'07"	Lead voice repeats line 1, followed by the low and middle voices singing along with the refrain.
0'14"	Introduction continues with the call-and-response overlap of the lead and supporting voices
	Line 2: *I heard the words from heaven say.*
0'17"	Refrain repeats.
0'20"	Line 2 repeats, followed by the refrain and a repeated third verse with refrain.
0'37"	*Rhymer* (lead voice) begins to improvise using the text of the "Lord's Prayer." Listen for the supporting voices continuing the refrain repetition throughout the rest of the example.

Source: "My Lord, Help Me to Pray," performed by Bruce Green, Clifton Green, and Tweedie Gibson and recorded by Peter K. Siegel and Jody Stecher, Nassau, Bahamas, 1965; from the recording entitled *Kneelin' Down Inside the Gate: The Great Rhyming Singers of the Bahamas*, Rounder 5035. Used by permission.

ETHNO-CHALLENGE (CD 3.8): Sing the refrain, "My Lord, help me to pray," along with the supporting voices, perhaps adding your own harmony pitches.

Cultural Considerations. Many hymns and spirituals common to the southern United States can be found in the Bahamas as well. The slaves of British Loyalists exiled after the American Revolutionary War brought these songs with them and maintained their performance in many contexts before and after slavery was abolished. The influence of the Baptist church, with its emphasis on energetic singing, emotionally extemporized sermons, and congregational participation, is especially pronounced. Anthems sung in church are the best-known reminder of the Bahamas' historical link with the United States.

The church's influence was felt in secular realms as well. Rhyming spirituals were most often sung by sponge fisherman who roamed the western coast of the island of Andros. Biblical themes were most common, though some songs focused on local events, such as a shipwreck. The spirituals are essentially narratives told through song rather than speech. The rhymer recounts the tale through his improvisations as the other voices provide harmonic and rhythmic support. The bass voice is likened to the earth while the upper voices are considered to be the sky. The rhymer weaves between the two with a rhythmic freedom akin to the ever-changing movement of wind or waves.

When the sponge-fishing industry declined, a major context for the performance of rhyming spirituals was diminished as well. Consequently, the art of rhyming now has a limited number of practitioners. Today, extemporized rhyming spirituals are most commonly heard at funeral wakes. Some professional groups, such as the Dicey Doh Singers, continue to perform rhyming spirituals, but their music has a slick polished sound intended to appeal to tourists. The raspy voices, improvised rhymes, and ambiguous harmonies heard in our example from the 1960s have been replaced with full voices, composed lyrics, and regular harmonic progressions. Nonetheless, though they have lost some of their raw energy, rhyming spirituals continue to be a distinctive aspect of Bahamian musical identity.

Arrival: Cuba

Only some 90 miles from Florida, Cuba remains a difficult destination for Americans today though tourism by the rest of the world is growing by leaps and bounds. This was not always so. Before the revolution in 1959, when Fidel Castro swept away the American-backed dictatorship of Fulgencio Batista, Cuba was a playground for rich North Americans wishing to dodge the restrictions on alcohol consumption imposed by Prohibition. Havana, wide open to liquor, prostitution, and gambling, was one of the most enticing cities in the Western hemisphere, with its grand hotels, homes, and casinos. One of Cuba's great attractions today is its "time capsule" atmosphere: colonial architecture, classic American cars, and an abundance of old-time Cuban music, the latter made famous by a 1990s recording and movie titled *The Buena Vista Social Club* featuring surviving musicians from an actual members-only club in Havana whose heyday was the 1940s.

An island slightly larger than Indiana or Greece with a population of eleven million, Cuba was first "discovered" by Christopher Columbus in late 1492 but largely ignored by the Spaniards, who found Hispaniola to the east more rewarding. At that time Cuba's inhabitants were the native Tainos and Arawak, but after the beginning of colonialization in 1511, when the Spaniards forced the native people to work the gold mines, rebellions, disease, and starvation reduced that population to only 5,000 survivors by 1550. The first African slaves arrived in 1522 to work the new sugar plantations, and while treatment was harsh, the Spanish permitted the slaves to maintain tribal groups and therefore a semblance of their original culture. In addition to sugar, the Spaniards began cultivating tobacco and raising cattle, but with little supervision, Cuba (and the Caribbean generally) succumbed to the chaos brought about by pirates, especially the British. Friction between Spain and the United States over Cuba led finally to the Spanish-American War of 1898, triggered by the explosion of the U.S. battleship *Maine* in Havana harbor early that year and made famous by Teddy Roosevelt's charge up San Juan Hill with his Rough Riders. Following direct American control until 1902, Cuba achieved independence but remained under heavy American influence. A series of harsh and corrupt regimes, culminating in that of Batista, led to the Cuban Revolution in 1959, instigated by Fidel Castro and the now iconic Che Guevara, followed by the ill-fated "Bay of Pigs Invasion" of 1961 and the Cuban Missile Crisis of 1962. Relations between the United States and Cuba, long severed, are now undergoing a slow rapprochement under Fidel's brother, Raul Castro. Whatever else we might say about its government, post-1959 Cuba has shown generous support for the traditional arts, particularly music, and now travelers to Cuba can enjoy performances by vintage musicians of the highest professional level.

What makes Cuba's music distinctive is its successful blending of European and African musical traditions. This mixing can be heard in a range of styles, from the mostly African **Santeria**, a syncretistic religion combining traditional African/Yoruba practices with Roman Catholicism, to genres such as *son* and ***guaracha***, which mix African rhythms with European melodies and harmony, to mostly European genres such as *danzón*. It was the middle ground combining Europe and Africa that gave rise to what came to be called the "Latin styles," a plethora of types and artists which spread widely from their original Cuban roots. This led to a musical "rage" for Latin-styled music, a trend that continues today, and was particularly reinforced by the rising popularity of "Latin" ballroom dance.

Site 6: Cuban *Son*

First Impressions. Easy going from the outset, this danceable piece of music starts with a guitar or related instrument, quickly joined by others including a trumpet and a variety of percussion instruments, including a prominent one with a sharp clap, another with a gentle scraping sound, and also some hollow-sounding drums. At first a group of men sing, but later a solo voice alternates with the group. Is it any wonder that Cuba attracts visitors, not just for its relaxed way of life and friendly people, but its music?

Aural Analysis. Field recorded around 1980 in Santiago, Cuba, in Oriente province where *son* was first created at the end of the nineteenth century, the group's instrumentation is much expanded from the original *son* groups, which consisted of just three instruments: *tres*, a guitar-like instrument with three courses of two strings each, **claves**, a pair of hardwood sticks struck together, and *maracas*, a pair of small gourds whose seeds create a "sheh-sheh" sound when shaken. After migrating to Havana early in the new century, *son* groups began adding more instruments, some African derived, such as the *marimbula* or *botija*, a wooden box with large metal lamellae plucked to provide bass pitches, and *bongos*, a pair of small single-headed drums, along with European derived ones, such as *timbales*, metal-framed drums of the military snare family, and trumpets or cornets. Additional

SANTERIA
An African-derived animistic belief system found primarily in Cuba and the United States.

GUARACHA
(pronounced *gwah-rah-cha*) A Latin American ballroom dance, as well as a song type emphasizing call-and-response vocal organization.

CLAVES
An instrument consisting of two sticks beaten together.

THE CARIBBEAN

Havana, Cuba street musicians play music for tips from the many non-American tourists visiting Cuba each year. (Left to right) *claves*, *tres cubano*, guitar, (front) *bongos*, (right) *marimbala* (bass lamellophone) (Shutterstock)

Two street musicians in Trinidad, Cuba, declared a World Heritage Site in 1988. *Claves* (left), *maracas* (right) (Shutterstock)

WORLD MUSIC: A GLOBAL JOURNEY

Rumba clave, the patterns used for *son* as played by the *claves* (a pair of wooden sticks)

	1	-	2	-	3	-	4	-	5	-	6	-	7	-	8	-
Rumba Clave (3+2)	X "1"	-	-	X "2"	-	-	-	X "3"	-	X "1"	-	X "2"	-	-	-	-
"Reverse" (2+3)	-	-	X "1"	-	X "2"	-	-	-	X "1"	-	-	X "2"	-	-	-	X "3"

A *güiro*, originally a scraped gourd—now often of wood—common throughout the Caribbean, including Cuba (Shutterstock)

instruments were gradually added, including the *güiro*, a gourd with ridges cut into the side which are scraped, the guitar itself, African-derived conga drums, and later, as *son* was transformed into an urban, big band form, piano and other jazz instruments as well.

The *son*, occupying a point that balanced African and European musical traits, became the progenitor of most music now labeled "Latin." The typical form, heard here, consists of an introduction sung in chorus by the players, followed by a section called the *montuno*, where a soloist alternates with the group. Following this, the instrumentalists begin a free interplay that probably reflects more of a jazz influence than the traditions of Oriente. Many

THE CARIBBEAN

scholars consider the *montuno* section to be the feature that was most influential on the many *son*-derived styles.

Titled "Soneros Son" and recorded by the song's creator, Pedro Fernandez of the group Estudiantina Invasora in Santiago de Cuba in 1978–1979 by ethnomusicologist Verna Gillis, the lyrics constitute an expression of pride by the author that "his songs" are known worldwide:

> Eso es mi Son, bailalo bién
> Es todo Cubano, gózalo mi hermano
> Ha paseado el mundo, mi Son Cubano
>
> This is my Son, dance it well
> It is purely Cuban, enjoy it my brother
> My Cuban Son has traveled around the world
> This is my Cuban Son

Although non-Latin musicians hear this song in duple or 2/4 meter, Cuban/Latin musicians hear it in "son clave." The *claves*, a pair of hardwood sticks creating the sharp rap so prominent in the recording, are actually articulating a cyclic pattern of five clicks, this being the typical "clave" for *son*. Almost certainly derived from an African iron bell pattern, the *son clave* emphasizes the subordinate beats more than the main ones. Using both your ear and the chart on p. 410 as a guide, count "one and two and three and four" while clapping at the correct points.

LISTENING GUIDE

CD 3.9 (4'42")

Chapter 11: Site 6
Cuba: *Son*

Vocals: Three male vocalists (lead and two background)
Instruments: *tres* guitar, guitar, acoustic bass, maracas, claves, trumpet, timbales, cow bell.

TIME	LISTENING FOCUS
0'00"	*Tres* guitar begins the performance.
0'06"	Timbales roll signals entrance of other instruments. Trumpet plays the main theme.
0'30"	Vocalists enter with polyphonic singing on the main theme. Note the reverse clave (also known as *son clave*) rhythm of the claves.
0'49"	Brief timbales fill.
0'52"	Trumpet returns.
1'15"	Voices return with repeat of lyrics.

1'33"	*Montuno* section begins. Note the "Eso es mi son cubano" repeated refrain. Listen for the improvisatory style of the trumpet.
1'36"	Note the appearance of cow bell with a complementary rhythm to the reverse clave pattern.
1'55"	Lead vocal sings in improvisatory style between the vocal duet's repeated refrain.
2'28"	Voices and cow bell drop out as the *tres* guitar takes lead melodic role in improvisatory style.
3'42"	*Tres* guitar plays repeated pattern to signal transition to trumpet melodic lead at 3'58".
4'00"	Voices return on *montuno* refrain. Trumpet plays lead improvisatory melody.
4'21"	Lead vocal returns to improvisatory style.
4'32"	Closing phrase.

Source: "Soneros Son" by Estudiantina Invasora from the recording entitled *Music of Cuba*. Recorded by Verna Gillis in Cuba 1978–1979, Folkways Records FW 04064, © 1985. Used by permission.

ETHNO-CHALLENGE (CD 3.9): Clap the reverse clave rhythm throughout the performance. Perform some vocal or instrumental improvisation during the *montuno* section, or sing along with the vocal refrain.

Cultural Considerations. The development of Cuban music is inextricably tied to dance, and while the various forms of Latin jazz, pop, and rock can stand on their own simply as music, their success is continuously reinforced by the prevalence of ballroom dance generally as well as programs such as *The Ohio Star Ball* and *Dancing with the Stars*. Modern ballroom dancers would rarely encounter old, genuine Cuban music like this track, but none would have difficulty in dancing the rumba (sometimes spelled rhumba) to it. Of all the Cuban-derived dances—including bolero, cha cha chá, and mambo—rumba is the most basic and easiest. But the terminology is confusing in that *rumba* (meaning "party") originally denoted a secular form of local dance music played primarily by African-derived percussion with singing. The misnamed "rumba craze" of the 1930s was set off by the popularity of a song called "The Peanut Vendor" (*El Manisero*) created from street vendors' cries by Moises Simons and first recorded by Rita Montaner for Columbia in 1927. Mislabeled "rumba" (actually it was a *son*), "The Peanut Vendor" led to innumerable imitations, some faster, some slower, all called "rumba." Rumba dance, however, only made use of the slower *bolero-son*.

The ballroom steps were only created later by Pierre Zurcher-Margolle and his partner, Doris Lavelle, then living in London, Zurcher-Margolle having observed local dancing in Havana during trips in 1947, 1951, and 1953. The basic "international" step pattern "breaks" (begins) on beat 2, as - 2 3 4 hold 2 3 4 hold, etc., whereas the American rumba patterns break on 1 (1 2 3 hold or 1 hold 3 4) in a box pattern.

While the *son*, with its *montuno* section, was the foundation for developments that led ultimately to *salsa* music (see Chapter 13, Site 9, *salsa*), two other types of music also associated with ballroom dances—the *cha cha chá* and *mambo*—must be considered. These

Cuban rhumba (or rumba) dancer Zulema peforms with a band at the Zombie Club in pre-revolutionary Havana, Cuba, in 1946 (Hulton Archive/Getty Images)

arise from the European-derived *danzón*, a genre popular among Euro-Cubans that gave rise to numerous musical offspring. Derived from old French *contredanse*, both the dance and its music reflected European harmonic and melodic traditions almost exclusively, but over time Cuban musicians increasingly made it their own, especially by infusing African-derived rhythms.

First, the *mambo*. In 1938 Cuban musicians Orestes and Cachao López created a *danzón* song titled "Mambo," which gave rise to many imitations, all termed informally "*danzón-mambo*." Cuban dancer Perez Prado became closely associated with this type of music in 1943, and after moving his group from Havana's La Tropicana to Mexico City in 1948, he and his musicians began recording many new "mambo" songs, and Prado evolved a dance style that came to be identified as "mambo." After success in Mexico, Prado and his followers brought the style to the United States where, during the 1950s, a "mambo craze" blossomed, centered at the Palladium Ballroom (the "Temple of Mambo") in New York City but also prominent in Los Angeles among Mexican Americans. American dance teachers, however, found Prado's choreography too difficult for social dancing and evolved named step patterns within reach of amateur dancers. Even so, mambo dancing was challenging, requiring dancers to break on beat 2 and also emphasize beat 4 in a complex syncopated pattern. The music for mambo had by then also absorbed characteristics of *son*.

Second, the *cha cha chá*. Zurcher-Margolle, who also created the *rumba*, observed during his 1952 visit a variant of mambo music that subdivided the fourth beat, and dancers moved their feet close to the floor, creating what was heard as a "cha cha cha" sound. Cuban composer Enrique Jorrin came to be closely identified with this type of music. Zurcher-Margolle and partner Lavelle then created named step patterns for a new ballroom dance that was easier than mambo, because it was danced as 2 3 4 and 1 (with the "cha cha cha" on beats 4 and 1), though American teachers came to view it as beginning on beat 1 (the "prep step" for international dancers). Quickly the new *cha cha chá* caught on and, like mambo and rumba, was adopted into the fixed curricula of ballroom dance studios. What happened after that awaits the discussion for Chapter 13, Site 9, *salsa*.

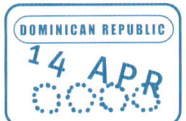

Arrival: The Dominican Republic

The island of Hispaniola is divided into two countries: French-speaking Haiti in the west and the Spanish-speaking Dominican Republic in the east. Whereas an African-descended populace dominates Haiti, the Dominican Republic's population is largely a mix of Spanish and African heritages. While African cultural influence is strong throughout the Dominican Republic, Dominicans prefer to emphasize their European roots and associate themselves with Hispanic culture, largely due to the cultural policies promoted by the former dictator Rafael Leonidas Trujillo Molina (r. 1930–1961). These policies instilled a fear of anything Haitian, especially anything associated with the widespread practice of *Vodou*. Trujillo's influence is still felt today, though many youth are embracing their African roots.

Site 7: *Merengue*

MERENGUE
A Latin American/Caribbean dance and music genre, originally from the Dominican Republic.

GÜIRA
(pronounced gwee-rah) A scraped metal idiophone commonly used in *merengue*. (Note: a *güiro* is a similar scraped idiophone made of gourd.)

Dancing to *merengue* music by a *merengue típico moderno* group led by accordionist Adolfo Diaz (Paul Austerlitz)

First Impressions. **Merengue** is fast-paced. The "scraping" sound of the **güira** is the primary timekeeper and perhaps the genre's most distinctive feature. The accompanying drum (called a *tambora*) plays in "bursts," with a thudding fundamental sound and interlacing slaps. The repetitive melodic line moves at a frenetic pace, pausing only when the voices enter. As with much Caribbean music, *merengue* is highly danceable.

Aural Analysis. The identifying feature of *merengue* is the pairing of the *güira* and *tambora*. The *güira* is a rasp idiophone, typically a bulbous gourd with rings cut into the surface. The "scraping" sound is produced when a piece of wood or metal is rubbed along the coarse outside face of the instrument. The *güira* provides the fundamental tempo and typically emphasizes the

THE CARIBBEAN

A group of *merengue* musicians: (left to right) accordion, *marimba* (bass lamellophone, sometimes called rumba box), *tambora*, and *güira* (scraped metal tube) (Paul Austerlitz)

Francisco Ulloa, one of *merengue*'s most innovative and prominent accordionists offbeats with a long "scrape." The *tambora* is a small barrel drum made with two thick leather faces and is held in the lap. Deep tones are produced by playing one face with a stick, while striking the other face with the hand creates slapping sounds. The "bursts" typical of the instrument are played with the stick and are followed by hand-slap punctuation. In rural performances, the *güira* and *tambora* not only provide the fundamental rhythm but are also frequently featured in improvisatory passages. Ballroom dance *merengue* styles do not generally include such vibrant improvisation on these instruments, however.

The melodic content in our recorded example is provided by a button-box accordion, as well as by the voices. The melody is rhythmically dense and contributes to the fast-paced feel of the music. The voices follow a call-and-response format, which is imitated by the accordion at the conclusion of its solo sections. The quickly repeated tone imitates the call, while the subsequent harmonic chords correspond to the group's response. Other styles of *merengue* may use guitars or saxophones as the primary melodic instruments.

Merengue songs are typically divided into three sections: *paseo*, *merengue*, and *jaleo*. These equate to an introduction, verse, and chorus. The *paseo*, or "walking" section, emphasizes the melodic instruments and often begins at a slower tempo, sometimes in free rhythm. This quickly leads to the *merengue* section, which is established by the *güira-tambora* rhythms. Vocalists sing different verses in this section followed by a refrain, the *jaleo*, which is repeated throughout the piece. The accordion (or saxophone) improvises its own *merengue* section and follows with a *jaleo* refrain before the voices return. This alternation between *merengue* and *jaleo*, which may be performed either by vocalists or instrumentalists, can continue indefinitely. The concluding *jaleo* often quickens in tempo as a sign that the performance is about to finish.

LISTENING GUIDE

CD 3.10 (2'03")

Chapter 11: Site 7
Dominican Republic: *Merengue*

Voices: Single male lead with supporting male ensemble
Instruments: Button-box accordion, *tambora* (barrel drum), *güira* (scraped idiophone)

TIME	LISTENING FOCUS
0'00"	The button-box accordion begins the performance.
0'02"	The *güira* enters, followed by the *tambora*. Listen for the contrasting timbres of the drum as one side is played with a stick (lower tone) and the other with the hand (higher "slap" sound).
0'12"	Listen for the *güira* briefly matching the rhythmic density of the button-box.
0'29"	Vocalist enters.
0'34"	Vocal ensemble responds. Listen for the transition to a quick call-and-response between the lead

	vocalist and vocal group. Note that the button-box is quieter and only sounds along with the group response.
0'47"	The button-box returns as the aural focus as the voices drop out. Listen for variations in the rhythmic pattern of the *tambora*.
0'58"	Listen for variations in the rhythmic pattern of the *güira*.
1'15"	Lead vocalist returns, followed by quick call-and-response section at 1'21.
1'29"	Listen for the button-box solo without the use of harmony.
1'38"	Listen for variations in the rhythmic pattern of the *güira*.
1'46"	Listen for the subtle return of harmony in the button-box part.
1'49"	Listen for the extended "scraping" of the *güira*.
1'57"	Example fades.

Source: "Apágame la Vela (Put Out my Candle)" performed by Nicolá Gutierres, Porfirio Rosario and Santo Pea, recorded by Verna Gillis with Ramon Daniel Perez Martinez, 1976, from the recording entitled *Raíces Latinas: Smithsonian Folkways Latino Roots Collection*, SF 40470, provided courtesy of Smithsonian Folkways Recordings. © 2002. Used by permission.

ETHNO-CHALLENGE (CD 3.10): Construct a scraper to imitate the sound of the *güira* and perform along with the example.

Cultural Considerations. While there are several styles of *merengue*, they are all generally categorized as either "folk" or "ballroom." A large orchestra, often backing a crooning vocalist, and a consistent *güira-tambora* rhythm, characterizes ballroom *merengue*. The ballroom form still follows the *paseo-merengue-jaleo* pattern but has less improvisational freedom. Ballroom *merengue* was strongly promoted during the Trujillo years as a "national" dance in order to help establish a unique Dominican identity. Today, long after the end of Trujillo's rule, *merengue* remains the most popular music in the country.

As with many Caribbean music genres, *merengue* also refers to a dance. Outside the Dominican Republic *merengue* dance experienced a short-lived "craze" during the 1990s but remains one of the highly codified dances of the American ballroom curriculum. The dance is a simple side-step in which the leg that follows drags on the ground. The modern form of the dance requires exaggerated hip movement from side to side, generally called "Latin (or Cuban) motion" by dancers. It is often danced in pairs, with the dancers' upper bodies poised in a standard ballroom dance position with one hand on the hip and the other held out at shoulder height. The dancers move to the left in a circle around the floor but may rotate in a single spot, which allows for numerous couples in a small space.

The origin of *merengue* and its associated dance is not entirely agreed upon, but many believe that the dance is a combination of West African circle dances and European salon dances. The side-step shuffle seems to evoke a time when slaves' feet were chained together while working in the sugarcane fields. The upper body movements mimic the dance positions of a French minuet. One of the step patterns in ballroom *merengue* is called the *ibo*, a term that, interestingly, refers to the Igbo ethnic group of West Africa. The music is also a blend of African and European elements. The *tambora* is believed to derive from similar West African instruments. The *güira* is thought by some to be a Dominican creation, while others consider it an innovation based on scraped gourd idiophones found in West Africa. The call-and-response vocal organization is reminiscent of West African vocal performance. On the other hand, the inclusion of the button-box accordion and the use of the guitar and saxophones as primary melodic instruments reveal musical connections with Europe.

Questions to Consider

1. Where do "African survivals" appear in music of the Caribbean? What makes them African?
2. How did differences in colonial rule affect the course of musical development in the Caribbean?
3. What role does music play in spirit possession in religions such as *Vodou* and *Santeria*?
4. Which Caribbean musics best exemplify the idea that music can express discontent and challenge authority? How are the examples chosen different in content and attitude?
5. How can you account for the fact that the most prominent music types in the Caribbean are popular in nature?
6. How has modern ballroom dance been influenced by music of the Caribbean? What ballroom dances derive from "Latin" music?

On Your Own Time

Visit the textbook website to find these resources for further exploration on your own.

Haiti

Book: Rouget, Gilbert. *Music and Trance: A Theory of the Relations between Music and Possession.* Chicago: University of Chicago Press, 1985.
http://press.uchicago.edu/ucp/books/book/chicago/M/bo5956162.html

Book: McAlister, Elizabeth. *Rara! Vodou, Power, and Performance in Haiti and Its Diaspora.*
http://rara.wesleyan.edu/
http://www.ucpress.edu/book.php?isbn=9780520228238

Website: Sacred Arts of Haitian Voodoo
http://www.amnh.org/exhibitions/vodou/

Audio: *Rhythms of Rapture: Sacred Musics of Haitian Vodou.* Smithsonian-Folkways: SFW40464, 1995.
http://www.folkways.si.edu/albumdetails.aspx?itemid=2364
http://itunes.apple.com/us/album/rhythms-rapture-sacred-musics/id151593754

Internet: Popular Artists from Haiti
Boukman Eksperyans
Boukan Ginen

Jamaica

Book: King, Stephen. *Reggae, Rastafari, and the Rhetoric of Social Control.* Jackson, MS: University Press of Mississippi, 2007.
http://www.upress.state.ms.us/books/612

Book: Bradley, Lloyd. *This Is Reggae Music: The Story of Jamaica's Music.* New York: Grove Press, 2001.
http://www.groveatlantic.com/#page=isbn9780802138286

Website: Bob Marley—Official Website
http://www.bobmarley.com/

Audio: *Legend: The Best of Bob Marley and the Wailers.* Tuff Gong/Island Records, 1984.
http://itunes.apple.com/us/album/legend-remastered-bonus-tracks/id406819

DVD: *The Harder They Come.* Dir. Henzell, Perry. New World Pictures, 1972.
http://www.imdb.com/title/tt0070155/plotsummary

Book: Veal, Michael. *Dub: Soundscapes and Shattered Songs in Jamaican Reggae.* Middletown, CT: Wesleyan University Press, 2007.
http://www.upne.com/0-8195-6571-7.html

Website: Jimmy Cliff—Official Website
http://www.jimmycliff.com/v-css/news/

Website: Carlos Jones—Official Website
http://www.carlosjones.com/

Internet: Popular Artists from Jamaica
Bob Marley
Jimmy Cliff
Peter Tosh
Bunny Wailer
Toots and the Maytals
Burning Spear
Lee "Scratch" Perry
King Tubby
Steel Pulse
Desmond Dekker
Sly and Robbie

Trinidad and Tobago

Book: Regis, Lewis. *The Political Calypso: True Opposition in Trinidad and Tobago.* Gainesville, FL: University Press of Florida, 1998.
http://www.upf.com/book.asp?id=REGISS98

Book: Hill, Donald R. *Calypso Calaloo: Early Carnival Music in Trinidad.* Gainesville, FL: University Press of Florida, 1993.

Book: Guilbault, Jocelyne. *Governing Sound: The Cultural Politics of Trinidad's Carnival Musics.* Chicago: University of Chicago Press, 2007.
   http://press.uchicago.edu/ucp/books/book/chicago/G/bo5298970.html

Website: National Geographic—Calypso
   http://worldmusic.nationalgeographic.com/view/page.basic/genre/content.genre/calypso_701/en_US

Website: National Carnival Commission of Trinidad & Tobago
   http://www.ncctt.org/home/

Website: Soca Monarch
   http://www.socamonarch.net/new/

Book: Dudley, Shannon. *Music from Behind the Bridge: Steelband Aesthetics and Politics in Trinidad and Tobago.* New York: Oxford University Press, 2007.
   http://www.oup.com/us/catalog/general/subject/Music/WorldMusicEthnomusicology/?view=usa&ci=9780195321234

Book: Stuempfle, Stephen. *The Steelband Movement: The Forging of a National Art in Trinidad and Tobago.* Philadelphia, PA: University of Pennsylvania Press, 1996.
   http://www.upenn.edu/pennpress/book/1853.html

Book: Dudley, Shannon. *Carnival Music in Trinidad: Experiencing Music, Expressing Culture.* New York: Oxford University Press, 2003.
   http://www.oup.com/us/catalog/general/subject/Music/WorldMusicEthnomusicology/?view=usa&ci=9780195138337

Internet: Popular Artists from Trinidad & Tobago
   Lord Kitchener
   Calypso Rose
   Mighty Sparrow
   Destra Garcia
   Bunji Garlin
   KMC
   Arrow
   David Rudder
   Rikki Jai

The Bahamas

Audio: *The Bahamas: The Real Bahamas in Music and Song.* Nonesuch Records: 79725, 1966.
   http://www.nonesuch.com/albums/the-bahamas-the-real-bahamas-in-music-and-song

Audio: *The Bahamas: Islands of Song.* Smithsonian-Folkways: SFW 40405, 1997.
   http://www.folkways.si.edu/albumdetails.aspx?itemid=2424
   http://itunes.apple.com/us/album/the-bahamas-islands-of-song/id151591784

Book: Charters, Samuel. *The Day is so Long and the Wages so Small.* London: Marion Boyers Publishers, 2002.
   http://www.marionboyars.co.uk/Amy%20individual%20book%20info/The%20Day%20is%20So%20Long.html

Book: Rommen, Timothy. *Funky Nassau: Roots, Routes, and Representation in Bahamian Popular Music.* Berkeley, CA: University of California Press, 2011.
   http://www.ucpress.edu/book.php?isbn=9780520265691

Internet: Popular Artists from the Bahamas
   Joseph Spence

Baha Men
T-Connection

Cuba

Book: Fernandez, Raul. *From Afro-Cuban Rhythms to Latin Jazz.* Berkeley, CA: University of California Press, 2006.
http://www.ucpress.edu/book.php?isbn=9780520247086

Book: Manuel, Peter. *Caribbean Currents: Caribbean Music from Rumba to Reggae.* 2nd edition. Philadelphia, PA: Temple University Press, 2006.
http://www.temple.edu/tempress/titles/1175_reg.html

Website/Audio/DVD: Buena Vista Social Club
http://www.buenavistasocialclub.com/

Website: Mamborama
http://www.mamborama.com/cuba_music.html

Website: Salsa and Merengue—Cuban Son Montuno
http://www.salsa-merengue.co.uk/VidTutor/rhythm/son_phrasing_part_one.html

Audio: *Cuban Counterpoint: History of the Son Montuno.* Rounder Records: R102013, 1992.
http://www.allmusic.com/album/cuban-counterpoint-history-of-the-son-montuno-r102013

Internet: Popular Artists from Cuba
Celia Cruz
Buena Vista Social Club
Los Van Van
Haila
César "Pupy" Pedroso
Arsenio Rodriguez
NG La Banda

The Dominican Republic

Book: Austerlitz, Paul, and Robert Farris Thompson. *Merengue : Dominican Music and Dominican Identity.* Philadelphia, PA: Temple University Press, 1997.
http://www.temple.edu/tempress/titles/1060_reg.html

Book: Sellers, Julie. *Merengue and Dominican Identity: Music As National Unifier.* Jefferson, NC: McFarland & Co., 2004.
http://www.mcfarlandpub.com/book-2.php?id=978-0-7864-1815-2

Book: Manuel, Peter. *Caribbean Currents: Caribbean Music from Rumba to Reggae.* 2nd edition. Philadelphia, PA: Temple University Press, 2006.
http://www.temple.edu/tempress/titles/1175_reg.html

Internet: Popular Artists from the Dominican Republic
Juan Luis Gerra
Milly Quezada
Antony Santos
Fernando Villalona
Omega el Fuerte

South America and Mexico: The Amazon Rainforest, Peru, Argentina, Brazil, Mexico

12

Background Preparation	424	**Arrival: Brazil**	439	Established by the ancient Incas in Peru at least by the thirteenth century, Machu Picchu, a ruined city at 9,000 feet/2740 meters in the Andes Mountains, was forgotten following the Spanish conquest in the early sixteenth century and only rediscovered in 1911 (M. Tyler Rounds)
Planning the Itinerary	426	Site 4: *Samba*	440	
An Inside Look: Martin Pereira Algarita	426	**Explore More: Carnival**	444	
Arrival: The Amazon Rainforest	427	Site 5: *Capoeira* Music	444	
Site 1: Amazonian Chant	428	**Arrival: Mexico**	449	
Arrival: Peru	430	Site 6: *Mariachi*	449	
Site 2: *Sikuri* (Panpipe) Ensemble	431	**Questions to Consider**	454	
Arrival: Argentina	434	**On Your Own Time**	455	
Site 3: *Tango*	435			

Background Preparation

In the Western hemisphere, Central and South America, as well as Mexico, are frequently overshadowed by the global attention given to the United States. While tourism is increasing steadily, most travelers choose the United States or islands of the Caribbean for their vacation destinations. Many areas south of the U.S. border are still regarded as "developing," but many great cities in these areas are quite cosmopolitan and as highly developed as cities in the United States and Europe. The region also boasts some of the world's most beautiful natural wonders, such as the Amazon—the largest river in the world—and its surrounding rainforests (mostly in Brazil); Angel Falls (Venezuela), the highest waterfall in the world; and the Andes Mountains, second only to the Himalayas in peak height and the longest system of high mountains in the world, running all along the western coast of South America.

While the generally accepted theory is that the indigenous populations of the Americas crossed from Asia, recent archaeological evidence indicates that there were people living in modern Brazil some 30,000 to 50,000 years ago and in Chile and Venezuela roughly 13,000 years ago. Though little can be said for certain regarding the activities of these earliest inhabitants, the ancient empires of the Western hemisphere, namely the Maya, Aztec, and Inca empires, are better known and continue to influence the cultural identity of the present populations of Mexico, Central, and South America. Remnants of these ancient civilizations are visited by thousands of tourists every year, and archaeologists work tirelessly to uncover clues to the cultural activities of these early indigenous peoples. Evidence of advanced knowledge in astronomy, mathematics, and agriculture, as well as of highly structured political and religious systems, dates to as early as 200 B.C.E. and suggests that at their peak each empire may have rivaled those of ancient China or Rome.

Spanish conquerors, however, put an end to the development of these civilizations soon after Christopher Columbus "discovered" the New World in 1492 C.E. Coupled with the

Perhaps Mexico's most famous Mayan ruin, the pyramid at Chichen Itza was begun about 900 C.E. and testifies to the advanced technological development of this early civilization (Andrew Shahriari)

SOUTH AMERICA AND MEXICO

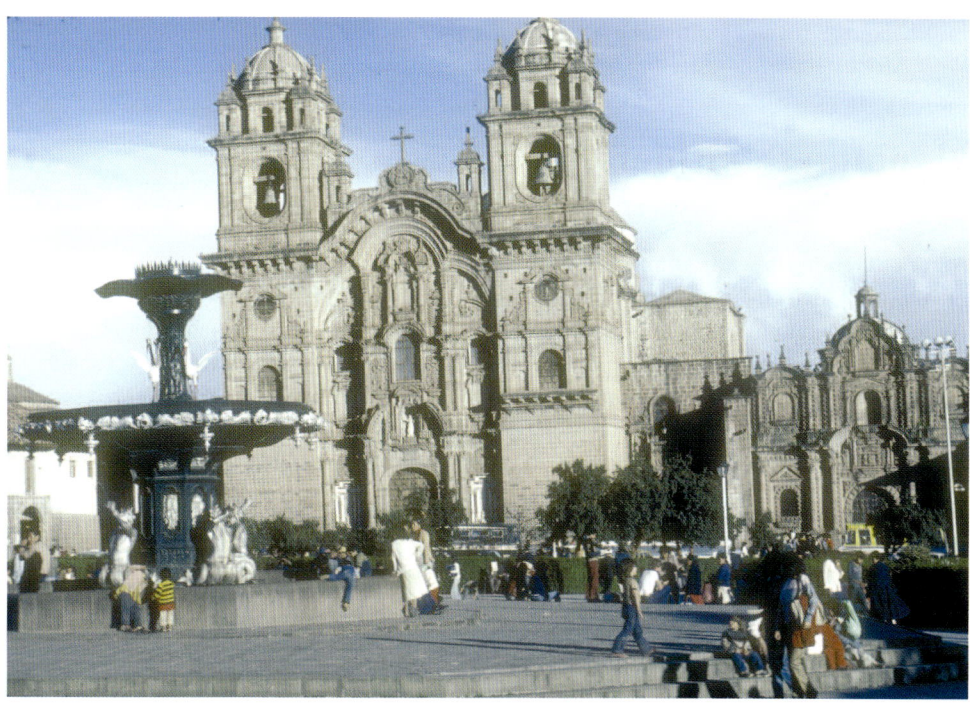

In Cusco, Peru, the Iglesia de la Compania de Jesus in the Plaza de Armas was built in the late 1570s and rebuilt later after an earthquake. Its large plaza is where festivals including music and dance occur frequently (Max T. Miller)

military conquests of the Spanish conquistadors, Old World diseases—such as smallpox and measles—decimated many indigenous populations who had no biological resistance to the foreign diseases. Throughout the region, Roman Catholic missionaries found fertile ground in which to establish new churches. By the end of the eighteenth century, the Spaniards had settled in far-reaching areas of North, Central, and South America that have since grown into some of today's largest cities, such as San Francisco, Los Angeles, Mexico City, Lima, and Buenos Aires.

In addition to subjugating native peoples, Spanish and Portuguese colonialists also brought many African slaves to the Americas to work in gold and silver mines, to raise cattle, and to farm plantations growing crops such as tobacco and sugarcane. Other European colonialists followed suit, and brought with them laborers from other colonized countries such as India and Indonesia, while the French transferred many prisoners to the region. Because of this, many areas of South America today, Guyana, Suriname, and French Guiana in particular, reveal strong cultural connections with non-European peoples. Eastern coastal areas, especially in Brazil, are densely populated with peoples of mixed African and Iberian ancestry (*mulattos*), while Central America and much of the interior of South America comprise mainly indigenous populations, many of whom also have Spanish ancestry (those of mixed ancestry are known as *mestizos*). The rainforests of Brazil remained largely immune to the influx of foreigners until the late nineteenth and early twentieth centuries. Rapid deforestation in the 1980s led to increased interest in the protection of wildlife and the preservation of the traditional lifeways of the many indigenous Amazonian tribes.

The musical activities of the diverse peoples of Central and South America reflect these historical interactions. Indigenous populations in the rainforests and in rural areas of the Andes preserve musical traditions believed to predate the arrival of Columbus. Music found in urban areas reveals influences from Europe, specifically Spain and Portugal, as well as West Africa.

Planning the Itinerary

The music of Central and South America, and of Mexico (geographically part of North America), comprises three major ingredients: Indigenous traditions, European-derived music, and African-inspired musical activity. The music of the Amazonian tribes and Andean rural communities dates to pre-Columbian times and has presumably remained little changed for centuries. Spanish influence is felt in numerous music traditions, especially those found in urban areas. African influence can be seen in the survival of African secular and religious practices, the creation of new instruments modeled after African ones, and in the use of musical traits, such as polyrhythm, commonly associated with various ethnic groups from Africa.

Martin Pereira Algarita

AN INSIDE LOOK

We created the ensemble "Impromptus" in 1985 while we were students at the Universidad Pedagogica Nacional de Bogota in the capital city of Colombia. Students from different academic disciplines began meeting at the campus to practice different styles of Latin American popular music just because we enjoyed it. We named ourselves after the Romantic musical form called Impromptus, meaning "spontaneous."

Through constant practice and exchanging musical experiences, including those from traditional styles, plus the creative urge of the group members, we found a common purpose, that of exploring new vocal and instrumental sonorities in search of a voice that would speak to the younger generations. As with all new tendencies, our group had both admirers and detractors. The fact that our director, Mauricio Rangel Valderrama, is the son and nephew, respectively, of Oton Rangel and Oriol Rangel, both considered among the best interpreters of Colombia's traditional music, did not make the evolutionary trajectory of this group any easier. Other members of the ensemble had also been nurtured by tradition and yet, by listening to groups from

Impromptus

other countries, particularly elsewhere in Latin America and the Caribbean, and focusing more on vocal styles, particularly the immensely popular ballads of the 1980s, we developed a style that we call "New Colombian Music." This could be appreciated from our first recorded work introduced in 1991. By then the ensemble had gained recognition and followers who continued the evolutionary path that "Impromptus" had started and expanded to reach a national audience. National competitions and festivals of this new music now take place in Colombia. Unfortunately, new media and means of

> communication seem to ignore the new styles. Moreover, the different genres of Colombian music, which are numerous due to the country's geographical location and diversity, are not equally appreciated. Andean-derived styles like ours do not seem to have the popular demand that the more popular *salsa*-like Caribbean styles have. Nonetheless, we will continue to assert our own voices.

Our introduction to the music of this region begins with a discussion of the Kayapó-Xikrin, an Amazonian indigenous tribe found in the rainforests of Brazil. Next we travel to the upper reaches of the Andes Mountains, where descendants of the ancient Inca civilization continue to play the *siku* (panpipes), which are believed to date from at least the thirteenth century. Moving to urban areas, we discuss the Spanish-influenced music of *mestizo* populations throughout Mexico and South America by examining the Argentinean *tango* and the Mexican *mariachi*. Finally, we turn to the coastline of Brazil, which is home to two of the clearest examples of African influence in South America: the unique martial arts dance form known as *capoeira* and the celebratory music of Carnival known as *samba*.

Arrival: The Amazon Rainforest

The Amazonian rainforest of Brazil is one of the largest remaining tropical forests on the planet. It is home to thousands of wildlife species, such as jaguars, toucans, and macaws, and numerous nomadic and semi-nomadic hunter-gatherer human communities. During the latter decades of the twentieth century, the Amazon became a flashpoint for environmental activities concerned about the earth's deteriorating ecosystem. Logging companies were destroying (and continue to destroy) millions of acres of rainforests and have consequently displaced many Amazonian peoples. Some of these groups were forced to integrate into modern society, while others retreated further into the rainforest. Still others, such as the Kayapó Indians, managed to resist the encroachment of the modern world by actively protesting against the intruders and organizing events that drew international attention to the plight of their peoples. Today, many Amazonians have managed to straddle both worlds by educating themselves about modern society while maintaining their traditional way of life. The romantic vision of the Amazonian Indian as a bare-footed, spear-toting, loin-clothed hunter-gatherer is no longer a realistic portrayal of the native population, who can often be found in T-shirts, hunting with rifles, and sitting in classrooms learning to read and write. Still, ceremonial activities based on traditional belief systems remain at the heart of the community life of each individual group of Amazonians.

There are many distinct tribes of Amazonian peoples, and cultural traits, such as language, dress, belief system, kinship practices, and so on, vary widely from group to group. Many commonalities do exist, however, and thus some general cultural tendencies can be represented by individual groups. In our case, we focus on the Kayapó-Xikrin, who live in the southwestern area of the state of Para in central Brazil, to gain a better understanding of the music of Amazonian peoples.

Site 1: Amazonian Chant

First Impressions. Our example begins with an "eagle cry," followed by group chanting. The singing seems to be part of a community ceremony or shamanic ritual—which is usually the case. To a non-specialist, the vocal performances of Amazonian tribes may seem indistinguishable from those of North American native groups, and indeed there are some parallel musical traits.

Aural Analysis. A first listening to an Amazonian musical performance reveals several identifiable features typical of the majority of Amerindian tribes of the Brazilian rainforests. Unison group singing is most common and is often unaccompanied. The singing is in a style characterized as chant and uses only a few pitches. Unaccompanied unison (monophonic) group chanting is not unique to Amazonian Indians, but it is a recognizable trait of most tribes of the Brazilian rainforest. Men and women usually sing separately, and indeed our example includes only male voices.

Many songs have a descending melodic contour, while others consist of only one or two pitches. A melodic drop-off usually closes a vocal phrase. The text setting is most often syllabic. The dynamic level is usually consistent, though shouting sometimes occurs but not usually as a central feature of the performance. Vocal pulsation (a slight periodic volume amplification) is sometimes employed to add a rhythmic element to purely vocal performances. Rattles, flutes, or small drums sometimes accompany these performances, though none are heard in this example. Handclapping and foot-stomping are also frequently employed to maintain a steady pulse during performance. Additionally, large sticks or hollow tree branches are sometimes pounded on the ground to add a rhythmic element.

Amazonian Indians (Kayapó-Xikrin) native to the Brazilian rainforest (Alamy)

Though the music follows a steady pulse, metrical units are frequently irregular as they follow the phrasing of the text rather than being organized into a set number of pulses.

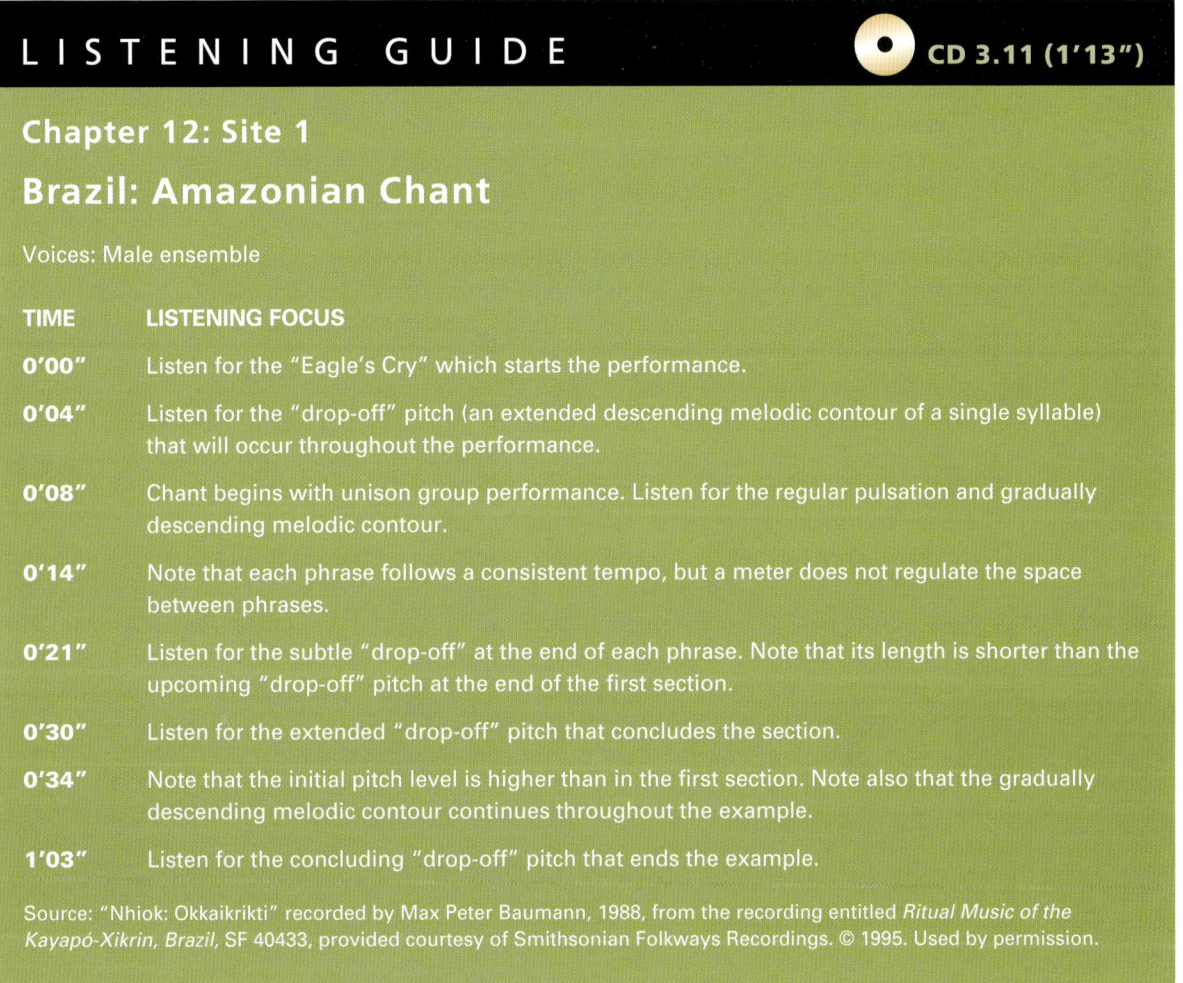

ETHNO-CHALLENGE (CD 3.11): A common speculation is that all indigenous populations in the Americas originally come from the same source. Compare some examples of chant traditions from other indigenous groups in the Americas (North and South) and draw your own conclusions as to the validity of this hypothesis.

Cultural Considerations. The music of Amazonian peoples is integral to their ritual activities. Some familiarity with these rituals is useful for a better understanding of the meaning of musical performance. The recording we have selected is the concluding section of a Kayapó-Xikrin naming ritual. Known as *takak-nhiok*, this ritual occurs in five stages over a period of five years. Each stage enables the initiates to participate in and gain new knowledge of a growing number of activities practiced by elder members of the community, such as feather handicrafts and hunting. The status of the initiates increase, and they are given secret knowledge regarding the community's history and belief system in the form of myths, dances, song, body-painting, and featherwork.

The concluding chant of the naming ritual begins at sunset and continues until dawn. It is identified by the opening call, which imitates the screech of a Harpy Eagle. The name-recipients, in this case female, form a semicircle with their backs to the setting sun. The male vocalists complete the circle while a select group of "jaguar men," generally the elder community leaders, dance counter-clockwise around the interior of the circle, approaching each female in turn with a symbolic "clawing" gesture that completes their naming. The Harpy Eagle's chant translates as: "The claws of the Harpy Eagle will claw the Nhiok / Breathe and come through the path / Breathe and keep seeing hummingbird's feathers being born." The reference to the hummingbird is significant: The Kayapó-Xikrin believe that the hummingbird is "the jaguar remedy" (*Ritual Music of the Kayapó-Xikrin, Brazil*, SF 40433, Washington, DC: Smithsonian Folkways, 1995, p. 59). The hummingbird is considered unique; indeed, it is the only bird capable of flying backward. As such, it is quick and elusive. Hummingbird feathers are burnt and mixed with a plant to produce an ointment believed to protect an individual from jaguars. The Harpy Eagle call proclaims the final stage of the initiation ceremony, the completion of which signals that the newly named participants have acquired a higher status among the community.

For most Amazonian tribes, music is an important means of communicating with natural and spiritual forces. **Totems** are acknowledged and respected through music. Shamans often use music to communicate with or appease spirits of the rainforest. Indeed, some tribes believe that songs are taught to them by these spirits through dreams. Music, then, is central to the lives of Amazonians and integral to their cultural identity. The chants of the Kayapó are integrally bound up with issues common to the realm of anthropology, such as kinship systems, social organization, and gender and age classifications. Many cultural aspects of the Kayapó are reflected in their music, as they are with any group, not just in the Amazon, but around the globe.

TOTEM
A plant, animal, or natural object used as an emblem for a person or group of people.

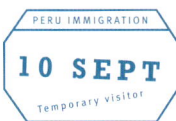

Arrival: Peru

Peru's landscape varies widely. Urban areas are found on the western coast, while much of the eastern interior is taken up by the tropical rainforests of the Amazon. Between these two zones are the highlands, where descendents of the ancient Inca Empire still live in adobe huts among llamas and alpacas, surrounded by the snow-capped mountains of the Andes. Peru's native and mestizo peoples form the majority of the population. Both Spanish and Quechua, an indigenous language formerly associated with the Inca Empire, are recognized as official languages of Peru.

The Inca Empire dates to roughly the thirteenth century and reached its peak in the last decades of the 1400s. Important centers of power and culture included the city of Cusco in southeastern Peru near Lake Titicaca, and the stronghold of Machu Picchu some 50 miles to the northwest and nearly 9,000 feet above sea level. Spanish conquistadors began arriving in the early 1500s and quickly toppled the ruling powers of the Inca, beheading the last Inca Emperor, Túpac Amaru, in 1572.

Though Inca heritage is still a vital aspect of the cultural identity of the native population, the Spanish influence is also felt in many ways. Roman Catholicism is especially prominent throughout the region, though in a form that reveals many influences from pre-contact religious systems. The numerous religious holidays associated with both Roman Catholicism and the earlier traditions provide ample opportunities for small- and large-scale festivals in both urban and rural areas. Among the most popular are Easter celebrations, which incorporate a variety of musical activities.

Site 2: *Sikuri* (Panpipe) Ensemble

First Impressions. Aside from the pounding drum beat, the breathy sound of the melodic panpipes, called **siku**, is the most distinctive feature of this example. The short repetitive melody, with its "calliope-like" timbre, sounds joyfully out of tune and is reminiscent of a carousel ride spinning non-stop.

SIKU
Panpipes common among indigenous populations from Peru and throughout the Andes.

Aural Analysis. The *sikuri* panpipe ensemble is common to many Andean communities throughout Peru and elsewhere in Andean South America. *Sikuri* ensembles normally have around twenty *siku* players, though the group in our example is larger, consisting of fifty-two musicians. The *siku* is made of several cylindrical reeds of varying lengths tied together to form one or two rows of pipes—in this case two. The performer holds these vertically and blows across the tops of the open pipes to produce breathy pitches, just as you would with a soda bottle: the shorter the pipe, the higher the pitch. Thus, they are open-ended flutes in the aerophone family.

One *siku* is not typically capable of playing all the notes of a scale. Rather, a second *siku* must complement it. The two performers use an interlocking technique to produce the entire melody. If, for example, the first player sounds the odd-numbered pitches, say 1–3–5, while the second player sounds the even ones, 2–4–6, then the two musicians must alternate in order to play pitches 1 through 6 consecutively. The musicians try to overlap their pitches slightly so that no gaps are heard between pitches. The breathy sound of the *siku* makes it easier for performers to smoothly connect successive pitches.

Another common feature of Andean music is the use of parallel polyphony. Parallel polyphony occurs when two melodic lines follow the same melodic contour but start on different pitches, thus moving in parallel but with a polyphonic structure as well. The most commonly used intervals between the two parallel lines are the fourth and fifth. The interval used here, however, is a third, which is typical of the Conima style of which this music is an example. Intentional tuning variances often occur, sometimes as wide as a quartertone or more, giving the music a slightly dissonant quality. As is typical of native Andean music, the melodic line is short and repetitive and features only minor variations.

In our example, a large bass drum (**bombos**) and a snare drum (*cajas*) provide a driving beat. Drums in Peru are often made with a llama- or alpaca-skin face and are struck with a wooden mallet. Different genres of *sikuri* performance use different types of drums; in fact, the bass and snare drum accompaniment heard here rarely occurs outside Easter celebrations. In most performances, occasional whistles are heard, most notably toward the end of the performance, to signal the musicians to increase their tempo.

BOMBOS
A large drum used in *sikuri* performances from Peru.

WORLD MUSIC: A GLOBAL JOURNEY

Descendants of the ancient Inca still live today in the Andes Mountains of Peru (Max T. Miller)

LISTENING GUIDE

 CD 3.12 (1'33")

Chapter 12: Site 2

Peru: *Sikuri* (Panpipe) Ensemble

Instruments: *Siku* (end-blown flutes), *bombos* (large drum), *cajas* (small drum)

TIME	LISTENING FOCUS
0'00"	Listen for the whistle used to call the musicians to attention and the sound of a few performers blowing quietly into their *siku*.
0'03"	Listen for the *siku* initiating the performance. Note the use of a homophonic structure (with parallel polyphony) throughout the performance.
0'05"	Listen for the *bombos* playing a regular beat. Note the number of pulses between each pause in the rhythmic pattern. Though not consistent, this pattern features two phrases with a short number of pulses (usually seven), and then a longer phrase (usually seventeen) that concludes with the end of the melodic phrase.
0'07"	Listen for the *cajas* entrance contrasting with the lower drum.
0'15"	First melodic phrase concludes.
0'18"	Listen for the pause of the lower drum. Note that this does not occur simultaneously with the end of the melodic phrase.
0'30"	Listen for the pause of the lower drum. Note that it occurs at the end of the melodic phrase.

SOUTH AMERICA AND MEXICO

> **0'41"** Listen again for the pause of the lower drum in relation to the end of the melodic phrase. Continue to note this relationship throughout the performance.
>
> Source: "Easter Music" by Qhantati Urui performed by the Conimeño Ensemble, recorded by Thomas Turino, Conima, Peru, 1985, from the recording entitled *Mountain Music of Peru: Volume 2*, SF 40406, provided courtesy of Smithsonian Folkways Recordings. © 1994. Used by permission.

> **ETHNO-CHALLENGE (CD 3.12):** Construct your own panpipe. Use the Internet to research how to do this.

An Andean panpipe and drum ensemble performs on stage at a university folk festival (Dale Olsen)

Cultural Considerations. Evidence of *siku* and other types of flutes dates to pre-Columbian times, while the many chordophones and brass instruments found today arrived only after the 1530s with Spanish conquistadors and Roman Catholic missionaries. The *sikuri* ensemble is most common among the Aymara-speaking peoples surrounding Lake Titicaca, the largest lake on the continent and the highest navigable lake in the world (at 12,500 feet above sea level). Living and farming in these highland rural areas requires collective effort and social cooperation, and scholars consider the *sikuri* ensemble a reflection of this social structure.

Sikuri is most often performed during monthly festivals associated with indigenous ceremonial rites that frequently are combined with Roman Catholic holidays. Instrumental performance is considered a male activity, while women generally dance or sing. During a *sikuri* performance, any man from the village can participate, regardless of his musical ability or familiarity with the tune. The emphasis of the performance is on social interaction rather than on a strict adherence to musical accuracy. The interlocking parts of the *siku* express the Aymara ideal of "playing as one."

12 WORLD MUSIC: A GLOBAL JOURNEY

The panpipes (*siku*) are among the most common indigenous instruments of the Andes

Inter-community festivals may feature several *sikuri* ensembles, each representing a different village. The performers dance in one or more circles around the drummers, who stand in the center. Friendly competitions often occur between the different ensembles as non-performers dance and cheer. The choice of a "winner" is based primarily on who has given the most energetic performance and on the general reaction of the crowd, rather than on strictly musical qualities. In short, the response of the community is the essential factor in determining a successful *sikuri* performance.

Arrival: Argentina

The pre-contact history of Argentina is sketchy. None of the ancient empires of the Americas held dominion over the territory, which was sparsely populated by hunters and gatherers and home to a few agricultural settlements. Spanish colonization of the region began in the early sixteenth century, with the first attempt at a permanent settlement, Buenos Aires, in 1536. Five years later the settlement was abandoned, due in part to conflicts with the indigenous populations. Eventually, the region was successfully colonized and Buenos Aires was resettled in 1580. In time, the growing city became an important port and gained a reputation as a haven for smugglers. By the middle of the eighteenth century its population had swelled to more than 20,000.

The British attacked the city in 1806 but were ousted only a few months later by a citizen army. Subsequent attempts by the British to overtake the city failed and indeed encouraged a strong patriotic sentiment among the city's inhabitants. However, in 1810 the people of Buenos Aires rebelled against the Spanish crown, and only a few years later they succeeded in gaining their independence. It is this spirit of rebellion that drives the **tango** in its purest form.

Site 3: *Tango*

First Impressions. *Tango,* both as a dance and as music, embodies passion. The original form of the dance it accompanies symbolically represents a battle between two men for the affections of a fickle woman. At one point in the dance, one of the male dancers lustfully looms over the helpless woman before she is torn away by the other jealous suitor. Even in its simplest form, the music evokes the predatory stares of the men and the indecisiveness of the woman through variations of dynamics, tempo, and phonic structure.

TANGO
A dance and associated music originating in Argentina.

Aural Analysis. *Tango* ensembles vary in size, and *tango* itself comes in a variety of styles. A distinctive feature of most *tango* orchestras is the inclusion of the *bandoneón,* a type of button-box accordion. The **bandoneón** was invented in Germany in the mid-nineteenth century by Heinrich Band and was brought to South America around 1890, initially in the hands of missionaries who found it a portable alternative to the organ. The instrument has two square wooden manuals (keyboards) separated by a bellows made of leather. Larger *bandoneón* have up to seventy-two buttons, but the distribution pattern does not follow the usual melody–chord dichotomy found on typical accordions. As the performer alternately compresses or draws out the bellows, air passes through a series of "free" metal reeds to produce the tones; thus, the *bandoneón* is a free-reed aerophone. Dynamic variations are produced by squeezing or drawing the air through the instrument more quickly for greater volume or more slowly for a quieter sound. In addition to the *bandoneón,* the violin, guitar, flute, and piano are frequently found in *tango* ensembles and a vocalist is often present as well.

BANDONEÓN
A type of button-box accordion.

Tango rhythms are frequently syncopated, meaning some accents fall between the regular beat. Our example employs a common *tango* rhythm by emphasizing the offbeats of the first and second pulses. In order to hear this, you must first find the regular pulsation to establish a meter, in this case a duple meter with four beats. The melodic line anticipates the first beat of each four-beat grouping; therefore, it is probably easier to find the first pulse by listening to the underlying chords. The tempo is rather quick and fluctuates frequently, as is typical of *tango.*

The syncopated *tango* rhythm falls within the four-beat grouping. Once you have established the meter by counting the four-beat grouping, divide this by saying "and" between each pulse, that is, 1&2&3&4&. The "and" division indicates the "offbeat." The *tango* rhythm, articulated by the underlying chords, displays a fairly constant pattern of 1&–&3–(4)–. The "2" beat is absent, as is the "4&." Most of the melodic phrases also begin on the "offbeat,"

The *bandoneón*, an accordion common in Argentina, is the most prominent instrument that accompanies the tango (Geoffrey Clifford/Getty Images)

typically the "and" of the third beat. This emphasis on syncopation creates an off-balance feel throughout the performance: the musicians constantly flirt with the regular beat, but never commit to it. Indeed, this aspect of *tango* music parallels the fickle affections of the female character in *tango* dance's symbolic courtship battle. Interestingly, in American-style ballroom *tango* dance steps begin right on beat 1, but in International style, many steps begin on the "&" following beat 1.

The indecisive seductions of the female *tango* dancer are also manifested through fluctuations in dynamics, tempo, phonic structure, and even key. Bursts of volume with strong chord accompaniment at a quick tempo contrast with soft, sultry, slow passages with only a single melodic line. Though *tango* music is dominated by minor keys, the performers will often slip in brighter passages that utilize major keys, again keeping the music off-balance. As the dancers embrace in a loving gaze characterized by a major key, they suddenly turn from each other as the music abruptly shifts back to minor. Such variations of mood are essential to the unique character of the *tango*.

LISTENING GUIDE

 CD 3.13 (1'54")

Chapter 12: Site 3
Argentina: *Tango*

Instruments: *Bandoneón* (reed aerophone, i.e., accordion)

TIME	LISTENING FOCUS
0'00"	Listen for the use of melody and accompanying harmony. Note the "tango" rhythmic pattern (1 & – & 3 – (4) –) articulated by the chord accompaniment.
0'09"	Listen for the slight *ritard* (slowing tempo) at this point. Note the variations in tempo throughout the example.
0'19"	Note that the "tango rhythm" briefly drops out.
0'26"	Listen for the contrasting melodic line of the lower harmony and the less-consistent use of the tango rhythm.
0'44"	Listen for the swell in volume. Note the varying use of dynamics throughout the example.
0'47"	Listen for the slowing tempo and decrease in volume.
0'51"	Listen for the high-pitched melodic trill and the absence of harmony.
0'53"	Listen for the contrasting harmonic pitch underneath the melodic line.
1'01"	Listen for the return of the tango rhythm in the harmonic accompaniment and the gradual increase in volume.
1'07"	Listen for the syncopated rhythmic patterns of the harmony.
1'15"	Listen for the swell in volume, slowing of the tempo, absence of the harmony, and loss of tango rhythm.
1'19"	Listen for the dramatic swell of the harmony and the contrasting solo melody that follows.
1'24"	Listen for the return of the tango rhythm in the supporting harmony.
1'44"	Listen for the final swell in volume, which signals the end of the performance.

Source: "El Choclo" (The Ear of Corn): *Tango Criollo* by René Marino Rivero, recorded by Tiago de Oliveiro Pinto, 1991, from the recording entitled *Raices Latinas: Smithsonian-Folkways Latino Roots Collection*, SF 40470, provided courtesy of Smithsonian Folkways Recordings. © 2002. Used by permission.

ETHNO-CHALLENGE (CD 3.13): Find an instructor in your area and take a tango dance lesson. You might also research various appearances of tango performance in movies and compare each version of the dance and musical accompaniment.

Cultural Considerations. Buenos Aires, Argentina, is the birthplace of *tango*. Since its resettlement in 1580 by Spanish sailors, this city has been a port of call for sea sojourners navigating around South America. As a hub of maritime trade for more than four hundred years, the city has attracted a variety of immigrants, primarily Spanish, but also Italian. Trade with European cities boomed after Argentina was officially proclaimed independent from Spain in 1816. By 1880, when it emerged as the capital city of Argentina, Buenos Aires was one of the most important economic and cultural centers of Latin America.

As often happened with port cities during the nineteenth century, the transient lifestyle of seamen encouraged a seedy subculture characterized by taverns and bordellos where sailors could unwind before heading to their next port of call. Knife fights and bar brawls over women were common occurrences among the *porteños* (people of the port area), typically initiated by inebriated sailors vying for the affections of a single seductive strumpet. *Tango* dance reflects these possessive relationships, originally casting two men and a woman in a sensual choreography with a distinctly predatory nature: the "vertical expression of horizontal desire," as it is often described. *Tango* music also suggests such seduction as the musicians thrust and parry through dynamic variations and tempo fluctuations, echoing the love triangle narrative of the dance.

Because of its lurid association with the vagabonds of the brothels, *tango* was disdained by aristocrats, who considered the music and its dance to be vulgar. Yet, the lure of bohemian nightlife attracted many, especially among the younger generation, who flocked to *tango* just as teenagers in the United States later flocked to rock 'n' roll. By the end of the nineteenth century, *tango* had captured the youthful passions of popular culture in Buenos Aires and quickly spread throughout Argentina and the urban centers of many South American countries (including Uruguay, from which our example derives).

The Argentine tango, unlike the regularized ballroom form, requires rapid changes of emotion, from control to inflamed passion (Jack Vartoogian/FrontRowPhotos)

The attraction to *tango* was not limited to South America. By 1910 *tango* was tantalizing the playboys and dilettantes of salons in Paris, France, and it soon made its screen debut together with Rudolph Valentino in *The Four Horsemen of the Apocalypse* (1926). Carlos Gardel (1887–1935) became an international superstar as *tango-canción* (*tango* song) was popularized on the radio and in the cinema. But in the United States, where puritan moralists have long considered dance to be sinful, Vernon and Irene Castle, who brought *tango* into the ballroom dance world, felt obligated to reassure readers of their *tango*-instructional booklets that this new and exceptionally sensual dance would not corrupt anyone's morals:

> The much-misunderstood Tango becomes an evolution of the eighteenth-century Minuet. There is in it no strenuous clasping of partners, no hideous gyrations of the limbs, no abnormal twistings, no vicious angles. Mr. Castle affirms that when the Tango degenerates into an acrobatic display or into salacious suggestion it is the fault of the dancers and not of the dance. The Castle Tango is courtly and artistic, and this is the only Tango taught by the Castle House instructors.
>
> (Elisabeth Marbury in Castle, 1914, p. 20)

The Castle version of tango codified the choreography of tango for ballroom dance contexts, which has become the foundation for its performance around the world today. Tango in social contexts, however, maintained more fluid and "salacious suggestion," particularly in Argentina where the dance originated.

By the 1940s *tango* had seduced every social class, but the Golden Age of *tango* was nearing its end. After World War II, rock 'n' roll pushed *tango* (as well as jazz) from the airwaves and dance clubs, although it still found an audience in Argentina and among many of the upper classes who had accepted it as the sultry side of ballroom dance. *Tango* never regained its former popularity, although composers such as Astor Piazzolla (1921–1992) helped to establish it as a music genre independent of the dance itself. Interest in *tango* briefly surged in the 1980s, and it has maintained its visibility to the present day, in part through the inclusion of tantalizing *tango* scenes in hit films such as *The Scent of a Woman* (1992), starring Al Pacino, and *Moulin Rouge!* (2001), starring Nicole Kidman and Ewan McGregor.

Arrival: Brazil

Brazil is the largest country in South America and home to roughly 186 million inhabitants. Our earlier visit to the Amazonian rainforests presented a stark contrast to the bustling activity of the urban centers that dot the eastern half of the country. Brazil's largest cities are mostly found along the coastline and include Rio de Janeiro, São Paulo, and Salvador. The country was colonized by the Portuguese, who began arriving in the region around 1500. They discovered a land rich in natural resources and with fertile soil. Within fifty years Portuguese colonialists began to import slaves from Africa to work on sugar, tobacco, and coffee plantations. Gold was discovered in the late 1600s, encouraging the enslavement of more Africans to work as miners. African populations were imported to Brazil for more than three hundred years, resulting today in the largest African Diaspora in the world.

Brazil became an independent nation in 1822. The government was then ruled by a succession of emperors descended from members of the Portuguese royal family. The abolition of slavery in 1888 was followed the next year by a revolution initiated by the military, which ousted the monarchy and created a federal republic in Brazil. The new government struggled to represent its diverse population equitably. Most of the political power resided with the wealthy landowners, invariably of European descent, while the vast majority of the population, either *mulatto* or of purely African descent, occupied the slum areas of the urban centers and had little or no political voice. By 1930 discontent among the masses had come to a head, while a collapse in the economy, brought on by the global depression that began in 1929, caused the landowning elite to lose confidence in their elected officials. A disgruntled military once again encouraged revolution, which was personified by the rise to power of a single man, Getúlio Vargas (1883–1954).

Vargas was a central figure in the revolution of 1930 and became president and ruled as an elected official until 1937. Rather than risk losing power, Vargas initiated a revolution of his own with the help of the military and with the support of the urban working and middle classes. He eliminated the congress and ruled by decree as a dictator for the next eight years. Vargas began many social and economic reforms that were, ironically, modeled after the policies of the Italian dictator Benito Mussolini, against whom the Brazilian military fought (in aid of the United States) during World War II. His *Estado Novo* (New State) encouraged a strong sense of a unified national identity among the masses and a feeling of pride in being Brazilian, no matter what a person's ethnic background or social class. His propaganda machine was instrumental in the promotion of *samba* as a music for all Brazilians.

Site 4: *Samba*

SAMBA
A popular music and type of dance from Brazil.

AGOGO
A double-bell found in Western Africa and used in African-derived musics in the Western hemisphere.

RÊCO-RÊCO
A notched scraper idiophone found in Latin American music traditions.

First Impressions. **Samba** is dance music. Its boisterous beat, wailing whistles, and shouting *sambistas* encourage the party atmosphere associated with its most notable context, Carnival (see below). The driving *samba* beat conjures up images of revelers parading through the streets of Rio de Janeiro in frenetic celebration. *Samba* music makes you move from the bottom of your feet to the top of your head.

Aural Analysis. *Samba* is strongly Afro-Brazilian, meaning that its musical characteristics are primarily drawn from African ingredients but have a unique Brazilian flavor. Polyrhythm underlies the instrumental organization; thus, the majority of instruments in *samba* are percussion. African-derived double bells *(agogo)*, tambourines, scraping instruments *(rêco-rêco)*, and drums, large *(surdo* or *bombo)* and small *(caixa)*, are all instruments commonly found in a wide variety of *samba* styles. The most distinct *samba* instrument is the friction drum *(cuíca)*, which is a membranophone that has its face pierced in the center with a long, thin stick. When the stick is pushed, pulled, or twisted, it rubs against the membrane to produce a unique squeaking sound. Call-and-response vocals, usually in Portuguese, are standard, and are generally accompanied by a guitar.

A prominent "*samba* rhythm," usually played by the largest drum or an electrified bass guitar, is what most differentiates the music from other Latin American dance musics. The *samba* rhythm is based on a standard duple meter but emphasizes the third beat by inserting a short pause just before it. In a four-beat pattern (though *samba* moves so quickly, it is typically thought of as having only two beats), the *samba* rhythm would sound on the first beat, the "and" of the second, and the top of the third beat, that is, 1–&3–. The rhythm is infectious and seems to call out: "Mooove your feet! Mooove your feet!" Other instruments add several other more rhythmically dense patterns to this fundamental *samba* groove.

LISTENING GUIDE

CD 3.14 (2'02")

Chapter 12: Site 4
Brazil: *Samba*

Vocals: Lead mixed ensemble and single male soloist
Instruments: Guitar, *cavaco* (high-ranged guitar), electric bass, *surdo* (low-pitched drum), *cuíca* (friction drum), *pandeiro* (tambourine), shaker

TIME	LISTENING FOCUS
0'00"	Example fades in. Listen for the underlying polyrhythm of the percussion and the consistent samba rhythm (1– &3–) of the electric bass and *surdo* (low-pitched drum). Note the contrasting middle-ranged guitar and high-ranged *cavaco*.
0'03"	Listen for the spoken dialogue of the solo vocalist.
0'10"	Listen for the mixed vocal ensemble entrance on the word "samba."
0'24"	Listen for the "squeaking" timbre of the *cuíca* (friction drum).
0'45"	Listen for the solo vocalist adding exclamations to complement the choral melody.
1'24"	Return to opening melody and verse.
1'52"	Example fades.

Source: "Agoniza, Mas Nao Morre" ("It suffers but doesn't die"), performed by Nelson Sargento, from the recording entitled *Brazil Roots: Samba*, Rounder CD 5045, 1989. Used by permission.

ETHNO-CHALLENGE (CD 3.14): Compare and contrast the varying styles of *samba* music.

Cultural Considerations. *Samba* traces its roots to Angola and the Congo in Africa. Its name is believed to be derived from the term *semba*, a Bantu word describing the distinctive "belly bump" found in some circle dances of the region. The navel is considered a spiritually significant body part, and contact between two navels symbolically links two dancers together. In Brazil, the *samba* folk dance begins with this gesture of bumping bellies as a dancer invites another dancer to enter the circle and dance together as one.

Initially, the ruling powers of Brazil viewed *samba* as a vulgar dance performed by slum-dwellers who lived in the *favelas* (slums) on the hills surrounding the city of Rio de Janeiro

Members of a *Gongada* from Minas Geraes perform during Carnival celebrations in Brazil (Welson Tremura)

At Rio de Janeiro's Carnival, the largest in the world, a gigantic float passes through the *Sambadrome Marquès de Sapucai*, an indoor arena for Carnival parades (Shutterstock)

Costumed drummers march in the Carnival parade of Montevideo, Uruguay (Shutterstock)

and in the *bairro*, a section of the city known as "Little Africa" due to the large number of African-descended inhabitants. The popularity of *samba* was especially visible during the Carnival season (see below), when music and celebration in the streets were more tolerated by government authorities. The driving rhythms of the music and the erotic appeal of the dance gradually attracted members of the rising middle class, many of whom were *mulatto* (of mixed African-Iberian ancestry), so that by the mid-1920s composing *samba* had become a full-time occupation for many talented artists. Each year, neighborhood associations would parade through the streets during Carnival playing music and dancing to popular *samba* melodies, usually composed by one of their own members. By the end of the decade, these associations were referring to themselves as *escolas de samba* (*samba* schools).

After taking power in 1930, Getúlio Vargas actively encouraged *samba* as part of his *Estado Novo* campaign to promote a unified Brazilian national identity. In 1934 he made Carnival an official national event and decreed that only *samba* schools legally registered with the government could perform in parades. He further encouraged *samba* and its association with Carnival by offering public funds to support the registered *samba* schools, which were strongly encouraged to create costumes and compose music that stimulated national pride by glorifying national heroes and promoting patriotic symbols. Though such overt nationalism has fallen out of fashion, public support of the *samba* schools and a focus on Carnival as the hallmark event of the Brazilian calendar year have remained.

Today, *samba* is nearly synonymous with Brazilian popular music. The term covers a variety of styles in much the same way the term *jazz* is used to describe a broad range of styles in the United States. The best-known styles, namely *samba-carnavalesco* (carnival *samba*), *samba-baiana* (Bahian *samba*), and *samba-enredo* (theme *samba*), are still associated with Carnival. Also popular is *samba-canção* (song *samba*), which is a staple of

Brazilian nightclubs and the origin of *bossa nova*, a particularly popular style for ballroom dance. Since the 1990s *samba-reggae*, the Brazilian version of Jamaican *reggae*, has become widely known as well.

Explore More

Carnival

Carnival is a pre-Lenten festival associated in the Americas with countries where Roman Catholicism was the primary religious tradition of the colonizers. The tradition originated in Europe but has come to be most associated with the grand parades and intense revelry of places such as Rio de Janeiro (Brazil), Port of Spain (Trinidad), and New Orleans (USA, where it is known as *Mardi Gras*).

Traditionally, Carnival celebrations were considered the last "party" before the forty days of Lent, during which Roman Catholics are supposed to renew themselves spiritually by abstaining from activities such as drinking alcohol, eating meat, dancing, and playing music. Weddings and other celebratory events were also forbidden during the Lenten season. The elite social classes held masked balls to indulge themselves before the commencement of Lent. Among the "common folk," outdoor festivals were held, which typically included a variety of "Carnival" games, jugglers, comedians, storytellers, and so on, much like the Renaissance Fairs of today. Among those to encourage the Carnival celebration were Gypsies (see Chapter 9), many of whom made their living by performing as entertainers and musicians.

The Carnival season, which typically lasted four or five days, was considered a time to "forgive and forget" any animosity between individuals, and the authorities also tended to be more lenient during the celebrations. This carefree attitude was transferred to the New World. The European colonialists maintained their tradition of masked balls and indoor revelry in many cities throughout the Caribbean, while the lower classes, most of whom were of African descent, were usually allowed to celebrate with outdoor activities. A common feature of these outdoor activities was the street parade, which has since become the highlight of nearly every Carnival celebration around the world.

The Brazilian Carnival celebrations are considered by many to be the pinnacle of the festivals held the world over. Thousands of people travel to Rio de Janeiro to participate in the non-stop partying that characterizes the Carnival Season (between February and March, depending on the date of Ash Wednesday). Body paint, confetti and streamers, lots of alcohol, and continuous dancing to the *samba* beat mark the annual activities, which are capped with a parade through the city center featuring the most extravagant costumes and floats found in any festival the world over. *Sambistas* dance through the city streets followed by batteries of deafening percussion. *Samba* schools compete for prizes based on their music performance, dance choreography, and costumes. Each school's performance is organized around a specific theme, typically one that promotes Brazilian identity and revolves around national, historical, or political figures and events.

CAPOEIRA
A dance that developed from a style of martial arts created by runaway slaves in Brazil.

Site 5: *Capoeira* Music

First Impressions. ***Capoeira*** is music with a groove. Whereas the *samba* music of Carnival pushes the body to a frenetic extreme, *capoeira* music embodies the laid-back attitude Brazilians often take during the rest of the year. The music constantly bobs and weaves as if the listener is relaxing on a small fishing boat along the Brazilian coastline. The waves

SOUTH AMERICA AND MEXICO

bring him closer and closer to shore, gradually picking up momentum as he casually steers himself onto the beach. Fluid motion is the general feel, but there is also a constant awareness that the waves can tip the boat at any moment.

Aural Analysis. Among the key features of *capoeira* music are the call-and-response organization of the vocal performers and the subtle polyrhythmic organization of the African-derived instruments. These instruments include the **pandeiros** (tambourines), *agogo* (double bell), *rêco-rêco* (notched scraper), and **atabaque** (drum), as well as the most distinctive instrument of the *capoeira* ensemble, the **berimbau** (musical bow). All of these instruments were recreated in Brazil by African slaves taken in particular from areas now comprising the modern Central African nations of Angola and the Democratic Republic of the Congo (formerly Zaire).

PANDEIROS
A hand-held frame drum with attached cymbals (i.e., a tambourine), used in *capoeira* music.

ATABAQUE
A drum of West African origin used in *capoeira* music as well as *candomblé* rituals.

BERIMBAU
A musical bow used in *capoeira* music.

The Brazilian *berimbau* (musical bow) played during a capoeira performance (Jack Vartoogian/ FrontRowPhotos)

445

Capoeira artists in the midst of "combat." *Berimbau* performers and other musicians are pictured in the background (Jack Vartoogian/FrontRowPhotos)

In our example, which is the *Capoeira Angola* style, three *berimbau* are played, to provide low, middle, and high parts. The *berimbau* is made from a wooden bow with a steel string. A piece of twine is looped around the base of the bow to attach a gourd resonator, which is pressed against the body to change the timbre and pitch of the instrument's sound. The smallest finger of one hand, usually the left for a right-handed player, balances the instrument on this loop during performance. A large coin or stone is held between the thumb and forefinger and is pressed against the string in order to change the acoustic length of the string and consequently alter the pitch. This coin is sometimes only lightly pressed against the string, so as to produce a buzzing timbre.

The other hand strikes the string with a small stick several inches long. This hand also holds a small wicker basket that encloses a handful of either pebbles or small seashells. The performer simultaneously shakes this rattle as he strikes the string of the bow with the stick. The timbre of the *berimbau* is much like the "boing" sound of a large spring. The use of the coin, rattle, and open string, along with the varied resonances produced by the gourd, allows the *berimbau* to provide a great variety of simultaneous timbres.

Though the vocalists carry the primary melody, the unique "springy" timbre of the *berimbau* is the focus of the dancing that this music typically accompanies. In the *Capoeira Angola* style, the lowest-pitched *berimbau* plays the basic pattern, while the middle *berimbau* plays a complementary rhythm. The highest *berimbau* ornaments these basic patterns with improvisation, paying close attention to the movements of the dancers.

The steady groove of the music is provided by the other instruments. The fundamental rhythm, 1–&3–4–, is set by the drum with three low tones and a "slap" on the fourth beat. This rhythm is common to most *capoeira* music as it corresponds to the basic **ginga** movement of the dancers (see below). The other instruments follow their own rhythms, being careful not to overshadow the fundamental beat or the sound of the *berimbau* trio.

As the music progresses, the tempo often gradually increases. The *berimbau* pattern will subtly shift throughout, urging the dancers to heighten their performance. The basic

GINGA
(Also, JENGA)
A back-and-forth motion used as the basis for *capoeira* dancing.

ginga pattern of the drum does not change, but the other instruments may shift their patterns, creating denser rhythms to correspond with the increased intensity of the music. The dynamic level typically remains constant, though the *berimbau* may increase its volume as the dancers "play" harder.

The vocal organization remains in call-and-response form throughout a performance. The text setting is primarily syllabic and has a descending melodic contour. The melody will change as the music progresses but generally keeps the same phrase length. The lyrics are generally sung in Portuguese, the national language of Brazil, and tend to focus on the dancers, the musicians, or other aspects of *capoeira* performance. Oftentimes the singers use symbolic language, such as describing a large dancer as a tall immobile tree, to prod the dancers to better or faster movements.

LISTENING GUIDE

CD 3.15 (3'26")

Chapter 12: Site 5
Brazil: *Capoeira* Music

Vocals: Single male lead and supporting male ensemble
Instruments: *Berimbau* (musical bow), *pandeiros* (tambourine), *atabaque* (drum), *rêco-rêco* (scraped idiophone), *agogo* (double bell)

TIME	LISTENING FOCUS
0'00"	Listen for the lead vocal "call" as the example fades in. Note the underlying polyrhythm along with the steady rhythmic pattern (1–& 3–4–) provided by the drum. Also, listen for the distinct two-pitch timbre of the *berimbau*.
0'06"	Listen for the group vocal response.
0'10"	Listen for the lead vocal "call" and subsequent group response. Note that this structure occurs throughout the performance.
0'21"	Listen for the change in melodic rhythm of the lead *berimbau* and subsequent emphasis on syncopated rhythms and divergence from emphasizing the basic pulse of the underlying polyrhythmic percussion.
0'50"	Listen for the lead *berimbau* returning to the basic pulse established by the underlying polyrhythmic percussion.
0'58"	Listen for the lead *berimbau* again emphasizing syncopated rhythmic activity.
1'08"	Listen for the return of the melodic rhythm of the lead *berimbau* heard at 0'21," and subsequent rhythmic improvisations.
1'19"	Example fades.

Source: "Saia do Mar Marinheiro" by Grupo de Capoeira Anglo Pelurinho, from the recording entitled *Capoeira Angola from Salvador, Brazil*, SF 40465, provided courtesy of Smithsonian Folkways Recordings. © 1996. Used by permission.

> **ETHNO-CHALLENGE (CD 3.15):** Construct a *berimbau*. Alternatively, provide the drum rhythm throughout the example. If possible, find a *capoeira* club in your local area and observe a practice session or performance.

Cultural Considerations. *Capoeira* is a unique form of dance that developed from a distinctive style of martial arts created by runaway slaves in Brazil. Before abolition, many slaves who escaped the oppression of the sugar and coffee plantations would take refuge in the mountains near the country's coastline. Not having guns or swords, they developed a martial arts system that drew upon various fighting styles from Africa. The system that was created, which is known as *compé*, emphasizes the use of the feet during combat. The movements are characterized by cartwheels, handstands, flips, and spinning motions.

After slavery was abolished in Brazil, many of the *capoeira* artists continued to utilize their skills as bodyguards for Brazil's social elite. Many others formed gangs, which led to *capoeira* being associated with street fighting and vandalism. The authorities, of course, frowned on such disturbances, so the gangs attempted to disguise their practice sessions and street fights by simultaneously performing music. Because the music and fighting styles were African-based, the European-descended officials were fooled into accepting the *capoeira* movements as an unusual dance style rather than a combat technique. Eventually, the inclusion of music in the performance of *capoeira* became standard practice, so that today the genre is often regarded as more of a dance style than a martial arts system.

A *capoeira* performance takes place in a *roda*, a large circle approximately 18 feet (5.48 meters) in diameter that is outlined by the *capoeira* musicians and other participants standing in observation of the dancers. The two dancers typically begin the performance by "bowing" to the *berimbau*, typically the lowest sounding one, which is usually played by the senior *mestre* (master) of the group. The dancers then perform opening movements intended to assess the abilities of their opponent. This initial section is described as "cooperative," because the opponents do not attempt to strike their partner but rather work together to execute interesting moves, such as back flips and back-to-back body rolls. Throughout the performance, only the hands, feet, and head of the *capoeira* artist are allowed to touch the ground.

As the performance progresses, the dancers slow their movements in conjunction with a shift in the music. This "control" section is intended to develop the strength and balance of the performers as they slowly move through cartwheels and handstands, still making little attempt to strike their opponent. Finally, the music urges the performers to move to the "confrontational" section of the dance, in which the *capoeira* artists execute their movements with full force. The objective during this section is to knock the opponent off-balance and send him to the mat or into the ring of observers.

The basic beat of the music, which is articulated as 1–&3–4–, corresponds to the dance movement known as *ginga*. This movement requires the performer to cross one leg behind the other and lean back before springing forward to repeat the same movement with legs crossed in the opposite direction. The *ginga* is the starting position for all strikes, because it allows the performer to keep in constant motion and attain more momentum from the back position as he strikes forward.

The music is intended to encourage the performers, and the vocalists prod the dancers to higher feats of skill and comment on the action. If, for example, a smaller opponent topples a larger one, the lead vocalist may sing about the "falling of a tree" to tease the defeated foe. The *mestre* may shift the music to bring a performance "down" if he feels the dancers' performance is becoming too competitive and is threatening to turn into genuine fighting. While novice dancers focus on the *ginga* rhythm, advanced performers focus on the sound of the *berimbau* to spur themselves to perform more intense choreography. The sound of the *berimbau* bobs in and out of the basic rhythm in much the same way the performers weave in and out of reach of each other's strikes.

Capoeira has achieved an international reputation in the past decade as a unique martial art worthy of inclusion in competitions around the world. *Capoeira* clubs are increasingly popular in the United States and throughout the Western hemisphere. Though there is no direct relationship, the similarities between some of the *capoeira* moves and break-dancing, popular in the United States in the 1980s and experiencing a resurgence of interest in the early twenty-first century, have helped bring the *capoeira* tradition to the attention of many young Americans, especially because *capoeira* artists sometimes integrate their moves into dance club performances.

Arrival: Mexico

Mexico is the fourth largest country in the Western hemisphere and has a population of 107 million. Mexico City, the largest urban area in the world today, with more than fifteen million people, is built on the ruins of Tenochtitlán, the center of trade and military activity of the Aztec empire, which dominated the region for nearly one hundred years. The Aztec era (1427–1521) remains an important source of cultural pride for much of the population, many of whom are direct descendents of the Aztec.

While the native heritage of the Mexican population is important, the influence of Spanish culture is also quite prevalent. Many of the soldiers of the Spanish explorer Hernán Cortés, who conquered the Aztec, intermarried with the native populations, as did the Spanish colonialists who followed in their wake. As a result, more than 80 percent of Mexico's present population is *mestizo,* that is, a mix of Spanish and native ethnic heritage. The influence of the *mestizo*'s Spanish ancestry is visible in many aspects of Mexican culture. The architecture of Mexico's churches, the fact that Spanish is the national language (though many indigenous languages continue to flourish, including Nahuatl, the language of the Aztecs, spoken today by more than a million people), and, certainly, Mexico's music are all indicative of strong Spanish roots.

Site 6: *Mariachi*

First Impressions. **Mariachi** is often a festive music. While sad and romantic songs are common to the genre, contagiously peppy performances, such as the audio example, are the more common conception of mariachi music. A single listen to this celebratory style can conjure images of confetti and firecrackers with revelers holding their margarita glasses high and singing along with sombrero-topped musicians.

Aural Analysis. *Mariachi* is heavily imbued with European musical characteristics. This is shown most obviously by its instrumentation, which incorporates such familiar instruments

MARIACHI
An entertainment music associated with festivals and celebratory events in Mexico.

VIHUELA
A small, fretted plucked lute from Mexico, similar to a guitar but with a convex resonator.

GUITARRÓN
A large fretted plucked lute from Mexico, similar to a guitar but with a convex resonator.

as the violin, the trumpet, and the guitar. Guitars appear in a number of forms, including the **vihuela** (small guitar) and **guitarrón** (large guitar), both of which have convex resonators. Frequent changes in instrumentation are characteristic of *mariachi* music as different instrumental sections are highlighted to produce contrasting textures. Melodic passages are exchanged between the violins and the trumpets, with the guitars as a constant rhythmic and harmonic accompaniment. Few percussion instruments are heard in *mariachi*, because the percussive sound of the guitarists as well as the handclapping and foot-stomping of the dancers (absent from the recording) usually provide enough rhythm.

Vocalists use a full, often operatic voice, complemented by the occasional yells and laughter of fellow band members, who chime in to help make the music more festive. During vocal sections, the violins and trumpets generally play a secondary role to avoid overshadowing the singer. Song texts often have romantic themes, but they may also be about work, as with our example, *Los Arrieros* (The Muleteers). Lyrics with political or religious references are less common. Due to the Iberian descent of mestizo musicians, Spanish is the language of the *mariachi* singer.

Another key feature of *mariachi* is the use of clear, often memorable melodic lines, such as the melody of "La Cucaracha" (The Cockroach), a well-known Spanish folk tune that became popular in Mexico during the early twentieth century. Modern *mariachi* bands typically use trumpets and/or violins to play the main melody. Shifts in tempo corresponding to variations in instrumentation are also common; for example, if performance of the main melody switches from violins to trumpet. These changes in tempo typically correspond with changes in the movements of dancers and are reminiscent of the frequent

A Mexican *mariachi* group performs at a North American wedding. (From left to right) violin, *guitarrón*, *vihuela*, guitar, and trumpets (Alija/Getty Images)

SOUTH AMERICA AND MEXICO

The bass range *guitarrón*

Left to right: The *vihuela*, *guitarrón*, and guitar common to *mariachi* ensembles tempo changes found in Spanish flamenco music. *Mariachi* music may follow a variety of meters, which are usually clear-cut and in duple or triple meter, occasionally shifting along with changes in tempo. Our example is a song style known as *son jalisciense*, which tends to be more rhythmically active than most *mariachi* music, with its frequent subtle shifts of meter and tempo.

Mariachi music is most often in a major key, which is characteristic of "happy" music in European-related music traditions. Dynamic variations result from changes in instrumentation, as the trumpet-highlighted sections are louder than those sections emphasizing the violins or vocalist. The form of our example includes many distinctive sections, essentially **strophic**, meaning that the music repeats with each new verse sung by the vocalist.

STROPHIC
In song lyrics, the use of distinct units (strophes) that have the same number of lines, rhyme scheme, and meter.

LISTENING GUIDE

CD 3.16 (2'30")

Chapter 12: Site 6
Mexico: *Mariachi*

Vocals: Single male lead with supporting male ensemble
Instruments: Violins, trumpets, mid-range guitar, *vihuela* (high-range guitar), *guitarrón* (low-range guitar)

TIME	LISTENING FOCUS
0'00"	Listen for the freely rhythmic melodic introduction of violins and trumpets in harmony.
0'03"	Listen for the entrance of the guitar trio accompaniment, followed by an increased rhythmic density in the melody.
0'05"	Listen for the declamations of the lead vocalist.
0'08"	Listen for the decreased rhythmic density and freer rhythm. Note the subsequent return of a rhythmically dense passage with a regular beat.
0'15"	Listen for the descending melodic contour and steady triple meter.
0'28"	Listen for the repeat of the descending melodic contour in triple meter.
0'41"	Lead vocalist begins first verse. Listen for the shift to duple meter and increased tempo.
0'44"	Listen for the violins and trumpets closing the phrase with a thick rhythmic density and syncopated accents that contrast with the beat of the vocalist and guitars.
0'47"	Melodic phrase repeats.
0'55"	Listen for new melodic material from the vocalist and supporting guitars.
1'03"	Listen for the syncopated rhythmic activity of the supporting guitars.
1'06"	Listen for the violins closing the melodic phrase and the subsequent repetition of the vocal line by the supporting vocal ensemble.

1'15"	Listen for the syncopated rhythmic activity of the supporting guitars.
1'19"	Listen for the trumpets closing the melodic phrase.
1'20"	Listen for the shift to the trumpets and violins as the opening melodic material returns. Also, note the vocal declamations of the lead vocalist. Compare this material with that at the beginning of the performance.
2'00"	Vocalist begins second verse.
2'24"	Example fades.

Source: "Los Arrieros" ("The Muleteers"), performed by Mariachi Los Camperos de Naticano, from the recording entitled *Raíces Latinas: Smithsonian Folkways Latino Roots Collection,* SF 40470, provided courtesy of Smithsonian Folkways Recordings. © 2002. Used by permission.

ETHNO-CHALLENGE (CD 3.16): If possible, attend a performance of a *mariachi* ensemble in your local area. Also, examine the portrayal of mariachi musicians in film history.

Cultural Considerations. While Mexico is much more than merely *mariachi*, it is the decorative *charro* suits, wide-brimmed sombreros, and dramatic serenades of the *son* singers that have come to characterize Mexican music to the outside world.

The origin of the term *mariachi* is unknown. One popular theory is that the term is a corruption of the French term *mariage* (meaning marriage), because the music was frequently found at weddings and other festive events. Others believe the name comes from an indigenous word referring to a type of social event that features dancers stomping on a wooden platform. Whatever the etymology of its name, *mariachi* first appeared in the southwestern state of Jalisco.

Various instruments found in *mariachi*, such as the violin, harp, and guitar, were originally brought by Spanish missionaries for use in church services but soon became common in secular musical activities as well. The early *mariachi* bands were primarily string bands, with the violin as the dominant melodic instrument. The harp was originally a principal instrument accompanying the violin, but with the addition of trumpets to the ensemble, the *vihuela, guitarrón,* and other guitars became the instruments of choice in part because they could be played with greater volume. The inclusion of the trumpet also encouraged the use of several violins in an ensemble, so that today it is common to see *mariachi* orchestras that include a dozen or more performers.

Early *mariachi* groups played primarily for festive events and in restaurants and taverns. These contexts are still common places in which to find *mariachi* music, as well as for private functions. Musicians serenade their patrons with the expectation that they will be paid for each song they perform. During the 1940s–1950s, *mariachi* reached its peak of popularity, as it was the featured music in a number of Hollywood films set in Mexico, as well as films from Mexico itself. As a result, the elaborately decorated *charro* suits and sombreros presented in these films have become the standard dress for *mariachi* musicians throughout

A *mariachi* (note instruments in background) mass at the Roman Catholic cathedral in Cuernavaca, Mexico

the country. In addition to these secular functions, *mariachi* has become common in many religious settings as well, including masses, communions, weddings, and even funerals. From about 1959 *mariachi* masses became prominent, especially at the Cathedral of Cuernavaca, a center for Liberation Theology.

Audiences in the United States temporarily lost interest in the music of Latin America following the appearance of rock 'n' roll, and thus *mariachi*, like *tango*, mostly slipped off the radar screen as far as North Americans were concerned. The most prominent North American pop star to promote *mariachi* in recent years has been Linda Ronstadt, whose album *Canciones de Mi Padre* (1987) includes many *ranchera* songs, *ranchera* being a style of *mariachi* that emphasizes vocal performance.

Questions to Consider

1. To what extent do each of the musics in this chapter reflect pre-Columbian, European, or African musical traits?

2. How does *siku* performance reflect community cohesion among Andean populations?

3. How does *tango* music reflect the essence of *tango* dance?

4. Is *capoeira* a dance or a martial art? Why might it be considered both?

5. How does *mariachi* affirm or challenge American stereotypes of Mexican culture?

6. How is the survival of indigenous music and culture related to the challenges of modernization and environmental degradation?

On Your Own Time

Visit the textbook website to find these resources for further exploration on your own.

The Amazon Rainforest

Book: Seeger, Anthony. *Why Suyá Sing: A Musical Anthropology of an Amazonian People*. Champaign, IL: University of Illinois Press, 2004.
   http://www.press.uillinois.edu/books/catalog/74ncw8sx9780252072024.html

Book: Olsen, Dale. *Music of the Warao of Venezuela: Song People of the Rain Forest*. Gainesville, FL: University Press of Florida, 1996.
   http://www.upf.com/book.asp?id=OLSENS96

Audio: *Ritual Music of the Kayapó-Xikrin, Brazil*. Smithsonian-Folkways: SFW40433, 1995.
   http://www.folkways.si.edu/albumdetails.aspx?itemid=2352

DVD: *Children of the Amazon*. Dir. Denise Zmekhol. ZD Films, 2010.
   http://www.childrenoftheamazon.com/

Internet: Popular Artists from the Amazon Region
   Marlui Miranda
   Mawaca

Peru

Book: Turino, Thomas. *Moving Away from Silence: Music of the Peruvian Altiplano and the Experience of Urban Migration*. Chicago: University of Chicago Press, 1993.
   http://press.uchicago.edu/ucp/books/book/chicago/M/bo3643710.html

Book: Mendoza, Zoila. *Shaping Society through Dance: Mestizo Ritual Performance in the Peruvian Andes*. Chicago: University of Chicago Press, 2000.
   http://press.uchicago.edu/ucp/books/book/chicago/S/bo3641137.html

Book: Olsen, Dale. *Music of El Dorado: The Ethnomusicology of Ancient South American Cultures*. Gainesville, FL: University Press of Florida, 2002.
   http://www.upf.com/book.asp?id=OLSENS02

Audio: *Mountain Music of Peru*. Vol. 2. Smithsonian Folkways: SFW40406, 1994.
   http://www.folkways.si.edu/albumdetails.aspx?itemid=2321

Website: Music from the Andes
   http://boleadora.com/andes.htm

Website: The Incas
   http://incas.homestead.com/

Internet: Popular Artists from the Andes

Los Kjarkas
Los Incas
Illapu
Quilapayún
Rumillajta
Savia Andina

Argentina

Book: Castle, Mr. and Mrs Vernon. *Modern Dancing*. Special edition. New York: World Syndicate, 1914.

Website: Argentina-Tango
http://www.argentina-tango.com/index.htm

Website: Tango Argentino de Tejas
http://www.tejastango.com/

Book: Denniston, Christine. *The Meaning of Tango: The Story of the Argentinian Dance*. Anova Books, 2008.
http://www.history-of-tango.com/history-of-tango-dance.html

Website: Ástor Piazzolla
http://www.piazzolla.org/

Internet: Popular Artists from Argentina
Carlos Gardel
Tanghetto
Carlos Libedinsky
Gotan Project
Bajofondo

Brazil

Book: Browning, Barbara. *Samba: Resistance in Motion*. Bloomington, IN: Indiana University Press, 1996.
http://www.iupress.indiana.edu/catalog/product_info.php?products_id=21462

Book: McGowan, Christopher, and Ricardo Pessanha. *Brazilian Sound: Samba, Bossa Nova, and the Popular Music of Brazil*. Philadelphia, PA: Temple University Press, 1998.
http://books.google.com/books/p/temple_univ_press?id=7MFD-EoTR7MC&dq=samba&source=gbs_navlinks_s

DVD: *Favela Rising*. Dir. Matt Mochary and Jeff Zimbalist. Magnolia Pictures, 2009.
http://www.favelarising.com/

Audio: *Getz/Gilberto*. Verve Records: 521414, 1964.
http://www.vervemusicgroup.com/artist/music/detail.aspx?pid=10366&aid=2856
http://itunes.apple.com/us/album/getz-gilberto/id44005

Website: Top 10 Carnival Festivals of the World
http://www.festivalpig.com/Carnivals-of-the-World-Top-10.html

Website: Virtual Capoeira
http://www.virtualcapoeira.com/

Website: Grupo Nzinga de Capoeira Angola (Portuguese)
http://nzinga.org.br/pt-br

Book: Talmon-Chvaicer, Maya. *The Hidden History of Capoeira: A Collision of Cultures in the Brazilian Battle Dance*. Austin, TX: University of Texas Press, 2007.
http://www.utexas.edu/utpress/books/talhid.html

SOUTH AMERICA AND MEXICO

Audio: *Capoeira Angola from Salvador, Brazil.* Smithsonian-Folkways: SFW40465, 1996.
http://www.folkways.si.edu/albumdetails.aspx?itemid=2378
http://itunes.apple.com/us/album/capoeira-angola-from-salvador/id82059632

Internet: Popular Artists from Brazil
Gilberto Gil
Caetano Veloso
Margareth Menezes
Daniela Mercury
Olodum
Clara Nunes
Chico Buarque
Ivete Sangalo
Virginia Rodrigues
Marisa Monte

Mexico

Website: Mariachi 4 U
http://www.mariachi4u.com/

Website: Mariachi.org
http://www.mariachi.org/

Website: MENC Mariachi Resources
http://www.menc.org/gp/menc-mariachi-resources

Book: Sheehy, Daniel. *Mariachi Music in America.* New York: Oxford University Press, 2005.
http://www.oup.com/us/catalog/general/subject/Music/WorldMusicEthnomusicology/?view=usa&ci=9780195141467

Audio: Nati Cano's Mariachi Los Camperos. *¡Viva el Mariachi!: Nati Cano's Mariachi Los Camperos.* Smithsonian Folkways: SFW40459, 2002.
http://www.folkways.si.edu/albumdetails.aspx?itemid=2818

Internet: Popular Artists from Mexico
Carlos Santana
Selena
Ritchie Valens
José Alfredo Jiménez
Vargas de Tecalitlán
Banda Machos
Pepe Aguilar
Banda el Recodo
La Arrolladora Banda El Limón
Tito Guízar
Molotov

Canada and the United States

13

Background Preparation	460	**Site 6: African-American Spiritual**	488
Planning the Itinerary	461	**Site 7: African-American Gospel Choir**	491
An Inside Look: Buddy MacMaster	463	**Site 8: Country Blues**	495
Arrival: Canada	464	**Site 9: "Nuyorican"** *Salsa*	499
Site 1: Cape Breton Fiddling	464	**Site 10: Cajun Music**	505
Arrival: The United States of America	467	**Arrival: Native American Reservations**	508
Site 2: Ballad-Singing	468	Site 11: Plains Indian Dance Song	510
Site 3: Old Regular Baptist Lined Hymn	471	Site 12: Native American Flute	514
An Inside Look: Hugh McGraw	476	*Explore More: Inuit Throat-Singing*	517
Site 4: Singing School Shape-Note Music	476	**Questions to Consider**	518
Site 5: Bluegrass	482	**On Your Own Time**	518

This 460 foot covered bridge, built in 1866 by James Tasker and Bela Fletcher at a cost of $9,000, spans the Connecticut River between Cornish, New Hampshire and Windsor, Vermont.

Background Preparation

For many of our readers this chapter covers what is essentially "home," the United States of America and Canada. Though Mexico is geologically part of North America, it is culturally part of South and Central America and thus was covered in the previous chapter. Formerly it was believed that the earliest people to inhabit North America, those who came to be called Native Americans, crossed the Bering Strait about 11,500 years ago, but recent excavations throughout the Americas have called this belief into question. Indeed, excavations at Meadowcroft, Pennsylvania, 30 miles/50 km south of Pittsburgh, have uncovered evidence of human civilization dating back to between 12,000 and 15,000 years. It is now thought that migrations from Northeast Asia could have begun 30,000 to 50,000 years ago.

By the end of the fifteenth century, Europeans—starting with Italian-born, but Spanish-backed Christopher Columbus—had found their way to what was called the New World, though there is evidence of earlier arrivals by Scandinavians in the late tenth century. From the early sixteenth century onward Spanish, Portuguese, French, Dutch, and English colonists came in increasing numbers. By the 1600s, England, France, and Spain had become the dominant powers in North America and the Caribbean. With the development of sugarcane and tobacco plantations, a need developed for large numbers of laborers. Because the number of colonists was still small, Europeans attempted to force Native Americans into slave labor. When this attempt failed, because Native American slaves resisted or died in the process, Europeans started importing slaves from Africa. The slave trade was at its peak from 1701 to 1810, though during that time the vast majority of Africans were sent to South America and the Caribbean rather than North America.

Ohio fiddler and fiddle maker Cliff Hardesty leads two friends playing guitar (center) and mandolin (left) in playing an old string band tune

Eventually people from all over the world began immigrating into North America, making the United States and Canada two of the world's most diversely populated countries. Indeed, it can be said that in North America everyone's roots are somewhere else (except perhaps for Native Americans). The experience of starting a better life in a "new world" imbued many immigrants to North America with a spirit of energetic optimism. Many brought and preserved musical traditions from their homelands, some of which can be observed to this day. But it is also true that what is truly "American" (in the broadest sense) is the result of a mixing of peoples and traditions, a hybridization process that created new forms of musical expression. Indeed, America's musical culture has long been one of its most attractive, influential, and lucrative exports.

North America's musical prominence is not borne of an immense population or size; the continent accounts for only about 13 percent of the earth's land surface and is home to only around 340 million people, a mere quarter of China's population, though the addition of Mexico's 111 million would change this somewhat. While Canada is the second-largest country in the world, its population of around thirty-three million is quite modest, about a quarter of Japan's population. Even the population of the United States, slightly over 300 million, is small in comparison not only to that of China but also to that of India as well.

Both Canada and the United States began as colonies of Great Britain, though parts of each were earlier under French control, and the southwestern United States was under Spanish control. Unlike much of the Caribbean and most of Central and South America, where the colonial powers were mostly Roman Catholic, North America was largely Protestant. The dominance of Protestantism had at least two results: first, a greater tendency to suppress the religious traditions of both Native peoples and African slaves, and second, the flowering of an incredible number of highly diverse religious groups, many of which developed unusual or innovative musical traditions

Planning the Itinerary

What *is* traditional North American music? Until recently, it would have been exclusively thought of as music from the British Isles, such as ballads and folk songs, fiddling and dance music, and some kinds of religious music. A broader view, however, must include Native American music, various African-American forms, and any number of other hybrid genres incorporating influences from Europe, Africa, Latin America, the Middle East, and Asia.

Despite this need for a broader perspective, it is of course still true that no tour of American "traditional" music would be complete without including the Anglo genres, even though many represent survivals more than they do American innovations. We will look at four such examples from the United States: a ballad, an archaic lined-out hymn, a singing school shape-note song, and a bluegrass song. While all of these typify the heart of Anglo-American culture, the traditions they represent remain little known to the general population. Sadly, it is possible to earn one or more degrees in music in most American institutions without being exposed to any (or more than a little) "traditional" American music. A foreigner arriving in the United States would be hard-pressed to locate any traditional styles, except perhaps bluegrass. Even that is mostly restricted to aficionados.

Canada's traditional music remains little known in the lower "48." What makes Canadian music distinctive is its abundance of Native American traditions. In addition, one

13 WORLD MUSIC: A GLOBAL JOURNEY

Picturesque Peggy's Cove near Halifax, Nova Scotia, Canada, attracts numerous visitors to its peaceful fishing village atmosphere during the summer

finds various traditions associated with the *métis* (i.e., people of mixed Native American and European ancestry). There is also, of course, much music that derives from the British Isles. The primary influence is Scottish, as seen in the relatively familiar fiddling and piping traditions, but there are also pockets of Gaelic culture. French traditions remain strong as well, more obviously in Quebec, but also in Nova Scotia. Canada is here represented with an example of Scottish fiddling from the Cape Breton area of Nova Scotia.

Among America's greatest musical treasures are the contributions of people of African descent. Indeed, most of the musics that have come to represent America's energy and innovation have been African American in origin. Because so many of these musics have been absorbed into "white" culture, it would not be too outlandish to describe the United States as an "Africanized" culture in which people of all races participate in and appreciate African-American forms such as jazz, blues, and gospel, and in which much commercial music has "black" roots. African-American music is represented by an old-time spiritual, a modern gospel choral song, and an old Delta blues.

People of Hispanic descent now constitute America's largest minority, as their population has recently surpassed the African-American population. Hispanics number at least thirty-three million and constitute some 12 percent of the population of the United States. They come from many places, though those from Mexico, Puerto Rico, and Cuba constitute the vast majority. Hispanics are dispersed throughout the United States, with major concentrations in California, Florida, New York, and of course in all states bordering Mexico. Their influence on American music is pronounced. For example, a great deal of Anglo-American ballroom dance music is of Cuban, Puerto Rican, Brazilian, Dominican, and Argentine origin. *Salsa* music, an energetic style that developed in New York among Puerto Rican musicians but based on Afro-Cuban music, along with dancing, has become widely popular.

The French-speaking Acadians in Louisiana—though originally from Canada—have also developed a distinctive music, known as *Cajun*, as well as its later offshoots, including *Zydeco*.

Because the ancestors of today's Native Americans were forcibly moved from their ancestral lands, and because their religious rituals and cultural activities were suppressed by zealous Christian missionaries and government bureaucrats, much traditional Native musical culture has been lost. Nonetheless, numerous kinds of Native American music can still be found throughout the United States. In recent decades interest in Native music has increased, as Native American flute playing and drum circles, both based on Native traditions but innovations nonetheless, have come to be associated with "New Age" spirituality. We have chosen two examples to bring about a discussion of traditional Native American music: a powwow performance in the Plains style and a performance of Zuni flute music from the Pueblo region of the southwestern United States. We also highlight the highly unusual "throat-singing" of the Inuit peoples from Canada and Alaska.

Buddy MacMaster — AN INSIDE LOOK

Buddy MacMaster, Cape Breton (Canada) fiddler

I was raised in a Gaelic-speaking home and was introduced to the old music of Cape Breton through the lilting "mouth music" of my mother. By the age of four I would "jig" tunes using sticks to pretend to play the fiddle. At eleven I found an old fiddle in my father's trunk and learned a tune that very day. By fourteen I was playing for local dances, often with another fiddler to reinforce the volume.

In Cape Breton you could recognize a player from Mabou if you heard him. Also somebody from the Iona area, Victoria County, you could know by their playing. That was in the horse and buggy days. I am from Judique, and I know that my style is somewhat different from that of Mabou. I formed my own style from listening to different players and trying to pick what I liked, trying to do what the better players were doing. Through the years I tried to be a dance player, as well as playing for concerts or house parties. So, I kind of combined all that. I tried to play lively and sweet, to put some expression in the music. I suppose I figured out for myself that music played sweet sounds nicer. I like to try to give the music a pretty good lift and try to make it sound sweet and good to listen to, as well as to dance to.

In Cape Breton, step dancing and square dancing have a lot to do with the way we play—we make it lively for the dancers. You have to give it a lift or a lively feel to make the dancers feel like dancing or performing better. When you see a dancer responding to your music, that puts you in a better mood to play. It's the same at the square dances; if you see the people enjoying themselves, it sure puts you in the mood to play.

I don't speak Gaelic myself, but I think the Gaelic had an effect on my music because my parents were Gaelic speakers. Gaelic is a musical language, and I think it comes out in the Cape Breton music.

I enjoy the Cape Breton music if it's played well. What's special about it? Well, it's cheerful, lively, and bright; and there's quite a variety of tunes—different kinds, like, airs and marches, strathspeys, reels, jigs, clogs, and hornpipes. If you are in the Cape Breton area of Nova Scotia, please watch for opportunities to hear some genuine fiddling by me or one of my many fiddling friends.

Arrival: Canada

Although larger than its neighbor to the south, Canada is in many ways not well known by Americans. As similar as Canada's heritage and lifestyle are to those of the United States, Canadians proudly maintain a distinct identity. Like the United States, Canada is a nation that has attracted immigrants from around the world, and is home to many Native American peoples (called First Nations by Canadians). Because Canada's population is small, the relative significance of non-European immigrants and First Nations people is much greater than in the United States. Also important is French Canadian culture, which, while centered in Quebec, is found elsewhere as well, such as in Nova Scotia. Canada's culturally modern and ethnically diverse urban areas contrast with rural areas, where more culturally uniform populations continue to maintain long-practiced traditions. Our example of Canadian music originates in one such rural area, Cape Breton Island in Nova Scotia.

Site 1: Cape Breton Fiddling

First Impressions. This familiar-sounding dance-like music, which hardly seems exotic at all, features a violinist (known colloquially as a *fiddler*) performing with piano and guitar

Buddy MacMaster, Canada's best-known fiddler, lives on Cape Breton, Nova Scotia, in maritime Canada and plays primarily music of Scottish origin (Buddy MacMaster)

accompaniment. This music may sound vaguely "Celtic," though this term usually points toward Irish music. If you feel the urge to dance, you wouldn't be alone, for the sounds of dancing feet would normally accompany such playing.

Aural Analysis. Buddy MacMaster, one of Canada's best-known and most-loved fiddlers, plays a jig in our excerpted example: "The Golden Keyboard." Jigs are associated with a dance form (also called jig) known for its vigorous rising and falling movements. Along with other types of Scottish dance music—such as hornpipes, strathspeys, and reels—jigs came to North America with immigrants who settled in Nova Scotia ("New-Scotland"), one of Canada's eastern maritime provinces. Jigs are metrically organized in 6/8 time, with each of the two main beats having three sub-beats (**1** 2 3 / **2** 2 3). A given jig tune might be known by several different names depending on locale, while two jigs of the same name can also be musically distinct.

This jig is in the key of E minor. Its range is limited to less than two octaves because most folk fiddlers only play in "first position," meaning that they do not slide their left hand toward the instrument's body to play a higher range of pitches. In spite of their length in performance, most jigs consist of just two or three short sections, each of which is eight measures long. To keep the piece going, fiddlers repeat or alternate these sections. This jig performance can be charted as A A B B A A B B A A, though some of the repetitions incorporate variations.

Violins, in spite of their association with European classical music, have also been domestic instruments for centuries. While it is true that famous violinists use instruments valued in the millions of dollars, "folk" musicians usually play locally made instruments or ones bought by mail order at a modest price. Because the violin (called the *fiddle* in folk music contexts) was so often used for indoor dancing, and because families with "properly furnished parlors" usually had a piano, it became customary for fiddlers to be accompanied by a pianist who improvised a simple chordal or figured part. When the parlors were large enough, friends and neighbors could dance as well as listen.

LISTENING GUIDE

CD 3.17 (1'37")

Chapter 13: Site 1
Canada: Cape Breton Fiddling

Instruments: Fiddle (violin), guitar, piano

TIME	LISTENING FOCUS
0'00"	Listen for the three different instruments: violin, guitar, and piano. Note the main melody in this opening section (A) and listen for its return throughout the performance.
0'09"	Melody (A) repeats. Listen for the steady compound meter (six pulses divided into two groups of three) in the melodic line.

0'17"	Listen for new melodic material (B).
0'24"	Melody (B) repeats.
0'32"	Listen for the return of the opening melody (A). Listen for the steady low-range pitches of the piano contrasting with the syncopated rhythms of the upper range chords and guitar.
0'39"	Melody (A) repeats.
0'48"	Listen for the return of the second melody (B).
0'55"	Melody (B) repeats.
1'03"	Listen for the return of the opening melody (A). Note the subtle addition of grace notes and a more aggressive bowing technique.
1'11"	Melody (A) repeats.
1'19"	Listen for the return of the second melody (B). Note that the violin plays with "double-stops" (playing two strings at once) to add a harmony pitch to the melody.
1'26"	Melody (B) repeats and example fades.

Source: "E Minor Jigs," performed by Buddy MacMaster, fiddle, and Mac Morin, piano, from the recording entitled *Buddy MacMaster: The Judique Flyer*. Stephen MacDonald Productions, Atlantic Artists SMPCD 1012, n.d. Used by permission.

ETHNO-CHALLENGE (CD 3.17): Find a "fiddle" and learn to play a few simple melodies.

PEURT A BEUL
(pronounced *porsht a boy*) An unaccompanied dance song with nonsense syllables used to substitute for fiddling.

Cultural Considerations. Atlantic Canada includes four eastern provinces: New Brunswick, Nova Scotia, Prince Edward Island, and Newfoundland. The population is relatively diverse, as it includes First Nations, particularly the Mi'kmaq and Maliseet, as well as French Acadians and a small community of African-descended people. The majority, however, are of British (especially Scottish) extraction. Many among this latter group are (or were) Gaelic speakers, and have maintained Gaelic song traditions to the best of their abilities. The traditional context for their music-making was the *cèilidh* (pronounced "kaylee"), a kind of house party. Along with singing, fiddle music was especially popular. Several kinds of dance, including solo Scottish step dance, were enjoyed at these parties, accompanied by fiddle if possible. If no instrumentalists were available, someone could sing these dance tunes using nonsense syllables, called **peurt a beul** (pronounced approximately "porsht a boy") in Gaelic; some call this "mouth music."

Cape Breton, from which our example originates, is an island separated from the mainland by the narrow Strait of Canso. Although Gaelic Scottish culture once flourished throughout Atlantic Canada, Cape Breton has come to be most closely identified with it. A revival in the Gaelic arts—part of an international Celtic revival—has made music and dance the primary markers of Scottish identity there. Today there is an active "Gaelic College"—actually a summer school for the arts—at St. Anne just north of Baddeck in central Cape Breton.

The fiddling tradition in Cape Breton consists primarily of Scottish dance music, particularly waltzes, reels, jigs, polkas, square dance tunes, and schottisches. Fiddle music found in Cape Breton is not purely Scottish in origin, however. There has been cross-pollination between the French Acadian and Scottish styles, and in recent years there have also been a number of innovative younger players who draw on a variety of traditions. Fiddling was in rapid decline by the 1960s, but the Glendale Festival of 1973 stimulated a broad revival. In addition, Rounder Records of Boston has released a great number of albums of Cape Breton fiddling, which helped bring the music to the attention of the wider public. Today Natalie MacMaster, Buddy's niece, has achieved an international reputation for playing updated Cape Breton fiddle tunes along with innovative compositions.

Map of Nova Scotia

Arrival: The United States of America

Because the United States is a country of immigrants superimposed on the original culture of Native Americans, American culture is of necessity highly complex. Beneath the appearance of a generic American culture—primarily its popular, mass culture—there are uncounted sub-cultures comprising people who identify with a particular language, religion, racial stock, or other factor. Within these communities, whose diversity continues to expand to include such formerly unknown groups as Karen and Mon from Burma and Nepalese expelled from Bhutan, are groups of people so completely insulated from mainstream culture that they live their original culture and never use English as well as groups that have become totally assimilated into American society, and every possibility between. This raises a challenge relative to what can represent the United States musically. Any answer is inevitably a compromise. Choosing to explore music unchanged from its foreign source (e.g., Persian music in the U.S.) makes for interesting reading but fails to enlighten on what "American music" means. Limiting ourselves to music that arises from the unique circumstances of the United States, that is, a music that could only result from the unique mixing here, creates a different set of dilemmas. "Jazz," for example, is considered distinctly American, but covers such a multitude of styles, both contemporary and historical, that no one audio example could capture its essence. A visitor to the United States seeking to know its music will have to make tough choices, and that includes us.

By size the United States, including Alaska, is equal to China, three times that of India, and only a little more than half of Russia. Their populations, however, are dramatically different, China having more than four times the population in the same space, India having more than 3.5 times the population in one-third of the space, while Russia has half the U.S. population in nearly twice the space. In terms of birthrates, China and India struggle to keep the populations from growing, Russia suffers from a flat growth rate, but much of the growth in the United States is from immigration, a factor that continues to increase its diversity, and consequently its definitions of what is "American music" as opposed to "music in the United States."

WORLD MUSIC: A GLOBAL JOURNEY

APPALACHIA
A geographic region of the eastern United States along the Appalachian Mountains, which extend from New England to the southeast in Georgia.

Of the immigrant cultures, the first to establish themselves were the English and Germans. Though German was considered as the national language of the new nation, English was chosen instead. Two areas of the United States have preserved traditional Anglo music more than others: New England and the Southern **Appalachians**. Much of the traditional culture of both areas is disappearing, however, as once isolated and relatively economically disadvantaged communities have increasingly been incorporated into "modern" American life. Nonetheless, a good deal of collecting of ballads, songs, and dance music over the last one hundred or so years has preserved important examples of the music that once was common but distinctive throughout these regions.

Site 2: Ballad-Singing

First Impressions. This track may strike you as rather plain and unexciting. It features an unaccompanied vocalist, who sings with little ornamentation or rhythm, and whose words are perhaps hard to understand. Nonetheless, it is an example of an old-time traditional ballad-singing field recorded in the 1950s, the influence of which is still felt in popular music today.

BALLAD
A song that tells a story, usually performed by a solo voice but representing different "speakers."

Aural Analysis. A **ballad** is a song that tells a story. Though sung by one person, it may incorporate both dialogue among two or more individuals and a narrator who comments on the story. The ballad we have chosen was recorded in Rhode Island sometime around 1950 by a Miss E. Price, who claimed to have learned the song from a friend living in Massachusetts. With the passing of her generation and a breakdown in the transmission patterns, most ballad singers today have to learn their songs from recordings and are better called "revivalists."

Listen carefully to our example and you will notice that the unaccompanied singer makes use of only five pitches—that is, a pentatonic scale. Some might hear this scale as sounding "minor" because the three notes A, C, and E outline a minor triad (three-note chord), but in fact pentatonic scales are neither major nor minor.

The text is a poem organized in stanzas of four lines each, but because the fourth line is repeated, the song actually has strophes with five lines. Though the basic meter is duple (divisible by two or four), sometimes there are extra words that seem to disrupt this flow. Ballad texts and tunes were all orally transmitted. Over time the words were sometimes changed, either when a singer sought to localize a song by changing place names or by bringing the story up to date, or when a singer made inadvertent changes based on misunderstandings or forgot something. One such misunderstanding occurred with a ballad called "The Burley Banks of Barbry-O": the song was originally about a low-class "rank [coarse] robber," but in America the "rank robber" became a "bank robber."

Many ballads concern stories that are depressing, even violent, and the ballad we have chosen is no exception. The recording's original liner notes summarize the story:

> A mother sees blood on her son's clothing and asks him "How it came?" At first the son avoids giving a truthful answer but finally [he] confesses the murder of his father, brother, or, in this New England version, brother-in-law. Then follow a number of questions, each one bringing out a new fact.
>
> (*Eight Traditional British-American Ballads*, 1951)

CANADA AND THE UNITED STATES

LISTENING GUIDE

CD 3.18 (1'29")

Chapter 13: Site 2
United States of America: Ballad-Singing

Vocals: Single female

TIME	LISTENING FOCUS
0'00"	Verse 1 begins. Listen for the higher concluding pitch (D) at the end of this "question" line.
	Line 1: *How came this blood on your shirt sleeve? Oh dear Lord, tell me . . . me . . . me.*
0'12"	Listen for the lower concluding pitch (G) at the end of this "answer" line.
	Line 2: *It is the blood of my old gray hound that traced that fox for me . . . me . . . me . . . that traced that fox for me.*
0'27"	Verse 2 begins.
	Line 1: *It does look too pale for the old gray hound. Oh dear Lord, tell me . . . me . . . me.*
0'39"	Line 2: *It does look too pale for the old gray hound, that traced that fox for thee . . . thee . . . thee . . . that traced that fox for thee.*
0'57"	Verse 3 begins. Listen for the change from "hound" to "mare" in the lyrics.
	Line 1: *How came this blood on your shirt sleeve? Oh dear Lord, tell me . . . me . . . me.*
1'10"	Line 2: *It is the blood of my old gray mare that ploughed that field for me . . . me . . . me . . . that ploughed that field for me.*

Source: "Edward," performed by Edith B. Price, from the recording entitled *Eight Traditional British-American Ballads from [the] Helen Hartness Flanders Collection*, Middlebury College, 1953. Used by permission.

ETHNO-CHALLENGE (CD 3.18): Use numeral or staff notation to transcribe this example. Also, seek out unaccompanied ballads (lullabies, nursery songs, etc.) known by members of your own family and compile a transcription collection of them.

Cultural Considerations. The ballad is one of Europe's most important song types, and its roots go back to medieval times. Ballads in continental Europe and the British Isles were primarily an orally transmitted folk form. With the rise of the Romantic Movement in the late eighteenth century, however, poets both major and minor began writing ballads. Among them were two of the greatest poets of the time: Johann Wolfgang von Goethe (1749–1832) and Johann Christoph Friedrich von Schiller (1759–1805). Some of these literary ballads were then set to music, most famously by Franz Schubert (1797–1828). Anyone who has taken a Western classical music appreciation class has no doubt encountered Schubert's ballad "Die Erlkönig" (1815). As with the traditional ballad, a single singer performs all the voices: a narrator, the father, the son, and the spirit of the Elf King.

British ballads were brought to the attention of British and American scholars by Francis James Child (1825–1896), Harvard University's first Professor of English. Between 1882 and 1898 Child published a five-volume collection, *The English and Scottish Popular Ballads*. Child compiled the verses (but not the music) of more than 1,000 ballads, mostly collected from printed and manuscript sources and not from living singers. "Edward," the example used here, is number 13 in the collection, and thus it is labeled "Child 13."

Though American students pored over the Child collection, none seemed to recognize that these very same ballads were part of a living American oral tradition and that singers throughout the United States (and Canada) were still singing them at home for friends and relatives. It took an English folksong collector, Cecil J. Sharp (1859–1924), to reveal this living tradition to Americans. Sharp's first visit to the United States took place during World War I and was followed by three more visits, during which he collected folksongs and ballads from singers in the Appalachian region. His publications, especially *English Folk-Songs from the Southern Appalachians* (1917), precipitated a gold rush in ballad and folksong collection throughout the United States. Most of the collectors, however, were professors of English, not ethnomusicologists, and because their goal was to collect texts, they usually paid little attention to the tunes. One important collector in New England was Helen Hartness Flanders, whose collection is housed at Middlebury College in Vermont and from which comes the present example, "Edward," collected in Rhode Island. It can be said that Sharp was especially responsible for this surge in collecting, which brought the new and little-known field of Folklore to prominence.

Cecil J. Sharp and assistant Maud Karpeles noting down songs from Mrs. Lucindy Pratt of Hindman, Knott County, Kentucky, September 1917 (Courtesy of the English Folk Dance and Song Society, London)

The golden age of collecting ended around 1950, and while there are still singers who know Child ballads, it is the progenitors of these ballads who were important in the development of American music, both in a generalized sense and especially in the popular realm. More recent performers, such as Jean Ritchie, a Kentucky-born singer who has been important in the "folk revival" movement, have continued to sing Child ballads, but usually accompanied by instruments, especially the Appalachian lap "dulcimer," a three-stringed fretted zither played flat on the lap or a table.

Site 3: Old Regular Baptist Lined Hymn

First Impressions. Some first-time hearers of Old Regular Baptist lined hymns are puzzled or even put off by these seemingly tuneless and meterless sounds. As with the previous track, you hear only unaccompanied singing but now by a group that seems unable to come together either melodically or beat-wise. This smudge of moving sound is occasionally interrupted by a male soloist who seems to be chanting rather than singing. However confusing it may be on first hearing, this track, which was recorded by Kentuckians living in Ohio, represents one of the most archaic kinds of music still heard in the United States: a form of religious song with roots going back at least as far as the seventeenth century.

Aural Analysis. "And Must This Body Die?" is an eighteenth-century hymn by the eminent English poet Sir Isaac Watts (1674–1748) and is sung here by members of Pleasant View Old Regular Baptist Church near Medina, Ohio, led by their Moderator, Elder Larry Newsome. The Moderator simply begins singing, without announcing the hymn, since only he has a copy of the hymnal, a small paperback book without musical notation. Members join in as they recognize the hymn. At the end of the first line, the moderator "gives out" or "lines out" the next line of text—but uses a melodic formula to do this, *not* the tune. Because of differences in timing and degree of ornamentation, the singers produce simultaneous variants of the same tune (i.e., heterophony). The singing is quite slow, and therefore the music has little sense of beat or meter. Performers simply sing from memory, without even knowing the name or origin of the tune, which has been passed down through generations.

The words of this hymn are both elegant and sobering, expressing the conviction that while the body is temporary, the spirit is timeless:

(Verse 1) And must this body die?
This mortal frame decay?
And must these active limbs of mine
Lie moldering in the clay?

(Verse 2) Corruption, earth, and worms, [accompanying audio ends here]
Shall but refine this flesh,
Till my triumphant spirit comes
To put it on afresh.

WORLD MUSIC: A GLOBAL JOURNEY

Elders and other members of Valley Home Memorial Old Regular Baptist Church in Kurtz, Indiana, sing a hymn during a service. The second man from the left "lines out" the hymn from a words-only songbook

LISTENING GUIDE

CD 3.19 (1'36")

Chapter 13: Site 3

United States of America: Old Regular Baptist Lined Hymn

Vocals: Single male lead and mixed male/female congregation

TIME	LISTENING FOCUS
0'00"	Listen for the single male lead initiating the verse in free rhythm. Note the melismatic text setting. Line 1: *And must this body die?*
0'10"	Listen for some members of the congregation joining the lead vocalist at the end of the first line.
0'13"	Listen for the lead vocal "lining out" the upcoming lyrics. Line 2: *This mortal frame decay?*
0'17"	Listen for the congregation joining the lead vocalist to sing the second line. Note the heterophonic structure.
0'32"	Listen for the lead vocal "lining out" the upcoming lyrics. Line 3: *And must these active limbs of mine*
0'36"	Listen for the congregation joining the lead vocalist to sing the third line.

0'57"	Listen for the lead vocal "lining out" the upcoming lyrics.
	Line 4: *Lie moldering in the clay?*
1'00"	Listen for the congregation joining the lead vocalist to sing the fourth line.
1'15"	Listen for the lead vocal "lining out" the upcoming lyrics.
	Line 5: *Corruption, earth, and worms.*
1'18"	Listen for the congregation joining the lead vocalist to sing the fifth line.
1'28"	Example fades.

Source: "And Must This Body Die," performed by a congregation led by Elder Larry Newsome, from the recording entitled *Grace 'Tis a Charming Sound: Pleasant View Old Regular Baptist Church in Worship*, privately issued on CD by Terry E. Miller and members of the Advanced Field and Lab Methods in Ethnomusicology Class, Kent State University, Spring, 2000. Used by permission.

ETHNO-CHALLENGE (CD 3.19): Sing along as if you were a member of the congregation.

Cultural Considerations. Martin Luther's attempt to reform the Roman Catholic Church was not the only cause of the Reformation. French theologian John Calvin (1509–1564) had ideas far more radical than those of Luther. He objected to most everything that was distinctively Roman Catholic, including vestments, stained glass, most Catholic rites, and everything sensual, such as incense, bells, and full-bodied music, especially with instruments. He asserted that only the **Psalms** of the Old Testament, being the "inspired word of God," could be sung in church. These, being prose, had to be put into regular poetic verse ("versified") to allow for singing. Calvin's influence on the continent was great, but his influence in the British Isles was greater.

In England momentous changes had already taken place. King Henry VIII, desiring a divorce from one of his many consecutive wives and being denied one by the Roman Catholic Church, broke from Rome in 1534 and created the Church of England. As Calvin's influence spread, England underwent a Reformation as well, which resulted in the founding of the "presbyterian-structured" Church of Scotland and a reform of the Church of England in conformity to Calvinist ideals. The "Presbyterian" form, which came out of an attempt to make the church less hierarchical, is a bottom-up system in which representatives are selected at four levels, from local to general: session, presbytery, synod, and general assembly. While these changes were occurring, the radical Protestant and anti-monarchist Oliver Cromwell took power in England. Cromwell executed King Charles I in 1649 and began attacking Catholicism throughout the British Isles, including Ireland. Eventually, Cromwell's reforms were overturned in England, and in 1660 the crown was restored, but Calvinism nonetheless continued to develop deep roots in Scotland's rocky soil.

It was in Scotland that a tradition of psalm-singing that is one of the roots of Old Regular Baptist singing in America first flourished. Cromwell had organized the Westminster Assembly of Divines, a conference to reform the Church of England toward Calvinism, which

PSALMS
A book of the Bible's Old Testament comprising texts praising God, used as the exclusive source for songs in strictly Calvinist churches.

ran from 1643 to 1648. In 1645 this conference published the *Directory for Publick Worship*, which prescribed how religious services were to be conducted. This book is not the first to document the performance practice of "lining out" a Psalm, but it was the first to sanction it. Because many church members lacked books or were unable to read, the writers of the *Directory* recommended that the "clerk" (pronounced "clark") or minister "read" the Psalm passage before it was sung.

This led to a performance practice in which a leader (called *precentor* in Scotland and *clerk* in England) gave out the line of text in a chant-like manner just before the congregation sang the line to the tune. In the United States this came to be called "lining out," because a leader "lines out" the words, one line at a time. Furthermore, when the Scottish congregation sang, they sang without accompaniment. Whereas Reformed churches on the continent allowed musical instruments, most of those in Scotland forbade them. Because their singing was unaccompanied and without harmony, it was quite slow and had no recognizable beat. Further, some singers fell behind, some added ornamentation, some thought the melody went up when others thought it went down. The result was a "sonic smudge" of simultaneous variants of the tune, or in technical terms, "heterophony."

These practices came to the American colonies almost immediately. Over time, and with the founding of various Baptist churches—a history far too long and complex to describe here—there was also a change from singing psalms to singing hymns, the difference being that psalms come from the "divinely inspired" Book of Psalms in the Bible's Old Testament, whereas hymns are poems of human creation and may reference the New Testament. Over a long period and as people migrated to the South and West after the Revolutionary War (1775–1782), isolated groups of Baptists found themselves in remote parts of Appalachia.

Interior of a Free Church of Scotland near Uig on the Isle of Skye has enclosed family pews. The three-tiered front area reserves the highest position for the minister, then for the elders, then the precentor, the latter being a male who "gives out the line" of the sung Psalms

CANADA AND THE UNITED STATES

Old Regular Baptist elders at Pleasant View Church near Medina, Ohio, prepare to baptize a new member after having broken six-inch thick ice

The Old Regular Baptists were officially founded in 1870 out of earlier Baptist groups in eastern Kentucky. There they continue to worship in a manner they believe was true of the first-century Christians, without instruments and observing most of Calvin's ideas on austerity and theology.

If this denomination originated in eastern Kentucky, why was the track recorded in Ohio? After World War II as the troops returned from Europe and the Pacific, jobs were hard to come by in Appalachia. There was little more than coal mining in Appalachia, but the burgeoning auto plants in Indiana, Ohio, and Michigan offered jobs and could be reached by car. Many people from the "hollows" of eastern Kentucky drove north and found manufacturing jobs in places such as the Detroit area, northern and central Indiana, and the Cleveland area. When enough Old Regulars settled in a new area, they founded a congregation, preferring to meet in a small building in the countryside even if they lived in nearby cities. That is true of Pleasant View Church, located amidst cornfields west of Medina, Ohio.

Hugh McGraw

AN INSIDE LOOK

I was born and raised in one of America's oldest and most enduring singing traditions, that of the *Sacred Harp*, a songbook first compiled by two fellow Georgians, Benjamin Franklin White and Elisha J. King, in 1844. Like a lot of other books, most of them now forgotten, the *Sacred Harp* was printed using a system of shape notes, by which the different pitches of the scale—fa, sol, la, fa sol, la, mi—are indicated by four different shapes, one for each syllable. Sacred Harp singers are the last holdouts in America of this old "fasola" system that goes back to early England. Because this book has always been popular around the South, it has been republished as the "*Original*" *Sacred Harp*, and I served on the revision committees in 1960, 1971, and 1977. In 1991 I served as General Chairman, and in fact I've contributed eight compositions to these editions.

For over fifty years I've traveled throughout the United States teaching this treasury of early American sacred music to all kinds of people. In 1982 I was honored to receive a National Heritage Fellowship Award from the National Endowment for the Arts for my work. Since then I've also appeared in two films, *Lone Riders* and Bill Moyers's documentary *Amazing*

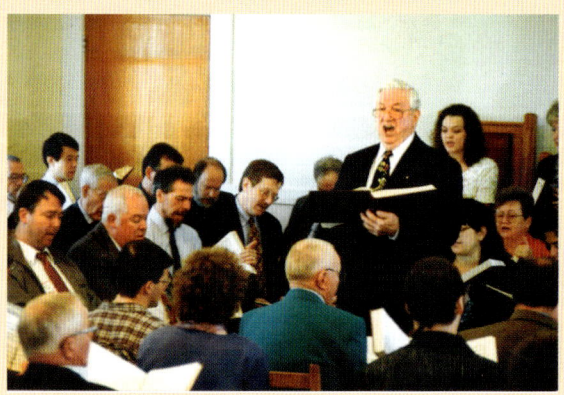

Hugh McGraw, Sacred Harp shape-note song teacher and singer, Bremen, Georgia

Grace. Since 1958 I've served as Executive Secretary of the Sacred Harp Publishing Company, Inc. in Bremen, which continues to publish this wonderful old book that has been central to my life. Sacred Harp singings are open to all, and I invite any of you to come join in the singing, the fellowship, and the great food served in our "dinner on the ground." You can find out where and when singings are held at www.fasola.org.

Site 4: Singing School Shape-Note Music

SINGING SCHOOL
A tradition of teaching four-part harmony techniques, earlier found in New England's towns and later in rural areas throughout the United States.

First Impressions. Arriving at a small wooden country church in rural Alabama near the town of Cullman on a hot June morning in 1971, I (TM) could hear the singing some distance away, because all the windows were wide open. Hopewell Primitive Baptist Church was surrounded on two sides by a cemetery, the likes of which I had never seen before. All the grass had been scraped away, leaving the ground bare. This practice, typical of the rural South, may be an African-derived custom also adopted by the white population. The singing I heard is also typical of the South, particularly northern Florida, Georgia, Alabama, Mississippi, and east Texas. People refer to it as *Sacred Harp singing* or *fasola singing*, terms that will be explained presently. Others may refer to it as "an all-day singing with dinner on the ground."

This track once again features unaccompanied vocalists, though this time their singing has an easily detectable beat. The first time through the song, they seem to be singing syllables, not words. Their tone of voice is quite nasal and strident, and the pronunciation has a Southern twang. After all sing a line together, each part comes in one after another and all four sing together to the end. One senses a certain enthusiasm not heard in the previous two tracks.

Aural Analysis. Among the many songs recorded that day was "Exhortation," a "fuging tune" composed by Eliakim Doolittle in 1800, using a hymn text written in 1709 by English poet Sir Isaac Watts, the same poet who wrote the Old Regular Baptist hymn. The title, "Exhortation," actually refers to the tune or musical composition, rather than the text; tunes are named because the same text may be used with more than one tune. The singers are arranged in a square, and each holds a thick, oblong book entitled *The "Original" Sacred Harp, Denson Revision*. A male singer first intones the three pitches of the triad that defines the key, which is written as A minor, though the pitch level is set for the comfort of the voices, as there are no instruments in the building to sound a pitch.

"Exhortation" is an example of one of the most interesting song types in this tradition, called a *fuging tune*. Although fuging tunes have a slight resemblance to a "round" (e.g., "Row, row, row your boat"), they are closer to the fugue, an instrumental genre of the Baroque period (*c.*1600–1750). Fugues begin with a single part called the "subject" that is then imitated by the second part, then the third, then the fourth, and so on (depending on how many voices the fugue has). Fuging tunes are not fugues, but after a first section in which all four parts sing together in harmony, a single voice part begins what sounds like a simple fugue. Usually this is the bass, which is followed by the tenors, then either of the upper two parts (called *counter* (alto) and *treble* (often pronounced "tribble")). The actual "melody" line (tune) is found in the tenor part, with the counter and treble providing harmonic parts; this was typical of virtually all singing school music. Fuging tunes first developed in England but became a favorite of the early New England singing schools.

In this example, all four parts begin singing simultaneously, but they use syllables, not words. The first time through the tune it is customary to sing these syllables, which are based on the syllables "fa, sol, la, fa, sol, la, mi" rather than the better known "do, re, mi, fa, sol, la, ti" used today. The singers then begin the first line of text, "Now, in the heat of youthful blood, Remember your Creator God." After these lines, the basses enter alone with the next phrase, "Behold the months come hast'ning on"; they are quickly followed by the tenors, then the altos, and finally the trebles, each "imitating" the original bass phrase. After all four parts have gotten back together, they continue to the end with the words "When you shall say, My joys are gone." The section with staggered entries, which resembles the beginning of a fugue, is customarily repeated.

While the music seems to be in a minor key, in fact it is in the Aeolian mode, one of the so-called "church modes" that preceded the development of the major–minor tonal system. The seven degrees of the scale are A, B, C, D, E, F, G, A. In A minor, the G would be sharp, but here it is natural, giving the scale an archaic sound. If you listen to the first and last chords, you will note that only two different pitches are sounded, A and E; the C that normally would be added to make the chord sound full is missing. Sometimes you also hear nothing but the interval of a fifth, which gives the music a hollow sound. The way the vocal lines move sometimes produces dissonance, caused by the clashing of neighboring pitches.

Hopewell Primitive Baptist Church near Cullman, Alabama, and its "scraped" (grassless) cemetery, site of an annual *"Original" Sacred Harp* sing

A male singer (standing) leads a song from *The "Original" Sacred Harp, Denson Revision* at an all-day singing at Hopewell Primitive Baptist Church near Cullman, Alabama

LISTENING GUIDE

CD 3.20 (1'30")

Chapter 13: Site 4
United States of America: Singing School Shape-Note Music

Vocals: Mixed male/female ensemble

TIME	LISTENING FOCUS
0'00"	Listen for the opening voice establishing a tuning pitch (A) with the *solfège* syllable "La," followed by other voices.
0'03"	Listen for the full ensemble beginning the melodic line using *solfège* syllables. Note the use of *solfège* syllables throughout the opening verse, the homophonic structure, and the consistent use of duple meter.
0'14"	Listen for the entrance of the low-range male voices (*bass*), followed by, respectively, the high-range male voices (*tenors*), low-range female voices (*counters*), and high-range female voices (*trebles*). Each "fuging" entrance follows on the second pulse after the preceding voice.
0'28"	Listen for the "fuging" entrances of each vocal range, heard in ascending order.
0'44"	Listen for the change to lyrics (not *solfège*) and the repetition of melodic/harmonic content.
0'57"	Listen for the "fuging" entrances of each vocal range, heard in ascending order.
1'11"	Listen for the "fuging" entrances of each vocal range, heard in ascending order.

Source: "Exhortation," performed by Sacred Harp singers at Hopewell Primitive Baptist Church near Cullman, Alabama, 1971. Recorded by Terry E. Miller. Used by permission.

ETHNO-CHALLENGE (CD 3.20): Sing a familiar tune using fa-sol-la *solfège* syllables. If possible, participate in a shape-note "sing" in your local area.

Cultural Considerations. Many of the early colonists in New England were members of "dissenting" churches—that is, denominations other than the Church of England. Most of these denominations were Calvinist, and some were far more radical than John Calvin himself had been. The "Pilgrims" who came to Plymouth in 1620—in whose memory Americans celebrate Thanksgiving—were dissenters, believing in congregational independence and sharing Calvin's austere views. Consequently, they and their brethren sang only the versified psalms, normally lined-out and sung heterophonically in a fashion similar to the performance of the lined-out hymn in Site 3 (see above).

By the end of the seventeenth century, voices in metropolitan areas such as Boston were raised against this practice, known then as the "Old Way of Singing." Ministers urged a turn away from what they felt was a moribund practice toward "Regular Singing," by which they

"Exhortation" from *The "Original" Sacred Harp, Denson Revision* composed in 1800 by Eliakim Doolittle notated in fa-sol-la shape notes

meant singing by note, in parts, and in meter. In order for this change to be accomplished, however, a number of elements had to fall into place first. There needed to be a system of musical notation, a set of compositions, singing books, and people to teach the congregations Regular Singing. These elements, which came into being during the first half of the eighteenth century, are still in existence today in the form of the "singing school."

The old singing schools were taught by "singing masters"—though admittedly some had mastered very little. During the last third of the eighteenth century, however, a number of singing masters appeared who were also composers, and some published their four-voice compositions in oblong-shaped tunebooks that became normal for singing-school music.

Each book began with a substantial singing tutorial that offered instruction on notation and singing. From the earliest times singers in New England used the syllables—what is called *solfège*—customarily used in England. Instead of the series of seven syllables known today (do, re, mi, fa, sol, la, ti, do), they used only four (fa, sol, la, fa, sol, la, mi, fa). In the singing schools it was customary to sing the syllables the first time the song was sung, before singing the verses.

After the Revolutionary War, many people migrated out of New England, and singing masters followed them. During the nineteenth century, singing schools were popular social events on the frontiers in the Midwest and the South. Around 1802 two clever singing masters, William Smith and William Little, authors of *The Easy Instructor*, created "shape notes," in which each of the four syllables of the "fasola" system had its own shape. *Fa* is a triangle, *sol* is round, *la* is rectangular, and *mi* is a diamond.

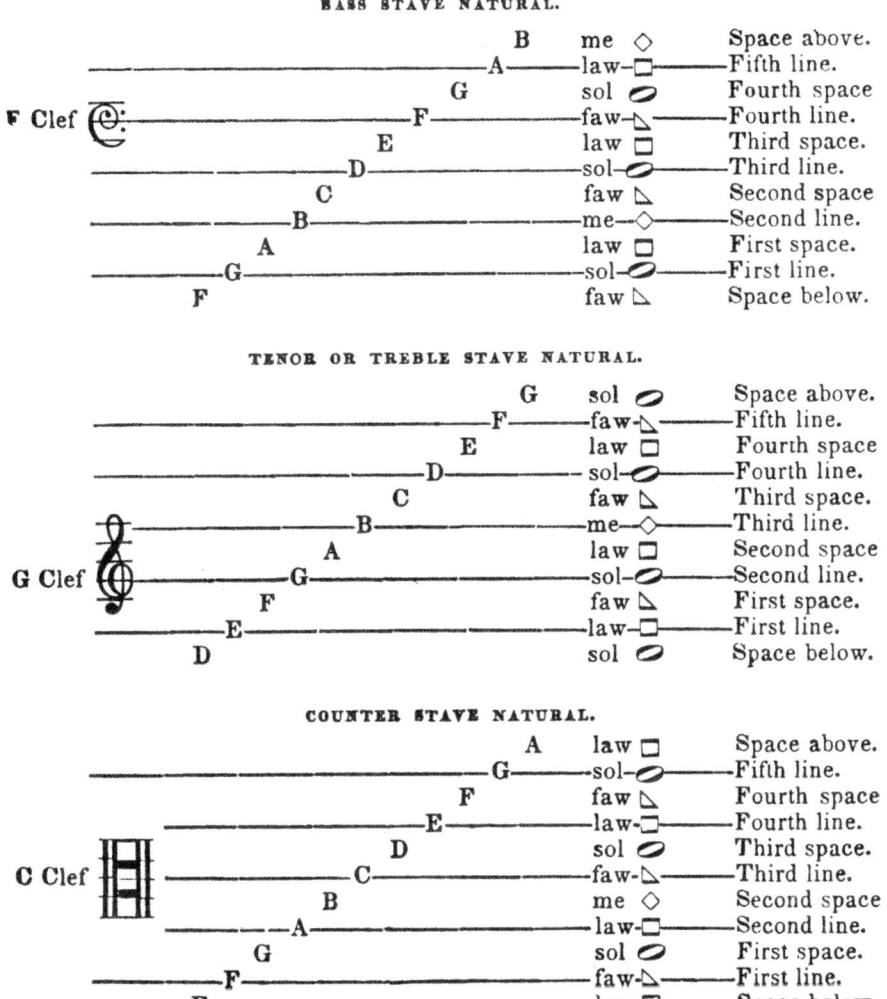

Chart from the singing tutor of *The "Original" Sacred Harp, Denson Revision* showing the succession of pitches and shapes in three clefs, from bottom to top: C clef, G clef, and F clef

After that, most singing schoolbooks were published in **shape notes**, a notation style that continues to be used to this day. Of the many collections published, the most prominent and successful was *The Sacred Harp*, compiled in Georgia by Benjamin Franklin White and Elisha J. King and published in Philadelphia in 1844. During the rest of the nineteenth century and through the twentieth, new editions were published. It became the custom to have annual "conventions" during which singers assembled to sing from *The Sacred Harp* at an "all-day singing with dinner on the ground" (i.e., a potluck meal sometimes served outdoors). This lively tradition continues into the twenty-first century throughout Georgia, Alabama, Mississippi, and parts of Florida, Tennessee, and Texas.

Sacred Harp singings are often held in rural Baptist churches, and because these only meet one weekend a month, the church is open for one-, two-, and three-day singings on the other weekends. The arrangement of the church pews, with the pulpit in the center, creates a square. With the pulpit moved away, there is seating for each of the four parts. Anyone

SHAPE NOTES
A music notation system that uses differently shaped "note" heads to indicate pitch.

WORLD MUSIC: A GLOBAL JOURNEY

Singers still gather once a year at Cabe's Cove Missionary Baptist Church in Tennessee's Great Smokey Mountain National Park to sing from M. L. Swan's *The New Harp of Columbia*, a seven-shape book from 1867

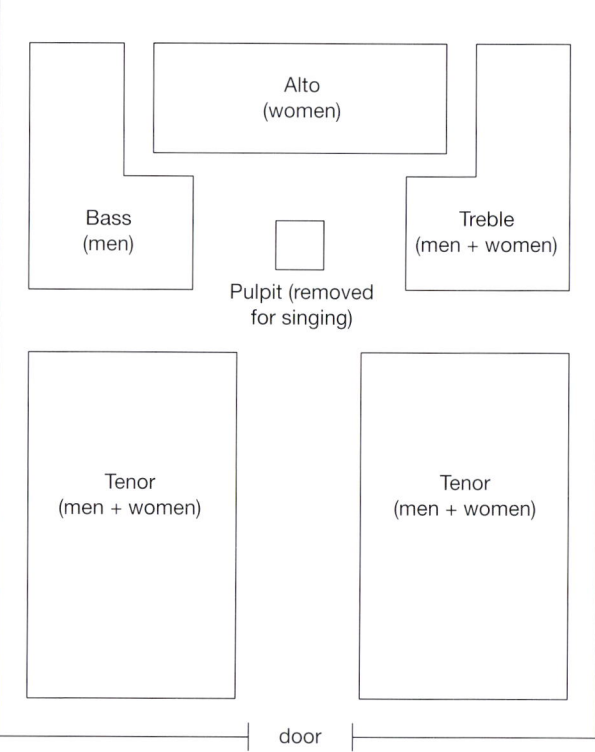

Typical seating plan for a *Sacred Harp* singing in a country church

who wishes to do so is offered a chance to come up front and lead two songs. When lunchtime comes, everyone spreads his or her food on long tables outside. Afterward, they continue singing until late afternoon. Similar singings have become popular throughout the United States since the 1980s, providing "northerners" a chance to sing this style music.

Site 5: Bluegrass

BLUEGRASS
A style of American folk music characterized by virtuosic instrumental performance and the "high lonesome" vocal style, in which a harmony line is sung above the main melody.

First Impressions. **Bluegrass** music is characterized by what is called the "high-lonesome sound": a high tenor harmony part over a baritone vocal melody, accompanied by a variety of stringed instruments. A bluegrass concert, typically a mix of "old-timey" tunes, "driving" instrumental solos, and the occasional gospel tune, is "down-home," a refuge from the hectic modern way of life. Perhaps you can picture the band in our recording set up under a gazebo in a town square on a sunny Sunday afternoon, surrounded by families on picnic mats.

CANADA AND THE UNITED STATES

A banjo player picks a tune during an outdoor wedding celebration in Nelson County, Virginia

A Bluegrass band plays at a folk festival (Lyn Pagsolingan/chickrawker.com)

Aural Analysis. Bluegrass music has clear melodic lines, simple harmonies, and a steady beat. Acoustic (non-electric) chordophones, namely the fiddle (violin), mandolin, banjo, guitar, and string bass, form the standard ensemble. Percussion instruments are rarely heard; the underlying rhythm is provided instead by the plodding bass line of a stringed bass or by the low strings of the guitar.

Each instrument has a unique timbre and different range. The bowed fiddle provides smooth melodies and countermelodies with frequent double-stops (the playing of two strings simultaneously) and sliding ornamentations. The other instruments are plucked, either with the fingers or with a plectrum. The five-stringed banjo has a "twangy" tone quality that contrasts with the mellow timbre of the six-string guitar. The banjo's unique timbre is due to the cowhide membrane used for the face of the resonator; this material brings out more high overtones than would be true of wood.

The bright timbre of the mandolin, the smallest instrument in the group, is primarily due to the high tension on the strings and the short neck, both of which contribute to the production of high, piercing pitches. The instrument has eight strings in four courses; this doubling of strings amplifies the mandolin's sound, allowing it to compete with the volume of the other instruments.

In vocal bluegrass music, the instruments play a secondary role, by supporting the voices with strummed harmony, "fills" (short melodic phrases played during pauses in the singing), and countermelodies (contrasting melodies played simultaneously with the vocalist at a lower volume). The string bass keeps the rhythm steady by playing on every first and third beat. The other plucked instruments often contribute to the rhythmic element by strumming on the upbeats (the second and fourth pulses), playing ornamented versions of the melody, or providing countermelodies.

Bluegrass musicians are expected to be highly skilled performers and often play extremely virtuosic melodic passages. Each instrumentalist (except the bassist) is given the opportunity to perform a solo during sections without vocals, in which they play their own version of the melody at a greater volume than the other instruments. This alternation of the voice with instrumental solo breaks provides a clear example of a strophic form.

In our example, each verse has eight pulses. The fiddle opens the performance, anticipating very closely the main melody sung by the vocalists in the next verse. The banjo takes the next solo break and is followed by a second vocal verse. The **mandolin** is next and is followed by the third vocal verse; the fiddle then returns, this time with a bit more improvisation. A fourth verse concludes the performance.

The vocal timbre of bluegrass music tends to be nasal, even pinched. This is characteristic of Appalachian vocal music in general, but the "high lonesome" tenor voice enhances this strained quality, as the vocalist intentionally sings in the upper reaches of his voice. The main melody is carried by the lower voice, while the harmony is usually a third or fifth interval above, moving in parallel motion. The texts usually focus on male–female relationships or on the difficulties of having to "leave home" or family in, for example, their beloved state of Kentucky. Our example, "True Life Blues," performed by Bill Monroe and the Bluegrass Boys, focuses on the hardships of married life—interestingly, from the woman's perspective, even though the vocalist is male.

MANDOLIN
A high-ranged fretted lute of Italian origin commonly used in bluegrass music.

CANADA AND THE UNITED STATES 13

Bill Monroe (Courtesy of BenCar Archives)

Brought from Italy, the mandolin became popular in the United States early in the twentieth century, later becoming a mainstay of Bluegrass music

LISTENING GUIDE

 CD 3.21 (2'36")

Chapter 13: Site 5

United States of America: Bluegrass

Vocals: Two males
Instruments: Fiddle (violin), mandolin, guitar, banjo, string bass

TIME	LISTENING FOCUS
0'00"	Listen for the violin lead playing "double-stops" (two-pitches simultaneously), followed by guitar, string bass, and banjo accompaniment.

485

0'19"	Voices enter with a homophonic structure. Listen for the main melody in the lower voice and the "harmony" in the upper voice.
0'38"	The aural focus shifts to the banjo. Note that the main melody is played in the lower pitches, while the upper pitches supply harmonic support.
0'55"	Listen for the audience applause.
0'56"	The aural focus returns to the vocal duet for the second verse.
1'15"	The aural focus shifts to the mandolin.
1'32"	The aural focus returns to the vocal duet for the third verse.
1'50"	The aural focus shifts to the violin.
2'09"	The aural focus returns to the vocal duet for the fourth verse.
2'22"	Listen for the decrease in tempo.
2'25"	Instruments pause for final vocal line and then conclude the performance.
2'29"	Listen for the audience applause.

Source: "True Life Blues" performed by Bill Monroe and the Bluegrass Boys, from the recording entitled *Off the Record, Vol. 1: Live Recordings 1956–1969*, SF 40063, provided courtesy of Smithsonian Folkways Recordings. © 1993. Used by permission

ETHNO-CHALLENGE (CD 3.21): Watch some video recordings of the Grand Ol' Opry that feature Bill Monroe and the Bluegrass Boys. If possible, attend a local folk festival.

Cultural Considerations. Bluegrass music is truly an American music. Its elements are drawn from a wide variety of American music traditions, including the "old timey" tunes of Southern Appalachia, gospel, blues, jazz, and even mainstream pop. Bluegrass was inspired by nineteenth-century American roots music but was created during the booming economic era of the post-World War II years. Radio and television were integral to bluegrass's early success, but they have since mostly shunned its presentation. Bluegrass musicians generally prefer being ignored by the mass media and pop culture, which represent the hectic lifestyle of the urbanite. For them, the perfect environment is an outdoor performance in which technology is kept to a minimum and the music, rather than the presentation, is the focus.

The main figure of the bluegrass tradition is Bill Monroe (1911–1996). Indeed, even the term *bluegrass* itself is derived from the name of Monroe's group, "Bill Monroe and the Bluegrass Boys," after their home state, Kentucky being the "bluegrass state." Many of the most famous bluegrass musicians, such as Earl Scruggs and Lester Flatt, were members of the Bluegrass Boys at one time, and all bluegrass musicians, from Doc Watson to Alison Krauss, acknowledge Bill Monroe as the standard for the style.

Bill Monroe was born and raised in Kentucky. His older brothers, Charlie and Birch, already played fiddle and guitar, so Bill learned the mandolin as his major instrument. As is typical of most bluegrass musicians, Monroe acquired his musical skills informally. His mother and uncle were his primary influences—indeed, Monroe always credited his unique "shuffle" sound to his Uncle Pen (Pendleton Vandiver), who played fiddle for local dances. Having grown up in Appalachia, Monroe was inspired by a variety of musical traditions associated with the region.

Shape-note singing strongly influenced Monroe's "high lonesome sound," with its upper-voiced harmony and nasal timbre. Gospel tunes became a standard part of his repertory. The instruments common to Appalachian string bands formed the basis for his own band. Monroe even claimed to have been inspired by the Scottish bagpipes, which, while not normally associated with Appalachia, were indeed known in the region due to the large number of inhabitants with Scottish ancestry.

The music traditions from which Monroe drew were associated with the white working-class rural populations of southern Appalachia. Beginning in the 1920s, large numbers of these Appalachians began migrating from rural areas to urban areas in search of work in factories. "Hillbilly" music, as the rural Appalachian music was then called, represented the life they had left behind. By mid-century, nostalgia for "country living" led to the popularity of radio and television broadcasts of this rural music, sung by groups such as the Carter family and later dubbed "country." The most important radio station in the South for country music was WSM in Nashville, which produced a program called "The Grand Ole Opry," because it followed a program of classical "Grand Opera" each week. Bill Monroe and his Bluegrass Boys became a prominent feature of this program, as well as of the subsequent television version. Monroe also released recordings of numerous songs, many of which, such as "Blue Moon of Kentucky," have become standards of the bluegrass repertory.

Discarding the "hillbilly" uniform of rustic overalls and worn-out shoes, Monroe dressed himself and his band in smart-looking suits and ties and donned clean, wide-brimmed cowboy hats. This polished stage presentation reflected the professional performances of the musicians in his band. Bluegrass, as the style was dubbed in 1956, was not "sing-along" music; it was concert music. The quick tempos and driving instrumental solos demanded exceptional virtuosity on the part of performers and serious attention from the listener. The solo breaks were infused with a competitive spirit, as performers vied to take the music to uncharted territory during each performance, an approach Monroe borrowed from jazz. Bluegrass had come to represent rural America, but with a sense of urban urgency.

Though overshadowed by the popularity of rock and roll, bluegrass acquired a large following during the 1950s and early 1960s. Interest in "folk music" surged in the mid-1950s with bands such as the Kingston Trio. The banjo became especially popular due to the success of folksinger Pete Seeger. Bluegrass became well known during this period, and musicians in particular gravitated toward its sound. Whereas the audiences for folk music performances were mostly made up of non-musicians, bluegrass concerts attracted musician-heavy audiences, who appreciated the high technical skills of the performers.

In 1965 the First Annual Bluegrass Festival was held in Fincastle, Virginia. At this event, Bill Monroe was deservedly dubbed the "father of bluegrass." Since then, bluegrass festivals and folk festivals in general have been the primary venues for the performance of bluegrass music. When the Coen Brothers' film *O Brother, Where Art Thou?* was released in 2000, many reconnected with Gospel bluegrass because one track on the film's soundtrack album featured veteran singer Ralph Stanley, originally one of The Stanley Brothers, a pair that was contemporary with Bill Monroe. Though a few somewhat bluegrass-based musicians have achieved success in the mainstream music industry, such as the Dixie Chicks and Alison Krauss, the majority of bluegrass musicians remain unknown to the general public. While "traditional" bluegrass continues to dominate the scene even today, since the 1950s there have been counter currents, collectively known as *newgrass*, associated with such groups as the Seldom Scene and the New Grass Revival.

Site 6: African-American Spiritual

First Impressions. This track, which sounds something like the Old Regular Baptist track (Site 3), once again features unaccompanied vocalists. Their singing is rhythmically rather free and without any clearly articulated meter, and the pitches they employ do not always sound "in tune." There is an almost improvisatory character to this performance. While it is religious in nature, it does not really sound like regular congregational church song.

Aural Analysis. This widely sung spiritual makes use of only five pitches within the narrow range of an interval of a sixth, rising a third from the central pitch and falling a fourth below it. The upper third, however, wavers between being major or minor and is closer to what is called a "neutral" third. These pitches, which are characteristic of African-American singing in general, are commonly known as **blue notes**. It is this ambiguity between major and minor that gives spirituals and many other forms of African-American singing one of their distinct flavors.

BLUE NOTE
A pitch not standard to the Euro-American tradition, believed to derive from West African tuning systems.

As is typical of spirituals, the words are simple, because they must be remembered. They also follow a structure in which stanzas are repeated with only a few words changed. Spirituals can have an unfixed number of stanzas, and these stanzas can appear in many different orders. This performance has three stanzas. The first line, "Come and go to that land," is sung three times, then completed with the phrase "where I'm bound." The second stanza substitutes "I have a savior in that land" for the first part of the first line, but finishes again with "where I'm bound." The final stanza begins with the phrase "Peace and happiness in that land."

Spirituals incorporate freely interpolated comments here and there, such as "woe." Inserting these extra sounds allows individuals to express themselves while remaining part of a group. These spontaneous interpolations also reflect the African-American attitude toward performance, which is not thought of as an exercise in lockstep precision but as a community event in which a certain amount of freedom is encouraged.

LISTENING GUIDE

CD 3.22 (2'30")

Chapter 13: Site 6
United States of America: African-American Spiritual

Vocals: Single male lead with mixed male/female congregation

TIME	LISTENING FOCUS
0'00"	Listen for the lead vocalist initiating the first verse. Note the use of a duple meter with slightly varying tempo.
	Verse 1: *Come and go to that land* (repeats three times)
	Where I'm bound.
0'03"	Listen for the congregation joining the lead vocalist to finish the line. Note variations of the melody sung by individuals at the beginning and ending of each line throughout the performance.
0'22"	Verse 1 repeats.
0'38"	Listen for the melody line concluding the first verse sung by some of the congregation, while others repeat the "Where I'm bound" line a second time before concluding the melody.
0'43"	Verse 1 repeats.
1'01"	Listen for the lead vocalist overlapping the start of the second verse as some members of the congregation conclude the first verse.
	Verse 2: *I have a savior in that land* (repeats three times)
	Where I'm bound.
1'21"	Verse 2 repeats.
1'39"	Listen for the lead vocalist initiating the third verse, followed by the congregation.
	Verse 3: *Peace and happiness in that land* (repeats three times)
	Where I'm bound.
1'59"	Verse 3 repeats.
2'17"	Listen for the lead vocalist beginning to recite the Lord's Prayer as the congregation continues to hum the melody of the song.

Source: "Come and go to that land," recorded by Terry E. Miller at Gethsemene Baptist Church. Cleveland, Ohio, 1986. Used by permission.

ETHNO-CHALLENGE (CD 3.22): Sing along as if you were a member of the congregation. If possible, attend a predominantly African-American "gospel music" church in your area.

A formal photo of the Fisk Jubilee Singers from Fisk University, Nashville, Tennessee, who began touring in 1871 to raise money for the struggling university. Their arrangements of "Negro spirituals" made the genre famous (From J. B. T. Marsh, *The Story of the Jubilee Singers*, London, 1885)

Cultural Considerations. While the term *spiritual* is usually associated with African Americans, it has also been used to denote a variety of Anglo pentatonic "folk hymns." But it was the African-American spiritual that caught the ears of travelers through America's South in the early nineteenth century, because its sound was so un-European. Although several scholars claimed these songs could not really be notated because of their free rhythms and non-European pitch intonations, several collections of transcribed spirituals were nonetheless printed during the nineteenth century. These notations, however, cannot capture the rhythmic and tonal subtleties of roots-style spirituals.

The spirituals constitute what is perhaps the oldest extant form of black singing in America. Because Protestant Christians almost always suppressed any Africanisms, particularly religious ones, slaves had to express themselves in a form acceptable to their masters. This meant singing something that resembled European melody, with a text in English, usually taken from the Bible. Most spiritual texts were sorrowful and looked forward to a release from earthly cares in Heaven. Some, however, were joyful, such as "Blow your trumpet, Gabriel"; this latter type of spiritual was often referred to as a *jubilee*. Many scholars have suggested that the texts of spirituals contained double meanings. For example, the words "Didn't my Lord deliver Daniel?" or "Steal Away" were perhaps coded expressions of the desire to escape from slavery.

Ironically, as spirituals declined in popularity in African-American culture toward the end of the nineteenth century, more and more outsiders came to appreciate them. During the twentieth century, "Negro spirituals" in many guises became a mainstay of American music; in arranged versions, they were sung by high school choirs and great black soloists such as Mahalia Jackson and Paul Robeson, and were played by bands and orchestras everywhere. Even classical vocal soloists often sang such spirituals in their programs, especially as an "encore."

CANADA AND THE UNITED STATES

The old-time spiritual, however, has not disappeared, as is attested to by our recording. In African-American churches, particularly Baptist ones, many different kinds of music representing different historical and style periods co-exist. One can encounter the old "Dr. Watts" or "long-meter" lined-out hymns that go back to the eighteenth century, the timeless spiritual, standard hymns from the nineteenth and twentieth centuries, and gospel songs of all sorts in numerous guises within a single service. The old-style spiritual is most likely to be heard during "Devotions," a brief period of preparation led by the deacons before or just after the main service begins. In a few churches these songs may also be accompanied by organ and piano.

Site 7: African-American Gospel Choir

First Impressions. On this track a full and enthusiastic-sounding choir accompanied by an electric organ sings a rhythmically active religious song, during a church service. Because it is so upbeat and joyful, this performance may not sound like typical American religious music to you. In fact, it may even remind you of "popular" music because of its strong rhythms and the style of the accompaniment.

Aural Analysis. As a visit to any record store will affirm, the bins marked "gospel" include two kinds of music, "white gospel" and "black gospel." The latter has had the wider appeal to audiences both inside and outside African-American churches. Indeed, there are now gospel choirs, especially on college campuses, whose members come from many backgrounds. African-American gospel has become, like jazz, everyone's music. The present

The Convent Avenue Baptist Church Inspirational Ensemble directed by Dr. Gregory Hopkins at the piano in "A Special Concert in Harlem" at the Convent Avenue Baptist Church, Harlem, New York City (Jack Vartoogian/FrontRowPhotos)

example was recorded at New Hope Baptist Church in Akron, Ohio, a typical urban, northern, African-American church. "God is Good All the Time," composed by Paul Smith, a local musician, has been the church's theme song for some years and is sung every Sunday.

The choir, made up of approximately thirty adult members, is accompanied by a Hammond C-3 electric organ. The old Hammond organ sound is still the preferred sound in African-American churches even though their electromagnetic tone-wheel technology dates to 1935 and was superseded by solid-state electronics in the 1970s. Combined with ordinary speakers or those with rotating drums made by Leslie, an acoustic piano, and oftentimes a drum set, the Hammond organ (B-3 club model or C-3 church model) provides accompaniments that range from straight "pipe organ" to nightclub stylings frequently played with much vibrato. Adding to the sound is the choir's clapping on beats two and four.

"God is Good All the Time" is a purely choral composition—that is, without a soloist—consisting of a main section lasting half the song, a middle section based around the word "Hallelujah," and a closing section that partly restates the main theme. Many other gospel compositions, however, feature a solo vocalist who alternates with the choir. Both kinds are heard during a typical service at New Hope Baptist Church. "God is Good all the Time" also exemplifies the predominantly joyful side of gospel. Other compositions may be much more subdued—at least at the beginning, though they usually become more animated and emotional by the end.

For choir members, gospel is an aural tradition, transmitted by the director to the singers through demonstration. While some directors write fairly complete scores mostly for their own use, others write only skeletal "charts" and some use no notes whatsoever. Singers rarely use any kind of score. Directors typically use their own arrangements, which are often derived from recordings. Accompaniments are provided either by the director or by a separate person and are mostly improvised from memory or based on an incomplete chart. Many directors also compose their own songs or create gospel-style arrangements of well-known hymns and "Negro spirituals." Stylistically, there is no attempt to distinguish gospel from the contemporary popular genres heard outside the church, for the secular and sacred sides of African-American music have long influenced each other.

LISTENING GUIDE

 CD 3.23 (2'01")

Chapter 13: Site 7

United States of America: African-American Gospel Choir

Vocals: Female ensemble
Instruments: Electric organ, piano

TIME	LISTENING FOCUS
0'00"	Listen for the electric organ as it plays once through the melodic content. Note the use of a duple meter with a steady tempo.

0'12"	Listen for the piano adding occasional melodic embellishments throughout the performance.
0'22"	Listen for the choir singing the refrain with a homophonic structure.
	Refrain: *God is good all the time, all the time.*
	God is good all the time.
	When I look and see, all He's done for me
	There's no cause to complain, I can truly say.
	God is good all the time.
	GOD IS GOOD ALL THE TIME.
0'45"	Refrain repeats.
1'09"	Listen for the choir singing the first verse.
	Verse 1: *Let's give him some praise.*
	Clap your hands, Clap your hands.
	Let's give him some praise.
	RAISE YOUR VOICE, RAISE YOUR VOICE.
1'12"	Listen for the choir and congregation clapping their hands on the second and fourth pulses of the meter.
1'25"	Refrain repeats. Note that the handclaps continue.
1'48"	Listen for the change in musical content.
	Verse 2: *Hallelujah, Praise the Lord*
	For He is good, all the time.
1'55"	Verse 2 repeats as the example fades.

Source: "God is Good All the Time," performed by New Hope Baptist Choir, from the recording titled *God is Good: The Total Musical Experience at New Hope Missionary Baptist Church, Akron, Ohio*, privately issued on CD by Terry E. Miller and members of the Advanced Field and Lab Methods in Ethnomusicology Class, Kent State University, Spring, 1998.

ETHNO-CHALLENGE (CD 3.23): Sing along as if you were a member of the choir. If possible, attend a predominantly African-American "gospel music" church in your area.

Cultural Considerations. The term *gospel*, besides referring to the first four books of the New Testament of the Christian Bible, refers to a complex of musical types running the gamut from simple, unadorned hymns sung dispassionately to elaborate, passionately sung compositions/arrangements involving a soloist and choir and multiple instrumentalists. "Gospel" music has a single root that, over time, split into separate histories for Anglo Americans and

African Americans. Although "white gospel" remains a major musical force in the United States, "black gospel" has not only attracted greater attention, but it has also become one of the prominent forms of American "popular" music. It has also been exported, as thriving gospel traditions found in the Caribbean, the United Kingdom, and Africa demonstrate.

As a musical term, *gospel* originally referred to the hymns and songs associated with American evangelism from the mid-nineteenth century onward. Gospel songs developed out of three sources during the first half of the nineteenth century: the simple but "correct" or "scientific" harmonies found in the hymns of white New Englanders such as Lowell Mason ("My Faith Looks Up to Thee") and Thomas Hastings ("Rock of Ages"), Civil War–era Sunday School songs (such as William Bradbury's "Jesus Loves Me"), and the songs used in evangelistic services from the Civil War onward, such as "What a Friend We Have in Jesus," "Softly and Tenderly Jesus is Calling," and "Jesus, Keep Me Near the Cross." The term *gospel* **hymn** (or *gospel song*) was coined in the early 1870s by Ira D. Sankey, the musical associate of evangelist Dwight L. Moody. Gospel hymns are always in a major key and are characterized by the presence of a verse–chorus structure, the use of mostly simple chords (though some have complex, chromatic chords), and by the use of *afterbeats*—that is, echo-like repetitions of short text phrases—heard while one part holds a long note. Perhaps the best-known gospel hymn is "The Old Rugged Cross" (music and verses by the Rev. George Bennard, 1913).

Gospel hymns have been spread worldwide by evangelists, but in the South they were taken into the shape-note singing school tradition in the late nineteenth century. But it was their absorption into the Pentecostal movement, founded in Los Angeles in 1906, that caused them to flourish among African Americans. Some of the standard gospel hymns were composed by African Americans, but these songs in their written versions were indistinguishable

HYMN
A "humanly composed" religious verse set to music.

With its pastor, the Rev. Benny Williams, singing solo, the Gospel Choir of New Hope Missionary Baptist Church, Akron, Ohio, is directed by Mr. Robert Nation during the Sunday service (Daniel Ledingham)

from white songs. One man, though, Charles A. Tindley, composer of "We'll Understand It Better By and By" (1905), brought black gospel hymns into the limelight. During this same period black street preachers began singing gospel hymns as part of their sermonizing, accompanying themselves on guitar. Among the best known of these preachers were Blind Willie Johnson and the Rev. Gary Davis, first active in the 1930s.

Standard gospel hymns, now treated as the starting point for increasingly free performances, developed into other new forms from the 1920s on, especially the vocal "quartet" (called "quartets" even though some groups had more than four singers). The most prominent black composer of the time was Thomas A. Dorsey (1899–1993), formerly a barrelhouse pianist known as "Georgia Tom." His gospel hymn "Precious Lord, Take My Hand" remains the virtual anthem of black religious music today. Solo gospel singers, the most famous of them including Mahalia Jackson, Clara Ward, and Marion Williams, brought gospel to the concert stage. Gospel performances involving choirs, often combined with one or more soloists, became increasingly prominent in the 1950s. During the 1960s vocalist James Cleveland brought choral gospel to prominence not just within the African-American community but for the outside world as well. Gospel music was increasingly influenced *by* and influential *on* popular genres. Indeed, much of black popular music, especially *soul*, derives ultimately from the old lined hymns and gospel performances of the churches.

Today "black gospel" mainly means choral music, with or without soloists. While it was originally associated with rough and ready street evangelists and "storefront" churches (small churches started in rented storefronts in the inner cities), over time it has been accepted by the mainstream denominations, including Baptists, Methodists, Roman Catholics, and even black Lutherans, Presbyterians, and Episcopalians. Gospel music remains one of the most exciting and creative of America's many musical expressions, and it is less and less restricted to the domain of black churches. Each year more and more colleges and universities add "gospel choir" to their list of official ensembles, and these attract students of every ethnic background. Gospel, like jazz earlier, has become an American music rather than a specifically African-American music.

Site 8: Country Blues

First Impressions. **Blues** music is raw. Though vocal prowess and musicianship are valued, the essence of blues music is emotion. Through his music and words, the blues musician reveals his innermost feelings, whether of sorrow, anger, joy, or lust. Even the first-time listener to real rural blues may recognize features, such as harmony and scale, that are the foundation of much rock and popular music around the world today.

Aural Analysis. Country or folk blues features a solo voice, typically male, and an accompanying instrument, usually a guitar but sometimes a harmonica. The vocal timbre is often gritty, and the singing is declamatory and interspersed with melismatic moans. The lyrics are primarily sung in the first person. The vocalist expresses his emotions frankly and often deals with serious subject matter.

The guitar acts as a second voice, responding to the vocal phrases with "riffs" that affirm the proclamations of the singer. Though based on European equal-tempered tuning, blues is characterized by the use of one or more "blue" notes, which fall between those pitches

BLUES
A secular folk tradition originating within the African-American community in the southern United States with lyrics commenting on life.

normally used in the Western tradition. These "blue" notes make the music neither major nor minor—yet suggestive of both—and create tension and an "edgy" sound that reflects the unsettled mood of the music. Though much of the more familiar "urban" blues music of today is quite polished, folk blues was always rough around the edges.

Most blues music uses a minor-sounding key, because minor keys are perceived to indicate sadness. The typical blues song, however, usually uses only five or six tones, with the second and/or sixth pitches of the scale being omitted. The "blues" notes are generally found between the fourth and fifth scale degrees or the sixth and seventh scale degrees. Pianists will use the "augmented" (raised) fourth and a flatted seventh to play these "blue" notes, because the pitches of the piano cannot be altered. The harmonic progression of most (but not all) blues follows a standard "12-bar blues" stanza form. Each "bar" comprises four beats. The first four bars correspond to the first vocal phrase. The phrase is typically repeated in the second four bars, while the poetic response is sung in the last four bars. The harmonic structure of the blues utilizes the I–IV–V chords (roman numerals are used to represent harmonic scale degree) in the following form:

```
Line 1 I - - - | I - - - | I - - - | I - - - |
Line 2 IV - - - | IV - - - | I - - - | I - - - |
Line 3 V - - - | IV - - - | I - - - | I - - - | (repeated for each succeeding stanza)
```

This structure is often modified, especially in the last four bars, frequently as V–V–I–I or by having the last bar be V, which acts as a "turn around" that leads into the next 12-bar stanza.

Robert Johnson – Studio Portrait (Hook Bros., Memphis, 1935. Copyright 1989 Delta Haze Corporation. All Rights Reserved. Used By Permission.)

The non-musician can think of these chord symbols as representing tension and release. I is home, the most relaxed and comfortable chord. IV increases that tension, but then returns home. V increases the tension even more before returning to the I chord. Listen for this release of tension in the closing phrase (V–IV–I–I) of the first verse, in which the vocalist proclaims, "Back to the land of California (V), to my sweet home, Chicago (IV–I)." The guitar arpeggios complete the verse on the home chord with a "turn around" shift to V leading to the next verse.

While the 12-bar blues is the standard model for performance, blues musicians frequently take liberties with various aspects of the form. Rhythmic flexibility is an essential feature—bars can be added or excluded and the tempo can be changed—and even the chord structure can be modified. In our selection, the tempo is roughly 92 beats per minute as the performance starts, but by the end it has increased to more than 104 beats per minute. Such fluid musical elements add tension and enhance the unsettled mood of much blues music.

CANADA AND THE UNITED STATES

LISTENING GUIDE

CD 3.24 (3'02")

Chapter 13: Site 8
USA: Country Blues

Vocal: Single male (Robert Johnson)
Instruments: Guitar

TIME	LISTENING FOCUS
0'00"	Guitar introduction.
0'06"	Vocalist enters as 12-bar blues progression begins (I). Following four-beat measures, the chord progression is

    First Line: I   IV   I   I

    Second Line: IV   IV   I   I

    Third Line: V   IV   I   I (with V "turn-around" change)

TIME	LISTENING FOCUS
0'17"	First lyric is repeated. Listen for the harmony chord change of second line (IV).
0'26"	Response lyric, "Back to the . . ." leads into third harmonic line (V). Note the vocal line implies the shift to IV harmony as guitar riff sounds. This is followed by a resolution (I) and "turn-around" chord change to V leading into the next verse.
0'36"	Repeat of the first verse.
1'05"	New verse, "Now, one and one . . ."
1'34"	New verse, "Now, two and two . . ."
2'02"	New verse, "Now, six and two . . ."
2'30"	New verse, "I'm going to California . . ."
2'54"	Closing phrase on guitar.

Source: "Sweet Home Chicago" from *The Complete Recordings*. Sony/BMG, 2008. Used by permission.

ETHNO-CHALLENGE (CD 3.24): Note the track times for the harmonic changes after the first verse. Listen for the 12-bar blues progression in the music of various blues artists, such as Robert Johnson, Son House, B.B. King, and Muddy Waters. In addition, you might research cover recordings by various artists of "Sweet Home Chicago," which is a blues standard.

Cultural Considerations. An appreciation of the blues requires only that the listener have empathy for the hurts, joys, desires, and frustrations the singer expresses through his music. Though the country blues originate from the experience of being an African American in a racist and unjust world, the music's heartfelt and realistic perspective on the fundamental emotions of all human beings have given it broad appeal around the world.

The roots of much African-American music can be traced to the field hollers and work songs of slaves who labored under the broiling sun in the South, especially Mississippi, Alabama, Georgia, Tennessee, the Carolinas, and Virginia, as well as Louisiana and Texas. Singing was commonplace among slaves, who were forced to work long, hot days on plantations and elsewhere. The singing, especially the work songs, provided distraction from the tediousness of the work, while the music's regular beat often helped organize whatever physical activity the slaves were engaged in, be it pounding rocks or tamping railroad ties. The vocal style and melodic and rhythmic freedom of these work songs and field hollers, as well as many of the songs themselves, became the basis for early blues, spirituals, and gospel songs among African Americans after Emancipation in 1865.

By the 1890s, the blues form had appeared in many places throughout the Deep South. The most famous blues came from the Yazoo River delta in northern Mississippi and are called the "delta blues." While the instrumentation and harmonic progression of the music were inspired by the folk ballad traditions of Europe, the three-line form and use of an instrumental accompaniment as a "second voice" were African-American innovations. The characteristic "blue" notes are believed to derive from African conceptions of tuning. Even the itinerant lifestyle of the "bluesman" is thought to have its roots in the West African *griot* (jali) tradition (see Chapter 10, Site 7).

The "troubled" life of the bluesman provided a major resource for the lyrical content of blues music. Lost loves, promiscuity, alcohol and drugs, the bluesman's nomadic existence, racism, and death are all common themes in the country blues. Many of the early blues artists were blind, such as Blind Willie McTell, Blind Lemon Jefferson, and Blind Blake. Being blind made life difficult for a black man in the Deep South, as finding work was nearly impossible. Many other early blues artists chose the lifestyle as preferable to hard labor that paid little. A weekend's music performance at a picnic or other event could earn them as much or more than a week's wages farming on plantations or building levees. For the country bluesman, the burdens of a nomadic life were preferable to the struggle to maintain a sedentary existence. Sleeping in railroad cars, shacking up with a female admirer for a weekend or two, and avoiding the law or racist thugs all became fodder for the bluesman's songs.

Many possible venues for blues performances existed in the early years of the twentieth century. Traveling tent and medicine shows often hired blues musicians to accompany them to attract audiences—particularly black populations, as the vendors themselves were generally white. Bluesmen frequently found work at house parties or in *juke joints*, the latter being the term for social clubs with a primarily black clientele. Brothels also commonly hired blues musicians to entertain and were one of the earliest contexts for blues pianists.

An important activity for the blues artist was playing in what are called *cuttin' heads* contests. These contests pitted musicians against each other in a kind of duel judged by the audience, which determined who was the better player. Competitions were a necessary way for a musician to demonstrate his skills and gain a reputation in order to find work. However, if a musician was "cut" (i.e., if he lost), he generally had to hand over his guitar to the winner. Losing meant a musician would have to earn, borrow, or steal enough money to buy back his guitar from the local pawnshop. For obvious reasons, these contests were a great incentive for musicians to develop their skills and expand their repertory.

The popularity of the blues was recognized by the budding music industry of the 1920s and 1930s, which released a slew of recordings by country blues artists. These recordings were a staple of the "race record" industry, which featured primarily black artists, whose recordings were sold to black customers. As the industry grew, blues musicians saw it as an opportunity to make some quick cash (musicians were paid a one-time fee for their services) and maybe gain some notoriety through a successful record.

When the Great Depression of the 1930s hit the Deep South, many rural workers moved to distant cities to seek employment. Northern cities, such as Detroit, Cleveland, New York, and especially Chicago, offered the greatest opportunities for work in factories and mills. As the black population

African Americans dance at a "Juke Joint" social venue. Notice the police observer (Photo by Wolcott, Marion Post, pub. 1939, courtesy of Library of Congress)

left the South, the bluesman found that his audience was disappearing. Consequently, he followed his patrons to the city where he adapted his music to his new situation. Our audio example, performed by country blues legend, Robert Johnson, reflects this "gold rush" to the big city, that is, Chicago, in its lyrical content. Artists such as Muddy Waters, Howlin' Wolf, and Elmore James gave the urban blues a jolt of energy, literally, by adding electric guitars and forming combo groups that included less portable instruments, such as drums and piano.

Creative use of the microphone gave great harmonica players, such as Little Walter and James Cotton, a new sound and a prominent role as soloists in many blues bands. Later this updated form of the blues came to be known as *rhythm and blues*. These innovations led to the development of a new genre in the 1950s, namely *rock and roll*. Early American popular artists, such as Elvis Presley, Jerry Lee Lewis, Chuck Berry, and Little Richard, based much of their repertoire on the blues forms, as did later successful rock bands from overseas, such as the Rolling Stones, Cream, and Led Zeppelin. Not only rock was influenced by the blues, however: much early jazz was played in 12-bar blues form, and the distinctive piano style called *boogie-woogie* was essentially piano blues.

Blues was perhaps one of the most influential musics of the twentieth century and today is still a prominent feature of America's musical landscape. Many contemporary blues artists, despite usually traveling with a band, maintain the rural roots of the music by performing solo pieces drawn from recordings made in the early years of the twentieth century. Older artists such as Robert Johnson, Charlie Patton, and Blind Willie Johnson are still revered as the models for performance and are legends of the genre.

Site 9: "Nuyorican" *Salsa*

First Impressions. This recording is perhaps more rhythmically complex than any of our other examples of music from the Americas. As danceable as it is listenable, it offers both African-derived polyrhythmic patterns and European- and jazz-inspired harmonies,

13 WORLD MUSIC: A GLOBAL JOURNEY

New York's Spanish Harlem around 1970 showing the area's many small shops (H. Armstrong Roberts/Retrofile/Getty Images)

A local *salsa* band plays on the stage of the Eastman School of Music in Rochester, New York

played in a crisp fashion with everything from brass "punches" to a florid, jazz-inspired flute solo.

Aural Analysis. Because the Caribbean is known for its cultural fusions, it comes as no surprise to hear European brass and the piano combined with a *slit-gong* wood block. Other instruments, such as the cowbell, are perhaps African in origin, but the clarinet, trumpet, trombone, string bass, and flute are European. This mixing of instruments representing different cultures (European, African, and Amerindian) is typical of the music we know as

500

salsa, a term that otherwise denotes a colorful, pungent sauce much associated with salty corn chips. Our example also includes a solo male voice that works in a kind of call-and-response pattern with the melodic instruments and a small chorus.

While the melody and harmony are Euro-American, with a clear influence from jazz, the whole metrical/rhythmic structure is from another source: Africa. True, the music is ostensibly in duple meter—4/4 time—but this is no march, with a heavy, obvious downbeat. Here and there beat 1 is easy to find, perhaps by focusing on the melody, but in other passages it is obscure. Accented sounds are heard on the offbeats, giving the music a highly syncopated feel. This is because the underlying organization is closer to African timeline patterns than to European meter based on units of four beats each (i.e., measures). The basic organizational unit in this music is a two-measure pattern called the *son clave*, which consists of either 3 + 2 or 2 + 3 beats played in a syncopated fashion (see Chapter 11, Site 6, Cuban *Son*). Other percussion instruments play their particular patterns in opposition to the *clave*, giving the rhythm section a changeable complexity that is as difficult to sort out as it is to ignore. Indeed, in many compositions, beat 1 is de-emphasized or even omitted, requiring the listener to feel the missing pulse in order to know where the measures begin.

Our example begins with a melody played twice by piano and string bass, underpinned by the *clave* pattern (2 + 3) played on a wood block (called a *slit-gong* because the block has a deep slit cut in it near one edge). As the piano-bass pattern is played twice more, a tall barrel-shaped, single-headed drum called *tumbadora* or *conga* enters, playing its own *tumbao* pattern accompanied by the *maracas* (rattles). When the brass instruments begin playing melody, the *timbales* also enter, these being a pair of metal-framed drums of European military origin. The pattern that the *timbales* play, called *cascará*, is categorized as a *palito* because it is struck on the side of the drum. After this, the solo voice alternates

Celia Cruz (left) and Tito Puente (right), two of the most famous artists associated with *salsa* (Jack Vartoogian/FrontRowPhotos)

13 WORLD MUSIC: A GLOBAL JOURNEY

Left photo: (front) a pair of *tumbador* or *conga* drums, (right rear) a pair of *timbales* or *pailas* drums with metal bell attached, (left rear) a pair of *bongo* drums

Right photo: (from top clockwise) *concerro* cow bell, *maracas* (shakers), *claves* (wood sticks), *shekere* (gourd shaker), and *güiro* scraper (Andrew Shahriari)

with brass "punches" and flute. Finally, a section begins in which the voice alternates with a chorus comprising several singers, while the *timbale* player adds a bell pattern.

Entitled "Quítate de la vía Perico," the song is a mock lament for someone nicknamed Perico (meaning "parakeet"). *Perico*, perhaps a local odd fellow, was sucking sugarcane while walking on the railroad tracks and, not hearing the train, was killed. After an opening that sounds like a train whistle, someone calls out "And here comes Perico again; let's have fun once more! And what a machine [locomotive], man." The vocalists then warn Perico in a sung "call": "Move away from the train track, Perico; the train is coming. . . . Later you may not say that you were not warned." In the response section the group sings, "If I had known that Perico was deaf, I would have stopped the train." The rest of the song more or less repeats these ideas, though we will spare you certain grisly details. This song was originally recorded by Puerto Rican musicians, including singer Ismael Rivera and band leader Rafael Cortijo Verdejo, but its text includes phrases associated with Cuba, not Puerto Rico. It is classified as a *guaracha*, a type of dance music derived from the *son*, and maintains the *son*'s *montuno* call-and-response section.

Cultural Considerations. The road that led to *salsa* started in Cuba, continued on to New York City, and then spread throughout the Americas, if not the world. Numerous factors account for its creation, and sorting them out properly requires understanding practically the entire history of Latin music in North America. First, we emphasize Cuba as the primary source for virtually all the styles of Latin music that developed elsewhere. In addition to influencing Americans visiting Havana before 1959, numerous Cuban musicians and band leaders either toured or moved to the United States to take advantage from the rapidly growing taste for Latin "pop," Cuban music that was adapted to the tastes of American popular culture. Among those exponents was Xavier Cougat, a Spanish-born immigrant to Cuba whose family moved to New York City in 1915. A band leader who first flourished during the "tango craze" of the 1920s, Cougat followed the changing tastes, and by the later

LISTENING GUIDE

 CD 3.25 (2'43")

Chapter 13: Site 9

Nuyorican (New York City): *Salsa*

Voices: Single male lead with mixed male/female supporting ensemble
Instruments: Trumpets, trombone, piano, electric bass, bongo and *conga* drums, *timbales* (membranophone), flute, shaker, *slit-gong* (wood idiophone), cowbell

TIME	LISTENING FOCUS
0'00"	Brass instruments open with a "train whistle" imitation.
0'04"	Listen for the piano and electric bass establishing an underlying melodic rhythm used throughout the main sections of the performance. Also, note the entrance of the *clave son* (2 + 3) rhythm on the *slit-gong*.
0'08"	Brass instruments imitate "train whistle" again. Also, listen for the *conga* drum briefly improvising in the background.
0'13"	Listen for the *timbales* accent just before the *conga* drum and shaker enter with a regular rhythm. Also, note a single strike on the cowbell.
0'22"	Listen again for the *timbales* accent just before the melodic instruments enter.
0'25"	Vocalist enters with extemporaneous spoken dialogue. Listen for references to "Perico," the subject of the lyrics.
0'42"	First verse begins. Listen for the piano and rhythm instruments accompanying the vocalist, while the remaining instruments punctuate the end of the lyric's phrases.
1'12"	Listen for a short instrumental break.
1'17"	Listen for the appearance of the backing vocals as the music moves to the *montuno* section.
1'21"	Lead vocalist improvises while the backing vocals provide a consistent "response" refrain.
2'11"	Listen for the new instrumental melodic material, which emerges as backing vocals sing a new refrain, "Perico!"
2'30"	Listen for the flute improvising in a new *montuno* section with melodic rhythmic support from the piano and percussion as the example fades.

Source: "Quítate de la vía Perico," performed by Tolú, from the recording entitled *Bongo de Van Gogh*, *Tonga* Productions TNGCD 8405, 2002. Used by permission.

ETHNO-CHALLENGE (CD 3.25): Keep the *clave* rhythm going throughout the performance. Additionally, visit a *salsa* club in your local area or take some *salsa* dance lessons.

1940s and 1950s emphasized what some would call "watered down" Cuban music. Another impetus to the spread of Latin music was Desi Arnaz, a Cuban-born musician and actor whose family fled to Miami in 1933. Long after marrying actress Lucille Ball in 1940, Arnaz, formerly a guitarist in Cougat's band and later a band leader in his own right, joined his wife for the long-running television series "I Love Lucy," in which he played Enrique "Ricky" Ricardo, a Latin band leader. Cougat and Arnaz, then, helped create the space for Latin music's popularity in the 1950s.

A more direct factor was the development of Latin jazz. This began in the 1940s when Cuban conga drum players began coming to New York, bringing with them the timeline patterns of Cuban *Santeria*, an African-derived religion that had syncretized with Roman Catholicism. Among them was Chano Pozo, a feisty Cuban drummer who teamed with jazz trumpeter Dizzy Gillespie, along with Machito (Frank Raul Grillo) and trombonist Juan Tizol to begin the evolution of Latin jazz, a history too extensive and complex for inclusion here. Although Pozo died only one year later (in a car accident), Latin jazz continued to develop parallel to the new crazes for rumba, mambo, and cha cha chá, both the dances and the music associated with them. By 1959, when Fidel Castro's Cuban Revolution ended tourism to Cuba as well as the migration of Cuban musicians north, the nation's attention was drawn from things Latin to the new craze for the idols of the "British Invasion," especially the Beatles. Yet Latin music in the United States continued to develop and flourish, though to more specialized audiences.

In the absence of new Cuban blood, the Latin music scene began a series of changes that lead directly to the emergence of *salsa* music. One major factor was the growing population of "Latinos" in New York City, the majority having come from Puerto Rico. This population began producing most of the upcoming Latin artists as well as provided a ready market for both concerts and recordings of Latin music. Responding to this need, Dominican band leader Johnny Pacheco and Italian-American lawyer Jerry Masucci founded Fania Records in 1964. Besides producing most of the successful Latin albums until the company's demise in 2005, the Fania All Stars, a group of the label's best musicians, toured widely, launching some of Latin music's greatest new artists such as Celia Cruz (Cuban born, died 2003), Willie Colon (New York born of Puerto Rican descent), Hector Lavoe (Puerto Rican born, died 1993), and Rubén Blades (Panamanian born). A third factor was the emergence of Santana, a Mexican-born rock guitarist who later pioneered the development of *salsa* and Latin fusion. Santana's 1971 concert before 40,000 people in Yankee Stadium was also a key reminder for the broader public of Latin music's continuing vigor.

The musical term *salsa*—otherwise a spicy, tomato-based sauce—was gradually applied to the Latin music that emerged in New York in the 1970s out of Cuban-derived *mambo*, *cha cha chá*, and Latin jazz. Although he rejected the term, preferring to call himself an exponent of Latin Jazz, many people consider *salsa*'s most famous exponent was Tito Puente (1923–2000), a "nuyorican" ("New York born Puerto Rican") classically trained at Julliard but later known as "The Mambo King" and the "King of the Timbales" for his work in most of the styles leading to and including *salsa*. Featured in films, known for live performances worldwide, and honored by institutions such as the Smithsonian, Puente became synonymous with *salsa*. Puente's music is among the most rhythmically complex Latin music ever recorded.

Finally, *salsa* continues its popularity today under a great variety of younger artists, both well known and obscure. Because *salsa* music is generally faster than *mambo* and much faster than *cha cha chá*, the ballroom steps associated with those dances are difficult to execute to this music. *Salsa* dance, while taught in most ballroom studios, remains outside the ballroom canon, but the steps are generally the easier ones borrowed or derived from *mambo*, but unlike *mambo*, where dance steps break on beat 2, in *salsa* they break on beat 1. Nonetheless, because of the rhythmic/metrical complexity of *salsa*, articulated by the *clave* pattern rather than European meter, even finding beat 1 can be challenging.

Site 10: Cajun Music

First Impressions. This is relatively simple music with an infectious beat and much forward drive, which places the accordion at the center. The singing is in French, though it sounds like French with a southern twang. Cajun music, like Cajun food, has attracted a growing number of followers and, like the spiciness of the alleged "Cajun sauces" served in many American restaurants, has a certain spiciness of its own. This is music that practically pushes you out of your seat onto the dance floor.

Aural Analysis. Besides the voices, only two melodic instruments are heard, the accordion and fiddle, but if you listen closely you will also hear the high, clear tones of a metal triangle. The accordion has just one row of melody buttons. Like the way the basic and inexpensive accordions usually mail-ordered from "up north" are used, the harmonies of Cajun music are simple—basically I and V (tonic and dominant). The melodic range is just one octave, rising a fifth above the tonic and descending a fourth below. Because such an accordion can be played in only one key, an instrument must match the singer's range. But much Cajun singing, as this example shows, is sung in the singer's upper range. The accordionist gives the vocal melody greater energy by repeating most notes.

A favorite Cajun expression is *laissez les bons temps rouler*, meaning, "let the good times roll"—but this sentiment masks the hard realities of life in southwestern Louisiana and seems contradicted by the sometimes distressing words to Cajun songs. Cajun musicians frequently quickly invent new songs to comment on local events and community scandals. Our example, entitled "The Blackberry Bush," deals with more general human foibles, as it concerns the misbehavior of a young woman who goes into the blackberry bushes with her boyfriend. They become lost in the briars—perhaps a metaphor for being lost in a broader sense.

TIME	LISTENING FOCUS
0'00"	Listen for the spoken introduction.
0'01"	Listen for each instrument in the opening musical material. Note the foot-stomping of the performers, which articulates the steady duple meter.
0'11"	Opening musical phrase repeats.
0'20"	Vocalist enters with the first verse. Listen for the violin imitating the melodic contour of the singer. Note that the accordion plays with a quieter volume whenever the vocalist sings.
0'30"	Listen for the aural focus returning to the instruments.
0'38"	Listen for new melodic harmonic material.
0'48"	Listen for the return of the vocalist for the second verse and the shift back to the "home" harmony.
0'58"	Listen for the aural focus returning to the instruments.
1'06"	Listen for the return of the secondary melodic harmonic material.
1'17"	Listen for the return of the vocalist for the third verse and the shift back to the "home" harmony.
1'26"	Listen for the aural focus returning to the instruments.
1'34"	Listen for the return of the secondary melodic harmonic material.

Source: "La talle des ronces," performed by Adam and Cyprien Landreneau and Dewey Balfa, from the recording entitled *Louisiana Cajun from the Southwest Prairies. Recorded 1964–1967, Volume 2*, Rounder 6002, 1989. Used by permission.

ETHNO-CHALLENGE (CD 3.26): Play the triangle's rhythmic pattern throughout the performance.

CREOLE
A term referring to populations of French descent that are found in the southern United States, primarily Louisiana.

Cultural Considerations. The term *Cajun* is a shortened colloquial form of *Acadian*, a word referring to the French settlers who first migrated to Atlantic Canada in 1605. Caught in the wrangling between the French and English during the seventeenth and eighteenth centuries, they were forcibly deported, starting in 1755, and scattered south to various places, including Louisiana, which was then still a French colony. Although many of the French returned to Canada during the later eighteenth century, several thousand who had gone to Louisiana remained there. Louisiana was also home to French-speaking peoples of African or mixed ancestry who came from the French islands of the Caribbean. Today the latter are called **Creoles**, though the term once referred to all French speakers. The Cajun community is concentrated in southwestern Louisiana from Lafayette westward to the Texas border.

The older and more traditional context for Cajun music and dancing was the home, where parties called *bals de maison* (house dances) were held. Visitors to Cajun country are now more likely to encounter the music on Saturday nights in public dancehalls. These dancehalls are called *do-do*, which means "go to sleep"—something parents probably said

CANADA AND THE UNITED STATES

Louisiana Cajun music played at a National Folk Festival

Cajun button-box accordion and player from Louisiana (Jack Vartoogian/ FrontRow Photos)

Cajun accordion (Shutterstock)

to their children before going to the dance. There, ordinary folks danced a great variety of styles, at least in the past—today, waltzes and two-steps predominate.

In the early days, long before accordions were available and before people could afford fiddles, Cajuns sometimes danced to wordless vocal melodies called *reels à bouche*, similar to the *peurt a beul* of the Gaelic Scottish of Cape Breton, Nova Scotia. Eventually, the presence of one or two fiddles became usual. After contact with German settlers, Cajuns absorbed the diatonic, single-row button box accordion, now the signature Cajun instrument. Contemporary Cajun music has also added electrical amplification, guitar, bass, and drums. At the same time, old-fashioned acoustic Cajun music has enjoyed a revival, because of tourism and the rise of folk festivals in the 1960s.

ZYDECO
Creole dance music that blends African-American styles with *Cajun* styles from the southern United States, primarily Louisiana.

The Creoles had much in common with the white Cajuns, and their music was sometimes indistinguishable from that of the Acadian French. But over time they blended elements from the Caribbean, of both African and Spanish origin, into their music. Since their parties were called *la la* or **zydeco**, the latter term came to denote the music of Creole Cajuns. Today's *zydeco* also shows influence from blues and even rock. While they use the same instruments as their white brethren, Creoles are more likely to add a metal washboard, called *frottoir*, which is played with thimbles, bottle openers, or other kitchen utensils.

Arrival: Native American Reservations

Many Americans would be surprised to learn that Native American (also, American Indian) reservations are found in more than half of the states of the U.S.A. Though the best-known reservations are found in southwestern states, primarily Arizona and New Mexico, there are significant reservations throughout the country, including the east and southeast. While many Native Americans choose to live on these reservations, more than two-thirds of the roughly nine million Native Americans in North America live elsewhere. Indeed, because of intermarriage with Anglo Americans and African Americans, many Native Americans are actually of mixed ancestry, have Anglo names, and live as the mainstream population does. The stereotypes of the old "Western" films resemble in no way modern Native American life.

The American Indian population is the most diverse ethnic "group" in North America. Though unified by their Native American ethnicity, their cultural practices vary greatly. Distinctions in Native American dress, subsistence patterns, spiritual beliefs, marriage customs, language, kinship systems, and so on, have intrigued anthropologists and linguists since the start of their respective disciplines. The earliest ethnomusicologists (1890–1930s) in the United States focused much of their attention on Native American musical traditions. With more than three hundred different tribes throughout North America, the research produced in the last one hundred years, while extensive, is still far from complete.

Scholars generally identify nine primary culture areas among the Native Americans of the United States, Canada, and northern Mexico: Southeast, Southwest, Plains, Plateau and Basin, California, Northwest Coast, Subarctic, Arctic, and Northeast.

Though a great variety of musical activity occurs throughout these regions, there are several qualified generalizations that can be made about most Native American music traditions. The foremost characteristic of Native American music is the use of the voice as the primary focus of performance. While instrumental traditions exist, vocal solos and group singing are most frequent in both spiritual and secular contexts. The use of **vocables** or non-lexical (untranslatable) syllables, such as *yaa, heh, daa, weh,* and so on, is common in many traditions. Vocables are often believed to hold a secret meaning that enables the performer to communicate with the spirit world. Drums and rattles are the most common instruments used to accompany the voice.

VOCABLES
Words considered only with regards to sound, not in terms of meaning.

Musical performance, even in secular contexts, usually has a spiritual or symbolic significance for the musicians. Many songs are believed to have been taught by spirits and animals through dreams and by other means. Nature is often an inspiration for songs, and many songs are intended to honor and respect the environment. Other songs relate the history of a community or great deeds of warriors from the past. The myths and legends of a tribe are passed on through song, and frequently music plays an important role in male–female relationships and courting rituals. Practically all traditional music is passed on orally from generation to generation.

Though Native American musical practices are quite diverse, we will focus on two distinct styles of performance. Both styles have become quite visible to the general public in the past few decades. First, the Plains Indian style is typical of singing practices originating among American Indian populations of the Midwest. It is the source for many of the musical traditions presented at Native American powwows, now the most common pan-tribal event found throughout the United States. The second style is represented by a courting song performed on the Native American flute by a Zuni musician from the Taos Pueblo region of the southwestern United States. This music has recently become closely associated with the "New Age" movement that has flourished since the 1980s.

Site 11: Plains Indian Dance Song

First Impressions. The striking features of this Plains Indian musical performance are the tense warble of the vocalists and the steady pounding drum sound, which almost seems to telegraph a message.

Aural Analysis. As with most Native American music, the voice is the focus of Plains Indian music performance. The singing style is chant-like, with a distinctive "cascading" or "terraced" melodic contour, which starts high and remains primarily on one pitch before falling to successively lower pitch levels. The range between the starting pitch of a phrase and the closing pitch is wide in the Plains style. Vocal pulsation, in which a periodic slight increase in volume is used to create rhythmic accents, is common, especially when vocables are sung. This pulsation creates a warbling sound on a single pitch but is not considered melisma, because melisma requires more than one pitch per syllable.

Vocal timbre varies among performers, but a strained sound is often desirable in the Plains singing style. Some practitioners will gently press on their throat to tighten the vocal cords in order to produce the preferred sound. This tense timbre is most strongly associated with the vocable sections, when the clear articulation is less important. During the translatable sections of performance, a tense voice and vocal pulsation is less noticeable as the extended vowels are fewer and the emphasis is on the text itself rather than the singing style. Group performances in the Plains style usually feature a leader who begins a vocal phrase and is followed shortly thereafter by the other voices, who either enter at the end of the

Located in northern Arizona, "Montezuma's Castle" is the best-preserved cliff dwelling in America. Consisting of twenty rooms, it was built by the Sinagua Indians around 1,000 years ago

leader's initial call or overlap the lead voice to complete the phrase. Group singing is most prominent during vocable sections, while the leader may either sing the translatable sections as solos or with the group.

A large double-sided frame drum is the most common instrument found in Plains group performances. The instrument can be round or edged, even sometimes square or octagonal. The drum is placed on a stand with one face upward. The drummers sit around the drum and strike the face with padded mallets. The beat is steady, often with an unequal (short–long) rhythm that imitates the sound of a heartbeat, symbolic of Mother Earth. The accents of the vocal pulsation and of the drum do not necessarily correspond, creating a polyrhythmic interaction.

LISTENING GUIDE CD 3.27 (1'34")

Chapter 13: Site 11

United States of America: Plains Indian Dance Song

Vocals: Male ensemble
Instruments: Double-sided frame drum (membranophone)

TIME	LISTENING FOCUS
0'00"	Listen for a single male beginning the performance with non-lexical lyrical content. Note the consistent "heartbeat" rhythm of the drum and the high range of the vocalist focusing on a single pitch (F).
0'04"	Listen for the descending pitch range of the lead vocalist, emphasizing two middle pitches (C, then B). Note that other vocalists join the lead performer.
0'10"	Listen for the descending pitch range of the lead vocalist, focusing on a low-range pitch (F).
0'19"	Listen for the single accent on the drum as the vocalists shift to singing lexical text beginning in a middle range and descending to a lower range. Note that the drum quiets its volume during the sung text.
0'27"	Listen for the drum's increase in volume.
0'33"	Listen for the return of non-lexical text and the melodic contour's return to the high range of pitches.
0'53"	Listen for the single accent on the drum as the vocalists again shift to singing lexical text.
1'00"	Listen for the drum's increase in volume.
1'06"	Listen for the return of non-lexical text and the melodic contour's return to the high range of pitches.
1'24"	Listen for the vocalists again shifting to singing lexical text as the example fades.

Source: "Rock Dance Song" performed by The Pembina Chippewa Singers. Recorded by Nicholas Curchin Peterson Vrooman, Turtle Mountain, North Dakota, 1984, from the recording entitled *Plains Chippewa/Metis Music from Turtle Mountain*, SF 40411, provided courtesy of Smithsonian Folkways Recordings. © 1992. Used by permission.

WORLD MUSIC: A GLOBAL JOURNEY

> **ETHNO-CHALLENGE (CD 3.27):** Diagram the melodic contour of the example. If possible, attend a powwow event in your local area.

POWWOW

A pan-tribal American Indian event celebrating Native American identity and culture, generally also open to non-Native Americans.

Cultural Considerations. The Native American group activity most open to the general public is the **powwow**. The modern powwow is a pan-tribal event central to maintaining the cultural identity of American Indians throughout North America. Public powwows are much like outdoor fairs. While music and dance performances are the central activity, there are also vendors selling jewelry, crafts, instruments, clothes, books, food, and so on. For non-Native Americans, powwows are the most available opportunity to experience Native American culture.

The powwow was created by several Plains Indian tribes in the mid-1800s. During this period, the influx of white settlers into the Midwest was contributing to the decline of traditional Native spiritual, social, political, and economic practices. At the same time, intertribal warfare had become greatly curtailed, because all tribes were threatened equally by the American military. As Native American populations dwindled, many groups were forced to resettle among other culturally distinct tribes.

The powwow events were created in response to these developments. They became a means of reinforcing the unity and strength of Native American culture in order to ensure its survival. The many social differences among tribes were acknowledged but were made

A typical inter-tribal powwow. The drum circle in the foreground provides the accompaniment for the dancers behind them

Typical of a powwow, dancers representing many tribes join together to celebrate their Native American heritage (Andrew Shahriari)

secondary to the Native American identity shared by all. The events have changed over the years, but since the 1950s they have functioned primarily as a means of honoring and expressing Native American identity within and outside the American Indian community. Powwows usually last between one and four days. The public events can be held outdoors or indoors, in parks, on college campuses, in gymnasiums, or in conference centers. Most are minimally advertised, and, as public events, are often free. Though variations in the proceedings occur, a powwow typically begins with a "Grand Entry" parade led by flag-bearers representing the participating tribes. These marchers are then followed by dancers, respected elders and tribal chiefs, and children.

Music and dance are the main focus of powwow events. Each tribe displays its unique traditions through regalia and performance. Intertribal dances are also common, usually using a basic toe-to-heel dance step that corresponds to the beat of the drum. The Plains style of singing is the most common musical accompaniment for these dances. Non-natives are sometimes encouraged to participate in these dances as well.

Other group dances also encourage intertribal participation. Social dances are common, such as the Round Dance, which is performed in a circle and based on a basic side-step motion. In Rabbit Dances, male and female dancers hold hands or interlock their arms as they dance to a love song and the beat of the drum. Contest dancing is a more specialized but important activity in which dancers competing for prizes and prestige dress in elaborate regalia with sophisticated symbolic meanings. The most successful of these dancers often perform outside the powwow context to earn a living, doing concerts and workshops around the United States and internationally.

Site 12: Native American Flute

First Impressions. If the sound of the Plains Indian drum is symbolic of Mother Earth, then the sound of the Native American flute represents the wind. This is the sound of sublime solitude, an escape from the hectic life of the city into a peaceful unity with nature.

Aural Analysis. Native American flute performance is one of the few solo instrumental traditions found among Native American peoples. Vertically blown flutes are more common than side-blown or transverse flutes and are made from soft woods such as cedar or other geographically available woods and materials such as bone, reed, clay, and metal.

While each flute is considered unique, the type that has become most popular is modeled after the courting flutes used by Plains tribes, which have five or six fingerstops or fingerholes that, when opened and closed, produce a melody. This flute is distinctive for its "bird," "block," or "saddle" ornament, which is tied firmly on to the sound-producing mechanism located just below the mouthpiece or blow-hole. This ornament is vital to the sound production as it channels the air flow across an edge to create the sound vibrations.

R. Carlos Nakai, Navajo/Ute, plays a Native American flute (Courtesy of Canyon Records; Photo by John Running)

CANADA AND THE UNITED STATES

Today, there are many genres of music incorporating the Native American flute, from solo works, to ambient, to classical, to jazz, to world fusion musical styles, as well as so-called "New Age," a marketing label applied to many modernized indigenous music traditions from around the world. Solo recordings frequently make use of nature sounds and "canyon" sound effects to emulate how the Native American flute may have sounded in its traditional context. The effect creates a "distant," transcendent sound as if the music were echoing through a great canyon.

While the music does not always follow an articulated steady beat, clear melodic phrases are the norm. Native American flute music in a solo context exhibits an indirect beat that may be felt rather than heard. Melodic ornamentation or embellishment techniques are varied among flute performers and are often dependent upon whether the music is traditional or contemporary in nature, as well as the cultural, social, and song-type contexts. A few of the ornamental techniques that may be heard within Native American flute music include trills, mordants, pitch bending, flutter tonguing, and the characteristic "pop" (quick ascending pitch) that is used to indicate the conclusion of a phrase, a sub-phrase, or the song itself. Vibrato (wavering of the pitch) is often heard on sustained tones. Most compositions use a scale of between five and seven pitches, with a range of little more than an octave. Overtones are not commonly used, though special effects are sometimes employed to imitate the sounds of birds or natural elements, such as the wind. Typical solo Native American flute music is quiet, with little dynamic variation.

LISTENING GUIDE

CD 3.28 (0'52")

Chapter 13: Site 12
United States of America: Native American Flute

Vocals: Male ensemble
Instruments: End-blown flute (aerophone)

TIME	LISTENING FOCUS
0'00"	Listen for the "breathy" timbre and "distant" reverberation of the flute. Note that the performance is in free rhythm, with each melodic phrase following its own sense of timing.
0'22"	Listen for a return to emphasis on the initial pitch (A). Note that the return to this "musical thought" is followed by entirely new melodic material.
0'47"	Listen for the closing pitch and the extended reverberation that follows.

Source: "Courting Song" performed by John Rainer, Jr., from the recording entitled *Music of New Mexico: Native American Traditions*, SF 40408, provided courtesy of Smithsonian Folkways Recordings. © 1992. Used by permission

ETHNO-CHALLENGE (CD 3.28): Transcribe this performance using numeral or staff notation.

Cultural Considerations. The flute is the most widespread melodic instrument found in Native American culture. The Plains Indian vertically held flute type has become most popular in the modern era but is only one of many types. The vertically held flute made of wood is the most common, since the resurgence of interest in American Indian flute traditions that began in the 1970s.

The renaissance of the Native American flute was brought about in particular by two people: Dr. Richard W. Payne, a physician from Oklahoma, and Doc Tate Nevaquaya, a Comanche visual artist, flute maker, and flute player. Throughout his life, Payne encouraged the playing and making of the flute among the Native American peoples, including Nevaquaya. Among the notable Native American flutists who play or played music in the traditional style, such as John Rainer, Jr.'s "Taos Pueblo Courting Song," include: Doc Tate Nevaquaya (Comanche), Belo Cozad (Kiowa), Kevin Locke (Lakota), Dan Red Buffalo (Lakota), Richard Foolbull (Lakota), Woodrow Haney (Seminole), and Tom Mauchahty-Ware (Kiowa/Comanche). Especially important in the renewed interest in flute making and playing was R. Carlos Nakai, who brought the Native American flute into the mainstream with his pivotal recording, *Canyon Trilogy*. Of Navajo-Ute heritage, and considered the premier performer of the Native American flute, Nakai is credited with creating a significant surge of worldwide interest in the Native American flute with his profound solo flute creations and his innovative cross-cultural, cross-genre musical collaborations with some of the world's finest musical artists.

This revival of interest has spurred much debate within Native American communities, as many who now play the flute are not of Native American ancestry. Flute circles and social clubs of Native American flute enthusiasts are increasingly popular and open to anyone. The premier Native American flute organization is the International Native American Flute Association (INAFA) whose goal is to foster the preservation, appreciation, and advancement of the Native American flute. Many Native Americans, such as R. Carlos Nakai, a co-founder of INAFA, support these organizations, taking the attitude that the instrument and its music are not the exclusive property of Native Americans but are to be shared with everyone. Others

Detail showing "bird block" on a Native American flute (Courtesy of Canyon Records; Photo by John Running)

take an opposing stance, asserting that the music has a sacred dimension and cultural value and thus is only appropriately performed by Native Americans.

Traditionally, among the Plains people, the flute was primarily used in courting rituals. Love songs were performed on the flute, which substituted for the voice. This usage dwindled to near non-existence by the end of the nineteenth century and is little practiced today. Another important context was storytelling. Often an elder would tell a story that ended with a moral, much like Aesop's fables in the Western tradition. When the story was finished, the storyteller would play the flute while the listeners reflected on the meaning of the story.

The main characters of these stories are often animals or natural elements, reflecting the importance that the environment plays in the cultural, social and spiritual lives of the Native American people. Native Americans believe that humans can learn much from their surroundings if they only pay attention. The "bird" ornament on the top of the flute is an example of the symbiotic relationship between people and nature, since Plains mythology states that the woodpecker is responsible for giving/gifting the flute to the people. Today, the Native American flute is frequently sold at powwow events, flute gatherings/festivals, and on the Internet, and it has become broadly representative of Native American musical identity.

Explore More

Inuit Throat-Singing

One of the more interesting vocal traditions to surface in recent decades is Inuit throat-singing. The Inuit, often referred to as Eskimos, live in several arctic areas of North America. Though modernization has considerably changed the Inuit lifestyle, hunting and fishing are still the primary means of subsistence as they have been for centuries. In the past, hunting expeditions would often last for more than a month. Throat-singing developed among the women of the Inuit communities as a means of entertainment during the long absences of the men.

Throat-singing among the Inuit (in contrast to the "two-tone" throat-singing found in Mongolia and elsewhere) is characterized by its deep, breathy sounds and rhythmically dense performance technique. Two women (sometimes four) face each other at a close distance, typically holding each other's arms. One woman leads while the other follows. The lead voice establishes a short, fast-paced rhythmic phrase, and the second voice is expected to interlock with this phrase in the gaps between the sounds. The performance is considered a kind of game. The first person who runs out of breath or who cannot keep pace with the other loses. Good performers will subtly change the rhythm of their phrases.

Many variations of the throat-singing style are found throughout Canada, the most commonly known type being *katajjaq* (pronounced "kawta-jock") from northern Quebec. In this style, the performers frequently imitate the sounds of nature and everyday life, such as the barking of dogs, the whistling of wind, or the buzzing of insects. For many years this tradition was strongly discouraged by Christian missionaries, but it is again finding popularity among the Inuit youth, who consider throat-singing an important means by which to express their cultural identity.

Questions to Consider

1. What is "American" music and what differentiates it from European or African music?
2. How does music from the British Isles underlie music surviving today in the United States and Canada?
3. Compare and contrast the performance of "lined" hymns and "shape-note" singing. What makes these types of music especially archaic?
4. How have Protestant Christian values influenced music in the United States?
5. Compare and contrast African-American spirituals and gospel music. What elements of each might reflect the African heritage of their creators?
6. How does blues music express the social conditions of African Americans in the United States?
7. Discuss the relationships and differences between the Cuban *son* (see Chapter 11, Site 6) and North American *salsa*.
8. How have the powwow and the Native American flute shaped the outsider's view of Native American culture?

On Your Own Time

Visit the textbook website to find these resources for further exploration on your own.

Canada

Website: Cape Breton Fiddlers
http://www.capebretonfiddlers.com/

Website: Cape Breton Fiddle Recordings
http://www.cbfiddle.com/rx/index.html

Website: Celtic Music Centre
http://www.celticmusiccentre.com/

Website: Cape Breton Live Radio
http://www.capebretonlive.com/news-old.htm

Internet: Popular Artists from Cape Breton Fiddling
Buddy MacMaster
Natalie MacMaster
Ashley MacIsaac
The Glengarry Bhoys
Jerry Holland

The United States of America

Ballads

Audio: *Jean Ritchie: Ballads from her Appalachian Family Tradition.* Smithsonian-Folkways: SFW40145, 2003.
 http://www.folkways.si.edu/albumdetails.aspx?itemid=2969
 http://itunes.apple.com/us/album/jean-ritchie-ballads-from/id82497122

Website: Child Ballads (Lyrics and Tunes)
 http://www.contemplator.com/child/index.html

Book: Child, Francis James. *The English and Scottish Popular Ballads, Vol. 1 of 5: The Child Ballads.* Charleston, SC: Forgotten Books, 2007.
 http://www.forgottenbooks.org/ (Search Child Ballads)

Website: English Folk Dance and Song Society
 http://www.efdss.org/

Website: English Folksongs from the Southern Appalachians
 http://www.traditionalmusic.co.uk/english-folk-songs/

Internet: Popular Artists from Appalachia (Ballads)
 Hedy West
 Jean Ritchie
 Appalachian Karma
 Appalachian Celtic Consort

Lined Hymnody and Shape-Note Singing

Audio: Indian Bottom Association. *Old Regular Baptists: Lined-Out Hymnody from Southeastern Kentucky.* Smithsonian Folkways: SFW40106, 1997.
 http://www.folkways.si.edu/albumdetails.aspx?itemid=2653
 http://itunes.apple.com/us/album/old-regular-baptists-lined/id118382349

Book: Dorgan, Howard. *The Old Regular Baptists of Central Appalachia: Brothers and Sisters in Hope.* Knoxville, TN: University of Tennessee Press, 2001.
 http://utpress.org/bookdetail-2/?jobno=T00085.01.01

Website: Encyclopedia of Appalachia
 http://utpress.org/Appalachia/

Website: Old Regular Baptist Churches
 http://pages.suddenlink.net/orb/orb/index.htm

Website: Singing Traditions of the Primitive and Regular Baptists in Appalachia
 http://www.library.appstate.edu/appcoll/research_aids/chogue.html

Website: Sacred Harp & Related Shape-Note Music
 http://www.mcsr.olemiss.edu/~mudws/resource/

Book: Cobb, Jr., Buell E. *The Sacred Harp: A Tradition and Its Music.* Athens, GA: University of Georgia Press, 2004.
 http://www.ugapress.org/index.php/books/sacred_harp/

Book: Eastburn, Kathryn. *A Sacred Feast: Reflections on Sacred Harp Singing and Dinner on thè Ground.* Lincoln, NE: University of Nebraska Press, 2008.
 http://www.nebraskapress.unl.edu/product/Sacred-Feast,673390.aspx

Website: Sacred Harp Musical Heritage Association
 http://fasola.org/

Website: The Sacred Harp Publishing Company
http://originalsacredharp.com/

Audio: *Fasola: Fifty-three Shape Note Folk Hymns: All Day Sacred Harp Singing at Stewart's Chapel in Houston, Mississippi.* Smithsonian Folkways: FW04151, 1970.
http://www.folkways.si.edu/albumdetails.aspx?itemid=685

Internet: Popular Artists from Appalachia (Lined Hymn & Shape-Note)
Tim Eriksen
Social Harp
Sacred Harp Singers
Word of Mouth Chorus
United Sacred Harp Musical Association

Bluegrass

Book: Rosenberg, Neil V. *Bluegrass: A History (20th Anniversary Edition).* Champaign, IL: University of Illinois Press, 2005.
http://www.press.uillinois.edu/books/catalog/35pyc6pm9780252072451.html

Book: Rosenberg, Neil V., and Charles K. Wolfe. *The Music of Bill Monroe.* Champaign, IL: University of Illinois Press, 2007.
http://www.press.uillinois.edu/books/catalog/66aqb3ty9780252031212.html

Website: Old Time Music
http://www.oldtimemusic.com/

Website: International Bluegrass Music Association
http://www.ibma.org/

Website: International Bluegrass Museum
http://www.bluegrass-museum.org/general/home.php

Website: Society for the Preservation of Bluegrass Music of America
http://www.spbgma.com/

Audio: *Classic Bluegrass from Smithsonian Folkways.* Smithsonian Folkways: SFW40092, 2002.
http://www.folkways.si.edu/albumdetails.aspx?itemid=2806
http://itunes.apple.com/us/album/classic-bluegrass-from-smithsonian/id261154690

Internet: Popular Artists from Bluegrass
Bill Monroe
Earl Scruggs
Doc Watson
Ralph Stanley
Alison Krauss
Ricky Skaggs
Lester Flatt
Béla Fleck

African-American Spirituals and Gospel

Audio: *Wade in the Water: African-American Sacred Music Traditions.* Smithsonian Folkways: SFW40076, 1996.
http://www.folkways.si.edu/albumdetails.aspx?itemid=3043

Audio: *Been in the Storm So Long: A Collection of Spirituals, Folk Tales and Children's Games from Johns Island, SC.* Smithsonian Folkways: SFW40031, 1990.
http://www.folkways.si.edu/albumdetails.aspx?itemid=2060
http://itunes.apple.com/us/album/been-in-storm-so-long-a-collection/id260727493

Audio: *Classic African American Gospel from Smithsonian Folkways*. Smithsonian Folkways: SFW40194, 2008.
http://www.folkways.si.edu/albumdetails.aspx?itemid=3201
http://itunes.apple.com/us/album/classic-african-american-gospel/id272149140

Audio: *In Him I Live - The Church of God and Saints of Christ*. Lyrichord: LYRCD7423, 1995.
http://lyrichord.com/inhimilive-thechurchofgodandsaintsofchrist.aspx
http://itunes.apple.com/us/album/church-god-saints-christ-in/id49304262

Book: Young, Alan. *Woke Me Up This Morning? Black Gospel Singers and the Gospel Life*. Jackson, MS: University of Mississippi, 1997.
http://www.upress.state.ms.us/books/815

Book: Boyer, Horace Clarence, and Lloyd Yearwood. *The Golden Age of Gospel*. Champaign, IL: University of Illinois Press, 2000.
http://www.press.uillinois.edu/books/catalog/62amk2pf9780252068775.html

Website: Negro Spirituals
http://www.negrospirituals.com/

Website: Sweet Chariot—The Story of Spirituals
http://ctl.du.edu/spirituals/

Website: Black Gospel
http://www.blackgospel.com/

Website: Gospel Music Workshop of America
http://www.gmwanational.net/

Website: Gospel Music Hall of Fame
http://www.gmahalloffame.org/site/

Internet: Popular Artists from African-American Spirituals and Gospel music
Mahalia Jackson
Sister Rosetta Tharpe
The Staples Singers
Aretha Franklin
Marvin Sapp
Yolanda Adams
Fairfield Four
The Winans

Country Blues

Book: Oliver, Paul. *The Blues Fell this Morning*. New York: Cambridge University Press, 1990.
http://www.cambridge.org/gb/knowledge/isbn/item1138125/?site_locale=en_GB

Book: Palmer, Robert. *Deep Blues: A Musical and Cultural History of the Mississippi Delta*. New York: Penguin Books, 1982.
http://us.penguingroup.com/nf/Book/BookDisplay/0,,9780140062236,00.html?Deep_Blues_Robert_Palmer

DVD: *In Search of Robert Johnson*. Dir. Chris Hunt. Sony Music, 1992.
http://www.imdb.com/title/tt0272834/

Audio: *Robert Johnson: The Complete Recordings*. Legacy Recordings (Sony/BMG Music), 1990.
http://en.wikipedia.org/wiki/The_Complete_Recordings_(Robert_Johnson_album)

Book: Lomax, Alan. *The Land Where the Blues Began*. New York: Pantheon, 1993.
http://culturalequity.org/alanlomax/ce_alanlomax_books.php

DVD: *The Blues*. Dir. Martin Scorsese PBS (Public Broadcasting System), 2003.
http://www.pbs.org/theblues/

Website: The Country Blues
http://www.thecountryblues.com/

Internet: Popular Artists from Country Blues
- Robert Johnson
- Charley Patton
- Son House
- Big Bill Broonzy
- Blind Lemon Jefferson
- Blind Willie McTell
- Blind Blake
- Skip James
- Blind Willie Johnson
- Lightnin' Hopkins
- Mississippi John Hurt
- Keb' Mo'
- Chris Thomas King

Salsa

Book: Washburne, Christopher. *Sounding Salsa: Performing Latin Music in New York City*. Philadelphia, PA: Temple University Press, 2008.
http://www.temple.edu/tempress/titles/1557_reg.html

Book: Waxer, Lisa. *Situating Salsa: Global Markets and Local Meanings in Latin Popular Music*. New York: Routledge, 2002.
http://www.routledge.com/books/details/9780815340201/

Book: Aparicio, Frances. *Listening to Salsa: Gender, Latin Popular Music, and Puerto Rican Cultures*. Middletown, CT: Wesleyan University Press, 1998.
http://www.upne.com/0-8195-5306-9.html

DVD: *Latin Music USA*. Dir. Pamela A. Aguilar and Daniel McCabe. PBS (Public Broadcasting System), 2009.
http://www.pbs.org/wgbh/latinmusicusa/#/en/hom

Website: Brown Planet—Musica Latina Fansite
http://www.brownplanet.com/

Internet: Popular Artists from Salsa
- Tito Puente
- Celia Cruz
- Arsenio Rodríguez
- Rubén Blades
- La India
- Oscar D'León
- Marc Anthony
- Fania All-Stars
- Eddie Palmieri
- Willie Colón
- Héctor Lavoe
- Johnny Pacheco

Cajun Music
Book: Kilpatrick, Blaire. *Accordion Dreams: A Journey into Cajun and Creole Music.* Jackson, MS: University of Mississippi Press, 2009.
http://www.upress.state.ms.us/books/1120

Book: Bernard, Shane. *Swamp Pop: Cajun and Creole Rhythm and Blues.* Jackson, MS: University of Mississippi Press, 1996.
http://www.upress.state.ms.us/books/715

Book: Brasseaux, Ryan André. *Cajun Breakdown: The Emergence of an American-Made Music.* New York: Oxford University Press, 2009.
http://www.oup.com/us/catalog/general/subject/Music/MusicHistoryAmerican/?view=usa&ci=9780195343069

Website: Cajun Music Hall of Fame
http://web.lsue.edu/acadgate/cajunmus.htm

Website: The Cajun French Music Association
http://www.cajunfrenchmusic.org/

Internet: Popular Artists from Cajun Music
Doug Kershaw
BeauSoleil
Geno Delafose
Clifton Cheneir
Balfa Brothers

Native American Music
Book: Browner, Tara, ed. *Music of the First Nations: Tradition and Innovation in Native North America.* Champaign, IL: University of Illinois Press, 2009.
http://www.press.uillinois.edu/books/catalog/55rxe7np9780252022210.html

Book: Browner, Tara. *Heartbeat of the People: Music and Dance of the Northern Pow-wow.* Champaign, IL: University of Illinois Press, 2009.
http://www.press.uillinois.edu/books/catalog/37cqb5fn9780252071867.html

Website: Powwows.com
http://www.powwows.com/

Website: Native American Music Awards
http://www.nativeamericanmusicawards.com/home.cfm

Website: Canyon Records
http://www.canyonrecords.com/

Website: International Native American and World Flute Association
http://worldflutes.org/

Website: Flutopedia
http://www.Flutopedia.com/contents.htm

Book: Stern, Pamela, and Lisa Stevenson. *Critical Inuit Studies: An Anthology of Contemporary Arctic Ethnography.* Lincoln, NE: University of Nebraska Press, 2006.
http://www.nebraskapress.unl.edu/product/Critical-Inuit-Studies,671852.aspx

Website: Inuit Gallery of Vancouver
http://www.inuit.com/

Website: Inuit Throat Singing
http://www.ubu.com/ethno/soundings/inuit.html

Online Video: Inuit Throat Singing Demonstration. Smithsonian-Folkways, 2004.
http://itunes.apple.com/WebObjects/MZStore.woa/wa/viewPodcast?id=402451316

Audio: *Heartbeat 2: More Voices of First Nation Women.* Smithsonian-Folkways: SFW40455, 1998.
http://www.folkways.si.edu/albumdetails.aspx?itemid=2423
http://itunes.apple.com/us/album/humma-ha-ba-ba/id151048359?i=151048808

Internet: Popular Artists from Native American Music
Robbie Robertson
Buffy Saint Marie
Martha Redbone
Verdell Primeaux and Johnny Mike
Red Earth
R. Carlos Nakai
Kevin Locke
Joseph Firecrow

Discovering Yourself Through Music   14

Up to this point, you have been listening to the music of *other* people in places mostly outside your own life and experience. Now is the moment to realize that *your* life is also bound up with music, that you are as "traditional" a person as any found in this book, and that your music, be it rap, ragtime, or Rachmaninoff, resonates within the larger culture in which you live. This chapter is offered as a guide to self-exploration through music. It introduces the techniques and tools used by ethnomusicologists to study music cultures. These same tools can easily by adopted by you to study your own musical traditions.

The chapter is divided into three sections: (1) music and self-identity; (2) researching your musical roots;, and (3) disseminating your findings. Essentially, these three steps are those followed by ethnomusicologists in researching any of the world's musics. The first step is conceptual, the second is the active fieldwork phase of collecting material, and the third involves sharing insights with a larger community. We suggest that you try out these three steps in your classroom or on your own, treating the first step as an extended research paper, the second as a project in field documentation, and the third as a live presentation for class (or another public forum) and/or as a possible publication.

Music and Self-Identity

At its core, identity is self-awareness. Self-awareness develops over time—indeed, infants do not initially have a sense of themselves separate from their mothers or their general surroundings. In addition to a personal identity, a child develops a social identity shaped by his or her socio-cultural environment. Interactions with others help the child understand the social categories or "groups" to which he or she belongs. This belonging is determined partly by biological factors, such as race and sex, but is largely determined by socio-cultural factors like religion, language, gender, economics, and politics.

Most people are unaware of how these social and personal identities are manifested through their behaviors in daily activities. When you wake up in the morning and put on a pair of jeans and a T-shirt, you may think nothing of it, but this simple act says a lot about the kind of person you are as well as your cultural upbringing. The same can be said for music. The kind of music that you listen to says much about the type of person you are and your cultural background. Music, as much as anything else, is a manifestation of the personal and social identities of an individual or group. The function of the music, its structure, and the context in which it is performed all reveal significant information about social values. Music reflects a community's identity and expresses "who they are." Essentially, what we have striven to do throughout this text is to "get to know" other people through their music.

But who are *we*? Turning the tables and trying to figure out how music reflects who we are is also important. Though our global journey has taken us to many places, we cannot realistically say that our chosen "sites" represent the music of all peoples of the planet. Our few selections represent only the kinds of music that stand out, to us, as most significant to the personal and social identities of the people who live in those regions. In addition to being choices made from our own subjective perspectives, the selections are limited in many other ways, too. The handful of examples that we have from India, for example, do not necessarily represent the types of music listened to by the majority of the Indian population. However, if you were to meet someone from India and ask, "What is Indian music?," our examples would easily qualify as appropriate representations of Indian culture to the outside world. Indian self-identity, both personal and social, is in part expressed through this music.

Let's look at American music as one expression of self-identity. If you are an American, what one example would you choose to reflect your "American" identity? Does rap define who we are as Americans? Britney Spears? Garth Brooks? Does the music of Mozart and Beethoven represent us, even though its origin is European? How about jazz? What kind of jazz? Which performer and from what style period? Defining "American" identity through one example of music is impossible, yet in this textbook (as in any other) we have only enough pages to focus on a few examples from countries often much larger than the United States, and frequently with histories much longer than our meager 230 or so years. Yet, through just a few music examples, the spiritual beliefs, political philosophies, moral values, attitudes, and activities of many aspects of life are revealed. No doubt, we are able to learn something about the people of other cultures and gain a greater understanding of who they are by studying their musical traditions. We can do the same by examining our own musical expressions.

So, how does music express your self-identity? Ask yourself some questions: What music do I like to listen to? What music do I like to perform (whether you are a musician playing for an audience or just singing to yourself in the shower)? Why does that music appeal to me? How does this music reflect me personally, my philosophy of life, my goals and desires, my spiritual beliefs, my personal history and life experiences? How does the music I enjoy reflect my social identity—that is, the friends I have, the organizations I belong to, the activities in which I participate? What does this music say about my cultural upbringing as an American? What stereotypes does it suggest about my personality and behaviors? Start with some of these questions and then try to pick one example that most accurately expresses all the facets of your self-identity. You will likely find this to be quite difficult. Trying to pick just one example to say to the outside world, "this is me," is a challenge for most. If it is for you, a little research may be in order.

Researching Your Musical Roots

Having situated yourself in a social context that ranges from being a Westerner, to being American/Canadian/British/South African/Chinese or whatever, to being a part of something much closer to home, it is time to ask what kinds of music express your own life and the lives of those around you, be they family members or friends. Sorting this out requires what we call *fieldwork*. Fieldwork is essentially the process of going into the environment in which a specific music normally occurs in order to observe musical activities and question individuals with knowledge of the tradition under study. **Fieldwork** is a method for studying music that is employed by ethnomusicologists wherever they work. It may include any or all of the following: (1) being an observer or participant-observer; (2) audio recording; (3) video recording; (4) still photography; (5) interviewing; (6) exploring the Internet, and (7) collecting and archiving of materials, be they instruments, books, recordings, or any other kind of memorabilia.

FIELDWORK
The study of cultural activity (e.g., music) in its normal human context.

Observation and Participant-Observation. Typically, a researcher observes musical activity from the sidelines, sometimes documenting it, sometimes merely absorbing impressions. Sometimes it may also be appropriate for the researcher to join in an activity, by learning to play an instrument, by dancing, or by singing. When you join in, you become what is called a *participant-observer*. In those circumstances, it is important for the researcher to maintain as much objective distance as possible. The researcher and the researched cannot become one, especially in the case of forays into religions.

Audio Recording. The equipment for making field recordings has changed dramatically over the last thirty years, having gone from analog recording—first on reel-to-reel tape, then on cassette—to digital recording on a variety of media. When one of the present authors (TM) began making field recordings in 1970, for example, stereo reel-to-reel tape recorders with twin microphones for stereo sound were considered state-of-the-art technology. After about 1980 audio-cassettes became the norm, and reel-to-reel recording retreated to the recording studio. Because they were much smaller and lighter, and the media (cassettes) were also small, cassette recorders were a great improvement on reel-to-reel. The costs came down too. A top-of-the-line Swiss reel-to-reel recorder cost $10,000 in 1970, while a comparable cassette machine cost less than $500 in the early 1980s. In the field, the lighter and simpler is preferable to the complex and heavy. Field recording is not to be confused with studio recording.

Since the 1990s digital recording has gradually superseded all forms of analog recording, and costs have once again fallen. Today a new generation of tiny, digital recorders has appeared. There are a great variety of inexpensive MP3 recorders, most of which record onto a built-in drive. Their drawbacks include the fact that MP3 files are highly compressed and that these machines only record using "automatic level control" (ALC). ALC's drawback is that it adjusts for the loudest sound at any particular moment. The presence of percussion causes it to change levels constantly, perhaps even making the melodic portion inaudible. Such recordings are uploaded to a computer and can be burned to a compact disc. At a much higher level are professional recorders (presently made by Edirol, Zoom and others) which record to SD cards and offer a variety of recording formats, from MP3 to 24-bit Wave or better. Although they have built-in microphones, they allow for external ones, as well as manual level control.

While the recording machine is obviously important, the choice of microphone is essential. The sound cannot be better than what the microphone can hear. One can use a pair of single-channel microphones or a single-point stereo microphone that allows some track separation. Microphone placement is extremely important for critical recordings, and researchers may need to experiment before choosing their setup.

Video Recording. Until about 1970 the only way to produce "moving pictures" short of a professional film crew was with a silent Super 8 film camera powered by a spring. Today most camcorders have built-in hard drives (low end models use memory cards) whose files are uploaded into a computer and can be burned onto DVDs. These eliminate the need for cassettes and provide exceptionally long-term recording without interruption.

The most important aspect of videography is the stability of the camera. Except when one needs to move around a subject, it is best to use a sturdy tripod to capture good images. A jerky video will not appeal to you, your audience, or your students. A common mistake amateur videographers make is to pan too fast and too often. Similarly, avoid overusing the zoom feature. On the other hand, images produced by simply placing the camera on a tripod and letting it run for hours will be excruciatingly boring to watch. Strive for smoothness and slowness of movement; do not emulate television music videos or commercial advertisements, with their obsessively fast scene changes. Try to capture some important details in close-ups, as well as having other footage that gives a sense of the bigger picture—the space and circumstances of a performance, including the audience.

Still Photography. There are currently two forms of photography, analog and digital, though few use the former now. Analog photos may be black and white or color; in either case, film is required. Print film produces negatives that are printed onto photo paper while slide film results in transparencies (slides) that can be projected onto a screen. Both forms can be scanned into digital format as well, though slides are better scanned with dedicated slide scanners. Digital cameras have advanced to professional levels, and today most people use this type. Even the "point and shoot" types are small and light and allow a great number of images to be captured on a single memory card.

For fieldwork, digital photography offers advantages over analog especially because of its ability to make good photos in dim light and at night using available light. While one could use flash units with analog cameras, on small cameras these were not strong enough to reach beyond about 10 feet. Digital cameras not only offer built-in flash but also the ability

Nguyen Thuyet Phong AN INSIDE LOOK

Although I was born in a rice-growing village deep in the Mekong River delta of southern Vietnam, I came from a family of skilled traditional musicians who performed the local ritual music in our province. My father began teaching me music at age five, and at age seven I began study with Tram Van Kien, a great master of the region, concentrating on both instrumental and vocal music. When I was seven my family sent me to a nearby market town where I continued my music studies while living in a Buddhist temple. By the age of twelve I had become proficient in many kinds of music, including instrumental music, ritual music, theater music, folksongs, and Buddhist chant. After that I studied at the University of Saigon, earning a Bachelor of Arts in philosophy and literature in 1972.

Most of these early years, however, were very stressful because of the war's increasing ferocity, and many times my family's village was bombed by American forces and our house destroyed. I was working in Japan when the war ended in April 1975 and the country fell into difficulties. Fortunately, France—Vietnam's former colonial ruler—accepted me, and in 1982 in Paris I was able to complete a Ph.D. in Musicology with distinction from the Sorbonne University, writing my dissertation on Vietnamese Buddhist chant. Eventually, 1984, I made my way to the United States and have lived here ever since. Although it is difficult to make a living performing traditional Vietnamese music, I have been fortunate to have been invited to play throughout the United States and in many other countries, including Canada, Norway, Netherlands, France, Germany, Switzerland, Italy, Korea, Japan, Singapore, Hong Kong, and Taiwan among them. In 1997 the National Endowment for the Arts awarded

Dr. Nguyen Thuyet Phong, director, Institute for Vietnamese Music and independent scholar

me a National Heritage Fellowship presented by the First Lady Hillary Rodham Clinton. My ensemble and I continue to perform live and make recordings. I also remain a scholar, writing books and articles, compiling compact discs, doing field research, and lecturing. I created the Phong Nguyen Collections currently preserved at the Library of Congress' Folklife Center and at Hobart and William Smith College's Global Education Center. Recently I had the honor of advising the National Conservatory of Music in Hanoi on creating the first program in ethnomusicology in Vietnam supported by an American-government Fulbright grant.

Presently I have made Vietnam my permanent home and am involved in creating and building a new university devoted to the study of traditional arts and culture. I feel that Vietnam has a bright future now.

---

to change film speeds so as to maximize the range of the flash. Whereas analog cameras require a supply of film, digital cameras require a supply of memory devices and a laptop computer into which photos are uploaded. Digital photos can be stored and saved in multiple formats and in large or small sizes, and can be uploaded and mailed electronically. Although most professionals shoot "raw," these images are extremely large, and most scholars can do fine with JPEG images; these can also be digitally edited to crop out unwanted material or alter the lightness/darkness or color balance.

Interviewing. Interviewing is essentially a conversation between the researcher and someone who can provide information and insights about the music under study. That person, sometimes referred to as an ***informant***, could be either a musician or simply someone familiar with the tradition. The information gleaned in an interview is subject to all the limitations of human conversation and thinking, however. Information provided spontaneously from memory may or may not be reliable. Other factors may also distort the information. For example, someone may tell the researcher what they think the researcher wants to hear, or they may attempt to manage a music's or culture's image by carefully selecting what facts they present. Regardless of these drawbacks, however, interviews can elicit valuable information.

> **INFORMANT**
> A person from whom a field researcher obtains information.

Especially in an initial interview, questions should be kept short and open ended, so as to encourage an informant to speak freely. Although it is wise to plan a series of questions in advance, researchers must also be prepared to alter the order of questions or take the conversation in unexpected directions if the informant seems interested in pursuing a particular topic. In short, the researcher should not try to control the informant.

There are two ways to preserve an interview: taking notes and recording. The latter is far better in that it produces an exact record of what was said, and allows the researcher not to be distracted by the process of writing things down. However, it is always necessary to get an informant's permission before recording commences. A recording is especially valuable if the informant sings or plays an instrument during the interview. In fact, if there is to be much performance, the researcher is better off videotaping the interview. Whatever technology is used, the researcher must strive to keep it out of sight and out of mind as much as possible, so as to minimize the informant's self-consciousness.

Collecting and Archiving. The conditions under which you keep recordings, photos, and other documents affect how long they last. When such materials are subjected to extremes of heat and cold, humidity and dryness, and other changes, they deteriorate faster. Instruments are particularly challenging because they take up much space and, when neglected, fall into disrepair because of broken strings, warped or cracked wood, splits in bamboo, cracked reeds, and so on. The most valued of resources are generally deposited at an archive, such as the American Folklife Center at the Library of Congress or Indiana University's Archives of Traditional Music, which is the nation's premier collection of ethnographic field recordings. Professional archivists maintain such collections to ensure their availability for future generations.

It is extremely important to "back up" your digital files, be they text files or photo files. Computer crashes cannot be predicted, and when they happen it may already be too late to recover lost data. You can back up your files on CDs, DVDs, an external hard drive, or through a backup service via the Internet. Anyone who has suffered in a computer crash knows how important this advice is.

To people like your authors, to whom the Internet came in adulthood, the information highway is nothing short of a miracle and beyond comprehension. Using a search engine such as Google or Bing, you can find information stored anywhere in the world in any language. Internet users must beware, however, that some information found there is unreliable.

Disseminating Your Findings

Discovering yourself through music is a challenging but ultimately rewarding experience. In the process of learning about your own musical roots, you undoubtedly learn much about other people who have contributed to the development of your self-identity. While this new knowledge is of great benefit for you, it may also be helpful for other people in knowing their own musical heritage as well. Disseminating your findings is an important way to help future sojourners learn from your experiences so that they can add new knowledge through their own inquiries rather than just repeating research you have already completed. There are many avenues through which to share your research, but the most pertinent ones in the field of ethnomusicology are (1) teaching, (2) performance, and (3) publishing.

Teaching. Many ethnomusicologists teach at institutions of higher learning around the world, but others also teach in less formal environments. Teaching is merely a matter of sharing knowledge with others. It can take place in a classroom, at a local worship center, as part of a community program, at a folk festival workshop, or just among family and friends.

A common way of teaching or of communicating information to peers is to give presentations. Researchers often present their findings by reading "papers" at professional conferences. Most scholarly societies hold such meetings. The larger professional organizations may have both an annual national or international meeting and a regional or chapter meeting. The latter are often more receptive to student papers than national ones. Upon receiving a "call for papers," the researcher submits an **abstract**, that is, a paragraph or so that explains their topic. If this is accepted, they are invited to present their paper at the conference; usually, their presentation is expected to last no longer than twenty minutes. Whenever possible, it is best for presentations to include audio and video examples of the music under discussion. This is particularly true when the audience comprises non-specialists. Presenters today often feel compelled to use PowerPoint in their presentations. This can enhance a presentation greatly, but if done improperly (e.g., too much text in the slides, irrelevant information or graphics, technical problems), it can detract from the presentation. Remember, when you project text on the screen, your listeners read that and may tune out the speaker, so it's best to follow the 6 × 6 rule, meaning no more than six lines of text with six or fewer words per line.

ABSTRACT
A brief summary of the contents of a book, article, or speech.

Performance. However useful audio and video examples may be, live performance is an even more effective means of teaching. For this reason, ethnomusicologists often invite "guest artists" to help them demonstrate a music tradition. Ethnomusicologists frequently find themselves in the role of manager or concert promoter as well. Through their research, they sometimes discover unknown artists of great quality, and they may wish to organize opportunities for these musicians to perform publicly. Arranging performances at local schools or community centers is usually easy to do. By getting a musician to perform in public, you are helping to preserve the music that artist represents and are providing the musician with an opportunity to share his or her musical talents with others.

Some researchers also learn to perform the music they study. Back in the 1960s Dr. Mantle Hood of the University of California, Los Angeles, advocated what he called "bi-musicality" as a method for learning about and presenting music. While you would normally not aspire to become "professional" in doing this, it can serve to draw you closer to the musicians and music under study and make your presentations far more interesting and credible.

Publishing. The most permanent means of disseminating knowledge about a music tradition is through print publication. With the advent of desktop and electronic publishing, this is far easier than before, but it should be understood that not all publications are equal. In academia a clear distinction is made between publications that are "peer-reviewed" or "refereed," and those that are not. Peer-reviewed publications—be they articles, books, or recordings—have been reviewed by one or more people with expertise in the field before being accepted. Most peer reviews are done "blind," that is, the reviewers do not know the name of the author under review. With regard to book publishing, there is also a distinction between legitimate scholarly presses that subject manuscripts to close scrutiny and review and so-called "vanity presses" that publish whatever an author submits in exchange, usually, for a payment or a guarantee of sales. Virtually anything written can find its way into some kind of print, physical or electronic, but being in print alone is not a guarantee of quality or reliability.

A further distinction is made between scholarly and commercial publication. Professors are expected to publish the results of their research in scholarly journals. Even though these journals pay nothing for articles, publication in them is often the basis for promotion, tenure, and pay increases. On the other hand, when ethnomusicologists do write for magazines and other commercial publications, they can expect to be paid. Authors of academic press books can expect—or at least hope for—royalty payments based on the number of copies sold. However, because academic publications are expensive to print and have limited sales potential, their authors rarely realize more than a token "profit."

Today many individuals have created their own personal websites where they maintain a collection of self-generated materials (e.g., their resume), family pictures, and so on. It is possible to upload the results of your own research onto your website. With today's powerful search engines, interested readers are increasingly likely to stumble on your work. This likelihood increases when your titles include the key words with which users will likely search. Social media websites, such as Facebook, can offer similar means of disseminating research, including photos, video, audio, as well as text. They also have the advantage of linking you to a network of people around the globe with similar interests in music and cultural study.

Where to Go From Here

Most readers of this book are likely students having their first experiences with the musics of the world. In writing the previous pages, we understand that most of you are unlikely to become practicing ethnomusicologists working in academia. And, considering the relative dearth of jobs in higher education for ethnomusicologists, we are not suggesting you change your major and join us. Still, we hope you will become aware of the music around you that is little known but may be important to your family, community, or ethnic group and decide to document it. Professional ethnomusicologists cannot be everywhere. The music you document may someday find its way into the local historical society, your family's treasure trove, your church's library, or your club's memento collection.

Documenting music may preserve its sound (and sights, if done with a video camera), but music that only exists in archives and is no longer heard live is not the same as a living tradition. Do what you can to encourage the continuation of the music you like or discover.

You might even consider learning it yourself. Most state arts councils offer small grants for "apprenticeships in the folk arts." These offer modest funds to a practitioner (called "the master artist") for passing on the tradition to a novice (called the "apprentice"). Because most "master artists" do not think of themselves as such, it will probably be up to you to obtain the application forms, fill them out, and encourage the master to make the application.

If you are (or become) a teacher, you can explore your community for individuals who carry interesting music traditions and bring them to the attention of others. Many states and localities offer modest funds to support appearances by artists in schools. These "tradition-bearers" can be brought to a school to present programs in classrooms or to give a concert for the whole student body. This recognition not only allows students to learn about individual musicians, it also can encourage these practitioners to continue performing, as their skills are sometimes otherwise little known or appreciated.

On a more modest scale, you can do your part to preserve diversity in the musics of the world by purchasing (not "file sharing") audio and video recordings of traditional music. You can attend concerts, workshops, festivals, houses of worship, and other venues where music can be heard live. Or perhaps you could purchase an instrument and buy an instruction book (or find a teacher) and learn to play it. There's no telling where you could go by following an interest in world music. The path you follow is entirely up to you.

Glossary

Authors' Note: As some of the transliterated words below are difficult to pronounce or have no English equivalent, we have included pronunciation approximations in parentheses following a number of the glossary terms.

A

A-AK: A Confucian ritual ensemble from Korea. (Chapter 7)

ABAKWA: An animistic belief system found primarily in Cuba. (Chapter 11)

ABORIGINES: A generic term for an indigenous population, often used to describe native peoples of Australia. (Chapter 4)

ACCENT: An emphasized beat. (Chapter 2)

ACCORDION: A bellows-driven free-reed *aerophone* with buttons or keys that enable a performer to play melody and harmony simultaneously. (Chapter 9)

ACOUSTIC: Term used for non-electric instruments. (Chapter 13)

ADHAN (Also, AZAN): The Islamic call to prayer. (Chapter 8)

AEROPHONE: Ethnomusicological classification referring to instruments that require air to produce sound; namely, flutes, reeds, trumpets, and bellows-driven instruments. (Chapter 2)

AFIRIKYIWA: An iron clapper-bell from Ghana. (Chapter 10)

AFRIKANER: A South African of Dutch descent. (Chapter 10)

AGOGO: A double-bell found in western Africa and used in African-derived musics in the Western hemisphere. (Chapter 12)

AKADINDA: A large, heavy log *xylophone* from sub-Saharan Africa, associated with the former kingdom of Buganda. (Chapter 10)

ALAP (Also, ALAPANA): The opening, freely rhythmic period of improvisation of *raga* performance in Indian classical music. (Chapter 5)

AL-'UD: See UD.

AMADINDA: A log *xylophone* similar to the *akadinda*, but with fewer pitches; from sub-Saharan Africa. (Chapter 10)

ANTHEM: A category of shape-note song that is *through composed,* meaning it has different music from beginning to end. (Chapter 13)

ANTHROPOLOGY: The study of all aspects of human culture, including music. (Chapter 1)

ANUDRUTAM: The first element of the *tala* in Indian classical music. (Chapter 5)

ANUPALLAVI: The second section of a *kriti* vocal performance from South India. (Chapter 5)

APARTHEID: The official South African policy of racial segregation, abolished in 1992. (Chapter 10)

APPALACHIA: A geographic region marked by the Appalachian Mountains, which extend throughout the eastern part of the United States. (Chapter 13)

APREMPRENSEMMA: A low-ranged *lamellophone* from Ghana. (Chapter 10)

ARABIAN PENINSULA: A geographic region in the Middle East that includes Saudi Arabia, Yemen, Oman, and the various smaller nations on the Persian Gulf. (Chapter 8)

ARADHANA: A South Indian festival. (Chapter 5)

ARAWAK: A pre-Columbian indigenous population of the Caribbean. (Chapter 11)

ATABAQUES: A drum of West African origin used in *capoeira* music as well as *candomblé* rituals from Brazil. (Chapter 12)

ATUMPAN: A pair of goblet-shaped drums often used as a speech surrogate by several ethnic groups from Ghana. (Chapter 10)

AULOS: A double-reed *aerophone* from Ancient Greece. (Chapter 3)

AVAZ: The improvised, non-metrical section of a performance in the Persian classical tradition. (Chapter 8)

AYATOLLAH: A high-rank clergyman in Islam. (Chapter 8)

AZAN: See ADHAN.

AZTEC: A pre-Columbian indigenous population found in central and southern Mexico. (Chapter 12)

B

BAĞLAMA: A round-bodied lute from Turkey. (Chapter 3)

BAGPIPES: A reed *aerophone* consisting of an airbag, *chanter* (melody pipe), and drone pipes. (Chapter 9)

GLOSSARY

BAIRRO: A poor housing area found in the city of Rio de Janeiro, Brazil. (Chapter 12)

BALAFON: A *xylophone* from West Africa often played by oral historians. (Chapter 10)

BALALAIKA: A triangle-shaped, fretted plucked lute from Russia. (Chapter 9)

BALLAD: A song that tells a story, usually performed by a solo voice and commonly associated with music from the Appalachian region of the United States. (Chapter 13)

BALS DE MAISON: A house party that typically has *Cajun* music as entertainment, found in the southern United States, primarily Louisiana. (Chapter 13)

BANDIR: A frame drum common to Turkish and Arabic music. (Chapter 8)

BANDONEON: A type of button-box accordion. (Chapter 12)

BANJO: A fretted, plucked lute from the United States, the resonator of which has a membrane face. (Chapter 13)

BANSRI (Also, BANSURI): A transverse flute from North India. (Chapter 5)

BANTU: An African linguistic category. (Chapter 10)

BAR MITZVAH: A Jewish "coming-of-age" ceremony. (Chapter 8)

BASHRAF: An Arabic musical form. (Chapter 8)

BASSER: The lowest vocal part in a *rhyming spiritual* performance from the Bahamas. (Chapter 11)

BATA: Ritual drums used in *Santeria* ceremonies. (Chapter 11)

BATUQUE: An animistic belief system found primarily in Brazil. (Chapter 11)

BAULS: A group of itinerant musicians from India, especially noted for their poetry. (Chapter 5)

BAYA: A small bowl-shaped drum that is one of the pair of North Indian drums known as *tabla*. (Chapter 5)

BAYIN: The Chinese organological system. (Chapter 7)

BEAT: A regular pulsation. (Chapter 2)

BELLOWS: An apparatus for producing a strong current of air; used with the Irish bagpipes, as well as the pump organ and other *aerophones*. (Chapter 9)

BERIMBAU: A musical bow used in *capoeira* music from Brazil. (Chapter 12)

BHAJAN: Devotional songs from India. (Chapter 5)

BHANGRA: A folk dance from the Punjabi region of north India/south Pakistan that is also the basis of a popular music style of the same name that developed in London, England. (Chapter 5)

BIBLE: The sacred text of Christianity. (Chapter 13)

BIN: A fretted plucked lute considered the origin of other popular lutes in India, such as the *sitar*. (Chapter 5)

BINO: A sitting dance typical of traditional music and dance performances from Kiribati. (Chapter 4)

BIRA: A spirit possession ceremony of the Shona ethnic group from Zimbabwe. (Chapter 10)

BIRIMINTINGO: The instrumental solo sections of a *jali* performance from West Africa. (Chapter 10)

BIWA: A fretted, pear-shaped plucked lute from Japan. (Chapter 7)

BLUEGRASS: A style of American folk music characterized by virtuosic instrumental performance and the so-called "high lonesome" vocal style, in which a harmony pitch is sung above the main melody. (Chapter 13)

BLUES: A secular folk music tradition originating within the African-American community of the southern United States. (Chapter 13)

BODHRAN: A frame drum from Ireland, played with a beater. (Chapter 9)

BOLERO: A Latin American dance and music. (Chapter 11)

BOLLYWOOD: An informal name for India's film industry derived from a combination of the words "Bombay" and "Hollywood." (Chapter 5)

BOLS: Mnemonic syllables corresponding to drum strokes in Indian drumming traditions. (Chapter 5)

BOMBARDE: A double-reed *aerophone* from France. (Chapter 3)

BOMBOS: A large drum used in *sikuri* performances from Peru. (Chapter 12)

BON: Festive dancing from Japan. (Chapter 7)

BONANG: A rack gong found in *gamelan* ensembles from Indonesia. (Chapter 6)

BONES: A small pair of wooden slats struck together to create rhythm. Common to folk music in the United States as well as Great Britain. (Chapter 9)

BOSSED GONG: A gong with a bump-like protuberance. (Chapter 6)

BOUZOUKI: A round-bodied lute from Greece. (Chapter 3)

BUGAKU: A Confucian ritual ensemble from Japan that incorporates dance. (Chapter 7)

BUNRAKU: A popular form of puppet theater from Japan. (Chapter 7)

BUZUK (Also, BUZUQ): A round-bodied lute from Turkey. (Chapter 3)

BYZANTINE CHANT: A chant style associated with the Greek Orthodox Church, centered on a complex system of *modes*. (Chapter 9)

C

CAIXA ("x" pronounced *sh*): A small drum from Brazil found in *samba* performances. (Chapter 12)

CAJAS: A small drum from Peru used in *sikuri* performances. (Chapter 12)

CAJUN: A term describing the cultural traditions, including music, of French-speaking Louisiana, USA. (Chapter 13)

CALL AND RESPONSE: A style of vocal organization characterized by having a leader who "calls" and a group that "responds." (Chapters 10 and 13)

CALYPSO: A popular music form from Trinidad characterized by improvised lyrics on topical and broadly humorous subject matter. (Chapter 11)

CANCIÓN: A general term for "song" in Mexico. (Chapter 12)

CANDOMBLÉ: A belief system combining animism and syncretized Roman Catholicism, found primarily in Brazil. (Chapter 10)

CANTAORA: A vocalist in Spanish flamenco music. (Chapter 9)

CANTE: A traditional Spanish style of singing incorporating a strained timbre and heavy use of *melisma*. (Chapter 9)

CANTINA: A social venue for drinking and dancing found in the Texas-Mexico borderland region of the United States. (Chapter 13)

CANTON: The term used for the states of the Swiss Federation. (Chapter 13)

CAPOEIRA: A form of dance that developed from a distinctive style of martial arts created by runaway slaves in Brazil. (Chapter 12)

CARANAM: The final section of a *kriti* vocal performance from India. (Chapter 5)

CARIB: A pre-Columbian indigenous population of the Caribbean. (Chapter 11)

CARNATIC (Also, KARNATAK): A term referring to the cultural traditions of South India. (Chapter 5)

CARNIVAL: A pre-Lent festival celebrated primarily in Europe and the Caribbean. Known as Mardi Gras in the United States. (Chapter 12)

CASCARÁ: A rhythmic pattern played on the *timbales* in *salsa* music. (Chapter 11)

CASTE SYSTEM: A system of social organization based on hereditary status found in India. (Chapter 5)

CÉILI: An Irish band that performs in a public house (pub) for entertainment and dancing. (Chapter 9)

CÉILIDH (pronounced *kay-lee*): A kind of "house party" associated with fiddling traditions in Canada, Ireland, and Scotland. (Chapter 13)

GLOSSARY

CELTIC: A subfamily of the Indo-European language family that is associated with the Scottish and Irish peoples of Great Britain. (Chapter 9)

CHA-CHA: A Latin American ballroom dance. (Chapter 11)

CHAHAR-MEZRAB: A metered piece in the Persian classical music tradition. (Chapter 8)

CHANTER: The melody pipe found on various bagpipes. (Chapter 9)

CHARRO: A style of suit worn by *mariachi* performers from Mexico. (Chapter 12)

CHASTUSHKI: A category of songs from Russia considered "playful." (Chapter 9)

CHÉQUERES (Also, SHEKERE): A gourd rattle with external beaded netting. (Chapter 11)

CHING: A pair of cup-shaped cymbals from Thailand. (Chapter 6)

CHIZ: The composed section of vocal performance in Indian classical music. (Chapter 5)

CHOBO: The narrator and accompanying shamisen performers of the Kabuki theater in Japan. (Chapter 7)

CHORD: The simultaneous soundings of three or more pitches. (Chapter 2)

CHORDOPHONE: Ethnomusicological classification referring collectively to the four types of stringed instruments: lutes, zithers, harps, lyres. (Chapter 2)

CHOU: The comic role-type in Beijing Opera from China. (Chapter 7)

CH'UN HYANG KA: The name of one of five stories performed in Korean *p'ansori*. (Chapter 7)

CIMARRONS: A term for escaped slaves from the Spanish-colonized regions in the Caribbean and Americas. (Chapter 11)

CIMBALOM: A hammered zither from Eastern Europe, commonly associated with Rom (gypsy) music. Also, the national instrument of Hungary. (Chapter 9)

CIRCULAR BREATHING: A technique used to maintain a continuous air flow in *aerophone* performance. (Chapter 4)

CITERA: A small zither from Hungary. (Chapter 9)

CLAVES: A pair of hand-held wooden bars used as percussion instruments in many African and Latin American music traditions. (Chapters 10 and 11)

CLERK (pronounced *clark*): A religious leader in Calvinist churches in the United States and Scotland. (Chapter 13)

COBZA: A pear-shaped lute from Romania. (Chapter 3)

COLOTOMIC STRUCTURE: The organizational system of *gamelan* music from Indonesia. (Chapter 6)

COMPARSA: A Latin American dance music. (Chapter 11)

COMPÉ: A martial arts style from Brazil that emphasizes striking "with the foot." (Chapter 12)

GLOSSARY

CONCERTINA: A small hexagonal accordion with bellows and buttons for keys. (Chapter 9)

CONGA (Also, TUMBADORA): A tall, barrel-shaped, single-headed drum used often in Latin American music. (Chapter 11)

CONJUNTO: A popular dance music found along the Texas-Mexico border in North America. (Chapter 13)

CONTRADANZA: A Cuban dance form. (Chapter 11)

CORROBOREE: A nighttime ritual performed by Australian aborigines. (Chapter 4)

CREOLE: A term referring to populations of French or mixed African and French descent that are found in the southern United States, primarily Louisiana. (Chapter 13)

CRESCENDO: A gradual increase in volume. (Chapter 2)

CROSS-RHYTHM: A "two-against-three" rhythmic pattern often found in polyrhythmic performance in sub-Saharan Africa and Latin America. (Chapters 10 and 11)

CUÍCA (pronounced *kwi-kha*): A small friction drum used in *samba* music. (Chapter 12)

CULTURAL REVOLUTION: A ten-year period (1966–1976) in China's history marked by severe social and political upheaval. (Chapter 7)

CUMINA: An animistic belief system found primarily in Jamaica. (Chapter 11)

CUTTIN' HEADS: A music contest found in African-American communities, typically involving blues musicians. (Chapter 13)

CZARDAS: A popular dance from Hungary. (Chapter 9)

D

DAN (pronounced *dahn*): The female hero role-type in Beijing opera from China. (Chapter 7)

DAN CO: A fiddle from Vietnam. (Chapter 6)

DAN KIM: A fretted plucked lute from Vietnam. (Chapter 6)

DAN TRANH: A plucked zither from Vietnam. (Chapter 6)

DAN TYBA (pronounced *dahn tee-bah*): A pear-shaped lute from Vietnam. (Chapter 6)

DANCEHALL: See DUB.

DANZA (Also, DANZON and DANZONETE): A Cuban dance form. (Chapter 11)

DARABUKA: A goblet-shaped hand drum common to various Turkish music traditions. (Chapter 8)

DARAMAD: The freely rhythmic opening and conclusion of a *dastgah* performance in the Persian classical music tradition. (Chapter 8)

DASTGAH: A *mode* or system of rules and expectations for composition and improvisation in Persian classical music. (Chapter 8)

DECRESCENDO: A gradual decrease in volume. (Chapter 2)

DEFINITE PITCH: A sound with a dominating frequency level. (Chapter 2)

DENSITY REFERENT: A reference pattern heard in polyrhythmic music, usually articulated by a bell, rattle, or woodblock. (Chapter 10)

DERVISH: Turkish word literally meaning "beggar," but often used to refer to Sufi Muslims. (Chapter 8)

DHIKR (Also, ZIKR): A ritual commonly performed by Sufi Muslims in which believers chant the names of Allah with the goal of entering a spiritually ecstatic state. (Chapter 8)

DHRUPAD: A category of vocal music from India. (Chapter 5)

DIAO: The *key* used in a music performance from China. (Chapter 7)

DIDJERIDU: A long trumpet made from a hollowed tree branch played by aborigines from Australia. (Chapter 4)

DILRUBA: A bowed lute from India. (Chapter 5)

DIZI: A transverse flute from China. (Chapter 7)

DOMBAK: A goblet-shaped hand drum used in Arabic music traditions. (Chapter 8)

DOMRA: A round-shaped fretted plucked lute from Russia. (Chapter 9)

DONDO (Also, DONNO): An hourglass-shaped pressure drum from Ghana. (Chapter 10)

DOUBLE-STOPS: The practice of playing two strings simultaneously on bowed lutes such as the violin. (Chapter 13)

DOULCEMELLE: A hammered dulcimer from France. (Chapter 3)

DR. WATTS: An informal term for a *lined hymn* employed in some African-American communities. (Chapter 13)

DREAMTIME: A term describing the Australian aboriginal spiritual belief system and concept of creation. (Chapter 4)

DRONE: A continuous sound. (Chapter 2)

DRUTAM: The second element of the *tala* in Indian classical music. (Chapter 5)

DUB (Also, DANCEHALL): Recorded music that emphasizes the bass and rhythm tracks so that a DJ can talk over the music through a microphone. (Chapter 11)

DUDA: Bagpipes from Hungary. (Chapter 9)

DUENDE: A Spanish word meaning "passion," which refers to an emotional quality considered essential in performances by Spanish flamenco singers. (Chapter 9)

DUFF: A small, single-headed drum, sometimes having snares, common to Turkish and Arabic music traditions. (Chapter 8)

DULAB: A compositional form found in Turkish and Arabic music. (Chapter 8)

DUNG CHEN: A long metal trumpet from Tibet. (Chapter 7)

DUNG KAR: A conch-shell trumpet from Tibet. (Chapter 7)

DYNAMICS: The volume of a musical sound. (Chapter 2)

E

ECHOS (pl. ECHOI): *Mode* used for Byzantine Chant. (Chapter 9)

EKÓN: An iron bell used in *Santeria* rituals. (Chapter 11)

EKTARA: See GOPIYANTRA.

ELECTROPHONE: Ethnomusicological classification that refers to instruments that require electricity to produce sound, such as the synthesizer. (Chapter 2)

EMIC: A term borrowed from linguistics, used by anthropologists and ethnomusicologists to describe the perspective of a cultural insider. (Chapter 3)

ERHU: A fiddle from China. (Chapter 7)

ESCOLAS DE SAMBA: Samba schools of Brazil. (Chapter 12)

ETHNOCENTRISM: The unconscious assumption that one's own cultural background is "normal," while that of others is "strange" or "exotic." (Chapter 1)

ETHNOMUSICOLOGY: The scholarly study of any music within its contemporary context. (Chapter 1)

ETIC: A term borrowed from linguistics, used by anthropologists and ethnomusicologists to describe the perspective of a cultural outsider. (Chapter 3)

F

FAIS-DO-DO (pronounced *fai-doh-doh*): Literally meaning "go to sleep," this term refers to a public dancehall that hosts performances of Cajun dance music. (Chapter 13)

FASOLA SINGING: A singing style that uses shape-note notation. (Chapter 13)

FAVELA: Poor housing areas in the hills around Rio de Janeiro, Brazil. (Chapter 12)

FIDDLE: A generic term used to describe a bowed lute. (Chapter 2) Also, a slang term for a violin. (Chapters 9 & 13)

FIESTA: A festival or celebration in Spain or Latin America. (Chapter 9)

FILMI (Also, FILMI GIT): Popular music taken from films in India. (Chapter 5)

FIRQA (pronounced *feer-kah*): Large orchestral ensembles consisting of traditional Arabic instruments from the Middle East. (Chapter 8)

FLAMENCO: A Spanish musical tradition featuring vocals with guitar accompaniment, characterized by passionate singing and vibrant rhythm. (Chapter 9)

FLUTE: A type of *aerophone* that splits a column of air on an edge to produce sound. (Chapter 2)

FOLKLORE: The study of orally transmitted folk knowledge and culture. (Chapter 1)

FORM: Underlying structure of a musical performance. (Chapter 2)

FREE RHYTHM: Music with no regular pulsation. (Chapter 2)

FRET: A bar or ridge found on the fingerboard of chordophones that enables performers to produce different melodic pitches with consistent frequency levels. (Chapter 2)

FRICTION DRUM: A type of drum with a membrane that is "rubbed" rather than struck. (Chapter 9)

FROTTOIR (pronounced *fwaht-twah*): A metal washboard used in Cajun-Zydeco music. (Chapter 13)

FUGING TUNE (pronounced *fyu-ging*): A category of shape-note song in which individual voices enter one after the other. (Chapter 13)

G

GADULKA: A spiked fiddle from Bulgaria. (Chapter 3)

GAELIC (pronounced *gaa-lik*): The indigenous language of Scotland. (Chapter 9)

GAGAKU: A Confucian-derived ritual ensemble from Japan. (Chapter 7)

GAIDA: Bagpipes from Bulgaria. (Chapter 9)

GAMELAN: An ensemble from Indonesia comprised primarily of *metallophones.* (Chapter 6)

GAMELAN GONG KEBYAR: An ensemble type from Bali, Indonesia, comprised primarily of *metallophones* and characterized by rhythmically dense performance technique. (Chapter 6)

GANJA: A Rastafarian word for marijuana, borrowed from the Hindi term for "herb." (Chapter 11)

GARAMUT: A slit drum from Papua New Guinea. (Chapter 4)

GARDON: A struck lute from Hungary. (Chapter 9)

GAT (pronounced *gaht*): The composed section of instrumental performance in Indian classical music. (Chapter 5)

GEISHA: A Japanese girl or woman trained to provide entertainment, including musical entertainment. (Chapter 7)

GHAWAZI: Term in Arabic cultures for female dancers who specialize in very rapid hip-shaking movements. (Chapter 8)

GHUNUR: A string of bells worn around the ankle, commonly associated with the Bauls of South Asia. (Chapter 5)

GLOSSARY

GIG: A slang term referring to a musical job or performance-for-hire. (Chapter 9)

GINGA (Also, JENGA): A back-and-forth motion used as the basis for *capoeira* dancing. (Chapter 12)

GONG AGENG: The largest gong of an Indonesian *gamelan* ensemble. (Chapter 6)

GOOMBAY: A type of folk music ensemble from the Bahamas. (Chapter 11)

GOPIYANTRO (Also, EKTARA): A single-stringed *chordophone* with a membrane base found in India and often associated with the Bauls. (Chapter 5)

GOSPEL: An American religious music tradition associated with Christian evangelism. (Chapter 13)

GRIOT (pronounced *gree-oh*): The French term for a wandering minstrel, often used to describe the West African *jali*. (Chapter 10)

GUARACHA (pronounced *gwah-rah-cha*): A Latin American ballroom dance, as well as a song type emphasizing call-and-response vocal organization. (Chapter 11)

GUIRO (pronounced *gwee-roh*): A scraped gourd *idiophone*. (Chapter 11)

GUITAR: A fretted plucked lute common to American folk and popular music, as well as Spanish flamenco and various other traditions. (Chapter 13)

GUITARRÓN: A large fretted plucked lute from Mexico, similar to a guitar but with a convex resonator. (Chapter 12)

GUQIN (pronounced *goo-chin*): See QIN.

GURU: A teacher or spiritual guide, primarily associated with Hindu traditions from India. (Chapter 5)

GUSHEH: Short composed melodic phrases found in Persian classical music. (Chapter 8)

GYPSY: See ROM.

H

HACKBRETT: A hammered zither from Germany. (Chapter 3)

HAJJ: The Islamic pilgrimage to Mecca, Saudi Arabia. (Chapter 8)

HALILE: A pair of cymbals found in Sufi Muslim music performance. (Chapter 8)

HANUMAN: The "monkey-hero" in the Indian epic, *Ramayana*. (Chapter 5)

HARHIRAA: A type of throat-singing from Mongolia. (Chapter 7)

HARMONICA: A free-reed *aerophone* common to folk music from the United States. (Chapter 13)

HARMONIC: An *overtone* produced by lightly touching a string at a vibrating node. (Chapter 7)

HARMONIUM: A free-reed pump organ. (Chapter 5)

HARMONY: The simultaneous combination of three or more pitches in the Euro-American music tradition. (Chapter 2)

HAWAIIAN STEEL GUITAR: A guitar style of performance characterized by sliding tones (portamento) and wide vibrato. (Chapter 4)

HETEROPHONY: Multiple performers playing simultaneous variations of the same line of music. (Chapter 2)

HICHIRIKI: A double-reed *aerophone* used in *gagaku* music from Japan. (Chapter 7)

HIGHLAND PIPES: Bagpipes from Scotland. (Chapter 9)

HIGHLIFE: A generic term describing urban popular music traditions found throughout sub-Saharan Africa. (Chapter 10)

HINDUSTANI: A term referring to the cultural traditions of northern India. (Chapter 5)

HOCKET: A performance technique in which performers trade pitches back and forth to create a complete melody. (Chapter 12)

HOMOPHONY: Multiple lines of music expressing the same musical idea. (Chapter 2)

HOSHO: A gourd rattle from Zimbabwe. (Chapter 10)

HOSSZÚ FURULYA: A long end-blown flute from Hungary. (Chapter 9)

HULA PAHU: Hawaiian dance songs using drum accompaniment. (Chapter 4)

HURDY GURDY (Also Tekerölant): A *chordophone* common in France and Hungary that uses a wheel turned by a crank to vibrate the strings. (Chapter 9)

HYMN: A "humanly composed" religious work. (Chapter 13)

I

IDIOPHONE: Ethnomusicological classification encompassing instruments that themselves vibrate to produce sound, such as rattles, bells, and various other kinds of percussion. (Chapter 2)

ILAHI: A Sufi Muslim hymn. (Chapter 8)

IMPROVISATION: An instrumental or vocal performance or composition created spontaneously without preparation. (Chapters 4–13, especially Chapter 5)

INCA: A pre-Columbian indigenous people from the Andes region of South America. (Chapter 12)

INDEFINITE PITCH: A sound with no single dominating frequency level. (Chapter 2)

INDEPENDENT POLYPHONY: Multiple lines of music expressing independent musical ideas as a cohesive whole. (Chapter 2)

GLOSSARY

INTERVAL: The distance between two pitches. (Chapter 2)

INUIT: The term for specific Native American populations that live primarily in Canada and Alaska; often referred to as "Eskimos." (Chapter 13)

IQ'A (pronounced *eek-ah*): Rhythmic *modes* used in Arabic music. (Chapter 8)

ISAN (pronounced *ee-sahn*): A term referring to Northeast Thailand and its regional culture, including music. (Chapter 6)

ISICATHAMIYA (pronounced *isi-"click"ah-tah-mee-yah*): A term meaning, "to walk like a cat," that is, stealthily, which describes a soft style of *mbube* all-male vocal performance from South Africa. (Chapter 10)

IST: The central or "home" pitch of a Persian classical music performance. (Chapter 8)

J

JALEO: Clapping and shouts of encouragement associated with a *juerga* ("happening") in Spanish flamenco music. (Chapter 9) Also, refers to the closing section of a *meringue* performance from the Dominican Republic. (Chapter 11)

JALI (Also, JELI; pl. JALOLU): Term for a Mandinka poet/praise singer and oral historian from Senegal–Gambia. (Chapter 10)

JALTARANG: An instrument from India, consisting of a series of small china bowls each filled/tuned with a different level of water and struck with a small beater. (Chapter 5)

JAMACA (pronounced *yah-mah-kah*): In Islam, word used for an important *mosque*. (Chapter 8)

JANIZARY (pronounced *ye-nis-air-ee*); (Also, JANISSARY or YENICERI): A corps of elite troops commanded by the Ottoman caliphs from the late fourteenth century until their destruction in 1826. (Chapter 8)

JATI: The final section of the *tala* in Indian classical music in which the number of beats in the cycle varies. (Chapter 5)

JHALA: Refers to a set of drone strings on Indian *chordophones*. Also, a reference to the climactic end of the *alap* section of *raga* performance in India. (Chapter 5)

JIG: A musical form in 6/8 time, popular both in British and in North American fiddle traditions (Chapters 9 & 13).

JING: The warrior role-type in the Beijing Opera from China. (Chapter 7)

JINGHU: The lead fiddle of the Beijing Opera's instrumental ensemble. (Chapter 7)

JINGJU (Also, JINGXI): Beijing Opera from China. (Chapter 7)

JOR: A regularizing of the beat in the opening section of *raga* performance in Indian classical music. (Chapter 5)

GLOSSARY

JUERGA (pronounced *hwair-ga*): An informal event associated with Spanish flamenco music in which the separation between musicians and audience is blurred. (Chapter 9)

JUJU: A popular music style from Nigeria. (Chapter 10)

JUKE JOINT: An African-American social venue serving alcohol and hosting dance music, typically *blues*. (Chapter 13)

K

KABUKI: Popular music theater form from Japan. (Chapter 7)

KAHUNA: A Hawaiian term for a ritual specialist. (Chapter 4)

KALIMBA: A *lamellophone* from sub-Saharan Africa. (Chapter 10)

KANG DUNG: A trumpet from Tibet made from a human thighbone. (Chapter 7)

KANUN: See QANUN.

KAPU: Strict taboo system from precolonial Hawaii. (Chapter 4)

KARNATAK: See CARNATIC.

KARTAL: Indian percussion instrument consisting of a steel rod struck by a horseshoe-shaped beater. (Chapter 5)

KASIDE: Freely rhythmic melismatic passages performed by a vocal soloist in a Sufi Muslim ritual. (Chapter 8)

KATAJJAQ (pronounced *kah-tah-jahk*): An Inuit throat-singing style from northern Quebec, Canada. (Chapter 13)

KATHAKALI: A classical dance drama from South India. (Chapter 5)

KAYAGUM: A plucked zither from Korea. (Chapter 7)

KECAK: A Balinese theatrical performance of the *Ramayana*. (Chapter 6)

KEMENCE (Also, KEMANCHEH or KEMANJA): A spiked fiddle common to Turkish and Arabic music traditions. (Chapter 8)

KERESHMEH: A type of metered piece in the Persian classical music tradition. (Chapter 8)

KEY: A tonal system consisting of several pitches in fixed relationship to a fundamental pitch. (Chapter 7)

KHAEN: A bamboo mouth organ from Northeast Thailand. (Chapter 6)

KHANEGAH: A type of Sufi Muslim monastery. (Chapter 8)

KHAWNG WONG LEK/KHAWNG WONG YAI: Respectively, the higher- and lower-ranged gong circles found in classical ensembles from Thailand. (Chapter 6)

KHON: A classical masked drama based on the Thai version of the *Ramayana*. (Chapter 6)

GLOSSARY

KHÖÖMEI: Throat-singing tradition from Mongolia. (Chapter 7)

KHRU: A Thai teacher; the term is linguistically associated with the word *guru* found in Hinduism. (Chapter 6)

KHRUANG SAI: A classical Thai ensemble characterized by stringed instruments and rhythmic percussion. (Chapter 6)

KHYAL: A category of vocal music from India. (Chapter 5)

KILT: A knee-length skirt made of wool associated with Scottish Highlanders. (Chapter 9)

KILU: A small drum from Hawaii, usually made from a coconut shell with a fish-skin face. (Chapter 4)

KISAENG: A professional entertainer from Korea. (Chapter 7)

KLEZMER: A European-derived dance music commonly associated with Jewish celebrations, influenced by jazz and other non-Jewish styles. (Chapter 8)

KOMUSO: Lay-priest associated with Zen Buddism from Japan who performed the *shakuhachi*. (Chapter 7)

KONI: A plucked lute from West Africa. (Chapter 10)

KORA: A harp-lute or bridge-harp performed on by *jalolu* from Senegal-Gambia. (Chapter 10)

KORAN (Also, QUR'AN): The sacred text of Islam. (Chapter 8)

KOTO: A plucked zither from Japan. (Chapter 7)

KO-TUZUMI: A small, hourglass-shaped drum from Japan that is held on the shoulder. (Chapter 7)

KRITI: A genre of devotional Hindu poetry from South India. (Chapter 5)

KUDUM: A type of kettle drum common to Turkish and Arabic music. (Chapter 8)

KUMBENGO: The sung sections of a *jali* performance from West Africa. (Chapter 10)

KUNDU: An hourglass-shaped drum from Papua New Guinea. (Chapter 4)

KUSHAURA: The "leading" rhythmic pattern of *mbira dza vadzimu* performance from Zimbabwe. (Chapter 10)

KUTSINHIRA: The "following" rhythmic pattern of *mbira dza vadzimu* performance from Zimbabwe. (Chapter 10)

L

LA LA: A Creole dance party. (Chapter 13)

LADYSMITH BLACK MAMBAZO: A popular vocal group in the mbube/isicathamiya style from South Africa. (Chapter 10)

LAGHU: The final element of the *tala* in Indian classical music. (Chapter 5)

LAM KLAWN (pronounced *lum glawn*): Vocal repartee with *khaen* accompaniment from Northeast Thailand. (Chapter 6)

LAM SING (pronounced *lum sing*): A popular music form from Northeast Thailand. (Chapter 6)

LAMELLOPHONE: A type of *idiophone* that uses vibrating "lamellae" or strips of material, usually metal, to produce sound. (Chapter 2)

LANGAJ: A ceremonial language found in the *vodou* (voodoo) tradition from Haiti. (Chapter 11)

LATA MANGESHKAR: Famous *filmi* singer from India. (Chapter 5)

LAUTO: A pear-shaped lute from Greece. (Chapter 3)

LAYALI: A vocal improvisational form in Arabic music traditions. (Chapter 8)

LIKEMBE: A *lamellophone* from sub-Saharan Africa. (Chapter 10)

LINED HYMN: An archaic form of singing found in Scotland and the United States, in which a leader "lines" out a verse and the congregation repeats it heterophonically. (Chapter 13)

LONG-METER SONG: An informal term for a *lined hymn*. (Chapter 13)

LUTE: A type of chordophone with a resonating body and a neck with a fingerboard that enables individual strings to sound different pitches. (Chapter 2)

LWA (Also, LOA): A category of deities in Haitian vodou (voodoo). (Chapter 11)

LYRA: A spiked fiddle from Greece. (Chapter 3)

M

MAGHRIB: A geographic region in North Africa that includes Morocco, Algeria, Tunisia, and Libya. (Chapter 8)

MAHORI: A classical ensemble from Thailand characterized by melodic and rhythmic percussion, stringed instruments, and a fipple flute. (Chapter 6)

MAKAM (Also, MAQAM): A *mode* or system of rules and expectations for composition and improvisation in Arabic classical music. (Chapter 8)

MAMBO: A Latin American dance and music form. (Chapter 11)

MANA: Term for spiritual power in the Hawaiian belief system. (Chapter 4)

MANDOLIN: A high-ranged fretted lute commonly used in bluegrass music from the United States. (Chapter 13) Also, the term for a medieval round-bodied lute. (Chapter 3)

MANEABA: Term for a communal meetinghouse in Kiribati. (Chapter 4)

GLOSSARY

MARACAS: A pair of small Caribbean gourd rattles with interior beads. (Chapter 11).

MARIACHI: An entertainment music associated with festivals and celebratory events in Mexico. (Chapter 12)

MAROONS: Anglicized term for *cimarrons*. (Chapter 11)

MASHRIQ (pronounced *mah-shrik*): A geographic region in the Middle East that includes Egypt, Israel, Jordan, Lebanon, Syria, and Iraq. (Chapter 8)

MASJID: Term for a local *mosque* in Islam. (Chapter 8)

MAWLAM (pronounced *maw-lum*): A professional *lam klawn* singer from Northeast Thailand. (Chapter 6)

MAWWAL: A vocal improvisational form in Arabic music traditions. (Chapter 8)

MAYA: A pre-Columbian indigenous group from Central America, primarily Mexico and Guatemala. (Chapter 12)

MBIRA: A general reference to lamellophones found throughout Africa. (Chapter 10)

MBIRA DZA VADZIMU: A *lamellophone* from Zimbabwe. (Chapter 10)

MBUBE: A choral style of typically all-male vocal groups from South Africa. (Chapter 10)

MEDIUM: The source of a sound, be it instrumental or vocal. (Chapter 2) Also, the term for a person in a possessed or trance state. (Chapter 10)

MEHTER: Ceremonial music of the Turkish *Janizary*. (Chapter 8)

MELANESIA: A collection of islands in the Pacific Ocean. The term is derived from Greek, meaning "black islands," a reference to the darker skin pigmentation of the majority population. (Chapter 4)

MELE (pronounced *meh-leh*): Poetic texts used in Hawaiian drum dance chant. (Chapter 4)

MELE HULA (pronounced *meh-leh hoo-lah*): Unaccompanied Hawaiian songs specifically associated with dance. (Chapter 4)

MELISMA: Term for a text-setting style in which more than one pitch is sung per syllable. (Chapter 2)

MELODEON: A small reed organ. (Chapter 9)

MELODIC CONTOUR: The general direction and shape of a melody. (Chapter 2)

MELODY: An organized succession of pitches forming a musical idea. (Chapter 2)

MEMBRANOPHONE: Ethnomusicological classification referring to instruments such as drums that use a vibrating stretched membrane as the principle means of sound production. (Chapter 2)

MENTO: A creolized form of ballroom dance music considered a predecessor to *reggae*. (Chapter 11)

MERENGUE: A Latin American dance and music form, originally from the Dominican Republic. Also, the term for the middle section of a *merengue* performance. (Chapter 11)

MESTIZO: A person of mixed Native-American and Spanish descent. (Chapter 12)

MESTRE: A Brazilian term for a senior *capoeira* artist considered a master of the tradition. (Chapter 12)

METALLOPHONE: An *idiophone* consisting of several metal bars graduated in length to produce different pitches. (Chapter 6)

METER: A division of music beats into regular groupings. (Chapter 2)

MICRONESIA: A collection of islands in the Pacific Ocean. The term, meaning "tiny islands," is derived from Greek. (Chapter 4)

MIHRAB: A small "niche" or focal point found in a *mosque,* used to orient Islamic worshippers in the direction of Mecca, Saudi Arabia. (Chapter 8)

MINARET: The tall tower of a *mosque*, used for the Islamic call to prayer. (Chapter 8)

MIXOLYDIAN: A medieval church *mode* that predates the "equal tempered" tuning system used today as the basis of Western music. (Chapter 9)

MODE: A set of rules or guidelines used to compose or improvise music in a particular tradition. (Chapter 5)

MODERNISM: In an academic context, a term for scholarship that emphasizes objective "truth" and objective description in favor of subjective interpretation. (Chapter 1)

MONOPHONY: Music with a single melodic line. (Chapter 2)

MORIN HUUR: A fiddle from Mongolia with a distinctive horse head ornament. (Chapter 7)

MOSQUE (pronounced *mosk*): A house of worship for Islamic believers. (Chapter 8)

MRIDANGAM: A barrel-shaped drum from India. (Chapter 5)

MUEZZIN: A person who calls Islamic believers to worship five times a day. (Chapter 8)

MUHAMMAD: Muslim prophet and Arab leader who during his lifetime (570–632 C.E.) spread the religion of Islam and unified a great deal of the Arabian Peninsula. (Chapter 8)

MULATTO: A person of mixed African and Iberian ancestry. (Chapter 12)

MULLAH: A low-ranking clergyman in Islam. (Chapter 8)

MUMMER: A type of street theater actor, usually in performances staged during the Christmas season. (Chapter 11)

N

NAGASVARAM: A double-reed *aerophone* from India. (Chapter 5)

NEY (Also, NAY): A vertical flute found in Turkish and Arabic music traditions. (Chapter 8)

NGA BOM: A double-faced drum from Tibet. (Chapter 7)

NODE: A point of minimum amplitude on a vibrating string. (Chapter 7)

NOH: Classical drama form from Japan. (Chapter 7)

NOKAN: A transverse flute from Japan. (Chapter 7)

NONGAK: Style of folk music from Korea associated with farmers. (Chapter 7)

O

ORGANOLOGY: The study of musical instruments. (Chapter 3)

ORISHA: A category of deity in the animistic spiritual belief system of *Santeria* and in other African-derived religious traditions. (Chapter 11)

ORNAMENTATION: An embellishment or decoration of a melody. (Chapter 2)

ORUS: A rhythmic pattern associated with an *orisha* in the *Santeria* religious tradition. (Chapter 11)

OSSIAN: Legendary Gaelic hero and bard of the third century C.E. (Chapter 9)

OTTOMAN EMPIRE: An empire centered in what is now Turkey that spread throughout West Asia, eastern Europe, and northern Africa from the fourteenth to the nineteenth century. (Chapter 8)

O-TUZUMI: A small, hourglass-shaped drum from Japan that is held at the hip. (Chapter 7)

OVERTONE: A tone that is heard above a fundamental pitch, and that is one of the ascending group of tones that form the harmonic series derived from the fundamental pitch. (Chapter 7)

P

PAHU: A single-headed cylindrical *membranophone* from Hawaii that stands vertically on a carved footed base. (Chapter 4)

PALILLOS (pronounced *pah-lee-yohs*) (Also, PITOS): A type of finger-snapping commonly found in Spanish flamenco music. (Chapter 9)

PALITO: The term for a rhythmic pattern played on the side of a drum in *salsa* music. (Chapter 11)

PALLAVI: The first section of a *kriti* vocal performance from India. (Chapter 5)

PALM WINE GUITAR: A popular music style from sub-Saharan Africa. (Chapter 10)

PALMAS: The term for the hand-clapping commonly found in Spanish flamenco music. (Chapter 9)

PAN: A musical instrument from Trinidad made out of a steel oil drum. (Chapter 11)

PANDEIROS: A hand-held frame drum with attached cymbals (i.e., a tambourine), used in *capoeira* music from Brazil. (Chapter 12)

PANORAMA: A steel drum orchestra competition held at the end of the Carnival festival in Trinidad. (Chapter 11)

P'ANSORI: Narrative vocal performance style from Korea. (Chapter 7)

PARANG: A Portuguese-derived music sung during Christmas season. (Chapter 11)

PARLANDO RUBATO: A term meaning "speech-rhythm," indicating a fluctuating tempo. (Chapter 9)

PASEO: The opening section of a *merengue* performance. (Chapter 11)

PENTATEUCH: See TORAH.

PENTATONIC SCALE: A scale consisting of only five pitches. (Chapter 2)

PEURT A BEUL (pronounced *porsht a boy*): Unaccompanied dance song with nonsense syllables used to substitute for fiddling. (Chapter 13)

PHIN (pronounced *pin*): A fretted plucked lute from Northeast Thailand. (Chapter 6)

PHLENG LUK THUNG (pronounced *pleng look toong*): A popular music form from Thailand. (Chapter 6)

PHONIC STRUCTURE: The relationship between different sounds in a given piece; this relationship can be either m*onophony* or some form of *polyphony*. (Chapter 2)

PI (pronounced *bee*): A double-reed *aerophone* found in the *piphat* classical ensemble of Thailand. (Chapter 6)

PIBROCH (pronounced *pee-brahk*): A form of Scottish bagpipe music with an elaborate theme-and-variations structure. (Chapter 9)

PIPA: A pear-shaped lute from China. (Chapter 7)

PIPHAT (pronounced *bee-paht*): A type of classical ensemble from Thailand characterized by the use of melodic and rhythmic percussion and a double-reed *aerophone*. (Chapter 6)

PITCH: A tone's specific frequency level, measured in Hertz (Hz). (Chapter 2)

PITOS: See PALILLOS.

POIETIC: The process of creating the meaning of a symbol. (Chapter 1)

POLYNESIA: A collection of islands in the Pacific Ocean. The term is derived from Greek, and means "many islands." (Chapter 4)

POLYPHONY: The juxtaposition or overlapping of multiple lines of music; the three types of polyphony are *homophony*, *independent polyphony*, and *heterophony*. (Chapter 2)

POLYRHYTHM: A term meaning "multiple rhythms"; the organizational basis for most sub-Saharan African music traditions. (Chapter 10)

PORTAMENTO: A smooth, uninterrupted glide from one pitch to another. (Chapter 4)

PORTEÑOS: A term for residents of the port area of Buenos Aires, Argentina. (Chapter 12)

POSTMODERNISM: A general term applied to numerous scholarly approaches that reject "modernism," with its emphases on objective "truth" and objective description, in favor of subjective interpretations. (Chapter 1)

POWWOW: A pan-tribal American Indian event celebrating Native American identity and culture, generally also open to non-Native Americans. (Chapter 13)

PRECENTOR: A song leader who recites the "line" of a *lined hymn* in Calvinist churches in the United States. (Chapter 13)

PROGRAMMATIC MUSIC: Music that has a "program"—that is, tells a story, depicts a scene, or creates an image (Chapter 3).

PSALMS: A book of the Christian Bible used as the source for many songs in Calvinist churches in the United States. (Chapter 13)

PUK: Drum used to accompany Korean *p'ansori* performance. (Chapter 7)

PYGMIES: A generic term applied to a diverse population of forest-dwellers in Central Africa. (Chapter 10)

Q

QANUN (Also, KANUN): A plucked zither used in Turkish and Arabic music traditions. (Chapter 8)

QAWWALI (Also, KAWWALI): Sufi Muslim devotional songs. (Chapter 5)

QIN (pronounced *chin*; also, GUQIN): A bridgeless plucked zither from China, the playing of which is characterized by the frequent use of overtones. (Chapter 7)

QUR'AN: See KORAN.

R

RADA: Ritual drums used in *vodou* (*voodoo*) ceremonies from Haiti. (Chapter 11)

RADIF: A collection of *gusheh* for each *dastgah* in Persian classical music. (Chapter 8)

RAGA: A mode or system of rules and expectations for composition and improvisation in Indian classical music. (Chapter 5)

RAKE AND SCRAPE: A folk music from the Bahamas. (Chapter 11)

RAMA: The central figure of the Hindu Indian epic *Ramayana*. (Chapter 5)

RAMAYANA: An Indian mythological epic about the Hindu god Rama found throughout South and Southeast Asia. (Chapter 6)

RANAT EK (pronounced *rah-nahd ek*): The lead *xylophone* of classical ensembles from Thailand. (Chapter 6)

RANAT THUM (pronounced *rah-nahd toom*): The supporting *xylophone* of classical ensembles from Thailand. (Chapter 6)

RANCHERA: A style of "country" *mariachi* from Mexico that emphasizes vocal performance. (Chapter 12)

RANGE: All the pitches that a voice or instrument can potentially produce. (Chapter 2)

RAQS SHARQI (pronounced *rocks shar-kee*): Middle Eastern dance form characterized as "belly dance" by outsiders to the region. (Chapter 8)

RASA: The mood or sentiment of an artistic expression in India. (Chapter 5)

RASTA: A believer in *Rastafarianism*. (Chapter 11)

RASTAFARIANISM: A religious belief system centered in Jamaica, which purports that the second coming of Jesus Christ has already occurred in the form of Haile Selassie, an Ethiopian king. (Chapter 11)

RAVANA: The villain in the Indian epic *Ramayana*. (Chapter 5)

RAVI SHANKAR: A famous musician and composer from India. (Chapter 5)

REBAB: A fiddle commonly found in gamelan ensembles from Indonesia. (Chapter 6)

REBEC: A spiked fiddle from France. (Chapter 3)

RÊCO-RÊCO: A notched scraper *idiophone* found in Latin American music traditions. (Chapter 12)

REEDS: A type of *aerophone* that uses a vibrating reed to produce sound. (Chapter 2)

REELS: A type of dance music found in Scottish and Appalachian music. (Chapter 13)

REELS À BOUCHE: An unaccompanied song used for dance music in the Cajun region of Louisiana in the United States. (Chapter 13)

REGGAE: A popular music form from Jamaica characterized by a rhythmic emphasis on the offbeat and by politically and socially conscious lyrics. (Chapter 11)

REGULATORS: The metal keys that "regulate" the drone pipes on the Irish bagpipes to produce different pitches. (Chapter 10)

RENAISSANCE LUTE: A pear-shaped plucked lute from Europe. (Chapter 3)

RHYMER: The lead vocalist in a *rhyming spiritual* performance from the Bahamas. (Chapter 11)

RHYMING SPIRITUAL: A vocal genre from the Bahamas. (Chapter 11)

RHYTHM: The lengths, or durations, of sounds as patterns in time. (Chapter 2)

RHYTHMIC DENSITY: The quantity of notes between periodic accents or over a specific unit of time. (Chapter 2)

RHYTHMIC MELODY: The complete musical idea of polyrhythmic music. (Chapter 10)

GLOSSARY

RIQQ (pronounced *rik*): A small, single-headed drum with pairs of small cymbals inserted into its frame (i.e., a tambourine), common to Turkish and Arabic music traditions. (Chapter 8)

RITARD: A musical term for slowing the tempo, normally at the end of a piece. (Chapter 2)

ROCK STEADY: A popular music form from Jamaica considered a precursor to *reggae*. (Chapter 11)

RODA: A circular area used for the dancers in *capoeira* performances. (Chapter 12)

ROM (Also, ROMANI or GYPSIES): An ethnic group originating in India characterized by a semi-nomadic lifestyle; popularly known as *gypsies*. (Chapter 9) *Rom* is also the term used for large paired cymbals from Tibet. (Chapter 7)

RUMBA (Also, RHUMBA): A Latin American dance and music form. (Chapter 11)

RYUTEKI: A transverse flute from Japan. (Chapter 7)

S

SACRED HARP: The most popular collection of *shape-note* songs. (Chapter 13)

SACHS–HORNBOSTEL SYSTEM: Standard classification system for musical instruments created by Curt Sachs and Erik M. von Hornbostel, which divides musical instruments into four categories: *aerophones*, *chordophones*, *idiophones*, and *membranophones*. (Chapter 2)

SALSA: A Latin American dance music form. (Chapter 11)

SAMBA: A popular music form from Brazil. (Chapter 12)

SAMBA-BAIANA: "Bahian samba" from Brazil. (Chapter 12)

SAMBA-CANÇÃO (pronounced *samba kahn-syao*): "Song samba" from Brazil. (Chapter 12)

SAMBA-CARNAVALESCO: "Carnival samba" from Brazil. (Chapter 12)

SAMBA-ENREDO: "Theme samba" from Brazil. (Chapter 12)

SAMBA-REGGAE: "Reggae samba" from Brazil. (Chapter 12)

SAMBISTAS: Dancers in the *samba schools* that parade during Carnival in Brazil. (Chapter 12)

SAMUL-NORI: A type of folk music from Korea. (Chapter 7)

SANDOURI: A hammered zither from Greece. (Chapter 3)

SANJO: An instrumental form from Korea. (Chapter 7)

SANKYOKU: A classical ensemble type from Japan, consisting of *koto*, *shakuhachi*, and *shamisen*. (Chapter 7)

SANTERIA: A belief system combining animism and syncretized Roman Catholicism, found primarily in Cuba and the United States. (Chapter 10)

GLOSSARY

SANTUR: A hammered zither from the Persian classical tradition. Often cited as the origin of hammered zithers found throughout Asia, northern Africa, Europe, and the Western hemisphere. (Chapter 3)

SARANGI: A bowed lute from India. (Chapter 5)

SAROD: A fretless plucked lute from India. (Chapter 5)

SAW U (pronounced *saw oo*): A Thai fiddle with a coconut resonator. (Chapter 6)

SAZ: A fretted plucked lute from Turkey. (Chapter 8)

SCALE: The pitches used in a particular performance arranged in ascending order. (Chapter 2)

SCHALMEI: A medieval double-reed *aerophone* from Europe. (Chapter 3)

SCHEITHOLT: A spiked fiddle from Germany. (Chapter 3)

SEMIOTICS: The study of "signs" and systems of signs, including music. (Chapter 1)

SHAH: The title formerly given to hereditary monarchs in Iran. (Chapter 8)

SHAKA ZULU (1787–1828): Leader of the Zulu ethnic group from South Africa. (Chapter 10)

SHAKUHACHI: A vertical flute from Japan. (Chapter 7)

SHAM'IDAN: A Middle Eastern dance in which the dancer performs with a large, heavy candelabrum with lighted candles balanced on the head. (Chapter 8)

SHAMISEN: A fretless plucked lute from Japan with a membrane resonator face. (Chapter 7)

SHANGO: An animistic belief system found primarily in Trinidad. (Chapter 11)

SHAPE NOTES: A music notation system from the United States that uses differently shaped "note" heads to indicate pitch. (Chapter 13)

SHAWM: A medieval double-reed *aerophone* from Europe. (Chapter 3)

SHENG: A mouth organ from China. Also the term for the male hero role-type in Beijing Opera from China. (Chapter 7)

SHIA: The fundamentalist branch of Islam. (Chapter 8)

SHO: A mouth organ from Japan. (Chapter 7)

SHOFAR: A Jewish ritual trumpet made of a ram's horn. (Chapter 8)

SIKU: Panpipes common among indigenous populations from Peru and throughout the Andes. (Chapter 12)

SIKURI: A type of ensemble from Peru, consisting of *siku* performers with accompanying drummers. (Chapter 12)

SINGSINGS: A cultural festival common to Papua New Guinea that comprises several ethnic groups performing indigenous music and dance traditions. (Chapter 4)

SINGING SCHOOL: A tradition of teaching four-part harmony techniques, found in rural areas throughout the United States. (Chapter 13)

SITA (pronounced *see-tah*): The wife of the Hindu God *Rama* in the Indian epic *Ramayana*. (Chapter 5)

SITAR: A fretted plucked lute from India. (Chapter 5)

SIZHU (pronounced *sih-joo*): An ensemble comprising "silk and bamboo" instruments from China. (Chapter 7)

SKA: A popular music form from Jamaica considered a precursor to *reggae*. (Chapter 11)

SOCA: A popular music style related to calypso music from Trinidad. (Chapter 11)

SOCIOLOGY: The study of human social behavior, emphasizing its origins, organization, institutions, and development. (Chapter 1)

SOLFÈGE: Mnemonic syllables corresponding to individual pitches in a scale. (Chapter 5)

SON: An Afro-Cuban music genre from Latin America. (Chapter 11)

SONG LANG: A clapper *idiophone* from Vietnam. (Chapter 6)

SON JALISCIENSE: A category of *mariachi* that features frequent subtle shifts of meter and tempo, making it more rhythmically active than most *mariachi* music. (Chapter 12)

SPIRITUAL: A term for religious folk music. (Chapter 13)

SPOONS: A pair of spoons struck together to play rhythm. (Chapter 9)

STEEL DRUM: A musical instrument from Trinidad made from steel oil drums. (Chapter 11)

STRING BASS: A large fretless plucked lute heard in many music traditions from the United States. (Chapter 13)

STROPHIC: A song form in which the music repeats with each new poetic verse. (Chapter 13)

SUFI (pronounced *soo-fee*): The mystical branch of Islam. (Chapter 8)

SUNNI (pronounced *soo-nee*): The mainstream branch of Islam. (Chapter 8)

SUONA (pronounced *swoh-nah*): A double-reed *aerophone* from China. (Chapter 7)

SURDO: A large drum used in Samba music in Brazil. (Chapter 12)

SUSAP: A mouth harp (lamellophone) from Papua New Guinea. (Chapter 4)

SYLLABIC: A text setting in which only one pitch is sung per syllable. (Chapter 2)

SYMPATHETIC STRINGS: A set of strings, most commonly found on Hindustani Indian chordophones, that vibrate "in sympathy" with the vibrations of other strings on the instrument. (Chapter 5)

SYMPHONIA: A medieval European instrument similar to the *hurdy gurdy*. (Chapter 9)

SYNAGOGUE: A Jewish house of worship. (Chapter 8)

SYNCOPATION: The accenting of a normally weak beat. (Chapter 2)

T

TABLA: A pair of drums found in Hindustani music from India. (Chapter 5) Also, a goblet-shaped hand drum found in Arabic music. (Chapter 8)

TAHMALA: A compositional form found in Turkish and Arabic music. (Chapter 8)

TAHRIR: A freely rhythmic section emphasizing melismatic performance found in Persian classical music. (Chapter 8)

TAI THU (pronounced *tai tuh*): A type of chamber music ensemble from Vietnam. (Chapter 6)

TAIKO: Generic term for *drum* in Japan. (Chapter 7)

TAKHT: A type of instrumental ensemble found in Arabic music traditions. (Chapter 8)

TALA: Rhythmic framework found in *raga* performance in India. (Chapter 5)

TAMBOO-BAMBOO: A type of ensemble developed after drums were banned in Trinidad, which used cane and bamboo tubes that were beaten with sticks and stamped on the ground. (Chapter 11)

TAMBORA: A small barrel-drum made with a thick leather face, commonly used in *merengue* from the Dominican Republic. (Chapter 11)

TAMBURA: A round-bodied lute used to provide the "drone" element in Indian classical music. (Chapter 5) Also, a term used to describe round-bodied lutes from Bulgaria, Croatia, and Serbia in Southeastern Europe. (Chapter 3)

TANBUR: A fretted plucked lute common to Turkish and Arabic music. (Chapter 8)

TANGO: A dance and associated music originating in Argentina, but now commonly associated with ballroom dance. (Chapter 12)

TAQSIM (pronounced *tahk-seem*): An instrumental improvisational form in Turkish and Arabic music traditions. (Chapter 8)

TARAB: Arabic word for a state of emotional transformation or ecstasy achieved through music. (Chapter 8)

TASLAM: A compositional form found in Turkish and Arabic music. (Chapter 8)

TAVIL: A pair of drums from India, often used to accompany the *nagasvaram*. (Chapter 5)

TEJANO (pronounced *teh-hah-noh*): Term referring to populations and cultural activities from the Texas-Mexico borderlands in North America. (Chapter 13)

TEJAS (pronounced *teh-hahs*): Native American name for what is now Texas in the United States. (Chapter 13)

GLOSSARY

TEKEROLANT: See Hurdy Gurdy.

TEKKE: A type of Sufi Muslim monastery. (Chapter 8)

TEMPO: The relative rate of speed of a beat. (Chapter 2)

TEMPO GIUSTO: A regular or "precise" metered rhythm following an unmetered section. (Chapter 9)

TEXT SETTING: The rhythmic relationship of words to melody; can be *syllabic* (one pitch per syllable) or *melismatic* (more than one pitch per syllable). (Chapter 2)

THEKA (pronounced *teh-kah*): The entire pattern or set of words (*bols*) for a given *tala* in classical Indian music. (Chapter 5)

TIMBALES: A pair of metal-framed drums of European military origin used often in *salsa* music. (Chapter 11)

TIMBER FLUTE: A wooden transverse flute from Ireland. (Chapter 9)

TIMBILA: A log *xylophone* from Mozambique. (Chapter 10)

TIMBRE: The tone quality or "color" of a musical sound. (Chapter 2)

TIN WHISTLE: A metal vertical flute from Ireland. (Chapter 9)

TOMTOM: A pair of tall, single-headed hand drums from Ghana. (Chapter 10)

TORAH (Also, PENTATEUCH, pronounced *pent-a-toik*): In Judaism, the first five books of the Bible, or more generally, all sacred literature. (Chapter 8)

TOTEM: An animal, plant, or other natural object used as the emblem of a group or individual, and strongly associated with an ancestral relationship. (Chapter 13)

TRUMPET: A type of *aerophone* that requires the performer to vibrate his or her lips to produce sound. (Chapter 2)

TUMBADORA (Also, CONGA): A tall barrel-shaped single-headed drum used in *salsa* music. (Chapter 11)

TUMBAO: A rhythmic pattern played on the *conga* in *salsa* music. (Chapter 11)

TUNING SYSTEM: The pitches common to a musical tradition. (Chapter 2)

U

UD (Also, AL'UD): A fretless, plucked pear-shaped lute found in Arabic music traditions. (Chapter 8)

UILLEANN PIPES (pronounced *il-en*; Also, UNION PIPES): Bagpipes from Ireland, called *uilleann* (meaning "elbow") because the performer uses an elbow to pump the bellows. (Chapter 9)

UKELELE: A high-ranged plucked lute from Hawaii. (Chapter 4)

UMBANDA: A belief system combining animism and syncretized Roman Catholicism, found primarily in Brazil. (Chapter 11)

URTYN DUU: A Mongolian vocal form described as "long song"; performers are accompanied by the *morin huur*. (Chapter 7)

V

VENU: A transverse flute from South India. (Chapter 5)

VIHUELA: A small, fretted plucked lute from Mexico, similar to a guitar but with a convex resonator. (Chapter 12)

VINA: A plucked lute from South India, often associated with the Hindu goddess Saraswati. (Chapter 5)

VODOU (Also, VOODOO): An animistic belief system found primarily in Haiti. (Chapter 10)

W

WAI KHRU: A teacher-honoring ceremony from Thailand. (Chapter 6)

WAULKING SONG: Work songs from Scotland performed while working with wool. (Chapter 9)

X

XYLOPHONE: An idiophone consisting of several wooden bars graduated in length to produce different pitches. (Chapter 10)

Y

YANGBANXI (pronounced *yahng bahn shi*): Chinese term for post-1949 Beijing Operas infused with communist and nationalist political messages; translated as "Revolutionary Peking (Beijing) Opera." (Chapter 7)

YANGQIN (pronounced *yang chin*): A hammered zither from China. (Chapter 7)

YENICERI: See JANIZARY.

YUE QIN (pronounced *yweh chin*): A plucked lute from China. (Chapter 7)

Z

ZAKIRLER: A specialist group of male vocalists who perform metered hymns in unison during a Sufi ritual. (Chapter 8)

GLOSSARY

ZARB: A goblet-shaped hand drum used in Persian classical music traditions from Iran. (Chapter 8)

ZHENG (pronounced *jeng*): A plucked zither from China. (Chapter 7)

ZIKR: See DHIKR

ZITHER: A type of chordophone in which the strings stretch across the length of the resonating body. (Chapter 2)

ZOUK: Popular music form from the French Lesser Antilles in the Caribbean. (Chapter 11)

ZURNA (Also, ZOURNA): A double-reed aerophone from Turkey and Greece. (Chapter 3)

ZYDECO: Creole dance music from the southern United States, primarily Louisiana. (Chapter 13)

Resources for Further Study

As comprehensive as this book seeks to be, there is no way to include enough material to cover all possible questions. Further, we have suggested that both teachers and students will supplement our Sites by constructing their own. Thirty years ago, when ethnomusicology was still young in American institutions and resources were severely limited, it was difficult to find information on many world music traditions. Today, with the explosion of available information and new technologies for delivering it, anyone can obtain further information on virtually any topic. Not all libraries will have a broad selection of print, audio, or video publications available, but anyone with access to the Internet will find it profitable to at least visit any of the better, more professional websites devoted to virtually any musical type or style in the world. The following, also found in part at the end of Chapter 1, is a guide to some of the available resources that will lead you to further explore the world's musics.

We have arranged these resources into four categories: (1) print materials; (2) visual materials; (3) audio materials; and (4) additional resources. Our inclusion of an item does not necessarily imply our complete approval of its contents, but does mean we feel it offers something of value. Our exclusion of an item does not signal our disapproval; we are attempting to deal with limitations of space and the limits of our own knowledge. We have also limited ourselves to materials in English.

Lastly, a word of caution about using the Internet as a research tool. While the Internet is quite a valuable resource, articles found on it are generally not "refereed" to ensure accuracy of content, so do not rely on the Internet alone. Nevertheless, using a search engine, such as Google or Yahoo, to get started on a topic of interest can save you a lot of time digging through hard copy bibliographies for more information.

Print Materials

Encyclopedias and Dictionaries

Randall, Don Michael, ed. *The Harvard Dictionary of Music,* 4th ed. Cambridge, MA: Belknap Press of Harvard University Press, 2003.

    Originally a slender book written entirely by one man, musicologist Willi Apel, this dictionary first appeared in 1944 and has undergone many revisions. The present volume supercedes the previous edition, called *The New Harvard Dictionary of Music.* This resource provides lengthy but broad articles, such as "East Asia," "Folk Music," and "American Indian

Music," but there are also short entries for particular instruments (e.g., "sitar"), ensembles (e.g., "gamelan"), and genres (e.g., "reggae"), though there are none on individuals.

Sadie, Stanley, and John Tyrrell, eds. *The New Grove Dictionary of Music and Musicians,* 2nd ed. 29 vols. London: Macmillan, 2001.

Originally a small encyclopedia published by Englishman Sir George Grove in the 1870s, the "Grove" (as it is known familiarly) was long biased toward England in particular and Europe in general. The advent of the twenty-volume first edition of the *New Grove* in 1980 was a milestone in the study of world musics, for the encyclopedia now included substantial entries by recognized scholars on most countries of the world. The second edition of 2001 incorporates those articles plus everything that had appeared in the earlier *New Grove American* and the *New Grove Dictionary of Musical Instruments*. Thus, the Grove now includes articles at the level of continent (or subcontinent), nation, genre, ensemble, instrument, and individual performer/composer/innovator.

The Garland Encyclopedia of World Music. 10 vols. New York and London: Routledge, 1998–2002.

This monumental encyclopedia, each volume having from 900 to 1,200 pages, is the first such work devoted entirely to the world's musics. Each volume has three sections: The first is an introduction that includes overview articles; the second, called "Issues and Processes," includes articles on specific questions or approaches; and the third is devoted to individual nations, cultures, or genres. Volume 10, entitled *The World's Music: General Perspectives and Reference Tools,* includes articles by individual scholars under the heading "Ethnomusicologists at Work," and a section called "Resources and Research Tools" that combines the bibliographies, discographies, and videographies of volumes 1 through 9, each of which is devoted to a single continent or subcontinent (e.g., South Asia). Each volume, save for volume 10, is liberally illustrated with photos, charts, and notations and includes a compact disc. The appropriate volumes will be cited under each of our chapters.

Books and Journals

World Music: The Rough Guide. 2 vols. (vol. 1: Africa, Europe, and the Middle East; vol. 2: Latin and North America, the Caribbean, India, Asia, and the Pacific). London: Rough Guides, Inc., 1999–2000.

While a few of the articles were written by known scholars and discuss traditional kinds of music, the bulk are devoted to contemporary forms, especially popular, revivalist, and innovative forms, with special attention to groups and individuals who make recordings. With its extensive illustrations, the two-volume set is nonetheless valuable for understanding at least certain aspects of each country's music scene. The Rough Guide has also produced a growing series of compact discs, mostly presenting popular and "worldbeat" forms.

Oxford University Press Global Music Series. 17 vols. Oxford: Oxford University Press, 2004–2005.

This series of short books, intended for a non-specialist audience, provides in-depth discussion of specific cultural areas as well as an accompanying CD of common musical types. The volumes have a strong "music education" approach, as one of the series editors, Patricia Shehan Campbell, is well known as a music educator specializing in world musics. Some of the volumes are mentioned below, but the areas covered include: East Africa, Central Java, Trinidad, Bali, Ireland, the Middle East, Brazil, America (United States), Bulgaria, North India, West Africa, South India, Japan, China, and more specifically *mariachi* music in the United States.

Shahriari, Andrew. *Popular World Music*. Upper Saddle River, NJ: Prentice Hall, 2011.
    After writing the first edition of *World Music: A Global Journey*, we realized how much more there was to say about popular music genres around the world. Given the size and scope of this text already, we could not offer such study here. Andrew, consequently, took up the challenge of writing a more complete review of popular world music with an emphasis on musical style and genre history. If some of our introductions to popular music, such as reggae and salsa, piqued your interest, consider further investigation with this complementary publication.

We would be remiss if we did not include a few texts specific to various world music traditions discussed herein. We have intentionally limited the list to just a handful of resources as some areas have a wealth of associated material, some of which the serious student will no doubt easily discover on his or her own. The sources listed below, however, are a useful starting point. We have organized them according to chapters in the current book.

Chapter 1 Before the Trip Begins: Fundamental Issues

Blacking, John. *How Musical Is Man?* Seattle: University of Washington Press, 1973.
Hood, Mantle. *The Ethnomusicologist*. Kent, OH: Kent State University Press, 1982 (New York: McGraw-Hill, 1971).
Nettl, Bruno. *The Study of Ethnomusicology*. Urbana: University of Illinois Press, 1983.
Myers, Helen, ed. *Ethnomusicology: An Introduction*. New York: Norton, 1992.

Chapter 2 Aural Analysis: Listening to the World's Music

Kamien, Roger. *Music: An Appreciation*, 4th brief ed. New York: McGraw Hill, 2002 (1990).
    The opening sections of any number of "introductory" Euro-American art music texts, such as Kamien's, are useful for understanding basic music terminology. The above-mentioned dictionaries also provide detailed discussion.
Kartomi, Margaret J. *On Concepts and Classifications of Musical Instruments*. Chicago: University of Chicago Press, 1990.
Sachs, Curt. *The History of Musical Instruments*. New York: Norton, 1940.

Chapter 3 Cultural Considerations: Beyond the Sounds Themselves

Barz, Gregory F., and Timothy J. Cooley. *Shadows in the Field: New Perspectives for Fieldwork in Ethnomusicology*. New York: Oxford University Press, 1997.
Clayton, Martin, Trevor Herbert, and Richard Middleton, eds. *The Cultural Study of Music: A Critical Introduction*. New York: Routledge, 2003.
Merriam, Alan P. *The Anthropology of Music*. Evanston, IL: Northwestern University Press, 1964. This text is particularly important to the "anthropology" branch of ethnomusicology and is considered fundamental to the field.

Chapter 4 Oceania: Australia, Papua New Guinea, Hawaii, Kiribati

Chenoweth, Vida. *A Music Primer for the North Solomons Province.* Ukarumpa, Papua New Guinea: Summer Institute of Linguistics, 1984.

Feld, Steven. *Sound and Sentiment: Birds, Weeping, Poetics, and Song in Kaluli Expression,* 2nd ed. Philadelphia: University of Pennsylvania Press, 1990.

Malm, William P. *Music Cultures of the Pacific, the Near East, and Asia,* 3rd ed. Englewood Cliffs, NJ: Prentice Hall, 1996 (1967).

Moyle, Alice M. *Songs from the Northern Territory.* Canberra, Australia: Australian Institute of Aboriginal Studies, 1974 (1967).

Moyle, Richard M. *Traditional Samoan Music.* Auckland, New Zealand: Auckland University Press, 1988.

Chapter 5 South Asia: India, Pakistan

Capwell, Charles. *The Music of the Bauls of Bengal.* Kent, OH: Kent State University Press, 1986.

Clayton, Martin. *Time in Indian Music: Rhythm, Metre, and Form in North Indian Rag Performance.* Oxford: Oxford University Press, 2000.

Kaufmann, Walter. *The Ragas of North India.* Bloomington: Indiana University Press, 1968.

_____. *The Ragas of South India.* Bloomington: Indiana University Press, 1976.

_____. *Sai Devotional Songs.* Tustin, CA: Sathya Sai Book Center of America, n.d.

Wade, Bonnie C. *Music in India: The Classical Traditions.* Englewood Cliffs, NJ: Prentice Hall, 1979.

Chapter 6 Southeast Asia: Vietnam, Thailand, Laos and Northeast Thailand, Indonesia (Java and Bali)

Becker, Judith. *Traditional Music in Modern Java: Gamelan in a Changing Society.* Honolulu: University of Hawaii Press, 1980.

Miller, Terry E. *Traditional Music of the Lao.* Westport, CT: Greenwood Press, 1985.

Morton, David. *The Traditional Music of Thailand.* Berkeley: University of California Press, 1976.

Nguyen, Thuyet Phong, ed. *New Perspectives in Vietnamese Music.* New Haven, CT: Department of International and Area Studies, Yale University, 1990.

Shahriari, Andrew. *Khon Muang Music and Dance Traditions of North Thailand.* Bangkok: White Lotus Press, 2005.

Spiller, Henry. *Gamelan: The Traditional Sounds of Indonesia.* Santa Barbara, CA: ABC-CLIO World Music Series, 2004.

Tenzer, Michael. *Gamelan Gong Kebyar: The Art of Twentieth-Century Balinese Music.* Chicago: University of Chicago Press, 2000.

Chapter 7 East Asia: China, Mongolia, Korea, Japan, Tibet

Garfias, Robert. *Music of a Thousand Autumns: The Togaku Style of Japanese Court Music.* Berkeley: University of California Press, 1975.

Heyman, Alan C. *Korean Musical Instruments.* New York: Oxford University Press, 1995.

Jones, Stephen. *Folk Music of China: Living Instrumental Tradition.* Oxford: Clarendon Press, 1992.

Liang, Mingyue. *Music of the Billion: An Introduction to Chinese Musical Culture.* New York: Heinrichshofen, 1985.

Mackerras, Colin. *The Rise of the Peking Opera, 1770–1870.* Oxford: Clarendon Press, 1972.

Malm, William P. *Japanese Music and Musical Instruments.* Tokyo: Tuttle, 1968 (1959).

Park, Chan E. *Voices from the Straw Mat: Toward an Ethnography of Korean Story Singing.* Honolulu: University of Hawaii Press, 2003.

Wichmann, Elizabeth. *Listening to Theatre: The Aural Dimension of Beijing Opera.* Honolulu: Hawaii University Press, 1998.

Chapter 8 The Middle East: Islam and the Arab World, Iran, Egypt, Sufism, Judaism

During, Jean. *The Art of Persian Music.* Washington, DC: Mage Publishers, 1991.

Nettl, Bruno. *The Radif of Persian Music: Studies in Structure and Cultural Context.* Champaign, IL: Elephant & Cat, 1987.

Picken, Laurence. *Folk Music Instruments of Turkey.* London: Oxford University Press, 1975.

Shiloah, Amnon. *Jewish Musical Traditions.* Detroit, MI: Wayne State University Press, 1992.

_____. *Music in the World of Islam: A Socio-Cultural Study.* Detroit, MI: Wayne State University Press, 2003 (1995).

Touma, Habib Hassan. *The Music of the Arabs.* Portland, OR: Amadeus Press, 1996.

Chapter 9 Europe: Greece, Spain, Russia, Scotland, Ireland, Hungary, Bulgaria

Bohlman, Philip V. *The Study of Folk Music in the Modern World.* Bloomington: Indiana University Press, 1988.

_____. *The Music of European Nationalism: Cultural Identity and Modern History.* Santa Barbara, CA: ABC-CLIO World Music Series, 2004.

Chuse, Loren. *The Cantaoras: Music, Gender, and Identity in Flamenco Song.* New York: Routledge, 2003.

Nettl, Bruno. *Folk and Traditional Music of the Western Continents,* 3rd ed. Englewood Cliffs, NJ: Prentice Hall, 1990 (1965).

Rice, Timothy. *May It Fill Your Soul: Experiencing Bulgarian Music.* Chicago: University of Chicago Press, 1994.

Slobin, Mark, ed. *Retuning Culture: Musical Changes in Central and Eastern Europe.* Durham, NC: Duke University Press, 1996.

Totton, Robin. *Song of the Outcasts: An Introduction to Flamenco.* Portland, OR: Amadeus Press, 2003.

Chapter 10 Sub-Saharan Africa: Ghana, Nigeria, Central Africa, Zimbabwe, Uganda, Senegal, The Republic of South Africa

Berliner, Paul F. *The Soul of Mbira.* Chicago: University of Chicago Press, 1993 (1981).

Charry, Eric. *Mande Music: Traditional and Modern Music of the Maninka and Mandinka of Western Africa.* Chicago: University of Chicago Press, 2000.

Chernoff, John Miller. *African Rhythm and Sensibility.* Chicago: University of Chicago Press, 1979.

Erlmann, Veit. *Nightsong: Performance, Power, and Practice in South Africa.* Chicago: University of Chicago Press, 1996.

Kisliuk, Michelle. *Seize the Dance! BaAka Musical Life and the Ethnography of Performance.* New York: Oxford University Press, 1998.

Locke, David. *Drum Gahu: An Introduction to African Rhythm.* Tempe, AZ: White Cliffs Media, 1998.

Nketia, J.H. Kwabena. *The Music of Africa.* New York: Norton, 1974.

Chapter 11 The Caribbean: Haiti, Jamaica, Trinidad and Tobago, The Bahamas, Cuba, The Dominican Republic

Béhague, Gerard H., ed. *Music and Black Ethnicity: The Caribbean and South America.* London: Transaction Publishers, 1994.

Hill, Donald R. *Calypso Calaloo: Early Carnival Music in Trinidad.* Gainesville: University Press of Florida, 1993

Johnson, Howard, and Jim Pines. *Reggae: Deep Roots Music.* London: Proteus Books, 1982.

Manuel, Peter. *Popular Musics of the Non-Western World.* New York: Oxford University Press, 1988.

Stuempfle, Stephen. *The Steelband Movement: The Forging of a National Art in Trinidad and Tobago.* Philadelphia: University of Pennsylvania Press, 1995.

Waxer, Lise. *Situating Salsa: Global Markets and Local Meaning in Latin Popular Music.* New York: Routledge, 2002.

Wilcken, Lois. *The Drums of Vodou.* Tempe, AZ: White Cliffs Media, 1992.

Chapter 12 South America and Mexico: The Amazon Rainforest, Peru, Argentina, Brazil, Mexico

Almeida, Bira. *Capoeira: A Brazilian Art Form.* Berkeley, CA: North Atlantic Books, 1986.

Clark, Walter Aaron, ed. *From Tejano to Tango.* New York: Routledge, 2002.

Marbury, Elisabeth. "Introduction." In *Vernon and Irene Castle's Modern Dancing.* New York: World Syndicate, 1914.

Perrone, Charles A., and Christopher Dunn. *Brazilian Popular Music and Globalization.* New York: Routledge, 2002 (2001).

Seeger, Anthony. *Why Suyá Sing: A Musical Anthropology of an Amazonian People.* Cambridge, U.K.: Cambridge University Press, 1987.

Sheehy, Daniel. *Mariachi Music in America: Experiencing Music, Expressing Culture.* Oxford: Oxford University Press, 2005.

Stevenson, Robert. *Music in Mexico: A Historical Survey.* New York: Thomas Y. Crowell, 1952.

Turino, Thomas. *Moving Away from Silence: Music of the Peruvian Altiplano and the Experience of Urban Migration.* Chicago: University of Chicago Press, 1993.

Chapter 13 Canada and the United States: Cape Breton, Appalachia, Ohio Valley, Mississippi Delta, Nuyorican, Cajun

Cantwell, Robert. *Bluegrass Breakdown: The Making of the Old Southern Sound.* Urbana: University of Illinois Press, 1984.

Cobb, Buell E., Jr. *The Sacred Harp: A Tradition and Its Music.* Athens: University of Georgia Press, 1989 (1978).

Crawford, Richard. *The American Musical Landscape.* Berkeley: University of California Press, 1993.

Flanders, Helen Hartness. *Eight Traditional British-American Ballads.* Middlebury, VT: Middlebury College, 1951.

Herndon, Marcia. *Native American Music.* Hatboro, PA: Norwood, 1980.

Koskoff, Ellen, ed. *Music Cultures in the United States: An Introduction.* New York: Routledge, 2005.

Nettl, Bruno. *Blackfoot Musical Thought: Comparative Perspectives.* Kent, OH: Kent State University Press, 1989.

Oliver, Paul. *Songsters and Saints: Vocal Traditions on Race Records.* Cambridge, U.K.: Cambridge University Press, 1984.

Peña, Manuel. *The Texas-Mexican Conjunto: History of a Working-Class Music.* Austin: University of Texas Press, 1985.

Periodicals

There are several periodicals devoted to the study of world music. Among the most prominent are: *Ethnomusicology: Journal of the Society for Ethnomusicology* (www.ethnomusicology.org/), *Ethnomusicology Forum* (www.bfe.shef.ac.uk/), *Asian Music* (asianmusic.skidmore.edu/academics/asianmusic), and *The World of Music* (www.uni-bamberg.de/~ba2fm3/wom.htm). Two invaluable websites, *The Scholarly Journal Archive* (www.jstor.org) and *Project MUSE* (muse.jhu.edu), provide online access to many scholarly journals.

The journals mentioned above are varied in content, but all often include reviews of books, recordings, and video documentaries. Membership to the organizations that publish these journals is usually less than $100US and cheaper for students. Membership provides access to electronic forums and contact lists that will allow you to network with ethnomusicologists around the globe.

Visual Materials

Video Collections

The JVC Video Anthology of World Music and Dance. 30 vols. (1990)

The original series of thirty videotapes and nine books was produced in Japan by JVC, and offered clips of five hundred performances from one hundred countries. While this collection is quite valuable, it is also heavily oriented toward dance and does not include some important kinds of music—for example, Javanese gamelan. With fifteen volumes on Asia and two on the Americas, the collection is obviously weighted away from the Western hemisphere. Furthermore, certain features, such as the section "Soviet Union," date the collection a bit. The volumes are arranged as follows: East Asia, 1–5; Southeast Asia, 6–10; South Asia, 11–15; the Middle East and Africa, 16–19; Europe, 20–22; Soviet Union, 23–26; the Americas, 27–28; Oceania, 29–30.

The JVC Smithsonian Folkways Video Anthology of World Music and Dance of the Americas. 6 vols. (1995)

Produced in the mid-1990s, this set of six videos and booklets offers 158 performances, making up for the paucity of clips from the Americas in the earlier set.

The JVC Smithsonian Folkways Video Anthology of World Music and Dance of Africa. 3 vols. (1995)

This set of three videos and booklets was produced in the mid-1990s and offers seventy-two performances from eleven countries in Africa.

The JVC Smithsonian Folkways Video Anthology of World Music and Dance of Europe. 2 vols. (1996)

Also produced in the mid-1990s, this set includes fifty-nine performances to supplement those in the original set.

Multicultural Media (www.multiculturalmedia.com) has produced a series of ten video documentaries on various topics. In conjunction with Lyrichord, Multicultural Media has also re-released a series of documentary films by Deben Battacharya.

Shanachie Entertainment Corporation (www.shanachie.com) has released numerous videos and DVDs, including Jeremy Marre's documentary series *Beats of the Heart*.

Audio Materials

It is not possible to list all the companies that produce world music audio materials. The following is a sampler of the best-known companies:

- ARCMusic (www.arcmusic.co.uk)
- Arhoolie (www.arhoolie.com)
- Auvidis (www.auvidis.com)
- Hugo Records (Hong Kong) (www.hugocd.com)
- King Records (World Music Library series) (www.kingrecords.co.jp)
- Lyrichord Discs (www.lyrichord.com)
- Multicultural Media (www.multiculturalmedia.com)
- Naxos Records (including the Marco Polo series) (www.naxos.com)
- PAN Records (Leiden, The Netherlands) Playa Sound Records (including the Air Mail Music series) (www.playasound.com)
- Rounder Records (www.rounder.com)
- Shanachie Entertainment Corp (including Yazoo Records) (www.shanachie.com)
- Smithsonian Folkways (www.folkways.si.edu)

Additional Resources

We have prepared a website to accompany this book: **www.routledge.com/cw/miller**. It includes additional listening examples and articles, plus photos and web links, among other features. The "On Your Own Time" sections found at the end of each chapter in this book are also intended as starting points for further explanation of world music and culture.

There are several institutions around the country with ethnomusicology programs for those that are interested in turning their interest in world music into a career. Most prominent among these is the program at UCLA in Los Angeles, California (www.ethnomusic.ucla.edu).

A complete list of programs can be found on the SEM website (www.ethnomusicology.org) under Resources (webdb.iu.edu/sem/scripts/guidetoprograms/guidelist.cfm).

Archives are also a source of much useful information. Notable among these are the UCLA Ethnomusicology Archive (www.ethnomusic.ucla.edu/Archive/) and the Ethnomusicology Institute at Indiana University (www.indiana.edu/~folklore/ethnomusicologyinstitute.htm). Again, check the SEM website for a more complete list.

Index

Page numbers for illustrations are in **bold** type.

a-ak music 218
Aborigines, Australian 62, 63–9
Acadians 463, 466, 467, 506
accent 29
accordion: *balalaika* ensemble 299; Cajun 505, 508; in *merengue* 416, 418; *tango* 435, **436**
Achim, Arnim von 5, 286
Adams, John 212
Adé, King Sunny (KSA) 348–9
Adeyeye, Adesanya 331–3
adhan (Call to Prayer) 55, 248–53, 256
Aeolian mode 477
aerophones 19–20, 62; double reed 20, 54, 57, **58**, 114
Africa: background 328, 329; European colonization of 329, 334–5; Islam in 248, 252, 328–9; languages 329, 340–1, 381; rhythm 29–30; tonal language 340–1; *see also* Central Africa; sub-Saharan Africa; *and individual countries*
African-American music: blues 76, 462, 495–9; gospel 462, 491–5; jazz 462; spirituals 29, 488–91
African influences: in the Caribbean 380, 381, 383, 384, 385, 388, 408, 410–11, 414; in South America 426, 427, 441, 445
African National Congress (ANC) 368
Afrikaners 367, 368–9

afrikyiwa 337–8
Afrobeat 349
agogo bells 331, 440, 445
Ahyoung, Olivia 398
Aida (Verdi) 263
akadinda music
Akan people 339
al-'ud see ud
alap in *raga* 100, 107
Albania 55, 248, 252
Alexander the Great 51, 55, 245, 287
Algarita, Martin Pereira 426–7
Ali ibn Abi Talib 248
amadinda 361
"Amazing Grace" 305, 308
Amazon rainforest 427–30
American Indians *see* Native Americans
Amin, Idi 359
Andrews Sisters 396
Andreyev, Vasily Vasilyevich 298–9, 301
Angola 441, 445
animism 62, 74, 151; in Australian Aboriginal cosmology 64; in Indonesia 165; in Mongolia 217; in sub-Saharan Africa 330
Anthony, Marc 504
Anthropology of Music, The (Merriam) 9, 42
anudrutam 110
apartheid 368, 371
arabesque 256
Arabic language 244

Arabic music 54, 55, 247–57, 263–8; modal system 248, 254–5, 264–5, 278
aradhana 112
archives and collections 530–1
Argentina 434–9; *tango* 427, 435–9
Arnaz, Desi 504
art music 31, 263, 297
arts, the 46–7
Asante (Ashanti) 343
Asch, Moses 13
Asia 55; *see also* Central Asia; South Asia; Southeast Asia
atabaque 445
atumpan drums 341, **342**
audio recording 9, 13, 45–6, 527–8
aulos 57
Australia 62, 63–9
Austro-Hungarian Empire 54, 282
Aymara 433
Aztec empire 424, 449

baglama 57
bagpipes: Bulgarian *gaida* **319**, 322; Irish or *uilleann* 304, 309–12; North America 308; Scottish highland 303–8, **304**, 487
Bahamas 378, 379, 404–7
balalaika 298–301
Bali 134; *Gamelan Gong Kebyar* 165, 169, 171–7; "Monkey Chant" (*kecak*) 177
Balkanska, Valya 319
ballad-singing, United States 461, 468–71

INDEX

ballroom dance 163, 379, 390, 408, 412–14, 444, 462; see also cha-cha-chá; mambo; merengue; rumba; salsa; samba; tango
bandoneón 435
Bangkok 132, 145–6, 154
Bangladesh 90, 92, 96–7, 123, 247
banjo: in bluegrass 484, 487; in Irish music 312
bansri 103
Baptish church 407, 474, 491; lined hymns 471–5; shape-note music 461, 476–82
Bartók, Béla 284–5, 315, 317, 322
Bauls 96–7
baya 102
beat, definition of 29
Beatles 106, 213, 504
Beats of the Heart (documentary series) 13
Becker, Dr. Judith 38–9
bedhaya dance 171
Beijing 189
Beijing Opera 47, 203–8
Belafonte, Harry 396
bell choirs 139
bells: afrikyiwa 337–8; agogo 331, 440, 445; cow 500
"Belly dance" (raqs sharqi) 267
Bengal 96–7
Benin 334, 383
Bennard, Rev. George 494
berimbau **445**, 445, 446, 448, 449
Berry, Chuck 499
bhajans 96, 116–20
bhangra 96, 127
Bharata Naatyam dance 113
bi-musicality 10
bino 81, 83–4
bira ceremony 358
biwa 57, 254
Blacking, John 9
Blackman, Garfield 397
Blackwell, Chris 348–9
Blades, Rubén 504
Blake, Blind 498
blue notes 488, 495–6, 498
bluegrass music 461, 482–8; festivals 487; vocal timbre in 484
blues: country 76, 462, 495–9; urban 496, 499

bodhran 313
Boers 367
Bollywood 120, 121–2, 127
bombos 431
bongos 408
Bonism 237
boogie-woogie 499
bossa nova 444
botija (marimbula) 408
bouzouki **58**, 58, 254; in Irish music 312
Bradbury, William 494
Brahms, Johannes 317
Brazil 379, 424, 425, 439–49; Amazonian chant 428–30; candomblé 334, 384; Carnival 440, 443–4; Kayapó-Xikrin Amazonian tribe 427–30; martial arts dance (capoeira) 427, 444–9; samba 427, 440–4
break-dancing 449
Brentano, Clemens 5, 286
Britten, Benjamin 165
Buddhism: China 191; Indonesia 165; Korea 217; Mongolia 213; South Asia 92; Tantric 237; Thailand 2–3, 151; Tibetan 234–8; Zen 227
Buenos Aires 438
Buganda 359
Bulgaria 55, 57, 318–22
Bulgarian Orthodox Church 319
Bulgarian women's chorus 319–21, 322
bunraki theater 223
Burke, Mary Lawson 83
button box see accordion
buzuq 58, **253**, 254, 256
Byzantine chant 287, 288–91
Byzantine Church 52–3, 55; see also Greek Orthodox Church
Byzantine Rite 52
Byzantium 51, 290; see also Constantinople; Istanbul

cai luong theater 144
Cajun music 463, 505–9
call-and-response; in Afro-Brazilian samba 440; in Bahamian rhyming spirituals 405; in capoeira music 445, 447; in Indian bhajan singing 117–18; Kiribati 83; in merengue 418; in Pygmy music 351, 352; in salsa 502; in sub-Saharan Africa music 330, 351, 352, 357, 369; in Vodu ritual 380; in Zulu choir 369
"Call to Prayer", Islamic 55, 248–53, 256
Calvin, John 473, 475, 479
calypso 379, 390, 391–7
Canada 302, 460, 461–2, 463; Cape Breton fiddling 462, 463–7
candomblé 334, 384
canon 12, 40
cante flamenco song 296
cantillation see chant
cantors 275
Cape Breton fiddling 462, 463–7
capoeira 427, 444–9
Caribbean 378–9; languages 378; slavery in 378–9, 393–4, 407–8; see also Bahamas; Cuba; Dominican Republic; Haiti; Jamaica; Trinidad and Tobago
Carnatic music 108–16
Carnival: Brazil 440, 443–4; New Orleans 444; Trinidad 390, 394, 396, 397, 401, 403, 444
cascará 501
castanets **293**
Castle, Vernon and Irene 439
Castro, Fidel 407, 408
Catholic Church see Roman Catholic Church
'cello 114
Celtic harp 307, 312
Celtic languages 284, 285; see also Gaelic
Central Africa 349–53; Pygmy music in 334
Central Asia 244, 248
cha-cha-chá 163, 313, 412, 413–14, 504
chant 2; Amazonian 428–30; Greek Orthodox (Byzantine) 287, 288–91; Hawaiian drum-dance 77–8, 80; Islamic call to prayer 55, 248–53, 256; Jewish liturgical 274–8; Sufi *Dhikr* ceremony 269–71; Tibetan Buddhist **49**, 237, 238; Vedic 93
chanter 305

573

chantwells 396
Chiang Ching *see* Jiang Qing
Chiang Kai-Shek 210–11
Child, Francis James 470
Chile 424
China 182, 183, 184, 189–213, 247, 467; arts in 47, 187; Cultural Revolution 190, 191, 210, 212; differences between North and South 190; dynasties 187; "folk music" 190; *guqin* 192–5; and Japanese music compared 223, 227; *Jingju* (Beijing Opera) 47, 203–8; musical instruments 49, 50, 57, 141, 190, 195, 197–9; narrative tradition 191; political influences 187, 191, 211–12; popular music 212, 213; *sizhu* ("silk and bamboo") music 141, 190, 195–203, 227; theatrical tradition 190, 191, 206–7; "traditional" music 189; Western influences 183, 189, 191; *Yangbanxi* (Revolutionary Beijing Opera) 191, 208–13
ching 148, 152
Chinggis (Genghis) Khan 213
choral music: African-American gospel 462, 491–5; Bulgarian women's chorus 319–21, 322; Kiribati 63, 81, 83–4, 85; Zulu 334–5, 369–72
chordophones 19, 21–2, 62, 70
chords 31
Christian missionary influences 62, 69, 74, 79, 85
Christianity 244, 250, 287, 329
Church of England 473
church modes 477
Church of Scotland 473
cimbalon 318
circle dances 353, 417, 441, 513
circular breathing 65
clappers: Chinese 205; Vietnamese *song lang* 141, **142**, 143
clapsticks: in Aboriginal music 64, 65–6; in Pygmy music 351; *see also* claves
clarinet 114, 391
classical music 6, 48; European 5, 12, 285–7; Iranian (Persian) 258–62; Southeast Asia 134;
Thai (*piphat*) 26, 146–52; versus folk music 5, 285–7; versus popular music 40; Vietnamese 141–5; *see also individual composers*
claves 408, 411
Cleveland, James 495
Cliff, Jimmy 385
cobza 57
Colombia 426
Colón, Willie 504
colonialism 62, 69, 85, 92, 329, 334–5, 378, 425, 439
colotomic structure, in Gamelan music 167, 171
Columbus, Christopher 378, 390, 404, 407, 460
comparative musicology 9, 45
composers 48
computers, use in fieldwork 531
conch shell trumpets 234, 238
Confucianism 194, 210, 217, 218
Confucius *see* Kong Fuzi
conga drum 391, 410, 501
Congo, Democratic Republic of 349, 441, 445; Mbuti Pygmy music 350–3
Constantine I, Emperor 51
Constantinople 52, 53, 290–1; see also Istanbul
Cook, Capt. James 74, 81
corroboree ritual **68**, 69
cosmology, Australian Aboriginal 64, 68
Cotton, James 499
Cougat, Xavier 502, 504
country music 487
cowbell 500
Cozad, Belo 516
Cream 499
Creole language 380, 381
Creoles 506
crescendo 31
Croatia 57
Crusades 53, 55
Cruz, Celia 504
Cuba 378, 379, 407–8, 462, 502, 504; *cha-cha-chá* 412, 413–14; *guaracha* 408; *mambo* 379, 412, 413; *santeria* tradition 334, 384, 408, 504; *son* 408, 410–12, 502
"Cucaracha, La" 450

cultural studies 10
culture 2, 4, 36–59
Cumina 384, 390
cymbals: Chinese 205; Thai 149, 152; Tibetan 234, **236**
czardas 31

Dahomey people 334
Dairo, I.K. 347
dan tyba 57
dance 46, 47; Australian Aborigine 69; Balinese gamelan 171, 175; "belly" (*raqs sharqi*) 267; Brazilian *capoeira* 427, 444–9; break-dancing 449; Cajun 506, 508; Cape Breton, Nova Scotia 465; Carnatic 113; circle 353, 417, 441; contests (Kiribati 85; Native American 513); Egyptian 267; Hawaiian *hula* 76, 77, **79**, **80**; Hungarian *czardas* 316; Indian *Kathakali* 47, 115–16; Irish 310, 311, 313; Israeli *klezmer* music for 273–4; Javanese *bedhaya* 171; jigs 465; Kiribati 81, 83–4, 85; martial arts (*capoeira*) 427, 444–9; Mbuti Pygmies 353; Native American 512, 513; Papua New Guinea 69, 73, 74; Scottish 305, 467; Spanish *flamenco* 292–7; sub-Saharan Africa 330; Sufi Mevlevi sect 271–2; Thai 163; *see also* ballroom dance; *bossa nova*; *cha-cha-chá*; *guaracha*; *mambo*; *merengue*; *rumba*; *salsa*; *samba*; *tango*
dancehall (dub), reggae 378, 390
dancehalls (*do-do*), Cajun music 506, 508
Dance song, Plains Indian 510–11
danzón 408, 413
Daoism 191
dastgah 259–61; compared to Arabic *maqam* 259
Davis, Rev. Gary 495
De Klerk, F.W. 368
de Lucíía, Paco 297
Debussy, Claude 165, 256
decrescendo 31
dejembe **24**

574

INDEX

density referent 338, 351; *see also* rhythmic density
Densmore, Frances 9, **10**
Dervishes, Whirling 271
Deux arabesques (Debussy) 256
Dhikr ceremony 269–72
dhol 127
dholak 124
Dicey Doh Singers 407
didjeridu 62, 63, 64–9, **65**
Diksitar, Muttusvami 112
Directory of Publick Worship 474
Dixie Chicks 488
dizi 195, **198**, 199
DJs in Jamaican music 390
dombak 262
Dominican Republic 379, 414; *merengue* 414–18
domra 300
donno 337
Doolittle, Eliakim 477
Dorsey, Thomas A. 495
double reeds 54, 57, **58**
Dreamtime (*The Dreaming*) 64, 68
drone 28; in Aboriginal music 65, 66; bagpipes 305; in Bulgarian women's chorus 320; in Carnatic *Kriti* 111; in Greek Orthodox chant 288, 289; in Hungarian *hurdy gurdy* 314, 315; in *raga* 100
drums: African 331, 332, 334, 334–45; *atabaque* 445; bongos 408; conga 391, 410, 501; Dominican Republic *tambora* 414, 416, 418; Egyptian *takht* ensemble 264; friction 440; Hawaiian 77, **79**, 80; Indian (*baya* 102; *dhol* 127; *dholak* 124; *mridangam* 111; *tabla* 100, **101**, 102, 106, 117, 124; *tavil* 114); Iranian *dombak* or *zarb* 262; Irish *bodhran* 313; Japanese *o-tuzumi* and *ko-tuzumi* 230–1; Japanese *taiko* 223, 231, 232–3; Korean *puk* 219–20; Native American 509, 511; Papua New Guinea *kundu* 70, 73–4; Peruvian 431; slit 62, 70; Thai 149; Tibetan 234; *timbales* 408, 410, 501; as

type of membranophone 24; *Vodou* ritual 381
drutam 110
dub (dancehall), reggae 378, 390
duff 264
dulcimer *see* zither, hammered
dung chen 234, 238
dung kar conch shell trumpet 234, 238
DVD *see* video recordings
dynamics 31; defined 18

East Asia 48, 90, 183–4, 187–9; *see also* China; Japan; Korea; Mongolia; Tibet
Easy Instructor, The (Smith and Little)
ecstasy states 267–8, 271–2
Egypt 262–8; *firqua* ensembles 265; *Takht* instrumental ensemble 263–7
electric guitar: in *jùjú* music 346; in reggae music 385–6
electronic keyboard 385
electrophones 19
emic (insider) perspective 36, 38
England 473
English Folk-Songs from the Southern Appalachians (Sharp) 470
English and Scottish Popular Ballads, The (Child) 470
environment, music and 43–4
equal-tempered tuning 26, 495
orhu 195, **196**, 197, 199, 205
Eskimos *see* Inuit
Estefan, Gloria 504
esthesic process 4
ethics 43
Ethiopia 388
Ethiopian lyre **22**
ethnic identity 41
ethnocentrism 4, 9, 36
ethnomusicology 8–13; defined 8; history of, in America 9–11; new theoretical perspectives 45; resources 12–13; technology and 45–6
etic (outsider) perspective 36, 38
Europe: art music tradition 31; ballads 469; classical music 5, 12, 285–7; general information

on 282–5; Islam in 248, 252; language groups 284–5; *see also* individual countries
European influence 62, 69, 74, 79, 83, 85, 369
exhortation 477

Fania All Stars 504
fasola singing 476, 480
Fernandez, Pedro 411
fiddle 55; bluegrass 484; Cajun 505, 508; Cape Breton fiddling 462, 463–7; in Chinese music 195, **196**, 197, 199, **204**, 205, 210; Egyptian 263; Irish 312; in Javanese gamelan 166; in Thai music **160**; in
Vietnamese music 141
fieldwork 9, 10, 11, 527–31; audio recording 9, 13, 45–6, 527–8; collecting and archiving materials 530–1; computer technology 531; dissemination of findings 11, 531–3; interviewing 530; observation and participant observation 527; publication of materials 532–3; still photography 528–30; video recording 528
filmi/filmi git 96, 121–2, 397
Finland, *kantele* zither **21**
firqua ensembles 265
First Nations *see* Native Americans
flamenco 292–7
Flanders, Helen Harkness 470
Flately, Michael 313
Flatt, Lester 486
Fleck, Bela 217
flute: Chinese *dizi* 195, **198**, 199; Egyptian; end-blown 55, **57**; Indian 103; Japanese **20**, 223, **225**, 228; Middle Eastern *ney* 55, **57**, 262, 265, 269; Native American 463, 509, 514–17; "Nuyorican" *salsa* 500; Oceania 62; `timber' 312; as a type of aerophone 19–20; Vietnamese 141
folk music 5, 6, 8, 322, 465, 469; American bluegrass 461, 482–8; Chinese 190; classical music

575

versus 5, 285–7; country blues 495–9; Hungarian 314, 317, 318; Islam and 253; Russian 298
folklore 9, 144, 470
Folkways 13
Foolbull, Richard 516
form 32
free rhythm 30
French culture and influences 286; *see also* Acadians; Cajun music
French *rebec* 55
fret 21
friction drum 440
frottoir washboard 508
fuging tunes 477
funk 347

Gabriel, Peter 126
gadulka 55
Gaelic language and culture 38, 301, 307, 310, 462, 466
gagaku (Japanese court music) 223
gaida **319**, 322
gamelan 39, 165; *Balinese gamelan gong kebyar* 165, 169, 171–7; Javanese court gamelan 165, 166–71, 177
garamut 70, 74
Gardel, Carlos 439
Garland Encyclopedia of World Music 12, 361
Garvey, Marcus 388
gat in *raga* 102–3, 107
Genghis Khan 213
German *Scheitholt* 55
Germanic language and culture 284, 285, 286
Ghana: history of 328; *ntahera* horn **20**, **37**; polyrhymthic ensembles 335–40; "talking drums" in 340–5
Gillespie, Dizzy 504
ginga dance movement 446, 448
Glass, Philip 165, 359
"God is Good All the Time" 492
Goethe, J.W. von 469
gongs 23; in Balinese *gamelan gong kebyar*; in Chinese music 205; as idiophones; Javanese Court Gamelan 166, 167, 168; in Thai music 146, 147, 149; in Vietnamese music 138–41

Gospel music 51, 462, 491–5
Graceland (Simon) 371, 372
"Grand Ole Opry, The" 487
Greece, Ancient 52, 55, 287; music theory 54, 245
Greek *bouzouki* **58**, 58, 254
Greek *lauto* 57, **58**
Greek *lyra* 55, **57**
Greek Orthodox Church 55; Byzantine chant 287, 288–91
Greek *zourna* 57
Grillo, Frank Raul 504
Growling Tiger, The 391
Guangzhou 189
guaracha 408, 502
güiro 410, 414, 416, 418
guitar 21, 62; in bluegrass 484; in country blues 495–6; *flamenco* 293, 294–6; Hawaiian slack-key steel 63, 76, 79; in Mexican *mariarchi* music 450, **451**, 453; in Nigerian *jùjú* music 346, 348; in reggae 385–6; Vietnamese **49**, 50, 141; *see also* ukulele
guitarrón 450, **451**
guqin 192–5
Guyana 120, 398
Gypsies (Rom/Romany) 55, 283, 296, 314, 317, 321, 444
Gypsy Kings 297

Haile Selassie 388
Haiti 379–80, 414; *vodou* (voodoo) ritual 335, 380–4
Haney, Woodrow 516
Hanoi, Vietnam 137, 138
Hapsburg Empire 54
harmonica 495, 499
harmonium 116–17, 124
harmony 25, 31; in African *mbira dza vadzimu* 355; in Kiribati vocal performance 83, 85
harp: Celtic 307, 312; *kora* 362–3; in *mariachi* music 453; mouth 23, 63, 70–3; as a type of chordophone 22, 70
Harrison, George 106
Hastings, Thomas 494
Hawaii 62, 74–80; drum-dance chant (*mele*) 77–8, 80; *hula* dance 76, 77, **79**, **80**; slack-key steel guitar 63, 76, 79; ukulele

76, 79, **80**; vocal performance 63, 77–8
Hebrides 38, 301, 307
Herder, Johann Gottfried 286
heterophony 31; in Baptist lined hymns 471, 474; in Vietnamese music 143
Hibbert, Toots 390
"hillbilly" music 487
Hinduism 92, 96, 118, 120, 151, 165, 175
Hindustani music 96, 97–107, 108
hip-hop music 29
history songs, Aboriginal 68–9
Ho Chi Minh City, Vietnam 137
Holy Roman Empire 54, 282
homophony 31
Homrong (film) 152
Hood, Ki Mantle 9–10, 165, 532
Hornbostel, Erich Moritz von 9, 19
hosho 355
hula dance 76, 77, **79**, **80**
hula pahu songs 80
Hungary 278, 285, 314–18; *hurdy gurdy* 314–16
hurdy gurdy 314–16
hymns: gospel 494–5; Greek Orthodox 288–91; lined 461, 471–5, 479; Sufi (*Ilahi*) 269; *see also* shape-note music

López, Orestes and Cachao 411

McAllester, David Park 10
McGraw, Hugh 476
Machito (Frank Raul Grillo) 504
McLaughlin, John 106
MacLeod, Morag 302–3
MacMaster, Buddy 463–4, 465
MacMaster, Natalie 467
McPhee, Colin 165
McTell, Blind Willie 498
Maghrib 244
Mahabharata 171
Mahavishnu Orchestra 106
mahori 147
makam see maqam
Making Music in the Arab World (Racy) 267
Malaysia 182, 247, 252
Malaysian *serunai* **58**

Mali kingdom 328
Malm, William 38, 40, 223
mambo 379, 412, 413, 504, 505
Manchester School of popular music studies 10
Mandela, Nelson 368, 371
mandolin 58, 114, 312, 484, **485**
maneaba 84
Mangeshkar, Lata 121–2
Manley, Michael 385
Mannette, Ellie 399
Mao Zedong 187, 190, 210, 211
maqam 254–5, 264–5, 278; compared to Persian *dasgah* system 259
maracas 400, 408
Marcano, Neville (The Growling Tiger) 391
mariachi 427, 449–54; instruments of 450, 453
marimbula (*botija*) 408
Marley, Bob 348, 385, 386, 388
Marre, Jeremy 13
martial arts dance (*capoeira*) 427, 444–9
Martin, Ricky 504
Marxist interpretation 45
Mashriq 244
Masnavi 259
Mason, Lowell 494
Mauchahty-Ware, Tom 516
mawlam singer 156, **157**
Maya Empire 424
mbira dza vadzimu 354–8
mbube singing 369–72
Mbuti Pygmies 334, 350, 350–3
medium 18–19; defined 18
Mehmed II 543
Melanesia 62, 69
mele poetry 80
melisma 30, 294
melodic contour 28
melody 27–8
membranophones 19, 24–5, 62
merengue 379, 414–18
Merriam, Alan 9, 42
Merrill, Robert 278
mestizo 425, 427, 431, 449
metallophones 167, 172, 174
meter 29–30; additive 322; Bulgarian 322; Korean music 222; *sizhu* ("silk and bamboo")

199; Thai music 147–8, 157; Vietnamese music 143
Mevlevi sect 259, 268, 271
Mexico 424, 462; *mariachi* 427, 449–54
Micronesia 62, 80
Middle East 52, 244–5; tuning system 26; *see also individual countries*
Minimalist movement 227
missionaries *see* Christian missionary influences
modal system: Arabic 248, 254–5, 264–5, 278; in Beijing opera 205; Byzantine chant 289; Indian classical music 98, 107; Persian *dastgah* 259–61; Vietnamese 142
modernism 10, 45
Mongolia 182, 183, 213–17; overtone or throat singing 214–17
"Monkey Chant", Balinese 177
monophony 31
Monroe, Bill **485**, 486–7
morin khuur 214, 215
Morocco 247
mouth harp 23; Papua New Guinea 63, 70–3
"mouth music" 466
"Mozart effect" 42, 43
mpintin 341
mridangan 111
Mu Kezhai 205
Muhammad 52, 248, 250, 251, 268
mulattos 425, 443
mummer players 379
music: and the arts 46–7; and culture 2, 4, 36–59; definitions of 2, 252–3; and emotion 267; and environment 43–4; and ethics 43; exchange and adaptation 49–59; and identity 40–1, 526–7; interpretation of 4, 45; Marxist interpretation of 45; and possession rituals 42; Queer Theory applied to 45; and ritual 39, 42; semiotic interpretation of 4; as speech surrogate 72, 340; and spirituality 42, 270–2; teaching of 48; and trance states 39, 40,

43; as universal language 3; use versus function 42; and value systems 40
music therapy 42
Music and Trance (Rouget) 42
musical iconography 47
musical literacy 48
musicology *see* comparative musicology; ethnomusicology
Mussolini, Benito 440
Mussorgsky, Modest 47
muzak 44

nagasvaram 114
Nakai, R. Carlos 516
Nanongkham, Priwan 135
Native Americans 9, 460, 461, 463, 466, 508–17; dance 512, 513; drums 509, 511; flute music 463, 509, 514–17; Plains Indian Dance song 510–11; powwow events 463, 509, **512**, 512–13, **513**; vocables 509, 510
Nattiez, Jean-Jacques 4
Nettl, Bruno 10, 32
Nevaquaya, Doc Tate 516
New Age movement 509, 515
New Grass Revival 488
New Grove Dictionary of Music and Musicians, The 12
ney 55, **57**, 262, 265, 269
Nhac Tai Tu chamber music 141–5
Nigeria 334, 345–9; *jùjú* music 334, 345–9
Nixon, Richard 212
noh theater 223, 228, 232
noise, distinguished from music 2
non kan **20**
non-musiqa 252, 253
North America: colonization of 460; Scots-Irish culture in 302, 308, 312; *see also* Canada; United States
North Korea 187, 217, 218, 221–2
notation systems 48; Chinese *jianpu* 201, **202**, 202; tablature 193; Tibetan Buddhist chant **49**; *see also* shape-note music
Nova Scotia, Cape Breton fiddling 462, 463–7
ntahera **20**, **37**

nusach see chant, Jewish liturgical
Nusrat Fateh Ali Khan 126, 127

o-tuzumi 230–1
Obey, Ebenzer 347
oboe, Thai (*pi*) **20**, 147
Oceania: defined 62; music in 62–3; *see also* Australia; Kiribati; Papua New Guinea
octaves 25–6
Oguchi, Daihachi 232
Old Regular Baptists, lined hymns 471–5
opera 46–7, 263, 286; Beijing (*Jingju*) 47, 203–8; Revolutionary Beijing (*Yangbanxi*) 191, 208–13
oral traditions 48, 62, 380, 382, 469, 470, 509
organology 19
"Original" Sacred Harp, Denson Revision 477
ornamentation 28
Ottoman Empire 54, 247, 248, 285, 319, 321
"outsider" knowledge 36, 38
overtone singing *see* throat (overtone) singing

Pacheco, Johnny 504
Padmasambhava 237–8
Pahlevi, Muhammed Reza, Shah 258
pahu 77, 79, 80
Pakistan 90, 92, 95, 122–7, 247; *qawwali* 97, 123–7
pan see steel band music
pandeiros 445
panpipes (*sikuri*) 427, 431–4
P'ansori 218–22
Papua New Guinea 62, 63, 69–74; *singsings* 73–4; *susap* mouth harp 70–3, **71**
parlando-rubato 315
participant observation 527
Pathet Lao 154
Patton, Charlie 499
Payne, Dr. Richard W. 516
"Peanut Vendor, The" 412
Pentateuch 276
Pentecostal movement 494
performance, as a means of demonstrating world music 532
Persia 97, 247, 258; *see also* Iran
Persian music 258–62; modal system (*dastgah*) 259–61; *santur* 55, 57, 259, 261, 262
Peru 430–4; *sikuri* ensembles 427, 431–4
peurt a beul 466
Phawnsak Sawng-saeng 160
Philip of Macedonia 51, 287
phin 160
Phong, Nguyen Thuyet 529
phonic structure 30–1
Phonogrammarchiv 9
photography, still 530
pi (oboe) **20**, 147
piano: boogie-woogie 499; in Cape Breton fiddling 465; intervals 27; in "Nuyorican" *salsa* 501; in *tango* music 435
Piazzolla, Astor 439
pibroch music 305
Pictures at an Exhibition (Mussorgsky) 47
Pike, Kenneth 38
pipa 19, 57, 195, 197–8, **198**, 199, 254
piphat music 146–52
pitch 25–9; Arabic/Turkish 255; defined 18; definite 25; indefinite 25; *raga* 98, 107; *sizhu* ("silk and bamboo") 199; Thai 147; Vietnamese 142
Plato 43
Plymouth pilgrims 479
poietic process 4
political influences: Chinese arts 187, 191, 211–12; North Korea 218, 222–3
Polynesia 62, 63, 74
polyphonic stratification 149
polyphony 31; independent 31; parallel 431
polyrhythm: in African music 330, 334, 335–40, 346, 351, 360, 361, 364; defined 330; *salsa* 499; in South American music 426, 440; in *Vodou* 380, 381
Pompuang Duangjan 164
popular music 5, 6, 8, 40; East Asia 212–13; India 96, 121–2, 127; Jamaican reggae 348, 385–90, 444; Nigerian *jùjú* 334; Southeast Asia 134, 154, 159–64
popular music studies 10; Manchester School 10
portamento, in Hawaiian music 77
Portugal 55, 379
Portuguese colonialism 439
positivism 10
possession ritual 42, 358, 383–4
postmodernism 10, 45
Poulenc, Francis 165
powwow events 463, 509, **512**, 512–13, **513**
Pozo, Chano 504
Prado, Perez 413
praise-singing/drumming 343, 362–6
Presbyterianism 473
Presley, Elvis 76, 213, 499
Price, Miss E. 468
primitive Baptists *see* shape-note music
programmatic music 47
Protestantism 461
psalm singing 474, 479; Gaelic language 38, 302, 473
Psalms 473
publication of fieldwork findings 533–4
Puento, Tito 504
Puerto Rico 378, 379, 462, 504
puk 219–20
Pygmies: defined 350; Mbuti 334, 350, 351–3

qawwali (devotional song) 97, 123–7
Queer Theory 45
quqin 192–5
Qur'an (Koran) 55, 248, 252

Rabbit dances 513
"race record" industry 499
Racy, Ali Jihad 267
rada 381
raga 4; defined 98; North Indian (Hindustani) 97–107; pitches 98, 107; "scales" in 98; vocal 103; *see also* Carnatic music
Raghavan, Shanti 94

Rainer, John Jr. 516
Ramakian 153
Ramayana 153–4, 171, 177
ramwong (circle dance) 163
range 27
rap 29, 390
raqs sharqi ("belly dance") 267
Rara performance 381
rasa (mood) 103, 105
Rastafarianism 388, 389
rattles: *hosho* 355; *maracas* 400, 408; Native American 509; *shekere* 24, **381**; as type of idiophone 23
rêco-rêco 440, 445
Red Buffalo, Dan 516
reeds: capped 57; double 54, 57, **58**, 114; as type of aerophone 20
reels 311
reels à bouche 508
reggae 348, 348, 379, 385–90, 444
Regular Singing 480–1
Reich, Steve 165, 359
rhymer 405, 407
rhyming spiritual 404–7
rhythm 28, 29–30; defined 18; free 30; *raga* 102, 107; syncopated 143, 401, 435–6; Vietnamese 143; *see also* polyrhythm
rhythm and blues 499
rhythmic density 30; gamelan performance 168, 172
Riley, Terry 359
Rimsky-Korsakov, Nikolai 297
Rio de Janeiro 439, 440, 444
riqq 264
Ritchie, Jean 471
ritual 39, 42; Amazonian 429–30; Australian Aborigine 62, 69; Jewish 274–8; sub-Saharan Africa 330, 358; Sufi *Dhikr* ceremony 269–72; Thai 149, 151–2; Tibetan Buddhist 234–8; Vietnamese 140, 144; *vodou* (voodoo) 334, 380–4
Rivera, Ismael 502
Robeson, Paul 490
rock and roll 499
rock steady 390
Rolling Stones 499
Rom/Romany (Gypsies) 55, 283, 296, 314, 317, 321, 444

Roman Catholic Church 52–3, 291, 473
Roman Catholicism 52, 408, 504; Peru 431, 433; in relation to Carnival 394, 444; relation to Vodou 383
Roman Empire 51–2, 282, 287
Romance languages 284, 285
Romania 55; *cobza* lute 57
Romanticism 5, 286, 469
Ronstadt, Linda 454
Rouget, Gilbert 42
"rounds" 31
rumba 163, 412, 413, 504
Rumi, Jalal al-Din Muhammad 271
Russia 182, 297–30, 467
Russian Balalaika Orchestra 299

Sabri Brothers 124, 126–7
Sachs, Curt 9, 19
Sachs-Hornbostel system 19
Sacred Harp, The (White and King) 476, 477, 481
Saigal, Kundan Lal 121
Saigon (Ho Chi Minh City) 137
St. Vincent **43**
salsa 51, 379, 408, 412, 462, 499–505
samba 427, 440–4
samba-reggae 444
samul-nori 222–3
Sankey, Ira D. 494
sankyoko chamber music 223, 224–7
Santana 504
santeria tradition 334, 384, 408, 504
santur 55, 57, 103, 259, 261, 262
sarangi 103
sarasvati vina 114, **115**
sarod fretless **22**, 99
Sastri, Syama 112
Sawa, George Dimitri 246
scale 27; pentatonic 27
Schalmei 57
Schiller, Friedrich von 469
scholarship, new theoretical perspectives 45
Schubert, Franz 469–70
Scotland 284, 301–8, 474; dance music 305, 467; fiddling 462; Gaelic culture 38, 301, 307, 466;

highland bagpipes 303–8, 487; history of 301–2; psalm singing 302, 473; *waulking* songs 302
scrapers: *güiro* 410, 414, 416, 418; *rêco-rêco* 440, 445
Scruggs, Earl 486
Seeger, Pete 487
semiotics 4
Senegal-Gambia 362–6; Mandinka *jali* 334, 362–6
serunai **58**
Shabalala, Joseph 371–2
shadow-puppet theater 47, 136, 149, 171
Shaka Zulu 329, 367, 371
Shaka Zulu (Ladysmith Black Mambazo) 371
Shakti orchestra 106
shakuhachi 223, 224, **225**, 228
Shamans 430
shami'dan 267
shamisen 223, **224**, 224, 225, 230
Shanghai 189
Shango 383
Shankar, Anoushka 107
Shankar, Ravi 106, 107
shape-note music 461, 476–82, 487, 494
Sharp, Cecil 470
shawm 57
shekere **24**, 381
Shia Islam 248, 250, 257–8
shofar 276, **277**
Shona peoples, *mbira dza vadzimu* music 354–8
Shorty, Lord 397
Siam *see* Thailand
sikuri ensembles 427, 431–4
"silk and bamboo" music *see sizhu*
Simon, Paul 371, 372
singing school shape-note song 461, 476–82, 494
singsings, Papua New Guinea 73–4
sitan **22**
sitar 103, **106**, 106
sizhu ("silk and bamboo") chamber music 141, 190, 195–203, 227
ska 390
skomorokhi 300
slavery 378–9, 393–4, 407–8, 425, 439–40, 448, 460, 498

Slavic languages 284, 285
Smith, William 480
Smithsonian Institution 9
soca 379, 390, 396, 397
socialist realism 22, 145, 218
solfège 98, 107, 480
son 408, 410–12, 502
son jaliciense 452
song: Australian Aborigine 64–9; Baul 97; blues 76, 462, 495–9; Cajun 505; calypso 390, 391–7; flamenco *cante* 296; Gaelic psalm 302; Hawaiian 80; India 113 (devotional 96, 108–13, 116–20; *filmi git* 96, 121); Kiribati 81, 83, 85; *Lam Klawn* 155–9, 164; *merengue* 416; Mongolian *urtiïn duu* 214–17; Native American 510–11; Pakistani devotional (*qawwali*) 97; reggae 348, 349, 379, 385–90, 444; shape-note 461, 476–82, 487, 494; *son jaliciense* 452; and speech distinguished 2–3; *waulking* songs 302; work 320, 498; see also ballad singing; call-and-response; chant; choral traditions; lined hymns; popular music
song lang 141, 142, 143
Songhai kingdom 328
soul music 495
South Africa, Republic of: apartheid 368, 371; background information 366–8; Zulu choral tradition 334–5, 369–72
South America 424–6; African influences in 426, 427, 441, 445; see also Argentina; Brazil; Peru
South Asia 48, 90–6, 247; levels of development 95; religions 92–3; social organization 93; see also India; Pakistan
South Korea 217, 218, 221, 222
Southeast Asia 48; background 132–3; bamboo instruments 134; bronze metallurgy 134; classical music 134; ethnic groups in 114, 134; Islam in 165, 170, 247, 252; levels of development 133; lowland versus upland peoples 134; popular music 134, 154; theater 47, 134, 136; see also Indonesia; Isan; Laos; Thailand; Vietnam
Spain 247, 291–7, 378, 407–8; Flamenco music 292–7; Moorish 55, 57, 291
Spanish influence in South America 425, 426, 431
speech: heightened 2, 252, 276, see also chant; and song distinguished 2–3; substitute (surrogate) 72, 340
spirituality 42, 62, 68, 270–2
spirituals 29, 379, 404–7; African-American 488–91; rhyming 404–7
Sri Lanka 120
Srinivas, U. 114
Stanley, Ralph 487
steel band music 379, 390, 398, 399, 400–4
Stillman, Amy Ku'uleialoha 75
Stockhausen, Karlheinz 217
Stravinsky, Igor 297
string bass 484, 500, 501
strophic form 452, 484
Stumpf, Carl 9
sub-Saharan Africa 328–75; call-and-response in 330, 351, 352, 357, 369; goblet drums (*djembe*) 24; lamellophones 23, 354–5; polyrhythm in 330, 334, 335–40, 346, 351, 360, 361, 364; see also Central Africa; Ghana; Nigeria; Senegal-Gambia; South Africa; Zimbabwe
Sufism 247, 250–1, 268–72; definition 250; devotional song (*qawwali*) 123–7; *dhikr* ceremony 269–72; Mevlevi sect 259, 268, 271
Süleyman the Magnificent 54
Sunni Islam 248, 250, 258
Suntaraphon Band 163
Suraphon Sombatjalern 164
susap 70–3, **71**
Susilo, Hardjo 39
"sympathetic" strings 99
syncopated rhythm 143, 401, 435–6
syncretism 383

tabla: Egyptian-Arab 264; Indian 100, **101**, 102, 106, 117, 124
tablature notation 193
tai tu ritual 144
taiko 223, 231, 232–3
takak-nhiok ritual 429–30
Takht instrumental ensemble 263–7
tala (*raga* rhythm): Carnatic 110; Hindustani 102, 103
"talking drums" 340–5
tamboo bamboo 396, 402, 403
tambora 414, 416, 418
tambourines 111; *pandeiros* 445
tambura 57–8, 98–9, **99**
tanbur **21**, 57, **58**
tango 427, 435–9; bandoneón accordion 435; syncopated rhythm of 435–6
Tantric Buddhism 237
Taoism 217
Taqasim 253–5, 256
tarab 267
tavil 114
Tchaikovsky, Pytor Ilich 297
teaching music 48
teaching world music 531–2
technology, and development of ethnomusicology 45–6
tekerölant see *hurdy gurdy*
tempo, defined 29
text setting 29; melismatic 29, 30; syllabic 29
texture see phonic structure
Thailand 9, 247; Buddhist tradition 2–3; classical music (*piphat*) 26, 146–52; history and background 134, 145–6; Khon 47, 149, 152; *lam klawn* repartee singing 155–9; northeast see Isan; popular music 159–64; *ramwong* 163; tuning system 26, 147; *wai khru* ceremony 149, 151–2
theater 45–6, 47; Chinese tradition 190, 191, 206–7; Japanese 223, 228–32; Southeast Asia 47, 134, 136; see also shadow-puppet theater
theka 102
Theodosius I, Emperor 51–2

throat (overtone) singing: Inuit 217, 463, 517; Mongolian 214–17, 238
Tibet 182, 233–8; Buddhist chant **49**, 237, 238; Buddhist ritual 234–8; overtone singing 217, 238
timbales 408, 410, 501
timbre 18–25; defined 18; instrumental 19–25; vocal 19
timeline patterns: in African music 336–7, 339, 501; in Afro-Cuban music; in Haitian music 381
Tindley, Charles A. 495
tintal 102
Tirunal, Svati 112
Tizol, Juan 504
Tokens, The 371
tom-tom 337
tonal languages 340–1
tone 27
Torah 276
Tosh, Peter 388
totemism 62, 64, 430
"traditional" music 8, 10; East Asia 189; Japan 189, 223; Vietnam 144–5
trance states 39, 40, **43**, 271–2
Trevor-Roper, Hugh 307
triangle, in Cajun music 505
Trinidad and Tobago 117, 120, 378, 379, 390; calypso song 379, 390, 391–7; Carnival 390, 394, 396, 397, 401, 403, 444; soca 390, 396, 397; steel band music 379, 390, 400–4
Trujillo, Rafael 414, 417
trumpets: Jewish *shofar* 276, **277**; in *mariachi* music 453; in *salsa* 500; Tibetan 234–5, **235**, 238; as type of aerophone 20; *vaksin* 381; see also didjeridu
Tuff Gong see Marley, Bob
tumbadora see conga
tumbi 127
tuning systems 25–6, 27; Gamelan 167; Thai 147; Vietnamese 142
Turkey 247, 268; *baglama* lute 57; *kanun* zither **26**; musical instruments, influences on Asia and Europe 55–9; *tanbur* lute **21**, 57, **58**; *zurna* 54, 57, **58**; see also Istanbul
Turnbull, Colin 350
Tuva, Republic of 213, 217
Tyagaraja, Sri 108–9, 112

ud 57, 253–4, 256, 263
Uganda 358–61
uilleann bagpipes 304, 309–12
ukoko 332
ukulele, Hawaiian 76, 79, **80**
Ungarisches Rhapsodien (Liszt) 317
United States 334, 379, 407, 460, 461, 467–8; ballad-singing 461, 468–71; ballroom dance 439; bluegrass music 461, 482–8; Cajun music 505–9; *capoeira* clubs 449; country blues 76, 462, 495–9; and Cuba 408; ethnomusicology 9–11; gospel music 51, 462, 491–5; Hispanic population 462; Islam in 248, 252; jazz 462; lined hymn 461, 471–5, 479; *mariarchi* music 454; "Nuyorican" salsa 499–505; shape-note song 461, 476–82, 487; spirituals 488–91; see also North America
urtïïn duu 214–17

vaksin 381
Valentino, Rudolph 439
value systems and hierarchies 40
Vargas, Getúlio 440, 443
Vedic chant 93
Venezuela 424
Verdejo, Rafael Cortijo 502
Verdi, Giuseppe 263
Vergleichende Musikwissenschaft 9
Verney, Frederick 36
vibrato: in Hawaiian vocal music 77; in Native American flute music 515
videorecording 528–9
Vietnam 132, 136, 137–45, 183, 247; Central Highlands Bronze Gong Ensemble 138–41; Chinese influences 49; cultural regions in 137; modal system 142; musical instruments 49–50, 57, 138, 141; *Nhac Tai Tu* chamber music 141–5; rituals 140, 144; theater 136, 137, 144; upland and lowland cultures 140
vihuela 450, **451**
viola 114
violin: in Carnatic music 111; Egyptian 263; in *mariachi* music 453; in *tango* music 435; see also fiddle
vocables, in Native American music 509, 510
vocal performance 29, 62; Australian Aboriginal 64, 65, 66, 67; bluegrass 484; Hawaii 63, 77; India 108–21; Kiribati 63, 81, 83–4; Korean narrative 218–22; Mbuti Pygmies 351–2; Mexican *mariachi* 450; "Nuyorican" salsa 501–2; Southeast Asia 134; sub-Saharan Africa 330; Sufi *Dhikr* ceremony 269–71; *takht* ensembles 263, 267; see also chant; choral music; opera; popular music; song
vocal range 27
vocal timbre 19
Vodou (voodoo) 334, 380–4

wai khru ceremony 149
Wailer, Bunny 388
Wang Wei 194
Ward, Clara 495
washboard 508
water-puppet theater 136, 137
Watson, Doc 486
Watts, Sir Isaac 471, 477
waulking songs 302
Wayang 47
Weavers, The 371
Weber, Alain **37**
Weinman, Zev 275
"Whirling Dervishes" 271
White, Benjamin Franklin 476, 481
Williams, Marion 495
"Wimoweh" 371
work songs 320, 498
World Music: The Rough Guide 12

INDEX

xiao 195
Xinjiang province 247
xylophone: Javanese 167; Thai 146, 147; Ugandan *akadinda* 359–61; Ugandan *amadinda* 361

Yangbanxi 191, 208–13
yangqin 195, **197**, 197, 199
Yoruba 334, 346, 348, 383, 408

zarb 262
Zen Buddhism 227

Zhou Xuan 213
Zikr see Sufism, *dhikr* ceremony in
Zimbabwe 353–8; *mbira daz vadzimu* 354–8
Zionism 273
zither: Appalachian lap 471; Chinese seven-stringed (*guqin*) 192–5; Chinese *yangqin* 195, 197, 199; hammered 21, 55–6, **57**; Hungarian *cimbalon* 318; Japanese *koto* 21, 223, **224**, 224–5; *kanun* **26**, 264; Korean *kayagum* 222; plucked 21; *santu*r 55, 57, 103, 259, 261, 262; as type of chordophone 21
zourna see *zurna*
Zuckerman, Ken 107
Zulu 367; choral singing 334–5, 369–72
Zumsteeg, Johann Rudolf
Zurcher-Margolle, Pierre 412, 413
zurna (*zourna*) 54, 57, **58**
zydeco dance music 508

Recorded Examples

CD 1

Chapter 4 Oceania

1. (Site 1) Australian Aborigine song with *didjeridu*, "Bushfire," by Alan Maralung, from the recording entitled *Bunggridj-bunggridj Wangga Songs, Northern Australia* recorded by Allan Marett and Linda Barwick, SF 40430, provided courtesy of Smithsonian Folkways Recordings. © 1993. Used by permission.
2. (Site 2) *Susap* from Papua New Guinea, "Badra from Buzi" ("Sounds of a *Susap*") performed by Amadu, recorded by Wolfgang Laade, Buji, Western Province, Papua New Guinea, 1964, from the recording *Music from South New Guinea,* Folkways 04216, provided courtesy of Smithsonian Folkways Recordings. © 1971. Used by permission.
3. (Site 3) Hawaiian drum-dance chant, "Kau ka hali'a I ka Manawa," performed by Noenoe Lewis, drum, vocal, and Hau'oli Lewis, calls, dance, from the recording entitled *Hawaiian Drum Dance Chants: Sounds of Power in Time.* SF 40015, provided courtesy of Smithsonian Folkways Recordings. © 1989. Used by permission.
4. (Site 4) Kiribati group song, "*Kai e titirou e matie,*" sung with clapping by men and women of Ititin Rotorua Dance Troupe, Betio Village, Tarawa Island, Kiribati, recorded by Mary Lawson Burke, 1981. Used by permission.

Chapter 5 South Asia

5. (Site 1) Hindustani instrumental *raga*, "*Raga* Ahir bhairav," played by Buddhadev DasGupta, *sarod*, from *The Raga Guide: A Survey of 74 Hindustani Ragas,* Nimbus NI 5536/9 (4 CDs and 196 pp. book), 1999. Used by permission.
6. (Site 2) Carnatic (South Indian) classical singing (*Kriti*), "Manasā! Etulörttunë" *Raga Malayamārutam, Rūpakam Tala*, composed by Sri Tyāgarāja and performed by Sri V. Ramachandran, vocal; Sri S. Varadharajan, violin; Ramnad Sri Raghavan, *mridangam*; Sri R. Balasubramaniam, *kanjira*; recorded at the 2002 St. Thyagaraja Festival by the Thyagaraja Aradhana Committee, Cleveland, Ohio, 2002. Used by permission.
7. (Site 3) *Bhajan* devotional song, "Parvati Nandana Gajanana," recorded by Terry E. Miller at the Sai Baba Temple, Longdenville, Trinidad, 1985. Used by permission.
8. (Site 4) *Qawwali* devotional song from Pakistan, "Jamale kibriya main hoon," performed

RECORDED EXAMPLES

by the Sabri Brothers, from *Musiciens Kawwali du Pakistan/Les Fréres Sabri/Musique Soufli, vol. 3*, Arion ARN 64147, 1991. Used by permission.

Chapter 6 Southeast Asia

9. (Site 1) Central Highlands bronze gong ensemble of the Jarai, Pleiku City, Pleiku province, recorded by Terry E. Miller and Phong Nguyen, from *Vietnam: Mother Mountain and Father Sea,* White Cliffs Media WCM 9991 (6 CDs and 47 pp. book), 2003. Used by permission.
10. (Site 2) *Nhac Tai tu* amateur chamber music, "Xuan tinh" ("Spring Love"), performed by Nam Vinh, *dan kim*, Sau Xiu, *dan tranh*, and Muoi Phu, *dan co*, recorded by Terry E. Miller and Phong Nguyen, from *Vietnam: Mother Mountain and Father Sea,* White Cliffs Media WCM 1991 (6 CDs and 47 pp. book), 2003. Used by permission.
11. (Site 3) Classical Thai *piphat* music, "Sathukan" and "Sathukan klawng" from *Wai Khru/The Traditional Music of Siam*, produced by The Committee of the College of Music Project, Mahidol University, Saliya, Thailand, 1994.
12. (Site 4) Northeast Thai *lam klawn*, "Lam thang san" (excerpts) sung by Saman Hongsa (male) and Ubon Hongsa (female), and accompanied by Thawi Sidamni, *khaen,* recorded by Terry E. Miller in Mahasarakham,Thailand, 1988.
13. (Site 5) *Luk thung* from northeast Thailand, "Sao Jan Kang Kop" sung by Phawnsak Sawng-saeng, from *Sao Jan Kang Kop*, JKC Marketing Co., Ltd, JKC-CD 157 (n.d.), used with permission.
14. (Site 6) Javanese court gamelan, "Udan Mas" ("Golden Rain"), from the recording entitled *Music of the Venerable Dark Cloud: The Javanese Gamelan Khjai Mendung*, Institute of Ethnomusicology, UCLA, IER 7501, 1973. Used by permission.
15. (Site 7) Balinese *gamelan gong kebyar*, "Hudjan Mas," recorded in south Bali by a *gamelan gong kebyar* ensemble, from the recording entitled *Gamelan Music of Bali*, Lyrichord CD 7179, n.d. Used by permission, Lyrichord Discs Inc.

Chapter 7 East Asia

16. (Site 1) The *Guqin* seven-string zither, "Yangguang sandie," performed and recorded by Bell Yung, Pittsburgh, PA, 2002. Used by permission.
17. (Site 2) The "Silk and bamboo" *Jiangnan sizhu* ensemble, "Huan Le Ge," recorded in Shanghai, People's Republic of China, 2007, by Terry E. Miller.
18. (Site 3) Beijing opera (*jingju*), "Tao Ma Tan (role), aria from *Mu Kezhai* (opera)," from the recording entitled *The Chinese Opera: Arias from Eight Peking Opera,* Lyrichord LLST 7212, n.d. Used by permission, Lyrichord Discs Inc.
19. (Site 4) Revolutionary Beijing opera (*Yangbanxi*), Scene 1,"A Rush Shipment," from the recording entitled *On the Docks: Modern Revolutionary Peking Opera,* performed by the "On the Docks" Group of the Peking Opera Troupe of Shanghai. China Record Company, M-958, n.d. Used by permission.

RECORDED EXAMPLES

CD 2

1. (Site 5) Mongolian throat singing, "*Urtïn duu: Sinder Mountain*," from *Mongolia: Living Music of the Steppes/Instrumental Music and Song of Mongolia*, Multicultural Media, MCM 3001 (1997). Used with permission.
2. (Site 6) *P'ansori*, "P'ansori, Ch'un-Hyang-Ka, Song of Spring Fragrance" sung by Mme. Pak Chowol with drum accompaniment by Han Ilsup, recorded by John Levy, from the recording entitled *Korean Social and Folk Music*, Lyrichord LLST 7211, n.d. Used by permission, Lyrichord Discs Inc.
3. (Site 7) *Sankyoku* Chamber Music of Japan, "Keshi no hana" from *Japanese Shamisen/Chamber Music (Jiuta) with Koto and Shakuhachi*, Lyrichord Archive Series, LAS 7209, 2010.
4. (Site 8) *Kabuki* theater, "Excerpt from *Dozyozi [Dojoji]*," performed by the Kyoto Kabuki Orchestra, recorded by Jacob Feuerring, from the recording entitled *Japanese Kabuki Nagauta Music*, Lyrichord LLST 7134, n.d. Used by permission, Lyrichord Discs Inc.
5. (Site 9) Buddhist ritual, "Genyen gi topa" ("In praise of Ge-nyen"), performed by the monks of Thimphu and nuns of Punakha, recorded by John Levy, from the recording entitled *Tibetan Buddhist Rites from the Monasteries of Bhutan, Volume 1: Rituals of the Drukpa Order*, Lyrichord LYRCD 7255, n.d. Used by permission, Lyrichord Discs Inc.

Chapter 8 The Middle East

6. (Site 1) Islamic "Azan" ("Call to Prayer"), by Saifullajan Musaev from the recording *Bukhara, Musical Crossroads of Asia*/Recorded, compiled and annotated by Ted Levin and Otanazar Matykubov, provided courtesy of Smithsonian Folkways Recordings, Smithsonian/Folkways CD SF40050, ©1991. Used with permission.
7. (Site 2) Arab *Taqasim* modal improvisation, "Maqam Kurd," performed by Ali Jihad Racy, *buzuq*, and Simon Shaheen, *ud*, from *Taqasim: Improvisation in Arab Music*, Lyrichord LYRCD 7374, n.d. Used by permission, Lyrichord Discs Inc.
8. (Site 3) *Dastgah Shur* for *santur* and voice, "Dastgah of Shour," performed by Mohamed Heydari, *santour*, and Khatereh Parvaneh, voice, from the recording entitled *Classical Music of Iran: The Dastgah Systems*, SF 40039, provided courtesy of Smithsonian Folkways Recordings. © 1991. Used by permission.
9. (Site 4) *Takht* instrumental ensemble suite, recorded by the Middle Eastern Ensemble of the University of California, Santa Barbara, directed by Dr. Scott Marcus, 2011. Used by permission.
10. (Site 5) *Dhikr* ceremony, "Sufi Hymn" (from Turkey), performed by the Jarrahi Dervishes. Recorded by J. During, Konya, Turkey, 1982, from the recording entitled *The Silk Road: A Musical Caravan,* SF 40438, provided courtesy of Smithsonian Folkways Recordings. © 2002. Used by permission.
11. (Site 6) Jewish *shofar* and liturgical cantillation, "Cycle of 10 Calls During Additional Service," by David Hausdorff, from the recording entitled *Kol Háshofar (Call of the Shofar)*, Folkways Records FW8922, provided courtesy of Smithsonian Folkways Recordings, 1957. Used by permission. "L'dor vador" sung by Dr. Peter Laki, recorded by Terry E. Miller, Kent, Ohio, 2005. Used by permission.

585

RECORDED EXAMPLES

Chapter 9 Europe

12 (Site 1) Byzantine chant, "Come, Faithful," from the recording entitled *Byzantine Hymns of Christmas,* Society for the Dissemination of National Music, SDNM 101, n.d. Used by permission.

13 (Site 2) *Flamenco*, "Alegrias," performed by Carlos Lomas and Pepe De Malaga, from the recording entitled *Andalusian Flamenco Song and Dance,* Lyrichord LYRCD 7388, n.d. Used by permission, Lyrichord Discs Inc.

14 (Site 3) *Balalaika*, "Yablochka," from the recording entitled *Eastern European Folk Heritage Concert: St. Nicholas Balalaika Orchestra,* private issue, 2003. Used by permission.

15 (Site 4) Highland bagpipes by the City of Glasgow Police Pipe Band, "The Royal Scots Polka" and "The Black Watch Polka" from *All the Best from Scotland/35 Great Favorites*, vol. 2, CLUC CD 77, n.d.

16 (Site 5) *Uilleann* bagpipes, Ireland, "The Lilies of the Field" and "The Fairhaired Boy," private studio recording by Eliot Grasso, 2011. Used by permission.

17 (Site 6) Hurdy gurdy medley of traditional tunes, performed by Sean Folsom, Ft. Bragg, CA, 2003 (private studio recording). Used by permission.

18 (Site 7) Bulgarian Women's chorus "Harvest Song" (originally published on Balkanton BHA 1293), from the CD to accompany book: Timothy Rice, *Music in Bulgaria: Experiencing Music, Expressing Culture.* New York: Oxford University Press, 2004. Used by permission.

Chapter 10 Sub-Saharan Africa

19 (Site 1) Polyrhythmic instrumental ensemble, "Fante Area: Vocal Band," performed by the Odo ye few korye kuw Vocal Band, recorded by Roger Vetter, Abura Tuakwa, Ghana, 1984, from the recording entitled *Rhythms of Life, Songs of Wisdom: Akan Music from Ghana,West Africa,* SF 40463, provided courtesy of Smithsonian Folkways Recordings. © 1996. Used by permission.

20 (Site 2) Talking drums, "Talking Drum," by Elizabeth Kumi, and Joseph Manu from the recording entitled *Rhythms of Life, Songs of Wisdom*, Akan Music from Ghana, SF 40463, provided courtesy of Smithsonian Folkways Recordings. © 1996. Used by permission.

21 (Site 3) *Jùjú* from Nigeria, "Oro Yi Bale" from *Bábá mo Túndé*, composed and arranged by King Sunny Adé and his African Beats. © 2010 Mesa/Blue Moon Recordings/IndigeDisc. Used by permission.

22 (Site 4) Pygmy song from the Democratic Republic of the Congo, "Elephant Song," performed by Mbuti Pygmies, from the recording entitled *Music of the Rain Forest Pygmies: The Historic Recordings Made by Colin M. Turnbull,* Lyrichord LYRCD 7157 (original recording, 1961). Used by permission, Lyrichord Discs Inc.

23 (Site 5) *Mbira dza vadzimu* Shona ancestral spirit song, "*Nyama musango*," performed by Elias Kunaka and Kidwell Mudzimirema (Mharadzirwa), recorded by John E. Kaemmer, Jirira, Zimbabwe, 1973. Used by permission.

24 (Site 6) *Akadinda* xylophone, Buganda *akadinda* song "*Gganga aluwa*" ("Gganga escaped with his life"), performed by Sheikh Burukan Kiwuuwa and his group of royal

akadinda musicians, recorded by Peter Cooke, Kidinda Village, Mpigi, Buganda, Uganda, 1987. Used by permission.

CD 3

1. (Site 7) *Jali* with *kora*, "Kuruntu Kallafa," performed by Salieu Suso with *kora*, from the recording entitled *Griot: Salieu Suso,* Lyrichord LYRCD 7418, n.d. Used by permission, Lyrichord Discs Inc.
2. (Site 8) *Mbube* vocal choir, "Phesheya Mama" ("Mama, they are overseas"), sung by the Utrecht Zulu Singing Competition, recorded by Gary Gardner and Helen Kivnick, 1984, from the recording entitled *Let Their Voices Be Heard: Traditional Singing in South Africa.* Rounder 5024, 1987. Used by permission.
3. (Bonus Track) *Isicathamiya*, Ladysmith Black Mambazo, "Because I Love You" from *Raise Your Spirits Higher,* Heads Up International, 2004. Licensed courtesy of Gallo Music International.

Chapter 11 Caribbean

4. (Site 1) *Vodou*, ritual excerpts from "Bosou Djo Eya (Mayi rhythm)," performed by Sociètè Jour M'alongè Fòc Nan Point Dieu Devant, recorded by David Yih, Carrefour, Haiti, 1987, and "Guantanamo Song (Rara Rhythm, Southern Style)," recorded by Elizabeth McAlister, Port-au-Prince, Haiti, 1993. From the recording entitled *Rhythms of Rapture: Sacred Musics of Haitian Vodou.* SF 40464, provided courtesy of Smithsonian Folkways Recordings. © 1995. Used by permission.
5. (Site 2) Reggae, "Torchbearer," performed by Carlos Jones and the PLUS Band, from the recording entitled *Roots with Culture,* Little Fish Records LF02912, 2004. Used by permission.
6. (Site 3) Calypso, "Money is King," performed by Growling Tiger and the Trans-Caribbean All-Star Orchestra, from the recording entitled *Growling Tiger: High Priest of Mi Minor—Knockdown Calypsos,* Rounder 5006, 1979. Used by permission.
7. (Site 4) Steel band, "Jump Up," performed by the Miami (Ohio) University Steel Band, from the recording entitled *One More Soca,* Ramajay Records. Used by permission.
8. (Site 5) Rhyming spiritual, "My Lord Help Me to Pray," performed by Bruce Green, Clifton Green, and Tweedie Gibson, recorded by Peter K. Siegel and Jody Stecher, Nassau, Bahamas, 1965, from the recording entitled *Kneelin' Down Inside the Gate: The Great Rhyming Singers of the Bahamas,* Rounder 5035. Used by permission.
9. (Site 6) Afro-Cuban *Son*, "Soneros Son," by Estudiantina Invasora from the recording entitled *Music of Cuba*, recorded by Verna Gillis in Cuba 1978–1979, Folkways Records FW 04064, © 1985. Used by permission.
10. (Site 7) *Merengue*, "Apágame la Vela" ("Put Out My Candle"), performed by Nicolá Gutierres, Porfirio Rosario, and Santo Pea, recorded by Verna Gillis with Ramon Daniel Perez Martinez, 1976, from the recording entitled *Raíces Latinas: Smithsonian Folkways Latino Roots Collection,* SF 40470, provided courtesy of Smithsonian Folkways Recordings. © 2002. Used by permission.

RECORDED EXAMPLES

Chapter 12 South America and Mexico

11 (Site 1) Amazonian Indian chant, "Nhiok: Okkaikrikti," recorded by Max Peter Baumann, 1988, from the recording entitled *Ritual Music of the Kayapó-Xikrin, Brazil,* SF 40433, provided courtesy of Smithsonian Folkways Recordings. © 1995. Used by permission.

12 (Site 2) *Sikuri* ensemble, "Easter Music," by Qhantati Urui performed by the Conimeño Ensemble, recorded by Thomas Turino, Conima, Peru, 1985, from the recording entitled *Mountain Music of Peru: Volume 2,* SF 40406, provided courtesy of Smithsonian Folkways Recordings. © 1994. Used by permission.

13 (Site 3) *Tango*, "El Choclo" ("The Ear of Corn"): *Tango Criollo*, by René Marino Rivero, recorded by Tiago de Oliveiro Pinto, 1991, from the recording entitled *Raíces Latinas: Smithsonian-Folkways Latino Roots Collection,* SF 40470, provided courtesy of Smithsonian Folkways Recordings. © 2002. Used by permission.

14 (Site 4) *Samba*, "Agoniza, Mas Nao Morre" ("It suffers but doesn't die"), performed by Nelson Sargento, from the recording entitled *Brazil Roots: Samba.* Rounder CD 5045, 1989. Used by permission.

15 (Site 5) *Capoeira*, "Saia do Mar Marinheiro," by Grupo de Capoeira Anglo Pelurinho, from the recording entitled *Capoeira Angola from Salvador, Brazil*, SF 40465, provided courtesy of Smithsonian Folkways Recordings. © 1996. Used by permission

16 (Site 6) *Mariachi*, "Los Arrieros" ("The Muleteers"), performed by Mariachi Los Camperos de Naticano, from the recording entitled *Raíces Latinas: Smithsonian Folkways Latino Roots Collection,* SF 40470, provided courtesy of Smithsonian Folkways Recordings. © 2002. Used by permission.

Chapter 13 Canada and the United States

17 (Site 1) Cape Breton fiddling, "E Minor Jigs," performed by Buddy MacMaster, fiddle, and Mac Morin, piano, from the recording entitled *Buddy MacMaster: The Judique Flyer,* Stephen MacDonald Productions, Atlantic Artists SMPCD 1012, n.d. Used by permission.

18 (Site 2) Ballad singing, "Edward," performed by Edith B. Price, from the recording entitled *Eight Traditional British-American Ballads from [the] Helen Hartness Flanders Collection,* Middlebury College, 1953. Used by permission.

19 (Site 3) Old Regular Baptist lined hymn, "And Must This Body Die," performed by congregation led by Elder Larry Newsome, from the recording entitled *Grace 'Tis a Charming Sound: Pleasant View Old Regular Baptist Church in Worship.* Privately issued CD by Terry E. Miller and members of the Advanced Field and Lab Methods in Ethnomusicology Class, Kent State University, Spring, 2000. Used by permission.

20 (Site 4) Singing school shape-note music, "Exhortation," performed by Sacred Harp singers at Hopewell Primitive Baptist Church near Cullman, Alabama, 1971, recorded by Terry E. Miller. Used by permission.

21 (Site 5) Bluegrass, "True Life Blues," performed by Bill Monroe and the Bluegrass Boys, from the recording entitled *Off the Record, Vol. 1: Live Recordings 1956–1969,* SF 40063, provided courtesy of Smithsonian Folkways Recordings. © 1993. Used by permission.

22 (Site 6) African-American Spiritual, "Come and go to that land," recorded by Terry E. Miller at Gethsemene Baptist Church, Cleveland, Ohio, 1986. Used by permission.

23 (Site 7) African-American Gospel Choir, "God is Good All the Time," performed by New Hope Baptist Choir, from the recording titled *God is Good: The Total Musical Experience at New Hope Missionary Baptist Church, Akron, Ohio.* Privately issued CD by Terry E. Miller and members of the Advanced Field and Lab Methods in Ethnomusicology Class, Kent State University, Spring, 1998.

24 (Site 8) Country Blues, "Sweet Home Chicago," from *The Complete Recordings.* Sony/BMG, 2008. Used by permission.

25 (Site 9) *Salsa*, "Quítate de la vía Perico," performed by Tolú, from the recording entitled *Bongó de VanGogh,* Tonga Productions TNGCD 8405, 2002. Used by permission.

26 (Site 10) Cajun music, "La talle des ronces," performed by Adam and Cyprien Landreneau and Dewey Balfa, from the recording entitled *Lousiana Cajun from the Southwest Prairies Recorded 1964–1967, Volume 2,* Rounder 6002, 1989. Used by permission.

27 (Site 11) Plains Indian Song, "Rock Dance Song," performed by The Pembina Chippewa Singers, recorded by Nicholas Curchin Peterson Vrooman, Turtle Mountain, North Dakota, 1984, from the recording entitled *Plains Chippewa/Metis Music from Turtle Mountain,* SF 40411, provided courtesy of Smithsonian Folkways Recordings. © 1992. Used by permission

28 (Site 12) Native American Flute, "Courting Song," performed by John Rainer, Jr., from the recording entitled *Music of New Mexico: Native American Traditions,* SF 40408, provided courtesy of Smithsonian Folkways Recordings. © 1992. Used by permission